The Last
Love Song

Also by Tracy Daugherty

Just One Catch: A Biography of Joseph Heller

Hiding Man: A Biography of Donald Barthelme

The Last Love Song

A BIOGRAPHY OF JOAN DIDION

Tracy Daugherty

St. Martin's Press ❧ New York

THE LAST LOVE SONG. Copyright © 2015 by Tracy Daugherty. All rights reserved. Printed in the United States of America. For information, address St. Martin's Press, 175 Fifth Avenue, New York, N.Y. 10010.

www.stmartins.com

Designed by Steven Seighman

Library of Congress Cataloging-in-Publication Data

Daugherty, Tracy.
    The last love song : a biography of Joan Didion / Tracy Daugherty. — First edition.
       pages cm
  ISBN 978-1-250-01002-5 (hardcover)
  ISBN 978-1-4668-7740-5 (e-book)
  1. Didion, Joan. 2. Novelists, American—20th century—Biography.
I. Title.
  PS3554.I33Z57 2015
  813'.54—dc23
  [B]

                           2015017162

St. Martin's Press books may be purchased for educational, business, or promotional use. For information on bulk purchases, please contact the Macmillan Corporate and Premium Sales Department at 1-800-221-7945, extension 5442, or write to specialmarkets@macmillan.com.

First Edition: August 2015

10 9 8 7 6 5 4 3 2 1

Making a book is the lighting of a candle.
This candle burns in memory of

Jo Anne Daugherty
Robert Homler
Christina Ward

Acknowledgments

Kit Ward, Colleen Mohyde, and Michael Homler made this book possible. My admiration for them extends well beyond their professional skills. Until the very end, Kit sacrificed her time for others, and Colleen and Michael stepped up with grace and fortitude during moments of great difficulty.

Ted Leeson and Marjorie Sandor taught me to write better sentences. They are not responsible for the embarrassments that remain on the page. Elizabeth Wyckoff was an indispensable researcher. Keith Scribner enthusiastically shared his ideas on the American dream with me. Jon Lewis was a fine companion through the filmic and historical back alleys of Los Angeles. Kerry Ahearn keeps alerting me to the whereabouts of the Dead Father—a way of finding true north. I am grateful to the staffs of the Bancroft Library, the New York Public Library, the UCLA Library, the Harry Ransom Center at the University of Texas, and the libraries at Columbia, Harvard, Princeton, and Texas State University for their help. Laura Wyss and Elizabeth Seramur conducted the photo research and editing. Dinah Lenney and Lyle Wilen made marvelous tour guides. The St. Martin's team, particularly Lauren Jablonski (tireless!), Carol Edwards, Meg Drislane, Amelie Littell, Steve Snider, Steven Seighman, Yolanda Pluguez, Dori Weintraub, Ivan Lett, Jessica Lawrence, Emily Walters, as well as William McNaull and Eric Rayman on the legal team, handled the book with extraordinary care during the copy-editing and production process.

I am grateful to the creative writing students at Oregon State University. For nearly three decades, they have energized me with their vitality and curiosity.

For his help with this book and for care and feeding, I am beholden to Tim Steele. I dearly miss him.

Below are some of the people who were kind enough to share their memories and thoughts, or point me in helpful directions. Any misunderstandings or errors of interpretation are mine, not theirs. For their extra generosity, I'd like to acknowledge Noel Parmentel, Rosa Rasiel, Dan Wakefield, Eve Babitz, Hunter Drohojowska-Philp, Josh and Foumi Greenfeld, Shirley Streshinsky, and Sean Day Michael. Their insights and stories were crucial to my understanding of the narrative. For permission to print previously unpublished material, my thanks to Philip and Amy Robbins, Margi Fox, and Roger W. Straus III.

Also, my gratitude to Don Bachardy, Weston Blalock, Christopher Buckley, William Burg, Janet Burroway, Phyllis Butler, Norman Carby, Jon Carroll, Larry Colton, Anna Connolly, Amy Cooper, Meghan Daum, Jim Desmond, Julie Didion, Willard Dixon, James Fallows, Carol Felsenthal, Jodie Ferrara-Adler, Gael Greene, Karl Taro Greenfeld, Linda Hall, Joan Haug-Smith, Carol Herman, Alex Ives, Boris Kachka, Sue Kaufman, Brian Kellow, Jonathan Lethem, Kel Munger, John Newhagen, Madeleine Noble, Joyce Carol Oates, Ivan Obolensky, Jay Parini, Harriet Polt, Claire Potter, John Ridland, Jill Schary Robinson, Gabriel Rummonds, Anna Schneider, Lynn Sharon Schwartz, Nora Sheehan, Gary Snyder, Matthew Specktor, Ben Stein, Susan Straight, Rob Turner, David Ulin, Paul VanDevelder, George Vazques, Lois Wallace, and Sam Waterston.

Finally, my love and thanks to Don and Debra Daugherty, Charlie and Joey Vetter, Jeanne Sandor and the rest of her lovely extended family, Willie and Alice, and most especially to Marjorie Sandor and Hannah Crum.

The consciousness of the human organism is carried in its grammar.

—Joan Didion,
A Book of Common Prayer

I think it is fair to say that the West has lost its place in the national imagination because, by some sad evolution, the idea of human nature has become the opposite of what it was when the myth of the West began, and now people who are less shaped and constrained by society are assumed to be disabled and dangerous. This is bad news for the American psyche, a fearful and antidemocratic idea, which threatens to close down change. I think it would be a positively good thing for the West to assert itself in the most interesting terms, so that the whole country must hear and be reanimated by dreams and passions it has too casually put aside and too readily forgotten.

—Marilynne Robinson,
When I Was a Child I Read Books

Look for it only in books, for it is no more than a dream remembered.

—Sidney Howard,
Gone With the Wind screenplay

The whole cosmology of America tends toward the West . . . the quenching of the sun in the sea.

—Christopher Hitchens,
"It Happened on Sunset"

Preface: Narrative Limits

One afternoon in late September 2011, I was riding in a cab from Central Park West to JFK, reading Christopher Hitchens's profile of Joan Didion in *Vanity Fair* magazine, when the cabbie, who had been muttering about the punishing price of gas, said wretchedly, "I don't know what happened to this country."

The cabbie was a transplanted Iranian. He complained about America's "wallowing" in ten-year remembrances of 9/11. Christopher Hitchens was dying. Didion would soon publish a book, *Blue Nights,* about the near impossibility of surviving everyone she loved. In prepublication interviews, she had hinted that this might be her swan song. "I used to say I was a writer, but it's less up front now. Maybe because it didn't help me," she told *Publishers Weekly.*

Ten years earlier, by coincidence, she had published *Political Fictions* on the day hijacked commercial airliners destroyed New York's World Trade Center towers and a portion of the Pentagon. *Political Fictions* excoriated America's ruling class: the politicians, the moneyed, and the media courting them while claiming to expose their corruption. Predictably, the book drew fire from political and media enclaves exploiting the events of 9/11 to censor speech or solidify their influence.

Coincidence is not something Didion much credited. And now, ten years later, within weeks of the 9/11 anniversary ceremonies, she was about to offer her account of the death of her daughter. An account of what it was like to leave no one behind. A totting up of the end.

Coincidence?

I don't know what happened to this country.

Already, from the Hitchens piece and other well-placed profiles, it was apparent that *Blue Nights* would not be read solely as a meditation on private loss. Given the timing, and Didion's reputation as a public pulse taker, her readers would receive the book as an elegy for everything those of us now living had experienced, including, perhaps, books themselves.

We are not adept at facing the ends of things in this country. But in the photograph accompanying the article on her daughter's demise, Didion did not try to evade the camera or conceal from it her physical and psychological losses. She confronted the viewer directly, the face of grief and desiccation. In shadow, against a creamy white couch, her right hand, veined and curled, resembled charred bone. And yet the viewer knew the shot was precisely posed in the manner of Irving Penn's old fashion layouts, for which Didion used to write captions—a sort of glamorous horror still. Who was she, really?

In the cab to JFK that day, I was not just idly considering Didion. In recent years, I had become—by coincidence, I sometimes thought, though I also distrust the concept—a literary biographer, and I had turned my ear to her. She was a powerful voice for my generation. Early in my career I had decided there was no point to literary biography if it did not seek to grasp what was said, and why, in a certain time. Unavoidably, this approach made the biographer an elegist, writing lamentations.

1

In the preface to *Slouching Towards Bethlehem*, her first nonfiction collection, published in 1968, Didion had written, "This book is called *Slouching Towards Bethlehem* because for several years now certain lines from the Yeats poem . . . have reverberated in my inner ear." Reportedly, in the preface to *Blue Nights*, she had written, "This book is called *Blue Nights* because at the time I began it I found my mind turning increasingly to illness, to the end of promise." The lines' echoes forged the link between her early career, when the culture's center seemed not to be holding and she was perhaps our keenest observer of the chaos, and her late writings, when she, like the readers who had matured with her, noticed her physical decline along with cataclysmic cultural shifts. Didion's readers knew *Blue Nights* would feature an idiosyncratic appraisal of grief. Additionally, her genius for and uncanny luck with timing inclined the book to be not just a harrowing lullaby but our generation's last love song.

A large claim. Yet a woman who had entitled one of her books *Slouching*

Towards Bethlehem and another *Democracy* had never shied away from making or accepting large claims, including the quiet insistence in her work that she had always spoken for us.

By nailing the naughtiness of American politics on the day two of its physical symbols were attacked, and by keening ten years later, exploring, as a blind person touches strange new skin, the mechanisms of mourning and irretrievable loss, she had told us who we are, who we were. She helped us admit things we intuited but rarely aired: the fragility of our national myths and the constant nearness of death. At its best, her prose surfaced suppressed emotions, causing in the reader vertigo, déjà vu, and yes, even the sensation of coincidence: the now and to come, the hidden and known, overlapping like warm and cold Pacific waves. So conceived, *coincidence* is an evocative word for what we have always been and what we are already losing. It is, like an evening tide, a thick and somber blue: for Didion, the color of our current moment.

2

In *Political Fictions*, Didion opened several essays with what Susan Sontag called the "generalizing impulse." For example:

> It occurred to me during the summer of 1988, in California and Atlanta and New Orleans, in the course of watching first the California primary and then the Democratic and Republican national conventions, that it had not been by accident that the people with whom I had preferred to spend time in high school had, on the whole, hung out in gas stations.

And:

> No one who ever passed through an American public high school could have watched William Jefferson Clinton running for office in 1992 and failed to recognize the familiar predatory sexuality of the provincial adolescent.

Rhetorically, these openings echo two of the world's best-known literary beginnings, in Jane Austen's *Pride and Prejudice* and Leo Tolstoy's *Anna Karenina*. Listen:

It is a truth universally acknowledged, that a single man in possession of a good fortune must be in want of a wife.

And:

All happy families are alike; each unhappy family is unhappy in its own way.

Didion's writing is more specific and personal, but like Austen and Tolstoy, she presents a confident speaker with a solid worldview offering verities about human nature and culture. That these verities are not true (or not *necessarily* true) is beside the point. The effort is to create a social context in which the characters we are about to encounter must be considered, and reveals the narrator's values. Since views of human nature and culture are notoriously subjective, such pronouncements are meant to be quibbled with, poked, and prodded.

Let me amend my earlier statement, then. That such verities are not true *is* the point.

In *Political Fictions*, what was most striking to longtime readers of Joan Didion was the presence of *confidence* and *verities* in her prose. After all, this was a woman who wrote in 1968, "We tell ourselves stories in order to live," but at some point, amid rising crime rates, a televised war, and a culture experimenting with sex and drugs, Didion began to "doubt the premises of all the stories" she had ever told herself. As an adult American, she said, she thought she "was meant to know the plot, but all I knew was what I saw: flash pictures in variable sequence, images with no 'meaning.'" With cult murders in the newspapers and rock songs on the radio insisting "love was sex and sex was death and therein lay salvation," she found she could no longer "believe in the narrative and in the narrative's intelligibility." At various times, between 1966 and 1971, she said,

I watched Robert Kennedy's funeral on a verandah at the Royal Hawaiian Hotel in Honolulu, and also the first reports from My Lai. I reread all of George Orwell on the Royal Hawaiian Beach, and I also read, in the papers that came one day late from the mainland, the story of Betty Lansdown Fouquet, a 26-year-old woman with faded blond hair who put her five-year-old daughter out to die on the center divider of Interstate 5 some miles south of the last Bakersfield exit. The child, whose fingers had to be pried loose from the Cyclone fence when she was rescued twelve hours later by the California Highway Patrol, reported that she had run after the car carrying her mother and stepfather and brother and sister for "a long time." Certain of these images did not fit into any narrative I knew.

Didion's *The White Album* explored American violence, American apathy, and American sexual mores in the 1960s and was filled with anecdotes—about the Black Panthers, Charles Manson, the Doors—that did not fit into the overarching story, familiar to us from old-school history books and popular culture, of American Promise and the American Dream. By using a collage structure and halting, repetitive sentences, Didion disoriented readers until we began to experience the senselessness she claimed to have felt during those years.

An awareness of narrative's limits characterized her immediate post-1960s fiction—the novels *Play It As It Lays* (1970) and *A Book of Common Prayer* (1977), which, like *The White Album*, were fragmented, hallucinatory, and obsessively repetitive. But with her nonfiction of the 1980s—*Salvador* (1983) and *Miami* (1987)—the attentive reader could detect a tentative, born-again belief that narratives, particularly overarching narratives that tell us how to live, *do* exist still, *do* make sense still, though more and more we have to look for them in unlikely places.

Salvador, Miami, and two later novels, *Democracy* (1984), about the fall of Saigon, and *The Last Thing He Wanted* (1996), covering the Iran-Contra years, prepared Didion's readers for the newly secure voice, reminiscent of her first novel, we encountered in *Political Fictions*. From 1963's *Run River* to a series of narrative breakdowns to the reinvigorated certitude of *Political Fictions*, Didion tracked American history as a reporter, novelist, and ardent reader, finding, losing, then finding again the stories imposed on our nation by time, history, and culture. Her late-in-life memoirs, *The Year of Magical Thinking* (2005) and *Blue Nights* (2011), investigations of aging, grief, and death, showed us more intimately *how we live,* and traced the inevitable life path of most Americans.

3

We think we know the woman behind the books. In her reportage, as in her essays and memoirs, Didion used her experiences to establish contexts and combine our national and individual stories. From the first, her work insisted that a single life contained the life of our times.

To discover what we *do* know about the woman, let's note a few things about the writer. First, recall her example of "the narrative," a well-known fable that tells us how to live. In Didion's version of the story, the princess is not caged in a castle or an evil stepmother's house, but in a "consulate." By slipping this unexpected word into a familiar trope, Didion highlights her literary sensibility. She doesn't care about magic kingdoms. She'd rather tour the embassies, the public squares surrounded by barricades and armored tanks. If *this* voice were to say, "It is a truth universally acknowledged," you'd know to pull on your army boots instead of your glass slippers. The truth you'd be chasing would be located more readily on a military test site than in a ballroom. And it would hardly be universal. Every writer's verities—Austen's, Tolstoy's, or Didion's—have their boundaries and particular terrains.

Second, Didion's "images" are barely images at all. She tells us she watched Robert Kennedy's funeral "on a verandah at the Royal Hawaiian Hotel." "Funeral" and "verandah" are rarely sentence partners; Didion provides no visual detail and, more crucially, no context to lessen the strangeness of the link. What was she doing at the Royal Hawaiian Hotel during Robert Kennedy's funeral? Was she alone? Did a crowd gather before a television set to watch the ceremony in sorrow? Was the TV propped on a wrought-iron table in the sun? What is the point of teasing us with the hotel if not to deliberately disorient the reader?

Third, the story Didion offers of the mother leaving her daughter near the last Bakersfield exit on I-5 is a variation of a particular American narrative. When the Joads left the road in John Steinbeck's *The Grapes of Wrath*, they exited near Bakersfield, hoping to discover the "pastures of plenty." The famous final scene in Steinbeck's novel depicts a new mother suckling a starving man like an infant, an image of maternal generosity undercut by Didion's freeway anecdote. The shocking story of the I-5 mom is made even more powerful, almost mythic, by the ghost narrative of *The Grapes of Wrath* haunting it. Paradise has rotted rapidly since the Joads. More broadly, Didion plays against the whole genre of American road stories, all of which, from Kerouac's *On the Road* to television's *Route 66*, hearken back one way or another to Steinbeck's novel, which played against the notion of the West as the final frontier.

I mention these examples to demonstrate that even as Didion frets about narratives in tatters, she is weaving narrative. She is carefully plotting a story, manipulating details, with a clear direction and a sense of who's in charge—Joan Didion, jittery, uncertain, but vivid and speaking with a distinctive Western voice. Her collages are not stitched of random scraps. Her roads do not dead-end. Her narrative breakdowns are mirages. Every piece fits, often in more or less conventional patterns.

4

In the foreword to *Political Fictions,* Didion tells us she spent her childhood and high school years among "conservative California Republicans" in Sacramento, "in a postwar boom economy." In other words, she grew up in a well-connected family surrounded by Okies and others like them who had weathered the Grapes of Wrath, who had managed to escape the fruit fields and achieve a modest prosperity, buying a few fields of their own, working for shipbuilders or aerospace companies or on test-site ranges or some other outgrowth of California's burgeoning defense industries. American Promise—in the shape of the war and its stimulus to the economy—had directly benefited these families and those, like the Didions, with serious ties to the land. They all had reason to believe in "the narrative" as the Cold War heated up and American consulates spread throughout regions we had liberated or conquered. As David Beers, the son of a fighter pilot, writes in his memoir, *Blue Sky Dream, Sputnik* was the "lucky star" for postwar kids in California, "its appearance in the darkness a glimmering, beeping announcement that we would not know want." In the 1950s, the GI Bill, housing loans, and government spending on computer development, aerospace, and foreign investment created what Beers calls the "Blue Sky Tribe," a new middle class that worshiped a "God [endorsing] progress, personal and national," and that believed it would live happily ever after in spotless, crime-free suburbs. Those invited to join the tribe—the people among whom Didion was raised—flourished in the new economy and voted conservatively in order to maintain it until the dream faltered in the 1980s.

In an early essay entitled "John Wayne: A Love Song," Didion sketched another version of this particular Western narrative. "John Wayne rode through my childhood," she wrote, determining "forever the shape of certain of [my] dreams." He suggested "a place where a man could move free, could make his own code and live by it; a world in which, if a man did what he had to do, he could one day take the girl and go riding through the draw and find himself home free . . . at the bend in the bright river, the cotton-woods shimmering in the early morning sun."

Later, when Didion claimed narrative lost its intelligibility for her, she was not speaking abstractly, as so many of her contemporaries were, about the craziness of the 1960s, the mass upheavals attending the Vietnam War protests, the sexual revolution, or the civil rights movement, though these events touched her. She was mourning the loss of a very specific story with its bright river and its cottonwoods, its silvery satellite stars beaming riches down on a tamed and temperate West.

Nor were the causes of her losses abstract, nothing as soggy as the notice our nation has borne in every decade of its existence that America had "lost its innocence" (how many times can innocence be lost?). No. Didion is as precise in her reporting as she is in her rhetoric and phrasing. Things stopped fitting for her when John Wayne, who was always and forever "supposed to give the orders," got cancer. An unexpected crack in the narrative. "I did not grow up to be the kind of woman who is the heroine in a Western," she laments, "and although the men I have known have had many virtues and have taken me to live in many places I have come to love, they have never been John Wayne."

Still later, she was "shocked and to a curious extent personally offended by the enthusiasm with which California Republicans . . . jettisoned an authentic conservative [Goldwater]" and rushed to "embrace Ronald Reagan," a less principled man, in her view. She registered as a Democrat, the first and perhaps the only member of her family ever to do so, she says. She does not list her problems with Reagan but makes it clear that, for all his Western posturing, he was simply no John Wayne.

For a while, after a dream fails, nothing seems to make sense. But Didion has never presented herself as a wide-eyed naïf. She admits that even as she fell for the John Wayne mystique, she understood that the world was "characterized by venality and doubt and paralyzing ambiguities."

Her prose is filled with little dodges like this: a subtle certainty in the face of doubt, hinting that we do not know the woman behind the books as well as we think we do. In part, the impulse to hedge reflects her Western upbringing (she comes from a family of gamblers). "I think people who grew up in California have more tolerance for apocalyptic notions," she once said, thinking of earthquakes, floods, and fires. "However, mixed up with this tolerance for notions in which the world is going to end dramatically is the belief that the world can't help but get better and better. It's really hard for me to believe that everything doesn't improve, because thinking like that was just so much part of being in California." More deeply, the paradoxes in her writing suggest her *real* interest is language, its inaccuracies and illusions, the way words imply their opposites, and the ways stories, particularly stories that tell us how to live, get told or don't. For all her fascination with American politics, the ostensible subject of much of her writing, George Orwell's politics of language grip her most. There is a trace of the literary critic in all of Didion's fiction just as there are echoes of nineteenth-century novelists—the omniscient, moral voice—in her later essays. And if, in the 1960s, her love of narrative structure led to a sense of betrayal (after all, one cannot be betrayed without first loving intensely), then that same love has allowed her to rediscover a coherent and ongoing American story.

5

It's a simple story she longs for. A moral story, with a clear beginning, middle, and end. A road trip with a final destination. A John Wayne movie plot. But she also knows that such a story could not possibly embrace something as vast, diverse, and shifting as American life. The "pastures of plenty" will always remain elusive. The emphasis, then, in both her nonfiction and fiction rests not on the longed-for story—which can never be told fully—but on the longing itself. Her sensibility. The ironies shaping her disorientation and desire, her dashed hopes.

On the page, Didion's sensibility is individual, "passive," "strange, conflicted," as well as communal. She attempts to speak for us all through the apparently self-defeating strategy of grounding her authority in weakness. In the confessional tradition of Montaigne, Didion admits her limitations and befuddlements up front, so readers feel they are in the presence of an unusually honest speaker. "I want you to know, as you read me, precisely who I am and where I am and what is on my mind," she says in *The White Album*. "I want you to understand exactly what you are getting: you are getting a woman who for some time now has felt radically separated from most of the ideas that seem to interest other people." This self-deprecatory statement is also a brassy declaration. Rhetorically, its function is to establish the narrator as someone with a unique consciousness, someone whose disengagement places her in a better position than anyone else to plumb contemporary life. She is an outsider whose singular, untainted perspective allows her to assume a public voice. Our responses to her persona tell us less about the woman behind the books than about ourselves.

Recall Robert Kennedy's funeral watched on a verandah of the Royal Hawaiian Hotel: a glimpse of Joan Didion? Perhaps, perhaps not. But the detail serves a *literary* purpose. American hotels, like American consulates, are outposts of U.S. values, especially in old colonial settings. Hotels appear often in Didion's work. They suit her persona. They establish contrasts (home and not home, freedom, restrictions, and loneliness) allowing her to mix public rituals with private insights and local politics—not to share her life, necessarily, but to expose communal currents, communal break points. Our response to *her* is more generally a test of *our* principles and concerns.

One more thought to bear in mind, and eventually we'll return to it: After the World Trade Center towers collapsed, many commentators, including Michiko Kakutani, a book reviewer for *The New York Times*, and Graydon Carter, the editor of *Vanity Fair*, wondered if irony might be dead. No one felt like laughing. Political cynicism seemed insensitive, maybe even unpatriotic. The attack and the ensuing debate over responses to it posed a challenge to the literary enterprise Didion had pursued since the 1960s.

Political Fictions, disparaging the corruption of America's governing class, hit the nation's bookstores on the day the towers fell. Irony? An example of why irony should be buried in the rubble (*we can't afford dissenting voices in a time of crisis*)? Certainly, the image of passenger planes deliberately smashing into office buildings did not fit into any previous American narrative.

6

"I belong on the edge of a story," Didion once said. Temperamentally, she is a reader, not an on-the-spot reporter or a stringer chasing witnesses down the street. In 1976 she signed on to cover the Patty Hearst trial for *Rolling Stone*. She wrote to the magazine's editor, Jann Wenner, that being in the courtroom on a specific day was not important to what she was writing. Wenner seemed dismayed at this news, but Didion insisted she was thinking of Hearst as an idea of California rather than as a defendant in a trial. She said she would probably spend more time in the Bancroft Library than she would in the courtroom.

Always, she has stressed the limits of traditional reporting: Rarely will a place reveal its past or a person tell you the truth. Most first-person accounts are predictable, self-serving, and bland (she has been especially scornful of the "insider" reporting practiced by Bob Woodward, who often gets chummy with his subjects and whose interviews, she argues, are leaks by officials spinning events). Rather, what's required of a writer is a thorough *investigation* of the public record. She feels that the surfaces of things—the stated claims of legal contracts, the walls and floors of gas stations, high schools—reveal as much as, if not more than, their depths. She abhors abstractions. Wary of interpreting behavior as a clue to character (the addiction, the sexual insecurity, the psychic wound repeating itself in each new relationship), she seeks, instead, fruitful inconsistencies. Thus, her careful *linguistic* construction of Joan Didion, her emphasis on the brute world's shaping of identities, on the importance of actions and facts—or, more accurately, the *forms* assumed by "facts" (documents, essays, architecture); her reluctance, especially in early work, to judge or qualify.

Given these attitudes, she leaves obvious potholes for a biographer, obstacles deepened by the apparently autobiographical material in her work: How much of it can be corroborated, dismissed, or augmented? What else is there to say? As of this writing, Didion is still living. Does a biography of a living person make sense? (At best, it can only smooth the ground for later, more comprehensive studies and must necessarily emphasize the writer's early development.) Is the proper distance for evaluation possible now? My hope has been that these questions would animate, not defeat, the project.

I put this hope to Didion, through her editor, Shelley Wanger. *Blue Nights* was about to appear. Joan was in the middle of publishing her book, so she could not really think about speaking to a biographer right now, Wanger replied, more or less as I thought she would. I said I understood; I'd ask again at a more convenient moment, knowing I might remain precisely or imprecisely on the edge of this story. Didion was known for granting access selectively to reporters. In a letter from the archives of the Lois Wallace Literary Agency, dated January 18, 1979, Maryanne Vollers had asked Didion if she would consent to being profiled in *Rolling Stone*. At the bottom of Vollers's letter, Didion had penciled, lightly, that this would not be possible. On another occasion, she had refused a scholar permission to quote from her work on the grounds that she didn't want people writing about her, and even more, she didn't want to *know* if people were writing about her. Since she was also, at this time, allowing her work to be reprinted and discussed in literary anthologies, her decisions seemed personal rather than categorical.

In *The Year of Magical Thinking,* she described an incident in a reception area of New York–Presbyterian Hospital, the night her husband died, when a social worker called her a "pretty cool customer." Her coolness was apparent in interviews she *had* given over nearly five decades in which she'd revealed little of herself, in which she'd crafted another persona, not entirely at odds with the Joan Didion in her formal writing but not completely consistent with it, either. In interviews, Joan Didion was generally looser, funnier—but just as deflective. "Clearly, I'd say anything!" she admitted merrily in 2011, on tour for *Blue Nights,* when pressed about nonanswers she'd offered in the past. Time and again, she'd repeat particular anecdotes, writerly wisdoms, and calculated confessions. Always, her interviewers noted her famously frail physique, her halting voice hovering just above a whisper. The details were accurate so far as they went, but their repetition tended to create what we think of today as a brand, and it was first promoted by Didion herself. In the preface to *Slouching Towards Bethlehem,* she had written, "I am so physically small, so temperamentally unobtrusive, and so neurotically inarticulate." This is the Joan Didion we would come to know, to the exclusion of all others, no matter what she said in interviews. Obviously, no reporter was going to get much out of her that she didn't want out. Fair enough. But it was important to bear in mind that she was always *working* her brand. In *Blue Nights* she declared, "[W]riting . . . no longer comes easily to me." The "no longer" suited her current narrative of diminishment (a condition belied somewhat by the power and suppleness of the prose), but the deeper effect of the statement was to reinforce the iconic image. Forty-three years earlier, she had written, "[T]here is always a point in the writing of a piece when I sit in a room literally papered with false starts and cannot put one word after another and imagine that I have suffered a small stroke." With a pretty cool customer, perhaps it was best to remain on the edge of the story, I thought. There is "bound to be friction between the inquisitive biographer and the subject who wants to control the narrative of his or her life," Carl Rollyson, author of biographies of Norman Mailer and Susan Sontag, once said. And after all, why *wouldn't* Didion oppose a biography? Much of her career had been devoted to exposing as illusions most of the conventional meanings we take from literature. I admired her fierceness on this point and recognized the contradictions knotting my project.

Ultimately, she chose not to cooperate. In her own work, she ceded as much weight to the correctly "perceived" as to the "accurately reported"—the point was to "get it right," she said. I have used her marker as my guide, as well as the advice of her old teacher Mark Schorer, who wrote in "The Burdens of Biography" that, in fact, living witnesses could rarely be trusted. The biographer must be a "drudge," a "trained scholar," and "an artist" in order to "bring shape out of the mass," he said. I make no claims to artistry, but ask the reader to accept Schorer's standard: "[B]elieve only the conduct of the narrative itself, and the resolution of its values."

In choosing Didion as a subject, I am offering a particular slant on literary biography. In the spirit of saying "exactly what you are getting," let me lay it out. There is the biographer who promises explanations by threatening to reveal a subject's secrets, who promises to *dish*. I am not that biographer. Nor will I live and die by psychological theories. When presented with the private correspondence, diaries, journals, or rough drafts of a writer, I remain skeptical of content, attentive instead to presentation. It is the construction of persona, even in private—the fears, curlicues, and desires in any recorded life—that offers insights. A writer forms her stories, but the opposite is also true. This is especially the case with Joan Didion, whose prime subject is the nature of narrative and who has often said she does not know what she thinks until she writes it down. The "women we invent have changed the course of our lives as surely as the women we are," she once wrote. Her work does not merely inform or misguide us about her; it enacts her on the page, reproducing her mental and emotional rhythms. Any serious work *about* her should seek to do the same.

Further, I trust that her literary methods will apply to *her* just as she pressed them on others—Joan Baez, Nancy Reagan, Dick Cheney, the "Joan Didion" in her novels—revealing the bedrock beneath layers of myth, gossip, PR, self-promotion, cultural politics, competing notions of human nature and the purposes of biography.

The central question is this: Does the life reveal the art, the art the life? In *The Miraculous Years,* a biography of Dostoyevsky, Joseph Frank said it is the "masterpieces" that make the "life worth recounting." My intent is to foreground my subject's masterpieces rather than treat them "as accessory to the life per se," and to trace her intellectual development.

Throughout my pursuit, I have kept in mind the limits of narrative, but, like Didion, I see no reason not to attempt what may very well end in failure. As Joseph Conrad, a writer essential to Joan Didion, taught us, even shipwrecks are instructive.

We read novelists, essayists, and memoirists for their views of the world. We read biographies of writers for an understanding of how they did their work and how the work evolved. In choosing Didion as a subject, I am abjuring abstractions ("the madness of the artist"), avoiding pat explanations of personal antics (booze, gender, trauma, even when they do inform the story), weighing conflicting testimonies, and scouring the public record for the underreported fact, the contradictory details.

Above all, in studying Didion, I am fashioning literary biography as cultural history as well as an individual's story. I take my cue from her long and varied career: Her life illuminates her era, and vice versa. If this were not so, a biography of Joan Didion would serve only prurience. Writing is the record we have of our time. Just as certain memories burn brighter with age—the day we were taken to get our first haircut, the day we left home, the day we got married—so, too, do the pages of our contemporaries, the marks they have made of our lives, cast us more vividly as immediate circumstances vanish and the record's uniqueness comes more to the fore.

PART ONE

Chapter One

1

Writers used to choose their pasts, before literary tradition began to erode in our culture. The Great Dead with whom writers would speak were invited to sit or snuggle beneath the bedcovers. Didion was a writer early. If, as a child, she did not yet know her companions, she tracked amenable traits and rhythms. She was born into a cultural atmosphere layered with Virginia Woolf (though she never warmed to her)—*A Room of One's Own* was published six years before Didion's first good cry; with Ernest Hemingway's *A Farewell to Arms;* with George Orwell's *Down and Out in Paris and London* and F. Scott Fitzgerald's *Tender Is the Night,* both arriving a scant few months before Didion opened her eyes for the first time; and with movies, America's fifth-largest industry then, associated with Didion's native California ever since Carl Laemmle established Universal Studios on a former chicken ranch in the San Fernando Valley.

At least, years later, this was the air Didion decided to breathe.

Her actual inheritance from both her mother and father was the wagon-train mentality of pioneers moving west until there was nowhere else to move: a view insisting that you left your dead where they fell, just as you left your past behind you, and wasted no days grieving, because by the time you've dried your dirty tears, some wind-borne calamity would have blasted the parcel you'd sought to claim. This was the romantic take on her inheritance Didion would spend a lifetime wrestling and debunking, though never to her total satisfaction. In California, girls of her era—she was born on December

5, 1934—learned of the Donner Party debacle, one of the state's foundational stories, from a volume entitled *History of the Donner Party: A Tragedy of the Sierra,* by a former teacher and attorney named C. F. McGlashan. It was first published in 1879—before California's legends "hardened," according to the foreword of an edition printed when Didion was six. In fact, Mc-Glashan was already glazing the legends. "I am haunted by the cannibalism of the Donner Party," Didion told Alfred Kazin in 1970, but McGlashan's account, one of the first narratives she was likely to know of the forty-odd people who perished in a Sierra snowstorm in 1846, "leaves much to be desired," said George and Bliss Hinkle in their foreword to the 1940 edition of McGlashan's book: "Its language is saturated with sentiment, and great stretches of the narrative are written in the pressed-flower-and-keepsake style of a young lady's album of the period."

McGlashan's sentimentality sweetened other twists on the tale, such as Julia Cooley Altrocchi's *Snow Covered Wagons: A Pioneer Epic,* published when Didion was two, and loved by girls her age as they came to be young readers. Altrocchi felt the story was "too important a part of western American history not to be set down in other forms—Why not write it down in verse?" In a preface to her book-length poem, she wrote, "I have made every effort to be accurate with all events and all people. Future research may shift the pattern here and there, but I believe that the design is essentially correct." Readers like Didion, an impressionable young descendant of one of the Donners' fellow travelers, were Altrocchi's ideal audience:

> *Foster has eaten the half-finished heart of Antonio . . .*
> *It is no longer the flesh of mortals,*
> *It is the flesh of a God–given beast*
> *Roasting in the fire!*

In time, Didion would reveal, both as a child writer and as a young professional, that what haunted her about the cannibalism of the Donner Party was not just the drama and despair of the story but also the fact that the story could be told "in other forms." It could be stylized. She may not have understood this concept as a girl, but she experienced its power. This is clear in the calm presentation of disasters coloring some of her earliest paragraphs. Eventually, she outgrew the sentimentality of writers like McGlashan and Altrocchi, but the tropes of the Donner tale, approached through a mythic veil, would never leave her. Beauty could be wrested from the apocalypse, and always in the middle of the storm, a courageous, moral person resisted (often by recording) the events.

As a slightly older reader, analyzing and not just absorbing pioneer stories, she learned further fine points of craft. She speaks of what she learned in her 2003 book, *Where I Was From,* ostensibly a meditation on California history. As she grew older, but while she was still a girl, she says, she turned from popular accounts of wagon-train crossings to primary sources, the diaries and journals of the pioneers themselves, including those of some of her ancestors. Death and rebirth, she saw, and redemption, were essential themes in the crossing myth: The old life must wither before a new one can begin. That she now understood this as a literary conceit did not alter the fact that she had also swallowed it as an almost biological truth about living. Further, she became aware of what she later called "a problematic elision or inflation, a narrative flaw, a problem with point of view" in the pioneers' autobiographies. She quotes a written account by the son of her great-great-great-grandmother Nancy Hardin Cornwall; he is relating the moment his grandfather left his mother to make the trek across the continent: "'Just ready to go, he entered his mother's parlor. She went out with him to his horse to say the last words and to see him depart. She told him that she would never again see him in this world.'" A precocious young reader, Didion began to wonder who was witnessing these incidents. From whose angle were these stories being told? In *Where I Was From,* she wrote, "[T]he actual observer, or camera eye, is often hard to locate," yet "the gravity of the decisive break demands narrative. Conflicting details must be resolved." Yes, and as an older writer, Didion would work hard to resolve conflicting details, but initially she was drawn by mystery, as children are: the mystery of the missing center, the dizziness of disjunctions, the off-kilter quality of not quite knowing what's going on while realizing it's "decisive." Elision, first encountered in the pioneers' testimonies, would become one of Didion's early signatures. It would even extend to her grammar: Often, she'd withhold a subject or verb until the end of a sentence, keeping the reader in suspense, suggesting that meaning—or resolving conflicting details—was not the point so much as worrying the music and rhythm of memory.

And always, there was the romance at the heart of the stories! In 1968, when she wrote in the preface to *Slouching Towards Bethlehem* that *"writers are always selling somebody out,"* what was it but a restatement of the pioneer family's stoicism in the face of decisive breaks? You leave your dead behind (you may even have to kill them yourself) in order to move on. When she told the story of the mother who left her child to die on Interstate 5 near the last Bakersfield exit, what was it but a crossing tale like *The Grapes of Wrath*: abandoning the weak one in the family, expecting her traces to be covered by wheel tracks?

2

Didion's first reader, her mother, Eduene Jerrett Didion, descended from Nancy Hardin Cornwall. Nancy followed the Donner-Reed Party west with her husband, Josephus Adamson Cornwall, a Presbyterian minister, whose refusal to abandon his books on the trail when travel got tricky often set his direction. It may have led him and his wife and children to split from the group at the Humboldt Sink in Nevada, hiking toward what is now Oregon's Willamette Valley. The family came from Arkansas, forerunners of the Arkies and Okies with whom Didion would attend school in the 1930s and 1940s; it would be an irony of history (and another puzzle for Didion to crack) that, during the Depression, descendants of the original immigrants would blame the newcomers for the region's decline.

When Josephus Cornwall married Nancy Hardin, he stood to inherit her father's land in Greenbrier, Arkansas, but he felt he had not earned the right to farm it. He'd never worked it. So, displaying the firm principles embedded in all the family stories Didion heard, he headed out on the old Oregon Trail with his wife and children. After splitting from the Donner-Reed Party, the family made its way to Applegate Creek in the Umpqua Valley, and Josephus built a small cabin there. That first snowy winter, they went without salt and bread but killed and ate forty-nine deer over a six-month span. In the flat, passive style of many family histories, composed dutifully by nonwriters (a style, conveying remoteness, depending on understatement, that Didion adopted to powerful effect), a genealogist named Diana Smith, writing for the Oregon Biographies Project, said of the Cornwalls' winter in the Umpqua Valley, "their supply of food becoming exhausted, they underwent intense suffering."

Three to four thousand Native Americans inhabited the area at the time, members of the Southern Molalla, Siuslaw, and the Cow Creek Band of the Umpqua tribe. Smith wrote, "Indians would visit [the Cornwalls] and pry around the house and on one occasion the father showed them a trunk filled with books, and they did not then molest the other trunks, thinking, probably, that they were also filled with books, for which they had no use." Twice now, Josephus's passion for reading had probably saved the lives of his family.

In *Slouching Towards Bethlehem,* in an essay entitled "On Keeping a Notebook," Didion claimed her first earnest writing was done at the age of five, in a Big Five tablet given to her by her mother "with the sensible suggestion that I stop whining and learn to amuse myself by writing down my thoughts." Her mother, Sacramento's assistant city librarian before she married, always encouraged her daughter to read. Didion's first foray was in fiction, a story about a woman hallucinating her demise in an arctic freeze, only to wake and find that she was, in fact, burning to death in the Sahara: a child's twist on crossing harsh terrains, an early awareness of irony, "a certain predilection for the extreme which has dogged me into adult life," she said in the essay.

She also said a desire to write tends to bloom in "lonely and resistant rearrangers of things, anxious malcontents, children afflicted apparently at birth with some presentiment of loss." She doubted her daughter, Quintana, not yet two when Didion published "On Keeping a Notebook," would ever take up writing because "she is a singularly blessed and accepting child, delighted with life exactly as life presents itself to her, unafraid to go to sleep and unafraid to wake up." This was a false glimpse of Quintana, as Didion surely knew even this early in her daughter's childhood. We will meet Quintana later. For now, the point is that Didion was already establishing her own frailty, a frailty that began in the cradle and led almost immediately to a need to write. To underscore the point, she distinguished her anxious, isolated self from her "sensible" mother and her "accepting" child (knowing, also, that her mother would read the essay and that Quintana might read it someday, too).

Clearly, Western pioneer myths, as well as family journals and diaries, were among Didion's first models of story craft. It's also clear that tales of courage in life's wild storms piqued her imagination. Her perception of her audience is less plain. When we hear that her mother supported her scribbling, we picture a welcoming reader, someone the writer would like to please, someone with whom she felt comfortable sharing her thoughts. Thirty-five years later, once Eduene was dead, Didion revealed that one of her mother's most common utterances—on any subject—was "What difference does it make?" She rarely dusted the house or made the beds because "they just get slept in again." Though she was "passionately opinionated on a number of points," she seemed to believe in nothing. So, in fact, Didion's first reader was removed, passive, and depressed; uninterested, perhaps often unresponsive. A tough audience. Possibly she got this way because of her own pioneer inheritance—as a girl in the upper Sacramento Valley (she was born in Tehama in 1910), she had witnessed her share of frontier justice, corpses swinging from tall trees in front of the courthouse. But the trigger for Eduene's temperament is less important than Didion's attempt to engage it with the notebook she'd received from the woman. A "certain predilection for the extreme": What else could reach a person for whom nothing mattered? How else to record events for a woman who doubted anything was worth recording?

Eduene is often an unspoken presence in Didion's prose. For example, in 1979, in a review of Norman Mailer's *The Executioner's Song,* a novel whose concerns include the lives of desert women, Didion wrote, "The authentic Western voice . . . is one heard often in life but only rarely in literature, the reason being that to truly know the West is to lack all will to write it down." It is easy to see her mother's listless shadow in the bones of that sentence (and to ponder the irony of her mother's gift of a notebook). There is a "vast emptiness at the center of Western experience," Didion wrote, "a nihilism antithetical not only to literature but to most other forms of human endeavor, a dread so close to zero that human voices fade out, trail off, like skywriting." Mailer's take on Western females impressed Didion with its dead-on accuracy: The women in the book are strong, depressed, unwilling to invest too much in words. They are "surprised by very little. They do not on the whole believe that events can be influenced. A kind of desolate wind seems to blow through the lives of these women."

As the daughter of such a woman, Didion may have felt hers was "one of those lives," so prevalent in the West, "in which the narrative would yield no further meaning." In the notebook essay, claiming impairment, she presented herself as the weak one in the family, the one discarded on the trail, perhaps seeing herself through her mother's eyes. Yet she was also the survivor, the journalist, the one who noted the loss. "I have already lost touch with a couple of people I used to be," she wrote near the end of the essay. And: in describing others, we attempt to trace ourselves. The "presentiment of loss" afflicting writers (and the children of Western mothers) is the sharp awareness of impending change and death, as clear as the color of day or the cold blue of an empty medicine bottle tossed from a covered wagon. The abandonment of the weak is the shedding of our own skin. So we leave our mark along the trail, though it makes little difference to those who come after us. A bent twig. A circle of rocks. A word in the sand. This is where I was from.

Didion never forgot she was a Westerner, never lost sight of her birthright's grammar and its relationship to a particular worldview. In the Sacramento Valley of her childhood, rattlesnakes were common. They were part and parcel of the paradise her ancestors yearned for. So it was that she learned to equate facts with objects on the ground, and proper behavior—ethics, morality—with their placement. In this world, abstractions got you killed. You always kept a snake in your line of sight so it couldn't surprise you. As a girl, Didion translated this advice to writing. Don't dither and overlook the facts. If you miss them, the facts will rise up and bite you. If you see a rattlesnake, kill it so it won't harm others. This, Didion's grandfather (a former Sierra miner) taught her, was the "code of the West." For her, it became a code of language: Nail the specifics. Imprecise expression was not just sloppy; it was harmful.

3

Snakes slithered around the Didion family cemetery when Didion was a girl but rarely ventured near the tombstones until she was a teen and vandals began ruining the graves, an activity that reached alarming proportions in the early 1980s, when someone dug up and stole a skull. The Matthew Kilgore Cemetery, east of Sacramento in Rancho Cordova, which became a rocket-manufacturing community for Aerojet General following World War II, was named after Didion's great-great-great-grandfather. He left Ohio and settled in Sacramento in 1855. From him was descended Ethel Mira Reese, who gave birth to Didion's father, Frank, on January 1, 1908. Two hundred and forty-five graves pocked the land near the American River Grange, among pyracantha, oleander, and wild blackberries, on what had once been Matthew Kilgore's 154-acre farm.

At the Kilgore Cemetery, Eduene Didion, dropping her usual diffidence, impressed upon her daughter the meaning of being a fifth-generation Californian: It lay in the sacrifices etched into the stones with the bold strokes of chisels; in words such as *faith, fidelity, courage,* and *integrity.* Didion's ancestors had come for the bounties of the land, spilled their blood among its blooms, and their burial in its soil anointed it—or so the story went. As an adult, Didion would learn that the family cemetery had been sold amid ugly bankruptcy proceedings, the way so many ranches in the valley had been sub-divided and auctioned off. So much for sacred ground. In November 2011, recounting for a Los Angeles audience the day her mother told her of the sale, Didion choked up. It was the "selling of what I had preferred to think of as heritage," she said: the end of the fairy tale, "a total collapse of the narrative." As part of that collapse, an auto-salvage yard, America Auto Wreckers, would set up shop next to Sacramento's Home of Peace Cemetery, antifreeze leaking and spreading into some of the oldest Jewish graves west of the Mississippi River; in the mid-1950s, the remains of more than five thou-sand pioneers would be exhumed from the Helvetia Cemetery and dumped in mass graves in order to accommodate urban growth. The old headstones would be scattered in people's backyards for children to play among. Per-haps at this point, Didion's mother began to relinquish what little faith she had had in the promise of California. Her depression grew, along with a grim recalcitrance. In succeeding years, she would threaten to leave the state "in a minute. Just *forget* it," Didion recalled.

As a child, though, Didion learned from her mother to revere the pioneer past, to bear solemnly the memories of those who had come before. Eduene may have doubted anything was worth recording, but as a mother she had to stick to family rituals; if nothing else, the family's social standing depended on an allegiance to the past. It was a descendant's duty to preserve the elders in the form of inscriptions, jottings in journals, as well as in the weavings and quilts, the smoothed rocks and blue glass bottles they left behind, objects lining the dark rooms of Didion's childhood homes. A quilt, a page of prose: Both were talismans, reminders of what is and is no more. Perhaps this is why Didion never kept diaries of her own: She was taught that writing was not self-expression or indulgence; it was history.

At the Kilgore, kneeling in the shadows of granite spires, Didion saw the costs of where she was from, the losses of so many parents and their need to mark the days of their children: "Our darlings," one year and nine weeks, two years and ten months, stillborn, here and gone.

Writing did not get more precise than in tombstone inscriptions. Beloved Daughter, Wife, and Mother, Born, Died. Facts, as lightning-sharp as the strike of a snake.

When she was twelve, and had been scrawling in notebooks for six or seven years, Didion discovered similarly sharp writing in the work of Ernest Hemingway. She had been going to the local library with a note from her mother saying it was okay for her to check out "adult" books (she had free reign in the library but "wasn't allowed to listen to the radio because there were scary things on it"—that is, fallout from World War II). Mostly, she read biographies. "I think biographies are very urgent to children," she would say later. They "told how you got from the helpless place I was to being Katherine [*sic*] Cornell, say." But then she read the first paragraph of *A Farewell to Arms*. She took the book home and *typed* the first paragraph of *A Farewell to Arms* on a solid Olivetti Lettera 22 typewriter. Four sentences, four commas, one hundred and twenty-six words, only twenty-three of which contained more than a single syllable. For the first time, another writer's rhythms filled her like a tide and she gave herself to the motion. It was a solemn cadence, like something you'd hear at a funeral. As in the crossing stories she'd first encountered, much of Hemingway's power came from leaving out information. "In the late summer of *what* year? *What* river, *what* mountains, *what* troops?" she asked herself. Unlike the pioneer mythmakers, Hemingway avoided abstractions. "I was always embarrassed by the words sacred, glorious, and sacrifice . . ." he wrote. "I had seen nothing sacred, and the things that were glorious had no glory . . ." He went on to say, "There were many words that you could not stand to hear and finally only the names of places had dignity." This was a new perspective on the past—what would the stories really say if you scratched out the words *sacrifice* and *courage*? If you stripped the stories to their place names? As she read more Hemingway—teaching herself typing skills by copying his "magnetic" words—she toughened her style. She began to hear a stronger music, to see a grander purpose, in writing, beyond just keeping records, though the impulse to note everything remained, along with the storm and the figure at its center. As Virginia Reed, a Donner Party survivor, wrote in a letter to one of her cousins, a passage Didion cherished and might have claimed as a credo, "I have not wrote you half the trouble we've had, but I have wrote you enough to let you know what trouble is."

Chapter Two

———— ❖ ————

1

The California of Didion's girlhood, during the Depression, offered enough open space to appear to be Eden still, especially to a child. The Sierra, where the Donners met their limits, still defied people's efforts to tame them. The moody weather of the Sacramento Valley, which dictated the inhabitants' physical and emotional rhythms, proclaimed daily its uncontrollability. In and around the Donner Pass, North America witnessed its heaviest snowfall, an average of thirty-seven feet a year. This formed an icy reservoir on the Sierra's western exposure, which melted annually around the first of May, filling and sometimes flooding the Feather, Bear, Yuba, American, and Cosumnes Rivers, offsetting the baked summers, nurturing wheat fields, rice paddies, and orchards, sprouting berries, sugar beets, melons, plums, tomatoes, peaches, pears, walnuts, olives, cherries, and grapes.

But this Eden was industrial. Silver irrigation pipes sprawled among wheat stalks sliced by whirring steel blades—and anyway, the wheat was beginning to thin. Bad planting practices had exhausted the valley soil. When Didion was a girl, the crusading writer Carey McWilliams lamented California's "factories in the fields"; his calls, in newspapers and books, for better care of the land and the people who worked it guided John Steinbeck's hand as he drafted *The Grapes of Wrath*. In the pioneer myths Didion grew up on, no mention was ever made of the gold rush as a technological enterprise, a drive to develop the mechanics of moving water across hostile terrain to support the miners. In her teenage years, Didion would hear from her mother, her teachers, and Sacramento's leaders that newcomers, the federal government, and corporate bosses from the East were ruining California's once-perfect environment, but, in fact, the land was already an android, artificial tendrils fused with the natural, sustaining an unholy agricultural system.

That life in the valley was not pure or preordained was impressed most directly on Didion by Sacramento's levees. From its founding, and through its early iterations, Sacramento City showed itself to be, in many ways, a poor idea. River floods devastated the place in 1849 and again in 1861 (perhaps one of the reasons Mark Twain decided not to stick around writing for *The Sacramento Union*). By early January 1862, twenty-three inches of rain had fallen in less than a month, melting some of the Sierra snowpack and driving most of the townspeople from their homes, among boxes, rotted goods, and debris, to a high spot known as Poverty Ridge, where squatting miners used to pitch their tents. A local paper, the *Marysville Daily Appeal*, reported that "stock of every kind could be seen passing downstream, some alive and struggling and bellowing or squealing for life."

By 1934, the year of Didion's birth, the levees had significantly reduced flooding. The Shasta Dam on the Sacramento River would be completed in 1945, emerging from within a grid of steelwork, cables, and scaffolding. The Wright Act, decades old by the time Didion was born, had chipped away at the natural flow of water by allowing farmers whose land did not abut rivers to organize irrigation districts to divert the moisture they needed from one area to another. Still, details such as those in the *Daily Appeal* of terrified cattle swept in torrents through the city seemed to belong to the present. Despite development, new technologies, and changing land uses, the politics and folklore of what some people still called Sacramento City ensured a living past, especially for a child with an imagination as vivid as Didion's. As a former boomtown, hunkered between Sierra miners digging for gold and San Francisco merchants spinning gold into ephemeral, expensive trinkets, Sacramento had developed a tough, opportunistic, and insular society. It was an overwhelmingly male society in the beginning, a town of squatters, gamblers, and dreamers lured by gold. In Didion's time, Sacramento still bore the traces and scars of this origin. Initially, the scarcity of women led men to idealize them, except for the ladies actually in their midst, often forced into prostitution, the ambivalence apparent in surviving saloon songs from the 1840s, such as "Sacramento Gals":

They're pretty gals, I must confess,
Nipping 'round, around, around;

And "Lordy-massy" how they dress,
As they go nipping 'round
On J Street . . .

The women's celebrated style boasted Sacramento's aspirations. It was a spot where rural treasure, extracted from the mountains, was forged by the magic of capital into luxuries destined for the drawing rooms of San Francisco. And each night that song could have been sung in a tavern called Didion's on Front Street, frequented by eye-catching women, and run by Frank Didion's great-grandfather.

As the initial crush of the gold rush receded, Sacramento's residents longed for more women to "civilize" the place, to provide moral ballast to the men's excesses. This longing, shaped into an unspoken civil policy, created a pinched and segregated social structure that lingered in the city well into Didion's maturity. In the 1950s, when Sacramento tried to annex several outlying communities, these communities resisted, in part because their citizens viewed Sacramento as a "cold" place, repressive and tolerant of brutal police tactics. The influx of women as a moral army also set the city's development patterns: The family unit was the pacifying force. Unlike farm life, which required many hands to do the work, city life, more centralized and diverse, operated as a series of interconnected hives. Subdivided lots and single-family dwellings checkerboarded the valley, making the buying and selling of real estate Sacramento's *real* business, and eventually giving Didion's family much of its income. Downtown, lavish hotels served as meeting spaces and stages for men just back from the mountains to strut their adventurousness. They struck the poses of literary figures from dime novels, newspaper stories, and railroad advertising circulars, which had seduced many of them into coming west in the first place. John Wayne prototypes: Daniel Boone, Davy Crockett (whom Wayne would one day play in a movie), Kit Carson, John Charles Frémont, the self-made man. While women kept order at home, men burnished their reputations as good-hearted hell-raisers or courageous loners ready to ride off into the sunset. Impromptu gambling halls came and went; the spirit of speculation was as thick as contagion. From the first, a boisterous, transient population pushing against pleas for greater order made nostalgia the city's dominant tone. As early as the 1850s, a newspaper editorial by E. C. Ewer mourned the loss of the good old days, "when the miners paid for everything in dust—when the red-shirted gentry were the nabobs of the land . . . Those days have passed, and with the change has come idleness, vagrancy, and coin as the circulating medium." This is the tone Didion would adopt for her first novel, *Run River,* about valley life, in 1963.

As she admitted later, the tone was not quite suitable. From the start, Sacramento was an ornery place with plenty of dead zones. Its government plazas displayed a ruthless efficiency of design, outpacing the politicians' capacities for matching it. That so many capital cities, where raw deals get made to enrich the whole, are ugly and lifeless at their cores reflects one of our oldest animal instincts: You don't want to eat where you shit.

2

Right away, Didion dreamed of getting out—or so she remembered years later. In fact, she remained fond of many places in and around Sacramento. Nothing awful occurred in her early childhood, but it was often a gloomy time spent in still, dark rooms. The first house she knew was on Highland Avenue, in a neighborhood now called Curtis Park, northeast of downtown. Her parents shared the house with her mother's folks. "The area was a streetcar suburb, built out between the 1880s and the 1920s," William Burg, the city's most ardent historian, told me. The no. 6 trolley cut through the neighborhood, past acres of hops and mint, ferrying a mix of laborers, bankers, and furniture salesmen; at night, just as mothers prepared children for bed, the outbound Twenty-first Street car clattered past tightly curtained windows. The houses, whether late Victorians, bungalows, or Tudors, had new sewer lines and were already being shaped by forces that would radically alter the look of Sacramento in just a few years. The most striking feature of the Didions' 1923 house was its massive carport. In fact, the streetcars were all but done. In 1947, Pacific Gas & Electric would sell off the last of its trolleys, and suburban growth exploded with the auto. The Didions had a large lot, elevated in case of floods, and the house (boxy, with thin windows blocking more light than they let in) sat well away from the street. But traffic was increasing. The Sacramento Aviation Company was expanding its operations here, recruiting more workers and their families, another sign of things to come.

The 1940 and 1941 city directories list the Didions' residence as 2211 U Street, a two-story 1908 Craftsman bungalow in Poverty Ridge, the former squatters' camp and flood haven. In the late nineteenth century, it had turned into a posh neighborhood of Queen Anne, Stick, and Colonial Revival four-squares. The Poverty Ridge house is the one Didion considered her true childhood home. It was near the Ella K. McClatchy branch of the public library—a children's library at the time—where Didion loved to read under towering, sunny windows.

In general, the neighborhood was still nice in the 1940s, but it was beginning to decline, as the suburbs drew many middle-class and wealthy families out of the city's center. The migration made for good housing prices in town, and the Didions, now with a second child, Jim, born in December 1939, almost doubled their square footage with the move, and got a five-space garage in the bargain.

"My father, when I was first born, he was selling insurance, but nobody was buying anything, so he'd play poker," Didion said. Gambling may have been lucrative for Frank Didion, but he continued to sell insurance through the Travelers Group well into the 1940s, even though his life in Sacramento was interrupted by the war and he had to leave town and return. City directories list a suburban address for his office. Frank Didion was a mediocre, or perhaps just a distracted, salesman; his real passion was risk. The place's speculative fever filled him. He loved not just poker but anything on which a sum could be wagered, a claim staked. He seems to have really hit pay dirt after World War II, cleaning up at a government auction, acquiring dozens of Royal manual typewriters, which he later sold at a profit, along with property—a fire tower, a few old mess halls, sitting on valuable lots now—and a military jeep, in which he would teach his daughter to drive. After the auction, he settled into the boom-and-bust rhythm of real-estate speculation, moving money from one account to another. *Dabble* was a word Didion associated with his professional activities. He was "fuzzy" about finances, she said. The family seemed to have plenty—the house was spacious, the kids never wanted for ice-cream cones, trips to San Francisco or Stinson Beach—but a feeling lingered that their privileges were wispy: myths and illusions, like the family's storied past. Frank was quiet and depressed—a good-looking man, though Eduene's family thought he had a weak mouth. He was quick to fix a drink to quell the smallest anxieties. Didion remembers him as "full of dread." She said that even at family parties, when he'd seem to enjoy himself playing ragtime piano, his bearing conveyed such tension, she'd run to her room and close the door. Frank's mother had died when he was young, in the 1918 influenza epidemic, and his father had married a dynamic woman named Genevieve, who spent more time on local politics than on raising her stepchildren. Frank's younger brother, Robert, lost an eye one summer in a fireworks accident in which Frank's carelessness seems to have played a part. Didion thinks he suffered guilt about this for the rest of his life. As an adolescent, restless, hunting distractions, he always hoped to work at the California State Fair but never measured up to the job. His greatest discipline was reserved for sports. He lettered in basketball in 1928 at Sacramento City College. But then, as an adult, his discipline dissipated; he was always seeking something for nothing. He'd go from the high-flown Sutter Club (he was not a member) to the seediest gambling joints. Late at night, he'd drive to the Nevada border to shoot craps. Until 1940, the riverboat *Delta King* offered floating card games and strong drink on the Sacramento River. Prohibition had only recently ended, and odd cocktails prompted by the liquor ban were popular. Since the quality of outlawed alcohol was suspect, creative bartenders had added flavorings, sweeteners, and leafy sprinklings to their furtive whiskeys. Now, while laying down his bets, Frank Didion happily imbibed whatever buddies set in front of him: gin slings, old-fashioneds, manhattans, and aviations. Lady Luck rode the river swells up and down, up and down, and Frank never tired of chasing her, as someone of romantic temperament might have put it. And why not? Family lore suggested the name Didion was a derivative of the French Didier, a variation of *desiderium*: "unfulfilled longing." In previous centuries, this longing had usually been spiritual in nature, though it often referred to a woman's yearning for a child.

Frank spent his childhood a few blocks from an eccentric white house at Sixteenth and H Streets, built in 1877 and featuring cupolas shaped like pastries, Victorian Gothic detail, gingerbread trim, and intricate door moldings. The house had once belonged to the Steffens family. As a boy, Frank befriended Jane Hollister, niece of the poet Lincoln Steffens, and was later a classmate of hers at Berkeley.

In 1903, the old Steffens house had become the Governor's Mansion. From that point on, every governor of the state of California lived in the house until Ronald Reagan in the 1970s. Like her father, Didion fell in love with this icon of nineteenth-century bohemianism, and like her father, she was always haunted by the conviction that its elegance meant the past was a lovely lost domain and the present a fallen state, dominated by petty, classless folk.

Eduene Didion preserved the genteel rituals of the past, holding ladies' teas for her friends and many relatives—endless Sunday aunts, Didion recalled.

One of them, her great-aunt Nell, habitually twisted the splendid rings on her fingers, snuffed cigarettes in a thick quartz ashtray, and told Didion that her grandmother was "nervous," "different." When Didion asked what this meant, Aunt Nell said it meant she couldn't be teased. Eduene, wearing an ankle-length red lace dress, passed around trays of butter cookies, slices of lemon on Wedgwood plates, and cream cheese and watercress sandwiches.

"Childhood is the kingdom where nobody dies": Didion had memorized this line from an Edna St. Vincent Millay poem and she thought of it, at tea, whenever one of the tottery ladies lamented the death of an old friend. To her, the notion of being alone, unattended, everyone close to you gone, was liberating and exciting, especially on these slow Sundays when the aunts came shuffling near, bathed in cloying perfume.

The rooms of the U Street house were filled with old muslin appliqués. There was a quilt stitched by Didion's great-great-grandmother during a plains crossing shortly after she'd buried a child on the trail. Photographs lined the rooms: a stone marker by the side of Nancy Hardin Cornwall's Umpqua cabin; Nancy's great-granddaughter, Edna Magee Jerrett, standing boldly on a bare Sierra outcrop. The house was mote-dizzy, dim, the curtains usually drawn: a museum stillness, a concession to Frank's "dread," which needed gentling, as well as a reverential nod to the relics. The silverware was tarnished, the wallpaper faded, the flowers in vases brittle and dry. For Didion, it was not quite like living with Miss Havisham, coming upon cobwebby cakes in the kitchen with spiders for icing, but she *did* breathe the dust her mother would not disperse, *did* live in the dark, *did* eat corn bread and relish from recipes hauled over mountain passes by people who, with one or two missteps, might have eaten one another. Didion's keen awareness of family ghosts and her home's tilt toward neglect caused her to envy her ancestors' heroics and to burn with shame that she could not match their examples.

Church did not ease her inadequacy. Eduene christened her daughter at the Trinity Episcopal Pro-Cathedral on M Street (where Eduene and Frank had married), and took her children to worship there each Sunday. Didion adored the elm trees dropping yellow leaves in front of the church, and perked up, smirking, whenever the priest compared Sacramento's agricultural riches to those of the Holy Land, but otherwise she took little from services beyond the beauty of the music and language.

Once she turned eleven, she announced she was done with church. Her mother's mother, Edna, educated in an Episcopal convent school, gave Didion an expensive Lilly Daché hat as an enticement to return to the fold. It didn't work, though it was one more lesson in luxury and taste, like the time she'd bestowed on the girl—when Didion was six and recovering from the mumps—some Elizabeth Arden perfume in a tiny crystal bottle wrapped with gold thread. Her house was another museum, lined with delicate seashells, coral, and seeds.

Whatever spiritual awareness Didion developed seems to have come from Edna's husband. Herman was the son of a forty-niner and a self-taught geologist whose livelihood depended on spotting the difference between serpentine and gold-bearing ores. In the language of geologic eras, in words such as *igneous, cretaceous,* and *magma,* Didion glimpsed the magnitude of time and its consequences for meaning and purpose. But these were abstractions, impossible to dwell on. Much more compelling was her awareness that her grandmother couldn't be teased or she'd cry. Often, Didion pushed her to the brink of tears just to watch.

Occasionally on the streets, Didion observed a weeping man or woman. By the late 1930s, more than fifteen thousand Sacramento citizens were unemployed. Many of them had worked in canning, which had all but collapsed. Hoovervilles appeared in parts of the city, spreading as winter freezes destroyed the valley's citrus crops, adding to the economic disaster. On rainy spring nights, as townspeople shored up the levees, it was possible for a child to notice differences between men for whom hauling the sandbags was merely a civic duty and those, more anxious and ragged, whose lives depended on the work. When she was twelve or thirteen, Didion asked her mother what social class the Didions belonged to. Eduene replied that the family didn't think in terms of class. "Class . . . is something that we, as Americans and particularly as Californians, were supposed to have passed beyond," Didion learned. But the main reason "we" don't think about class was implicit in Eduene's answer: We don't *have* to.

The Didions and their extended families—Jerretts, Reeses—were prominent in town, and always had been: ranchers, bankers, saloon keepers, sheriffs. When Didion was a child, her grandfather was a local tax collector. His wife, Genevieve, would become president of the Board of Education; eventually, an elementary school would be named after her. Another Didion sat on the district court of appeals. "They were part of Sacramento's landed gentry," William Burg told me, "families who called themselves agriculturalists, farmers, ranchers, progressives, but they were the owners, not the ones who got their hands dirty."

For all its visibility and influence, the family felt prosaic, muted, sad to Didion, even as a girl. Clerks and administrators: hardly the heroes of old, surviving starvation and blizzards. Furthermore, the progressives' hold on

Sacramento's fortunes had weakened in the Depression and with the restrictions of Prohibition—a real blow to the valley's hops growers. The land was ripe for tragedy, or the perception of it. When Didion was eight, the grand Buffalo Brewery, just blocks from her house, closed for good. It had been a palace of beer since the late 1880s. During Prohibition, the brewery temporarily halted production, but reopened the year of Didion's birth, following the law's repeal. It marketed drinks in cans but could never recapture its lost sales. The progressives got nervous. The place's shuttering was not just a business failure; it was the end of an era, a threat to a way of life. A whiff of decadence clung to the gentry. When the WPA approved loans for public works in Sacramento, prompting construction of the Tower Bridge across the Sacramento River, green-lighting forty-six new buildings (including the high school Didion would attend) as well as runways at local airports, the Didions benefited from the uptick in business, but they would never acknowledge the federal government's role in the changes. To admit the influence of outsiders, Easterners, *government men,* would suggest limits to one's proud independence. In 1936, construction began on McClellan Air Force Base (then called McClellan Field). Mather, another local airfield, reopened after a dormant period. These developments were good news economically, but they brought an influx of workers from afar, began to change the city's look and feel, and gave the Didions one more reason to cherish their glorious past and embrace whatever seemed inviolable about the present.

The Sunday aunts did their best to keep the past rolling. Miss Pearl Didion was busy with the Saturday Club, founded in 1893 to sustain classical music in Sacramento. Genevieve Didion was a powerful engine propelling the Camellia Society and eventually created a Camellia Grove in a park across the street from the state capitol, in honor of the valley's pioneers. Her efforts were part of the progressives' attempts to boost their *own* spirits by revising history—among other things, recasting the city's founder, John Sutter, not as the economic opportunist he was, but as an agricultural dreamer.

In addition to music and flower clubs, Sacramento had a literary society, but no Didions seem to have joined it.

For a time, Didion's literary activities stayed in her bedroom. Soon after becoming obsessed with tales of the Donner Party, she set a framed picture of Donner Pass on her dresser. In *Run River,* she writes of a woman "whose favorite game as a child" was "'Donner Party,' a ritual drama in which she, as its originator, always played Tamsen Donner and was left, day after day, to perish by the side of the husband whose foolish miscalculations had brought them all to grief." We're invited to wonder if the Donner Party game occurred to Didion much earlier in life than during the writing of her first novel.

Theatricality and drama appealed to her as much as writing—playacting was fun and seemed to suggest something true about people, in a family whose emotions were often masked (Didion said her mother gave a "successful impersonation of a non-depressed person," a magnificent performance).

"I wanted to be an actress," Didion said. "I didn't realize then that it's the same impulse [as writing]. It's make-believe. . . . The only difference being that a writer can do it all alone."

Declarations, evasions, confessions lay at the heart of drama. Didion's desire to capture accurate dialogue led her to leave her bedroom clutching her notebook. She'd go skulking in hallways, behind half-closed doors, eavesdropping on adults, recording their remarks. On the whole, the Didion family disappointed her in this unwitting project. For example, Didion's grandfather, her father's dad, "didn't talk," she recalled. "I don't think my grandfather knew my or my brother's names, he would always address us as 'hey you.'" And the conversations were rarely dramatic. "If you were born in Sacramento and bragged about the place, you were 'puttin' on airs,'" William Burg told me. "If you were a little uncomfortable about the city, it was easier to sell it to outsiders. A slightly disdainful aspect was an appropriate class attitude." In Didion's earliest essays on Sacramento, her disdain is apparent, but the attitude was not useful in her initial dialogue exercises. Still, she liked secretly gathering details. "There used to be a comic strip when I was little called Invisible Scarlet O'Neil," she recalled. "Invisible Scarlet O'Neil was a reporter. She would press a band on her wrist, become invisible and cover the story invisibly. And everybody would be amazed that she had gotten the story." And so Didion, gripping her notebook, would run and hide behind a tree, stalking the big folk.

In moments when she was all *too* visible—forced to go to church or attend a tea or other family gathering—her mother dressed her in "muted greens and ivories, dusty rose, what seems in retrospect an eccentric amount of black," she wrote. She inherited her great-grandmother's black lace mantilla. If Didion's memory is correct, her mother seems to have planted the idea in her daughter's mind that she was too delicate and sensitive for her own good, in the manner of all the family women. She had a sad and anxious personality— "my mother says"—from the day she got home from Mercy General Hospital with all its hovering nuns. She was said to have her dead grandmother Ethel's eyes, "eyes that reddened and watered at the first premonition of sun or primroses or raised voices, and I was also said to have some of her 'difference,' her way of being less than easy at that moment when the dancing starts . . ." It's true she didn't eat much as a child. Her mother fashioned a ritual to try to induce her to swallow her food—the "clean plate club," she called it, prompting Frank to yell one night, "She's not a human garbage can." In fact, Didion's meager appetite may have been an act of rebellion rather than a result of her frailty, a form of eating disorder (Didion later thought so). She admitted Eduene found her willful and difficult—so much so that if Eduene could have done it all over again, she might have stuck her daughter in a boarding school. This suggests steeliness beneath the quiet delicacy. Eduene had given her daughter a notebook to stop her "whining," but the notebook tugged her toward an inner life, a private world brewing storms beyond her mother's control. The myth of the weak one, the one who would have been left on the plains, was a way of convincing the girl she *needed* dark rooms, silent afternoons, the fussing of Sunday aunts. In truth, it was Eduene who needed the assurance of family rituals ("My mother 'gave teas' the way other mothers breathed," Didion wrote). With carte blanche in the adult sections of the library, with gifts of expensive perfume and fancy hats whenever she had an illness or required persuading, Didion, it appears, was more pampered than impaired.

She had a cousin named Brenda, a year and a half younger, the daughter of her mother's sister Gloria. Her favorite game with Brenda was "going page by page through an issue of *Vogue* and choosing what to 'buy,'" she once wrote. "Brenda could buy whatever she wanted from the left-hand pages; I was limited to the right. The point was to see which of us could assemble, given the options only as they turned up, the most desirable wardrobe." It thrilled Didion to imagine herself a woman wearing expensive clothing. She also liked controlling her cousin. If Brenda chose an item Didion didn't want her to have, she would reject it on a pretext, claiming it was unfair to use an editorial page, say. "I was the older cousin. We would therefore do it my way," Didion said. What Brenda preferred "never, not ever, not once . . . crossed my mind." She loved to scare Brenda by scripting scenarios for the two of them in which they were about to step into an elevator bound for perdition.

Perhaps Didion wanted to punish her cousin: Brenda adhered to the family rules enforcing decorous meals and the need to make a "perfect white sauce"; she was more willing to accept the "delicacy" myth, going to bed promptly at six-thirty each night; she agreed to play the Snow Princess by the Christmas tree each year, to the delight of all the parents. Or perhaps Didion was trying to enlist her cousin in precocious rebellion (a stance repeated many years later with Quintana: forcing a child to embrace adulthood before she was fully prepared for it). Didion was ready to take her place in the world. No yellow vegetables for her. No cookies and milk. She wanted a cocktail. Observing her father's tendencies, she'd take a leaf of iceberg lettuce, mix it with crushed ice in a stemmed glass, and pretend to drink like a grown-up.

Didion made other friends in town, notably Nancy Kennedy, whom she'd met when they were both five and starting ballet classes at Miss Marion Hall's Dancing School. Nancy was the sister of Anthony Kennedy, who would eventually become a U.S. Supreme Court justice. Since there wasn't a gap in their ages, Didion was less inclined to control the relationship with Nancy, though its pleasures suited her to a tee. The girls liked dressing up in their ballet costumes (especially for their performance in *Les Petites*) and enjoyed trying on clothes. Together, they once modeled outfits in a charity fashion show. Didion joined a Girl Scout troop. She recalled being pressed to sing to shut-ins in an asylum just outside Sacramento. The songs included such lyrics as "lilies of the valley line your garden walk" and "that will happen only when the angels sing." One of her troop mates told me that Didion was probably thinking of a medical facility called Weimar, north of the city, which treated tuberculosis patients. The place revealed to Didion the possible dangers of becoming an adult, but she still longed for the finish line of her childhood.

Twenty-four, her mother told her when Didion asked what was the best age to be. Eduene was twenty-four when she married, twenty-four when she gave birth to Joan. Twenty-four, she said, was her "lucky number" (for her, as for her husband, life was a floating casino). Grown-up talk was one thing Didion could share with her mother. Eduene would drag dusty boxes out of closets and show her daughter the red velvet cape with the white fur collar she wore at her wedding reception, as well as her older tea dresses.

From these glimpses of her mother's fashionable past, and from magazine pictures, Didion concocted romantic daydreams. These were not about princesses or magical coaches, but of paparazzi chasing her through some exotic locale, maybe Argentina (a place she had seen in *Vogue*), while she, in a sable coat and dark glasses, pursued a divorce from her wealthy husband. Her great-grandmother's black lace mantilla seemed to materialize out of these dramas and suggest their immanence.

She constructed literary fantasies, too. "I kept playing around with writing and imagining being a writer, which usually involved having a quote-unquote Manhattan penthouse," she said. "That was my image of being a writer."

3

San Francisco was not Manhattan—parts of it looked like Sacramento, only bigger—but the romance of the place was palpable, especially in the Paul Elder display windows and flower stands across from Union Square, home of jewelry shops and stores that sold books, art supplies, furniture, apparel, and sweets. On one family trip to the bayside city, Grandmother Edna bought violets for Didion and Brenda and ordered Dungeness crab Louie at El Prado. Eduene and Gloria wondered if the girls were getting so spoiled that they'd have nothing to look forward to in life. Said Edna, "Let that be the greatest of your worries."

Though more than seventy thousand dockworkers had lost their jobs, and men had died in labor strikes (roughly half the city's population belonged to unions), the visitors from the valley saw no trouble—Didions didn't think about class—gawking instead at seagulls in the fog, Bauhaus and Beaux-Arts buildings, banana boats anchored just west of the Third Street Bridge and freighters under footlights. They breathed the odors of rotting timbers, roasting coffee, raw sugar; marveled at the brand-new Golden Gate Bridge. Begun in 1928, Grace Cathedral (later under the unconventional leadership of the Right Reverend James Albert Pike, whom Didion would one day write about as a true California eccentric) remained unfinished, its spire a rusty rib cage. Always, Eduene left a contribution for its completion in the mite box.

In the 1920s, as a slender ingénue, Eduene had attended afternoon tea dances in the Garden Court of the Palace Hotel, sipping wine tea, nibbling handmade scones with Devonshire cream, and flirting with suitors. Her daughter's view of the city was awash in splendor. Didion felt she'd missed a magical world; in her mind's eye, department stores and hotels became the towers and ramparts of a castle in the clouds.

She'd stand at the water's edge, trying to imagine the bottom of the bay. Maybe, when she grew up, she wouldn't be a writer in New York. Maybe, instead, she'd study the oceans. She dreamed of leaving for Hawaii on the steamship *Lurline,* a voyage every woman of breeding and taste made at least once. With its palm trees, sweet drinks, and flowered necklaces, Hawaii was an even better place than Argentina to divorce a rich husband.

As she gazed out to sea, she wondered what had happened to Amelia Earhart. The headline in the *San Francisco Chronicle* read LONELY OCEAN STILL HOLDS SECRET OF AMELIA'S FATE. Like the pioneers of old, she had set out romantically in her fragile contraption, never knowing if she'd make her destination.

When they weren't visiting the city, the Didions made frequent trips into the parched Central Valley. There, the family owned land. In the scant shade of fruit trees, watching dark-skinned men in straw hats pick crops beside white women, men, and children, Didion recognized links between California and more southerly climes. A heat-shimmery harshness infested the place. Everything was close to the bone. This was the *real* California.

Didion knew its legacies through her grandfather Herman. He had become a civil engineer and an attorney after leaving the Sierra mining camps, and he had also become a writer, composing technical treatises such as *The Theory of Real Property Valuation* as well as writing local histories. His accounts included brief mention of migrant workers lynched in insular towns.

In a series of articles for *The San Francisco News,* John Steinbeck also wrote of Central Valley drifters "hated" by the locals, living in shelters of "corrugated paper" and tents the "color of the ground." These *News* pieces were run-ups to *The Grapes of Wrath.* Published in 1939, around the time Didion got her first notebook, Steinbeck's novel dared to declare its origins in advocacy, its roots in reportage. Didion never claimed Steinbeck as an influence, but his ruminations on the valley matched hers, if from a different political angle, and must have reminded her of her grandfather's writing (additionally, her paternal great-great-grandfather once organized grape growers in Florin County and owned twelve thousand acres of fruit trees). Stories like Steinbeck's, and the consequences of life in California for the descendants of the first waves of Okies, hover behind Didion's early essays. Steinbeck's documentary approach, like that of Dorothea Lange with her photographs, or James Agee and Walker Evans in *Let Us Now Praise Famous Men,* remained a model of how to frame political subject matter. In the 1960s and 1970s, critics would call Didion, along with Tom Wolfe, Norman Mailer, and Hunter S. Thompson, a pioneer of the New Journalism, in which the reporter inserted herself into the story as its centerpiece. In fact, the observational stance—the witnessing ethic—of Didion's essays, and her tough tone, scrappy as the Christmas tinsel waving on Sacramento's streetlights, shared as much DNA with the proletarian writing of the Great Depression as it did with the celebrity showstopping pieces of Mailer, Wolfe, and Thompson.

Chapter Three

———————— ❧ ————————

1

When Pearl Harbor was bombed on December 7, 1941, Sacramento mobilized. By two P.M., McClellan Field was scrambling hundreds of Curtiss P-40s and B-26 Marauders for flights to Alaska, where they would be prepped for battle. Thomas Monk, the city's mayor, ordered security details to guard the levees in case the mainland was attacked. On December 8, the mayor mandated citywide blackouts. Three days earlier, Didion turned seven. The festive atmosphere surrounding her birthday celebration soured quickly and then the world went dark. In the past, in San Francisco or on Stinson Beach, Didion, staring out over the waves, had mentally navigated Hawaii's shores. The place loomed large in the minds of well-to-do Californians: a paradise within easy cruising distance. But now it was a smudged spot in the atlas. A territory called "War."

After the attack on Hawaii, Didion's father was assigned by the U.S. Army Air Corps to travel from Fort Lewis in Washington State to Durham, North Carolina, and finally to Peterson Field in Colorado. He would take his family with him, fragmenting Didion's formal schooling from the end of first grade until the fourth. Military records indicate that Frank Didion joined the National Guard in 1939. His family had a long history with the Guard; his uncle Edward Reese served with distinction in the Guard's hospital corps in San Francisco following that city's massive earthquake and fire in 1906. It did not escape the Didions that military enlistment was often a conduit to business opportunities. Frank would remain in the military much of his life, working for the Selective Service as a procurement officer in Sacramento, becoming a major in the Air Corps, and finally retiring at the rank of lieutenant colonel in August 1965.

In his early thirties when the United States entered World War II, Frank stayed stateside, helping the army settle financial affairs. Specifically, he wrapped up outstanding World War I–era contracts, clearing the path for *new* business.

What this meant for Didion was saying good-bye to her friends. From now on, she'd experience reading not as something you did in school, but something you did on your own wherever you were: a secret pleasure. "I tended to perceive the world in terms of things read about it," she said. "I [had] a literary idea of experience, and I still don't know where all the lies are."

In Tacoma, Washington, housing on base and even in town was overcrowded because of the sudden arrival of so many soldiers. Eduene scrambled to find accommodations for her family, going every morning to the army housing office to try to claim a room somewhere. Didion remembered seeing her mother cry for the first time one day outside the housing office. "Meanwhile, we were living in a hotel with a shared bathroom," Didion recalled. "It was in sort of a nice part of town. I don't think it was a bad hotel, but it was a period in American life when hotel rooms didn't necessarily come with bathrooms. So my mother, I remember her emptying an entire bottle of pine-scented disinfectant into the bathtub every time she gave us a bath." Eventually, the Didions found a single room to rent in a nearby guesthouse. "It's an adventure," Eduene told her daughter, trying to be cheerful. "It's wartime, it's history, you children will be thankful you got to see all this."

Soon, Frank was transferred to North Carolina to sort through army records at Duke University. He traveled ahead. Eduene followed sometime later with the children. They took a train to Union Station in Los Angeles and from there caught the Southern Pacific's Sunset Limited, stopping once in New Orleans, spending a night at the St. Charles Hotel, a much finer establishment than they had known in Tacoma. The train was jammed with military personnel. Often Eduene and the kids were forced to stand in the couplings between cars, inhaling smoke and the smell of grease. One day, while the train was stopped on its way through the Southwest, a young sailor got off, bought a bottle of Coke for Eduene and a Navajo bracelet for Didion. Eduene thanked him graciously. Even in wearying circumstances, she was determined to keep up a respectable appearance, wearing a plaid seersucker suit, spectator pumps, and sometimes, when she could get them—as in New Orleans—white gardenias in her hair. She dressed her daughter in cardigans and pleated skirts. Her usual "non-depressed" performance slipped into sternness on the road, stiffened by the effort not to be humiliated. As for Didion, in the midst of confusion, her love of drama got plenty of nutrition. Her mother was right: This *was* an adventure. The sailor said he had survived the downing of the USS *Wasp*.

In Durham, the Didions again lived in one room, this one in a house owned by a Baptist preacher and his family. In the evenings, Didion would sit on the house's wide wooden porch, listening to cicadas, sipping a Grapette or eating peach ice cream straight out of quart cartons with the preacher's hulking daughters, hoping to play with their *Gone With the Wind* paper dolls. They never let her.

In sweltering midafternoons, other children on the block slithered under back stoops to eat dirt rich with clay, using a piece of raw potato as a spoon. Eduene told Didion the kids did this because of a physical condition called pica. "Poor children do it," she said. The clay satisfied some craving untouched by their regular diet. "You never would have learned that in Sacramento," Eduene said with a doubtful sense of accomplishment.

Sometimes during this uprooted period, Didion attended local schools; other times she didn't (she skipped second grade altogether). Later, she would say she missed absorbing certain fundamental skills, such as subtraction, which she never mastered. She *did* learn, by rote, the poem "In Flanders Fields" for Armistice Day commemorations, wearing a stiff red poppy to class, pinned to her dress, but making little connection between the heroics of World War I, viewed on scratchy film strips in visual-aids rooms, and the military regulations her father endured on each new base he visited.

One day, near the end of the family's stay in North Carolina, Eduene noticed her baby boy, Jim, reaching for something through the bars of his playpen: a copperhead, making its way through the room, eventually leaving, possibly to cool itself in the shade of a back stoop where the neighborhood children cradled their raw potatoes.

At Peterson Field in Colorado Springs, Didion first saw war. Though the family found decent housing here—a four-room bungalow—and Didion's routine was steadier, with regular classes at Columbia School and a Brownie troop, the base was spartan, its movements paced to the grim precision of emergency measures. The field was still being developed; many of its landing strips were temporary, lanes of dust kicked up by razor winds in eye-piercing gusts. Tar-paper barracks lined the perimeter, along with a small Officers' Club. Inside the club, in the late afternoons, Didion would sit, mesmerized by a display of fake blue rain behind the bar. About the time the Didions arrived, the field was named after 1st Lt. Edward J. Peterson, who had crashed here when the left engine of his twin-engine F-4 failed. He had been pulled alive from the flaming wreckage but later died of his burns. Didion heard stories about him, hushed and incomplete and in passing, and probably thought of him each time a noisy B-24 Liberator landed, rattling the house's windows. She recalled writing a letter to her grandmother about the field's new name, and she remembered how "pilots kept spiraling down through the high thin Colorado air. The way you knew was that you heard the crash wagons." Hard work, sacrifice, and terror: the rhythm of conflict. Uncertainty ruled the days. Though the bungalow was nice enough, Eduene refused to unpack the family's belongings. What difference did it make? she wondered. "Orders" could arrive at any moment, sending them packing. What were these "orders"? Did someone knock at the door with them? Whatever they were, they kept life tense, and they flattened Didion's mother. In certain blue hours, Eduene roused herself. At base barbecues, she wore flowers in her hair. She made her daughter give a soldier apple-blossom soap as a going-away present the day he got transferred. She gave her daughter a copy of Emily Post's book of etiquette and taught her how to accept and decline formal invitations. She told her daughter that after the war the family would move to Paris, where Frank would study architecture at the Sorbonne.

At Peterson Field, Didion encountered John Wayne. It was in a Quonset hut, and it was midafternoon. Outside, the wind was hot, stirring the yellow columbine. The B-24s were rumbling. It was the summer of 1943. The movie was *War of the Wildcats*, and it was love at first sight. His gestures, his voice, his deference toward women, his slow stoicism . . . together, if all this didn't add up to "orders," it's what "orders" should have been. In an unsettled time, Wayne's firm presence was just what the world needed. He was more confident than the men she had known, but he had that familiar, easy pioneer spirit. When he told the girl in the movie he would buy her a house at the bend in the bright river, Didion knew right where she belonged.

2

In essays, memoirs, and interviews, Didion has always underplayed her family's itinerant period as a factor in her development as a writer, but we should not dismiss it so casually. A number of experiences, working with and against her memories of Sacramento, coincided then to seed her future style.

In Colorado Springs, the bungalow's garden backed up to a psychiatric hospital. Didion used to take her notebook to the hospital grounds to record snippets of anguished dialogue. Discussing her memories of these episodes in *Blue Nights,* she ended with a flourish stylistically pleasing, but frustrating in its refusal to examine the emotional impact of sneaking around listening to people in pain: "I did not at the time think this an unreasonable alternative to staying in Sacramento and going to school." This sentence, a neat rhetorical feint, was reminiscent of *The White Album,* written over thirty years earlier, when she elided her *own* psychiatric evaluation. In the title essay, she said her alienated condition did "not now seem . . . an inappropriate response to the summer of 1968."

The *Blue Nights* account reinforces the image of the lonely writer obsessed with loss first seen in "On Keeping a Notebook." Just as, in the essay, she distinguished her discontented self from the more reasonable, better-adjusted people around her—her mother, her daughter—she said in *Blue Nights* that her four-year-old brother "scouted the neighborhood, and made friends" in Colorado while she brooded alone over dark doings in a scary place and dreamed up stories. No doubt the frequent moves isolated her, made her an outsider, and deepened her natural reserve (a schoolmate told her she was "military trash"). But more profound changes were afoot.

For one thing, her little brother wasn't the only one meeting new people. On the grounds of the psychiatric hospital, Didion wasn't always alone. Several afternoons, the daughter of a resident doctor accompanied her on her eavesdropping missions. This girl also carried a notebook and captured talk through open windows. At the end of the day, the two spies would convene to see who had gotten the best bits. Writing, then, was a social activity, and Didion was competitive about it.

She never forgot she was the daughter of a woman who "gave teas," yet here she was among tar-paper shacks, dirt runways, training aircraft, trucks, and jeeps. Her mother wasn't wrong: She was seeing things she would never see in Sacramento, but much of the time she wasn't sure what she saw. *Just looking* was no longer good enough. The act of watching required backstory and judgment. Her descriptive powers were tested by alien objects, incidents, and details, but more than this, she was glimpsing a world of men. She was not tempted to become a tomboy, but she saw how Sacramento had cosseted her. It's no surprise that, in just a few years, she would be receptive to Ernest Hemingway. The appeal was not just his style but the subjects on which he turned it—many of them familiar to her now.

Through solitary doggedness, Didion began to fashion a literary purpose. Like Invisible Scarlet O'Neil, she was a reporter. Her methods were surreptitious. She was not trying to write war stories, but stories of people suffering inner torment.

Not "an unreasonable alternative," not "an inappropriate response": From the beginning, certainty was one of her strengths, no matter how often she denied it (looking back, she called it "false bravery"). A young woman who could write, early in her career, that "for some time now [she had] felt radically separated from most of the ideas that seem to interest other people" is a woman comfortable with her voice on the page, a writer already experienced and confident despite her protests of frailty, and a woman in no way interested in apologizing for her point of view.

This point of view firmed up in wartime as she followed her father around the country. Only by leaving Sacramento could she begin—consciously or not—to glean she was a Westerner with firm Western attitudes: a stance she would develop more aggressively as she grew older, became more aware, and pursued writing as a vocation. "As far as my sense of place, I idealized Sacramento during those years," she once said. "I was just yearning to get home."

This did not mean her literary fantasies rejected Manhattan; one of her favorite pastimes on the army bases was reading *Mademoiselle* and *Vogue*. One day, in Colorado Springs, "we were snowbound," Didion recalled, and she and her mother were looking through a magazine. "*Vogue* used to have a contest for college seniors [offering a trip to New York], and my mother . . . pointed it out to me as something I could win when I got old enough."

Despite her early portraits of writer as isolated, maladjusted child, her memory of her mother's encouragement shows how bookish the family really was; she had tacit permission to pursue the pleasures of her notebook. Several members of her mother's family wrote verse. With Eduene's editorial help, Didion's maternal grandfather, Herman Daniel Jerrett, published in 1915 with a small Sacramento press a slender volume entitled *California's El Dorado Yesterday and Today*, dedicated to "my dear mother who crossed the plains with her parents and relatives in their own train of fifteen wagons, leaving their old home." In 1963, the year Didion published her first novel, he released *Hills of Gold*, again with a small press in Sacramento, tackling, he said, "historical questions of a controversial character."

In *Where I Was From*, Didion referred to her grandfather as an "innocent" from the mountains, but she adored him. He was much on her mind during her childhood exile from Sacramento. The importance of his literary activity lay not just in modeling for her the possibility of being a writer but also in teaching her to reject certain delusions. Inadvertently, he cast doubts on the family legacy. For example, in *California's El Dorado Yesterday and*

Today, he called California's crops sources of "enthusiasm and pride" for the state, and irrigation a "necessity for the production of fruits." He wrote this as a major California landowner whose fields depended on irrigation, while managing the Loon Lake Water and Power Company, which set irrigation policies. Many years passed before Didion could see past the surface of her grandfather's text to his self-interest. This process of rereading and rethinking what she thought she knew would eventually help her write *Where I Was From.* The habit of questioning, of comparing what she knew with fresh experiences and alternative viewpoints, began to take root on the road from Washington to North Carolina to Colorado.

If the world went dark for Didion during Sacramento's blackouts just days after her seventh birthday, darkness seemed to assume a personal shape and intent while she was eight years old and living in Colorado. One day, during a fire drill at the Columbia School, her right temple began to ache and she experienced the sensation that something had been "taken out of the middle" of her vision. She had lost something "mentally" as well. It was not just a headache. It "brutalize[d] me," she said. The school called her mother, who took her home. Didion lay listless in bed. Her conversation drifted. After a while, Eduene took her to the infirmary at Peterson Field, where an Air Corps doctor prescribed an enema, useless in relieving the pain.

Maybe her mother was right after all. Maybe she *did* need the quiet of darkened rooms and the fussing of Sunday aunts.

Didion learned that her grandmother, her mother, and her father had all suffered from migraines most of their lives—"those sick headaches my family brought west with the seeds." She had inherited the malady. It worsened during her adolescence and young adulthood, and though she would eventually learn to live with the recurring pain, she would never be entirely free of it. As recently as 2011, she would tell a filmmaker, interviewing her for a documentary, "I have [a migraine] right now. I have to fight for certain words. I can see you, but if you were to hold up a sign . . . I couldn't read the sign, probably."

"It seemed to me that my life was totally unmanageable because it could be taken over at any time by a headache," she said. This helplessness, compounded by not knowing when the next set of "orders" would upend the family's life again, disconcerted Didion, but it may have fed her self-image as a perversely "special" child whose main solace was writing. Nothing could motivate a person to become a "lonely rearranger" of things as much as sudden visitations of pain.

3

"My sense was that we lived in the only possible place where we could be, that we paid this immense price to be there. That sense was part of who I was," Didion said. Before Washington, North Carolina, and Colorado, she did not question the "immense price" paid by her ancestors in their arduous continental crossings. California was the "only possible place" for her family because her family had fought so hard to secure land there. But after seeing a bit of the continent, after returning to Sacramento, only to have fallen behind in school, the "dumb girl" in class, ostracized by social circles formed while she was gone, she began to perceive *she* was the one paying an "immense price to be there." Her ancestry was a burden and a trap. What had happened to her mother's promise of Paris? Eduene said her husband felt the family had an obligation to return to California.

Didion *was* happy to scan the flat horizons again (claustrophobic, all those mountains and trees!), happy to run through the tule fog in the winter and feel the summer heat. It made her strangely content when it rained so hard that the Natomas, the low-lying highway out to the airport, flooded. The land seemed to float. "There was a certain way that possibilities would seem to open up when the sun went down on really hot days," she recalled years later.

It was near the end of 1943 when Eduene and the kids returned to Sacramento. Frank went on to Detroit to settle more defense contracts. "I think Mother just couldn't face looking for another room in Detroit," Didion said. Eduene's mother and father took them in, in the house on Highland Avenue, while Frank served out the war. Didion attended the Arden School. "When the school was first built, it was in the middle of nowhere," Kel Munger, a reporter for the *Sacramento News and Review*, told me. "It was mostly for the ranch and farm children—the *white* children. Of course, the kids of the people who actually worked the land were Mexican. The city didn't integrate the schools until Didion was much older." Already, in 1943, the "middle of nowhere" was showing signs of becoming suburbia: a development the Didions hated.

Didion connected with none of her teachers. The "idea that I was smarter than other people" was "very rapidly punctured," Didion said. She felt she "didn't get socialised" because of the family moves. She withdrew at school. She couldn't be cheered at home. She had little in common with her brother, who loved to chase his bouncy boxer dog through streets and fields, and had a chipper disposition.

She took to missing the bus after school and walking home so she could pass a commercial greenhouse. The silence, the closed-in heat, the way the sloped glass panes focused diffuse sunlight appealed to her. She'd offer a nickel to buy a pansy, hoping the greenhouse keeper would let her spend the rest of the day there. He told her a nickel wouldn't cut it. She was "using up the air."

Often, migraines sent her to bed. On weekend outings, she'd cry and say she was afraid of the ski lift. She was afraid of rivers and sinkholes, afraid of snakes, afraid of the violence in comic books. The bridge over the Sacramento River? It was going to come crashing down someday. She exasperated her mother. Eduene couldn't promise her she would always be safe. What did promises mean to a woman who felt that nothing mattered? Eduene would sit across the table from her daughter in the kitchen, playing double solitaire. Shouldn't a mother teach her little girl to iron? To scramble an egg? "If you never learn how, you'll simply never have to," Eduene explained with a shrug, tossing another card onto the discard pile.

"It was mystifying to my mother why I was so despondent," Didion said. In an early essay, "On Going Home," she wrote, "We did not fight. Nothing was wrong. And yet some nameless anxiety colored the emotional charges between me and the place I came from." With Eduene, also despondent, often distant, she began "a guerilla war we never understood."

From Detroit, Frank brought Didion three silk twill handkerchiefs purchased at the J. L. Hudson Company. A saleswoman there had told him all the fashionable young girls these days wore them around their necks: orange, brown, and emerald green. Frank had never bought his daughter a gift—not without his wife's prodding. Didion was overwhelmed by the beauty of the silk, and even more awed by the fact that her father considered her a young lady. She sat with him for lunch: cracked crab and iced tea in a silver pitcher. A proper grown-up now, she reached for the pitcher to fill her glass and dropped the heavy thing, splashing tea all over the table. It was the mistake of a child, not the act of a young girl deserving gorgeous silk handkerchiefs. She ran to her room and locked the door.

4

The world war had been good to Sacramento. Though the Didions complained about the cosmetic and social changes spurred by war-related development, they prospered from it. McClellan Field had become enormously important to the war effort and helped establish the Sacramento Valley as a future center of weapons research and industry. Following Pearl Harbor, most of the B-25s and other U.S. Army Air Corps planes sent to the Pacific theater were prepared at McClellan. In just a few years, Aerojet-General would build a facility in nearby Rancho Cordova. Founded by Caltech scientists, Aerojet began manufacturing jet-assisted takeoff rockets in 1941, giving extra boosts to airplanes operating from aircraft carriers. The company's arrival in Rancho Cordova, and its need for worker housing, would be a boon to the Didion clan, which owned several hundred acres in the area.

Housing revitalized downtown as well. A resolution adopted by the Sacramento City Council on June 26, 1942, indicates that J. Frank Didion, Joan's grandfather, "Tax Collector of the County of Sacramento," conveyed to the county a large tract of land between A Street and the American River, profiting handsomely.

Buoyed by the defense industry, many of the Okie families in the Central Valley left the migrant camps, renting and even buying small houses in growing communities and towns. Okie kids jammed the hallways of Arden School. Didion picked up their characteristic drawl, the slightly nasal register, the flattening of vowels, and the tendency to stretch one-syllable words into two. As late as the 1970s, in a television interview with Tom Brokaw, Didion's accent sounds unmistakably "Okie" to an Oklahoman. As she grew older, her voice lost that Great Plains edge, though not the habit of trailing off, as if she were speaking into the wind. Whether this was another Dust Bowl influence, her natural reticence, or a combination of the two, it's hard to say. But it stood in contrast to her confident handwriting, which settled into its lifelong gait around this time, the phrases pressed hard into the page like inscriptions in stone, straight lines with leafy *g*'s and *t*'s crossed backward, tempting the reader to turn and start each sentence again.

At school dances, the music had a rough twang now, a beat like the thumping of an old flat tire, a lilt of gospel, a gumbo of folk and blues. Okie tunes: country, swing, a little black holler church, and proto-rock pierced by Scots-Irish despair. Above the exhilarating tempos, emptiness threaded through the melodies. It was minor-key moroseness tricked up as sexual urgency, and in the coming decade, Didion would track its spread through American culture.

In the Elks Clubs and town halls of the valley, safer Midwest music—square dance reels—played most Friday and Saturday nights. At dances, parades, sports events, at the state fair in the summers (fireworks sizzling above the worn old levees), Didion renewed old friendships and made new bonds.

She reconnected with her cousin Brenda. She caught up in school. Perhaps her knowledge now of what lay beyond the flat horizon prompted her to take greater interest in global events. The Spanish Civil War. Hitler's march into Poland. The founding of Israel. A massacre in a country called El Salvador. FDR's New Deal was a fraught topic at her aunts' supper tables. It was socialism, they said, stunting the West's pioneer spirit. Republican business leaders in town, including the Didion men, took up the Christian libertarianism of the California preacher James W. Fifield. Fifield claimed that the "blessings of capitalism come from God."

His sacred entrepreneurship inspired Didion's great-uncles when they opened a service station at Seventh and H, guided her uncle Robert when he established Didion Hardware on D Street, led Genevieve Didion when she planted camellias for tourists by the courthouse. These were fine examples of living up to "our heritage," Didion said in her eighth-grade graduation speech at Arden School, delivered to a room full of Okies in June 1948. The speech had been developed with the help of her mother and grandfather, using themes straight out of the latter's book *California's El Dorado Yesterday and Today* ("We had an irrigation problem, so we built the greatest dams the world has known," Didion wrote). Her mother helped her choose the perfect outfit for her performance, a crystal necklace and a pale green organdy dress, "a color that existed in the local landscape only for a few spring days when the rice first showed," she said.

The speech impressed her teachers. "There's a lot of mystery to me about writing and performing and showing off in general," she said later. Her confidence had been boosted by the fineries she wore (from then on, she never underestimated the power of fashion and style in presenting herself, publicly, as a writer), and by the conviction that her audience—most of them first-generation Californians, whose parents had been living in sod huts on the Great Plains just a few years ago—sorely needed the lessons she offered. How often had the Sunday aunts started a conversation by saying, "The trouble with these *new* people"? Then they'd blast the Dust Bowl natives who had come to California seeking handouts. Pioneer families like the Didions understood real work and taking pride in their work. They understood what it meant to "live up" to one's heritage.

The summer following her graduation speech, before classes began at California Junior High, Didion lived with her family on Walnut Avenue, on land apparently purchased by her father for subdividing and selling. It was "a downright rural region in the 1940s," William Burg told me. "Sheep ranches and rolling hills: the housing stock there now is a mixture of mid-century single-family homes and mansions with horse property. The first shopping malls in the Sacramento area were built a bit north of this neighborhood." Most of the land was divvied up from large old family ranches, Rancho Del Paso and others.

Didion recalled watching her brother on hot summer mornings take a shovel to the hardpan with the intention of digging a swimming pool on the property: a child's version of development fever (as an adult, Jim would follow his father into the real-estate business). Even utopia could not escape the postwar boom. In newspaper photographs, Didion said, Hawaii was now a place of "well-fed Lincoln-Mercury dealers relaxing beside an outrigger at the Royal Hawaiian Hotel."

One summer night, while the family was vacationing at Stinson Beach (where Didion, wearing a frayed bathing suit puckered with safety pins, would take a sack of nectarines to a nest of rocks above the surf and play solitaire), Didion told her parents she was going to take her little brother to a square dance. Her folks were playing cards with friends in their rented cottage and paid scant attention to what she said. She dropped Jimmy off at the dance at the Greyhound station—an old railroad depot with stucco walls and a steep slate roof—then hurried past the Two A.M. Club and Café, beyond faded signs for Coca-Cola lost among wild geraniums, and down to the water's edge. She had been writing stories about romantic suicides, people wandering San Francisco's streets before leaping off the Golden Gate Bridge or people walking into the sea. She "wanted to know what it would feel like" to head into "the big nasty surf," so, clutching her notebook, she put her head down and aimed herself in the general direction of Hawaii. "It was dark," she said. "I walked into the ocean thinking I'll get an idea of it by the time my knees are wet." A huge wave picked her up and rolled her onto the sand. "I got out. I picked up my brother and went home." It didn't come to anything. She wasn't serious about suicide. It was a literary experiment. She *was* serious about trying to grasp why a woman like her mother, with money and good looks, surrounded by family and friends, should "have so much trouble getting through the afternoon"—this sentiment appears in an early short story, "The Welfare Island Ferry." The story paints a melancholy portrait of a "small woman in a bright dirndl skirt and high-heeled straw mules." As the day wears on and the temperature approaches one hundred degrees, she wonders why on earth she should give a damn about the men's golf scores at the country club or about her husband and children or about anything at all. "[B]aby," she asks her daughter, "you ever afraid of the dark any more?"

5

"I would have to say the rivers are my strongest memory of what the city was to me. They were just infinitely interesting . . . I mean, all of that moving water. I was crazy about the rivers," Didion told Rob Turner, editor of *Sactown* magazine, in 2011.

In the way of adolescents, whose development requires testing limits, Didion shed many of her childhood fears during her junior high and high school years and enjoyed skirting danger. In the winters, flooding fascinated as much as terrified her now: the distant sound of dynamite on the levees, sheets of muddy water cresting thorny banks, hordes of ranchers and their children migrating through city streets to take shelter in school gymnasiums. In the summers, she joined friends in challenging the rivers for the thrills they'd release. In an essay entitled "Holy Water," she wrote about being seventeen years old and getting "caught, in a military-surplus life raft, in the construction of the Nimbus Afterbay Dam on the American River . . . I remember that at the moment it happened I was trying to open a tin of anchovies with capers. I recall the raft spinning into the narrow chute through which the river had been temporarily diverted. I recall being deliriously happy."

"The generation she was close to as a teenager, people who could describe Didion's personality then, mostly died in the 1980s," Kel Munger told me. "There *are* still a few Didions in town, but they don't like to be tracked down."

This was not entirely true, but the family members who responded to me were too young to have anything other than hazy recollections of their cousin.

Joan Haug-West remembered her classmate Joan. Haug-West remained in Sacramento and became a college English teacher, often assigning Didion's essays to her students.

"She was in a higher social class than I was—though most of us were more aware of race than class," Haug-West told me. "I knew a relative of hers sat on the Board of Education, and you didn't get a position like that unless you had money and influence. And she was friendly with Nancy Kennedy. I once heard Nancy talk about how her brother—it may have been Anthony—tried to stick a Coke bottle down the garbage disposal. Well, you know, very few people in town even *had* a garbage disposal back then."

Didion was a frequent supper guest at the Kennedy house. There, she sat among lawyers, lobbyists (one of whom, Artie Samish, later went to jail for tax evasion), and oil company executives. Kennedy's parents loved to quote Dickens and Shakespeare in the midst of casual conversations. "We had a very vibrant, active household," Anthony Kennedy once said. "My mother always had to set . . . extra places at the dinner table because people would come from out of the city, from out of the state to see [my father] and consult him. He was a great attorney."

When she wasn't greeting CEOs or hurtling down rapids, Didion attended meetings of the Mañana Club—the "rich girls' sorority," Haug-West called it. It was sponsored by the public school district. According to its bylaws, its aim was to promote democracy, charity, and literature—specifically, the reading of poetry. Nevertheless, a legal opinion written in the mid-1960s by a California appellate court stated that the Mañana Club practiced a "process of selection designed to create a membership composed of the 'socially elite.'"

To be admitted, girls had to be sponsored by three members; they had to have reached the ninth grade and to have maintained a C average during the previous semester, and they had to have read at least two books not prescribed as compulsory by the school system. Once a candidate had been proposed for membership and survived a "Rush Tea," the club's Admission Committee would "investigate all girls, and then select however many the officers have decided should be brought in."

Didion recalled her initiation in the Governor's Mansion one night. She was friends with Nina Warren, daughter of Governor Earl Warren. Nina, dubbed "Honey Bear" by the national press corps, was a year ahead of Didion in school. Didion loved visiting her because the house was full of large, high-ceilinged rooms in which "one [could] imagine reading . . . or writing a book, or closing the door and crying until dinner," Didion said. The initiation rite consisted of being blindfolded in Nina's bedroom and subjected to insults by the club's older members. Didion was shocked when Nina—"by my fourteen-year-old lights the most glamorous and unapproachable fifteen-year-old in America," Didion wrote—said Didion was "stuck on herself."

As a new member, she received a gold pin in the form of an *M*, with Mañana spelled out on the front in blue enamel letters. She was to wear it or keep it in her possession at all times. To others, outside the club, this may have fortified the impression that she was "stuck on herself." To Joan Haug-West, Didion seemed unnaturally shy. "I rarely heard her voice in school," she said.

Today, C. K. McClatchy Senior High School, in a posh area of the city known as Land Park, seems an oasis of seriousness and calm just off a busy boulevard, its tall windows reflecting rows of Italian cypress trees flanking its walls, its red tiled roof sloping low over Art Deco and California Mission detailing in the building's tan stone and dark brown woodwork. McClatchy marked "a very tedious time in my life," Didion said. How could she not want to heave whenever she walked across the plaque in the front entrance (passing two ridiculous stone lions on either side of the steps), proclaiming McClatchy's devotion to "Truth-Liberty-Tolerance" and its loyalty to the "Native Sons of the Golden West"? How frequently could she repeat, in class, the products of our Latin American neighbors? Must she recite, once more, Euripides: "I tell myself that we are a long time underground and that life is short, but sweet"? Did she have to hear, again, a local band butcher "How High the Moon" at some damp, dreary dance, and then walk home alone in the fog?

Worst of all was phys ed ("Sex Class"). There, she had to listen to the Nice Girls insist it was wrong to kiss boys "indiscriminately" because that was "throwing away your capital." Given the boys she met at McClatchy, Didion didn't think it was *possible* to kiss "discriminately." If you were "indiscriminate enough to kiss any one of them you might as well kiss them all," she decided.

Often, in her room, she lay in the dark with a cold washcloth over her eyes. The discomfort of her periods heightened the throbbing migraines. In public, she'd try to deny the pain. She'd sit in a classroom with tears on her face. The "pain seemed a shameful secret," she wrote, "evidence . . . of all my bad attitudes, my unpleasant tempers."

She still loved stage acting but was offered little range in local productions because she was so tiny. At school, and at a small repertory theater downtown, she took children's roles—including that of Babette in Lillian Hellman's wartime melodrama, *Watch on the Rhine*. At one point in the play, a character says, in Babette's hearing, "The Renaissance Man is a man who wants to know . . . what made Iago evil?" Didion remembered this reference to Iago and would use it, many years later, to open her second novel, *Play It As It Lays*.

Eugene O'Neill was a favorite. "I was struck by the sheer theatricality of his plays. You could see how they worked," she said. "I read them all one summer. I had nosebleeds, and for some reason it took all summer to get the appointment to get my nose cauterized. So I just lay still on the porch all day and read Eugene O'Neill. That was all I did. And dab at my face with an ice cube."

She memorized speeches from *The Member of the Wedding* and *Death of a Salesman*. She tackled *Moby-Dick* but "missed that wild control of language. What I had thought were discursive [passages] were really these great leaps. The book had just seemed a jumble; I didn't get the control in it." On the other hand, Theodore Dreiser's *An American Tragedy* knocked her out. She locked herself in her room one weekend and read it to the end. She was amazed to learn that a story's accumulating power did not always grow from a spectacular style. *Suspense* was a necessity. And Henry James's sentences, so intricate and complex, nearly paralyzed her. "[He] made me afraid to put words down," she said. One of the "discouraging things is that every word you put down limits the possibilities of what you have in your mind. [James] somehow got all of the possibilities into every sentence"—those multiple qualifications!—"and I really did not think I could do that."

From James, Didion learned how the mind decodes existence, sifting possibilities, balancing what it fears with paradoxical recognitions of pleasure. For a young reader, this was a new revelation of what fiction could do. No other form of human thought could touch it.

Her fears now had less to do with collapsed bridges than with changes in her body and awareness that others responded to those changes. She became obsessed with news stories about Suzanne Degnan, a six-year-old on the North Side of Chicago who had been kidnapped from her bed by a college boy, hacked up in a sink, and scattered into the city's sewer system. The gory details recalled aspects of the Donner Party stories, but there was nothing natural about this tragedy. Though the victim was only six, the crime seemed to have something to do with sex, with female and male and the unpredictability of that mix.

Didion's notebook jottings—the ocean walkers, the romantic suicides—were doom-laden and dark, her imagination drawn to extremes that *needn't have been* but *were*, toward mysteries of human impulses at their starkest. The sea strolls and kidnap stories had pioneer elements, traces of the outsider, the wayward and the lost, the emptiness and promise of back roads and branching trails, but the choices weren't as clear (*take this cutoff or don't?*) and the consequences less obvious than cannibalism (*hacked up and scattered into the sewer system?*). Self-invention, yes, manifest destiny—but reckless now. Mean. No sacrifice, no courage, no glory. The most celebrated of Didion's early essays mimed epic struggles reduced to splintered glimpses of *modern* American tragedies.

And, in part, her evolving imagination had to do with the adolescent's penchant for thrills. Donner Pass had become a popular spot for juicing and joyriding. At fifteen and a half, Didion earned her learner's permit, attacking the roads in an old Army jeep her father had gotten at auction. On weekends, she'd drive friends up switchbacks in the Sierra, from Sacramento to Lake Tahoe and back again, six or seven hours, buzzed by alcohol and flirting, risking wrecks or DUIs. On some nights, the fog was so thick, she could see the road only if one of her friends got out and walked in front of the headlights along the highway's white center stripe. She was experiencing a new sort of narrative: the aimless American road story.

On simmering afternoons, she drove to the family cemetery and sat undisturbed, listening to country music on the radio, staring at the chipped monuments and dreaming up sad new stories. The boneyard was more companionable than the dusty house sickly sweet with dying flowers, her father's legal papers scattered on tables, countertops, chairs.

At some point during this period, the family moved into a new residence at 500 Hawthorn Road, near the present Fair Oaks Boulevard, a secluded three-bedroom house built in 1935. Didion also spent many days in her step-grandmother's splendid neoclassical home at 2000 22nd Street—"a great house" with "proportions . . . a little different" for Sacramento, she said. That is, it was extremely large and slightly off-kilter, with pedimented dormers and balustrades. Didion discovered new hangouts. The Guild Theater in Oak Park. Vic's Ice Cream. The Crest (formerly the crumbling old vaudeville house the Hippodrome). The Woolworth on K Street, where teens gathered for food and sodas. The nation's first Tower Records. The first Shakey's Pizza. Boys took Good Girls—those who would "do it"—to the Starlite Drive-In. The

Nice Girls went to the Senator Theater downtown. Didion loved the smell of paint in her uncle Bob's hardware store, the Duncan yo-yos and palm-size flashlights he sold to little kids. In the rear, Rosie Clooney warbled "This Old House" on a big old radio. Occasionally, Didion and her friends sneaked over to the West Side and ate spicy tacos with their fingers.

She loved gas stations. There was the grand old Shell at Seventh and L, the men in white uniforms and bow ties; the O'Neil Brothers' five locations in town, offering "crankcase service" and "vulcanizing." Okie boys, Arkies, slouched around the hot, oily lots wearing T-shirts and greasy jeans, smoking, talking cars. Scary, intriguing—the kinds of boys Bill Clinton would remind her of years later. "They had knocked up girls and married them," Didion wrote, driving all night to Carson City for a five-dollar ceremony "performed by a justice of the peace still in his pajamas. They got jobs at the places that had laid off their uncles."

In the evenings, she liked to sit in the grass out by the Garden Highway (this area would become a primary setting for *Run River*), watching the sun set over waterfront ranches. Already, she knew the ranches were about to disappear, their lots subdivided and sold.

6

"In a gentle sleep Sacramento dreamed, until perhaps 1950, when something happened," a young Didion wrote at the height of her place-bound romanticism. "What happened was that Sacramento woke to the fact that the outside world was moving in, fast and hard. At the moment of its waking Sacramento lost, for better or worse, its character."

"That's a false portrayal of the city," Rob Turner told me. Mel Lawson, a longtime Sacramento High School teacher who knew Didion as a girl, agreed. "I don't see any loss of character, only change," he said. Before World War II, "this was essentially a town of shopkeepers, retired farmers, state workers, salesmen, operators of small plants like dairies, sheet-metal works, lumber yards and such. No big industries." What Didion meant by loss of character, he thought, was the erosion of the city's old power structure. In the old days, "it was fairly easy to pinpoint who was in it," he said. "One with any degree of perception had to be in Sacramento only a short time to know pretty well who ran the place," including "Joan's Aunt Genevieve [*sic*]."

At McClatchy High School, despite her shyness, Didion didn't always need a hall pass to get where she wanted to go. If she wasn't the most popular girl in school, she was the kind of girl the most popular girls in school wanted to hang with. She was pretty and smart, with a pageboy haircut and high-collared blouses; her writing skills and ambitions were already apparent. People felt better about themselves around Joan Didion. She was funny. Quick.

Looking back, she liked to say she didn't do well in high school. She was frail, she'd say. Always frail. Isolated and uninvolved. Several times a month, her migraines *were* debilitating. She had her family's tendency toward silence. Constantly, she questioned herself. But in yearbook pictures, she beams, appearing robust, her face full, almost chubby.

She was a member of the Rally Committee (by no means the smallest on the team, male *or* female), and wore a bulky white sweater with a big Mc-Clatchy *M* on the front. She served on the Sophomore Ball and Junior Prom committees. She was a Student Council member. She joined the Science, Press, and Spanish clubs. She worked on the yearbook, *The Nugget,* and the school newspaper, *The Prospector.*

She got an after-school job with the society desk at *The Sacramento Union,* for which, she was thrilled to learn, Mark Twain had once written. "I wouldn't call [it] reporting," she said of her first professional stints. "People wanted reports of their upcoming weddings in the paper the weekend of the wedding. And so they would send you accounts of what the bridesmaids were going to wear and stuff like that, and you would write it up." On her own, Didion was learning it was possible to write about California in a nonboosterish way, as Josiah Royce had in *The Feud of Oakfield Creek,* a novel based on the Sacramento squatter's strike of 1850, and as Frank Norris had in *The Octopus.*

It's hard to imagine what she might have sent *The Nation* (apparently, the manuscript has been lost), but she did submit a piece and received a prompt rejection. Already she felt the tension between making a name for herself at home and succeeding in the bigger world. In later years, she enjoyed recounting an anecdote involving one of her great-aunts and her mother. "We were talking about some people that we knew, the Johnston family," Didion said. "And my great-aunt said, 'That Johnston boy never did amount to anything.' And my mother said, 'He won a Pulitzer Prize.' It was Alva Johnston, who won a Pulitzer Prize when he was working for a newspaper in New York. And my great-aunt did not even look up. She was playing solitaire, and without even looking up from her game, she said, 'He never amounted to anything in Sacramento.'"

7

On April 25, 1952, she arrived home from school and found a letter waiting for her. She dropped her sweater and books on the hallway floor. The letter said:

> Dear Joan,
>
> The Committee on Admissions asks me to inform you that it is unable to take favorable action upon your application for admission to Stanford University. While you have met the minimum requirements, we regret that because of the severity of the competition, the committee cannot include you in the group to be admitted. The committee joins me in extending you every good wish for the successful continuation of your education.
>
> Sincerely yours,
> Rixford K. Snyder,
> Director of Admissions

Didion reread the letter, trying to will a revision of it. Then she ran upstairs to her room, locked the door, and wept into an old robe on the floor of her closet. All of her friends who had applied to Stanford had been admitted. She had a "sharp and dolorous image of . . . growing old" in the house, she wrote later, "never going to school anywhere, the spinster in *Washington Square*." She went into the bathroom, sat on the edge of the tub, and briefly considered swallowing several old codeine and Empirin tablets from the medicine cabinet. She pictured herself gasping in an oxygen tent while a sorrowful Rixford K. Snyder hovered over her in the ICU.

Perhaps the worst humiliation was knowing that the question of getting into the "right" school, "so traditionally urgent to the upwardly mobile," had never come up in conversations with her family. There was no stronger indication that, for all its history and influence in old Sacramento, the Didion family's "social situation was static" now. Later that evening, when she told her father her disappointing news, he simply offered her a drink.

PART TWO

Chapter Four

1

In 1953, Frank Didion was referred to Letterman General Hospital at the Presidio in San Francisco for study, tests, and treatment following what his daughter discreetly called "manifestations of . . . tension." These manifestations included emotional withdrawal, heavy drinking (mostly bourbon highballs), and long silences. He littered the house with blueprints of shopping malls he would never build. He exhibited intense xenophobia, insisting the name Didion was not French, despite his family's origins in Alsace-Lorraine; the French were untrustworthy. His daughter remembered him staying at the hospital for "some weeks or months." (The year before, an executive order had given the Veterans Administration the "responsibility for hospitalization for those members or former members of the uniformed services"—like Frank Didion—"who had chronic diseases.")

The hospital changed its spots frequently as military culture evolved. Initially, it developed from rows of tents erected to treat sick and wounded soldiers returning from the Spanish-American War in 1898. Just after the turn of the century, a three-hundred-bed facility was completed, and by 1918, Letterman was the army's largest general hospital. Its medical staff pioneered the use of several orthopedic devices (including the "Letterman Leg"), physical therapy treatments, and—fortunately for Frank Didion—experiments in a field only then being recognized by the military, psychiatry. At the time, according to the army's Office of Medical History, the "modern concept of personality development was not widely known or accepted." The military had only vaguely identified trauma as a legitimate medical condition, such as "alienation" or "nostalgia," a "species of melancholy, or a mild type of insanity, caused by disappointment, and a continuous longing for the home."

On weekends, Eduene would leave Sacramento, pick up her daughter at the Tri Delt house in Berkeley, where she was attending the University of California, and visit Frank at the hospital. They'd go to lunch. He'd only eat oysters. At area parks, he loved to watch pickup baseball games, and he liked to walk from Golden Gate Park back to the Presidio in the evenings. Didion recalled strolling with him, once, across the Golden Gate Bridge (and worrying later that a depressed person should not be allowed to walk alone across a precarious and foggy path). On Sunday nights, the ladies left Frank in the hands of the "mind guys"—his name for his doctors.

The "mind guys," many of whom were occupational therapists, untrained in psychiatry, had at their disposal a hydrotherapy plant in one of the building's basements. When made available to neuropsychiatric patients in a "scientific manner," it produced "most satisfactory results," according to a Surgeon General's report. The acronym ADL—activities of daily living—became familiar to the patients, the idea being that patients needed to be as independent as possible in their personal routines. "Reality Testing Situations" (work assignments, social planning, ordering bread from the Alcatraz bakery) were encouraged. Generally, psychiatric patients were given what the hospital termed a "Total Push Program," consisting of strenuous physical activity, recreation, and work. They were accompanied at all times by a physician. Talk sessions with psychiatrists were rare, as there was a shortage of trained doctors (most carried caseloads of thirty or more). Frank *did* later tell his daughter a particular "woman doctor" had been very helpful to him, prompting him to discuss the loss of his mother.

Probably he failed to quit bourbon highballs during his hospital stay, as each Friday afternoon the Letterman Officers' Club opened its doors to doctors and patients for a happy hour. There, among old adobe walls, waves of wounded GIs from Korea rolled toward the bar, some on gurneys. At sundown, flags were lowered, trumpets blared, and cannon were fired.

Frank was not restricted to neuropsych. He could leave the S-1 Ward any time he wished, wander uphill from Crissy Field to the main gate, and catch a trolley or the Muni no. 45 into San Francisco, though he did not much care for the city. The hillsides were canopied with orange California poppies and eucalyptus trees swaying in cool ocean breezes, lizards and salamanders scurrying among ice plants. These long walks, away from family, away from the amputees and the tuberculosis and malaria sufferers in the wards, may have done as much as anything to ease his "tension."

Years later, his daughter's writing would teach readers to seize the odd detail. Here's an odd detail about the Letterman General Hospital: James Alexander Hamilton, a graduate of Berkeley and of Stanford's medical school, received his training there; a former chief of the assessment services of the OSS, the forerunner to the Central Intelligence Agency, Hamilton would one day establish a drug-testing laboratory at the California Medical Facility at Vacaville, a male-only state prison. Briefly, Letterman housed Dr. James E. Ketchum, who would go from San Francisco to the Edgewood Arsenal's Medical Research Laboratories in Maryland, where, as chief of the Psychopharmacolgy Branch, he was "given pretty much a free hand," he said—along with a large congressional budget—to pursue mind-control experiments on human subjects using LSD, THC, and a long-acting atropine compound called BZ.

That Letterman General Hospital engaged in questionable medical experiments is certain; in 1955, a Letterman official wrote to Walter Reed Hospital, asking about the protocols for obtaining "permission" from patients on whom certain "test doses" were to be tried. This letter surfaced in the early 1990s during the Congressional Advisory Committee on Human Radiation Experiments hearings, which acknowledged that the "Army and the CIA had conducted LSD experiments on unwitting subjects" in the 1950s and 1960s. It's unlikely that Frank Didion had anything to do with such experiments, but he was among the population from whom the "unwitting subjects" were drawn: a military man, willing to serve; sick, accepting of treatments; a veteran, for whom financial compensation to the family could be dispatched with no questions should anything misfire.

To mention these odd details in connection with Frank Didion's treatment for depression at Letterman General Hospital in 1953 is to risk losing hold of our narrative. Yet in little more than a decade after her father's convalescence in San Francisco, Didion would be intrigued by the fact that San Francisco seemed to be the epicenter of LSD's spread across the United States; intrigued enough to mention in one of her best-known early essays, "In Bed," that Sandoz Pharmaceuticals first synthesized LSD-25 in its search for a cure for migraines, from which she still suffered once or twice a week; intrigued enough to travel to San Francisco's Haight-Ashbury neighborhood to witness a group LSD trip; intrigued enough to note that the press blamed what *Time* magazine called the "counterculture" for the lysergic craze, while it was in medical facilities and government labs that two of the counterculture's emerging leaders, Ken Kesey and Allen Ginsberg, first took the drug.

In fact, losing hold of the narrative, in a California whose true nature seemed increasingly clandestine and nefarious, was how Didion would make her name as a reporter. Writing about Patty Hearst, she would say that in contemporary America, wildly disparate events often carried the "*frisson* of one another, the invitation to compare and contrast."

So, for example, if Dr. James Alexander Hamilton, as described in a CIA memo dated May 29, 1963, was conducting research at Vacaville under "MK-ULTRA Subproject 140," and if MK-ULTRA Subproject 140 included funding to support a "new series of experiments on 100 prisoner-subjects," and if the CIA admitted to Congress that this research was "cover activity relating to independent work of Dr. Hamilton," were we not invited to compare and contrast this information with the fact that Donald DeFreeze, once an informer for the L.A. Police Department, was a prisoner-subject at Vacaville, that he would later christen himself "Cinque," found the Symbionese Liberation Army, and kidnap Patty Hearst? Were we not invited to note that the Symbionese Liberation Army never made any sense, politically or ideologically, even in a politically and ideologically unstable period, *except* in terms of the world of covert affairs, experimental drugs, domestic spying, mind-control studies, law enforcement's cozying up to organized crime, and espionage and counterespionage? Were we not invited to wonder about the fact that Congressman Leo Ryan of California, one of the CIA's staunchest critics, publicly identified Dr. James Alexander Hamilton as a CIA station agent in September 1978, and was murdered two months later in Guyana, near a former CIA training ground, by members of Jim Jones's Peoples Temple who had once offered themselves as hostages to the Symbionese Liberation Army in exchange for Patty Hearst, and who would subsequently die in a bizarre mass mind-control ritual? Were we not invited to marvel at the fact that not far from Haight-Ashbury, in the years just prior to the explosion of the LSD culture there, the CIA established a safe house under the supervision of a narcotics officer and former spy named George Hunter White, a safe house tricked up as a bordello? There, prostitutes brought unknowing customers drinks laced with LSD while White, sitting on a toilet, sipping martinis, observed the effects behind a two-way mirror. This "study" was known as Operation Midnight Climax.

Were we not invited to wonder what had happened to the narrative?

The degree to which the counterculture was just the culture, manipulated by people at the highest levels of what Dwight Eisenhower had called the "military-industrial complex," to test the limits of human behavior and its susceptibility to control; the degree to which the eventual waning of the love-and-peace movement occurred not because rebellion lost steam, but because the power structure moved on to other forms of weapons R&D and assaults on human will; the degree to which drugs, technology, and infrastructures first developed for military application and then flooded into a society unable to absorb them while grappling with the consequences of continuous wars—this is a history yet to be accurately rendered.

Meanwhile, in the 1960s, Joan Didion, native of a state whose "climate, habits, and modes of life," according to its Board of Health, were "well-calculated to break some link in reason's chain, and throw into confusion even the best balanced properties of mind," would begin to document cracks in the country's official narratives, cracks she had first noted upon leaving her sheltered world in Sacramento in 1953 and going off to college, a departure that seems to have precipitated her father's breakdown and his stay at Letterman General Hospital. In time, Didion would distinguish herself as one of the most incisive chroniclers of the sixties, a period whose legacy now appears to rest in its questioning of what does or does not constitute mental illness.

2

Between June 1952 and February 1953, after her rejection from Stanford and before her provisional acceptance to Berkeley, Didion, depressed, picked up a few classes at Sacramento Junior College and listlessly dated a boy whose only passion appeared to be golf. "[M]y aversion to outdoor games normally approaches the pathological," she once wrote, but she was drawn to this boy precisely because their differences allowed "dramatic possibilities" good for a spiky diversion.

She spent her evenings at drive-in movies. In the afternoons, she'd visit the family cemetery, sit in the car staring at chipped-wing angels, listening to country tunes and radio evangelists broadcasting from Tulsa. At the time, the most powerful Tulsa preacher, syndicated on five hundred AM stations nationwide, was Billy James Hargis. "All I want to do is preach Jesus and save America," he'd say. He saw his "Christian Crusade" as a weapon against "Communism and its godless ways." "Is the school house the proper place to teach raw sex?" he'd shout, and rant against public institutions poisoned by Reds whose plans to wreck America lay in eroding the country's morals. Among his supporters were the patriot-preacher Carl McIntire and Maj. Gen. Edwin Walker of the John Birch Society (Eduene Didion greatly admired the Birchers, she told her daughter). Allegedly, Lee Harvey Oswald would attempt to assassinate Walker in 1963, seven months before he was arrested for killing President Kennedy. When gaps appear in the narrative, conspiracy tales rush in to fill them.

In the summer of 1952, Billy James Hargis's sermons, rattling through the tinny speakers of Didion's car, presaged left- and right-wing violence, had she known. What she knew was that the shouting sounded like annexation debates in downtown Sacramento, one side arguing the city's responsibility for the poor, the other screaming, "Commies!" The dullness of the chatter paralyzed Didion so intensely, she simply watched one day as a rattlesnake slid among tombstones past her feet while she sat half in, half out of the car. Later she failed to warn anyone about the awful creature, violating her grandfather's code of the West.

Mark Schorer, Harvard educated, sophisticated in manner and dress, was the closest thing to an Easterner Didion had ever met, though in fact he was born in Wisconsin. A Midwesterner through and through—his finest achievement would be his biography of the Midwest American writer Sinclair Lewis—he seemed *credentialed* as an Easterner by virtue of his cultural knowledge and aesthetic refinement. By the time Didion took his classes at Berkeley in literature and creative writing, he was a literary star, having published a handful of short stories, many of them in *The New Yorker*, a study of William Blake, and a highly influential critical essay, "Technique as Discovery." Graduate students clamored to get into his writing seminars and undergraduates packed his classes on European and American literature.

Another Harvard alum, James D. Hart, best known now for his *Oxford Companion to American Literature*, taught Didion the American classics she hadn't already read on her own. In Henry Nash Smith's classes, she deepened her familiarity with Henry James. She recoiled from D. H. Lawrence, irritated by him "on almost every level," she said. "The writing was so clotted and sentimental" (she may have disliked him also because she failed to complete an assigned paper on him; each time she contemplated her Incomplete, she wanted to "heave," she confessed to a friend). Her classmates in English 106A were reading Céline, Beckett's *Waiting for Godot*, Bellow's *Augie March*. J. D. Salinger was all the rage. The boys in the class dismissed female writers on the grounds that they had no experience of war. Male novelists were granted a "social tradition" in which to operate, Didion discovered: "Hard drinkers, bad livers, wives, wars, big fish, Africa, Paris, no second acts." "A woman who wrote novels had no particular role," she said. "Women who wrote novels were quite often perceived as invalids, Carson McCullers, Jane Bowles, Flannery O'Connor, of course. I didn't much like it." On the other hand, she, too, was drawn to big fish and Paris; with the exception of George Eliot, the women she read did not impress her stylistically. The invalid role, invisible as Scarlet O'Neil, had always suited Didion. The Berkeley campus was a "big, anonymous place" into which she could melt. This pleased her. She soon recovered from the sting of failing to make Stanford. A friend of hers in Palo Alto asked her to write a paper for him on Joseph Conrad's *Nostromo*. She did and he got an A on it. For the same paper at Berkeley, Didion received a B-. Who was getting the stricter education? Going to Berkeley was like "waking up," she said, though she would never claim to be a "legitimate resident in any world of ideas."

"The Muse . . . / In distant lands now waits a better time," Bishop George Berkeley had written in 1752, envisioning the unspoiled Western world as an excellent place to cultivate "Arts and Learning." The California campus, named for him, nestled beneath sere, oak-dotted hills, its green lawns and white stone walls shaded by eucalyptus, alder, and flowering plum trees whose ripe fruit burned red as fevered skin. The petals of pink geraniums blew across cobbled walks mixed with flecks of deep blue lily of the Nile. The carillion in Sather Tower, known as the Campanile, tolled the stations of the day. At the end of each term, Didion stood among the smooth plane trees lining the Campanile Esplanade and listened to the bells play Rudyard Kipling's "They're Hanging Danny Deever in the Morning," a melancholy tune about a British soldier executed for murder. His punishment enforced discipline among the troops: Presumably, the song edified students sweating their final exams.

In the evenings, Didion wandered across the bridge over Strawberry Creek, past Doe Library, out Sather Gate, and into "the city of unfinished attics and stairs leading to strange towers," as Ishmael Reed would later say of the small community. A low throb of traffic animated the foggy streets and the air was sweetened with star jasmine. Behind the Claremont Hotel, dirt roads led into the hills; through Strawberry Canyon and Orindo Park, she hiked cool ravines padded with moss overlooking the flat part of town, with its factories and auto-repair yards, and, beyond that, the wide expanse of San Francisco Bay.

Despite the pleasant anonymity and the beauty of the campus setting, Didion felt nostalgic about her parents' house and she worried about her father. She had been in such a hurry to grow up, but on holiday visits home she painted her old bedroom bright pink, as if to seal it in the lead-based color of childhood. Standing in the kitchen, she'd eat waffles and apples, reflect on the sadness of the valley, with its dwindling hops fields (decimated since Pearl Harbor, when Japanese ranch hands had been interned), rummage through kitchen drawers, finding now-worthless food ration stamps. She'd note the yellow haze in the sky over Sacramento, an overcast indolence she termed "earthquake weather," and she'd remember, almost fondly, quarrels with her mother—what about?; nothing, nothing at all—and the long silences between them afterward. She found old keepsake boxes stuffed with broken seashells and pressed nasturtiums. She remembered going into San Francisco to see Alfred Lunt and Lynn Fontanne at the Geary Theatre in *O Mistress Mine* and wishing the whole world was a glib and overheated comedy for kids. She remembered broken levees, kilns burning in the night; shabby Chamber of Commerce parades—"fifteen dentists on fifteen palominos," she'd write; sitting with her father as he drank quietly in the Senator Bar downtown, ordering her lemonade with grenadine; the sound of silver dollars in her father's fingers; the smells of sherry and vermouth in the kitchens of her mother's friends, who nipped in secret just a little each day.

What else did she remember? Hiroshima. Hearing about it, she'd thought of a line from Episcopal liturgy: "As it was in the beginning, is now and ever shall be, world without end." She remembered her mother on the phone with one of her aunts, planning a tea, advising her it was *never* a mistake to buy a hat. She remembered dawns, getting up as the last stars faded, expecting flames to streak across the sky from a Nevada test shot.

On these visits home from Berkeley, her wistfulness soon dissolved into valley lassitude, the immense flatness of the place offering endless directions, all alike. "The landscape has a fantastic, strong, and depressing effect," she'd remark years later. "There is no way you can live up to the landscape. The works of man mean nothing . . . against [it]." A Conradian notion. "It's so awesome and clearly it can be wrenched apart in a millisecond by an earthquake."

In the meantime it was being subdivided by her father and his cronies. NO SEWER BONDS, said the signs. VETS NO DOWN. LOW F. H. A.

On the Southern Pacific's City of San Francisco, she'd return to campus, eager to resume her studies. But then homesickness hammered her again. Her classmates' easy teasing was wildly different from the pointed stillness in her parents' house. Gossip and small talk were simply beyond her. So were golden tans. She'd sit in her room, knitting a sweater for her father, or she'd lie awake, hearing the Campanile strike. She'd pity herself, a "humorless nineteen-year-old."

As she wrote in *Run River*, "It was as if she had stumbled alone across the plains and found that everyone else had already arrived, by TWA."

Out-of-staters appalled her; without thinking, they'd toss burning cigarettes from the windows of speeding cars. Didn't they know California was a tinderbox? Hadn't they heard of the Santa Ana winds torching the air? What was wrong with Eastern boys and Jewish kids with their fast talk and vulgar jokes, their sermons about trade unionism and democratic socialists? What was wrong with the Sigma Chis, convinced a whispered double entendre would get a girl so hot that she'd slip into the hills with them (after first stopping at a Shattuck Avenue drugstore for a discounted box of condoms)?

Didion's reserve and her faint pallor intrigued certain boys, lured by the challenge of cracking her silences and discovering her withheld mysteries. Soon, though, they'd be bored with her or terribly confused. She was simply *quiet*. In the mornings, she'd schlump to class in a dirty old raincoat, fingering bags of peanuts in her pockets.

Her rejection from Phi Beta Kappa nearly put her on the bus back to Sactown for good. She couldn't compete with the Pasadena social queens or quote Camus off-the-cuff at late-night mixers, so she had counted on her intelligence to distinguish her at Berkeley. But she had performed unimpressively in Psychology 1B, History 17A—even in the geology class she should have aced, thanks to her grandfather. When her grades arrived at her parents' house inside the self-addressed envelopes she had turned in to the registrar, she felt a marked loss of innocence. Quiet diligence and good manners would not exempt her from comparison to others and the need to prove her worth.

She pledged Delta Delta Delta ("Let us steadfastly love one another") and moved into the three-story sorority house on Warring Street. This gave her an identity and new friends: Barbara Brown, daughter of Pat Brown, California's attorney general and soon-to-be-governor, and Didion's roommate, Shirley Stephenson, a decorative arts major from Hayward. Didion was uncomfortable living among sixty girls gossiping about 7Up-and-bourbon kisses in the backs of waxed jalopies. These were the girls Simone de Beauvoir had in mind when she characterized Didion's generation following a campus visit one spring: "I looked at the athletic-looking young people, the smiling young girls . . . and I thought that certainly . . . there were no more than one or two who were concerned about the news of the day. They sometimes say that America is the land of youth. I am not so sure. Real youth is that which exerts itself in forging ahead to an adult future, not that which lives confined with accommodating resignation in the limits assigned to it."

Didion was *in* the world of Freddies and Sallies (as the Greeks were called on campus) but not *of* it; neither was she intimate with the Beats living up in the hills. "I came out of what was called the 'Silent Generation,'" she'd say later. "The whole bottom line was that we didn't really think there were any social answers to the problems of humanity." In a retrospective essay, she'd write, "The mood of Berkeley in those years was one of mild but chronic 'depression,'" a projection, perhaps, of her personal disengagement.

As with the sermons of Billy James Hargis, campus speech predicted coming violence, had the "Silent Generation" paid attention. Clark Kerr, Berkeley's chancellor, was overseeing the transformation of California's higher education from an agricultural base to a Cold War orientation. The university system flourished (and became, for a time, the finest in the world) with moneys devoted to weapons R&D. The year Didion entered Berkeley, California's defense contracts totaled $2.1 billion, tops in the nation. Kerr liked to joke that his job was to "provide parking for the faculty, sex for the students, and athletics for the alumni," but, in fact, he was tasked with militarizing academia. To this end, he envisioned a "multiversity" structured around separate research interests proceeding independently and often competing for federal grants. As he'd write in *The Uses of the University*, a profoundly influential text on U.S. education in the early 1960s, "There are several 'nations' of students, of faculty, of alumni, of trustees, of public groups. Each has its territory, its jurisdiction, its form of government. Each can declare war on others; some have the power of veto." Such language, shaping his thinking since the early 1950s, led to a specific campus layout. Whereas previously the Campanile had served as the university's center, with the library and classroom buildings forming a quadrangle, thereby encouraging students to mingle, the campus in Didion's time was beginning to fragment. Departments enlarged and disciplines split off into huge new buildings, erasing the old pedestrian paths. Some of the new structures straddled deep ravines, offering no gathering spaces. Kerr claimed his vision formed a "happy home" for the "intellect," a place where it could cozy up to the "ideological giants" (governments and businesses) who "rend the world with their struggles." But soon he grasped the unintended consequences of his efforts. In 1963 he admitted, "[T]he undergraduate students are restless. Recent changes in the American university have done them little good . . . Lack of faculty concern for teaching"—given the faculty's heavy research burden and dependence on private funding—"endless rules and requirements, and impersonality are the inciting causes." It was no coincidence that Berkeley gave rise to the Free Speech Movement in 1964 and witnessed some of the decade's most withering campus violence. If Didion's class was silent, it formed the first invisible wave of unrest: in 1952, as part of campus replanning, humanities students (those most engaged in analyzing language and ideological agendas) were located closer to Sather Gate, traditionally the spot given to off-campus groups for soapbox speeches and pamphleteering. Over a period of just a few years, this area would become the gathering place for a small, fertile subculture waiting to explode, especially when, in the early 1960s, Kerr and other campus officials tried to restrict speech. (These days, the space just outside the gate has been paved over and has the feel of a pedestrian mall at a strip shopping center.)

Had Didion attended to various orators while strolling past Sather Gate, she might have worried about Stalin's death and its effect on U.S.-Soviet relations; might have heard murmurings about a French military botch in Vietnam; might have noted the loss of bipartisanship in California politics. Richard Nixon had tarred and feathered Earl Warren with "New Dealism," introducing fresh levels of cruelty into the state's public speech. From California's shores, these toxic inflections would soon sweep the nation. The old agricultural elite was giving way to political candidates handpicked by investors in Lockheed and Douglas.

From the window of her room, Didion could see the construction of the Bevatron among alder, pine, and blue gum trees in the Berkeley-Oakland Hills: corrugated metal sidings, poured-in-place cement, topped by an impervious dome. The Bevatron was a particle accelerator, 180 feet in diameter, designed to create antiprotons to test the hypothesis that every particle in the universe had a corresponding antiparticle. It utilized a ten-thousand-ton iron magnet, a liquid hydrogen bubble chamber, and several large measuring devices called "Frankensteins." Its windows glowed an eerie deep blue at night. From the Bevatron, weird messages tumbled downhill: radiation, PCBs, beryllium, cesium-137, uranium-238, cobalt-60. A beautiful, terrible syntax, hypnotic in its dullness, began to seed local speech. Bruce Cork, a radiation specialist in Berkeley's Department of Physics, described the new facility this way: "The Bevatron requires an intense source of high-energy protons. The machine should accept monoenergetic protons for a duration of approximately five hundred microseconds once every six seconds. To satisfy the requirements of small loss due to scattering by gas in the accelerating chamber, a 9.9-mev linear accelerator has been built and operated." The jargon storm, the passive voice, the evasive verb tenses would become the dominant mode of American speech in the late twentieth century. The effect would be to erase agency and accountability (Richard Nixon had already smuggled these stratagems into politics in his 1952 "Checkers" speech, a desperate and successful attempt to shield his misdeeds).

In one of her classes, Didion had read *The Education of Henry Adams.* She perceived the connection between Adams's musings on the Dynamo and the Bevatron's presence on the hill. In the Universal Exposition in Paris in 1900, Adams had witnessed massive electrical generators in Machinery Hall and become convinced that technology had replaced the "moral force" of the church (best expressed in Gothic cathedrals such as Chartres, with its lovely blue windows devoted to Mary). For centuries, the Virgin's moral force had consisted of righteous power, eroticism, and hope, now more efficiently combined in the "vertiginous speed" of the machines. "The planet itself seemed less impressive" in the face of the Dynamo, Adams wrote in 1918. Similarly, in the shadow of the Bevatron, the globe seemed more vulnerable than before. In a poem entitled "Prayer to the Virgin," Adams wrote prophetically, "Seize, then, the Atom! rack his joints! / Tear out of him his secret spring! / Grind him to nothing!"

Night after blue night, the Bevatron ground away among the pines.

Didion was more fascinated by the facility's flashing lights than by its cultural impact, but links and revelations stirred her as she read. For instance, Adams had written of the Dynamo that it was basically an "ingenious channel for conveying . . . the heat latent in a few tons of poor coal." This dovetailed with Conrad's sagas of the Eastern seas, and the extraction of coal from treacherous climes, using cheap labor and exploitative economics. She wasn't sure how or why but she knew this information, knotted in some mad way, indicating the madness of human affairs, had a bearing on the Bevatron. Language and history were keys to understanding not only the past but also what was happening on the hill outside her window.

3

"The whole way I think about politics came out of the English Department," Didion told a reporter for Berkeley's *Daily Californian* in 2001. "They taught a form of literary criticism which was based on analyzing texts in a very close way. If you start analyzing the text of a newspaper or a political commentator on CNN using the same approach of close textual analysis, you come to understand it in a different way. It's not any different from reading Henry James."

In 1953 she was wary of the New Critical method. The New Criticism "depends on over-interpreting everything," she would say. "I think most writers don't analyze where [their work] comes from." But tracking the work's origins is a different kettle of fish from deconstructing a writer's use of language, and she applied herself diligently to parsing others' words, absorbing the nuances of verb tenses, syntax, point of view, selection, and omission. "I still go to the text," she said in 2002. "Meaning for me is in the grammar. . . . I learned backwards and forwards close textual analysis."

The development of her interpretive apparatus coincided with a love of existential philosophy. "I was very excited by Sartre in particular, by the whole idea of existentialism, which I ended up probably interpreting erroneously for my own purposes," she said. "I took it to mean that we should accept the meaninglessness of the world and still live in it." Her mother's refrain, "What difference does it make?" inclined her to this view. Now she had academic backing for her fatalism.

If the world was pointless but we had to live in it, we did so by investing importance in objects, people, ideas, and social roles. How and why these things came to embody the meanings we gave them—this was the burden of analysis, a way of decoding life's grammar. In novels, *comedies of manners* depended on seeing beneath the social niceties, separating what people said and did in public from who they were in private. Reading life was no different. Eduene's teas, the pioneer talismans, the fashions in *Vogue*, the power hierarchy in Sacramento had forced Didion to view life as theater. The logical next step was to strip away the costumes.

"Mark Schorer . . . helped me. I don't mean he helped me with my sentences or paragraphs—nobody has time for that with student papers; I mean that he gave me a sense of what writing was about, what it was for," Didion said.

In his landmark essay, "Technique as Discovery" (1948), Schorer advanced the New Criticism. The content of novels was less important than the "form and rhythm imposed" on them by the writer's techniques, he said. Technique not only "*contains* intellectual and moral implications . . . it *discovers* them," transforming the "world of action" into "texture and tone," creating a new and unique area of human experience. Didion now grasped Hemingway's appeal for her: His "early subject, the exhaustion of value, was perfectly investigated and invested by his bare style," Schorer wrote.

Furthermore, he said, writers expose their subjects *through* style: Didion built a career on this argument. Writing was not polemical. It was a kind of music, with major and minor keys.

For Schorer, *point of view* was the main technique propelling a writer "toward the positive definition of a theme." No one manipulated point of view better than Joseph Conrad. In *Heart of Darkness,* the horror swallowing Marlow and Kurtz is made more terrible by its passing from one person to the next and finally to the reader. The book's theme is not the madness it depicts, but our *complicity* in it, manifested by the point of view, making us the recipients of an old and tragic tale. We are charged with the awful responsibility of knowledge. In a similarly framed novel, *Victory,* written in the early twentieth century, Conrad insisted ours was an age "in which we are camped like bewildered travelers in a garish, unrestful hotel," sharing each other's stories. Didion would appropriate Conrad's perception and imagery—specifically, the "unrestful hotel"—as often as she could.

Victory dazzled her and became "maybe my favorite book in the world," she said. In the years ahead, she would reread it whenever she began to write new fiction. It "opened up possibilities" for novel structure. She said, "It's not a story the narrator even heard from someone who experienced it . . . so there's this fantastic distancing of the narrative, except when you're in the middle of it, it remains very immediate. It's incredibly skillful." She would employ a distanced point of view in *A Book of Common Prayer, Democracy,* and *The Last Thing He Wanted.* From *Victory,* she would also take a preoccupation with colonialism, remote island settings, hotels, underhanded business, shadowy world-traveling heroes attempting to rescue strong but doomed women.

Schorer demonstrated for her how one writer births another. In 1954 he published a novel, *The Wars of Love,* which borrowed its structure from the master. "I am not a central character," the narrator announces. "I am less important in this story than any of the others." In stating this (apparent) truth, Schorer's narrator takes a page from Conrad's tellers, but he's less subtle—naturally, his denial is a forceful assertion. His sensibility dominates the tale, a raising of narrative heat. Didion took note.

"I begin in this unpromising way . . . reader, to give you fair warning which is your right," says Schorer's man.

Didion's variation, fifteen years later: "I tell you this not as aimless revelation but because I want you to know, as you read me, precisely who I am."

Schorer's narrator says of a particular public figure, "[Y]ou know the name." "[Y]ou remember the names," says the peripheral narrator of *The Last Thing He Wanted.* Didion read Schorer's novel shortly after it appeared; she found it academic and stuffy, but she admired its shape. Clearly, his channeling of Conrad and its impact on her were immediate and lasting.

"*Victory* seems to me a profoundly female novel," she has said. How can a novel related by a seaman about a boorish hotel keeper, male brigands, and the coal and shipping trades be "female"? Didion explained, "[I]f style is character—and I believe it is—then obviously your sexual identity is going to show up in your style." In *Victory*, "you're seeing [the story] from a distance which is very like the distance in real life," she said. It's "told to you by someone who heard it from somebody else." For Didion, then, *structure* fashions *style*, a reflection of *orientation* and therefore of *character*. Here we have gossip based in hearsay, a disengaged relationship with the subject (the worldly affairs of men), an evaluative impulse, and a desire to pass lessons on to others. She located the "female" aspects of Conrad's novel in grammar and syntax rather than in biology, culture, and politics. Small wonder that, in little over a decade, she would clash with ardent feminists over the nature of female experience.

Schorer's creative writing course paralyzed Didion. "We were constantly being impressed with the fact that everybody else had done it already and better. It was very daunting to me," she said. Phyllis Butler, one of her classmates, remembered her as quiet but intense, a good performer of her work, which stood out in a group of extraordinarily talented students (including Butler, who went on to a successful writing career). To get into the course, students had to submit a one-page essay to Schorer. "You hoped he would like it, and a lot of people got turned down," Butler said.

"I was so scared in that class I couldn't speak. I felt too shy and too inadequate," Didion recalled. "[I had] a terror that any sentence I committed would expose me as *not good enough*." She completed only three of the required five stories. Her classmates, many of them older than she was, wrote witty and entertaining anecdotes. Conrad had hardened her conviction that "there was more to be learned" about life "from the *dark* journey." Her peers' concerns—marriage, work, the struggle for day-to-day contentment—seemed prosaic. "[I]t had not yet struck me in any visceral way that being nineteen was not a long-term proposition," she said years later. She failed to engage her compatriots in the glories of point of view, frame tales, the possibilities of intimacy and distance. "A lot of people don't get as excited about these things as I do," she told an interviewer. She dreaded showing up at noon each Monday, Wednesday, and Friday at Dwinelle Hall.

In class, Schorer stressed "sociological history," Butler told me. "'Understand your society,' he'd say. 'If you can capture your time in your writing—as Verdi did in his operas, for example—you've made a real contribution.' He also warned us, 'If you want to get published, it's difficult to come from California.' He felt there was a real East-West divide in the literary world."

Eventually, Didion completed a short story she felt pretty good about. It wasn't Joseph Conrad—she wasn't prepared to scale Mount Parnassus, so she stayed in the valley and wrote close to home.

She tried reporting for the campus newspaper. W. H. Auden began a West Coast tour in the fall of 1953. His recent poetry, about a culture driven "mad" by excess and war, intrigued Didion. He had defined the present as the "Age of Anxiety." His poem "September 1, 1939," whose images of "blind skyscrapers" and flashings of light amid an "odor of death" would be widely disseminated on the Internet following the World Trade Center attack in 2001, was quoted frequently in Berkeley bars. In it, he described the decade of Didion's birth as "low" and "dishonest," a snuffing of America's "clever hopes."

Perhaps Didion feared what he had to say about her generation's prospects. She was "absolutely terrified" of him, his smoker's cough and baleful eyes. She said, "I couldn't think of any questions [for him]. I had written some down but they seemed too stupid." She stammered and went white and mute during this meeting with Auden, her first official interview.

Chapter Five

1

By sophomore year, Didion had fled the chaotic Tri-Delt house and moved into a five-bedroom, twelve-bath place at 2520 Ridge Road, across from Etcheverry Hall, near old stucco apartment suites with scalloped balconies tucked among avocado and apple trees, Italian cypress, silver birch. She shared the house with three other girls, including Corrine Benson from Marin County and Didion's sorority roommate, Shirley Stephenson. Stephenson's decorative arts enthusiasms meant Mondrian murals were tacked to the closet doors and stylized animals crawled across kitchen walls. An abstract mobile hung from the living room ceiling, its sharp edges frightening Didion whenever she got up for any reason in the middle of the night. She felt her friends had staked out each corner of the house before she'd had a chance to move in.

If not quite at home on campus, she was settled in her rituals. She was part of a student coterie in the English Department invited to faculty digs. One night, one of her teachers got sloppy drunk and revealed his bitterness at academic drudgery and university regulations. Didion was stunned to learn her mentors shared some of the same adult disappointments she'd seen in her family's house while growing up. The serious English majors were expected to go to graduate school. Didion did not share this ambition. Though she felt like an imposter among her peers, her teacher's drunken screed strengthened her reluctance to remain in academia. For the time being, though, she hoped to secure an undergraduate teaching assistantship with Thomas Parkinson, a poet and Yeats scholar fascinated by the fledgling Beat movement. Parkinson was the son of a laborer who'd been blacklisted in the San Francisco general strikes in the 1930s. He was active in campus politics. He was particularly sympathetic to the struggles of his female students, whose fellowship opportunities were limited and poorly funded compared to their male counterparts'.

In the summers, Didion pursued a tepid romance in Sacramento with a boy she referred to in letters to friends only as Robert or Bob. Robert's uncle owned a Lincoln-Mercury dealership in Bakersfield, and his family had large oil, cotton, and uranium shares. In Bakersfield, the Lincoln-Mercury dealers—Haberfelde, Kitchen-Boyd—were major power brokers, hosting lavish parties, establishing fine arts collections, and controlling city politics. Robert had declared his enduring love for Didion and hoped she would marry him once she graduated from Berkeley. He insisted Bakersfield's future was boundless—Ford was about to introduce a new Continental sure to sell like hotcakes. For a starter home, the couple could purchase a modest ranch-style house in the suburbs, the type of acreage her father hoped to develop now that he was out of Letterman and dabbling again in real estate.

Four years after World War II, Americans had bought 21.4 million cars, 20 million refrigerators, 5.5 million stoves, and 11.6 million television sets. They had moved into one million new housing units. Simone de Beauvior, on the same trip to the States as her Berkeley visit, said the developing American suburb was "rigid," "frozen," "closed." She decried the "serried rows of ranch houses, painted in pastel colors, each with its own picture window and its garden, each equipped with a deep freeze, oil furnace, and automatic washer, spring[ing] up in the wilderness." But the nation was buying the dream.

The dream was sold, hard, in *Good Housekeeping, Mademoiselle,* and other magazines. Bob could use the glossy ads featuring well-coiffed wives in his courtship ritual. Ironically, in 1939, *Mademoiselle* had established a promotion encouraging college-age girls to delay keeping house and to pursue a professional path. It was called the guest editor program. Each year, twenty girls were chosen from fifteen hundred applicants nationwide to be flown to New York for a month to work with the magazine's editors on an August college issue. To apply, students submitted work fitting the magazine's needs in their personal area of interest: fiction, nonfiction, fashion, advertising. The girls got hands-on publishing experience and the magazine's advertisers got firsthand feedback from its target audience.

In 1953, Sylvia Plath was picked to be managing guest editor. She was two years older than Didion; otherwise, early on they would have competed for many of the same opportunities. In a letter to her mother, Plath summed up her experience at *Mademoiselle*: "I have, in the space of six days, toured the second largest ad agency in the world and seen television kitchens, heard speeches there, gotten ptomaine poisoning from crabmeat the agency served in their 'own special test kitchen' and wanted to die very badly for a day." She fictionalized her New York adventures in *The Bell Jar;* had the novel been published in time (it appeared under a pseudonym in Britain in 1963 and in the United States in 1971), Didion would have had reason to be skeptical of ranch house kitchens, not to mention magazine work. In 1955, submitting an early draft of a short story, she applied for *Mademoiselle*'s guest editor slot in fiction and got it.

2

Didion's first glimpse of Manhattan, from an Idlewild bus into town, was obscured by spring rain, but that fact was more exotic than her old penthouse dreams. It didn't rain in Sacramento in the late spring or summer. Her dress was too thin. She'd known it the instant she'd stepped off the DC-7 in Idlewild's makeshift terminal and sensed the moisture in the air—warm air tinged with mildew.

It was May 1955. She'd just completed her junior year (temporarily excused from taking her finals). A national magazine had recognized her talent. Later, in "Goodbye to All That," one of her finest early essays, she'd say "one of the mixed blessings of being twenty . . . is the conviction that nothing like this, all evidence to the contrary, has ever happened to anyone before."

The bus took her to the Barbizon Hotel for Women on the corner of Lexington and East Sixty-third Street: twenty-three stories of elegant Gothic Revival, Moorish, and Renaissance touches carved into coral brick and sandstone. Since 1927 a "women-only" establishment, whose patrons were expected to be pedigreed, stylish, and chaste, the Barbizon, said *Vanity Fair,* was "the city's elite dollhouse." *Mademoiselle* and other fashion magazines toasted it as the *only* place "ambitious, discriminating young women" would want to stay in New York: Anyone who was anyone wanted to be a "Barbizon girl."

Most of the hotel's seven hundred guest spaces were tiny and spare. Didion spent her first night in the Barbizon with a sudden fever and a cold from the rain and the room's freezing temperature. She did not know how to turn the air conditioner off. She was afraid to call the desk and ask someone to come up and help her because she did not know how much she should tip the hotel employees. So she wrapped herself in wool blankets and telephoned Bob. She told him she could see the Brooklyn Bridge from the window of her room. In fact, it was the Triborough Bridge. A single red rose and a work schedule lay on her pillow; the following morning she would meet the magazine's editors and all of her fellow "Millies."

Among the other guest editors that year were Jane Truslow, who would marry Plath's old boyfriend, Peter Davison; Janet Burroway, who would publish several well-regarded novels; Gael Greene, eventually a restaurant critic for *New York* magazine; and Peggy La Violette from Berkeley, with whom Didion was especially close.

Greene and Burroway said they had only vague memories of Didion. She kept herself small. "I remember Joan as something between shy and scared. But you never know when 'shy' is 'private,'" Greene said.

"I would say, consulting a faulty memory, that I did find her a touch aloof, intelligent at an intelligent distance," Burroway explained. But in no sense was Didion a "quivering creature." "She struck me as a very self-possessed young woman. Of course, I was a quivering contradiction of ambition and clumsiness myself, so I may certainly have failed to recognize that in her."

Mademoiselle's main conference room, on the sixth floor at 575 Madison Avenue, where the guest editors first got to know one another and received their initial assignments from the staff, had "one whole wall" fully mirrored, Burroway recalled. The other walls were decorated "in a black and cream wallpaper of Victorian ads, ladies in bustled dresses. This is where Betsy Talbot Blackwell [the magazine's editor] greeted us that first day with her fur stole, cigarette holder, and 'We believe in pink this year.'"

Burroway shared with me several excerpts from letters she sent her parents from New York. They cover in detail the group's activities and impressions.

May 31: "Interviews with *Mlle.* editors, all of whom were nice and helpful except for Miss McNeil, Merchandising Editor, who is a very tough cookie and not about to be impressed. . . . Had lunch at the Ivy Room of the Hotel Drake. . . . French and gold-leaf ritzy, filet of sole 3.95, coffee .50, ice cream .70. . . . We're going to Columbia campus tomorrow morning to have pix taken for the aug. issue. Gave us skirts, blouses, and shoes to wear. We have to give back the skirts and shoes, but I think we keep the blouses."

The photo shoot took place at 6:45 at Baker Field. The girls sat in the bleachers, squinting into the sun, wearing "man-tailored" long-sleeved cotton shirts with buttoned collars and woven stripes. Didion's pageboy is immaculate, her smile easy and wide, her face turned to the right—her preferred pose. It framed a slight dimple in her left cheek. Jane Truslow would write in her guest editor column that whenever the GEs got together, "creative energy crackled like summer heat lightning," but in these pictures the girls look sleepy and disoriented.

June 3: "The magazine is funny . . . ½ the office is writing it & ½ advertising it—there's even a dept. for publicizing *Mlle.* publicity. . . . Ridiculous."

"It was the first time I'd ever worked in an office," Didion said, years later, "except for *The Sacramento Union,* which wasn't a real office because it was *The Sacramento Union.*"

By June 7, the drudgery of writing and rewriting dull copy, having it "ripped to pieces" by the editors in tedious group conferences was setting in. Burroway wrote her mother, "*All* the GEs are disappointed and disillusioned, most of them more so than I."

June 9: "We sat in a 3-hour editorial conference rehashing ideas and style; then I took all the editorials and the conference notes, put each on a yellow card, shuffled and rearranged & tried to put them together to please everybody. It wasn't easy."

In the evenings, back at the Barbizon, sitting around the lobby on Oriental carpets under antique English lanterns, the GEs gossiped about the magazine's editors. One was Cyrilly Abels, the homeliest woman in the office, all the girls agreed. She wore wool crepe dresses clinging tightly to her bosom. She was unforgiving: She kept a box of Kleenex by her desk for girls who withered under her raw, critical gaze. Others included Polly Weaver; Rita Smith, the plump, alcoholic-splotchy sister of Carson McCullers ("Sistah has ruined my *life!*") and crying shoulder for Terry Southern, who called her seven or eight times a day; the "ridiculous" Miss Blackwell, always wearing formal hats at her desk, given to cataclysmic coughing—she'd be into the vodka by noon each day, her glazed eyes fixed on the Georgian chandelier in her office. The GEs traded stories they'd heard about Barbizon legends—Grace Kelly dancing in the hallways in her nightie; *Vogue* models splitting finger sandwiches in the lobby with dumpy girls from the Katharine Gibbs Secretarial School; J. D. Salinger seducing Barbizon babes at a nearby drugstore and then sweeping them off to naughty Greenwich Village. Homesick, the girls talked about where they'd come from—Arizona, Indiana, Ohio. They admitted they loved and hated New York.

In their monastic rooms at the Barbizon, the girls discovered ironing was unavoidable, even in the Big Apple.

Didion's view of Manhattan—a swirl of luxury, romance, and punishingly hard work—never wavered from her first impressions that summer (in her twilight years, she would choose to live in an apartment just blocks from *Mademoiselle*'s former editorial offices). Privately, she was delighted to be thousands of miles from Sacramento and her suitor, but for her profile in the magazine's August issue, she wrote, "Joan spends vacations river-rafting and small-boating in the picture-postcard atmosphere of the Sacramento Valley." Her "interests" included "almost any book published," she said, and "publishing a book of my own."

On June 14, staff paired the GEs with celebrities, fashion designers, and literati—among them, T. S. Eliot, Malcolm Cowley, Frank O' Connor, Gore Vidal, and S. J. Perelman. The assignment was to interview these folks for a segment in the magazine called "We Hitch Our Wagons." Didion was told to compose a brief profile of Jean Stafford. The session went much better than her Q&A with Auden back at Berkeley. "Certainly I was more socially anxious than Joan" during the interviews, Burroway told me. Stafford was big and wild-haired, friendly and relaxed. Didion sat demurely, prim beside her subject, wearing a long paisley skirt and a collarless blouse, tightly clutching a notebook. She was struck by Stafford's claim that the short story "seems better suited to the age" than novels: "Novels seem to be almost irrelevant these days." Stafford wrote three hours daily and believed getting a story accepted for publication was worse than rejection because it's "such an exposure and you're always convinced that the thing is terrible . . . only the thrill of knowing you're writing as well as you possibly can makes it worthwhile." Didion's profile of Stafford marked her first appearance in a national magazine.

We "discover[ed] to our delight that the famous are fun to meet," Jane Truslow chirped in her guest column. In a letter home, Burroway complained about a "disgusting cocktail party" at Miss Blackwell's: "You wouldn't believe so many famous people could be so dull," she wrote.

Joan Gage, another former GE, recalled "champagne and caviar" at Blackwell's soirees, "a strolling accordion player, a view of Central Park, a side chair once owned by Lincoln that no one was allowed to sit on and a cork floor that was badly scarred by the spike heels we wore. In her bedroom, free books sent for BTB's perusal [stood] in three-foot high stacks on the floor."

The GEs completed most of their work for the magazine in the first two weeks of their stay. On June 24 they toured the United Nations. They sat in Dag Hammarskjöld's chair: a crash course on world politics. The chair's language button was locked on Russian. Then they got to sightsee and play, getting their hair cut (by world-famous stylist Enrico Caruso), going to dances on the roof of the St. Regis, going to the theater to see *The Bad Seed*, attending a fashion show at Trigere's, visiting the ad firm of Ogilvy, Benson, and Mather, touring the press room of *The New York Times* and the NBC television studios, dropping by a private screening of Bob Fosse's movie *My Sister Eileen* at Columbia Pictures. A photograph in the college issue shows Didion and a fellow GE "receiv[ing] instruction in skin care from beauty expert Mala Rubenstein." The girls sit in front of big round mirrors, wearing towels on their heads, patting their faces in imitation of the looming Mala. Didion looks shrunken and pouty.

The group attended a College Clinic at the Astor "where fashion scored a touchdown," said Truslow. "Warner's offered us new hope for a slim-hipped future by showing us their miraculous 'Merry Widows.'" Everywhere they went, *Mademoiselle* "provided several escorts for each of us, not just one prince apiece." "We were made gifts of, stuffed into, or ushered along to ogle the fashions," Burroway said. "*[S]tiletto, sheath, cinch* . . . Underneath each of us wore the bra that conjured Amazons . . . stitched in stiff concentric circles to a point."

"Goodbyes . . . were bad at the office," Burroway wrote her mother on July 1. "I am feeling pretty generally overwhelmed."

For the return trip to California, Eduene had arranged for Didion to travel across the continent by train, including stops in Boston, Montreal, and Chicago. It would be an excellent education, Eduene said. En route, Didion wrote a series of letters to Peggy La Violette, who'd stayed in New York. However reticent Didion may have appeared publicly, the letters reveal a brash young woman sure of her intelligence and charm, impatient with most strangers, whom she considered commonplace and uninteresting. She was posing in the letters—the Barbizon girl loosed upon an unsuspecting world. But she was also certain of her ambition and talent.

She left the Barbizon for Grand Central Station on the morning of Friday, July 1. Beneath the starry dome, she couldn't persuade anyone to carry her bags or help her with directions, so she stood weeping in a bustling crowd. She was embarrassed to be crying so hysterically, but her tears brought action. A kind young man scurried over, took her bag, and helped her check it. (A few years later, she would write of a woman in *Run River*, "[she] was strong enough to make people take care of [her].")

On the trip to Boston, she was forced to sing Armenian folk songs with a circle of girls headed to an outdoor camp in the Massachusetts woods. Alighting in the city, she ate a sandwich at Schrafft's, drank a bland milk shake, and found the experience so disagreeable that she was determined to phone her mother and demand an immediate flight home. Her letters to La Violette seethe with melodramatic impatience. At her hotel, she fell asleep fully dressed on her bed and did not wake until ten-thirty the following morning. After breakfast, feeling somewhat better, she took a subway to Cambridge and Harvard and walked around the Boston Public Garden. Later, as she was watching the swan boats, a man approached her and made several rude remarks. That was it: Boston, off the list.

That night, she caught the Montreal Red Wing to Quebec and stayed at the Château Frontenac. The trip was trying. The train cars were sad and dirty, she said. A young man made passes at her and an older gentleman, worried about her traveling alone, offered to take her to his village so she could meet his family, especially his younger brother, who'd marry her in a minute, he said. She escaped to the dining car. She described the waiter to La Violette as an Uncle Tom. By now, she was beginning to feel like Daisy Miller, an emblem of American innocence in the Canadian outback.

She was thrilled to reach Chicago: tea at Marshall Field's! She put on flats and walked the lakefront. She bought a collection of Katherine Anne Porter's short stories and was pleasantly surprised by their complexity. Bob sent her a letter by special delivery. She couldn't tell if he was clueless or canny in his cooing imprecations. She told La Violette she felt like Ingrid Bergman in *Gaslight*.

Back on the train, she found the beauty of Colorado boring, but the flat, white, alkaline plains of eastern Utah, crossed by dried-up rivers, appealed to her "essentially monochromatic" personality.

And then she was back in Sacramento, in the listless arms of her family.

She missed New York. She couldn't stand being home. Downtown, stores selling paperback books were springing up on every block; other than that, everything seemed frozen in time.

Bob pressured her to be queen of the Lincoln-Mercurys. Her refusals were neurotic, he said. He understood her better than anyone. He knew she loved him. She said the most terrible things to him, but her cruelty made him cling to her all the more.

She needed to go to Berkeley to finish her finals, but she didn't want to. Almost desperately, she took a summer job writing wedding notices for *The Sacramento Union*. Journalism? Her editor told her it consisted mostly of clipping and rewriting, with a different slant, articles from opposition papers ("County Board of Supervisors Lauds North Area Realtors for Plan to Raze Slum, Construct Howard Johnson's").

She sat in the house, trying not to fight with her mother. Her bedroom was ugly. *Why* had she painted her walls "Pastel Cyclamen"? It hadn't turned out: an awful pink, making her cringe. Her periods laid her low. She told La Violette she had regular headaches, and she implied they might be psychosomatic.

The Society Editor at the *Union* decided to get married and asked Didion if she'd like to be her full-time replacement at the paper. After two years, she'd earn $125 a month. Great—and on top of that, marry Bob? The fellow wouldn't relent. She could just see herself moving to Kern County, driving a new Ford each year, hanging out at the country club, bored to her bones, slipping into boozy, sad affairs with other women's husbands.

In August, the *Mademoiselle* college issue graced Sacramento newsstands. Didion's relatives snapped it up. An editor at Henry Holt, noting her desire to publish a book, wrote to offer her a "sympathetic reading." If only she had a manuscript!

Between Bob and Henry Holt, Berkeley and the Society Desk, she lived the mixed messages of the "Millies." "Capture a man . . . and a career," said one of the magazine's ads: All you had to do was wear Dacron. "When you live out of a suitcase . . . take Tampax along."

All the Bobs in all of Kern County couldn't hold a candle to what she had seen. And what she'd seen, readers would come to witness. Didion's path through society pages and fashion magazines put a unique stamp on her writing, and her writing would become synonymous with the New Journalism. It was a literary style *valuing* style, coinciding with fashion and the reading practices of the New Criticism. No object was too trivial to be analyzed; *everything* was design. Clothing, jewelry, furniture: More than just accoutrements, they were signatures, cultural markers, indicators of the present and the future, means by which life *could be read*. Conrad—that most "female" of men—had understood this even better than Miss Blackwell had. A storehouse of "beads, cotton cloth, red kerchiefs, brass wire, and other trade goods" was called a "fetish," he said, "because of the spirit of civilization it contained."

And so fleeting!

Oscar Wilde said fashion is "a form of ugliness so intolerable that we have to alter it every six months." Didion knew she was writing elegies ("Nothing matters"). The champagne, caviar, and accordion music could not last.

In the late 1970s, *Mademoiselle* stopped the guest editor program. In 1980 it suspended its poetry and fiction contests. In 2001 the magazine ceased altogether. And what of the ambitious girls who had gathered in the summer of 1955 to burn like lightning? We all know what happened to the poetry winner. And: "I was shocked and thrown off balance when Jane Truslow died," Burroway said. Now Truslow is just a footnote to stories of Sylvia Plath. "Such a fully lovely and alive person, so little impact," Burroway said. "We are all wisps in the wind."

3

Grief passes.

"A night of memories and sighs / I consecrate to thee," wrote the poet Walter Landor. What did he mean by these lines in his elegy for a dead young girl? Clearly, said Didion's teacher, he meant that however overwhelming and necessary mourning may be, it is, like all human experience, finite. The teacher had gone on to say, "A *night*, not a matter of a lifetime, a matter of some hours."

Read it for yourself. Close textual analysis. *I'll expect your papers on Wednesday.*

She was back at Berkeley, trying to shake off her hangover from the inert second half of the summer. Fights with Bob. Mediocre productions at the Music Circus—*South Pacific* again! *Carousel* again (though it did make her weep)! Gordon MacRae and Shirley Jones at the state fair. The highlight of August was when her father roused himself to trade in the family's 1950 Ford for a '54 Sun Valley, pale shrimp in color, with matching upholstery and a glass top.

Mademoiselle should have been the season's glory, but the issue came and went; already, Didion felt like a has-been.

She had completed her finals from the term before. She had purchased five yards of mulberry gray wool, along with a *Vogue* pattern for a couturier coat, and sewn the coat and a matching skirt. She had hoped to make a cocktail dress of striped silk to show her sorority sisters she was just as fashionable as they were despite the fact that she'd abandoned the Tri-Delt house, but once classes started, she lost steam.

She had wanted to take another short story–writing class and a course on Conrad's novels, but the English Department determined she'd used up her electives. She was *required* to finish English 155 (Chaucer), Anthro 120 (the peculiarities of Incan grammar), and Psych 168 ("Abnormal"—the only class she liked). She feared she'd be at Berkeley for another hundred years.

Over the summer, Mark Schorer's students had read his new novel. In Dwinelle Hall they debated its themes: *Was* there freedom of choice in life— really? One member of the group said no and declared himself a Trotskyist. They kicked around Graham Greene's latest novel, *The Quiet American*: subterfuge, international intrigue, U.S. empire building.

Meanwhile, once a week, Didion fended off the rakish comments of Professor Caldwell, who asked her to his office to discuss Edmund Spenser.

It was a long way from mirrored conference rooms. Berkeley sophistication consisted of small coffee shops on Walnut Street where World War II vets spent the afternoons telling eighteen-year-olds stories of combat and prostitution; Sather Gate, where pro- and anti-McCarthyites cleared their throats at one another; and the Cinema Guild Theatre, tucked into the corner of the Sequoia Apartments building on Telegraph Avenue. The Guild showed foreign features (Renoir's *Grand Illusion*), smart Hollywood comedies (Preston Sturges's *Unfaithfully Yours*); the theater's program director at one time was Pauline Kael, before she made her name as her generation's most important and infuriating movie critic. At the Guild, Didion saw Marlene Dietrich in *The Blue Angel* and wept at *The Bicycle Thief*.

Didion figured the California Republican Party was dead for 1956, so she remained politically inactive. That year, the only campus event remotely subversive was a "particularly vigorous panty raid," said Seymour Martin Lipset, a sociology professor. In just a few years, women's underclothing would become a political symbol, but for now it was a source of harmless fun—unless you were a former *Mademoiselle* intern, in which case, it was a career path.

Up in the Berkeley Hills, boys and girls danced naked at night among trees exploding with lights. Such were the rumors: a perverse afterglow of the

Bevatron's throbbing through the blue gums and alders, as if society had to produce an antisociety, just as protons could not exist without their opposites. The Beats, the avant-gardists, the Berkeley Gothics with their stream-of-consciousness "poetry," their orgies, yoga, and chemical enhancers—Didion couldn't stand them. Not that she knew any of them, but the very *thought* of what she'd heard disgusted her.

At the time, Allen Ginsberg shared a cottage with Jack Kerouac on Mount Tamalpais. All around them, in the woods, the sharp, fresh smell of mint. They sat on the rotting porch among wild rosebushes and tomato vines, drinking, smoking, chatting with pals—"Zen lunatic drunks," Kerouac said. Ginsberg was writing his "Footnote to Howl!" and chanting "Holy! Holy! Holy!" Occasionally, he'd go grocery shopping in town, imagining Walt Whitman sizing up the stock boys. Near the cottage, Gary Snyder, planning a Buddhist pilgrimage to Japan, sat in his shack on a tatami mat, drinking tea, reading D. T. Suzuki, Han-shan, and Philip Whalen. He wrote poems titled "For a Far-Out Friend" and "Song and Dance for a Lecherous Muse." The poems celebrated getting "high" on a woman's body and being "hooked" on books. At a reading at the Poetry Center in March 1956, Kenneth Rexroth introduced Snyder by saying he'd met a woman who wanted to know if Snyder was a "real poet or is he just one of those people who object to everything?"

"This is very important," Snyder told me one afternoon. "We thought we had won. In Northern California, the intelligentsia, such as it was, had given up on Trotsky and Stalinism early, but it had not given up on radicalism. So we were embracing anarchy, Kropotkyn—it was a wonderful environment, but hardly anybody else in the United States thought that way, even in New York, for at least another ten years." By *writing* anarchy, Snyder and his buddies believed they would bring it about.

For Didion, writing was not a matter of communing with the spirit of the forest, sparking revolution, or buzzing with Eros. It was deadlines, cut-and-paste jobs, pleasing Saks Fifth Avenue.

Not only did she have nothing to do with the Beats, she had, during senior year, less and less contact with the sorority or anyone not connected to *The Occident,* Berkeley's literary magazine. The writers formed a "clique," said Gabriel Rummonds, a former editor. "A small group of students and their friends had hold on staff positions and authors who were published. It was hard for an outsider to join." John Ridland agreed. He had won a Phelan Scholarship in Poetry and would pursue a distinguished literary career, but the staff ignored everything he sent them. In 1956, the year Didion took the reins, *The Occident* reflected austerity, fastidiousness, and morbid self-regard. Humor had never been its strong suit—satire was reserved for *The Pelican*, another campus publication (*pelican* was a derogatory student term for coeds). The high-minded *Occident*, established in 1881, and counting Jack London among its illustrious contributors, shunned silliness. In 1949, Jack Spicer described a campus reading by *Occident* writers: a "ghostly symposium, five poets holding forth on their peculiar problems. One will say Magic; one will say God; one will say Form. When my turn comes I can only ask an embarrassing question: 'Why is nobody here? Who is listening to us?'"

As editor, Didion brooked no sandals or beards, no "pseudo-avant garde" nonsense. The inexperience of her coworkers revolted her. "The trouble with you, Didion," said one scornful young staffer, "is that you admire the *professional*." He "considered my concern with punctuation and my enthusiasm for Henry James a sellout to the English Department," she said.

"I tried to be friendly with her but got no encouragement," said Harriet Polt, another editor. "I recall her sitting on the floor at a staff meeting, my saying hello or something of the sort, and her just mumbling. She was a very shy, tiny thing, mouselike."

Nevertheless, she set up a card table in front of the library and tried to persuade students running to class to stop and purchase the issue. Joan Haug-West, her old high school classmate, now a Berkeley coed, remembers Didion sitting in the sun, quietly persistent. The magazine's business manager, an army vet and former researcher at *Time*, fought with Didion over promotional tactics. Card tables were fine, he said, but he had plans to raise *The Occident*'s national profile. He believed it should compete with *The Partisan Review*. Didion thought him psychotic. One morning he phoned her at eight o'clock, insisted she rush to Eshleman Hall for a meeting. She hung up on him. She'd been suffering from a migraine for three days and had to go to Cowell Hospital for some codeine.

"It is not professional, of course . . . but several of the pieces in the magazine are very close to being professional and indicate substantial promise in their writers," Thomas Parkinson wrote in a review of *The Occident* in the *Daily Californian*. He singled out Didion's first published short story and praised its "first rate" prose.

In "Sunset," Didion test-ran themes and circumstances she'd return to eight years later in her debut novel. The story opens with an overture reminiscent of *A Farewell to Arms* (and also of lyrical passages in Steinbeck's *The*

Long Valley or *The Grapes of Wrath*) in which the California heat assumes a presence stronger than any of the characters. Laura, a Central Valley native, descendant of pioneers, is married to a Midwestern businessman named Charlie ("And that had made all the difference," the narrator says; Charlie is a projection of the young golfer Didion dated just after high school). Laura has been away from California for a dozen years. She's depressed. Her husband's desire to see her father's grave in her family's cemetery irritates her, reminding her how much has changed since she left: "She even felt that she belonged to a different generation" now. Worse, she may as well not exist. She feels she could "fuse with the yellow fields, dissolve into the late summer twilight." Her marriage has been "completely without motivation or continuity" and she can easily "imagine that Charlie was not beside her." She cannot, or will not, talk to him about the source of her recent fragility—the belief that she has been spiritually "disinherited" by her father's death and the loss of family property.

As a teenager, Laura felt she was better than anyone else. Her father told her so: "But it was necessary to be polite to all the others, because that was really the final test of how much better you were, and that was how one got along in this world." The family had "pushed across the mountains a century before, broken across the Sierras and made the dry fields grow. 'You're the heiress to that entire century,' [Laura's father] had said harshly, 'and you'd better be damn proud of it.' She had felt it a grave responsibility."

Here is the story's autobiographical core. When teenaged Laura takes tennis lessons and insists she's not playing to win, her mother says, "Lauriebaby, everybody plays to win." Eduene to a tee. In the next line, Didion drops the narrative mask and reveals herself: "[H]er mother, of course, had been right." The line's confidence has nothing to do with Laura.

Didion shared with her character a sense of slipped tradition. Charlie is an early version of Ryder Channing, the entrepreneur and sly suitor in *Run River,* who knows California's future lies in betraying its past—a past in which he has no stake. Charlie is older than Laura, "already at the age when the idea of death was beginning to gnaw at the fabric of his daily life," patient with her petulance and cruelty. He is probably "going to die" before she does: the first of Didion's many tragic males. "[S]he could not face finding any fear, any weakness, in the man she had married for his strength," the narrator says, showing Didion's hand perhaps more than she realized at the time.

As the couple strolls among the tombstones, contemplating how much of the land has been sold, Laura sounds for the first time in Didion's printed prose the major theme of future writings, a precursor to Didion's contention that the center cannot hold, a twenty-one-year-old's prescient and permanent shock: It "was as if the rules under which she had lived her entire life had been arbitrarily declared invalid."

4

Didion wanted to be *literary,* not academic. This was hard at Berkeley. She wanted access to San Francisco's cultural events but had no car. Worst of all, because she was so quiet, the boys in her writing course thought they were smarter than she was.

One night she borrowed a dress from her roommate, Corrine. She had a date with a boy from Schorer's class. He was going to take her on the F train to dinner and a play in the city.

Corrine's dress smelled of Corrine's perfume, a scent Didion associated with a tenor voice singing "The Bluebird of Happiness" on a scratchy radio. Corrine liked to lie awake in her room, listening to this song, a local station's late-night sign-off.

The boy took Didion to a French family restaurant, where they ordered coq au vin—standard fare for UC students out on the town, yearning to be European. After the play, on the train back to Berkeley, he told her he liked her dress and asked why she'd not worn it before. She didn't admit she'd borrowed it to please him. He pulled a Dylan Thomas paperback out of his pocket and began to read aloud. "'It was my thirtieth year to heaven,'" he recited, then paused to explain, "It was his thirtieth birthday."

Didion nodded.

Playing dumb with poets: Surely this was not the way to be literary.

5

Fellow *Occident* editor Harriet Polt recalled, "Of course I was awfully jealous when she got the *Vogue* gig—and surprised, as she seemed so withdrawn."

First prize in *Vogue*'s Prix de Paris contest for young writers was one thousand dollars in cash or "two wonderful weeks in Paris," winner's choice. Finalists had to be college graduates. They were automatically screened for their potential as employees of Condé Nast Publications.

"[H]ow crazy I was to get out of California," Didion said. "The first time I came to New York it was so thrilling to me I just thought I had to get back . . . so I threw myself into the *Vogue* contest." She didn't believe she had a chance: The writing assignments were much more fashion-minded than those for the *Mademoiselle* competition. "Expect the contest *not* to be a cinch—it isn't," the magazine warned applicants. "Expect to give it time and some of your best thought."

Writers were evaluated for their "grasp of subject matter; presentation" and "demonstration of special skills." They were required to provide a six-hundred-word personal statement and short essays on a range of topics, such as "Why should fashion be important to a woman?" "Have you a clothes philosophy?" and "What clothes would you take" to exotic locations such as Europe or California?

In 1951, two years before marrying John Fitzgerald Kennedy, Jacqueline Bouvier won the Prix de Paris with an essay entitled "People I Wish I Had Known." She wished she had known Charles Baudelaire, Oscar Wilde, and Serge Diaghilev, "poets and idealists who could paint sinfulness with honesty and still believe in something higher." Her fantasy was to be a "sort of 'Overall Art Director of the Twentieth Century,' watching everything from a chair hanging in space." This was the sort of thing the magazine wanted. Jackie was its girl.

By November 1, 1955, Didion had mailed her application, parroting the magazine's verbal style and current enthusiasms—for jersey jumpers and striped oversweaters, coral jewels, blond cotton poplin, and "red, red, red!"

By January she was among the contestants invited to enter the second round of the competition. She was asked to "[g]ive ideas for a newspaper advertisement, window displays, fashion show" or to "[w]rite a profile on a personality . . . which would be of interest to readers of *Vogue*." Recently, the magazine had published an article entitled "Four Architects Helping to Change the Look of America," by Aline B. Saarinen, who profiled her husband, Eero, as well as Gordon Bunshaft, Philip Johnson, and Mies van der Rohe. She extolled the International Style. Van der Rohe's "unshakable sense of moral righteousness is like a Puritan's," Saarinen wrote. Nonsense, Didion thought. More convincing to her was the men's professional cattiness: "So-and-So is covering the country with a thick chocolate ooze," said one fellow of another. This sounded like a Sacramento real-estate debate. She could do this!

She wrote a profile of William Wilson Wurster, a prominent San Francisco architect and dean of Berkeley's architecture school. He resisted the steel and glass of the International Style, dismissing van der Rohe's "sheer, sleek" boxes in favor of local materials, indigenous shapes, and unassuming exteriors sensitive to the climate. He installed large picture windows in his houses, bringing the landscape into rooms as a central design element. For good or ill, the West had embraced suburbia, so Wurster did, too. In essence, he championed what Didion hoped to escape by writing about him: the California ranch house, with its automatic washers churning in the wilderness.

She submitted her essay in mid-March. On May 15, she heard she'd won first prize. She did not want to go to Paris (her mother had promised her Paris after the war, and Paris had turned out to be a lie). She wanted a job in New York. Jessica Daves, *Vogue*'s editor in chief, offered her a position at forty-five dollars a week, despite the fact that, during the interview, Didion had been running a fever of 102 and said even less than usual. She'd be expected to spend several months reading back issues, familiarizing herself with the magazine's layout, interests, and style, in preparation for writing promotional copy.

Bob did not believe she was going to leave. This was madness, he said. "[H]ell hell hell hell hell," she wrote Peggy La Violette. She was sick of classes, sick of her sorority sisters, sick of the Ridge Road house. If she ever saw another Mondrian print, she'd heave. No one reacted when she told them, "Go to hell!" Her friends were used to her moods.

Back in Sacramento, her mother puttered around not cleaning house; her father puttered around not earning a living—all pleasant enough in its paralyzing way, and perfectly routine. The family would eat in silence: roast beef or pork ordered from the Corti Brothers meat counter. Didion read alone in her bedroom, filched stationery from her father's Air Force recruiting office (she figured if taxpayers had to foot the bill for military supplies, she was damn well going to use them), and returned to Berkeley not refreshed, precisely, but calmer, at least for a while.

Her mother did not remember encouraging her as a child to apply for the *Vogue* contest. No matter. Her father knew it was a gamble, setting off for New York, a single young woman in a highly competitive field. Sometimes gambles paid off. His philosophy was simple: She can't play if she's not sitting at the table.

The trouble was, she had to graduate. She'd overlooked her Milton requirement.

The English Department agreed to let her commute from Sacramento once a week during the summer to discuss with a professor the cosmology of *Paradise Lost*. This would earn her the needed credits. On Fridays, she caught a Greyhound bus through Richmond and Crockett, past the C&H sugar plant, or she took the City of San Francisco train. The food on the train was rancid, soups from hell, and the tinted bus windows made a "grayed and obscurely sinister light" of the fires of the oil refineries around Carquinez Strait, she said.

Finally, on June 2, Professor Henry Nash Smith wrote her that he was returning her papers and turning in to the registrar a grade of A. He said, "I would like to tell you . . . how excellent I think your handling of the critical topics is. I believe you have truly remarkable abilities as a critic. Perhaps you have comparable abilities as a writer of fiction, but the story in the current *Occident* is the only piece of your fiction I have seen, and I am not sure I think it equal, as fiction, to the level you maintain in criticism."

Chapter Six

———————— ❧ ————————

In the fall of 1956, just shy of her twenty-second birthday, Didion felt her future lay in New York as a writer of fiction. She was aware of her naïveté. In the *Vogue* personnel office, filling out a profile sheet, she answered the question "What languages do you speak?" with "Middle English" and knew she was in over her head.

The editors for whom she worked had no idea what it was like to survive on forty-five dollars a week. "I can remember asking if someone could get me a discount on a polo coat, because I needed a winter coat, and she said, 'Oh sweetie, a polo coat is all wrong for you, put yourself in Hattie Carnegie's hands, she does wonderful things for small people.' Put yourself in Hattie Carnegie's hands! So I kept feeling even poorer than I was," she said.

She charged food at Bloomingdale's gourmet shop (but when could she ever pay?).

Women were required to wear hats in the office—a dress code Didion ignored. One day the company nurse, a "Miss K," caught her in the coffee room to tell her, "You lose ninety per cent of your body heat in your head." Didion understood. She'd been warned: Play the game.

Didion said that the personnel director, Mary Campbell, a former gym teacher and Condé Nast's personal secretary at one time, "would stop me in the hall to ask me if I'd called my mother, and if I said, 'Not since last Tuesday,' she'd say, 'Come into my office right now and call her.'" Every morning, Nurse K "would line up little cups of phenobarbital for you if you came in nervous. You could take naps in Miss K's office."

Rosa Rasiel, another aspiring young writer at the magazine, offered Didion space in the small apartment she shared with her sister Naomi on East

Seventy-ninth Street. She was struck by Didion's ambition: It was clear she didn't want to write "commercial stuff, in any sense of the word," and yet she wanted to be financially independent. She'd enter ad firms' slogan contests, penning phrases—"Colgate toothpaste is as fresh as an apple in your mouth."

"I was trying to write a novel at night," Didion recalled. "I did not see a career for myself on the staff of a magazine because I had no interest in the politics involved. I had no interest in dressing right and doing all of the things that you had to do if you were on a career track."

In those days, New York subway seats were covered with a tight straw weave that would rip a girl's nylons if she didn't first smooth her skirt along the backs of her legs. It was hard to remember to do this on early mornings, groggy as she rushed to work. Didion washed her hair every day "in an era when *no one* did that," Rasiel told Linda Hall for *New York* magazine. "She'd do it even in the dead of winter, and then she'd put on a black velvet cap that tied under the chin and go to work, and by the time she got there, her hair would be dry. And like most of us then, she had one pair of good shoes. But she would wear her sneakers and carry her shoes to work in a bag, long before anyone else did that."

Rasiel once asked Didion, "Doesn't your hair freeze, going out in the cold with a wet head every day?" Didion "ruffled the ends of her semi-pageboy," Rasiel said. "'Well, this morning it *did* crackle a bit,' she replied."

Sullen boys lined up each day outside the Lexington Avenue entrance to Grand Central Station, smoking and watching the women who went into the Graybar Building, where *Vogue*'s offices were. Despite her uneasiness with this, and with the magazine's corporate ethos, Didion "liked being there," she said. Her office mate Sue Delman, heiress to a shoe fortune, was pleasant and friendly (though the office itself, a cubicle with two desks beneath a cracked ceiling, brightened only by a travel poster Scotch-taped to the wall, depressed Didion). The smells of Madame Rochas, Disrissimo, and Arpege perfumes adrift in the corridors kept her floating, and the people couldn't have been more colorful. Other staffers included Despina Plakias Messinesi, a longtime travel editor, who had once ridden a donkey to breakfast at the Ritz to call New Yorkers' attention to a Greek war-relief effort; the mysterious Palma—a "Gorgon always called only by her last name," Rasiel said—who essentially served as Jessica Daves's bodyguard; and Mary Campbell, who didn't give a damn about fashion.

The office politics were morbidly entertaining ("The late fifties at *Vogue* . . .

represented the madwoman's last hurrah," Mary Cantwell, one of the magazine's writers, said). The secretaries were called "researchers," so they wouldn't realize they were secretaries. *Neurosis* was in, though the staff thought the fashion editors too shallow to be neurotic. The writers (the "verbals") didn't trust the photographers (the "visuals"), and the visuals thought the verbals were dowdy. "Well, it's a *look*," the editors would say wearily of a dress they hated but had to feature because the manufacturer advertised heavily in the magazine.

After work, if she'd received a little money from home, Didion might walk with coworkers to a nearby Chock Full o' Nuts for a toasted cream cheese sandwich, head to Barneys for a drink or to Henry Halper's for egg salad, or go to the Thalia or the Beverly to catch an old movie.

One morning, assigned to study back issues, Didion dusted off February 1, 1941. She came across a piece by John W. Vandercook, "All Eyes on Hawaii." Writing of Hawaii's "façade," he suggested its "nostalgic, Polynesian past, like a bee in amber, is somehow miraculously preserved, yet it is oddly not inconsistent with admirable hotel accommodation." But the truth was, Hawaii hosted "the largest concentration of regular Army troops in the United States." It was not quite the paradise it seemed. A maritime fortress, it was the Pacific coast's "one sure sanctuary," a place of "calm security," Vandercook said: "Neither the Army nor the Navy is the least bit worried" about an attack.

Didion wept. The irony was too great to bear and she missed the smell of the salt air, the sunshine, the fog, the thrill of Pacific distances. She was a stranger in New York. Her life here wasn't real. Was she lying to Bob or herself when she told him on the telephone that she'd be in New York only until Christmas, maybe Easter—at any rate, no more than a few months?

In "Goodbye to All That," she says she'd stroll past the Seagram Building fountains after work, feeling their foamy spray on her face; she'd peer through the barred windows of brownstones, seeing sweaty cooks hunched over vast industrial stoves—surely on the floors above, beautiful women were lighting candles for dinner or drawing warm water for their children's baths; she stopped at a fruit stand and stood, braced and chilled, eating a peach very, very slowly.

Somewhere in this city, teeming with soldiers home on leave from Korea, lining up on Broadway with discounted tickets for the plays, there was a John Wayne just for her, or a Howard Hughes, reclusive and mysterious, offering glimpses of extraordinary worlds.

No, her New York life wasn't real. Someday she'd pay for these pleasures. She *did* miss her flat horizons. But she wasn't sorry she'd come. After all, in her family, she was the latest in a long line of women given to "opaque bewilderment and moves to places not quite on the schedule." Years later, she'd reflect, "I was never a fan of people who don't leave home. . . . It just seems part of your duty in life."

PART THREE

Chapter Seven

———— ✿ ————

1

The woman we know from the books was about to emerge, but she felt she was "in a coma." "I could quote a lot of English poetry—that's what I did in college—and I could give you the house and garden imagery of a lot of English novels. You could have asked me what the Boer War was and I couldn't have told you."

Didion's selling herself short: She came to *Vogue* equipped with discipline, a passion for reading, a keen attentiveness, a grounding in the history of the West, and a sensitivity to quirky locutions. She came with an old-fashioned work ethic—you *fought* for your territory. She did not abide idleness or education for its own sake or the view that pragmatism sullied the soul.

"[I was] a good deal of trouble," she said, looking back. "[S]kirts too long, shy to the point of aggravation, always the injured party, full of recriminations and little hurts." At *Vogue,* she was initially limited to promotional copy—"the kind that was sent to stores as advertising support"—thirty lines at most, usually eight or so, hacked at by her editor.

Once a career has taken root, its seeds are hard to trace: In retrospect, its flowering seems inevitable. Surely, Joan Didion, piercing observer, fierce stylist, oddly sexy and reluctant pop icon, leaped fully blown into the hippie-dippie sixties, exposing our hypocrisies, our sloppy thoughts.

In fact, when she first settled in New York, "She was a) hard to know, b) very shy, and people, being stupid as they are, underrated her," said Noel Parmentel, who'd soon be a central figure in her life. "Practically everybody I knew underrated her. She just didn't register on the screen."

"I . . . tended my own garden, didn't pay much attention, behaved—I suppose—deviously," Didion said. "I mean I didn't actually let too many people know what I was doing."

An instructive aside: In 1973, John Gregory Dunne accused Pauline Kael of misunderstanding how movies are made, how careers unfold, how *art gets done*. In a letter to Kael warning her of his attack, he said, "I think you're the best movie critic in America, but I'm not altogether sure that's a compliment." The problem, he said later, is that an "implacable ignorance of the mechanics of filmmaking . . . prevails in all of Kael's books. . . . Few critics understand the roles of chance, compromise, accident and contingency in the day-by-day of a picture."

Similarly, Didion watchers tend to ascribe to her levels of agency, guile, and foresight she just didn't have. For example: Her early writing "captures the turbulence of a culture in upheaval," one reviewer said; it "impose[s] some order on . . . American mayhem," another wrote. Or as Jonathan Yardley, *The Washington Post*'s former book review editor, said, she "had her eyes on the nation" and "dared" to say what she saw.

These assessments—like the claims I made in the prologue to this book— aren't wrong, but they suggest a deliberative approach simply not present in Didion's daily writing of the 1950s and early 1960s. Her first important essays, written across several years for various assignments, composed in volatile emotional weathers, and under varying editorial strictures, did not come ready-made from a *Vogue* dress pattern—length, width, and color all laid out. Nor did their appearance make Didion an instant star, coaxing fire from her Smith Corona, the way Jimi Hendrix pulled flames from his Stratocaster.

If Didion sold her young self short, and critics gave her too much rope, the truth of her professional beginnings and subsequent fame is much more complex and fascinating.

Later, she understood how helter-skelter the process had been. "[In 1969] I was starting a column for *Life*, and we happened to be in Hawaii," she told Meghan Daum in 2004. "I had to write my first column introducing myself, and right then the My Lai stuff broke. So I called my editor at *Life* and said I want to go out to Vietnam, but he said, 'No, some of the *guys* are going out. You just introduce yourself.' And I was so angry that I introduced myself in a very un-*Life*-like way." That is, she was, or appeared to be, uncomfortably personal in a formal column (we'll look at the column later). "*Life* at that time had eleven million readers and I got an awful lot of feedback, a lot of it negative, and a lot of it more responsive than I could deal with. Then *Play It As It Lays* came out shortly after, which was read as autobiographical, although it wasn't, and so between *Play It As It Lays* and that column, I was getting a lot of that [popular attention]. It was kind of a burden."

She's not admitting how titillating it was, in 1969, for a woman to write about abortion, divorce, S&M, orgies, and drugs, especially if she appeared to be talking about herself. Women saw her as emotionally available; men fantasized more lurid access.

How crafty was she in choosing her subjects? How lucky? How did she get her breaks? How did the timing work? These questions can be answered only by studying her *Vogue* years, from 1956 to roughly 1966, though she contributed occasional columns after that. Until her relationship with *The New York Review of Books*, begun in 1973, her ties to *Vogue* formed her longest-lasting bond with a particular magazine. This commitment clicked when the slicks had power and she was a pup. In the meantime, the "advantages" of writing a novel at night, in secret, after a day in the fashion trenches were "probably . . . precisely the same as the disadvantages," she reflected later. "A certain amount of resistance is good for anybody. It keeps you awake."

2

Didion upped her salary from forty-five dollars a week to sixty-five or seventy. "At *Vogue*, she worked hard because they knew how good she was and made her do all of the heavy lifting," said Parmentel. Eventually, she "conned" the *Vogue* Promotion Department into thinking it was reasonable to expect only one ad every two weeks from a copywriter. The schedule gave her time to freelance for other magazines. She had an office, a telephone, and messenger service. Marshaling these resources, she fired off pieces to *Mademoiselle* and *Gentlemen's Quarterly*. The first one bit, not the second. At one point, she had six positive responses to queries she'd mailed, to places as diverse as *Commonweal*, *The Nation*, and *The Reporter*.

Rosa Rasiel left *Vogue* for graduate school at Columbia. When she moved out, Didion spent a year living in the cellar of Mildred Orrick's apartment. Orrick was a well-known fashion designer celebrated for introducing dance leotards as items of casual clothing and promoting flared coats once wartime fabrics restrictions eased.

Eventually, Didion rented an apartment in the East Nineties, "furnished entirely with things taken from storage by a friend whose wife had moved away," she wrote in "Goodbye to All That." The apartment was a third-floor walk-up at 1215 Park Avenue, across the street from the Armory, between Ninety-fourth and Ninety-fifth streets. She had a fireplace, shuttered windows, air conditioning, high ceilings and white walls, one bedroom and a kitchenette, for $130 a month—a tough amount to make, even freelancing. She hung a map of Sacramento County on the living room wall to remind herself of water. New York had rivers, but they weren't . . . well, *rivers*.

She bought Victorian walnut marble-top tables to add to the furniture she'd borrowed from her friend. To Peggy La Violette, she identified this friend as "Noel," her "old love." She remained involved with him off and on during her years in New York; exactly when she stopped considering him her "love"—if she ever *really* did—is unclear. (By now, Bakersfield Bob was history.)

Parmentel "has never been credited in Didion profiles because he has never (until now) agreed to go on the record about their relationship," Linda Hall wrote in *New York* magazine in 1996.

For over a year I requested an interview with this mysterious man, whom Hall had described as a "hard-drinking, anarchic, verbal gymnast." I got no answer, and then one day a charming voice on my answering machine said, "I owe you an apology. I didn't answer you 'cause I didn't want to talk to you, but everyone 'cept me thinks I *should* talk to you, so I will." A year or so later, he invited me to his lovely house in Fairfield, Connecticut, for a lengthy chat. He promised to meet me at the railway station carrying a copy of *The White Album* so that I'd know who he was: "We'll 'meet cute,' as in an old Hitch movie."

Later, when we'd settled on his screened porch with glasses of white wine, he said he "hadn't wanted to think about Joan again after what she's been through," but, once upon a time, he "knew her better than anybody in the world."

Noel E. Parmentel Jr. was born in Algiers, Louisiana, an old Victorian-era section of New Orleans west of the Mississippi River, in 1927. His mother had worked for the Veterans Administration. Besides having rivers in common, a love of Victorian houses, and a parent in the army, Didion and Parmentel shared temperaments. "I had a theory that if I could understand the South, I would understand something about California, because a lot of the California settlers came from the Border South," Didion said. Parmentel was her man.

Except he was not so easy to understand. His friend Norman Mailer saw him as an "arch-conservative but a marvelously funny guy" ("I must love him, otherwise I'd kill him," Mailer said). Historian Kevin Smant saw him as a "non-conservative," a wolf in sheepskin prowling the *National Review* offices, and writer Julia Reed remembered her mother dismissing him as "drunk, of course."

"[A]nyone who knew anything about New York . . . knew Noel," Dan Wakefield wrote in *New York in the Fifties.* He "was the most politically incorrect person imaginable. He made a fine art of the ethnic insult, and dined out on his reputation for outrageousness. In print, he savaged the right in the pages of *The Nation,* would turn around and do the same to the left in *National Review* [he once called *The Village Voice* a 'little Leftist don't-do-it-yourself affair'] and blasted both sides in *Esquire*—and everyone loved it."

"Well, Dan had some fun with me in his book," Parmentel said, "but it was accurate."

After a stint in the Marines, Parmentel attended Tulane University and the University of Minnesota before heading for New York. "I could have gotten my Ph.D. at Columbia, but instead I got my education at the West End Bar—a much better choice," he said.

Parmentel would pace Wakefield's "small, cluttered apartment on Jones Street, rattling the ice cubes in his glass of bourbon, clearing his throat with a series of harrumphs, and pronouncing who was a phony and who was not, like some hulking, middle-aged Holden Caulfield with a New Orleans accent," Wakefield wrote. "Most people, in Noel's harsh opinion, were phonies but he delighted in discovering the few who were not."

His search for authentic companionship took him down byways and into the back rooms of literary publishers, theater directors, and filmmakers—and to "about six parties a day. Too many," he said. "Everything happens at parties, and that's how I met people. My wife finally filed for divorce, and who could blame her?"

In his white suits, he was a seductive figure, with a large frame and a "shock of light brown hair falling over his wide brow," said Wakefield. He befriended Carey McWilliams and William F. Buckley Jr., Mailer, and the film documentarians Richard Leacock and D. A. Pennebaker. Like Didion, he had a "conservative streak that was real," said Jim Desmond, who worked as a cameraman for Leacock and Pennebaker. "He was no redneck, but he *knew* all those guys. He knew the stuff from the top right down to the crap. He could cross any class line there was. I mean, he took me *beagling* in New Jersey once!"

On a trip down South with Parmentel, the actor Sam Waterston learned "he'd been a rake-hell and a rogue in his youth, and it seemed to my innocent eyes that everyone who was anyone in the Garden District had been in love with him at one time or another."

In New York, he was a raconteur, prankster, gadabout, and one of the city's finest writers. "His style . . . was that of an axe-murderer," said John Gregory Dunne. Parmentel was perhaps the best *teacher* of young writers on the island. "[H]e was as close to a mentor as anyone I have ever known," Dunne wrote. "I arrived in New York in 1956 [full of] right-minded and untested opinion. I met him at a party, he insulted the hostess and most of the guests, and left. . . . In the polite, middle-class Irish Catholic circles in which I grew up, a guest did not call his hostess 'trash.' Neither did a guest, when introduced to a Middle-European count, say pleasantly, 'Scratch a Hungarian and you'll find a Jew.'" Parmentel was "like a stick of unstable dynamite," Dunne admitted, but he said Parmentel "taught me to accept nothing at face value, to question everything, above all to be wary. From him I developed an eye for social nuance, learned to look with a spark of compassion upon the socially unacceptable, to search for the taint of metastasis in the socially acceptable."

When Parmentel met Didion, he knew right away she was no "phony."

"As I remember it, Joan met Noel at a party we went to at John Sack's, courtesy of a college acquaintance, Steve Banker, who lived in the neighborhood and invited us to John's," said Rosa Rasiel. Banker had gone to Harvard with David Halberstam, J. Anthony Lukas, and Sydney Schanberg. John Sack had been a war correspondent in Korea.

"At the party, Joan and I got to talking about a gin mill in Berkeley I used to hang out at when I was a Marine," Parmentel told me. "We hit it off. I could see right away that she was different and special. The *best* sense of humor. And a wonderful bullshit detector."

Afterward, "Noel was around a lot," Rasiel said. (He lived very near them, in a railroad flat on Ninety-third Street.) "From the beginning, he called Joan 'That mouse.'" He became "Joan's eminence grise, her taskmaster," she said. He convinced her that World War II did *not* start with Pearl Harbor. He took her to meetings of the Village Independent Democrats and to parties at Bill Buckley's or Alexander Liberman's. He taught her to be skeptical, in print, even of her most cherished ideals, as when he dismissed the young Republicans he met each week in the White Horse Tavern, and of whom he was quite fond, as "the acne and the ecstasy."

"One evening, while Joan's mother was visiting New York, Joan invited me to dinner, I think as a buffer, since Noel was expected," Rasiel recalled. "I don't remember whether he ever called or showed up. I do remember Mrs. Didion saying, when he was about half an hour late, 'I don't know that I'd bother.'"

When Eduene *did* finally meet him, her sole pronouncement was, "He's too big."

At first, Parmentel wasn't quite sure what to make of Joan Didion. "I never saw ambition like that," he said. "Not ambition as in hanging out at Elaine's. I mean, Joan would work twelve hours a day at *Vogue* and twelve hours a night. It was ferocious. Flabbergasting. In the culture she was from, girls didn't go to New York and work like that."

In California, her family's fabric was beginning to unravel. Her parents called to say her grandmother Edna had collapsed, unconscious, on the sidewalk in front of her house. That night, in Sutter Hospital, she died of a cerebral hemorrhage. Wistfully, as though hearing a distant radio through an open window somewhere, Didion remembered Edna's old stories: in wartime, working the line at the Del Monte cannery, weeping with a migraine; knitting cashmere socks for the Red Cross to send to boys at the front; spending afternoons in Sacramento window-shopping at Bon Marché, buying a cracked crab for supper, and taking a cab back home.

She left Didion fifty shares of Transatlantic stock. Her will instructed her granddaughter to sell the stock and buy something she wanted but couldn't afford—food, a hat, cocktails after work.

Didion hunkered over her typewriter. From the window of her office, high above Lex, she could see TIME and LIFE spelled out in signs above Rockefeller Plaza.

The next deadline was nigh.

"Action verbs!" yelled Allene Talmey.

Didion couldn't believe it: She had grown up reading this woman in *Vogue*, and now she worked for her. A graduate of Wellesley, Talmey had been at the magazine since the 1930s, after writing for *The Boston Globe* and the *New York World*, and editing for the old *Vanity Fair*.

Each morning now, Didion walked into Talmey's office with several lines of copy. The editor wore a big ring; aquamarine and silver, it reminded Didion of her great-aunt Nell, and she sat mesmerized, trembling, as the ring flashed across her pages. With a blunt pencil, Talmey scratched out words. She would "get very angry," Didion said. A previous apprentice had told Mary

Cantwell, "The first few weeks [with Talmey] . . . well, my dear, I used to go home, sit in the tub, and *weep*. My dear, the bathwater was pure salt." Not everyone lasted with the fierce old editor, but those who did got a splendid education.

Didion's captions had to fit the magazine's layout—blocks of text, thirty lines long, each featuring sixty-four characters. Very demanding. "On its own terms it had to work perfectly," she recalled.

"I would have her write three hundred to four hundred words and then cut it back to fifty," Talmey said. "We wrote long and published short and by doing that Joan learned to write."

An early example: "All through the house, colour, verve, improvised treasures in happy but anomalous coexistence. Here, a Frank Stella, an Art Nouveau stained-glass panel, a Roy Lichtenstein. Not shown: A table covered with brilliant oilcloth, a Mexican find at fifteen cents a yard."

"It is easy to make light of this kind of 'writing,'" Didion wrote many years later. "I do not make light of it at all: it was at *Vogue* that I learned a kind of ease with words (as well as with people who hung Stellas in their kitchens and went to Mexico for buys in oilcloth), a way of regarding words not as mirrors of my own inadequacy but as tools, toys, weapons to be deployed strategically on a page."

To Peggy La Violette, Didion described Talmey as sharp and nasty; later, in interviews, she expressed her gratitude for the woman's teaching. "Run it through again, sweetie, it's not quite there," Talmey would say. "Give me a shock verb two lines in. Remember the Rule of Three: three modifiers per subject. Prune it out, clean it up, make the point."

"We were connoisseurs of synonyms. We were collectors of verbs," Didion said. "We learned as reflex the grammatical tricks we had learned only as marginal corrections in school ('there were two oranges and an apple' read better than 'there were an apple and two oranges,' passive verbs slowed down sentences, 'it' needed a reference within the scan of the eye) . . . Less was more, smooth was better, and absolute precision essential to the monthly grand illusion."

3

At photo shoots, Didion learned that the "traditional convention of the portrait, which was that somehow, somewhere, in the transaction between artist and subject, the 'truth' about the latter would be revealed" was false. "In fact, what occurred in these sittings, as in all portrait sittings was a transaction of an entirely opposite kind," she said. "[S]uccess was understood to depend on the extent to which the subject conspired, tacitly, to be not 'herself' but whoever and whatever it was that the photographer wanted to see in the lens." At the time, it may not have occurred to Didion that a writer's *verbal* portraits of people traced highly subjective truths, as well, but with a hungry eye she watched intensely the "little tricks," the "small improvisations, the efforts required to ensure that the photographer was seeing what he wanted": covering the lens with a veil of black chiffon, changing dresses, altering the lighting.

4

The night novel hung in strips of pages, taped together, on the wall of Didion's apartment near her map of Sacramento County. Whenever she finished a scene, she would tape or pin it to the others in no particular sequence. Sometimes a month, maybe two, would pass before she'd run her fingers through the strips. They rustled like snakeskins. *Harvest Home* was her working title; homesickness, her spur.

5

Among her writer friends, drinking was "part of the texture of life in general" in 1950s New York, Didion said. "I mean, it wasn't just writers. It was people across the board. People who worked in offices, people who worked in advertising agencies." At *Vogue,* "we'd routinely have a drink at lunch."

And then *after* work, neighborhood bars offered "drinks for fifty cents and you'd think, 'Wow, my god,' and you'd sit there and be pissed to your eyeballs," said John Gregory Dunne.

Didion met Dunne one night in 1958—"it was not long after *Sputnik,*" Parmentel recalled. He introduced them. At the time, Didion was living in Mildred Orrick's basement. She made dinner. "Noel told her, '*This* is the guy you ought to marry,'" Dan Wakefield said.

"It's true," said Parmentel. "I *did* tell her that. He was a good catch. His family had a good deal of money. The Dunnes were the Kennedys of Hartford. He was a nice guy, though he had some of those Irish shortcomings—temper, drink."

"Greg," as Dunne was known, wrote for *Time*. As his dinner date that night, he brought a charming woman named Madeleine, the daughter of Lloyd Goodrich, the director of the Whitney Museum. "I adored Greg," Goodrich—now Madeleine Noble—told me. "He was a very complex person—just the way he'd later come off in his books. Often, we'd go to hear Mabel Mercer together after work." For hours, they'd sit in the Byline Room and "down dry martinis."

Right away, at dinner, Dunne took to Didion. "He made me laugh," she said. "[H]e was smart and funny . . . and we thought the same way about a lot of things." For instance, neither believed they were particularly imaginative; their strength as writers lay in *responding* to their immediate surroundings. "I've thought of myself that way since I was a little girl," Didion said. Dunne said he understood this.

Prodded by Parmentel, who saw her tendency to withdraw as a professional liability, Didion had been trying to overcome her shyness. "I decided it was pathological for a grown woman to be shy," she said. "I began pushing myself to make a contribution. Instead of being shy, I became 'reticent.'" Her love of acting came in handy. It was useful to consider life a series of performances and to discover suitable roles—writing, sewing, cooking. To this repertoire, she now added "Jamesian distance."

Alcohol helped. Over drinks at dinner, she warmed to Greg Dunne. She liked his *heft*, his blue eyes, his gentle voice, slightly raspy, with just the trace of a lisp. Parmentel helped, too. He entertained the table, kidding Dunne about his Catholic boyhood. Didion's Western directness disarmed Dunne. According to him, after Parmentel left Didion's apartment, Madeleine passed out in a chair (she doesn't remember this). Didion fixed him red beans and rice, the great Southern standard. This is what men *liked*, right? "We talked all night," he said.

Didion's early *Vogue* pieces make explicit reference to unhappy domestic arrangements. She writes of being with a man who would whirl into the apartment, ask her to fix him a drink, and wonder why she hadn't cleaned the place. She'd stare at him and say nothing. She'd refuse to type his letters. He'd forget to ask her how she felt at the end of the day. "*Noli me tangere*, sweetie," he'd say, and slip out again.

This man had an irritating habit of trying to convince her he knew her better than she knew herself by telling her what she wanted—whether she wanted it or not.

He once told her it didn't matter whether you took care of somebody or they took care of you; it was all the same. The fact that this may have been a mature way of viewing life didn't matter to her. It still made her angry. Sometimes now "the world takes on for me the general aspect of a painting by Hieronymus Bosch," she wrote. "The tulips on Park Avenue appear to be dirty."

Above all, she feared her *own* feelings. Perhaps her ambitions were skewed. "[W]e are fatally drawn toward anyone who seems to offer a way out of ourselves," she wrote during her period with Parmentel. "At first attracted to those who seem capable of forcing the hand, we then resent their apparent refusal to understand us, their failure to be both Svengali and *someone to watch over me.*"

"The truth is, I did a lot for Joan and she did a lot for me," Parmentel said. "She tried to sober me up. It was hopeless. Then she tried to get me to write all the time, and that was hopeless, too."

At twenty-four—her mother's best year—she was sick of the world. Her novel kept fattening, shedding its skins. Allene Talmey tossed most of her words on the floor. And her Southern knight—well, where the hell was he *this* time?

Invited out for drinks—*Yes, five minutes. Get your ass over here!*—she'd rise from bed, slide the wet cloth off her head, and rush to the corner for a fifth of Jack. She couldn't risk missing anything, and yet after most parties, she was disappointed she'd gone. At dinner in a restaurant, aware of a man's flirtatious glances from the next table over, she overdid her slightest gestures. She couldn't help it; it was an automatic response. On the streets, waiting for a walk signal, she'd stare at a man to see if she could make him stare back at her, and then she'd move on with indifference. The confidence boost never lasted. Small favors for friends, their most innocuous requests, overwhelmed her. Everyone bored her.

She remembered a party in an apartment on Bank Street in the fall of 1956, when she'd first arrived in New York. In retrospect, what most surprised her that night was meeting *Democrats*! A grad student from Princeton tried to seduce her by suggesting he had a "direct wire to the PMLA, baby"; a Sarah Lawrence girl cooed about J. D. Salinger—she could tell from his work he had a Zen-like ability to see into her soul. Now, one more Zen remark at a party and she'd scream. By the way! someone had told her recently. Miss Sarah Lawrence? She seems to have pledged her soul to an electronics engineer.

———

One hot June evening, Didion attended a party at Betsy Blackwell's apartment for current and former *Mademoiselle* guest editors. It was the year Ali MacGraw became a GE; Didion would come to know her as Diana Vreeland's assistant. Years later, she and MacGraw would renew their friendship in California. But that night at Miss Blackwell's, Didion was not much in the mood to talk to anyone.

A power failure had knocked out the air conditioning. Miss Blackwell was drunk. The new GEs were eager, bright, and giggly: dreaming of penthouses, Argentina, sable coats. "Jamesian distance" couldn't calm Didion's nerves. The parade had moved on without her.

Chapter Eight

—————— ❁ ——————

1

Didion gave notice at *Vogue*.

Mademoiselle had been looking for a new college editor, someone to run the GE contest, read manuscripts, ride herd on the girls. Didion fit the bill. A former GE and now an *old woman*, she knew the ropes.

She'd done a few freelance pieces for *Mademoiselle*, including a travel brief on Carmel. Her long hours at *Vogue* meant she struggled to meet *Mademoiselle*'s deadlines. Polly Weaver, the editor, had become impatient with her. Still, it was Weaver who recruited her to oversee the college issue. She admired the girl's drive and knew she was juggling too much.

So in mid-summer of 1959, Didion told the frumpy Miss Daves, *Vogue*'s managing editor, that she'd decided to leave. Miss Daves shocked her by making a counteroffer: "Feature Associate." What would she say to that? She'd still be working with Allene Talmey, but she'd be writing articles instead of promotional copy. Her adjusted salary would top *Mademoiselle*'s bid. She'd be expected to start just after Labor Day.

Didion had a new piece in the *Mademoiselle* pipeline, scheduled to run in January. After the big betrayal, she'd still have to work with Polly Weaver.

She went to bed with a migraine.

Mademoiselle had asked her to return to her alma mater and report on "Berkeley's Giant: The University of California."

On the brink of a new decade, the magazine was more playfully innovative

than any of its competitors. While Luce publications predicted a stable period ahead, with prosperity and material contentment for all, *Mademoiselle*
had grasped the Beats' rumblings as an overture to mania.

The magazine's advantage was its freedom to explore subjects its peers
wouldn't touch. Words didn't sell it. Readers bought *Mademoiselle* for the
photographs and fashion bulletins, so the editors had considerable latitude
in choosing fiction and assigning topics. In its pages, Didion found herself
bumping up against the Beat writing she had so despised in college. Allen
Ginsberg, William Burroughs, Lorraine Hansberry, Norman Podhoretz,
François Truffaut, and Christopher Logue offered readers hopes and future
fears.

The January 1960 issue ran a feature called "Seven Young Voices Speak
Up to the Sixties." "Whatever one may think of them, certainly if more voices
like these speak up, lively and idiosyncratic, we may look forward to the decade with cheerful curiosity," the magazine declared. Later, Joyce Johnson
remarked that this particular issue of *Mademoiselle* gave "several thousand
young women between fourteen and twenty-five" a "map to a revolution."

Ginsberg wrote, "Everybody should get high for the next ten years."
Burroughs reduced America's values to "plastic, all hues, inflatable and
deflatable, for the Pause that Refreshes, helicopters and every kind of motor
vehicle. Gadgets, contrivances in dazzling number and variety, all mute and
odorless."

At Berkeley, Didion failed to see insurgencies. "Call it the weather, call
it the closing of the frontier, call it the failure of Eden; the fact remains that
Californians are cultivating America's lushest growth of passive nihilism right
along with their bougainvillea," she said. The current crop of college kids
was irresponsible, unmotivated, "totally unequipped," marked by an "absence
of drive."

In the library, or a sorority lobby, she *did* occasionally encounter vague
disquiet. "Everyone I meet is the same," one coed confessed to her. "I don't
know what I expected, but sometimes they make me tired." This is hardly a
foretaste of campus riots; with hindsight, it's tempting to say Didion didn't
get what was brewing. She projected her own lassitude onto people she met
and witnessed only what she wanted to see (her critics have *always* charged
her with this). On the other hand, the coed's remark shared page space with
a column of ads urging girls to "get top jobs" as secretaries, trained by Katharine
Gibbs, the Berkeley School, Grace Ball Secretarial College, Wood Secretarial
School, Grace Downs, the Powers School for "poise and self-assurance." Not
precisely a map to a revolution.

Instead of saying Didion missed the boat, we could just as easily—and more accurately—say she refused to buy "the times they are a-changin'" hype (already ubiquitous before the sixties began). Besides, her brother, Jim, was a Berkeley boy now, and fairly typical: happy-go-lucky, having fun. "We were all oblivious right up until the Free Speech Movement began in '64," the writer Larry Colton, a Berkeley alum, told me. "After that, it was impossible to ignore what was happening."

The changes Didion *did* record, she observed with detachment: "Berkeley has had a part in producing such diverse phenomena as Allen Ginsberg and the first atomic bomb," she wrote. *Howl* and the *Enola Gay*: the word *nihilism* seems eerily on the mark.

In retrospect, Didion's piece is most notable for its accompanying photographs, taken by Ted Streshinsky, a man who would play a pivotal role in her career, and for homesickness, her obvious longing for the California air smelling of "eucalyptus and salt water and January's first fruit blossoms." She gave her readers a taste of the nostalgia flooding her first novel, a "yearning for California so raw that night after night, on copy paper filched from my office and the Olivetti Lettera 22 I had bought in high school with the money I made stringing for *The Sacramento Union* ('Big mistake buying Italian,' my father had advised, 'as you'll discover the first time you need a part replaced'), I sat on one of my apartment's two chairs and set the Olivetti on the other and wrote myself a California river," she said.

2

Glimpses of the future Didion are scattered like keepsakes throughout the pages of *Vogue* in the early 1960s, particularly in the "People Are Talking About" column. A collage of celebrity sightings, clues to cultural hipness, commercial trends, the latest politics, comments on fashion, hot movies and books, the regular feature consisted of unsigned snippets arranged to form an eye-catching layout. Mary Cantwell said it was a "nightmare" searching for interesting material month after month. Didion told Peggy La Violette it was one of the "silliest occupations going." Nevertheless, the column forced her to suss out overlooked subjects or find new approaches to topics beaten to death. It gave her space to indulge her obsessions and turn them into cultural touchstones.

Allene Talmey took credit for "People Are Talking About," but Didion wrote many, if not most, of the pieces for it, beginning in 1960. Some bits are conspicuously hers; in other instances, it's hard to determine whether she suggested or wrote a piece. In any case, the column shows us the parade of men, women, trends, and objects she watched back then: JFK and Jackie, "leading a rebellion in beauty"—after Jackie, the "insistence on a certain nose, a special profile, is dead"; spy movies, *Dr. No, Fail Safe, The Manchurian Candidate;* the launching of Telstar; Cuba; the humor, "neither topical nor punchy, but simply human," practiced by Woody Allen and a set of edgy new comics; the atomic bomb; Willem de Kooning; Greasy Kid Stuff, a "hair tonic marketed by a couple of college students in Miami"; the "sleepiness of the enlarged—like a spleen—television news" and "local reporters who rarely ask the singularly important sensible question"; Buckminister Fuller; the John Birch Society, about which Didion knew a thing or two from her mom; interstate highway signs: "Have Wife With Gun Must Travel"; Marilyn Monroe, a "profoundly moving young woman"—the "waste seems almost unbearable if out of her death comes nothing of insight into her special problems; no step towards a knowledge that might save, for the living, these beautiful and tormented"; Tony Richardson and Vanessa Redgrave (who would play Didion onstage more than forty years later in *The Year of Magical Thinking*); Barbra Streisand; Warren Beatty; Henry Fonda, "looking like a man ridden . . . with desultory anxiety about fallout," hugging his intriguing daughter, Jane; the construction of the Guggenheim; protest marches organized by "threatened" people dragging their "monstrous" children with them through shabby urban battlefields.

It's obviously Didion who, in the midst of movie star profiles and fashion news, pauses to call our attention to slang or some slice of professional jargon warping or enriching American speech: the "satisfying rightness of the baseball phrase 'clutch play' used in any season to describe an instantaneous heroic move"; the "double-talk adjective, 'counterproductive,' used by Washington officials to describe those ideas that sound superb but wouldn't be"; "'elliptical,' a word necessary in describing a satellite in orbit"; "'Flash,' the word that replaces 'Kick' for anything that relieves monotony"—specifically, "flash" referred to the effects of LSD, as Didion would discover; and "zortz"— the word for "freshness in Los Angeles . . . as in 'This thing's got zortz." Apparently, this last one didn't catch on.

Didion's first "People" piece, in the November 1, 1959, issue, covered the Olympic Winter Games at Squaw Valley. The column is unsigned, but it's clearly Joan Didion fretting about "developers blast[ing] miles of ski runs out of the forest." Clearly, it's Joan Didion on the streets of Reno observing "ranchers' sons in Brooks Brothers suits and Stetsons . . . everyone speaking in the Oklahoma drawl, now the accent of the far West." She told game-bound readers where to eat on the mountain passes, how to arrange a ski trip on Donner Summit. Of course she knew from her father about the prized casinos. Hotels? When choosing, parents, keep in mind that children like "their mountains" pristine, "as if the remnants of the Donner Party just limped through," she wrote.

In 1960 she turned her ear to campaign speeches. Among the speech writers she profiled were Herbert G. Klein, a "41-year-old Californian with a sooth-ing touch" who wrote for Richard Nixon; JFK's man, Theodore C. Sorenson, "a gentle-mannered, but hard-headed lawyer" capable of a "pungent phrase." Didion's study of public texts and the personalities behind them honed the skills necessary for her later pieces in *The New York Review of Books*, as well as for her novels *Democracy* and *The Last Thing He Wanted*.

She keyed in to the changing vocabulary of international violence—"the tripping sound of 'plastique,' which in Paris means bombs"—and displayed an early impatience with what would soon be called the "counterculture": in "such Greenwich Village places as The Bitter End," where Bob Dylan per-formed, young people "[go] in for sentimental binges" on "social problems," she wrote, honoring songs such as "Brother, Can You Spare a Dime?" and "Times Gettin' Hard, Boys, Money's Gettin' Scarce," as though "every-one there [was] longing for the lovely Depression they were too young to know."

She tucked mini book reviews into the column, declaring Flannery O'Con-nor a "young writer with an uncompromising moral intelligence and a style that happily relies on verbs, few adjectives, and no inflationary details"; reiterating in public what she often said in private—that J. D. Salinger was "irritating"; warily praising William Burroughs's "dope dreams" (while dis-missing most of the Beats); noting, without comment, John Steinbeck's No-bel Prize; and absorbing Wright Morris's meditations on "what it means to be a Westerner"—in Didion's words, "unable to extricate the reality of the past from the myth of Manifest Destiny."

The young American writer who seemed to touch her most profoundly, in a surprisingly personal way, though his European-inflected sensibility couldn't have been more foreign to her, was John Hawkes, whose *The Lime Twig*, she said, left her "helpless" and compulsive under the assault of its "imaginative brilliance," unable to awake from its near hallucination and the rattlesnakes it freed in her mind. This was reading as dark eroticism.

Late in 1961, she delighted in discovering a little-noticed, "engaging" book, *I Want to Quit Winners*, by Harold S. Smith Sr., who ran Harold's Club in Reno and who, "exploring the vagaries of his career," Didion said, "wrote precisely, 'You play them as they lay.'"

In certain pieces, we overhear Didion's chats with Parmentel—when she writes glowingly of Barry Goldwater or complains of JFK's "fence-sitting" or asserts that "our economy, and consequently our Federal revenues" would be better off if we would "scale down our steeply progressive Federal income tax rules."

The column lets us follow her to the Thalia or Loew's, theaters earning more money—at last!—from the films they showed than from candy bar sales: Maybe it was going to be a great decade for Hollywood.

In Ingrid Bergman's performances, Didion sees how "part of the boredom in some of her movies lies in her habit of withdrawing even in front of the camera. She becomes, then, as remote as though her emotional life was fainting" and suggests "an apparent hesitation on the shore of sex." In these lines, written in 1959, we witness the initial (if unintended) conception of Maria in *Play It As It Lays*, published eleven years later.

The seeds of other novels appear in the furrows of the white spaces in *Vogue*. On page 761, in the May 1960 issue, we find juxtaposed a reference to nuclear testing and a lengthy mention of Hawaii, both obviously written by Didion, and both central to the project evolving, twenty-four years later, into *Democracy*. That book's collage structure gives its pages a sleek, spare look reminiscent of the "People" column.

Naturally, *Harvest Home* (ultimately *Run River*), the novel she was writing while composing "People" each month, kept popping up in the pieces. In addition to the "blue sky" elegy in the Olympics travelogue, we find, one year before the novel appeared, a rant against the "forced breaking up of the big San Joaquin Valley ranches: the bitterly fought, possibly suicidal result of a land reform law which says that anyone receiving Central Valley Project water must dispose of holdings over one hundred and sixty acres." The dying of the California ranches, and the loss of the social norms supporting them, is the novel's primary tragedy.

Vogue's screed against California water laws is followed by a loving portrait of a proton magnetometer, a geologic instrument no doubt evoking for Didion her ancestor Herman Jerrett and his stoic life in the Sierra.

Her first signed article for *Vogue*, a gloss on jealousy ("passion for the documentation of irrelevant detail is characteristic of the afflicted"), appeared in the June 1961 issue. Similar pieces followed—meditations on nostalgia, emotional blackmail, and self-confidence. One of her best-known early essays, "On Self-Respect," a centerpiece in *Slouching Towards Bethlehem*, made its first appearance in *Vogue* in August 1961. It came about, "improvised . . . in two sittings," because "the magazine had a piece that had been assigned, and the title was on the cover," she recalled. "And it didn't come in! But the cover had already been printed." She wrote the piece to a "character count," since the pages had been laid out in advance. Covers, layouts, and her peers' glacial work habits dictated much of what Didion wrote in those days.

"She was better than all of them, far above those people in every way," Parmentel says now. "A lot of her colleagues at *Vogue* were jealous of her. This little nobody from Sacramento shows up in her little dresses and outshines them all. She's smarter. Mannered. Better-bred. No bullshit."

She was starting to get noticed around town. In a gossip column in the August 1962 issue of *Esquire*, among mentions of W. H. Auden, Evelyn Waugh, and Hugh Kenner, this little tidbit appeared (probably planted by Parmentel): "Joan Didion, the fantastically brilliant writer and *Vogue* editor . . . at 26, is one of the most formidable little creatures heard in the land since the young Mary McCarthy."

But she was working without a plan, except for Condé Nast's month-by-month demands, and her editor put a heavy stamp on all her early pieces. It's instructive to read Allene Talmey's articles and learn, for example, that Didion's fondness for withholding a telling detail until the end of a paragraph is a favorite Talmey move. We see it in a profile of various theater people: Talmey describes a suite of offices consisting of "beat-up desks and usually an old container for coffee on the radiator." She concludes, "The only curiosity about all this is that these are the offices of the three producers." In future essays, Didion ran with this syntax: the wry, slightly formal, asidelike quality of the final flourish.

The nature of these early assignments—tossed to Didion at the last minute, randomly or because she was simply around to pick up the slack when others flubbed a deadline—gave her a reputation as a "personal" essayist. "A lot of people read these pieces and . . . people would come to me for, like, advice, and I hated it," she recalled. Later, "I quit writing those pieces because I couldn't take this Miss Lonelyhearts role." At the start of her career, she couldn't foresee she would end up, late in life, with readers once again seeking her advice—this time on grief and bereavement.

Chapter Nine

———— ❖ ————

1

In her early twenties, Didion was already grieving the passing of an old way of life. She worked that grief into her first novel. By now, she recognized and admitted to friends that she was "[d]istinctively dolorous by nature." Most of her friends did not know how to react to this. Noel Parmentel and Greg Dunne were just about the only ones who had "perfect pitch for [her] absurdities." On her twenty-third birthday, in 1957, Parmentel had altered a jacket of Henry James's *The Tragic Muse*. It now read *The Tragic M(o)use*. He slipped the jacket inside a Henri Bendel box along with a gray plastic rodent sporting a red ribbon on its tail and left the box outside her door. For the rest of the day, it was hard for her to play the "East End Avenue Ophelia."

On another occasion, this time within a month of Jack Kennedy's election to the presidency, she sat with a friend in an uptown movie theater, weeping as John Wayne, in the role of Davy Crockett, told a Mexican beauty, "A man's gotta live," and, "Republic is a beautiful word." She could not stop snuffling "by the time the battle was done, and Wayne lay on the cold, cold ground, bleeding as no one has bled since Janet Leigh in *Psycho*." At that point, the "last white woman walked out of the Alamo . . . She had soot on her face, and she was carrying her child, and she held her head high as she walked past Santa Anna into the sunset. So conspicuous was my sniffling by then that you could scarcely hear the snickers from my neighbors, a couple of young men from *Esquire*, both of whom resembled Arthur M. Schlesinger Jr.," Didion wrote.

These lines appeared in *National Review*. Though broadly humorous, the anecdote makes clear that, for Didion, the coronation of the handsome young Democratic president signaled America's decline—the country was an ashen-faced white woman with nowhere to go, surrounded by dark-skinned hooligans. Meanwhile, those nasty liberals from *Esquire* laughed as the fortress fell: "They don't make 'em like Duke on the New Frontiers."

Parmentel had introduced her to the folks at *National Review*. In its pages, mostly in book reviews, she expressed her dismay at the straying of the nation and perfected the tone of lament that would center her first novel.

Fictions of domesticity and suburban blah by Sloan Wilson and John Updike prompted this from Didion: "There was once a day when we not only expected men to disappear but allowed them to do it with grace (*Daddy's gone to get a rabbit skin to wrap his baby bunny in*), to escape without cracking up: men on the run opened the China trade, struck silver in the Comstock, followed dirt roads to sell pots and pans and trombones." No more. Duke, we hardly knew ye!

John Cheever hit the proper note for her in stories of "lost money and lost families": "I suppose that Cheever and my mother and I belong to the last generations in America with a feeling for the unbearable pull of the Chinese fan, the Canton fish plates; I am told that this sense of inextricable involvement with the past occurs infrequently even in my own generation," she wrote. "All of this means, perhaps, that Cheever is the matchless chronicler of a world that my children will never understand, a world caught in the ruins of a particular stratum of American society that somewhere along the way, probably during the 1920s, lost its will."

Perhaps most explicitly in a review of Evelyn Waugh's *The End of the Battle*, published in March 1962, we hear Didion pondering the roots of her literary sensibility: "Every real American story begins in innocence and never stops mourning the loss of it," she declares. "[T]he banishment from Eden is our one great tale, lovingly told and retold, adapted, disguised, and told again, passed down from Hester Prynne to Temple Drake, from Natty Bumppo to Holden Caulfield; it is the single stunning fact in our literature, in our folklore, in our history, and in the lyrics of our popular songs." But mourning the loss of Eden leads to dolor. Now, in the mid–twentieth century, with the recognition that reclaiming Eden is impossible without forking over a theme-park admission fee, the only escape from dolor is a "sense of the absurd, the beginning of a kind of toughness of mind; and to win that particular victory is to cut oneself irrevocably loose from what we used to call main currents of American thought." This is so because "hardness of mind

is antithetical to innocence, it is not only alien to us but generally misappre-
hended. What we take it for, warily, is something we sometimes call cynicism, sometimes call wit, sometimes . . . disapprove as 'a cheap effect,' and
almost invariably hold at arm's length, the way Eve should have held that
snake."

Said as only a whip-smart California conservative surrounded by Camelot's
press agents could say it.

This sophisticated and poignant struggle to find an effective American
voice could not be pried from her conviction, formed in childhood, that "there
are no more great journeys and possibly no more great vows." As she worked
to finish her first novel, she wondered if it was still worth it, at this point in
America's life, "to trouble to write a novel at all."

The *National Review* offices clashed vigorously with *Vogue*'s. From a woman's world to a world of (mostly) men; from mirrored conference rooms to
residential apartments redesigned as editorial bull pens but retaining the
claw-foot bathtubs of their former lives. The rooms overlooked a dingy inner
courtyard filled with trash (one morning, a tenant on a floor above pitched
his old bedsprings out the window, startling Whittaker Chambers, who had
just started at the magazine). Loose toilet paper rolls shared desk space with
Underwood typewriters, pinned-together galley sheets, a broken coffee
machine, and notes about the proper use of an en dash or when to lowercase
the word *Federal*. Takeout boxes from l'Armorique, Billy's Steakhouse,
and Nicola Paone's littered the floors around scattered pages from *Human
Events, The New York Times, The Washington Post*, and the Communist *Daily
World*. Over the clacking of the Underwoods, raised voices debated whether
fluoride was a Commie conspiracy or a conservative horror story, whether
Robert Welch, of John Bircher fame (and one of the *Review*'s initial investors),
really *had* accused Dwight David Eisenhower of being a foreign agent, or—
later—whether Goldwater's statement "I would remind you that extremism in
the defense of liberty is no vice. And let me remind you that moderation in
the pursuit of justice is no virtue!" was code for his support of the John Birch
Society. By that point, William F. Buckley Jr. had declared the Birchers the
lunatics of the Right and had distanced the *Review* from their libertarian
rhetoric.

The *Review* recruited Didion because it was "(correctly) perceived to be
too New York–East Coast oriented," according to Priscilla Buckley, WFB's
sister and the magazine's managing editor. Didion's Western perspective was

a plus. Also, though conservative, even libertarian, in her outlook, she was politically rough. "What was important to Bill in editing *National Review* was that the writing be distinguished," said Priscilla. "It seemed to him more important that a writer write beautiful prose than that the writer be a movement conservative. Indeed some of the people we published never were conservatives. Young John Leonard certainly was not. . . . Some started out as conservative, or perhaps as nonpolitical, and ended up as flaming liberals, Garry Wills, Joan Didion and . . . John Gregory Dunne among them. What they had in common was that all of them were prose stylists. And *National Review* profited from their skills, at least for a while." In fact, Ms. Buckley thought Didion did some of her very best work for the magazine: "[H]er prose, while always careful, was more relaxed, even impish" in the *Review,* funnier than it would be later, she said.

Didion was quite comfortable in this world of men. It was her father's world—a world of hierarchy and "orders," no bullshit—and her father had always been her biggest supporter. "My God, did he love and appreciate his daughter," Noel Parmentel said. "He liked me because I'd introduced her to people like the Buckleys and helped her get where he thought she belonged. He was unhappy, inwardly, but he had that kind of fierce male loyalty. And Joan—he thought she could do no wrong."

In the early 1960s, the Grand Central subway line was in particularly poor shape. The cars were dirty and badly ventilated; the lights went out frequently. Traveling to the *Review's* offices was hard on Didion, but some days she appreciated *NR's* relaxed chaos better than the chicer spaces of *Vogue.* She was tired of the gossipy intrigue in the hallways of Condé Nast. S. I. Newhouse had purchased *Vogue* and *Mademoiselle* and moved *Mademoiselle* into new offices in the Graybar Building. In the reorganization, many venerable editors left, voluntarily or otherwise, including Cyrilly Abels. It both amused and depressed Didion that even with a new staff, the ethos at *Mademoiselle*— "hysterical smallness"—didn't change. Occasionally, Didion still wrote pieces for *Mademoiselle* and grumbled that, given *her* druthers, the editors wouldn't cut her *fingernails,* much less her paragraphs. As for *Vogue,* it took a "good deal of unpleasantness" to finally get her name on the masthead.

Vogue alluded to politics as lightly as possible. Presumably, it took no sides. It presented its glamorous models against shadowy social backdrops—a floating vacuum catered with gin and canapés. *National Review* rolled up its sleeves and took a swing at just about everybody. Going back and forth on the dirty subway cars, Didion shuttled between these poles.

She took assignments from *Commonweal* and *The Nation.* "Nothing if not eclectic!" she'd quip to friends. She waffled between dismissing her freelance pieces as trivial and wanting to collect some of them into a book. She dreamed of calling the book *The Sweet, Swift Years,* after a line by William Saroyan: "I just turned a corner and the sweet, swift years were gone."

Didion's years in New York had exposed her to sophisticated media centers working to standardize journalistic expression. She had come from California with a different view of the press. Personalized advocacy was the norm at *The Los Angeles Times* under Harrison Otis and Harry Chandler; the paper did not report on California life as much as dictate it. Didion never questioned this stance, and it fit with the folks at *National Review.* At the same time, at the fashion magazines, she was learning to be more nuanced (she started at *Vogue* in a media atmosphere just coming to terms with the ruins of McCarthyism). Into this mix, she also brought her academic experience, a love of literary style. Her doggedness and ambition came from feeling herself an outsider with no possibility of being admitted into the club—as Nick Carraway said of himself, Gatsby, Daisy, and Jordan, "[We] were all Westerners and perhaps we possessed some deficiency in common which made us subtly unadaptable to Eastern life."

In the years ahead, the marriage of the Western press's PR savvy (using "news" to promote personal agendas) and the Eastern press's risk-averse professionalism (pursuing profits from multiple sectors with a pretense of objectivity) would create modern American politics, image-driven, filled with verbal codes. Didion, familiar with the turf on both coasts, and a skilled reader of texts, was perfectly primed to interpret the age.

2

In her pale blue office on the twentieth floor of the Graybar Building, Didion would sit staring at the twilight, wondering if Noel would show that night. She'd start a letter to her mother and not finish it (cheerily, Eduene had informed her that her brother had joined the Fijis at Berkeley and was *living it up!*). She'd thumb through an old issue of *Variety.* She'd watch the secretaries stand in the hallways playing with their makeup cases. Finally, she'd ring for the elevator.

The store windows on her walk home were padlocked and dark. She avoided the furniture outlets. It wouldn't do to look at furniture. Furniture was for families.

A series of short stories she wrote in the 1960s, cross-checked against details in her letters as well as slices of life in the "People" column, let us walk her home on these late evenings after work. The stories, which Didion admitted contained raw, undigested material from notes at the time, notes full of "everything I saw and heard . . . rough and inchoate," revealing "what I actually had *on my mind* . . . in New York," obsessively repeat experiences, scenes, patterns of behavior. The details are vivid, always the same, and are echoed, again, years later, in *Play It As It Lays*.

As one of her acquaintances puts it, most of these details concern "a romantic figure in . . . white suits, the doomed hero who all the women fall for": Noel Parmentel "is in all of her fiction." Years later, an angry Parmentel would agree. He would threaten a lawsuit against Didion for writing about him in a direct, "hostile," and unvarnished manner.

Her short stories about those years are uncharacteristically impressionistic. They capture her general feeling instead of offering a day-by-day accounting of facts. When reminded of the stories, particularly of their world-weary atmosphere, Parmentel could not recall specifics, but he agreed that the sketches were probably accurate. "That's what we did then. We went to parties," he said. "I was tall and single! Full days every day and full nights every night. I drank too much. Everybody drank too much. Sometimes I was over the top. But oh! What a memorable time it was!"

Waiting in her apartment after work were the chapters of her novel, fluttering limply in the air-conditioned breeze. She couldn't face them. A couple days of cool morning fog had made her long more than ever for the smell of eucalyptus. She'd pour herself a bourbon on the rocks and sit in the dark. After a while, maybe she would or maybe she wouldn't hear "Honey chile!" and a pounding at her door. He sounded like an Atlanta radio station. Depending on how much he'd had to drink, he'd fall into her bed still wearing his raincoat and ask her to hold him, or he'd insist they go to a party. If they went—somewhere in the East Sixties, say, where he knew a girl, *a girl with really pretty legs*, or a place down by the Frick—it would always be the same: At first, everyone would be enchanted by his noisy arrival and then, after a few drinks, he'd insult someone and none of them could wait for him to leave. He'd drag her to another gathering and they'd wind up on someone's busted-spring couch at dawn, stale-mouthed, too hungover to fight.

"In 'Goodbye to All That,' she says she stayed up all night with Noel—he's unnamed in the piece—and called on a friend at four in the morning to go to the White Rose Bar. That was me," Dan Wakefield said. "They knew I was always up for that."

Maybe afterward, Noel wouldn't show for days.

The stories "Coming Home," "The Welfare Island Ferry," and "When Did Music Come This Way? Children Dear, Was It Yesterday?" document a vexed dynamic.

She would press a suit coat he'd left in her closet—a kind of magical gesture to draw him back to her, or she'd have his dirty shirts and the striped bedsheets laundered. He'd *have* to come back for his shirts. Late one evening, he'd call to say he was someplace uptown, an important appointment, and he'd be there in forty minutes—no, fifty . . . maybe a couple hours—or maybe she could meet him in a bar down in the Village. She'd throw her raincoat over her nightgown and rush into the streets. Over beers, he'd tell her she needed more color in her face. She needed to *see* people. She only wanted to see him. A little later, *she'd* be the one suggesting they stop at a party. He could use a mood lift, the excitement of new people, she said. New people? He'd *met* all the new people. He'd already slept with most of them. He owed them money.

The story about sleeping with all the "new people" got "attached to me," Parmentel admitted, because "Oleg Cassini—he was always with Grace Kelly or Jackie Kennedy—made a joke once that he went to a party and realized he'd slept with everybody in the room. I was repeating that story."

Some mornings, walking to work, Didion would spot young mothers coming from the Donnell Library, wheeling home Winnie-the-Pooh books in baby carriages. She tried to imagine the women's lives. Cut daffodils in vases on dining room tables, lacquer trays, checkbook registers perfectly up-to-date. And the babies. It was hard to believe any of the *femmes du monde* at Condé Nast would ever have babies. Most of them were trying *not* to.

Throughout the day, every day, there was sobbing in the ladies' rooms. There were "rumors of abortions, all of which seemed to have been performed in Hoboken," Mary Cantwell said. "Fetuses were swimming in the sewers of New Jersey." Sometimes, after miscarriages, fetuses were quietly disposed of by doctors in the old Doctors Hospital, which was also pegged as a drying-out center for many editors when word got out that if you didn't catch them early in the day, they wouldn't be able to hold a coherent conversation with you.

One morning, one of Didion's colleagues told her she needed an abortion *and* she'd heard the district attorney's office had found her name on a "party girl" list making its way around town. She made a deal to rat out the good-time racket in exchange for the DA's arranging a legal D & C at Doctors Hospital. Didion would use this incident in a scene in *Play It As It Lays*.

It wasn't Doctors Hospital, but at Columbia-Presbyterian on East Sixty-seventh Street where Didion took *her* anxieties. An internist there whose mother-in-law had once been editor in chief at *Vogue* calmed her whenever she came to him frantic because her period was a day late. *Blue Nights* mentions the day he told her she'd need a ticket to Havana, his way of saying her rabbit test indicated an abortion might be in the cards and he would arrange it.

But there's a revolution in Cuba, Didion protested, uncomprehending.

The doctor misted plants on the bookshelves in his office. There's *always* a revolution in Cuba, he told her. Within days, she started bleeding. All night she cried—from relief, she thought. Then she realized she *wanted* a child.

In the mornings, now, the baby carriages near Donnell Library made her ache. On the evenings when Parmentel didn't arrive, she'd cut baby-food ads out of the paper and tack them to the wall beside her bed. In *Blue Nights*, she calls her sudden longing for a child a "tidal surge." She'd stare at the babies' eyes and imagine the children were hers. She'd burrow into blankets and squeeze her pillow.

It was clear. She needed not to attend more parties but to assert control, the control of a woman who could keep a checkbook.

Maybe they'd *feel* better if they got married, made some plans, she said to Parmentel. He demurred. Or he'd turn the talk from babies to sex.

What if she got pregnant? she asked him. He made it plain she'd be on her own.

(The question, "*Did* Didion ever get pregnant in New York?"—relevant because abortion became a central subject in her first three novels—her friends politely chose not to answer.)

She imagined being done with Parmentel, saying to him from now on they'd just be buddies.

What if the Queens tunnel started to crack one day while she was in it? What if a gas main exploded beneath her feet?

She thought of men she suspected of wanting her, men who liked her. Greg Dunne. They met for lunch occasionally, talked about writing. She enjoyed the affected way he greeted her with "Howdy," more like a Texan than an Eastern Irish Catholic (in fact, he said "Howdy" because he'd been a stutterer as a boy and still tripped on the word *hello*). They were comfortable together. They had a fine time, even if he *had* voted for JFK. One afternoon, he confessed to her that he loved poking around mailboxes in brownstone lobbies to discover who lived where. Serendipitously, he had located Tammy Grimes and Henry Fonda. She joined him for a round of snooping. They laughed a lot, and he told her he looked forward to their next lunch.

She wasn't eating much these days. Her stomach was usually upset. She had a yeast infection and often ran a fever. Sometimes she'd stare at a plate of pasta and it would look like a nest of snakes.

Nicky Haslam, an interior designer hired by *Vogue*'s Art Department, said that, in the office, Didion "spent most of every morning in tears following a disastrous evening, but by afternoon had put on lipstick and Fleurs de Rocaille, transforming herself into the most desirable, delicious, funny, and perceptive dinner date."

On visits to her parents in Sacramento, she'd sit in her old bedroom, remembering fireworks in the summer skies during the state fair; the marbled columns in old San Francisco hotels; her mother's warning, "All the fruit's going," during a flood when Didion was a girl; drinking beer or vodka and orange juice in the desert as a teenager, smelling of chlorine, sweat, and Lava soap, snuggling into a boy's shirt stiff with dirt and starch. She couldn't stand to stay in Sacramento, but she didn't want to return to New York. Her father told her it was okay to go back. He'd remind her she had to sit at the table to play. Years later, her mother told her she'd acted so listless on these visits, Eduene feared she was dying and just didn't want to tell them.

Always, it seemed, she got a run in her stockings on the flights back east. Her neck would hurt from sleeping against the window. She feared the landing gear wouldn't work. Invariably, New York was cold upon arrival, but then within days the heat would top ninety and people would pull ice cubes from tumblers of bourbon and run them along their arms.

One day, she found herself standing in the rain near Grand Central Terminal, trying to flag a taxi. It seemed she'd been standing there for hours without realizing it. A man came up and spoke to her. She started to cry. She feared she would never move from that spot.

Another day, she had thrown up after lunch. Once she got home, she emptied an ice tray into her bed. Maybe she could *freeze* the damn migraine.

3

"One incident I remember was very shocking to me," Parmentel recalled. "I said [to Joan], 'You ought to do a piece on the grand old hotels. She did and sent it to, I think, *American Heritage*. They sent it back, and she cried and cried and cried. I couldn't believe how hard she was taking it. She said this made her feel like when she hadn't been admitted to Stanford. I felt so bad for her that I sent the piece to somebody I'd met at *Esquire* and said, 'For Christ's sake, publish this thing—it's breaking her heart.' And they did."

A little later, during the excitement surrounding the founding of *The New York Review of Books*, he recommended Didion to Jason Epstein. "What do I want with some little nobody who writes for Buckley?" Epstein responded.

Throughout this period, to cheer her up (and perhaps to take some pressure off himself), Parmentel urged her to take short trips, eat a little, put on weight, get a bit of color into her skin. In the fall of 1962, she flew to California to vote in the Republican primary for a man named Joe Shell who was running against Richard Nixon. Nixon was too liberal for her. "Those Okies she grew up with were getting educated and taking over, and she was contemptuous of them," Parmentel said.

This act of pioneer citizenship gave her a glow, but soon it was gone. Off and on, she'd figured things were stalled with Parmentel, and the job at *Vogue* had "tapped into a certain vein of discontent," she said, "a definite sense that I was marking time, not doing what I thought I should be doing, which was finishing a novel that then existed only in pieces Scotch-taped to the walls of my . . . apartment."

Could she start over? Do something different?

Despite her ambition and drive, she had refused to believe she was locked into the consequences of her decisions. Like a gambler, she liked to keep her options open. Another way of saying this, she realized, was that she didn't want to grow up.

When she'd first got to New York, she had taken a correspondence course through the University of California Extension on shopping-center theory, a gesture in the direction of staying flexible—staying young—and *having it all*. She wanted to write fiction, but she was not deluded into thinking literature would pay the bills; if she could collect the capital and develop a series of regional centers in the West, lining up a department store as a mall's major tenant, or maybe even a neighborhood center or two with a supermarket chain as the anchor, she could fund her writing habit—she *was* her father's daughter! (As she dreamed of this, she recalled summer days in California with her brother, Jim, building model villages with matchboxes along the banks of irrigation ditches, planning the tiny cities' growth, watching them crumble into the ravines.) In her early days at *Vogue*, she'd sit on Irving Penn's studio floor reading *The Community Builder's Handbook*. Her colleagues didn't see the beauty of her plan—all those tasteless prefab buildings (beloved of the West, with so much space to fill). But she understood the value of malls: They were the same everywhere, "equalizers" in the "sedation of anxiety." The problem with her plan was not tastelessness or the difficulty of raising the scratch. A few months in New York taught her there were challenges unaccounted for by theory: government regulations, unions, the mob.

So she sought another direction. "I was bored . . . and I was having trouble with the novel . . . and I was tired of living this way, and so I decided to become an oceanographer," she recalled. She had always been fascinated by marine geography and "how deep things are." "So I went out to Scripps Institute to try to find out how to implement this and, of course, I learned that I was so lacking in basic science that I would have to go back to the seventh grade and start over."

Going back to seventh grade would certainly be a way of not growing up, but it was impractical. What she'd been avoiding was this: The desire to remain a child, untouched by consequences, was the real problem, a difficulty none of her New York friends seemed willing to face. It turned out that her body was ahead of her mind in grasping at least one practical course of action.

She tacked another baby-food ad to her wall.

On the "bad afternoon" when her break from Parmentel became official, she understood the terror of adult life: It was the need to make promises against an "amoral vacuum." "Making anything at all matter has never been easy," she wrote years later, recalling that day.

"Goodbye to All That" suggests *she* made the break. Dan Wakefield remembered it differently. "Noel came over to my place the day he convinced her he was never going to get married and have children," he told me.

In any case, she hoped she and Noel could stay friends. He was certainly a boon to her professionally.

She didn't comprehend how he could just stand there, listening to her so unmoved. He told her a lot had happened to him before he knew her, and "nothing much touched him anymore." She said she never wanted to get the way he was. "Nobody wants to," he said. "But you will."

4

Greg Dunne's apartment on East Eighty-fourth Street, in a block of flats built in the late 1930s, faced south and overlooked an identical building across the street managed by the same property owner. From his window he could see into an apartment just like his, with a decorative fireplace and the same number of light fixtures (four bulbs in the living room, three in the bedroom, and two in the kitchen). In *Vegas* (1974), a book Dunne described as a "memoir" as well as a "fiction which recalls a time . . . real and imagined," he said that while living in this apartment he discovered he had a "capacity for voyeurism" similar to a "virus lodged in [his] upper respiratory system." (In a letter to journalist Jane Howard, he admitted the phrase "real and imagined" was a ruse, designed to hide the book's autobiographical core.)

He had just broken up with a Catholic girl, who always said the Act of Contrition after sex in case she died in her sleep, when he realized what an unobstructed view he had into the apartment across the street and how bountiful that view could be. The tenant was a "large, good-looking woman of perhaps thirty, very tall, nearly six feet, long blond hair, well-proportioned figure," he wrote. Every afternoon, she opened her window, "turned the stereo on loud, made herself a drink, took off her clothes and then stark-naked, using her drink as a baton, began to conduct Mozart's Concerto #5 in A-Major."

She took his mind off *Time*. She changed his after-work routine. Now, instead of popping into funeral homes on the East Side "to see if anyone famous had died" or loitering around brownstone mailboxes, he rushed right home to his window: "She required total concentration."

Possibly in *Vegas* he exaggerated his snooping habits, as befits (one supposes) a fictionalized memoir, but in interviews Didion confirmed his proclivities and affirmed how much she enjoyed playing along with him (Invisible Scarlet O'Neil).

His love of sharing adventures with her would reach its peak over twenty years later in Los Angeles when, researching locations for the movie *True Confessions*, based on his novel, he visited the L.A. morgue at two in the morning with two homicide cops. "There must have been five hundred bodies in there," he said. "They're stacked in the cold room on Tiffany blue stretchers—you know, the light blue color of Tiffany boxes—five stretchers to a tier. The smell isn't too bad, but it's a little high, so you smoke a cigar. The whole thing just blew me away. It just blew my mind. I came home and woke Joan up and said, 'Babe, this is something you've got to see.'"

In *Vegas,* Dunne laid out a scene in which he told Didion about the woman in the apartment across the street. The thing was, he hadn't seen her in a while and he worried about her. Weeks ago now, she'd left all her lights on (*four in the living room, three in the bedroom, two in the kitchen*) and they were beginning to sizzle out. What if something had happened to her? Perhaps one of those randy fellows he'd spied in her bed . . .

Didion urged him to tell the building's super. He waffled. How could he do that without revealing his addiction to *watching*? Didion prodded him: Maybe she overdosed. On what? Dunne asked.

"Don't be obtuse," Didion said.

Shamed, Dunne went to the super. It turned out that the woman had eloped.

But that's not the point of the story. The point is, Didion pressured Dunne to confide in the super one morning in his apartment. She'd come home with him the night before. Together, they "sat and stared" at the missing woman's window, "neither of us saying a word," Dunne wrote, "until exhaustion finally took us to bed with each other for the first time."

John Gregory Dunne, born May 25, 1932 in West Hartford, Connecticut, always attributed his writing abilities (and his reporter's voyeuristic tics) to his childhood stutter. "I listened to the way people talked, becoming in the process a rather good mimic, and grew so precociously observant that my mother once complained that I never missed a twitch or a droopy eyelid or the crooked seam of a stocking," he wrote. He also learned to express himself well on paper, fearful that if he was called upon to recite, the nuns in St. Joseph's Cathedral School would respond to his stammers with raps of the ruler. "The joke . . . was that the nuns would hit you until you bled and then hit you for bleeding," he said.

He had been named after Archbishop John Gregory Murray of St. Paul, Minnesota, who had married his parents, but the nuns—Sister Theodosius,

Sister Barnabus, Sister Marie de Nice—witnessed more devilry than angelic behavior from him.

The fifth of six siblings ("we divided into the Four Oldest and the Two Youngest"), he carried, along with the rest of his family, "a full cargo of ethnic and religious freight," he said. Irish Catholics in a neighborhood of wealthy Protestants, they were made to feel like outsiders. Dunne grew up quietly resentful. Every Christmas, he felt humiliated when his mother made him line up with his brothers and sisters, "their faces scrubbed and shiny, to hand out oranges and shoes to the needy," knowing the Protestant kids (the Yanks) made little distinction between those giving and those receiving the charity. His grandfather, a potato-famine immigrant, had been a butcher, and though eventually his labor nicely positioned the family (he worked his way up in the community, from "steerage to suburbia," Dunne said, becoming a bank president), the neighbors never let the Dunnes forget they were nouveau riche, still living in Frog Hollow, the old Irish section. Once poor, always a pauper.

"[I was] slightly ashamed of my origins, patronizing toward the Irish still on the make," Dunne admitted. In that time and place, class was everything. "Don't get mad, get even": On public occasions, the community's leaders liked to repeat this key to success. For Dunne, the motto was "Get mad *and* get even."

Didion always thought West Hartford was not so different from Sacramento, which is why she and John got along so well.

"Poppa," Dunne called his grandfather. "[H]e had an enormous influence on my brother and me," Dominick Dunne said. "It was as if he spotted us for the writers we would one day be. He didn't go to school past the age of fourteen, but literature was an obsession with him. He was never without a book, and he read voraciously. Early on, he taught John and me the excitement of reading. On Friday nights we would often stay over at his house and he would read the classics or poetry to us and give us each a fifty-cent piece for listening."

Dunne's father became a heart surgeon. The family moved into a large house on Albany Avenue with a six-car garage. They hired "help"—not the "coloreds" the Yanks employed, but "wayward" Catholic girls from the House of the Good Shepherd. These girls worked until someone got them pregnant— "as my mother was the dispenser of Kotex, no missed period went unnoticed," Dunne wrote.

With six kids in the house, family life was full of "sniper fire." Like the nuns at school, the elder Dunne was a "quick man with a strap" and John's older brother Dominick—"Nick," everyone called him—caught the worst of the old man's rage. Nick preferred staging puppet shows to playing sports or hunting. He liked Mrs. Godfrey's dance classes. His father would call him a "Sissy" and beat him with a wooden coat hanger.

When the old man turned on John, John made it a point not to cry. He'd giggle and his younger brother, Stephen, afraid of pushing their father to his limit, "would do my crying for me," Dunne recalled. This seemed to be Stephen's role in the family. His mother used to say he "played life on the dark keys."

Sometimes he'd ask Dunne if he ever felt depressed. Sure, Dunne said. The brothers agreed that Heath bars, Oreos, and a day in bed were the best cures for the "jits."

"Greg," John's classmates called him at school because there were so many Johns. Or "Googs"—an early nickname, origins lost.

When Dunne was fourteen, his father died of a ruptured aorta. He was fifty-one years old. In the morning, the boy kissed his father good-bye on his way to school, and when he came home that day, the first thing he saw were oxygen tanks on the back porch. The family placed the body in a casket in the living room and surrounded it with candles. At night, when the mourners had filed out of the house, Dunne crept downstairs in his pajamas and stood staring at his father's face. He waited for the fingers, wrapped in a rosary, to flinch, waited to hear a breath. "I listened for a heartbeat, as years later I would bend over my daughter's crib and listen for her heartbeat," he wrote.

He was forced to mature swiftly. His training involved curbing the temper he'd inherited from his father. At the hospital, his father had fired interns and nurses in the midst of surgery if he felt they did not measure up to his standards. Already, Dunne knew *he* was just as exacting with people.

When his mother found a box of condoms in his room, she feared he would become sexually misguided with no man in the house. He had bought the condoms not quite knowing what to do with them, prompted by fantasies of the Polish girls who took business courses in high school "and worked in the factories of East Hartford and who were said to fuck."

His mother sent him to Portsmouth Priory, an exclusive boarding school in Rhode Island. The monks were "very worldly," he recalled. One day, one of them made him take down his pants and paddled his ass with a rubber hose because he'd played hooky. For the rest of his life, Dunne thought the fellow queer.

He liked the "pageantry" of Mass and he liked confession—"alternately rais[ing] and lower[ing] [his] voice every Saturday when [he] slipped into the confessional, a midget basso or a midget soprano depending on the week that was." Like his future wife, he had a theatrical temperament.

He spent much of his time at Portsmouth Priory crafting short stories modeled after O. Henry's urban fables. One of his efforts concerned a burglar who left a Bible wherever he stole and who spent the pilfered money on his ailing mother's medical bills. Years of Catholic education had taught him to accept as a given the "taint on the human condition." He filled his stories with losers, with down-and-outers.

Portsmouth failed to mute his sexual curiosity. According to *Vegas,* the older boys from New York talked about a club called the Lido in Times Square, and a pair of sisters, dime-a-dance hostesses there, who'd laid half the boarding school boys in the East. Like everything else, Dunne realized, sex boasts were all about class.

One evening, after sitting through rollicking tales of the Stork Club and La Rue, he was asked—challenged, really—by one of the cocky New Yorkers, "Where you from?" "Hartford," Dunne said (after a long day of classes, dropping the *t* and *r*'s in the manner of the lace-curtain Irish, "Ha-fod," giving himself away). "I think I've heard of it," the boy said with a nasal whine, signaling his fine breeding.

One weekend, Dunne managed to get to New York with a pack of hungry boys. Wearing his maroon school blazer, he bought a dollar's worth of tickets to the Lido. He stood and watched women smoke cigarettes. The women were too young to be as ravaged as they looked. "Though it was three years after Hiroshima and seven since Pearl Harbor, the only song on the jukebox seemed to be 'Praise the Lord and Pass the Ammunition,'" he wrote. He returned to Portsmouth still a "cherry."

His father had always insisted his children enroll in the best colleges in the East. The eldest brother, Richard, went to Harvard. Nick attended Williams. When John's time came, his mother and his aunt Harriet pressured him to realize his father's wish. "Hartford was a Yale town," he said. His mother "had always wanted a son to go to Yale . . . [and] Yale was where the Yanks went." But his anger at the Yanks' condescension had hardened into Frog Hollow defiance and he rebelled by going to Princeton. "I was just a tight-assed upper-middle-class kid . . . [with] this sense of Ivy League entitlement," he said years later.

On his entrance essay, he wrote that in college he hoped to meet "contacts who might help me in later life."

At Princeton, he developed a jaded sophistication, but the pose didn't free him of class resentments. Everyone he met was grooming himself for a vice presidency at Procter & Gamble ("Princeton in the Nation's Service"), except, perhaps, for his even *more* ambitious classmate, Donald H. "Rummy" Rumsfeld.

The boys all claimed to be sexual "swordsmen." At parties in nightclubs in New York, he was reminded of the cocky Portsmouth kids and his awkward evening at the Lido. At one such affair, in his sophomore year, his brother Nick introduced him to a motion picture press agent named John Foreman, who was showing off a young actress, Grace Kelly. She had just appeared with Gary Cooper in *High Noon*. Later, Foreman would become a friend and professional connection; already, the Hollywood crowd Nick courted proved lucky for Greg.

Four days shy of his twenty-first birthday, Dunne "finally made contact" with one of the legendary sisters he'd been hearing about since Portsmouth, he wrote. He said he called her from a bar in Times Square, made his way to her Fifty-second Street flat, near the mobbed-up cafés, and paid twenty dollars to lose his virginity among Salvation Army chairs and a couch. The woman had Ivy League school pennants pinned to her walls, and a photograph of Princeton's a cappella choir, the Nassoons.

In 1954, Dunne graduated with a degree in history. At his mother's insistence, he applied to the Stanford Business School, but then he changed his mind and volunteered for the draft. Nick had been a war hero, earning a Bronze Star for saving a wounded soldier in Felsberg, Germany. "John was always fascinated by that period of my life," Nick said, but if Dunne hoped to trump his brother's accomplishments, or simply compete with him, he was soon disillusioned. In basic training at Fort Chaffee, Arkansas, he learned the army was a "constituency of the dispossessed—high school dropouts, petty criminals, rednecks, racists, gamblers, you name it—and I fit right in," he said. Before then, he had not spent much time with America's "white and black underclass." He told George Plimpton, "I grew to hate the officer class that was my natural constituency. A Princeton classmate was an officer on my post [at Fort Carson, Colorado] and he told me I was to salute and call him *sir*, as if I had to be reminded, and also that he would discourage any outward signs that we knew each other. I hate that son of a bitch to this day. [Later] I took care of him [in print]."

Revenge, and the settling of class scores, would always supply him with literary fuel.

Dunne served in a gun battery in Wertheim, Germany, near the Czech border. There, he said, military training consisted mostly of learning "to appreciate whores."

In 1959 he went to work for *Time* in New York. He was twenty-seven years old. He had been bouncing around Manhattan, working as a messenger for an ad agency, living with four roommates in a fifty-six-dollar-a-month town house in the Silk Stocking District. "Every failure in New York" populated the place, he said: "A guy who had failed the New York bar exam twice, and failed a third time while he was there, was typical."

At night, he ate Hydrox cookies and swilled milk in his room while trying to write a novel about a movie director. Sometimes he'd slip out, on his own, to a piano bar. There, watching the desperate singles hoping to make contact, he could spot the latest fashions, hear the newest pickup lines. Social research. Once, in a club in the East Fifties, he saw Warren Beatty "tinkling the ivories"—before he was a star and before he'd "started going to bed with household names."

Dunne got a job at *Industrial Design* magazine, writing several hours a day in a cubicle on Fiftieth Street facing St. Patrick's Cathedral. He'd lied about his reporting experience (he concocted a résumé claiming he'd worked on a Colorado Springs daily). He parlayed this into the position at *Time* through a woman he was dating. She was seeing a writer in the magazine's business section. The Luce men were all Ivy Leaguers and looked after one another.

At *Time*, Dunne earned $7,700 a year, writing about stocks and bonds, about which he knew nothing. In the evenings, "waiters from the Tower Suite, on top of the Time-Life Building, rolled in buffet carts with beef Wellington and chicken divan and sole and assorted appetizers and vegetables and desserts," he said. Liquor was dispensed in "prodigious quantities." Hotel rooms "were available for those suburbanites who had missed their last train, or would so claim to their wives when in fact all they wished was an adulterous snuggle with a back-of-the-book researcher." There were "limousines to take us home, Carey Cadillacs for most, but I secured a company charge account at Buckingham Livery, which used only Rolls-Royces, and when I turned in my expense accounts no one objected. It was not journalism, but it was fun."

Eventually, he moved into better digs on East Seventy-third Street. Occasionally, his brother Stephen, who was hoping to become an art designer, shared the apartment with him.

According to his friend and colleague Calvin Trillin, Dunne was the "most creative gossip at the magazine." He "was always discovering two people who worked for *Time* necking in some place you'd never go, like Washington Heights. His typical sentence would begin, 'I just *happened* to be going through the lingerie department of Bloomingdale's yesterday, when who should I see . . .'"

"I was a jerk," Dunne said flatly.

His new lover was alarmingly frail. Headaches every week (he knew what that was like), weight fluctuating from little to less, fingers trembling, snapping like sparrows' beaks whenever she wanted to stress a point. She seemed increasingly distressed at the lack of discipline and order in the lives of her friends. Perhaps for this reason, she relished imposing her will whenever she could. When her cousin Brenda got married, "I was still trying to run the game, make the rules, have it my way," she admitted. "There would be at Brenda's wedding, I promised her, nothing banal, nothing ordinary. . . . I had decreed: there would be . . . checked gingham and wreaths of daisies." Right up until the guests were seated, Didion was hastily disporting the wreaths.

It was the sense of "great calm and order"—the *relief* of it—in the Hartford house of Greg Dunne's mother that made Didion think, "I want to marry him," she said.

He had invited her to dinner one night in New York, one of those weeks of parties and more parties and another round of drinks, martini lunches and editorial meetings, bars smelling of disinfectant, sugar, and chocolate, rips in the hem of her plaid silk dress and no safety pin to keep it taut, and he had said he was going to spend the weekend with his mother in Connecticut. Would she like to come?

"The minute I got into this house," Didion said, "[I] felt peace and well-being. . . . There were meals. There was a closet full of organdy tablecloths on long rollers—the way they came back from the French laundry, under tissue." Here, away from deadline pressures and tedious chatter about people's publishing advances, their editor this, their agent that, she and Dunne could share anxieties about their novels in progress without any fuss. They sat by the hearth at night, stoking the wood, close and warm in wavering circles of light.

Chapter Ten

1

Possibly it was in the Graben Hotel in Vienna, while on assignment for *Time* in November 1960, that Dunne caught the clap. He remembered being back in New York, a week later, at a black-tie party with a crowd watching the Kennedy-Nixon election returns and telling his date he "couldn't"—he had a "small problem of Teutonic origin." The woman told him she had a similar malady. The times they were a-changin'. Or maybe not.

In any case, as *Time*'s newly appointed "Saigon-watcher," he flew to Indochina and "fornicated for five weeks," he wrote. "I didn't even know where the countries were, so I asked *Time* if they'd send me there. I was a bachelor, so I said I'd take my vacation there . . . if they'd pay my air fare, and they said okay." Eventually, in "what now seems a constant postcoital daze, I floated to the nascent realization that the war beginning to metastasize in Vietnam was a malignant operation."

He met David Halberstam, Neil Sheehan, and Peter Arnett. "I respected these guys . . . and they were all saying things are not like the Pentagon says they are." He was confused. On the flight over, he'd thought his job was to "set straight the local reporters whom [his] editors thought had gone native." Later, he was grateful when Halberstam "overlook[ed] this impertinence."

He met a former colonel in the Turkish Air Force who had been recruited by the CIA for the Bay of Pigs invasion. This man had come to Vietnam to work off his contract following the Cuba fiasco. From his chopper, he said, what he saw was "all shit." Dunne tried to shake the chill of this with sweet drinks at Saigon's Cercle Sportif or with whores in Cholon.

His fascination with prostitutes, instilled in him in the army, had not abated. This could have been a sore spot, given his growing bond with Didion. Still, he indulged only when he traveled. Most months, his Vietnam reporting consisted of sitting at his desk in Manhattan, tailoring for mass consumption weekly cables sent to the office by the Southeast Asia bureau. The biggest problem with his assignments was the novel he was trying to write—he could never get to it.

Meanwhile, despite a strict nightly regimen, Didion was struggling to give shape to *Harvest Home*. She was thinking of retitling it *In the Night Season*. Perhaps the trouble lay in the story, which didn't much interest her. What interested her were sunsets and heat, neither of which she was able to enjoy on Manhattan's Upper East Side. There was always something missing. In an instant, the days got dark. Before writing in the evenings, she'd stroll to the Columbia-Presbyterian Hospital, one of the few vantage points in the city where the disappearing sun could be witnessed in its fullness. On the weekends, she'd walk to the Hudson to be in the presence of moving water. She knew homesickness, more than plot, tickled her prose, but a novel needed a plot. She'd stolen, as a kind of dresser's dummy for her narrative, an incident she'd read about in the *Times,* a one-inch story about a man in South Carolina on trial for killing the foreman on his farm. Perhaps the trouble lay in the incident—maybe it wouldn't translate to Sacramento. Perhaps the trouble lay in the characters. Lily and Martha, the women in the story, were not nearly as interesting to her as Everett, Lily's husband, but what did she know about a man's point of view? Perhaps the trouble lay in her work ethic. "I start a book and I want to make it perfect, want it to turn every color, want it to *be the world*," she'd reflect years later. "Ten pages in, I've already blown it, limited it, made it less, marred it. That's very discouraging. I hate the book at that point."

In Dunne's apartment, she'd pull out the Wicker Dale Spode his mother had given him—dinner plates, salad plates, butter plates painted with blue flower petals and roses—and she'd cook for them, and they'd sit together on his black chintz couch (also a castoff from Mama) and bemoan the miseries of fiction.

To add to his worries, Dunne was certain he was on a collision course with his editors at the magazine. His immediate boss, Otto Fuerbringer, bought the Pentagon's view of Vietnam, and so did Henry Luce, but Charley Mohr, the ground reporter whose cables Dunne edited each week, was telling a different story. Mohr's doubts confirmed Dunne's suspicions, formed on his visit to Indochina, that the American effort was faltering. Soon, Dunne was not going to be able to smooth things over with his bosses by softening Mohr's tone or leaving out certain details. It would be a matter of reporting accurately or deliberately lying to the public.

2

When Didion had typed around 150 manuscript pages, arranged so that sunsets didn't *utterly* overwhelm incident (though she wanted the novel "to be very complicated chronologically," she said, "to somehow have the past and present operating simultaneously"), she sent the pages to a publisher. The answer came back no. She mailed the pages again. Same result.

She cried on the subways. She wept in Laundromats. Someone had told her to breathe into a paper bag when the tears got to be too much and she felt herself hyperventilating, but the bags smelled of onions or the sweet afterscent of apples. It no longer cheered her to buy crab boil at her favorite Czech market in the East Eighties. "A friend would leave me the key to her apartment in the West Village when she was out of town, and sometimes I would just move down there, because . . . the telephone was beginning to bother me," she wrote of this period in "Goodbye to All That." "I remember one day when someone . . . came to pick me up for lunch there, and we both had hangovers, and I cut my finger opening him a beer and burst into tears, and we walked to a Spanish restaurant and drank Bloody Marys and *gazpacho* until we felt better."

The most memorable image in "Goodbye to All That" is the "fifty yards of yellow theatrical silk" hung across her bedroom windows because she "had some idea that the gold light would make [her] feel better." In fact, the loose curtains only got "tangled and drenched in the afternoon thunderstorms."

She had moved out of her Park Avenue apartment, leaving "everything in it, even my winter clothes and the map of Sacramento County I had hung on the bedroom wall to remind me who I was," she wrote. "[I]t was all breaking up."

Noel Parmentel took the Park Avenue apartment. *Her* new place was a four-room floor-through at 41 East 75th Street, across from the Whitney Museum. Beneath her was a nursery school. "[T]hese dwarfs would go out into the garden at odd hours of the day, and they would all scream," she said. She had two garden chairs, lent by friends, and a double mattress and box spring. She had her unfinished manuscript. She would live with it fiercely.

No, said a third publisher. Then a fourth.

She'd meet Dunne for long lunches at a Chinese restaurant near the Time-Life Building. "Its specialty is being two blocks away," he'd say. She enjoyed his ease with the city, the way he could turn almost anyone—waiters, fellow diners—into an audience for his stories and jokes. The staff at this particular restaurant knew him well. He'd wave a finger and summon a martini—unless it was a Wednesday or a Thursday, when the magazine's weekly deadlines howled in his ear. Then the waiters would bring a white wine spritzer or a club soda. The lunches were less enjoyable than they used to be because of Charley Mohr's gloomy cables. Also, like Didion, Dunne was beginning to feel restless and stale in the trenches, everyone talking about the books they were writing, only they weren't really writing them, or if they were, they couldn't get them published, and—oh!—the people *getting* published were just the worst sorts of folks—it was like being snowbound in a village full of nuts.

After Didion had unsuccessfully peddled her manuscript to half a dozen publishers, she appealed to an old friend. "The usual suspects all turned it down, so I more or less nagged Ivan into publishing it," Parmentel told me. "Ivan" was Ivan Obolensky.

He was a distinguished gentleman. ("He used to say, 'Everybody who comes from Russia claims he's a prince,'" said Parmentel. "But he really *was* a prince.") His small imprint was solid and well respected. He gave Didion a contract—"just to get me off his back," Parmentel joked. She felt lucky. In fact, she could not have wound up with an editor more at odds with her sensibilities.

Ivan Sergeyevich Obolensky was born to a Russian prince in London in 1925. He was the grandson of John Jacob Astor IV, said to be the richest man in the world when he died on the *Titanic*. Educated at Yale, formerly a navy pilot, Obolensky formed a publishing company with David McDowell in 1957. "I wrote this book, *Rogue's March*, and David and Donald Klopfer and Bennett Cerf [at Random House] thought the world of it," Obolensky told me. "David was my editor and I figured, What the hell, why don't we start our own house? So I scared up ten thousand dollars."

McDowell had befriended James Agee through Father James H. Flye at St. Andrew's School in Sewanee, Tennessee. At Vanderbilt, he met the young writer Peter Taylor. McDowell had a penchant for "pounding the sidewalks and just plain selling the books," said James Laughlin, a poet and the founder of New Directions. This, along with his links to Southern authors, put McDowell and Obolensky on the map. Under their imprint, Agee's *A Death in the Family* appeared posthumously. It won the Pulitzer Prize and became a bestseller.

McDowell left the firm in 1960. For a while, Obolensky carried on. "I didn't like the publishing business," he says now (subsequently, he became a financial analyst specializing in oil and gas, high-tech industries, nuclear power, metals and minerals). "It was a disappointment all around. A disaster. No matter what you do, it's a cash-and-carry situation. Publishers never get credit for what they do and authors always feel put upon." He lost over a million dollars in the field.

"To be very frank, I never liked her," Obolensky said of Didion. "She was fixed on herself, a stick-in-the-mud, a diamond that needed to be faceted. But she had good people working for her and they led me to believe she would be a fine author to have. 'She's the greatest thing since Post Toasties,' they said. I relented. I thought, Well, we've got a backlist, we're okay, and I'd be delighted to publish this first novel.' And what we did for her, we did flat out. The presentation on the page, the margins—everything was perfect."

Titles were the first sign of trouble: Neither *Harvest Home* nor *In the Night Season* was remotely commercial, Obolensky argued. He came up with *Run River*. "What does it mean?" Didion asked him. "It means life goes on," he replied. Didion said, "That's not what the book is about."

He urged her to change her style. "I felt she was too precious. She didn't have any punch or balls. I like fists and chins, stomp and gouge." Obviously, editor and author were miserably matched.

"She had total disregard for anything that was not borne for her, with her, or by her," Obolensky explained to me. "Doing anything for her was like throwing a rock in a pond."

Later, in interviews, Didion would admit she "didn't know how to do anything at all" with this novel: "I wasn't accomplished enough."

"Right. Sheer indulgences," Obolensky said. "Flashbacks and stream of consciousness . . . certain people love it. But I felt it was extraneous and the book suffered—she suffered—for it. She lost ground on stuff she didn't have to lose ground on. There was very little she would change. We were very professional and we were good and we were writers. But she was filled with her own magnificence—and that's always a loss for the author."

With her thousand-dollar advance, Didion took a two-month leave of absence from *Vogue* to finish the book. "That's why the last half is better than the first half," she said. Parmentel critiqued the pages for her; she'd argue with him but almost always decide he was right. Obolensky hired a young freelance editor, Carol Houck Smith, to streamline the story. Smith couldn't get anything past him, Parmentel said.

"I kept trying to run the first half through again, but it was intractable," Didion said. "It was set. I'd worked on it for too many years in too many moods."

"Moods? I don't know what her private life was like," Obolensky reflected. "If you're an introspective writer, it shows, and she wasn't. She wasn't a refreshed human being."

"Obolensky had a wonderful party for *Run River* at his town house," Parmentel recalled. Despite the editor's battles with his author, "by then, he'd got the bit in his teeth and said, 'This is going to win a Pulitzer.' He went all out for her. If Joan's complained about him since, she's an ingrate.

"Bobby Short came to the party. Billy Graham came to the party—the fighter, not the preacher. And Montgomery Clift—he was drunk."

"You've written a great American novel," Parmentel told Didion. He didn't miss the fact that her character Ryder Channing, all smooth talk and suits, alcohol and charm, was his spitting image.

3

The rough drafts of what became *Run River,* archived now in the Bancroft Library at Berkeley, confirm Didion's perception that her ambitions outstripped her abilities, though the book is hardly the failure she later considered it to be. Its evocations of the Sacramento Valley are achingly vivid, and if the book's nostalgic tone is mired in misunderstandings of California history, it still conveys passion and grievous loss.

Early versions of the story emphasized the lives of valley men more than women, a focus on social *change,* on builders and promoters. Subsequent drafts tilted the narrative toward mothers, sisters, and daughters, who, more than the men, experienced the *effects* of "progress" in the most intimate social realms. This perceptual shift gave Didion's theme greater nuance: *"Things change. Your father no longer tells you when to go to bed, no longer lulls you with his father's bourbon, brought out for comfort at Christmas and funerals."*

Had Didion augmented this angle of vision with a more intimate point of view, she might have achieved her desire to present the past and present simultaneously, to show how thoroughly nostalgia can grip an individual sensibility. Instead, she played with chronology in draft after draft, fracturing time, resequencing events, calling more attention to the hand of the author, cutting and pasting, than to the minds of her characters.

Run River is set on a postwar California ranch. Lily and Everett McClellan are the grandchildren of pioneers. They were married by a justice of the peace whose son spoke with a thick "Okie voice: *Ain't she the prettiest little bride . . .*" This voice, the nasal grate of the interloper with no links to local soil, mocks Lily's and Everett's dream of paradise. Their dream founders in the state's transition from agriculture to industry, self-reliance to profligate consumerism. Everett has "little interest . . . in using the land" responsibly; he wants "only to have it." He cannot grasp that the American economy is shifting—money is made from money now, and the land is just an afterthought. Lily is trapped in a cycle of meaningless social events where other desperate women "talk about their diets and their children and their golf scores, display their even dispositions and their gold charm bracelets, and . . . go home to take off the bright clean linen dresses, to lie on hot sheets and wait patiently for the day to begin again."

Children of privilege, of increasingly seductive consumer choices, Everett and Lily have lost the Old West notion of setting a strict code and living by it. Their families have realized the goal of "*lots of land / Under starry skies a-bove*" but in the new postwar economy, for a new middle-class generation, the "pastures of plenty" are no longer stakes in the future, but parcels to buy and sell and buy again. The stars are not to be wished on, but invested in; they are satellites manufactured by local industries.

It's not that earlier generations behaved better than Lily and Everett; alcoholism and infidelity *always* defined ranching life, in Didion's version of history. It's that the elders were more discreet with the knowledge of others' foibles, and cleverer at cleaning up the messes. The new generation's fumbling is a shocking erosion of social etiquette.

Didion's interest in language and American narratives appears in the book's imagery and echoes of earlier literary works: in the social satire reminiscent of Edith Wharton; in the Gothic description of the McClellan family's decline, as in the fall of Poe's Ushers; in the detail of the burned-out light on the McClellans' riverfront dock, a sharp counterpoint to Daisy's light at the end of *The Great Gatsby;* and of course in the road trips—brief, failed attempts at escape into destinies less obscure. At one point, following an abortion (the *final* end to the Old Way of Life), Lily rides a Greyhound bus through the San Joaquin Valley, in an afternoon heat scorching "towns so

clean that the houses and the buildings seemed . . . on the verge of demate-
rializing; there was the sense that to close one's eyes on a Valley town was to
risk opening them a moment later on dry fields, the sun bleaching out the
last traces of habitation, a flowered straw hat, a neon advertisement which
had blinked a moment before from a wall no longer visible." This moves beyond the Joads' weary disillusionment. It is Eliot's wasteland transposed on
the sunny promise of the West.

Though Didion resisted strict chronology, she did offer, at Obolensky's
insistence, a relatively straightforward presentation of events. Her familiarity with American literary tropes implies belief in a national tale, or several
chapters of it, peopled with familiar types (the pioneer, the adulterer, the
wastrel brother, the thwarted housewife, each has a name vaguely redolent
of the area's past, but, in fact, more suited to Hollywood—Knight, Everett,
Ryder—underscoring Didion's longing for a simple, moral story. There is even
a snake in this garden, in the novel's opening scene). At the end, Lily wonders what to tell her children about their suicide father: "She was not certain
that he had been [a good man] but it was what she would have wished for
him, if they gave her one wish." Despite her despair, this first Didion heroine dreams of John Wayne, of fairy tales offering people chances to indulge
their whims or live out their destinies.

Didion's later novels would wrestle more directly with the nature of
narrative—specifically, with narrative's limits—but in *Run River* we see the
seeds of this obsession: two distinct narrative concepts tussle in the book,
stemming from the pioneer families' confrontations with history. *"We could
make the reasons,"* Everett thinks, wondering how he might defend his murder
of a real-estate speculator: that is, we can write the story ourselves, or rewrite
it, to suit our self-perceptions. Narrative as open destiny, the American dream
of self-invention: a *gambler's* outlook.

On the other hand, Lily believes it's a little *"late for choosing . . . quite as
if it hadn't always been."* As the spawn of pioneers, they are prisoners of the
past, their roles already written, their narrative function clear: to uphold and
extend tradition. Lily's worst failure is her inability to understand the role of
ranch wife. She is locked into a rigid fate but has no inkling of how to fulfill
it on her way to the end.

It is striking that this novel, written on the cusp of a volatile new decade,
offered no sense of the social tremors appearing in other works of the time,

in the political writing of the Beats, say, or in Grace Paley's short stories about restless wives and mothers, just then beginning to appear, or in Philip Roth's first novel, *Goodbye, Columbus,* hinting at the gender battles to come, or in Walker Percy's bomb-haunted *The Moviegoer.* For the Didion of *Run River,* cataclysmic social change had already occurred. The Apocalypse had come. Time—narrative—had been warped beyond repair: "The future was being made . . . right here in California," Ryder Channing announces while chopping up valley ranches.

The future was being.

Past, present, and to come—*coincidence*—pressure-packed into a single, world-altering phrase. In the economic boom of the 1960s, this apparently airtight formulation (*we can have it all—right now!*) would open unforeseeable gaps in the national narrative.

Forty years after publishing *Run River,* Didion would declare the novel tainted with a "tenacious (and, as I see it now, pernicious) mood of nostalgia." Falsely, the book equated "change" with "decline," blind to the fact that Californians had *always* been "willing to traffic [their] own history" for economic gain. There *was* no "old" California to lose. Ever.

Her reconsideration appeared in *Where I Was From.* The self-critique was brave, pitiless, and incisive, but it did not credit *Run River*'s real achievement, which was, as she admitted sotto voce, to present a "not inaccurate characterization of the way Sacramento, or for that matter California itself, felt to a child growing up during the postwar boom years, the late 1940s and early 1950s."

"[F]or my family," read one half of Didion's dedication of the novel—the folks who suffered to acquire and work the land and were now in danger of losing it (though how must her family have felt about the book's portrait of inbreeding among old California ranching families, with its implication of planting insanity?).

"[A]nd for N," read the rest of the dedication. If this was an acknowledgment of Noel Parmentel, then the book's epigraph, an excerpt of Robert Lowell's poem "Man and Wife," was a good-bye note to him. Didion quoted only a section of Lowell, details pertinent to the book's plot—broken intimacy, madness, homicide. What she didn't quote (but Parmentel must have known it) was the poem's evocation of a soulless New York, literary types outdrinking one another in a hot Village apartment.

4

"A member of Vogue's *staff for the past several years, Joan Didion grew up in California, and lives, now, there and in New York. Her first novel,* Run River, *has just been published by Ivan Obolensky."*

This contributor's note appended "American Summer"—an article examining longings for innocence and the bitterness of young adulthood—in the May 1963 issue of *Vogue.* Its reference to living in California part-time precedes by over a year Didion's *actual* move back west but indicates she was not remaining quiet about her disillusionment with Manhattan. While finishing the second half of *Run River,* she often flew to Sacramento on night flights. The planes were nearly empty, seven or eight men, maybe, about half of them wearing short-sleeved shirts, ready for the beach, the other half still dressed for the East.

She could work undisturbed in her parents' house. They didn't ask her questions. They barely spoke to one another, or at all.

The air and the light—late into the evenings—stirred memories of Stinson Beach when she was a child: driving up the coast with her folks to watch Spencer Tracy movies at an old theater in Bolinas; screaming at a black widow beneath her mother's lawn chair at the beach cottage while her mother played solitaire. The strength of these memories only enriched the "tenacious" nostalgia webbing her novel.

After a few days, she'd miss the purple twilights of New York—slipping out to dinner in a silk dress, or watching the sun rise on someone's terrace while torch singers crooned from the hi-fi just inside the apartment.

She'd catch a late flight back east: the same guys in the same rumpled shirts.

She felt neither here nor there, which did not mean she had no obligations to her job or to friends. A Katherine Mansfield line strayed, often, into her mind: "[T]here are moments when I feel I am nothing but the small clerk of some hotel without a proprietor, who has all his work cut out to enter the names and hand the keys to the willful guests."

On June 15, *Kirkus Reviews* noted, of *Run River,* "While the scene here is California, the climate seems more somnolently southern in character: the fretful dissolution; the faintly incestuous family relationships; the bourbon; the sex down on the levee; and the soft singsong of 'baby' and 'Everett baby.'"

Guy E. Thompson, of the *Los Angeles Times,* had also noticed "the appearance in California of a novel genre formerly indigenous to the decaying South," singling out *Run River*. "As California wines are designated by the European type they most resemble, so must California novels be named for the established novelists they simulate. In which case this is Faulkner-type," Thompson wrote. "Many consider the California product less robust than the original—so will readers."

In addition to nostalgia, the novel was suffused with Noel Parmentel. It could not have sat well with Didion to have this pointed out to her repeatedly in print.

On balance, the reviews were tepid. *The New Yorker*'s response was typical: "Miss Didion's first novel," about a "childish creature who drinks too much, enjoys frequent crying spells, and takes every chance that comes along to be unfaithful," shows her "to be the possessor of a vigorous style," the magazine said, but her style was "wasted on her characters" who seemed like "human leftovers." "Miss Didion writes of people who get through life instead of living it."

Sales were disappointing, too. West Coast readers, the book's natural target, may have been confused by all this Southern talk. Literary insiders were puzzled, as well, by the book's appearance with a publisher best known for its Dixie list.

In Sacramento, a lot of people "seemed to think that I had somehow maligned them and their families," Didion said. Maybe she *couldn't* go home again. The novel was "only read by about ten people . . . you know, not only was it not a commercial success, it wasn't by any means, I don't think, a success on its own terms."

At exactly this moment—the summer of 1963—Buddhist monks in Vietnam began immolating themselves before the world's television cameras, protesting persecutions by the Ngo Dinh Diem administration.

Now, thought Charley Mohr, surely *Time*'s editors will stop airbrushing my dispatches. In early August he prepared a piece on Madame Ngo Dinh Nhu. He tied her family to government corruption in Saigon. America's investment in the Ngo family was shortsighted, he said, self-defeating. For well over a year, said David Halberstam, Mohr had been insisting that the "war was not even being fought, let alone being won" and the "Ngo family, rather than being a fine instrument of American anti-Communism, was . . . rotting, archaic." Mohr's new piece made a bulletproof case: "[T]he venture in Vietnam" was folly.

When Greg Dunne received Mohr's cables, he quailed. Halberstam: "[Henry] Luce's vision of mission and truth called for one kind of story"—despite the Buddhist crisis—and "the file from Mohr called for another."

Dunne believed Mohr: He'd been there. Furthermore, he'd served in the army; he knew war was all about class *here at home*. Forget the fucking domino theory.

To please his editors, Dunne "tried to thread the needle." He wrote a story using some of Mohr's information, "attempting to get in as much about the arrogance and insensitivity of the family as possible, while, of course, not entirely surrendering Fort Saigon," Halberstam said.

When Mohr saw the watered-down piece, he erupted. He fired off a letter denouncing Otto Fuerbringer's pro-Diem bias. Furious, Fuerbringer ordered a story about the "young, immature American press corps" in Vietnam; their liberal sympathies were misleading the public, he believed. Additionally, he assigned Dunne to write the next week's Vietnam piece without the use of cables from Saigon.

Halberstam got the details from Didion and Dunne:

> All week, colleagues kept coming by to laugh and congratulate Dunne on his good fortune in getting the Vietnam assignment. He was very nervous about it, even more so on Friday, when a strong file came in from Mohr that began: "Vietnam is a graveyard of lost hopes." . . . Dunne agonized over [what to do], went out for a drink with his fiancée . . . Joan Didion, and proceeded to get very drunk.

The couple went to the Chalet Suisse on West Fifty-second Street and ordered fondue. "There's no way *Time* is going to print this story," Dunne said miserably.

"Write it the way he sent it," Didion urged him.

He shook his head.

Halberstam: "He decided he would not return to the office but would call in sick. Miss Didion stiffened his spine; if he were a man, he would go back and write the truth, which he finally did, half drunk, staying up most of the night, turning out the worst piece of writing he had ever done for the magazine but keeping it faithful to Mohr's file."

The "story was of course completely turned around" once the senior editors got hold of it. Instead of a losing war effort, there was "light at the end of the tunnel." On Dunne's original copy, Fuerbringer had written, "Nice."

With Didion's support, Dunne asked to be relieved of Vietnam assignments. From then on, he was given minutia to cover. An expected raise never came through.

Dunne had saved the October 19, 1962, special issue of *Life* magazine devoted to the "Call of California: Its Splendor, Its Excitement."

He had always "dreamed of being an adventurer," he said, and of going to someplace exotic, like Thailand, where there was "a whisper of opium and there were women always called sloe-eyed, wearing *ao dais* and practiced in the Oriental permutations of fellatio."

His daydreams mushroomed in the Charley Mohr fallout. When his fantasies lit on California, they didn't altogether dissipate. He was *engaged* to a Californian. If her permutations weren't "Oriental," they were sufficiently complex to have kept his interest for half a decade.

"The longing in man's heart for a better life has driven him throughout history to seek out a brighter land," *Life* proclaimed. California! "Its only limitations rest within the power contained in the burning sun . . ."

The magazine hailed the Golden State's visionaries: Clark Kerr, educator; Joan Baez, a "tuneful source of . . . wistful intensity"; Robert Di Giorgio, agriculturalist, whose "modern methods of skillful management" were poised to lead America's march to prosperity in the 1960s.

Dunne knew from his dealings with editors, and from conversations with Didion, that California's stories were not nearly as simple as Luce would have them seem. Perhaps stronger, stranger narratives were waiting to be uncovered out west.

Of course, *marriage* was an adventure, but to hear the couple talk, they viewed their coming nuptials as just another assignment. Block it out, bring it in on time. What's the angle? Get it right. The first public announcement of their engagement appeared in the editor's notes column of *National Review*.

"[W]e did not guarantee to each other at the end of the first week that we would still be married at the end of the second," Dunne recalled.

"I don't know of many good marriages," Didion said. "I don't know of many not-good marriages, either." *What difference does it make?* It's an "exercise in self-improvement." Like keeping a notebook.

This certainly wasn't the grand passion she had shared with Noel Parmentel. No thunder and earthquakes. She had decided pragmatism offered better long-term benefits than passion. Good-bye to all that.

"It wasn't so much a romance as *Other Voices, Other Rooms*," Didion admitted. The reference was to Truman Capote's 1948 novel, in which a rather effeminate, tale-telling lad pursues a distanced and troubling friendship with a moody tomboy (Capote and Harper Lee as played by Dunne and Didion).

She contemplated Dunne's spying, his eavesdropping—hobbies, he said, "without emotional investment." She feared he was "clinically detached": a useful quality for a reporter but maybe not so good around the house. Still, the fact of his reporting explained his centrality to her life. He was a writer. He was *there*. On the ground. He knew what *on the ground* meant. How could she not be married to a writer? Who else would put up with *her* self-absorption?

She loved the way, when he thought he was alone, he'd loosen his tie and stand in front of the mirror, singing nasally, "Who can I turn to / When nobody needs me?" He was utterly, hopelessly tone-deaf.

5

"Marriage, writing, who could figure it out? It was easier for the guys. I remember, we all thought, I'd like to be a guy writer," Didion's friend Jill Schary Robinson told me. "Male writers—like Greg Dunne—they had mystique and access. Oh my God. They were surveyors of their land and of their society, and they *caught* it. And they could do something we couldn't do. They could *fight*. Girls were supposed to be polite.

"The thing about Joan is, she never questioned, 'Am I a writer?' even when she was about to marry Greg. So many of us took so *long* to say, 'This is what I do and to hell with everybody else'—*I'd* abandon projects left and right to fall in love with another idiot or work on someone's political campaign. But Joan was designed *to do this*, the way a Ferrari is designed to do what it does."

Nevertheless, Didion had to sit in the shadows, engine idling, watching "the guys" race toward the Guggenheims: Philip Roth, Josh Greenfeld, Brian Moore. Her novel languished on bookstore shelves. Tacitly, she felt, women were not in the game.

This was not a protofeminist stance. "She never got involved in the movement because she was beyond that, anyway," Robinson said. "Joan was just Joan. Of course, where she grew up made that possible. She was so independent. She didn't seem strangled by family or conventions of any sort."

In literary New York in the 1960s and 1970s, female role models—those who successfully balanced work, independence, and personal fulfillment—

were rare. Who could a young woman turn to? Djuna Barnes? "I'm in a serious decline and the young dykes are driving me crazy," she'd say, "but should I recover, perhaps they'll hear from me."

Lillian Hellman? She posed regularly for *Vogue* and appeared at all the literary parties, but her reputation seemed to rest largely on Dashiell Hammett, for whom she'd become the professional keeper of the flame. The pleasure she took in this role made Didion uneasy.

Mary Bancroft? Didion took great delight in *her*: a true free spirit, a child of money (*The Wall Street Journal*), a former CIA spy, companion to Carl Jung, Allen Dulles, and Henry Luce. Everyone in the publishing industry hoped to snap up her memoirs. But again, her luster seemed linked to the men she'd drawn.

The women in Greg Dunne's family wondered how *this* little thing had snared their baby boy. *She wasn't one of them.* "My mother had a party for us [in Hartford] and we had a hundred and twenty-five people," Dunne recalled. "There were one hundred and twenty-four Catholics and Joan."

His engagement saved him, gave him something to think about on those ruinous days at his desk.

Time assigned him to cover "by-elections in Lichtenstein, Scandinavian sexual mores, and Common Market agricultural policy." For one piece, he was forced to compose the sentence "How small is a small tomato?"

On November 2, 1963, Ngo Dinh Diem was brutally assassinated in Vietnam.

Three weeks later, in San Francisco, Didion entered a grand four-story edifice on Post Street. It was the home of Ransohoff's, a department store selling itself as "San Francisco's independently owned specialty shop, traditionally known for quality and fashion." Alfred Hitchcock had chosen the store for a key scene in his 1958 film, *Vertigo*. Despite its chattering crowds, airy ceilings, and spacious aisles, the place felt intimate, even cozy.

Didion had come to purchase a wedding dress—backless, white, short, made of silk.

On leaving the store, she heard that John Kennedy had been shot in Dallas.

In the following days, in newspapers and magazines, the amount of column space given to Jackie's wardrobe at the moment of the assassination was astonishing. Her pillbox hat and strawberry pink double-breasted Chanel wool suit dominated many accounts of the Kennedy shooting. The suit was described yet again when Jackie insisted on wearing it, stained with blood, at Lyndon Johnson's swearing-in on Air Force One, just before flying back to Washington, D.C.

At JFK's funeral, Jackie, the *Vogue* girl, the Prix de Paris winner, became the nation's mother, stiffening the spines of her children; she became the nation's mourner, dignified in her grief, proudly bearing the public's sorrow; in years to come, she bore the nation's memory and myths, crafting the story of Camelot.

Women may not have been *in* the game, but women were what the game was all about.

"It's when a woman is thirty—give or take a few years—that she comes at last into her personality. Her hour has struck. From then on begin the magnificent years, the beginning of youth with its frustrations and crotchets drained away—the nerves, suspense, suffocations finally gone. In that 'soft green meadow' of time, a woman emerges from the dream enclosing her, into an era of equanimity and realism." These words, probably written by Didion, appeared in *Vogue* four months before the thirty-four-year-old Jackie Kennedy lost her husband.

Didion was twenty-eight at the time, on the verge of marrying, of leaving New York and starting a new life.

"At thirty she knows what the teen years were meant for: a preparation for something fascinating to come," the *Vogue* article stated.

Accompanying the article was a large picture of Jackie, taken through a car window streaked with rain. The lengthy, complex caption, jeweled with a literary reference, was almost certainly the expression of the once and future Californian:

> The time was right for her, no doubt about that. We wanted to grow up. She came along, and suddenly we forgot about the American girl—that improbably golden never-never child who roved through the world's imagination with a tennis racket, an unmarred make-up, and some spotty phrase-book French—and fell in love instead with the American woman, a creature possessed of thoughtful responsibility, a healthy predilection for the good and the beautiful and the expensive, and a gift for moving through the world aware of its difficulties, its possibilities, its

large and small joys—the kind of American woman who at her best can be, as Henry James once said, "heiress to all the ages."

Jackie. Joan. Ready to leap—or thrust by circumstance—toward whatever came next.

6

In *Vertigo*, Kim Novak's character leaps from the bell tower of the mission church at San Juan Bautista. At another point, Jimmy Stewart's character dresses her up to be the woman he wants her to be—in Ransohoff's. He has fallen in love with a phantom, a woman who never existed.

In choosing to buy her dress at Ransohoff's and to recite her marriage vows in the mission church at San Juan Bautista—hardly a coincidence—Didion turned her wedding into an elaborate movie reference.

Hitchcock's love of voyeurism must have appealed to the groom. After all, he said his first intimacy with his bride-to-be had followed a spying incident, in a scene reminiscent of *Rear Window*. Later, in her essay "The White Album," Didion would describe her general response to the late 1960s, in the first years of her marriage, as "vertigo." Perhaps the movie in-joke, involving mistaken identities, fictional characters, paralyzing phobias, and a suicide attempt beneath the Golden Gate Bridge (recalling Didion's fears for her father during his days at Letterman) was the couple's way of hedging their bets: a little self-conscious levity masking a serious commitment.

Around forty people, mostly Dunne's family, with the exception of his aunt Harriet, a devout Catholic who objected to the ceremony (Dunne was marrying outside his faith), attended the wedding on Thursday, January 30, 1964.

Dunne had not, until that day, met Didion's mother. Eduene walked up to him and said, "You know those little old ladies in tennis shoes you've heard about? Well, I'm one of them." (For Christmas that year, Dunne gave her "the entire John Birch library, dozens of call-to-action pamphlets, boxed," Didion said. The Eastern Catholic and the Western libertarian warmed to each other swiftly.)

The church, dedicated in 1812, located at the foot of the Gavilan Mountains, was the largest of the California missions. A stone dove, representing the Holy Ghost, hovered above a large font in a central aisle situated between short wooden pews. The church's bloodred floor tiles, made of stone and cement, had been dried outdoors before being laid; as a result, skittish animal tracks marked them. The curved interior arches, painted white and earthy tan, had been decorated by a sailor who'd jumped ship in Monterey in 1816. He became the first American citizen to settle in California.

Didion did not want a formal procession. The ghosts of the pioneers and the natives they had conquered were enough for her. She wore her short backless dress and cried softly throughout the ceremony behind a large pair of sunglasses. Dunne wore a navy blue suit.

Given her fascination with geology, she probably knew that the San Andreas Fault ran through the mission grounds, along the base of the hill below the cemetery. The 1906 earthquake had collapsed a side wall of the church; the damage was still evident on the day of the wedding (the wall would not be fully repaired until the late 1970s). The couple stood at the altar along with the best man, Dunne's younger brother, Stephen, who would one day commit suicide. They were joined, as well, by Dunne's four-year-old niece, Dominique, a flower girl. She would one day be strangled to death. Cognizant of the family drama—aware that, to parents, a child's marrying is "the classic betrayal"—and overwhelmed by the odds against happiness in life, Didion promised Dunne that, if necessary, they would release each other before "death do us part."

A reception followed the wedding at the Lodge at Pebble Beach, a one-story log cabin–style inn overlooking the ocean. The couple honeymooned first in a bungalow at the San Ysidro Ranch in Montecito, toasting each other in the sprawling indoor spas, admiring the blossoms along the highways, and then, bored, fled to the Beverley Hills Hotel on Sunset Boulevard. California was every bit the luxurious adventure Dunne had thought it would be.

It's intriguing to think that at the Beverly Hills Hotel the couple might have watched on a television the Beatles' first performance on *The Ed Sullivan Show*, on Sunday, February 9. Possibly they found the Beatles, with their prim suits and neatly groomed long hair, silly. But a new music was about to sweep aside the old, the innocence of the Beatles' early lyrics—"I wanna hold your hand"—shadowed by the sexual urging of bass and drums. Rock 'n' roll wasn't fresh in 1964, but the Beatles put a stylish face on it (*Vogue* was a fan), spreading its subversive undercurrents far across and deep into the culture: black gospel, rhythm and blues, Dust Bowl laments laced with Anglo-Irish warrior screams. Within a few years, the Beatles' double record, popularly known as *The White Album*, would disorient and fascinate Didion; she'd find it ominous and disturbing, emblematic of the decade's darkest eddies. By 1968, the adolescent eagerness of "From Me to You" had given way to "Cry Baby Cry." The honeymoon was over. During this same period, the nostalgia in Didion's prose would sharpen to a razor edge and finally flake away. Eventually, she'd offer *her* version of *The White Album*, a verbal mirror of the horror in the Beatles' least-played, but arguably most important track, the sound collage "Revolution 9," a mash-up of car wrecks, protest shouts, burning buildings, gunfire, warfare, weeping babies.

Back in New York, after the honeymoon, Didion returned to what people were talking about:

The Cassius Clay–Sonny Liston fight in Miami. Days before the bout, Clay had posed for photographers with the Beatles ("So who *were* those little faggots?" he asked after the shoot). Like pop stars, he seemed dismissible, a garrulous clown—but with edgy undertones, especially when, a day after upsetting Liston in the sixth round, he changed his name to Cassius X and then to Muhammad Ali. What *was* the Nation of Islam?

The American Supermarket, an art show planned for the Upper East Side gallery of Paul Bianchini and Ben Birillo. The space would resemble a small supermarket featuring a painted bronze watermelon by Billy Apple, a plastic turkey by Tom Wesselmann, and dozens of chrome eggs by Robert Watts. In particular, Andy Warhol's paintings of Campbell's soup cans would surely confound patrons as to what was art and what was junk and *what difference did it make?*

A young short story writer named Donald Barthelme, about whom there was notable literary buzz. His first collection, *Come Back, Dr. Caligari,* was scheduled for publication in April and was already being hailed as bold, crazy, wildly innovative. Warhol had taken pictures of Barthelme in Times Square; the photos appeared in *Harper's Bazaar* along with shots of other writers, dancers, and painters to watch.

People were *not* talking about *Run River.*

Joan Didion was not a writer, dancer, or painter to watch.

How could she get traction on—or even begin—a second novel with "a lot of people talking to [her] all the time about their advances"; with all the glib, faux-intellectual chatter in the bars? One day, Dylan Thomas was all the rage. Then it was Auden. Then it was Yeats. "The Second Coming," the center giving way—what the hell did these green, gloomy writers know about the Apocalypse?

And then there was Noel, apparently happy to gad about town giving people "unshirted hell about their ethnic backgrounds, social proclivities, and general *raisons d'etre*." This was his description of a character in Jack Gelber's play *The Apple,* a "drunken reviler of all and sundry," reportedly based on him.

Come to Norman's party, he'd say to Didion. Ginsberg will be there. C. Wright Mills. Tiger Jones. Mobsters and beauties.

She couldn't stand it. She wouldn't go. New York had palled for her, altogether. "[One day] I stopped riding the Lexington Avenue IRT because I noticed for the first time that all the strangers I had seen for years—the man with the seeing-eye dog, the spinster who read the classified pages every day, the fat girl who always got off with me at Grand Central—looked older than they once had," she wrote in "On Keeping a Notebook."

She felt bone-weary. How had that happened? When? Everything that had seemed within her reach, the curiosities around every corner, the heady smells of "lilac and garbage and expensive perfume," drifted away from her.

And what about this *marriage* of hers? One Monday morning, she ducked into Saint Thomas Church—perhaps for relief from the crowds, all those fur-wrapped ladies walking their toothy little terriers. In the nave, she saw a book by James Albert Pike, *If You Marry Outside Your Faith.* The bishop said it was an error to marry outside your faith and that a person had a moral obligation to annul such a godless union and forget any promises she may have made in the heat of her wrong.

It was the kind of thing Noel might have said to her as a joke—not really joking.

Stunned, she fled the church.

Come on, come to Norman's party.

How could she *miss* the parties, even the bad ones? The putrid wine, the stupid talk. Ad agents. Democrats. Rejected novelists, convinced they'd find their muse in central Mexico. Everyone was scrabbling to find a niche.

"[I] could not walk on upper Madison Avenue in the mornings, and . . . could not talk to people and still cried in Chinese laundries," Didion wrote in "Goodbye to All That." "I could not even get dinner with any degree of certainty, and I would sit in the apartment on Seventy-fifth Street paralyzed until my husband would call from his office and say gently that I did not have to get dinner, that I could meet him at Michael's Pub or at Toots Shor's or at Sardi's East."

Paralyzed, maybe. But she got to a lot of movies. She had a regular film column now in *Vogue*. "Goodbye to All That" portrays her as full of despair during this period, but the column reveals that she was also having a good deal of fun at the filmmakers' expense. Her persona on the page was light-hearted, confident, and sassy. Of the movie *Captain Newman, M.D.*, she said, "Its main liability is its script, the drift of which is that the mind has no mountains, no cliffs of fall, which can not be painlessly eroded if you'll only just lie down there and let Gregory Peck (M.D.) and Angie Dickinson (R.N.) shoot you a little more sodium pentothal."

In fact, she may have been having a better time than her husband. It seems he could not count on dinner. At work, he was bored out of his skull with the Common Market and the financial distress of tiny monarchies. One day in April, he called Didion to ask if she'd mind if he quit his job at *Time*. Go ahead, she said. Absolutely. He could freelance. She could freelance.

He asked for a six-month leave of absence. To maintain cordiality, and to keep the door open in case the freelancing didn't work out, he wrote Otto Fuerbringer a note. They'd had their disagreements, he said, but he'd greatly valued his years at the magazine. Fuerbringer replied, "What disagreements?"

It's clear from Didion's movie reviews that, for some time, she had considered (or toyed with) joining the business of Hollywood. "I could sit through [this movie] only by wondering who in the screening room was involved with whom, and what they fought about," she wrote in March 1964 (the movie was *The Guest*).

"*What a Way to Go* is supposed to have cost six million dollars, which averages out to about a million and a half a laugh," she figured.

A few months later, she wrote, "Although I assume that someone, somewhere, lived through the fall of 1963 quite unaware that down on the west coast of Mexico, in Puerto Vallarta, John Huston was making *The Night of the Iguana*, the notion suggests a detachment so sublime as to border on the schizophrenic." Actually, what "suggests . . . detachment" is Didion's unironic belief that every individual on the planet was hanging on the latest scrap of gossip about the motion picture industry.

Had she wandered down to Horatio Street some evening around six or seven o'clock, ducked into Jimmy Baldwin's apartment at number 81, and sat with the people there, including her friend Dan Wakefield, she might have been reminded, in a galvanizing way, that not *every* writer in New York put a sizable advance in front of a love of words. She might have been shaken out of the fashionable weariness and insider professionalism glutting Condé Nast. If only briefly, she might have stopped dreading others' success and dreaming of flight to Tinsel Town.

But to most of Si Newhouse's toilers, Horatio Street was terra incognita. From a distance, Baldwin's bourbon-and-Bessie-Smith ethos echoed the Beats, though this was a grievous misconception. The Beats were dilettantes to many of the writers squeezed into Baldwin's hot and airless rooms. "Everyone's sitting around—all the white people—with this kind of deference and worship and fear [of Baldwin]," said the novelist Lynn Sharon Schwartz. "And he was slightly hostile but that was okay . . . it was a very, very tangled and delicate situation." The racial tension could not be separated from the literary—or human—camaraderie. "He was sounding off about . . . injustice, and very well, and we were all feeling guilty," Schwartz said.

"The American soil is full of the corpses of my ancestors!" Baldwin might shout. "My right to live here . . . how is it conceivably a question now?" Something was certainly at stake here—socially, literarily—but, you know, didn't it smack, somehow, of the Nation of Islam? What was *happening* in this country? Better to work late in the Graybar Building, dream of a Goldwater White House, watch the secretaries pack up their lipstick at the end of the day, and stare at the elevator lights.

Or better to go to the movies.

It seemed to Didion that American filmmakers had lost their bread and butter. The fine noir dialogue punching up so many black-and-white underworld pictures had been stolen by the French.

"Who'd you call?" "The cemetery, just in case you get careless."

When was the last time Hollywood had come up with something *that* fresh? French directors were making a much better job of it now than the West Coast studios.

Hollywood seemed to have mistaken seriousness for dim-wittedness. Movie stars were movie stars "precisely because we know them so well," Didion wrote—what moron decided they should *vanish* into their roles and actually *act*?

But the bottom line was this: "She knew exactly what she was doing and she knew how to get it done," said Dan Wakefield. That's why she studied the pictures so closely. "She's one of the smartest writers I know in terms of money. She and Greg couldn't earn enough from their books to live the way they wanted to live, and they wanted to live well."

She couldn't build shopping centers; the ocean-dream had sunk; so "she knew they'd have to work for the movies."

Wakefield wasn't surprised to get a letter from her one day saying she and Dunne had decided to go to Los Angeles for six or seven months. They would sublet their place. On April 24, 1964, she wrote that she was going to get tan and she would try not to be her "creepy self."

In Los Angeles, Dunne's brother Nick worked in television. He could connect them. Westerns had come to the small screen—just when the great John Ford seemed to have forgotten how to make them.

She was *really* in the doldrums now, eager to move but not quite ready. She had to pay off Con Ed, disconnect the phone, make the final rounds of parties.

Anxiety crept into her movie reviews. "[S]ome things just aren't as funny as they once were," she wrote. She couldn't relax enough to enjoy the goofiness of *The Pink Panther*. For her, the movie's sole achievement lay in staging "the only seduction ever screened . . . with all the banality of the real thing."

Presumably, her husband still wasn't getting many dinners at home.

"Goodbye to All That," a brilliant elegy to youth, romantic idealism, and the New York of Didion's apprenticeship, is an example of the author working her brand. Nothing in the piece is not true, but it highlights her vulnerabilities to the exclusion of everything else. This strategy reinforces the themes of naïveté and loss. It is why the essay is effective. But because Didion purports to be writing about herself, the reader is invited to ask if the piece fully reflects who she was at the time—in spite of the fact that Didion never intended full disclosure.

For her, all appearances to the contrary, confession was not the point of the essay. Yet for a reader, even a sympathetic reader willing to grant Didion her intentions, the issue is unavoidable. This is the paradox of autobiography, a paradox Didion pushed to extremes.

"Goodbye to All That" is in no way diminished by the biographer's curiosity. The essay suggests she left New York in 1964 in the grip of a melancholy breakdown: "[T]here was a song on all the jukeboxes on the [U]pper East Side that went 'but where is the schoolgirl that used to be me,' and if it was late enough at night I used to wonder that." Biography helps us recognize that nostalgia had been Didion's primary emotional register since she was a child. This was nothing new. New York was not over for her. The option to return after six months remained wide open.

Too, Didion nursed a contrarian streak. At Berkeley, she had defied her teachers' expectations of going to grad school. Now she would thumb her nose at those insisting a writer *had* to be in New York. "If you weren't in New York, you were nobody," said Jill Schary Robinson. "We were all made to feel that way."

So Didion would leave.

It *was* a counterintuitive move, given the solid career she had established in Manhattan—though, there again, she was not in danger of losing much at this point; she would continue to write movie and book reviews for *Vogue* over the next couple years from her home in California. The risk had more to do with America's perception—by which I mean the view of establishment critics—as to art's true center. Harold Rosenberg wrote, "If New York is the site from which art history is launched, to be present there would seem indispensable to the creation of an art that matters. One who fails to respond to the New York note is considered to be an exile from both past and future." Artists of any sort, including writers, who opted for "regionalism," he said, were engaging in a "revolt of geography against history."

PART FOUR

Chapter Eleven

1

CAUTION: CONSTANT LAND MOVEMENT.

Signs warning visitors of the ground's erratic instability ring the Harden Gatehouse at Portuguese Bend, where Joan Didion and John Gregory Dunne settled in June 1964. Here, at the southern tip of Los Angeles County's Palos Verdes Peninsula, domelike hills rise more than 430 meters above the sea, rolling, falling steeply. The topsoil slides—always—sheeting the coast with bentonite, a clay mineral made from weathered volcanic ash capable of absorbing vast amounts of water, losing its cohesiveness, and destabilizing the surface even further. Geologists posit the area's first major landslide at about 37,000 years ago. In our time, the land began to lose its grip again in 1956, initially shifting five inches a day over a two-year period. The danger did not stop real-estate developers from building more than 150 homes by 1961, digging seepage pits and installing septic systems in the trembling earth. When cracks began to appear in the houses' foundations, outraged home owners filed the nation's first class-action suit incurred by a geologic event, suing the County of Los Angeles, alleging that the landslide was caused by the construction of Crenshaw Boulevard. The court found the county liable even though it failed to establish negligence. Meanwhile, the land went on eroding.

Modern development began on the peninsula in 1913, when a New York investor named Frank Vanderlip envisioned a community of horse ranches on land first taken by the Portuguese from the Gabrielinos-Tongva Tribe and then stolen by U.S. entrepreneurs. Thus, the history of Southern California.

Didion's new home, the Harden Gatehouse, at 5500 Palos Verdes Drive South, was built in 1926 by Vanderlip's sister, Ruth, and her husband. A grand villa had been planned for the forty-eight acres of coastal land abutting the house's grounds, but the Depression quashed that vision. This would be the first of the spectacular abodes Didion and Dunne would occupy in the Los Angeles area from 1964 to 1988. "Joan definitely had the real estate gene from her family," said Josh Greenfeld.

"Joan put an ad in the paper saying that a writing couple was looking for a house to rent," said Dominick Dunne. "A woman replied, offering an attractive gatehouse on an estate on the sea at Palos Verdes and explaining that the main house had never been built, because the rich people who commissioned it went bust. The lady wanted $800 a month. Joan said they were prepared to pay only $400. They settled at $500."

This lady was the wife of Dick Harden, Ruth's son, who would become Didion's new landlord. Dunne found him eccentric and unpredictable, likable (he'd leave strawberries and baskets of sweet peas on their doorstep), but often uncomfortable to be around.

The Tuscan-style house, on a lot of just under two acres, initially had four bedrooms (it now has five) and a large living room with a stone fireplace and vaulted ceilings—over five thousand square feet. In Didion's day, blocky brown wooden beams curved over arched doorways and rectangular columns painted adobe tan or white, defining the rooms. The tiled floors were cool and dark. Rounded windows opened onto the sunset and salt-scoured willows glittering with reflected light from granite outcrops curving down to the shore. A swimming pool has since been built where Didion kept a wisteria box garden. The house was angled toward the ocean, with a view of Catalina Island, away from the public road, which was always under repair. Pieces of marble, imported for the never-built villa, lay scattered among tall palms on the lawn. A low wall topped with sloping red tiles surrounded the property.

At the entrance to the drive stood an imposing stone arch draped with ivy; in it was set a ten-foot-high wooden gate trimmed with fleur-de-lis spikes and a ship's bell jutting out from the wall.

At twilight, peacocks cried. They roamed the grounds aggressively, displaying their blue-green grace. Of an evening, Didion and Dunne would sit with iced drinks on a tiled back terrace, watching the peafowl prance. Hummingbirds and flycatchers flitted in and out of peach trees and low-hanging olive limbs. Glare from the Point Vicente lighthouse (said to be haunted by a woman whose lover had been lost at sea) raked the rocks below.

Sometimes the couple walked the shoreline, spying wreckage from the Greek freighter *Dominator,* sunk in a storm in 1961, just off Rocky Point. Occasionally, Dunne walked Didion down to the beach, among jagged tide pools teeming with hermit crabs, sea urchins, starfish, and anemone. They'd go swimming, skirting kelp beds by a submerged reef in Abalone Cove and timing the waves just right—"Feel the swell! Go with the change!" Dunne would shout—to be swept into a cave along the shore. Didion was afraid but exhilarated, reminded of shooting the rapids of the American River in Sacramento.

For shopping, laundry, and other errands, Dunne preferred the nearby village of San Pedro to the tonier community center, with its Spanish Mission–style houses and landscaping by the Olmsted Brothers, some eight miles distant. San Pedro, built on a foggy, shallow waterfront dubbed by its Portuguese discoverers the "Bay of Smokes," was a sleepy town of bars, former canneries, and shuttered whorehouses once catering to personnel at the Naval Auxiliary Air Station and at the LA-55 Nike missile battery where Crenshaw dead-ended. The missile site was more successful as a movie backdrop in sci-fi films than as a defense against phantom Soviet bombers.

On Liberty Hill, at Fourth and Beacon, Upton Sinclair had been arrested for reading from the Bill of Rights during a 1920s longshoremen's strike.

In his rented Chevy II Nova station wagon, Dunne cruised past scrap yards, the box houses of day laborers and shipbuilders, Croatian and Sicilian restaurants, and taverns such as TJ's and the Dew Drop Inn. San Pedro had always welcomed a diverse population, including, recently, army private Jimi Hendrix and a grifter from West Virginia named Charlie Manson, looking to pimp local girls.

Dunne itched to uncover the tainted lives inside the bars' moist, dark walls (that old Catholic teaching!). He'd gaze across the harbor to the Port of Los Angeles, at Terminal Island's oil tanks, freight cars, cargo berths, container ships belching low-grade bunker fuel into the air: fish, sulfur, rotting plankton. He began to understand the pleasures of driving: spying from just behind the wheel, sealed from the world's meanness, girded by speed.

On Friday mornings, he'd step out of bed and into the old Crane shower with its stainless-steel handle, wash quickly, and then wake his wife, who'd be sleeping, he wrote, in "her blue Dacron crepe nightgown." They'd brew coffee, sip a cup or two, and head north in the station wagon, circling the peninsula, toward Palos Verdes Estates. Friday was the day *The New Yorker* arrived at Portuguese Bend, sometimes as much as three weeks after the issue's appearance in the East.

To get to Chavez Ravine, they'd take the Pasadena Freeway. Beverly Hills, where Nick lived, required them to negotiate the Harbor Freeway and the San Diego Freeway. When they returned to the Bend late at night, often the fog was so dense, Didion would leave the car, walk along the road's center stripes, guiding Dunne home, just as her high school friends used to get *her* down from Donner Pass.

It was a "nutty idea that we could write for television," Didion said in an interview in *The Paris Review* in 2006. "We had a bunch of meetings with television executives, and they would explain to us, for example, the principle of *Bonanza*. The principle of *Bonanza* was: break a leg at the Ponderosa. I looked blankly at the executive and he said, Somebody rides into town, and to make the story work, he's got to break a leg so he's around for two weeks. So we never wrote for *Bonanza*. We did, however, have one story idea picked up by *Chrysler Theatre*. We were paid a thousand dollars for it."

Nick Dunne arranged a few initial meetings with TV people. "In Hollywood, if you were related to someone, you'd have no problem getting work," said Jill Schary Robinson. Tim Steele, a former ABC executive, told me, "Hollywood was always a nepotistic society. Mothers, fathers, brothers, sisters—no one frowned on that. It *helped*. It's true that, in the pictures, writers weren't terribly well respected, but even writers could gain respect if they had somebody opening doors for them. Plus, there weren't that many people in it—making pictures is a small business. And once you're in the system, it's hard to get out. People just like going to the same people—the devil you *know*, right? You can get by for a long time by just being okay at what you do, if you're not arrogant.

"Every event, every social occasion, is business, and you learn how to behave," he added. "There's lots of parties in people's houses—this keeps it small-townish."

Didion's training in Sacramento, the etiquette she had learned as a girl, helped her see the cues not only to social acceptance but to professional ascendancy (though she was never not aware of Fitzgerald's line from *The Last Tycoon*: "We don't go for strangers in Hollywood"). Of life for women in the upper reaches of the entertainment community, she wrote:

> [It was] quite rigidly organized. Women left the table after dessert, and had coffee upstairs, isolated in the bedroom or dressing room with demitasse cups and rock sugar ordered from London and cinnamon

sticks in lieu of demitasse spoons. On the hostess's dressing table there were always very large bottles of Fracas and Gardenia and Tuberose. The dessert that preceded this retreat (a soufflé or mousse with raspberry sauce) was inflexibly served on Flora Danica plates, and was itself preceded by the ritual of the finger bowls and doilies.

Her brother-in-law's wife, Lenny, was a superb hostess, well versed in the rituals, though she suspected her efforts were useless. She feared her husband, Nick, was a hack. Frank Sinatra teased him about this, late nights in the Bistro or at the Daisy (Dominick and Sinatra had gotten crosswise on a television program they'd done together). Nick's career seemed limited, as well, by his medium: He produced TV shows in a town where the motion picture was king.

Humphrey Bogart had brought him to California to produce a TV show called *The Petrified Forest*, which also starred Lauren Bacall. Bogart had met Nick while working at NBC in New York and recognized a fellow blue blood; beneath his tough-guy persona, Bogart was an Andover boy. One day, on one of Nick's early trips to Los Angeles in the mid-1950s (Lenny was still in New York), he gushed to his new friend, "God, I love to look at movie stars!" "Come to dinner," Bogey said. That night, Nick met Lana Turner, Judy Garland, David Niven, Henry Fonda, Spencer Tracy, Frank Sinatra. "I thought I'd died and gone to Heaven," Nick said. "They just sort of took me in. They accepted me as though I was one of them." From then on, he became a dedicated name-dropper (and any account of his life risks imitating him). "I called Lenny: 'We've got to move out here! It's incredible!' It was everything I wanted."

It wasn't Lenny's dream. Born Ellen Beatriz Griffin, an Arizona ranching heiress, she liked New York. She had lived for a while at the Barbizon and hoped to be a model. Now, Nick's Hollywood zeal alarmed her a little. But she packed up her baby, Griffin, and joined her husband in a beach house in Santa Monica, rented from Harold Lloyd. Nick had quit NBC and gone to work producing CBS's *Playhouse 90*.

Immediately, Lenny stepped in as his social conduit. "She was totally comfortable with who she was. I was never comfortable with who I was," Nick said. "My opinion of myself was nothing. I believed I was everything [my father] had said." But now movie stars were coming to his home. Lenny, dark-haired and slender, with sexy bangs and smart, steady eyes, naturally attracted people; Nick was good-looking, too, with a genial smile and a pale full-moon face. They gave lavish parties. "People said they were climbers," said Mart Crowley, author of *The Boys in the Band*, the movie version of which Nick would produce. "Lenny and Nick's parties were a veritable Who's Who of Hollywood. If they were famous and they were hot, they were at the Dunnes'." Included among these guests were François Truffaut, Vincente Minnelli, Natalie Wood, Diana Lynn Hall. And there weren't just picture people. "David Hockney," Crowley recalled. "Stephen Spender. Christopher Isherwood was always there."

"[It] was the best place to be at that moment in time," Nick said. His Santa Monica neighbor, just up the road at Louis B. Mayer's old house on Palisades Beach, was Peter Lawford, Jack Kennedy's brother-in-law. The Kennedys were "made" Irish—what the Dunnes had always striven to be; in 1950, through a college girlfriend, Nick had wrangled an invitation to the wedding of Robert Kennedy and Ethel Skakel. Bobby and Jack dazzled him. In Santa Monica, he was awed by the Kennedys' treatment of Lawford: They'd fly in and demand to use his house for trysts. They'd say, "'Get the girls, Peter. Get the blow, Peter. Tell Sinatra we can't come, Peter, we're staying at Bing Crosby's instead.'" Nick had heard about the boys' evenings with Marilyn Monroe in the house's back bedrooms. By the time the president was slain, he regarded the Kennedys the way Nick Carraway viewed Tom and Daisy in *The Great Gatsby*: "They were careless people . . . they smashed up things and creatures and then retreated back into their money or their vast carelessness, or whatever it was that kept them together, and let other people clean up the mess they had made."

Still. The call of California.

Nick moved his family into a white Georgian house on Walden Drive in Beverly Hills. The parties continued. For his tenth wedding anniversary, in April 1964—around the time his brother Greg requested a leave of absence from the Luce empire—he threw a Black and White Ball, based on the Ascot scene Cecil Beaton had designed for *My Fair Lady*: "Dancing 10:00 p.m., Black Tie, Ladies please wear black or white," said the invitations. Hydrangeas filled the house, wrapped around specially built white wooden trellises. A tent was raised on the lawn. Two orchestras played after a late supper. Among the many guests were Dennis Hopper and his wife, Brooke Hayward, Ronald and Nancy Reagan. *Vogue* photographer Bob Willoughby snapped Truman Capote dancing with Tuesday Weld. (Two years later, in New York, Capote would famously replicate the ball; he did not invite Nick or Lenny.)

When Nick's brother and sister-in-law arrived in town, he worried about the fit they'd make. Palos Verdes? And that goddamned *station wagon*! (Nick drove a black convertible Mercedes-Benz.) Didion wouldn't know a French dress if it bit her. She confessed she felt relieved at four P.M. each day when she didn't dip physically—she'd almost *always* had a hangover in New York. And now, more parties? But, honey, this is *business*. . . .

At night she would walk the road's center stripes, parting the fog with her arms. In the bathroom, she rummaged through the medicine cabinet, looking for something to ward off her migraines. Her husband switched back and forth between television programs, one showing an evangelist shouting at people in wheelchairs, the other featuring an actress discussing the pleasures of "balling." With the window open, she and Dunne would lie in bed in the dark, listening to the surf, trying to conceive a child.

2

"The freeway is forever!"

On the radio all summer, this slogan rode the static. If you didn't like the city's traffic, said one talk-show host, you could "go gargle razor blades."

In her second novel, Didion would offer unforgettable freeway scenes, but in fact she feared the roads at first, the Chevy Nova not armor enough to reassure her she was safe. She had reversed and reenacted the pioneer trek across the continent, west to east and back again. It was the nature of the trail to be surrounded by casualties.

Dunne, on the other hand, appreciated the egalitarian drift of the merging lanes, speed and anonymity the great equalizers. It's when you exited, into Silver Lake, Alhambra, Bell Gardens, South-Central, Beverly Hills, that you plunged into the world of class, social politics, one-upsmanship, the grids of misery and privilege.

On the freeway, along the matrices of the area's original railway lines, space became time (the experience of *passing through*) and place motion. Much of the road planning was new when Didion and Dunne arrived (a 1960 *Life* magazine article spoke of "ribbons of freeway . . . gradually tying the city's scattered pieces together"). People were split on what car culture was beginning to do to Los Angeles. Old residents argued that highway designers treated the "space between [destination] points [as] a social wasteland devoid of human significance." *Local* meant nothing. But young drivers said they'd bonded under siege: Look, we're surviving this rush hour together! It's our *weather*, our low- and high-pressure systems!

The inescapable truth was this: Los Angeles was *the* twentieth-century American city, the first city whose physical layout and social order owed its patterning entirely to a real-estate- and petroleum-based economy. Didion would catch its tenor in *Play It As It Lays*, conceiving of American life as a series of "audacious lane changes," a hurtle "straight on into the hard white empty core of the world."

For men and women here, at the heart of American business, commuting defined each day. A transitional act, getting from point to point, assumed front and center. It was like turning a footnote into the main body of the text.

Transitions seemed to be the order of the day. Old Hollywood was becoming New Hollywood (though the phrase "New Hollywood" would not become press parlance for another few years). All over town, Didion recoiled from people's anxieties about the change.

"What was happening was, the studios were dying, but they didn't necessarily know it," said Tim Steele. "This all went back to a pivotal moment in 1948. The antitrust decree was the beginning of the end. It said you couldn't vertically integrate the movies. You couldn't make *and* distribute them. The studios had to divest themselves of parts of their process. So Paramount, for example, divested itself of its theaters. It became the nucleus of ABC-TV. Film studios began to make television programs, stretching themselves thinner than before." Former power blocs, economic strongholds, splintered. The old master players had turned feeble: Adolph Zukor, of Paramount, was ninety-one in 1964; Jack Warner was seventy-two; Darryl F. Zanuck, at Twentieth Century–Fox, had just turned sixty-two. If the studio heads were slower and stiffer, the tools of the trade had gotten lighter. "Better technology meant the movies began to be mobile," Steele said. "Till then, the movies didn't like to go anyplace. That's what the back lots were all about." Another move toward decentralization.

For newcomers like Didion and Dunne, these shifts made reading the cues—personal, professional—trickier than it might have been: One day's verities vanished the following afternoon. Each Monday morning, there was a new ass to kiss.

"When the Old Hollywood fell apart, it devastated the social scene," said Jill Schary Robinson. Her father, Dore Schary, was the first writer to become a studio head (MGM). She had grown up in the "dream factory," along with other children of the traditional patronage system: Candice Bergen, Mia Farrow, Marlo Thomas, Tina Sinatra, and Shelley Wanger, daughter of Joan Bennett and producer Walter Wanger. Eventually, Shelley would become Didion's book editor at Knopf.

In the forties and fifties, Hollywood was "like a little neighborhood," said Marlo Thomas. "[W]e used to call it 'the Village.'" Eve Babitz—soon to be Didion's friend, a source of great entertainment to her—said the girls at Hollywood High were "too beautiful for high school"; they "were the downfall of any serious attempt at school in the accepted sense, and everyone knew it."

Life was aphrodisiac. And then it fell apart. But not so you'd know it at first. You had to catch the cues.

A year before Didion came to town, Kurt Niklas opened the Bistro on Canon Drive, bankrolled by sixty people at about three thousand dollars a pop. Nick Dunne was an original investor, along with Jack Benny, Tony Curtis, Otto Preminger, Frank Sinatra, and Alfred Bloomingdale. An "unassuming little Beverly Hills restaurant," according to the *Los Angeles Times,* serving "perfectly cooked" capellini, "impeccable" onion soup, and "wonderful clams casino." It appeared to be the latest extension of Old Hollywood glamour, catering to the Reagans, the Kennedys, actors and producers. In 1962 the Daisy, a private discotheque, opened on Rodeo. Its exclusive membership fee jumped from $250 a year to $1,000 as its popularity grew and it burnished the Hollywood legend. "Compared to The Daisy, all other discotheques are slums," Dan Jenkins wrote in *Sports Illustrated.* "It is a place where this great montage of thigh-high miniskirts and glued-on Jax pants are doing the skate, the dog, the stroll, the swim, the jerk, the bomp, the monkey, the fish, the duck, the hiker, the Watusi, the gun, the slop, the slip, the sway, the sally and the joint. Like all good Beverly Hills children, Daisy dancers never even sweat."

But the signs of change were apparent: an edgy knowingness (celebrities need someplace "evil" to go, Jack Hanson, the Daisy's owner, was quoted as saying), a sweet, smoky smell in the parking lot, a "hip" sneer in people's greetings, a rawness in table manners. The night it became most apparent this was *not* the Old Hollywood was the night Frank Sinatra paid the Daisy's maître d', a gentle man named George, fifty dollars to walk up to Nick Dunne's table, tap him on the shoulder, and punch him in the face: "Oh, Mr. Dunne, I'm so sorry about this, but Mr. Sinatra made me do it . . ."

"I was the amusement for Sinatra," Nick said later. "My humiliation was his fun." Here was the social order's devastation, the brave new world. Now, Hollywood power meant having the ability to "make a decent man do an indecent act."

Or perhaps none of this was true.

Perhaps New Hollywood *was* the Old Hollywood, just as California had never really changed. Was the "Lost Village" just a sloppy game of nostalgia? Styles and manners altered . . . but the fundamentals?

In *Blue Nights*, Didion casually mentions sitting one afternoon at the "corner banquette" of the Bistro, at a spot usually reserved for Sidney Korshak. By way of identifying Korshak, she quotes the producer Robert Evans: "Let's just say a nod from Korshak, and the Teamsters change management. A nod from Korshak, and Vegas shuts down. A nod from Korshak, and the Dodgers suddenly can play night baseball."

In fact, all coyness aside, Didion knew quite well who Sidney Korshak was. He was a fixture in Old Hollywood—and now in the New—part of a group of Eastern European Jewish men originally from Al Capone's Chicago Outfit. They had moved west to launder money in real estate, casinos, and lavish hotels, and to get in on the "flickers," the fledgling motion picture industry. They had extended their reach into the state's Democratic and Republican parties. Hollywood insiders referred to them as the "Kosher Nostra."

People called Korshak "the Myth," "the Fixer," or they simply called him a "mob lawyer" (reportedly, Robert Duvall's character in *The Godfather* was based on him). Nick had been to several parties at his house—each time shocked by the armed guards beneath the trees; along with Nick, Korshak had been one of the Bistro's initial investors. His corner banquette, table three, was known as Korshak's office. There, on a specially installed telephone, he had numerous "furtive conversations" with "such corporate titans and political lions as Al Hart, Lew Wasserman [head of Universal/MCA, along with Jules Stein], Paul Ziffren [a Democratic Party player, who'd made a killing selling assets seized from Nisei families in internment camps], Pat Brown, and Gray Davis," journalist Gus Russo reported. "There were also confabs with 'Dodgers people' such as Walter O'Malley and team manager Tommy Lasorda." Korshak had helped evict the squatters in Chavez Ravine so that Dodger Stadium could be built; as the Dodgers' "labor consultant," he was "responsible for keeping the cars parked, the lights on, and the food service employees behind the concession stands"—while drawing up stadium contracts for his pal Beldon Katleman, owner of the El Rancho Vegas casino. Katleman was a regular at Nick Dunne's parties and balls.

When Korshak wasn't dining in the Bistro, people vied to be seated at the notorious table three just for the thrill of it (Didion was no exception). *Here's* where Hollywood's deals got done. When he bustled in, the office was open for business. Niklas would seat him, get him a drink, escort starlets to the table so they could kiss his cheek.

"Along with his pal Lew Wasserman"—who nudged Ronald Reagan to become president of the Screen Actors Guild to do *his* labor bidding under the guise of anti-Communism—"Korshak ran the town," Tim Steele told me. "Anytime there was a problem, he was involved. He was the Teamsters' lawyer. The Teamsters were so powerful because in Hollywood you can't get anything done without a truck."

And you couldn't have the New Hollywood without the flooring of the Old. Sometimes it was hard to tell the gangsters, the politicians, and the movie stars apart (for example, as one of Jules Stein's MCA clients, Ronald Reagan got an early break in an Iowa nightclub controlled by the Chicago Outfit).

As the daughter of a gambler, Didion knew the *look* of deals being made, that little twitch of the mouth, masking supreme confidence. Raymond Chandler once said movie moguls at a luncheon look "exactly like a bunch of topflight Chicago gangsters moving in to read the death sentence on the beaten competitor." There was a "psychological and spiritual kinship between the operations of big money . . . and the rackets," he said. "Same faces, same expressions, same manners. Same way of dressing and same exaggerated leisure of movement."

They were gamblers in a town that loved to play.

"We were forced to sit in a house together and write to make a living, and neither one of us, I think, thought we could do it," Didion said. On top of that, "I had no idea how to be a wife. In those first years I would pin daisies in my hair, trying for a 'bride effect.'" She sounds, here, like Lily McClellan in *Run River*. "[B]oth John and I were improvising, flying blind."

Already, "crapshoot" had become their favorite metaphor for marriage. They'd joke to lessen fears about the pressures they faced. "We needed . . . money because neither one of us was working," Didion said.

She'd kept her reviewing gig, but *Vogue's* enthusiasm for the pieces she filed began to wane. Was she being punished for not staying in New York? In retrospect, she'd hint that she was fired either because a senior editor disapproved of the films she chose or because her review of *The Sound of Music* suggested lesbian diddling between Julie Andrews and the Mother Superior.

In fact, the review asserted no such thing; Didion said the movie was "like being trapped on a dance floor and crooned at by a drunk." "Take back your Alps," she wrote.

Didion's real problems with *Vogue* were the magazine's push for greater revenue and its discovery of Pauline Kael. Kael was offered a column. From the beginning, the women did not see eye-to-eye. Of the Jane Fonda movie *Cat Ballou,* Kael wrote, "It will probably be a big success, and it's so much better than a lot of movies around that, relatively speaking, it deserves it." In the following issue, discussing *The Sons of Katie Elder,* Didion appeared to take a swipe at her compatriot: "This is an old-fashioned action Western, the kind *Cat Ballou* tried so dismally to make fun of." Shortly afterward, she stopped reviewing for *Vogue.*

The bigger issue for Didion was Si Newhouse's more aggressive conception of what the magazine business should be. "At the time I began working for *Vogue,* there was a clear understanding that it was not a magazine for very many people," Didion told Meghan Daum. "It had 250 to 350,000 subscribers and then a large pass-along readership, but it was specifically designed as a magazine for not very many people. [Later,] once . . . Newhouse had bought it and settled in, that was no longer the way the magazine was conceived. It had to build circulation all the time. If you're building circulation all the time, you're going to have a different sort of magazine"—that is, a watered-down product with wider but blander appeal.

In her first year at Portuguese Bend, Didion wrote three short stories based largely on her New York miseries. She had no particular passion for the short story as a form. "I was suffering a fear common among people who have just written a first novel: the fear of never writing another," she said. "I sat in front of my typewriter and believed that another subject would never present itself. I believed that I would be forever dry. I believed that I would 'forget how.' Accordingly, as a kind of desperate finger exercise, I tried writing stories."

Years later, she said she discovered, quickly, that she had "no talent" for stories, "no ability to focus the world in the window." But in a letter to the actor Buzz Farber at the time, she expressed satisfaction with at least one of the pieces; she had carried off a first-person point of view, normally a difficult challenge for her, she said. As an aside, she told Farber she didn't like stories about children because such stories were generally self-indulgent.

Didion's pieces—family dramas and lovers' tales—were vague, heavy on exposition, quite conventional in shape. The characters were listless, unsympathetic ("[S]he had gone [to the party] only because the soft April twilight saddened her and made her want someone to buy her dinner"). The stories met rejection, from *Harper's Bazaar, Esquire, The New Yorker, The Atlantic Monthly,* and *Redbook.* Rust Hills, then fiction editor for *The Saturday Evening Post,* did accept "Coming Home," in retrospect an obvious run-through for "Goodbye to All That" ("When she heard the door close she got up, pulled off the blue silk slip and put on a nightgown, smoked a cigarette until it burned her fingertips, and then took two phenobarbitals from the bottle in Charlie's medicine chest").

The story is about a woman in a crumbling relationship with a peripatetic man. She has had an abortion because he did not want the baby: "When she was almost asleep she was able to conjure up an image of the baby, not her own unknown baby (she did not think about that) but the loved baby in [a] baby-food advertisement."

Writing these stories, far from New York, made her realize once more just how happy she was to be away from Noel's unpredictability. But there was another reason for her feeling of relief: "There's a rush to opinion in New York that is kind of destructive, particularly to young writers," she saw. "It's very incestuous."

She was glad to be gone. In truth, she had not held the New York intelligentsia in very high esteem. "Well, of course—her father was anti-Semitic," Josh Greenfeld explained; her dad's asides, his little jokes, may have deepened the estrangement she felt in the East.

In any case, she began to feel that one of the great things about Los Angeles "was you didn't see other writers and editors. You saw a broader range of people."

The appearance of "Coming Home" in the July 1964 issue of *The Saturday Evening Post* began a fruitful six-year relationship between Didion and the magazine, during which time she'd write some of her finest essays. Between 1964 and 1969, Didion and Dunne would publish more than fifty pieces there, sharing a column between them, "Points West." It would be the most reliable source of their income. (Their first year in Los Angeles, she and Dunne would earn less than seven thousand dollars from their freelancing; in the following few years, they'd average around eight thousand from magazine work.) A "sense of impending doom" always hovered about the *Post,* Dunne wrote—it was financially imperiled because "Middle America read the magazine, but wasn't buying the products advertised therein; the people whom the advertising was designed to reach didn't read the magazine;

change the magazine and you lost the readers." The managing editor, Otto Friedrich, fought with his publisher; a mild insanity seemed to inflict the management (once, at a dinner for Vietnam's Madame Nhu, the editorial director consistently referred to her country as South Korea).

But because the magazine was slowly failing, it was willing to try anything: a lucky situation for the writers, at least for a while. "Respect was grudgingly given, but once granted, the editors would follow you out onto the longest limb," Dunne wrote.

A far cry from Tinsel Town. Out here on the movie lots, said Jack Warner, writers were simply "schmucks with Underwoods."

In 1964, literary cachet still counted for something in certain Hollywood neighborhoods. The novel was a powerful cultural force. *Everyone* wanted to be Christopher Isherwood—and Isherwood knew it, too, at every party he attended.

Run River had not made Didion a novelist. She was just another person who'd published a book. She'd not made a mark in the pictures. The "fit" Nick worried about—Palos Verdes, the Nova—it was vexing.

Whom did he put them with?

The first time he'd had his brother and sister-in-law over, at a small outdoor Sunday lunch, he'd invited only two other guests, both book people with a toe in the movie pond: Helen Straus, Didion's literary agent at the time (she'd started in the Story Department at Paramount, then founded the literary wing of the William Morris Agency), and Gavin Lambert, an openly gay expatriate English writer who'd published a book of short stories about Hollywood's down-and-out modeled after Isherwood's *Goodbye to Berlin*. He'd written the screenplay for *Sons and Lovers*, so he, too, was trying to make a niche for himself somewhere between the literary and Technicolor.

In that spirit, and encouraged by his brother, Dunne went to work on a project—maybe a book, maybe a screenplay, or maybe it would serve as a treatment for something else—*product*, that was the thing. He called it *Show Me a Hero* (after Scott Fitzgerald's line "Show me a hero and I will write you a tragedy"). It was about a woman named Marjorie caught in a Cold War right-wing plot. Her husband, a spy, is thrown into a Communist prison. A handsome young reporter from *Tempo*, a *Time*-like rag, gets wind of the story and falls in love with Marjorie. She "reciprocates carnally in a midwinter tryst in either a cottage on Fire Island or a suite at the Radisson Hotel in Minneapolis, a plot point to be worked out later," Dunne wrote. In the end, the heroine is left to choose between love and duty to her husband.

The love story against a backdrop of conspiracy sounds more like Didion's Conradian mind than Dunne's, and in fact a letter from Dunne to H. N. "Swanie" Swanson, a legendary Hollywood agent who'd represented William Faulkner, Raymond Chandler, James M. Cain, and Ayn Rand, among others, says Didion cowrote the film treatment with him.

The letter is dated February 13, 1965, and is notable for two reasons: It is the first record we have of collaboration between Didion and Dunne; it indicates that their screenwriting partnership began immediately after their move to California in the summer of 1964. Second, the point of the letter is to withdraw the treatment from circulation in favor of a novel. Dunne had just signed a contract with Harper & Row. His belief that a movie of *Show Me a Hero* would be worthier, financially *and* critically, if it proceeded from the sale of a book, rather than from the direct sale of a screenplay, suggests the cultural power of novels.

Dunne's letter doesn't mention that, late in 1964, Didion had taken the film treatment to William Morris. A roomful of agents had offered the couple, as "constructive criticism," only the advice that they "make the margins a little wider."

This was typing, not writing; Dunne was grateful for the Harper & Row contract. He told Swanson he and Didion had no further plans for collaboration—she was working on a novel of her own, he said. In the meantime, if Swanson would consider representing Dunne's TV scripts, or his idea for a series . . .

The problem was, he had not written any TV scripts. He had not even *seen* a TV script. He and Didion had plunged into writing for the screen without pausing to study procedures and formats. Years later, Dunne recalled, "We were coming out of [the Daisy] one night about 2 o'clock in the morning, and some drunk actor was having a fight with his girlfriend, and he threw a script at her. And I picked up the script. It was a television script. It was the first script I'd ever read."

They began to go to screenings, clutching pencils and pads of paper. They diagrammed movie sequences. "Basically the terminology is easy," Dunne said. He named "three different things. Fade in. Cut to. Another angle."

In the next several years, beginning with their sale to *Chrysler Theatre*, they would shed their naïveté about the writing and pitching of scripts. They would witness green-lighted projects go dead, watch other writers take credit for their ideas, get paid for abandoned work, and understand this was simply business. The distinction between *literary* and *commercial, success* and *failure* (on a project-by-project basis) dimmed in their minds. They did not buy the sentimental view that the pictures had destroyed the literary talents of Faulkner and Fitzgerald. Almost gleefully, Dunne would come to accept the old Hollywood adage: "If you're going to be a whore, you can't complain about getting fucked."

3

"We were crazy about it. We just loved it. I didn't even notice that six months had slipped into a year," Didion said. "It was just easier to do everything, like take your clothes to the laundry." Dunne extended his leave of absence at *Time*. He ordered a six-cylinder Mustang convertible, poppy red, from the Ford factory at River Rouge. Didion took to wearing black-and-white sleeveless dresses—they would have been too thin in New York. The couple was getting into the So Cal spirit.

As he had done in Manhattan, Dunne haunted piano bars, trend spotting. "[N]o one goes to a piano bar except to get laid," he said. The first thing he discovered was that L.A. piano bars were filled with "ad guys from New York, Buckskin fringe, the kind of watch that tells the time in Caracas [and] Djibuti . . . Spritzer guys, a little Perrier water over the Almaden to cut the California taste," the kind of guys who checked their Maldive chronometers and said they had to "catch the noon bird back to New York." The women in these places all had a couple of ex-husbands and El Dorados with about thirty-two payments left on them. One day, at a bar, Dunne met a pro football player who spent eight thousand dollars a year on his wardrobe ("I'm into three-piece suits this fall . . . Part of the image I'm trying to project is a clean-cut guy in a certain kind of car.") Dunne was certain he was getting the L.A. vibe.

Didion liked to study the city from the other end of the social scale, at fund-raisers and gallery openings. While Dunne kept a voyeuristic eye on the lowlifes and strivers, she took him to mingle with movers and shakers. This was the strength of their partnership.

Sometimes it seemed to them, though, that they would never fathom how pawns advanced across the board. One night, at a gala dinner, Didion watched, amazed, as Dorothy Buffum Chandler wheedled Jules Stein into contributing $25,000 toward the construction of her Music Center. In return for his gift, she said, she would offer Stein "twenty-five thousand dollars' worth of free publicity" in her little family paper, the *Los Angeles Times*. The exchange was remarkable for pulling together the political and business interests of Downtown and the Westside, two communities traditionally at odds. Downtowners thought the Westside a place where people exchanged "too many social kisses," a way of saying it was too Jewish. The tête-à-tête at dinner exemplified a commingling of power and grace the "landed gentry" of Sacramento would have admired but could never quite achieve.

Didion feared she would never acquire the L.A. touch. She was not the accomplished hostess her sister-in-law was. "You want a different kind of wife," she would tell Dunne in the open Mustang on a late drive back to Portuguese Bend after a party. The refinery flames off the San Diego Freeway burned away the night fog. "You should have married someone more like Lenny."

"If I wanted to marry someone more like Lenny I would have married someone more like Lenny," Dunne would say.

At home, Didion sat on the closed lid of the old Victorian toilet and swallowed a phenobarbital.

She began to lose more weight. Her wedding ring kept slipping off her finger. She wore it on a chain around her neck.

She urged Dunne to join her in "planning meetings." They'd sit together with legal pads, state a problem they needed to solve, and then decide to drive to Santa Monica for lunch.

This seemed to work as well as any other strategy. As six months slipped into a year, they began to feel more at ease at affairs around town. They were less dependent on Nick. It turned out, literary cachet was not difficult to achieve in a place where no one read books. People were lazy and took you at your word.

Socially, it helped that Lenny considered Didion a work in progress. Lenny volunteered at the Colleagues, a charitable organization for unwed mothers. Show business ladies donated their previous year's wardrobes to the Colleagues for an annual fund-raiser. Didion looked sufficiently waiflike; Lenny set aside Natalie Wood's castoffs for her. They fit perfectly. Dunne recalled a "white Saint Laurent evening dress, a water-colored satin Galanos evening dress, and a yellow wool bouclé coat by Edith Head that had been part of Natalie's wardrobe for *Love with a Proper Stranger*."

"Outsiders . . . had to be thoroughly vetted before receiving passports into that closed community," Dunne wrote. Natalie Wood's wool bouclé coat was as good a pass as you could get. Soon, Didion and Dunne were dining regularly with Wood and her husband R. J. Wood charmed Dunne, using a table knife as a mirror, holding it up to her mouth while fixing her lipstick. He loved her stories of the old days when the studios took care of *everything* . . . like the time (oh, you remember, she'd say) when Nick Gurdin killed a man, driving drunk, and the studio buried the manslaughter charge . . .

On evenings like this, it was easy to believe you could toss the *plans.*

It would be oversimplifying matters to say that Dunne's brother Nick loved the Old Hollywood dream, and as hashish and blue jeans replaced cocktails in the discotheques, he lost his footing. But there *is* some truth to this. "Everything was changing," he lamented. "People were starting to smoke pot. I was shocked and disapproving when someone lit up in our house one night . . . evening dresses were giving way to miniskirts. . . . Hairdressers started to be invited to parties. Dances changed. The foxtrot was out. The twist was in. . . . Cole Porter was out. The Beatles were in."

As his brother's fortunes rose around town, Nick floundered, drinking too much—he reminded Didion of some of her New York pals—hoping people would forget his spat with Sinatra. By now, he and Lenny had three children, Griffin, Alex, and Dominique. Nick was so busy socializing, he rarely saw them. "The nanny would have the meal with the kids," Griffin recalled. "The adults would check in, you know, have a little something with us, maybe. But then they'd go out for dinner and dancing. Or we'd be up in the bedroom hearing them getting hammered and just having a fantastic time."

When the Beatles came to play the Hollywood Bowl in the summer of 1964, Nick took his kids to meet the moptops at the Brentwood house of Alan Livingston, Capital Records' president. In the garden, four-year-old Dominique curtsied, as her mother had taught her, when she shook Paul McCartney's hand. She amused the musicians, whose charm lay in their jokey boisterousness. It was another clash of old and new. Queasy, Nick snapped a picture for posterity.

Meanwhile, Didion's ardent support of Barry Goldwater posed a major social challenge in the mostly liberal Democratic circles she found herself in. People argued with her that the war in Vietnam was immoral; through Dunne's *Time* experiences, she'd become unhappy with the *effort,* but she figured "a series of such [military] encounters around the world was just part of the way that our future was going to be." If nuclear weapons might expedite things, they ought to be considered.

Dunne joked about her archconservative values, but he couldn't keep a cap on her passions as the Republican National Convention approached. It was to be held in San Francisco's Cow Palace from July 13 to July 16. Didion was furious at the way Ronald Reagan and Richard Nixon maneuvered to steal the spotlight from the "true" conservative, Goldwater. Two years earlier, a self-pitying Nixon had declared the country wouldn't have him to kick around anymore, but he had gotten himself a prime-time speech at the convention and his ambitions were clear. Reagan, on the stump, used a mix of Red baiting, trumped-up anger at "the Eastern elite," and nostalgia to enthuse crowds, and California Republicans seemed to fall for it. Didion's anger flared at parties, followed by long silences.

A few weeks before the convention, she and Dunne flew back to New York for a Goldwater rally in Madison Square Garden. William Buckley was there, seated in a one-thousand-dollar box; all of the attendees "with the possible exception of Senator Goldwater" appeared eager to "kiss the hem of his garment," Dunne wrote. "It was an idolatry that Mr. Buckley gave no sign of thinking either unjust or untoward," even though, from the perspective of a new Californian, it was anachronistic. Republican power had shifted to the West.

An ugly tone characterized the rally, presaging the San Francisco event and American political style ever since. Dunne noted "the repeated droll allegations in the Garden that liberals were double-gaited, limp-wristed, and generally so light on their feet they could dance on a charlotte russe."

"The stench of fascism is in the air," California governor Pat Brown warned the press in San Francisco as the Republican convention gaveled to order. At Goldwater's instigation, 70 percent of the convention delegates voted down a platform plank affirming the constitutionality of the recently passed Civil Rights Act.

While authorities in Mississippi were still searching for the bodies of James Chaney, Andrew Goodman, and Michael Schwerner, cheerful shouts caromed off the Cow Palace walls. "The nigger issue" was going to sink LBJ, a Republican aide told one reporter.

"A new breed of Republican had taken over the GOP. As I watched this steamroller operating in San Francisco, I had a better understanding of how it must have felt to be a Jew in Hitler's Germany," said Jackie Robinson, the baseball player and special delegate that year for Nelson Rockefeller. "The convention was one of the most unforgettable and frightening experiences of my life." He was appalled when Rockefeller was booed as a moderate Easterner. Several times that week, Robinson felt physically unsafe.

An African-American television reporter named Belva Davis and a fellow black journalist were chased out of the Palace by delegates yelling, "Niggers! . . . I'm gonna kill your ass!" "The throng began tossing garbage at us: wadded up convention programs, mustard-soaked hotdogs, half-eaten Snickers bars. . . . Then a glass soda bottle whizzed within inches of my skull," Davis said.

Fury at the Civil Rights Act was matched by the Republicans' anger at the media. NBC newscasters Chet Huntley and David Brinkley felt distinctly threatened when trapped in the elevators at the Mark Hopkins Hotel with delegates muttering under their breath that they were "crypto-liberals!" One day, one man said to another, in Brinkley's hearing, "You know, these nighttime news shows sound to me like they're being broadcast from Moscow."

This was all the result of the "greatest campaign in history," according to Richard Nixon's introduction of Goldwater as Goldwater accepted the party's nomination for president. Goldwater's speech fanned the week's violence. He swore the country would not "stagnate in the swampland of collectivism" or "cringe before the bully of Communism." It would not bow before the "false prophets" reversing the "tide of freedom" by expanding civil rights. This new legislation, he suggested, opened America's streets to "bullies and marauders."

At dinner parties and Hollywood gatherings, Didion shocked some of her fellow guests when she said she would vote for Goldwater again and again if she could. He was a principled man in the mold of the pioneers, of John Wayne, and that was that.

She shared the Republicans' disgust with the "liberal media." The "unspoken, unadmitted" bias in papers like *The New York Times* hit readers "like so much marsh gas," she argued. "[M]onkeys," she said, must be in charge of the Teletypes.

A few months before the convention, Universal Studios released the last Hollywood film Ronald Reagan would ever star in, Don Siegel's *The Killers*. Perhaps more than the convention, or any of Reagan's speeches for Goldwater that year, *The Killers* bared the methods by which Hollywood money and myths would enter mainstream American politics.

Joan Didion would understand this dynamic better than any other writer in the country. Partly as an attempt to secure her own survival in L.A., she had studied the culture shaping Reagan. She saw Old Hollywood's slippage and grasped the anxiety this would cause a man like him. Further, she saw the effects of change on the nexus of fashion, style, and the process of narrative formation that would manufacture Ronald Reagan as a leader for his time (in the interim, it was no coincidence that *another* Californian, Richard Nixon, had moved American politics toward greater cynicism).

In *The Killers*, Reagan plays a mob boss. The movie was made on the cheap. The sets were obviously fake. Universal's color processing left the scenes washed-out and flat. "By the early 60s, the classical Hollywood filmmaking of the 30s and 40s had become mummified," the critic Charles Taylor wrote. "*The Killers* reeks of this calcification." No place in the movie "seems like anywhere that anyone real could actually exist . . . In other words, its relation to the Hollywood films that had preceded it is exactly the relation of Reagan's white-picket fence vision of America to the real thing—a false, shallow copy stripped . . . to its basest motives."

The movie's plot? It was about how "a hood can become a respectable businessman." (Just as, twenty years later, the Nicaraguan "Contras" would become "Freedom Fighters.")

As Didion had learned, reading the A-lists, Hollywood had *never* distinguished hoods from respectable businessmen. Reagan's early career had depended on blurring his vision; he never made a distinction between above or below-the-line deal making. Nor would he—or anyone else here—question the need for the "show to go on," even if the means had "mummified" and the stage sets were cardboard.

For the time being, Didion's grasp of these cultural forces and future consequences remained nascent; she observed their manifestations mostly in the increasingly sad figure of her brother-in-law. In his desperation to retain Old Hollywood glamour and the respect of powerful friends, he was becoming a "fake," Nick admitted.

Meanwhile, Didion's return to New York for the Goldwater rally had further convinced her that she and Dunne had made the right decision in moving to California. People's assumptions, back east, that she would rush to embrace Manhattan again irritated her. New York was so *sentimental* about itself, like a lush hamming it up, convinced no one couldn't love her. New Yorkers' rote perceptions of L.A.—"smog," "kooky cults"—were shockingly shallow. In a reversal of Nixon and Reagan, who saw California's political process as a model for the rest of the nation, Easterners viewed "plastic" Los Angeles as a metaphor for all that was wrong with the country.

Back in Portuguese Bend, Dunne, still an Eastern boy, referred to his new home as "Lotusland" and was quickly corrected by his guests. At dinner, a visiting New Yorker complimented a Hollywood hostess's chiles jalapeños and chicken mole. "You cook New York," she said. "Mexico, actually," the hostess replied. Didion wasn't a Lenny-level hostess, but she was learning. The recipes she'd once copied for *Vogue* came in handy.

She reflected: *Vogue* had given her a style even when she'd chafed against it. She'd had to follow it closely to satisfy the magazine's editors. This year in Portuguese Bend, the problem she'd experienced trying to write film treatments, short stories, and scripts was dearth of style. Nothing to give her direction. No Allene Talmey. Just the ocean surf breaking below, the shifting of the land beneath the road, the wind in the trees. After parties in town or dinners at home, she'd listen, she'd read, trying to *hear* California. For example, Raymond Chandler on the dreaded Santa Ana winds: "On nights like [this], every booze party ends in a fight. Meek little wives feel the edge of the carving knife and study their husbands' necks. Anything can happen."

Chapter Twelve

————— ❖ —————

1

When anything can happen, everything is already over.

That's how 1965 felt to Nick Dunne.

"Everything was getting wilder. The pressures of social success with its incessant party going began to change me," he wrote later. "I started being unpleasant to Lenny, the person I most cared for." One night, Afdera Fonda, Henry's then wife, told Nick at a party that he "was not important," that he was there "on a pass . . . without significant achievement." "[I] couldn't look at Lenny," Nick said. "I knew she was ceasing to love me. . . . I had turned into an asshole and *that* was how I had come to be perceived."

On a different night, Nick dragged Lenny to another party she hadn't wanted to go to. Afterward, they "were in the Mercedes, and the top was down," he wrote. "We drove in silence for a while and then she told me she wanted to separate from me. I was devastated. I had to stop the car on Sunset Boulevard. I cried. I begged. But she had made up her mind, and she had made plans."

Didion and Dunne sided with Lenny through all that followed, though they remained friendly with Nick.

He moved into an apartment on Spalding Drive in Beverly Hills, by no means a step down. It had a "multipaneled mirrored dining room that could be bathed in red or blue light," he wrote. Perfect for amorous evenings after dancing in the clubs.

Initially shocked by pot and rock 'n' roll, he now applied himself to exploring their limits. It was more important to be "groovy" than glamorous.

As the months passed, he grew his hair longer. He went to Malibu beach parties where a rather inept local band, the Byrds, played under wind-whipped tents. He saw a new act called the Doors at a grimy little club called London Fog. He hung around the singer. His apartment became a hip "stop-by, a drop-in kind of place," he wrote. Harrison Ford, an unknown actor working as a carpenter, "came by for a smoke." One day, the Doors' Jim Morrison "stopped by to look at himself" in the dining room mirrors. "He closed the shutter doors behind him," Nick said. "He turned the blue lights on, then the red lights, then the blue and red together, turning this way, turning that."

Eve Babitz, one of Morrison's lovers, said he was a fat kid who'd lost a lot of weight doing speed. He never could believe how beautiful his body had become.

That day in the dining room, he looked at himself "from thirteen different angles," Nick said. "I always thought he exposed himself, but I was never really sure. Then he left."

Lyndon Johnson defeated Barry Goldwater in a landslide. His campaign had frightened the public, presenting Goldwater as a lunatic capable of destroying the planet. LBJ's most effective television spot showed a little girl plucking daisy petals as a countdown commenced. Two, one, zero, and then a mushroom cloud swallowed the child.

Just weeks after the Republican convention, Johnson had announced that North Vietnamese torpedo boats had attacked two U.S. Navy ships in the Gulf of Tonkin, the USS *Maddox* and the USS *Turner Joy*. Though Senator Wayne Morse of Oregon questioned the veracity of this claim, Johnson's speech further alarmed the public. Perhaps a change in the White House would not be wise if war was about to escalate.

Didion was not alone in thinking dirty tricks were at work. The timing of Johnson's news was just too neat.

Meanwhile, up the road at her alma mater, protests against the war had intensified. Peace marches these weren't. "Hot damn, Vietnam! Hot damn, Vietnam!" Norman Mailer shouted at a yelling crowd one day in the spring of 1965 while he rapidly paced Berkeley's lower athletic field. "Only listen, Lyndon Johnson, you've gone too far this time! You are a bully with an air force, and since you will not call off your air force, there are young people who will persecute you back. It is a little thing, but it will hound you into nightmares and endless corridors of night without sleep. It will hound you."

Mailer's appearance was the latest in a series of campus events signaling the end of the Silent Generation's reign. Joan Baez showed up with an old guitar to sing "We Shall Overcome." Gary Snyder read poetry. Prior to that, Berkeley faculty and students had arranged bus caravans to San Francisco to picket Goldwater's convention.

Shortly thereafter, a student named Mario Savio, a veteran of the Freedom Summer voter registration drives in Mississippi, somewhat reluctantly led the Free Speech Movement, lashing back at Clark Kerr's restrictions of political activity on campus. Savio gave a galvanizing speech, trouncing Kerr's view of the university as a "mechanism held together by administrative rules and powered by money."

"There is a time when the operation of the machine becomes so odious, makes you so sick at heart, that you can't take part; you can't even passively take part, and you've got to put your bodies upon the gears and upon the wheels, upon the levers, upon all the apparatus and you've got to make it stop," Savio said.

Inspired by Savio's words, Ralph Gleason, the *San Francisco Chronicle*'s music critic and soon-to-be cofounder of *Rolling Stone* magazine, wrote, "Literature, poetry and history are not made by smooth jowl and blue suit. They are made with sweat and passion and dedication to truth and honor."

Governor Brown did not agree. He pressured Kerr to quash the campus turmoil, at any cost.

Didion could not take the protestors *or* the administrators seriously. Berkeley was not a battlefield; Sather Gate was hardly the entrance to the City of Dis. Rich kids were not revolutionaries nor were the provost and deans the last garrison between civilization and perdition. The demonstrations and the backlash were a game of self-delusion, allowing each participant to claim high purpose and go merrily on his way.

Neither side respected the spirit of Bishop Berkeley, for whom the school had been named. To *be* is to be *heard*, he had said. Let be. Instead, there were bullhorns, tear gas, posturing, and pedantry. Didion still believed what she had thought when she was a student at Berkeley in the fifties: Humanity's problems were not political, nor could they be solved by political action. The problem was the intractable human heart.

Norman Mailer should have known that. (She believed Barry Goldwater knew that, which was why she had voted for him—he never would have tried to regulate the world into a happier place.) Mailer's ranting she found silly, but she had the greatest respect for his writing. In his prose, he said the "right things," she wrote in a review of *An American Dream* in the April 20, 1965, issue of *National Review*, within weeks of his appearance at Berkeley.

His public persona had done him no favors with the critics. Most dismissed the novel as melodramatic and repugnant. By contrast, Didion hailed the book as the "most serious New York novel since *The Great Gatsby*." She saw Mailer succeeding at what she had failed to do in her short stories: capture the stench of decadence in America's upper and middle classes. She admired his directness, his confidence, even if it did lead to absurdities, such as "[it was an] unmitigatable fact that women who have discovered the power of sex are never far from suicide." At least here was a writer trying to say *something*. She thrilled at the novel's noir romance, as when Rojack, the narrator, says of a lover, "[her] breast made its pert way toward what was hard and certain in my hand."

(In years to come, Didion remained one of Mailer's few female contemporaries who refused to disparage his portrayals of women or his depictions of danger and violence in sex. Some critics would view *her* heroines as masochistic and her males as hard cases.)

Mailer was so pleased by Didion's review, he wrote William F. Buckley: "What a marvelous girl Joan Didion must be. I think that's one conservative I would like to meet."

Eventually, at a party when she was back in New York, Noel Parmentel introduced her to him. When Mailer first glimpsed her striding across the room, he said, "She's a perfect advertisement for herself."

Didion perceived a "general erosion of technique" in the published fiction she read. "Experimental" stories, stream-of-consciousness writing emulating the Beats, and improvisational prose—it all made her "nose bleed," she said.

"[I]mprovisation is no art but a stunt" she declared in *National Review*. "[V]ery few of these [experimental] writers are opening any doors at all, preferring instead to jump up and down shrieking imprecations at the locksmith." *Catch-22*, she said, displayed "real vacuity." (It had become a bible of sorts on the front lines at Berkeley.) J. P. Donleavy and Thomas Pynchon failed for her because they refused to "follow or think out the consequences" of what they wrote. They would not "go all the way with anything," preferring instead to flit "any way [their] fancy led." To throw a "picaresque character into a series of improvised situations"—which is what she saw most of the "new fiction" doing—"is to stay as clear of a consistent point of view as one possibly can," she wrote. Perhaps not only fiction but also the campus protests, the issues of free speech, were on her mind when she added:

> Everyone wants to tell the truth, and everyone recognizes that to juxtapose even two sentences is necessarily to tell a lie, to tell less than one knows, to distort the situation, cut off its ambiguities and so its possibilities. To write with style is to fight lying all the way. Nonetheless, this is what must be done or we end up maundering. We tell nothing. To tell something, really tell it, takes a certain kind of moral hardness.

With great sadness, she identified another problem: People talked about movies now more than they talked about novels, and they did so in the *way* they used to talk about novels, analyzing and arguing their merits to an absurd degree. In a shockingly short time, literary cachet seemed to have lost its luster.

2

Passé or not, fiction remained paramount in Didion's mind even when she went to the movies.

Lilith, a Robert Rossen film released late in 1964, caught her eye. She did not think it very good, but certain scenes—of a "well-dressed, high-strung young woman" playing gin rummy in a mental hospital—teased her thoughts. For Didion, the problem with the movie was its insistence on answering the question, What is wrong with Lilith? This was a little like the Berkeley protesters asking, What is wrong with the world? and believing that, once they knew the answer, they could fix everything.

It was a little like her father's "mind guys" swearing by Letterman's hydrotherapy units when probably a bourbon highball at happy hour was just as effective.

Quite possibly, what was wrong with the world was the conviction that something was wrong with the world—specifically, people's "refusal to believe that the irrational might prevail" just as easily as the "rational." In a review of *Lilith* in *Vogue* (one of the last regular reviews she filed with the magazine), Didion wrote that the "irrational" was not a damaged version of the orderly; it was simply "something quite different." To ask, "What makes Lilith schizophrenic?" was like asking, "What makes Iago evil?" or "Why Auschwitz?"

"I wonder if to ask is not beside the point," Didion wrote.

Six years later, her second novel would begin with a woman in a mental institution declaiming, "What makes Iago evil? some people ask. I never ask."

3

In May 1965, Mary Bancroft wrote Didion from New York to say she'd appreciated Didion's piece on *An American Dream* in *National Review*. On May 9, Didion replied with her thanks. Only about six people in the country seemed to have liked Mailer's novel, she quipped.

A series of letters to Bancroft followed from Didion and Dunne; these, along with Dunne's letters to various editors and agents detailing his literary projects, allow us to trace the couple's life during the period spanning what the slicks called Freedom Summer to the Summer of Love.

It's clear that, in spite of warming to her new life in California, Didion felt separated from the literary world. She told Bancroft her "constitutional inferiority" had surfaced and infected everything. A visit from Dunne's old pal Calvin "Bud" Trillin reinforced the conviction that she was missing out. *The New Yorker* had sent Trillin to cover the Berkeley protests. This was *Didion*'s territory. She was skeptical of Trillin's ability to really "get" the story, especially when he wrote long and fast between breakfast and drinks and swimming in the ocean.

Tom Wolfe was another interloper getting a lot of mileage out of the West, writing about California car culture. Didion found his prose hit-or-miss—his editors were too lax with him, she thought—and when he sent Dunne a business letter on colored construction paper, she wondered about his sexuality.

She told Bancroft she heard from Noel Parmentel only when he was particularly high or particularly low. She worried about him. Apparently, he was carousing somewhere in the South with Richard Leacock, making a documentary about the Ku Klux Klan. In the wake of the Civil Rights Act and Malcolm X's murder, the South might not be the best place to be right now, even for a Southerner, she thought. But Noel had a genius for worming his way into places where he probably shouldn't be.

She probably shouldn't have been in Mexico earlier that year—not with Trillin and Wolfe eyeing her turf—but she had talked *The Saturday Evening Post* into sending her to a suburb of Mexico City to visit the movie set where John Wayne and Dean Martin were busy filming interiors for *The Sons of Katie Elder*. The Duke in the flesh! But he had just been diagnosed with lung cancer and was shooting the movie against his doctor's orders. He insisted on doing his own stunts. The man truly was a hero.

"John Wayne: A Love Song" recounts Didion's experiences at Estudio Churubusco and firmly establishes the Didion we would come to know on the page: the gambler's daughter, the outsider, the trenchant observer of telling gestures. For example, Wayne—his face "in certain ways more familiar than my husband's," Didion writes—observes "the Code" at a commissary lunch of *huevos con queso* and Carta Blanca beer, the Code of Movie Star, the Code of American Man: he "wiped his mouth, pushed back his chair, and stood up. It was the real thing, the authentic article, the move which had climaxed a thousand scenes in 165 flickering frontiers." But in the late afternoons, Didion saw him turning to the oxygen inhalator he'd tucked away on the set. She heard his racking cough. He had a bad cold. He had a tire around his middle.

After puncturing Hollywood pretenses—her own as well as the reader's—Didion ends her essay with the lure of nostalgia. Longing will not let us go, even when we know better, and this is what makes "John Wayne: A Love Song" a signature Didion piece: It becomes an elegy not just for an individual but for an era.

One night at dinner, on an ordinary evening, "an evening anywhere," Didion says, she and Dunne had a "lot of drinks" with Wayne and his wife, Pilar. Wayne, too, was ordinary by now, just a guy wrapping up a job. "And then something happened. Suddenly the room seemed suffused with the dream." Three mariachis came and serenaded the table with "The Red River Valley." Wayne lifted his wineglass "almost imperceptibly" toward his wife. The guitar players "did not quite get the beat right, but even now I can hear them, in another country and a long time later, even as I tell you this," Didion writes. Here we have it: the persistence of longing despite a discordant rhythm; the awareness of loss and the gesture of recovery in making a story to pass on to others; no, not just to others—to "you." This is as personal as can be.

Something else: that contrarian streak. Wayne was adamantly pro-war. He was rumored to be a member of the John Birch Society. Just as she was becoming a Hollywood insider—though she never would have perceived herself so ("Oh yeah, she became the *ultimate* insider," said her friend Ben Stein)—Didion chose to profile a figure despised by her new liberal friends, a proponent of views bucking cultural trends.

Never mind Bud Trillin: In context, "John Wayne: A Love Song" was *Didion's* piece on Berkeley's unrest, though she never mentions the campus. Her ode to the cowboy is the Silent Generation's last hurrah. Her finest early essays would all be distinguished by a stubborn refusal to tack with the prevailing winds.

In Mexico City, at week's end, she and Dunne were grumpy and tired. She may have caught Wayne's cold, and even then it might have borne a flu that would linger through the spring. The days were hot, the streets thronged with Texans drunk on money and margaritas. Every stranger the couple met told them they *had* to see the new anthropological museum. Dunne had no interest. He argued with Didion about it. Finally, one evening at around six o'clock, she set off alone. "I have found my way around *plenty of museums* without you, never you fear," she yelled at her husband, and slammed the hotel door. Wall plaster crumbled into dust at her feet.

The massive Pedro Ramírez Vázquez building, made of volcanic stone, overwhelmed her: a modern edifice with the power of a ruin, brutal and timeless. Her encounter with Wayne had put her in a pensive mood; similarly, the museum's giant Olmec head, its jade bats and stone fountains impressed *the ephemeral* on her, the way objects tend to outlast their makers, leaving behind only faint, flawed glimpses of history. She stood for a long time in front of a fountain, the tourists' chattering fading behind her. The shattering of the water, the prickles of drops on her face, brought to mind the word *immolation*.

That evening, over drinks, she made up with Dunne. She told him she might like to spend more time in Mexico, maybe a few months in the Yucatán. "Two months might be stretching that particular role," he said, and she laughed. He had caught her. Her dreaminess. Her nostalgia for Lost Domains. She knew he was right. They ordered more drinks and listened to an orchestra play "The Yellow Rose of Texas" for a group of good ol' boys in the corner.

Later, while poring over a map of Mexico, looking for the Yucatán Peninsula (Dunne may have been humoring her), they were captivated by the words *Quintana Roo,* the name of a territory on the peninsula's eastern side—an unexplored wilderness. They promised each other that if they ever had a daughter, they would name her Quintana Roo.

"[S]he cradles herself in her own arms, as women do when they are cold," Alfred Kazin wrote in a profile of Didion in *Harper's* magazine.

She was cold a lot in the spring of 1965 after returning from Mexico City. She had a stubborn flu. In late March, this flu seemed to culminate in a case of blindness. She told Mary Bancroft that for nearly six weeks she lost vision in one eye.

In his profile, published a few years later, Kazin said this "traumatic blindness" occurred "after a miscarriage."

At first, the doctors at the Beverly Hills Clinic thought she had arsenic poisoning. They tracked her history of migraines and the various drugs she had taken to control them, including self-administered histamine injections ("You don't *look* like a migraine personality," one doctor told her). They noted her heavy drinking and her reliance on Pall Malls. They tested her, suspecting multiple sclerosis. She interpreted this as their way of saying they didn't know what it was. It might or might not go away, they said. It might chronically affect her eyes, her legs, her speech. Or it might not. Cortisone shots might or might not help. They forced her to sit in one waiting room after another, listening to Muzak, "Mountain Greenery" over and over.

She phoned *National Review* in New York and said she was having a nervous breakdown. She couldn't file her scheduled book reviews.

Eventually, her eyesight returned.

"I had, [at this] time, a sharp apprehension not of what it was like to be old but of what it was like to open the door to the stranger and find that the stranger did indeed have the knife," Didion would write of her medical ordeal in *The White Album*. "[T]hings which happened only to other people could in fact happen to me."

4

Didion's brother, Jim, didn't know what to make of Dunne on those occasions when the couple traveled up the Central Valley to visit Didion's family in Sacramento. "Joan's husband," he'd call Dunne to his face. Dunne was "uneasy" in the house, Didion wrote, "because once there I [fell] into their ways, which [were] difficult, oblique, deliberately inarticulate." He was stunned by Eduene's habit of not cleaning (once, with his finger, he wrote the word D-U-S-T on tables and countertops in every room; no one noticed). "[W]e appear to talk exclusively about people we know who have been committed to mental hospitals, about people we know who have been booked on drunk-driving charges, and about property, particularly about property, land, price per acre and C-2 zoning and assessments and freeway access," Didion said. On one visit, when Jim failed to engage Dunne on the topic of sale leasebacks, the men slumped into an awkward silence. So "[w]e miss each other's points, have another drink and regard the fire," Didion wrote.

Back in Los Angeles, the Dunnes got invited to parties now without Nick's aid. "Joan and John were tremendous celebrity-fuckers," Josh Greenfeld said. "The thing is, they really knew how to work a party. They'd go through a party in twenty-five minutes and talk to everyone they had to talk to, and go."

Connie Wald, widow of producer Jerry Wald (*Mildred Pierce*, *Key Largo*) and hostess par excellence, became very important to Didion. Didion studied Wald's dinner gatherings: buffets of "red" chicken, roast pork loin, gnocchi, spaghetti puttanesca, all laid out in the dining room of her Dutch Colonial house in the heart of Beverly Hills. The Dunnes were seated next to Gore Vidal, Gene Kelly, Rosalind Russell—A-list all the way.

She met Tom Wolfe. He seemed androgynous to her, not a "fairy," she told Mary Bancroft, but something entirely new.

She did everything possible to get invited to Christopher Isherwood's house in Santa Monica. Isherwood thought the Dunnes "were strivers," said L.A. art critic Hunter Drohojowska-Philp, a view confirmed by Isherwood's diaries. "Mrs. Misery and Mr. Know-All," he called them. Didion "spoke in [a] tiny little voice which always seems to me to be a mode of aggression. Or an instrument of it, anyhow; for it must be maddening in the midst of a domestic quarrel. She drinks quite a lot. So does he." After one party, he noted, "Those tragic and presumably dying women, Lenn Dunne and Joan Didion were around, no doubt feeling as sick as they looked. How can they martyr themselves by going to these get-togethers? Is it really preferable to staying home? Are they so afraid of loneliness?"

Isherwood's longtime partner, Don Bachardy, told me, "Well, it was obvious why Chris didn't warm to Joan. She doesn't like fags. Really—I always thought, What's she doing, married to John? I've never been as cruised by anyone as I was by him. He wouldn't take his eyes off my crotch. He always seemed very queer to me, and so did his brother Nick. I couldn't understand how John could be so obvious about it. It was embarrassing to me. And Joan was around the whole time. She had to know. Women who are married to queers or who find out later . . . it has to be very peculiar for them. And it's easier to blame the queers than the husband."

Bachardy's remarks should be taken with heavy pitchers of salt; they're best understood in light of Dunne's class background, which made him feel perpetually excluded from whatever was happening, intensely curious about experiences he might be missing. Hence, his voyeurism, his reporting, his fascination with crime and prostitution (obsessions he would play out in his fiction), with getting invited to every party in town, a need he shared with his brother Nick (who, as it happened, admitted his bisexuality shortly before his death in August 2009).

What made a good party back then?

"Harrison," Eve Babitz told me. She meant Harrison Ford: beautiful young actors not yet sure of themselves. "And Joan, of course. The best cook, ever."

Babitz charmed Didion and always made her laugh. She was a writer and artist, the goddaughter of Igor Stravinsky. In 1963 she'd posed for one of the most famous photographs in modern art history, playing chess, nude, with Marcel Duchamp on the occasion of his retrospective show at the Pasadena Museum of Art.

She became an "art groupie/art model" around L.A. "In every young man's life there is an Eve Babitz. Usually it's Eve Babitz," said her friend Earl McGrath. For a while, she worked for Ahmet Ertegün at Atlantic Records, designing rock album covers. She met Didion through McGrath, a quintessentially L.A. creature, dabbling in a bit of everything—movies, music, art. "Mostly, he was supported by his wild Italian wife, Camilla," Babitz said. Camilla was the daughter of a countess. Footloose with pots of money, "Earl just poked around L.A.," Babitz said. He was one of Nick Dunne's great friends. "What he really wanted to do was cast movies with people like Harrison. He'd flit here and there. He'd pop into my lover's apartment unannounced at seven every morning. 'Oh, hello, Earl.'"

Like Didion, Babitz grasped the importance of style: Watch styles change, she thought—in fashion, music, cars ("Kandy-Kolored Tangerine-Flake Streamline Baby"), culinary and aesthetic tastes—and you're a step ahead of everyone else in predicting where the culture will go. What "serious" intellectuals dismissed as passing fads was, in fact, the ball game. For example, "Marilyn Monroe was [a] role model," Babitz pointed out. But then Hollywood abandoned the "Rubenesque" woman. "Marilyn had died [and] all the skinny girls were coming out and then when the Beatles came the skinny girls took over . . . the girls on the Sunset Strip. The girls that would go every night and get all dressed up and wear gloves and fake eyelashes and, you know, Jax dresses . . . it was just about sex."

It's striking that Nick Dunne, enchanted with the Old Hollywood, and Eve Babitz, eager to tweak it any way she could, both marked with great melancholy a cultural sea change timed to the Beatles' arrival in the States. And though, of course, Hollywood had *always* been about sex, it had gotten harder, and this could end only one way.

Many of the girls Babitz saw on the Sunset Strip wound up at night at the Chateau Marmont, a 1920s-era hotel modeled after the Château d'Amboise in France's Loire Valley. The hotel was situated between Beverly Hills and Hollywood. The old movie studios used to rent rooms at the Marmont as safe havens for their stars' bad behavior. "I mean, it was built for, you know, peccadilloes," Babitz told the writer A. M. Homes. "You know, if you want to commit suicide, if you want to commit adultery, go to the Chateau. It was the height of elegance."

Inside the hotel's walls, among the crushed velvet sofas, the glass chandeliers, and the tiny elevators lined with signs (IN CASE OF EARTHQUAKE, REMAIN CALM), guests could embrace the illusion that the Strip was *not* just sex; it kept its noirish charm; the ghost of Marilyn might waltz through the door any minute.

Visiting New Yorkers loved to stay there because they could believe they'd landed in Europe rather than in Los Angeles.

Earl and Camilla McGrath lived in the Marmont. "When I was growing up . . . the hotel was always part of our lives," Griffin Dunne said. "You know how some families have these uncles, they're not really their uncles, but you say uncle. Our uncle was a guy named Uncle Earl . . . Earl and Camilla lived in the fifth-floor penthouse. . . . [It was] the largest terrace space in Los Angeles. . . . If you're a kid it's like going to a castle."

Sometimes, on weekends, Nick picked up the kids and took them to the Marmont. Occasionally, there, he'd meet his brother and sister-in-law. They'd sit and drink, trade gossip. To Didion, life was beginning to feel once more like an endless debauch, but she was also not immune to feeling left out, and she appreciated it when a party was *well done,* brought off by a consummate performer. Magical evenings, like those at Connie Wald's, helped mitigate sadness and ease the burden of the tawdry.

Her greatest melancholy had to do with her longing for a child.

One afternoon, an acquaintance she'd met at a party invited her to her Malibu home. They sat together on the terrace, overlooking the sea, drinking wine and trying to catch a bit of sun. The woman told Didion her husband had been born the night the *Titanic* went down. This sentence struck Didion as the kind of line she might use in a fiction (if only she were *writing* fiction!), but she couldn't keep hold of it; she was more intrigued by the woman's confession that she'd like to rent out her house and be with her children, who lived in Paris now. Didion told her she wished she could afford the one thousand dollars a month to rent the house. "Someday you will," the woman said. "Someday it all comes."

Hungover slightly, Didion drove back to Portuguese Bend. Before going home, she stopped at a supermarket and overheard a checkout clerk telling a customer she had no choice but to divorce her husband because he had a seven-month-old baby by another woman. Didion nearly crumpled with dread "because I wanted a baby and did not then have one and because I wanted to own the house that cost $1,000 a month to rent and because I had a hangover," she said.

4

On August 11, 1965, in the Watts neighborhood, a white Highway Patrolman stopped a black driver on suspicion of driving while intoxicated. The officer called for backup; a growing crowd felt the police were using excessive force (especially when the driver's mother and brother arrived, heightening tensions). People began to throw rocks and chunks of concrete. Soon, cars were aflame. A police sergeant, Ben Dunn, said South-Central Los Angeles looked "like an all-out war zone in some far-off foreign country. It bore no resemblance to the United States of America." Thousands of National Guardsmen were mobilized to restore order.

Noel Parmentel, who'd come to town to visit the Dunnes, insisted they go down there.

Later, Didion would write coolly in her essay "The White Album" of the fires that burned at night, visible for miles on the freeways; she'd interview Huey Newton, cofounder of the Black Panthers, who said of the riots, "Black people had been taught non-violence; it was deep within us. What good, however, was non-violence when the police were determined to rule by force?" (Newton would become a Hollywood favorite, invited to parties, posing for photos with Dennis Hopper and Jane Fonda, and producers such as Bert Schneider [*Easy Rider, Five Easy Pieces, The Last Picture Show*], looking to snag a little street cred). What Didion didn't say in "The White Album" was that she spent the evening in Watts cowering in the backseat of the car, afraid she'd be shot by a National Guardsman, while Parmentel ran into the streets, shouting, "Press! Press!" (He *did* have legitimate press credentials at the time, from his work with *CBS Reports* and Richard Leacock on the documentary *Ku Klux Klan—Invisible Empire*.)

Parmentel got lost in the chaos. Worried, Didion and Dunne returned to Portuguese Bend, where they found Dick Harden prowling the grounds with a shotgun big enough to bring down a "goddamned elephant," Dunne said. "I'm going to be ready in case people come out here," he insisted.

Thirty-six hours later, Didion located Parmentel in the Chateau Marmont, where he was telling riot stories to a roomful of starlets. Then he was off to San Francisco with a lady friend to hang out with the editors of *Ramparts* magazine on a houseboat off Sausalito. He'd be back, he said. Upon his return, he drank and roamed the house, telling terrible jokes in mock Yiddish, grousing about Bobby Kennedy, griping about his mother, berating Didion for her shallow celebrity life. How *square* she'd become!

She'd retreat to her bedroom to smoke and calm herself with sewing. Or she'd whip up a meal in the kitchen, though this was not terribly soothing, as something was always boiling over or thickening too fast. She found she was only happy at the typewriter or polishing silver; otherwise, she felt paralyzed. She loved Noel, but she couldn't wait for him to leave.

According to Dunne, on Parmentel's last night in California, the two men squared off in a bar at three in the morning, arguing about the life the Dunnes had chosen, and threatened to kill each other with chairs. Parmentel disputes this.

Shortly before his plane took off the next day, the three old friends embraced and said they must get together again.

Years later, on the back of a framed picture she'd had hanging on the wall, Didion discovered a scribbled note to her from Parmentel (clearly meant to be found in the mists of time during some move or moment of change). It accused her of behaving badly toward him: "You were wrong," it said.

That fall, after "John Wayne: A Love Song" appeared in the August issue of *The Saturday Evening Post*, she received a note from Wayne. "The Old Duke" was gratified, he said. It did a fellow good to be written about that way by a woman.

Chapter Thirteen

———— ❖ ————

1

Something was happening in the Central Valley. Sid Korshak had "his ear to the ground," Dunne wrote in a pocket notebook. In Sacramento, Anthony Kennedy—the future U.S. Supreme Court justice and brother of Didion's childhood friend Nancy—was preparing to work as a lobbyist for Schenley Industries. (Schenley, a liquor producer, would soon be charged with delivering illegal kickbacks to restaurants in California and New York.) Like Korshak, like Robert Di Giorgio, Kennedy was worried about laborers in the fields.

What had them all stirred up was a secular saint or little tyrant—depending on whom you talked to—named Cesar Chavez. With Dolores Huerta, he had founded the National Farm Workers Association. On September 8, 1965, when Filipino laborers mounted a strike against grape growers in Delano (pronounced De-*lay*-no), Chavez supported them. He emerged as a compelling leader and local media magnet, a figure of resistant humility with sad eyes and stumpy legs.

On the long drives up and down the valley to visit Didion's family—"like driving four hundred miles on a pool table"—Dunne wondered, along with his wife, what the real stories were, the narratives beneath the headlines. While Burt Bacharach, Herb Alpert, or the 5th Dimension dithered from the car radio, as dust scratched the bottoms of the clouds and brown bodies bobbed up and down against the blue ridges of the Coast Range, the couple talked about doing a magazine piece on Chavez. Dunne's novel was nowhere—he'd written fifty or so bland pages. Perhaps a few days in the fields, a little reporting, would refresh him. In Sacramento or Portuguese Bend, he collected newspaper profiles of Chavez, articles on the workers, interviews with the growers: "Cesar is a mystic—he's always reading books on evolution." "The growers say the strike is just a battle, not the war. . . . "

Dunne wrote his literary agent, Carl Brandt, in New York, that in California's Central Valley the mythology of the thirties was at work in the sixties. Nothing had changed. Time had stopped. It was very much a story worth exploring.

So was Vietnam. Don McKinney, the Dunnes' editor at *The Saturday Evening Post*, had hinted that the magazine might send them out if they wanted to go—given Dunne's experience with the subject and given that the war had intensified following the North's attack on Pleiku, along with Operation Rolling Thunder, LBJ's massive new bombing campaign.

Dunne wasn't sure. His wife knew the valley's history, its social peculiarities; she told him stories of coming to the valley as a child, eating short ribs and plucking cherries from her father's bourbon cocktails in Gilroy, the "Garlic Capital of the World," where even the hotel napkins smelled of processed garlic. With her help, he might make a richer story than he could with Vietnam. He liked the idea of working with her. He picked up another article on Chavez and underlined the following passage: "It was rough in those early years," Chavez said. "[My wife] Helen was having babies and I was not there when she was in the hospital. But if you haven't got your wife behind you, you can't do many things. There's got to be peace at home. So I did, I think, a fairly good job of organizing her."

2

Didion was trying to have a baby, she told her friend Diana Lynn. It was New Year's weekend, 1966. The Dunnes had joined Lynn, her husband, Morty Hall, president of KLAC radio, and another couple, Howard and Lou Erskine, on Hall's "motor-sailer" for a getaway to Cat Harbor, just off Catalina Island. Howard Erskine was a television producer and performer. Diana Lynn was a once-promising movie star who had set aside her career for marriage and motherhood by the time Didion met her.

In 1951, Lynn had starred with Ronald Reagan in the film *Bedtime for Bonzo*. Reagan played a professor determined to prove that good morals, emotional stability, and a solid upbringing trump genetics in the well-being of a child. His proof was a chimpanzee, raised with the help of Lynn as a surrogate mother. Lynn entertained Didion with stories of how much more personable the monkey was than Reagan.

On the boat that weekend, the couples were always "having or thinking about having or making or thinking about making a drink," Didion wrote in *Blue Nights*. Adoption came up. Lynn had been adopted as a child. The Erskines had adopted a baby. Didion's pregnancy frustrations prompted Lynn to suggest she consult Blake H. Watson, a pediatrician at St. John's Hospital in Santa Monica.

"[T]he next week I was meeting Blake Watson," Didion wrote, eliding much of the narrative. "When he called us from the hospital and asked if we wanted the beautiful baby girl there had been no hesitation: we wanted her."

Whether or not she'd suffered a miscarriage the previous spring, she and Dunne wondered if a physiological problem prevented them from conceiving. In *Vegas*, in possibly the worst prose he ever wrote, Dunne describes a sperm test he took. He places the scene, chronologically, years after it actually occurred, but the logistical details—getting to the doctor by driving east "on Palos Verdes Drive. South on 26th Street in San Pedro. Onto the Harbor Freeway"—establish the time frame.

In a medical clinic on Wilshire Boulevard, he "sat in a stall trying to coax some heft into [his] flaccid member," he wrote. The doctor pronounced him perfectly healthy.

In a letter to Mary Bancroft, dated March 30, 1966, Didion mentions a recent hospital stay. She was getting final tests, she says, to settle the question of adoption. (As a contingency, the couple had already started adoption proceedings, according to a January 8 letter from Dunne to Carl Brandt.) In 2005, Didion would tell journalist Susanna Rustin that she and Dunne had been "[u]nable to have children of their own." There may be doubt, or at least some confusion, about when this condition was confirmed and whether it was *always* the case. Like Didion's fiction, Dunne's novels make several references to miscarriages, abortions, uteruses "not strong enough . . . to hold a child to term," or "incompetent" cervixes. At any rate, in the early months of 1966, the couple decided adoption was their best alternative.

On March 3, 1966, the baby they would adopt with "no hesitation" was born.

Didion told Bancroft she was exceedingly happy getting tests in the hospital. While there, she reread William Burroughs's *Naked Lunch* and picked up his latest novel, *The Soft Machine*. *The Soft Machine* had the effect of "a migraine attack, after pain and nausea and unwanted images have battered the nerve synapses until all connections are lost." The book's voice roved back and forth across centuries between modern Mexico and Panama and the Mayan empire, reminding Didion of the Pedro Ramírez Vázquez building, the giant Olmec head. She lay in her room envisioning banana rafts and hyacinths, overgrown jungles, strange albino creatures blinking in the sun. Burroughs's tropical imagery took her "not only back but ahead in time, to what seems to be the end of the world." She was reminded of T. S. Eliot's *Four Quartets*: "In my beginning is my end" and "Time present and time past / Are both perhaps present in time future / And time future contained in time past." More than ever, the name Quintana Roo, a lush openness, an unclocked mystery, seemed right.

3

"L'adoptada . . . M'ija."

One way to limit and control a narrative is through legal systems.

Tyrants know this (possibly saints do, as well). Writers know this. So do adopted children and their parents.

California Family Code, Section 8700–8720 states that "[e]ither birth parent may relinquish a child to the department, county adoption agency, or licensed adoption agency for adoption by a written statement signed before two subscribing witnesses and acknowledged by an authorized official." Section 9200 (a) ensures that this arrangement "is not open to inspection by any person other than the parties to the proceeding and their attorney and the department, except upon the written authority of the judge of the supreme court."

Accordingly, Quintana Roo Dunne's adoption, facilitated by Blake H. Watson, was private. Names and details were sealed according to California law and they remain sealed, though a caseworker's error at the time allowed the Dunnes to learn the birth mother's name and vice versa.

In *Blue Nights*, Didion speaks disparagingly of Quintana's birth family. Her nephew Griffin has called them, publicly, a "troubled lot." Since neither Didion nor Griffin Dunne has offered much in the way of detail, I felt obligated to try to locate the birth family to see if their story illuminated anything about Didion. Two separate private investigators, working on my behalf, concluded there was no legal path around California Family Code. No records of the birth family existed in the L.A. County civil index. Bad news for my book but soothing to me as a citizen, just as stories broke about the National Security Agency's invasions of privacy and Barack Obama began to resemble an aggrieved Richard Nixon.

In the case of California adoptions, who would blame *any* family wishing to limit the narrative? That word: *relinquish*. Right there in Section 8700–8720. Eventually, it would haunt Quintana—and the grieving mother of *Blue Nights*.

A "written statement signed": like executing a book contract.

4

In the mid-1960s, the preferred narrative was *We chose you*.

Positive. Proactive. A comfort to the child.

What the narrative didn't address—a howling silence no boy or girl failed to perceive—was that if *we* chose you, *someone else* chose to make you available to us.

To relinquish you.

Family law.

Blake Watson understood the narrative, and he understood how to arrange matters around it so that nothing interfered with the story. He was not just any pediatrician. In his lifetime, he would deliver more than thirteen thousand babies ("I have never gotten over it—that flicker of life," he'd say). His patients included Greta Garbo, Judy Garland, Elizabeth Taylor, Carol Burnett, and Ethel Kennedy. He was in the intensive care unit with Robert Kennedy the night Kennedy got shot; Ethel was four months pregnant with her eleventh child. Watson gave her a sedative. He overheard Jackie say to her, "I think you should feel as much of the pain and misery now as you can stand. Better now than later."

On March 3, 1966, in the late afternoon, Blake Watson phoned the house at Portuguese Bend. Didion was taking a shower. Dunne took the call. "I have a beautiful baby girl at St. John's," he said. "I need to know if you want her." Dunne rapped on the bathroom door. Didion sobbed at the news.

The baby's mother, eighteen and unmarried, lived in Tucson, but she had been staying with relatives in California. The Dunnes didn't meet her. They received solid assurances that the woman's health was good.

Despite the likelihood that Didion's parents did not fully approve of the adoption—one of Dunne's novels includes a colonel-like figure who "did not trust the uncertainties of unknown blood. He believed in a continuum of heirlooms and family silver"—Watson arranged all the paperwork. An hour after his phone call, Didion stood at the nursery window in St. John's Hospital staring at "an infant with fierce dark hair and rosebud features," she said. The baby was seventeen hours old. She was tucked into the arms of a nurse wearing a surgical mask. A pink ribbon curled across the infant's pale head. A band around her wrist told her story: "N. I." No Information, the hospital's standard ID for babies being adopted.

Didion had the start of another story: a name, Quintana Roo. Once upon a time.

We chose you.

"Once she was born I was never not afraid," she would write.

To the child through the nursery's glass partition, she whispered, "You're safe."

When Quintana was five or six years old, she asked Dunne again and again to tell her the story of the nursery. It was after visiting hours, he'd say. Your mother and I went to the hospital and we were offered the choice of any baby in the place. No, not that baby, we said. Not that baby, not that baby . . . *That* baby! The one with the ribbon!

"Quintana!" Quintana would shout.

And then she asked him to tell it again, to do "*That* baby," the baby with the ribbon.

In 1977, in an essay called "Quintana," Dunne used the word *fierce* to describe the initial impression the baby made on him. In 2011, in *Blue Nights*, Didion wrote "fierce" to convey the baby's immediate impact on her. Together, the Dunnes locked in a family story. Presumably, they intended the word to be positive, suggesting a fighter struggling into the world under tough circumstances, an indomitable spirit. But the word is ambiguous. Saint. Little tyrant.

A "singularly blessed and accepting child," Didion wrote within months of Quintana's birth.

"[W]atching her journey from infancy has always been like watching Sandy Koufax pitch . . . There is the same casual arrogance, the implicit sense that no one has ever done it any better," Dunne wrote a few years later. He said she had "panache."

These lines also entered the accepted narrative. What windy silences Quintana may have heard in them, we'll never know.

On the evening of March 3, after saying good-bye through the glass to their fierce new companion, the Dunnes stopped in Beverly Hills to tell Nick and Lenny the news. The child's family had roots in Arizona—maybe a good omen. Lenny loved Arizona. Perhaps Lenny could take a dress to the hospital from the Colleagues for the child's unwed mother. She pulled ice from a crystal bucket and offered to make drinks. "Making celebratory drinks was what we did in our family to mark any unusual, or for that matter, any usual, occasion," Didion wrote. "In retrospect we all drank more than we needed to drink."

In our family.

We all drank.

We were always "having or thinking about having or making or thinking about making a drink."

And we chose *you*.

The silences in *Blue Nights,* noticed on repeated readings especially in the passages on Quintana's entry into the family, ring louder and louder: "In my beginning is my end."

Lenny dropped more ice in Didion's drink and said she'd go with her to Saks to buy a layette: "Saks because if you spend eighty dollars they throw in the bassinette."

It hadn't occurred to Didion that she would need a layette, or a bassinette.

For three nights, Quintana remained in the nursery at St. John's Hospital. Didion writes of waking in the early mornings to chills, listening to the surf on the rocks beneath the house at Portuguese Bend. She dreamed and she imagined she'd left her baby behind, asleep or hungry in a drawer, while she'd gone off for dinner or a movie: "And worse yet, worse by far, so much worse as to be unthinkable, except I did think it, everyone who has ever waited to bring a baby home thinks it: *what if I fail to love this baby?*"

She couldn't believe she was about to be given this bundle—babies were what you *lost* on the trail, the weak ones you left in the weeds, not what you gained.

Dunne imagined Quintana's mother everywhere, bereft and ghostly, lurking, peering through fences or the leaves of trees. He imagined bad genes burbling in the baby's DNA. *The Dictionary of Literary Biography* cheered him: In it, he found "Quintana, Manuel José. Spanish poet, patriot, and Liberal, 18th century." A good association. Another fine omen.

He told Mary Bancroft that Didion was stunning those first three days, preparing for Quintana's arrival at Portuguese Bend. She got on the phone and was like a gambler calling in IOUs, he said, lining up bassinettes, thermal blankets, weighing scales, and playpens. Now they had about five of everything. They could barely move in the house.

Often paralyzed and depressed on an ordinary day, Didion was energetic, focused, and frighteningly efficient in an emergency.

The peacocks cried the day Quintana came from the hospital, warm in a silk-lined cashmere wrapper. "*What if you hadn't been home when Dr. Watson called?*" Quintana asked her mother years later. "*What would happen to me then?*"

Below the house, skirting rocks, waves crashed, a hollow roar, in the cave on the point.

"*Do the peacocks,*" Quintana would beg, or "*do the apple trees.*"

She meant "read to me." Almost from that very first night, Didion recited poetry to get the baby to sleep. Wallace Stevens's "Domination of Black" ("I heard them cry—the peacocks") or T. S. Eliot's "Landscapes" ("Swing up into the apple tree").

In the evenings, Didion set Quintana in her bassinette next to the wisteria in the box garden and sterilized bottles for the baby's formula.

At night, with the child asleep or not asleep, the ocean was alternately wild and calm—its power evoking for Didion a favorite passage in the explorer John Lloyd Stephens's account of his discovery of the Mayan city of Copán: "It lay before us like a shattered bark in the midst of the ocean, her masts gone, her name effaced, her crew perished, and none to tell whence she came, to whom she belonged, how long on her voyage, or what caused her destruction."

One night, in secret, Dunne bounced Quintana carefully in his hands. He carried her to a tiled sink inside the house, held her under a trickle of water, and gave her a personal christening. He didn't want to chance her dying before a formal ceremony, and awaking, terrified, in limbo.

Afterward, he announced in passing to his wife, "I just christened the baby." He didn't expect her to share his superstition—it was more *that* than faith—but he didn't want an argument, either.

She wasn't up for a fight. Between migraines and the baby's wailing at night, she was relieved to swallow some phenobarbital and fall into bed. She was also taking ergot, she wrote Mary Bancroft. Ergot was commonly prescribed to reduce heavy menstrual bleeding. It was also recommended before and after miscarriages.

Most nights, Dunne didn't sleep much, either. One morning at dawn, Didion awoke and saw him in the yard, hurling mushy peaches at the peacocks to get them to shut the hell up. The baby, he couldn't do anything about.

5

In *Blue Nights,* Didion swears it never occurred to her she couldn't take an infant to Saigon (Don McKinney, of *The Saturday Evening Post,* had firmed up an offer to send them). She says she went so far as to plan the trip, buying pastel linen dresses and a flowered parasol. In the end, she says, the Dunnes canceled the Vietnam assignment only because her husband had to "finish the book he had contracted to write about Cesar Chavez."

This wouldn't ring true in any case, even if we didn't know, from Dunne's letters to Carl Brandt, that the Chavez book was not a sealed deal until several months after Quintana was born, and only after much cat and mousing between two publishers vying for rights to the material. Nor was it clear whether Dunne would be writing the story, or Didion, or both.

The *Blue Nights* narrative is this: I was woefully unprepared to be a mother. Clueless. I would have taken my baby to Saigon—can you believe it?

Unprepared, no doubt. Clueless she was not. She was a steely professional, not about to let motherhood get in the way of her career. Absolutely, she would have taken her baby to Saigon. Around this time, Robert Silvers at *The New York Review of Books* was asking Mary McCarthy if she'd like to report on the war. Initially, she turned him down, but eventually she did fly to Southeast Asia. In *The Atlantic Monthly,* Frances FitzGerald had published on Vietnam, to much fanfare. Didion was itching to become one of the few females covering the story of the time.

What stopped her was the fact that Quintana would be a ward of the court until September, when the adoption was finalized. She could not be transported out of state, much less out of the country. So by default, the grape strikes became the couple's story.

They had another problem: Their landlord wanted them out of the house. The addition of the baby was bad enough. But what he *could not* abide was the help they'd acquired (Dunne told Mary Bancroft that Joan *had* to have assistance with the kid; she couldn't stop writing—they needed the money).

They'd hired a teenage girl named Jennifer to help feed the baby, and they'd hired a maid, an illegal named Arcelia, to clean the house. It was Arcelia's extended family that angered Dick Harden—he'd *already* put up with a damn stray gamecock, he said, abandoned no doubt by "Mexicans on the run," and now the place was literally *crawling* with Spanish speakers.

"*L'adoptada. . . . M'ija.*"

"*Qué hermosa . . . Qué chula.*"

The Dunnes would have to be gone by May first.

Vibora—the *one* Spanish word every Angelino understood. "*[V]ibora* in Los Angeles meant snake and snake in Los Angeles meant rattlesnake," Didion wrote in *Blue Nights*. On the afternoon a social worker showed up in Portuguese Bend to evaluate the adoption candidate in her home environment, Arcelia at one point dropped the garden hose, screamed, "*Vibora*," snatched up the baby, and ran inside the house.

A perfectly normal West Coast home.

Eleven days after Quintana was born, Bobby Kennedy arrived in the Central Valley to meet Cesar Chavez. He didn't want to do it. His assignment on the U.S. Senate's Subcommittee on Migratory Labor was the least glamorous of his roles; involvement in a regional agricultural squabble wouldn't help him politically—the rest of the country didn't give a damn about these strikes. On the flight from Washington, Kennedy kept pressing Peter Edelman, his point man, asking, "Why am I dragging myself all the way out to California?"

Ever after, the official story, promoted by Arthur M. Schlesinger Jr., Jack Newfield, and others, says RFK was so thoroughly charmed by Chavez, so taken with his saintliness, that "his head [caught] up with his heart" and he was, from that moment on, determined to see justice in the fields.

The truth was more complex. Dunne wrote, "The Kennedys sponged up ideas, and implicit in Chavez was the inexorable strength of an idea whose time had come. Kennedy's real concern for the farm workers helped soften his image as a self-serving keeper of his brother's flame and in turn plugged Chavez into the power outlets of Washington and New York. For the first time Chavez became fashionable, a national figure registering on the nation's moral thermometer. Robert Kennedy and Cesar Chavez—the names seemed wired into the same circuitry, the one a spokesman, the other a symbol for the constituency of the dispossessed."

Following the publicity surrounding Kennedy's visit, the Dunnes had all the more reason to broker a deal for a magazine piece, maybe even a book, about Chavez. Dunne wondered if *The New Yorker* was a possibility—it tended to publish "long." He told his agent some of the things he'd seen while traveling up and down the valley: students from Berkeley sitting on railroad tracks, trying to stop grape shipments; Walter Reuther singing with picketers "We Shall Overcome." He said the growers' attitude toward the fieldworkers was a kind of domestic colonization.

Finally, in June, Brandt wrote Dunne that *The Saturday Evening Post* would pay $2,500 for anything up to five or six thousand words; he told him not to stint on expenses. No promise of a book deal—Dunne should test the "desirability" of that idea.

Dunne wasn't sure even *this* agreement was firm; he pitched pieces on Hawaii's "big waves" and the aftermath of the Watts riots, just in case the Chavez deal fell through, but neither Brandt nor Don McKinney responded.

Brandt's letter came to the Dunnes' temporary new digs at 155 Fifth Anita Drive in West Los Angeles. It was the home of Sara Mankiewicz, Herman Mankiewicz's widow. She had scheduled a six-month trip and was happy to rent the house. She packed away her china, along with her late husband's Academy Award for *Citizen Kane* ("You'll have friends over, they'll get drunk, they'll want to play with it").

On the day Didion left Portuguese Bend, she was harried and on her own. Dunne had hit the road with the San Francisco Giants, writing an article on Willie Mays for *The Saturday Evening Post*. She borrowed Lenny's station wagon, packed it tight, settled Quintana in the backseat along with the teenage Jennifer, said good-bye to the gamecock in the yard, and drove to Fifth Anita Drive.

Dunne called her from a sad hotel room in Houston. He was miserable. The Astrodome looked *nothing like* a baseball stadium. It was Andy Warhol, when what you wanted in a ballpark was James McNeill Whistler. He'd made no headway with Mays. He knew Mays had adopted a child in 1959, and he tried to find common ground with him by talking about Quintana. No go. Mays seemed weary of white reporters always bringing up *race*, always insisting that sports was a perfect metaphor for America. Bullshit. Didion sympathized with her husband's difficulties, but after all, he was not sitting there with a crying child, among unpacked boxes in a big strange house. He was not staring at tax forms, wondering if day help could be deducted.

It was here, on Fifth Anita Drive, that she threw a reception following Quintana's official christening at St. Martin of Tours Catholic Church in

Brentwood. She served watercress sandwiches, fried chicken, and champagne, showed off the baby's new dresses—dozens and dozens of them on tiny wooden hangers in the closet—and, along with her friends, filled the house with cigarette smoke. Most of the women were dressed like Jackie Kennedy, in trim Chanel suits, or they wore Jax jerseys or Lilly Pulitzer shifts, and David Webb bracelets: Connie Wald, Diana Lynn, Lenny. Didion had finally arrived as a Hollywood hostess.

A few days later, the Dunnes received a letter from Henry Robbins, a senior editor at Farrar, Straus and Giroux. He would be going to Los Angeles for a few days, he said, and he'd like to meet them. He admired their magazine writing. He'd be staying at the Chateau Marmont.

On the warm night in June 1966 when she first met Henry Robbins, "I thought so little of myself as a writer . . . that I was obscurely ashamed to go to dinner with still another editor, ashamed to sit down again and discuss this 'work' I was not doing," Didion wrote in the introduction to her essay collection *After Henry* (1992). She felt poor and put-upon in spite of the fact that she was living in Brentwood (a sort of Beverly Hills for those who didn't want to seem pretentious by living in Beverly Hills), that her baby had just received sixty christening presents, and that she wore a black silk dress to dinner at the Bistro and then for drinks and music at the Daisy. She felt poor because, though the Dunnes regularly charged meals at the Bistro, they did not believe they could afford to tip the valet, so they parked their car on Canon Drive. The house they'd decamped to was "borrowed." She was drowning in laundry, and the couple's income from writing had amounted to only $305.06 in the previous three months.

With Robbins that night "we got drunk," she wrote, and "before the summer was out" he had "signed contracts with each of us, and, from that summer in 1966 until the summer of 1979," when he died of a heart attack in the Fourteenth Street subway station in New York, he served as Didion's book editor. (Actually, Didion got the dates wrong; she did not sign with Robbins until a year after their meeting.)

Robbins had an "epic" bearing, said his niece Margi Fox, an "unusual gift for nurturing," a "warmth" in his eyes that could give a listener "the sense that there were only two of [you] in [a] room full of people." The writer Wilfrid Sheed once called him a saint. Michael Korda, in his memoir, described him as a madman with an incendiary temper. In fact, he was a workaholic with a weak heart, too many debts, and a passionate love of literature.

Initially, he was more intrigued with Dunne than with Didion, perhaps because of Dunne's reportorial experience at *Time* (a job he had finally relinquished). And Robbins had not traveled to California just to meet the couple. His brother was a labor lawyer in San Francisco; through him and through media coverage of Bobby Kennedy's visit, Robbins had become enamored of Cesar Chavez. He talked with the Dunnes about the story they planned for *The Saturday Evening Post,* and he went to Delano, originally to see if he might sign Chavez to a book contract. A letter from Robbins to Chavez, dated July 5, indicates he had decided it would not be feasible for Chavez to write his own story, given how "incredibly busy" he was; it would probably be better to relate the tale "through a professional reporter (like John Gregory Dunne)." He concluded, "The enclosed check is my personal contribution to your strike fund, a token of my support for the great work you're doing." Effectively, the letter and check became Dunne's passport into Chavez's world.

Anthony Kennedy, attorney for Schenley Industries, The Bistro Restaurant, Los Angeles, 11 June 1966: $29.45.
Sidney Korshak, labor attorney, The Daisy, Los Angeles, 13 June 1966: $33.90.

So begins Dunne's list of expenses for his Chavez project.

Field hands had marched on the capitol in Sacramento in April. Governor Brown ignored them. He went on vacation to Frank Sinatra's Palm Springs home. Immediately afterward, Chavez signed a "Recognition Agreement Between Schenley Industries and the National Farm Workers Association," arranging for collective bargaining. Korshak signed on behalf of Schenley. Forget the governor. Chavez was getting what he wanted because he'd upset the liquor producers. Apparently, when liquor gets nervous, mob lawyers and future Supreme Court justices discover they have a great deal in common.

Following Robbins's letter to Chavez, on July 12, the Dunnes drove to Delano to see what all the fuss was about. TIRED, HUNGRY, CAR TROUBLE, NEED GAS? SHOP IN DELANO! said a sign on the outskirts of town. Dogs covered with flies nosed around dry alkaline ditches. Children played in the dust. The valley heat was punishing.

The Dunnes had stopped in Bakersfield and picked up a couple of cardboard hand fans given out by local mortuaries. One side of each fan featured a handsome black couple holding a baby: "A Joyous Family." The other side advertised funeral arrangements: "A Friendly, Courteous Service. Protect Your Loved Ones."

The couple had left Quintana with Didion's parents in Sacramento, but at some point during the several weeks they spent in Delano, coming and going, singly or together, they had Quintana with them, in the Stardust Motel (now a Travel Inn) just west of Highway 99. In 1970, in Room 44 of the Stardust, at two o'clock one morning, Chavez would sign the historic bargaining agreement between the farmworkers and Giumarra Vineyards, America's largest table-grape supplier. This forced the hand of other growers, twenty-six of whom signed contracts with the workers—an early major victory for Chavez.

In 1966, Delano was a town of about fourteen thousand. It didn't take long to get the lay of the land. Randomly, one night, in a draw-poker parlor called Divina's Four Deuces, near the Southern Pacific railroad tracks, Dunne asked a local what he thought of the grape strikes. "This used to be a good town before," the man said. Dunne wrote, "It turned out that he meant before the construction of the freeway leveled the red-light district."

Delano was Didion's book to write. Dunne acknowledged as much on the dedication page, thanking Chavez, Ted Streshinsky, the photographer on the project, and "most of all, Joan Didion, who has been there for five generations."

She was the one with grape growers in her family. She was the one who knew Anthony Kennedy. She was the one who understood the first place to stop would be a draw-poker parlor.

On July 15, a letter to Didion from Dick Kluger, a senior editor at Simon & Schuster, asked if "you are working on a book about the strike." He wondered about its status and expressed interest in acquiring it.

New motherhood wouldn't have stopped her from writing the story (it didn't stop her from *going* to Delano). She seems to have given her husband a gift, perhaps because she'd already published a book and now he needed to get untracked.

In any event, *Delano* is shadow Didion, a kind of corollary to *Run River*, the other side of the valley.

Which is not to diminish Dunne's reportorial acuity. His notebooks, papers, and rough drafts of *Delano*, archived now in the UCLA Library Special Collections, show him to be a thorough and disciplined man on the beat, far more alert at the detail level than Didion. If she was better at emotional nuance and the big picture, he was a collector of the almost overlooked, and he was at ease with people. It earned him their trust, got him the story.

In the valley today, little of the old Chavez hope remains. As Dunne foresaw with cutting accuracy, in the 1960s martyrdom would seem the only resolution to the nation's problems. If that didn't mean literal assassination, as in the case of Bobby Kennedy, it meant the eventual shunning of heroes. "People, issues, and causes hit the charts like rock groups, and with approximately as much staying power," he wrote. "For all the wrong reasons, Chavez had all the right credentials—mysticism, nonviolence, the nobility of the soil. But . . . saints generally fail and when they do not, the constant scrutiny of public attention causes a certain moral devaluation. Enthusiasm for a cause is generally in inverse proportion to actual involvement."

At the Filipino Community Center in Delano, just east of Highway 99, where Chavez gave some of his fiercest speeches ("In Ingles!" he'd exhort his followers—speak "in Ingles" so the reporters will understand!), no placards, statues, or artifacts mark the workers' history now. In the large meeting room with light green walls and a scuffed brown wooden floor, a nice young Filipino man told me he'd heard of Chavez but didn't know much about him. The meeting room had been turned into a day-care center for seniors, some of whom reminisced about the strikes while playing bingo.

The old Stardust hasn't changed much. The rooms are tiny, with gritty brown carpets, giant TV cabinets, and twiglike lamps sticking out of walls painted the color of urine. Nothing to honor Chavez's ghost. Up and down the valley, the dust haze in the air, reflecting the sky's light back at the sky, nearly obscures taco trucks and tractors, signs for palm readers and casinos. Flocks of swifts circle "Cowschwitz" (the Harris Ranch feedlot). A helicopter flying low over fields, with a long, thin sprayer slung to its bottom, buzzes a tall grain elevator next to wooden shacks. Men in heavy plastic suits move among crops, spreading smoky pesticides. "The soil [here] has been engineered to precision," Verlyn Klinkenborg has written. "This is no longer soil. It is infrastructure."

The California Aqueduct, running along I-5, drawing water from the Sacramento River delta, has caused the entire valley to slump, buckle, and sink; the United States Geological Survey has called this the "largest human alteration of the earth's surface."

Constant land movement.

On or around June 20, 1966, Shirley Streshinsky moved down the valley on a train from San Francisco. Her husband, Ted, a freelance photographer who often worked for *The Saturday Evening Post*, was already in Delano. "He had proposed a story on Chavez. John had as well, and the two of them were assigned to work together on the story," Shirley told me. "Those were luxury days for photojournalists, before magazines started saving money by sending out the writer to get the story, the photographer to follow up and provide photos." In the 1960s, "for magazines like *The Saturday Evening Post*, where photographs were an important *part* of the story, the photographer and the writer were to work together, and the magazine gave them enough time to consult with each other and talk through what the story was."

Shirley and Ted had married just days before, on the sixteenth. A Berkeley alum who abandoned a political science career to document the major issues of the day, he had met Didion a few years earlier, when *Mademoiselle* assigned him to take pictures for her article on the Berkeley campus. Shirley was a journalist and had stayed in San Francisco right after her wedding to finish a story.

"Joan picked me up at the train station" in Delano, she recalled. "I remember that one of my first questions to Joan was something like, 'Is Chavez genuine?' And her answer was something like, 'I think so.' At least I remember her reaction to be positive. We met John and Ted, and from then on my memories are sort of strobe light–like. We went to one of the watering holes for the farm labor movement"—this would have been People's Bar on the Garces Highway. It was "an old bar with pool tables. The main office was an old storefront. It had a big room, battered wooden floors, a bare-bones type of place where the major figures had gathered, along with workers and others. I'm not sure if [community organizer] Saul Alinsky was there, but I seem to remember him. Certainly Cesar was, and Dolores Huerta. My memory is standing in a large circle that encompassed the room, arms linked and hands held, singing 'We Shall Overcome.'"

Over the next several days, Didion impressed Shirley as "a knowledgeable daughter of the West, of the Central Valley, of its history and its long struggle over water rights. One way you can tell a true Westerner: she's the one who—when winters are too dry and too many days in a row are excessively beautiful—begins to worry about the snowpack in the Sierras." Didion and Dunne spoke obsessively of Quintana, she said, "with the real pleasure of new parents."

Didion had gone from the valley to *Vogue* and now she was back at the edge of the continent, where she'd first started scribbling in a Big Five tablet. Alongside her husband, she interviewed Yugoslavian grape growers, SNCC members and students down from Berkeley, fresh from the war protests, looking for a new cause to embrace. They'd help and hinder Chavez, she thought: enthusiastic, energetic but eternally romantic, a setup for dread and disillusionment. These kids made him feel a hundred years old, Dunne told her.

They were both aware of people posing as journalists but who, in fact, seemed to be taking pictures of the real journalists, noting their movements. They were also aware of people posing as supporters of the workers but who, in fact, seemed a little too brusque with the cops, giving them cause to move in and break up assemblies.

On some days, Dunne felt he was watching a thirty-year-old film reel.

"Who is this fellow, Saul Alinsky, meeting with Chavez?" a man in a crowd yelled at the cops one day. "People don't have a clue who he is. All they know is he's got a name like a bomb thrower."

Teamsters referred to the farmworkers as "the Vietcong."

Students moved through the throng, handing out pamphlets: "Agriculture is the very foundation of our nation." Didion could have given them her eighth-grade graduation speech.

She discovered that many of the field supervisors were the sons of Dust Bowl Okies—men like her old high school classmates—who had started working for the grape companies as pickers and moved their way up. They saw themselves as badasses now.

One afternoon, a Tulare County deputy sheriff stopped Dunne on a road beside a vineyard and asked to see his credentials. "I see you got a sunburn last Monday," the man said. Dunne knew then that he'd been watched. "And that little lady with you in the red dress—that your wife?" the deputy said. "She really wilted."

"Because I had been tired too long and quarrelsome too much and too often frightened of migraine and failure and the days getting shorter, I was sent, a recalcitrant thirty-one-year-old child, to Hawaii," Didion begins her essay "Letter from Paradise, 21° 19' N. 157° 52' W." In fact, she was sent to Hawaii by *The Saturday Evening Post*, perhaps initially to write the "big waves" piece Dunne had proposed to Don McKinney a few months earlier.

Dunne went with her. In *Delano*, his version of the trip goes like this: "In early August 1966, I decided to leave the Valley . . . I flew to Honolulu for ten days, glad to get away for a while from the heat, the bitterness, and the self-righteousness on both sides of the freeway in Delano."

The thrust of Didion's essay is that she lacked the "temperament for paradise," but it was a relief to the couple to sit by the pool of the Royal Hawaiian Hotel sipping frozen daiquiris. (Quintana was still with her grandparents.) People told wonderful stories. In the days of nuclear testing on the Marshall Islands, just after the Second World War, admirals and congressmen entertained Ernest O. Lawrence, designer of Berkeley's cyclotron and a key member of the Manhattan Project, at the Royal Hawaiian. Then they'd all fly to the Eniwetok Atoll to sit in beach chairs with coffee and sandwiches and witness the shots. In 1952 the first hydrogen bomb test obliterated the Elugelab islet near Eniwetok.

Oh yes, people had stories. People still remembered. Didion recalled her nights in Berkeley, hearing the hum of the Bevatron. Nearly twenty years later, she would open her novel *Democracy* with flashes of nuclear dawns on the scattered, pearl-like islands: "[S]omething to see. Something to behold. Something that could almost make you think you saw God . . ."

All day on Hawaii's hot sands, Hollywood vacationers read scripts or synopses of television shows. "They do not describe what they are doing as 'reading,'" Didion said. "They describe it as 'doing some reading.'" A good portion of the tourists at the most lavish hotels had just "done Carson"—that is, they'd had a recent guest spot on *The Tonight Show*.

On the beach in front of the new Kahili Hilton, the Rolling Stones, not yet as famous as they would be, sat glumly, "pale and bored, and facing away from the sea," disappointed that fans had not flocked to find them despite round-the-clock broadcasts by KPOI-Honolulu revealing their location. They ordered drinks with floating orchids and signed a napkin for a little girl. Didion noticed that when the girl left, she forgot the napkin, along with her soaked towel.

One morning, Didion left the Royal Hawaiian and took a bright pink tour boat from Kewalo Basin to Pearl Harbor. Amid the "sleazy festivity" of the tourists, at the site of the listing *Utah* and the spot where the *Arizona*'s gun turret broke the smooth gray waves, she began to cry. Later, she would write, "[S]omeone just four years younger than I told me that he did not see why a sunken ship should affect me so, that John Kennedy's assassination, not Pearl Harbor, was the single most indelible event of what he kept calling 'our generation.' I could tell him only that we belonged to different generations."

At the time of her initial visit to Pearl Harbor, she had just come from the Central Valley, from the heat and the air of her childhood. The Japanese attack on Pearl Harbor had wrenched her from that early innocence, blacking out her world, taking her for the first time from the valley—memories borne in on her as she bobbed in the little pink boat beside the *Utah.* The father of those war years—the Pearl Harbor dad—was perhaps the last stable father she had known, in his crisp uniform, in the grip and surety of his duty. Not the Letterman father. Not the desperate gambler.

From Pearl Harbor, she made her way to the National Memorial Cemetery of the Pacific, known locally as the "Punchbowl" or the "Hill of Sacrifice." Ancient lore mentioned human offerings to pagan gods on the edge of the volcanic crater. Underneath the crater, World War II–era tunnels remained, where gun batteries had once been installed. It may have occurred to Didion that U.S. militarization of these islands was a provocation to the Japanese, in some sense making the attack on Pearl Harbor inevitable, in some sense providing an inevitable excuse for Hiroshima. *As it was in the beginning, is now and ever shall be, world without end.*

Near a rim of the crater overlooking Waikiki, Didion noticed the latest human sacrifices, fresh graves marked with temporary plastic identification cards spattered with mud: military dead shipped from Vietnam. A man cut grass in the mist.

Down the hill, she wandered into hordes of sailors, nineteen, twenty years old, on R & R that week from the carrier *Coral Sea*, personnel from Schofield Barracks, and young Marines on their way to Okinawa and from there to Vietnam. The next wave of offerings to the gods.

They were cruising the strip clubs and the pinball arcades up and down Hotel Street, whistling at "girls with hibiscus in their hair," popping into tattoo parlors and massage studios. For the time being, this was as close as she would get to Saigon.

Dunne dreaded the return to Delano. He had learned something here in the islands, talking to fellows from the Longshoremen's and Warehousemen's Union. Since 1945, he was told, mechanization had reduced Hawaii's sugar workforce from 35,000 to 10,500. Chavez's agitation in the valley would only hasten the growers' move toward machinery. Cesar was ensuring his own doom, the doom of his movement, the ultimate sacrifice of the people who had placed all their faith in him.

Back in the valley, Quintana in tow, the Dunnes interviewed a physician from Fresno who tended the farmworkers. He told them about a recent visit he'd made to an apartment in town. "Inside were a mother and seven children. The stench of putrefying, necrotic tissue filled the interior," he said. "A baby of eighteen months lay asleep on the bare floor in front of a blazing gas heater. The mother lay sick on the couch. She had delivered her seventh baby at home, with the aid of a neighbor lady, several days before I arrived. There was a considerable loss of blood. I wondered who would take care of the children when she died."

While Didion fed Quintana in a room at the Stardust, Dunne walked to the People's Bar, hung out, talked to the volunteers from Berkeley, listened to them sing to a strike song on the jukebox, "El Corrido de Delano." Someone had tacked to the wall a cartoon depicting the Di Giorgio ranch as an octopus. Wet newspapers on the floor carried the latest reports of Ronald Reagan's gubernatorial campaign—if elected in the fall, he promised to correct the weaknesses of Pat Brown and Clark Kerr, and root out all the radicals at Berkeley.

One chilly late-summer night, near the end of the Dunnes' stay in the valley, in the foothills of the Sierra, Dunne watched a "California golden girl," probably a student, seduce a "panicky young farm worker" from Mexico. The girl "worked hard and loyally for Chavez," but "no amount of good faith on her part could bridge the chasm of social and sexual custom" between her and the young man. The encounter was bound to end badly, Dunne thought, just like the long, dusty struggle for justice: "I remember the boy still desperately picking on his guitar even as he was being led off to the bedroom"—maybe the last love song he'd ever sing.

Chapter Fourteen

—————— ❖ ——————

D idion had not shuttered her Royal KMM typewriter in the excitement of arranging her daughter's adoption or planning stays in Delano. Just before and during this period, she wrote one of her most enduring essays, "Some Dreamers of the Golden Dream," originally titled "How Can I Tell Them There's Nothing Left" and published in *The Saturday Evening Post* in the May 7, 1966, issue.

For nearly two years, she had been reading lurid headlines out of the San Bernardino Valley, MOVIE CALLED BLUEPRINT FOR DENTIST'S DEATH; MOTEL ROMANCE LOVELESS ON HIS PART; MRS. MILLER CALLED "USER OF PEOPLE." These teasers summed up a tawdry and apparently unremarkable bedroom-community episode. Nevertheless, the incident had drawn the attention of ace crime reporters from across the country. On September 5, 1965, Ruth Reynolds of the New York *Daily News* wrote, "Seldom has a jury been called upon to deliberate two points of view quite so divergent as those presented to twelve Californians last March at the end of the trial of Mrs. Lucille Maxwell Miller, 35."

The San Bernardino Valley "lies only an hour east of Los Angeles by the San Bernardino Freeway but is in certain ways an alien place . . . haunted by the Mojave just beyond the mountains, devastated by the hot dry Santa Ana wind that comes down through the passes at 100 miles an hour," Didion wrote as a preface to *her* version of Lucille Miller's story. In the mid-nineteenth century, Mormons streaming out of Utah, seeking escape to the sea, established irrigation canals in this basin—now commonly called the Inland Empire—and began to grow oranges, corn, and cabbages. "It was then and there"—based upon cultivating water where water naturally tended to dissipate—"that the phenomenon of modern Los Angeles began," wrote one historian.

Didion understood this history, and it would be the *real* subject of her essay.

After World War II, when young couples seeking affordable mortgages were seduced into the highway sprawl among savannalike grass, king snakes, and coyotes crying in canyon washes, the San Bernardino Valley inherited the coastal communities' troubles. It became an American lab experiment, a combination of Levittown and Appalachia, of industry and agriculture, of stolen water and prefab structures. In a country often hailed sweetly as a melting pot, the Inland Empire was the real thing, with all the grit, grease, and grievance the term suggested.

There were gun shops and mini-malls. Office parks. Hindu mortuaries tucked among pepper trees. Here and there, on the edges of mobile-home factories, the wreck of an old chicken ranch. A roadside motel had buildings shaped like a tee-pee (the Wigwam Motel). Freight yards. Bible stores. The Striptease Hall of Fame. Sanctuaries lined with bleachers and beer stands housed the local religion: high school football, practiced as brutally here as anywhere in the nation.

Hollywood sent its screenwriters to the valley to dry out or to meet impending deadlines. Among the brittle weeds of Victorville, Herman Mankiewicz finished the first draft of *Citizen Kane*. Truckers humping contraband stopped and burned their manifests in tangled mesquite. In San Berdoo, in 1948, the same year the McDonald brothers opened their first "Speedee Service" restaurant, a gang of desert-begrimed, disgruntled World War II vets formed a motorcycle club and named it after the U.S. Army's Eleventh Airborne Division: Hells Angels, hitting the highways for freedom.

It was here that Didion chose to set what would become the inaugural piece of her first nonfiction collection, in a landscape whose history she knew so well that she didn't have to mention the past; instead, she hinted at it to imbue a series of anecdotes with more general significance, convincing the reader that what happened in the San Bernardino Valley exposed America's soul.

What happened in the San Bernardino Valley was that a woman apparently burned her dentist husband alive in a Volkswagen one night after going to the market for milk. Police said she drugged him and deliberately set the blaze, motivated by her affair with a prominent local lawyer and inspired by the plot of *Double Indemnity*. Lucille Miller claimed the flames were accidental, sparked by a jostled gas can after the car jerked mysteriously off the road. Her husband was asleep in the front seat, having taken a combination of Nembutal and Fiorinal for depression. He'd been suicidal, she said, overwhelmed by their mortgage and his debts. Far from wanting to kill him, she'd tried repeatedly to save him. "What will I tell the children, when there's nothing left, nothing left in the casket?" she'd cried after glimpsing her husband's char through the Beetle's windshield. In particular, she was concerned about her sensitive daughter, Debbie, fourteen years old at the time.

On March 5, 1965, the jury found Lucille Miller guilty of murder in the first degree. She was remanded to the California Institution for Women at Frontera.

Didion's interest in the Millers lay less in the crime—a common enough tabloid story, she admitted—than in their restlessness for a happier life and their disappointment: pale echoes of the pioneer trope. An age-old California story was playing out again, the ancient legends abetted by the romance of the movies, whose dialogue people unwittingly mimicked in their talk of true love, affairs of the heart, crimes of passion.

"October is the bad month for the wind, the month when breathing is difficult and the hills blaze up spontaneously," Didion wrote, linking the land's distress with human frailty, establishing Lucille Miller's crime as something more than a crime: This is the land of unpredictable blazes; nothing can stop what is going to happen, what has always happened. "There has been no rain since April. Every voice seems a scream. It is the season of suicide and divorce and prickly dread, wherever the wind blows." In her opening aria, before even mentioning dentistry, debt, VWs, and sex motels, Didion has locked in her narrative.

Should we doubt her authority to tell this story, she says, "It might have been anyone's bad summer, anyone's siege of heat and nerves and migraine and money worries." You and me, reader, we've been there, too. Who can say no? The voice is so certain and *knowing*. She has enlisted our complicity.

"[It] was a bright warm day in Southern California, the kind of day when Catalina floats on the Pacific horizon and the air smells of orange blossoms," Didion wrote:

A seventy-year-old pensioner drove his station wagon at five miles an hour past three Gardena poker parlors and emptied three pistols and a twelve-gauge shotgun through their windows, wounding twenty-nine people. "Many young women become prostitutes just to have enough money to play cards," he explained in a note. Mrs. Nick Adams said that she was "not surprised" to hear her husband announce his divorce plans on the Les Crane Show, and, farther north, a sixteen-year-old jumped off the Golden Gate Bridge and lived.

Oh. *That* kind of day.

This is a masterful paragraph, combining random incidents so matter-of-factly, they don't seem random at all. Instead, they are unmistakable warnings of the inevitable "prickly dread."

In fact, it was only Didion's *view* of the events that was inevitable, shaped by her narrative. When the piece appeared in *The Saturday Evening Post* (along with a full-page ad for Volkswagens and a profile of Benjamin Spock talking babies and bombs), many inland residents quietly seethed at her sketch of their lives. As a seventeen-year-old university freshman in Los Angeles, novelist Susan Straight was assigned to read the essay: "I now learned how others saw us: 'the country of the teased hair and the Capris and the girls for whom all life's promise comes down to a waltz-length white wedding dress and the birth of a Kimberly or a Sherry or a Debbi and a Tijuana divorce and a return to hairdresser's school.'

"I lay awake all night, thinking of my friends and their parents," Straight said. She admired Didion's "elegance and precision and genius" but found the essay "painful" and unpitying in its class judgments.

"The future always looks good in the golden land, because no one remembers the past," Didion's essay insisted.

That's just wrong, says one inlander: "The guys I worked with . . . Get any three of them together in the pumphouse waiting out a rainy day and they would talk the whole time about who got paid the least for a day chopping cotton back in West Texas or Arkansas."

And all that teased-up hair Didion talked about? Forget it. The Inland Empire was "full of hot exciting young babes that never saw the inside of a hairdressers' school and whose residual fumes rock stars are probably still writing songs about."

In 1991, Lucille Miller's daughter, Debra, wrote Didion a letter concerning "Some Dreamers of the Golden Dream." "It helped to make you famous but it's my life," she said. Following her mother's incarceration and subsequent history, she'd suffered years of cocaine addiction and misery.

On a later occasion, in Los Angeles, she happened to meet Didion at a signing. Didion inscribed a book to her: "For Debra Miller—who knows better than anyone I know the ambiguity of the written word."

On March 5, 1965, when the jury pronounced Lucille Miller guilty of murder in the first degree, little Debbie had stood in the courtroom and shouted, "She didn't do it! She didn't do it! I'll never see my mother again!"

Quintana was three weeks old when Didion hit her deadline for finalizing the San Berdoo article for *The Saturday Evening Post*. "I never sleep the night before a piece closes. I always get up to check it," she said.

At the last minute, she doubted her accuracy about certain details and drove to the San Bernardino courthouse for the better part of a day to look up facts. It was the first time since bringing Quintana home that she'd left her infant's side.

PART FIVE

Chapter Fifteen

1

I am talking here about a time when I began to doubt the premises of all the stories I had ever told myself . . . I suppose this period began around 1966 and continued until 1971," Didion wrote. These dates match precisely the years she rented, for four hundred dollars a month, a sprawling, spooky house at 7406 Franklin Avenue, just south of the Hollywood Hills and north of Sunset Boulevard. "The place [was] vast," said John Gregory Dunne. It was "on the lines of an abandoned fraternity house."

Or a raddled old Barbizon. How life had changed.

It sat in the middle of the block, in a neighborhood shedding its former existence for an uncertain new direction. "Bette Davis had [once] lived on one corner, Preston Sturges on another [his widow, Sandy, would become a friend]; the Canadian consulate was a block away, the Japanese consulate at the time of Pearl Harbor [was] across the street," said Dunne. Now many of the glamorous old houses—plumbing busted, roofs eroding, paint chipping off the window shutters—were turning into communes. Rock 'n' roll bands moved into them, or fly-by-night self-improvement groups. A few wealthy octogenarians, refusing to countenance change, hung on in the area, eyeing newcomers angrily as nurses pushed them in their wheelchairs past newly minted warehouses, dilapidated bungalows, and pastel apartments choked with dusty oleanders. "Now the pimps and junkies were beginning to take over Hollywood Boulevard, a block south. There was a whorehouse in a brand-new high-rise down the street, Synanon owned one house in the neighborhood, a Dr. Feelgood was dispensing amphetamines like gumdrops in another, and the former

Japanese consulate, boarded up, was a crash pad for a therapy group," Dunne observed.

The clay tennis court behind the Dunnes' house had started to sprout weeds.

Mold grew in the crevices of some of the twenty-eight rooms *inside* the house, but this Havisham-like touch was offset by the place's genuine charm: tall French windows, sunny, open rooms (with plenty of space for Didion's Chickering piano, inherited from her family), and solid wooden floors. In the basement, rag rugs and "a vast Stalinist couch" lured dust, Didion said. Hundreds of copies of *The New Masses* moldered in a dark corner.

In the spacious kitchen, she hung a copy of a Karl Shapiro poem she had long loved. Its verses celebrated the West's ability to renew itself: "It is raining in California, a straight rain / Cleaning the heavy oranges on the bough."

Sometimes at night, she thought she heard rattlesnakes outside her bedroom window. Peering through the glass, Dunne scanned the nearby dry wash with a flashlight and told her it was nothing. A leaky faucet. Paper in the wind.

Physically surrounded by the scars and adornments of a changing story— Old Hollywood flaking under the New—Didion roamed the vicinity with wary fascination. It was yet another Lost Domain. The boarded-up consulate across the street epitomized for her not just the transformation of the block but also the country's fickle moods. In her essay "The White Album," the example she would offer of a story we once told "in order to live" began "The princess is caged in the consulate." Every morning from her smudgy windows, she could see the terms of this story. Fairy tales had fled the neighborhood along with trust when California locked its Amerasian children inside filthy internment camps.

And *now* look where we were: Just a few blocks away, a genuinely classy (if eccentric) American folk hero, Howard Hughes, hid inside a tacky Art Moderne house with chicken wire webbing its windows while kids tripping out of their heads trashed the street outside. Bette Davis had been ousted by the Mamas and the Papas. The young singers shared rooms on Franklin Avenue, up the block from the Dunnes. Since March, when their single "California Dreamin'" topped the record charts, they had been greeted in the press as New Hollywood royalty. Their presence in the neighborhood attracted groupies, hangers-on, Scientology advocates, strangers of every sort, and promoted a *no ownership* ethos. Free love, free food, open doors: Rock 'n' rollers hiked the Hollywood Hills chanting these generous mantras. In Laurel Canyon, nearby, there "were more pop stars than you could count," said Michelle Phillips, one of the group. "Everybody knew everybody . . . [W]herever you could fit a little wooden house . . . there were friends dotted over the hillside and right up to the edge overhanging the great, wide, shimmering city." Where old money had once run horses in the hills (Jeanette MacDonald, Nelson Eddy, Maurice Chevalier), one-hit, three-chord wonders now buzzed the rocky ravines on little tabs of acid. Even the gurus of freedom worried about where this "lifestyle" might lead. Phillips saw a "lot of thin, insipid girls . . . Flower Children, we called them . . . moving in and out" of people's rooms. Her fellow Mama, Cass Elliot, would soon buy a house and sling pillows all over the floor for "masses of friends and 'well-wishers.'" She was "pretty consistently ripped off," Phillips said. "People used to write on her walls: messages, loving graffiti, pestilent stuff. Problems arrived inside the house wearing pants or shorts or nothing at all. Cass was so easy to intrude upon."

Intrusion was the rhythm of Franklin Avenue. One day, Didion came upon a stranger in the entrance hall to her house. "What do you want?" she asked him. He said nothing until he saw Dunne on the stair landing. "Chicken Delight," he blurted. Didion had ordered no food and his hands were empty. He drove away in an unmarked panel truck. "It seems to me . . . that during those years I was always writing down the license numbers of panel trucks," Didion wrote, "panel trucks circling the block, panel trucks parked across the street, panel trucks idling at the intersection. I put these license numbers in a dressing-table drawer where they could be found by the police when the time came."

If the new spirit of *anything goes* attempted to slip through her foyer, the spirit of the past sent dusty clouds through the open door of her basement. She wondered what all those *New Masses* said about the history of her house. One day, Dunne asked their landlord about the magazines. He was a friendly middle-aged fellow named Dan James, a distant relative of Frank and Jessie. In the thirties and forties, he said, he had been a member of the Communist Party. He had become political working in the Oklahoma oil fields—some of those old Okies were pretty damn radical!—and began to attend Party meetings once he'd made his way to Hollywood. He met Charlie Chaplin and worked as a screenwriter on the set of *The Great Dictator*. Oh yes, he said, Franklin Avenue had seen plenty of raucous Party squabbles.

Susceptible to vertigo even on a good day, Didion was dizzied by the strange contradictions of her street, the odd and frightening loveliness of her house. She sought distraction by driving to area theaters and sitting through biker films. Lately, they had become a popular, if derided, movie subgenre. Right away, she saw that they, too, were a mix of old and new: the Beat sensibility married to the code of the Hollywood Western. Yearning lay at their core: longing for freedom and simple principles by which a man could live (and they were *all* about men). The acting was atrocious, the cinematography amateurish, but the landscapes in which they unspooled, the broad, open vistas, were stunningly gorgeous. Didion's reactions to the movies were as paradoxical as the films themselves. She saw them as markers of the time—the anguish of valuing an old way of existence while craving a new style of life. On the one hand, they represented everything she feared: a further dismantling of the Lost Domain, Old Paint made roadkill by a Harley. On the other, she enjoyed their decadent textures, familiar to her from Old Sac, from her days slumming in valley gas stations.

While biker movies filled L.A. theaters, Ronald Reagan was taking the oath of office in Sacramento: another contradictory image. Old Hollywood's last gasp; the grinning cowboy had trounced Pat Brown on the promise of halting the changes taking place. Just as Communists had once infiltrated the film industry, he said, Reds were now ruining California's college campuses.

In November 1966, at a Los Angeles dinner honoring the governor-elect as well as the regents of Berkeley, H. R. Haldeman, later Richard Nixon's chief of staff, toasted Reagan as "the man who will bring a big breath of fresh air to the university." Seated at one of the tables, Clark Kerr knew right away that one of the new governor's first acts would be to fire him as university president. Reagan saw him as weak for not punishing student protestors more harshly. Shortly after dinner, one of the regents whispered to Kerr a sentence Didion might have swiped as a motto of the years she'd spend on Franklin Avenue: "Before this is all over, you're going to be covered in blood."

2

Didion worked in the mornings in a nearly empty bedroom with piles of books and a chair. She kept her needlepoint handy in case she got stuck on a piece. Down the hall, Dunne typed his notes from Delano and began to shape them into a narrative. He still had no book contract, but he hoped to get more than a *Saturday Evening Post* article out of the grape strikes. Back in February, when his agent, Carl Brandt, had sent his observations on Chavez's movement to editors at Farrar, Straus and Giroux, most responded negatively, citing the difficulty of selling a book on such a dry-dust topic—it wasn't "big ticket," one said. Henry Robbins agreed, but he admired Dunne's writing and he'd fallen under Chavez's spell. He wanted to see something happen, and he encouraged Dunne to think beyond the boundaries of a magazine piece.

Dunne was scheduled to fly to Houston at the end of January to cover the first *Apollo* launch for *The Saturday Evening Post*. Didion had her assignments for the magazine, too, and she'd been tinkering with the start of a novel. But between going to Ralph's Market to shop for the baby each day and feeding her, she didn't feel much like a writer. Besides, a torched VW in San Berdoo wasn't remotely as glamorous as a domed baseball diamond or rockets to the moon.

Three or four days a month, migraines sidelined her. She'd spend a day in bed, leaving Quintana in the care of her teenage nanny. She took Dexedrine and drank gin and hot water to dull the pain. In retrospect, she'd see this period as a "troubled time," but she also noticed that major stressors—plumbing disasters, accidents—didn't cause her paralysis. "Tell me that my house is burned down, my husband has left me, that there is gunfighting in the streets and panic in the banks, and I will not respond by getting a headache," she said. "It comes instead when I am fighting . . . a guerrilla war with my own life, during weeks of small household confusions, lost laundry, unhappy help, canceled appointments, on days when the telephone rings too much and I get no work done and the wind is coming up." Key here is "work." The headaches were related to her writing and her sense of herself as a writer. Armed with this insight, she was able to massage her malady—she "learned when to expect it, how to outwit it, even how to regard it . . . as more friend than lodger."

In late December, while Dunne stayed behind to work on his Chavez story, she took Quintana to her parents' house in Sacramento. Everyone agreed the baby was a charmer. "Delano?" Didion's mother said when Didion told her about the project. "Nobody wants to read about Delano. Modesto, maybe."

Alone one morning in the Franklin Avenue house, Dunne walked downstairs and found the dining room filling with water. A pipe had burst. The ceiling had turned to soggy plaster. The following day, he returned from a trip to the grocer's and sensed immediately that something was wrong. Had another pipe split? No. "The door on the Victorian commode had been wrenched off its hinges, and the desk drawers in the living room were thrown open and the contents strewn on the floor," he said. Every room had been cased. "Is there anyone in this house?" he called. He touched nothing—the out-of-date passports, the expired New York apartment leases, carbons of letters he "wished [he] had never written," scattered across the floor—and called the police. Three hours later, officers arrived. Bored, they told him a similar break-in had recently occurred down the street; it was probably some kid looking for drug cash. Luckily, nothing major was missing. They dusted for fingerprints while Dunne smoked and made himself a drink. There wasn't much they could do, said the cops. Dunne glanced anxiously out his windows. "I had never noticed so many strangers on the block," he said.

In early January 1967, Dunne sent Brandt and Robbins a rough draft of the magazine version of his strike story. Robbins thought it a "superb job of reporting," with a strong "visual sense of what it's like in the fields." He was eager to give Dunne "comments and suggestions for expansion." He wanted to see a book, if only he could convince his colleagues at FSG. Meanwhile, Brandt had been busy stirring up interest in Dunne. Dick Kluger at Simon & Schuster, unaware of Robbins's involvement with the writer, wrote Dunne on January 4, "I keep waiting and hoping to hear about Cesar and Company. Can you, will you, advise what, if anything, has happened to the project?"

For a few days, at least, the grapes would have to keep, as Dunne tracked *Apollo*. On January 27, two days prior to his scheduled trip to Houston, he drove to the North American Aviation plant in Downey, California. There, engineers had designed the *Apollo* capsule. He crawled inside a full-size mock-up of the spacecraft. He ate some of the astronauts' food—it was even worse than the K rations he'd been served in the army. He was told there were seventy-eight cubic feet per man inside the cramped capsule—plenty of room, as the average male coffin had only twenty-eight.

The engineers' confidence made him giddy. In no time, moon shots were going to be routine, they said: "You can run a Greyhound bus line up there." By 1985 we'd be making round-trips to Mars.

What if something went wrong inside the spacecraft? Dunne asked. No problem. The survival factor clocked in at 99 percent.

Two days later, on the launching pad at Cape Canaveral in Florida, fire swept through the *Apollo 1* capsule, killing astronauts Gus Grissom, Edward White, and Roger Chaffee. Dunne canceled his Houston trip. He happened to be driving on the Hollywood Freeway when he heard about the fire on the radio. He recalled the engineers' swagger, their armor of invulnerability—almost of immortality, they seemed to think. He said the *Apollo* disaster "was as if Achilles had fallen down the cellar stairs."

In March, Quintana turned one. Almost coincident with her birthday, both her parents were about to secure major book contracts.

Robbins had convinced Roger Straus to approve a three-thousand-dollar advance for the grape story (Dick Kluger, at S&S, was furious, feeling he'd been played). Delighted, Dunne listed possible titles. He fancied *In Dubious Battle* but feared Mr. Steinbeck might object.

Robbins wrote to say, "And now that you're with FSG—how about bringing your charming wife along?"

Didion had taken their daughter to Sacramento, to celebrate Quintana's birthday with Frank and Eduene (and to distance herself from the fact that she was not writing much). In her parents' house, surrounded by her grandmother's hand-painted teacups, she felt protected; sheltered from deadlines, contracts, proposals. As a child, she'd been in a rush to grow up and go away, but now she liked to return and luxuriate, briefly, in the illusion that the world had not changed—that it *would* not change for her daughter.

She lit the candles on a large white cake. The adults drank champagne while the baby plowed through strawberry-marshmallow ice cream. Later, warm and content, sleepy, Didion pressed her face against Quintana's through the thick, fat slats of the crib.

Squelching his anger at Dunne over the Chavez dealings, Dick Kluger wrote to ask if he'd like to propose a book on the space program. Dunne declined; eventually, both Tom Wolfe and Norman Mailer produced books on the astronauts.

The "New Journalists," as Wolfe would call them, competed fiercely for the same subjects, many of them—car culture, hippies, NASA, Las Vegas—featuring Western settings or connections. "When I started writing in what became known as my style, I was trying to capture the newness and excitement of the West Coast thing," Wolfe said. "It's where all the exciting youth styles were coming from. They certainly weren't coming from New York. Everything I was writing about was new to the East Coast."

On March 22, Dunne wrote Henry Robbins, chasing a rumor that Wolfe was doing a piece on Ken Kesey and the acidheads. He wondered if Robbins knew anything about this, as it was a matter of some interest to them.

His wife had decided to go to the Haight.

3

"I had not been able to work in some months, had been paralyzed by the conviction that writing was an irrelevant act, that the world as I had understood it no longer existed," she said. "If I was to work again at all, it would be necessary for me to come to terms with disorder."

As she would write in the famous opening to her essay "Slouching Towards Bethlehem," "San Francisco was where the [country's] social hemorrhaging was showing up. San Francisco was where the missing children were gathering and calling themselves 'hippies.'"

Taking their cue from the Doors, the baby boomers shouted, "We want the world and we want it now!" Didion was intrigued and appalled.

The most privileged, pampered, studied, and commercially targeted group in American history, the boomers were a massive workforce in the eyes of corporate executives. Madison Avenue saw a crowd of consumers. In order to channel their emergent desires, government agencies and medical boards tracked every twitch, blink, and speck of saliva. Behaviorists argued with psychiatrists who quibbled with law enforcement over the care and well-being of America's kids. Biologists debated nature versus nurture, stimulus-response units, and organicism. The Woodworth Personal Data Sheet, Binet's IQ test, Rorschach's inkblots, the Thematic Apperception Test, the Minnesota Multiphasic Personality Inventory, Dr. Spock, and Captain Kangaroo spoon-fed boomers daily doses of themselves.

Overfed, resentful of the poking and prodding, the children puked it all up. Many decided to go missing. And then they wanted more, but on *their* terms. The world had tried too hard to shape them. They decided to change the world.

The testers had failed to maintain control. They'd fumbled the testing tools. How had this happened? Didion wondered.

Perhaps the starting point was 1946: Persuaded by data sheets that the American populace was crippled with neuropsychiatric disorders, the U.S. Congress signed into law the National Mental Health Act, budgeting $4.2 million to study dysfunctions and to treat their manifestations through medicine. In this context—in tandem with the military's aim to develop mind-control drugs—two Bay Area psychologists, working with Oakland's Kaiser Hospital, published a study arguing that mental patients receiving psychotherapy fared no better after nine months than patients getting no treatments; mood-enhancing drugs, then, might be a profitable area of research. The primary author of this study was a young man named Timothy Leary.

In this context, Max Rinkel, a psychiatrist at the Massachusetts Mental Health Center, ordered a shipment of LSD-25 from Sandoz Pharmaceuticals and dosed his colleague Robert Hyde to see what would happen. At the American Psychological Association's convention in Cincinnati in 1951, Rinkel reported that Hyde had become paranoid on the drug, hearing imaginary doors slam shut.

In this context, the Rand Corporation as well as various Veterans Administration hospitals, conducted lab experiments with mind-altering drugs. In Menlo Park, California, Dr. Leo Hollister, recruited by the CIA for MK-ULTRA, administered psilocybin and LSD to a volunteer subject named Ken Kesey.

By now, it's well documented that Kesey, Leary, and other pranksters let the goodies out of the bag. At least for a while, the lab men were no longer in charge of hallucinogen-based social experiments.

Old Hollywood was flashing: Cary Grant dropped acid more than sixty times. "I have been born again," he said. Christopher Isherwood dosed himself under the direction of Dr. Sidney Cohen of UCLA and the Veterans Hospital in Los Angeles. Even Henry Luce tried the drug on a visit to California. He conducted an invisible orchestra on a lawn one night.

Aldous Huxley, a lifelong quester for the ideal intoxicant and the author of *The Doors of Perception*, from which Jim Morrison took the name of his band, died, on the day JFK was shot, believing he had found in LSD the key to the cosmos. He used a William Blake quote as the epigraph to his book: "If the doors of perception were cleansed everything would appear to man as it is, infinite." He once told Timothy Leary that Western culture would experience a profound revolution in consciousness if "wisdom drugs" could be given to cultural "elites"—artists, economists, intellectuals—who would then disseminate their visions throughout society.

With the help of Kesey, Allen Ginsberg, Gary Snyder, Alan Watts (who praised drug-induced mysticism on his Bay Area radio show), the Grateful Dead, and pioneer outlaw chemists, primarily Owsley Stanley, Leary went Huxley one better. He dispensed "wisdom" on the streets at about two dollars a pop.

Cheap rents, the proximity of Berkeley, and state-of-the-art labs at nearby VA hospitals combined to make San Francisco's once-blighted Haight-Ashbury neighborhood a grand ballroom for mind expansion. "People are beginning to see that the Kingdom of Heaven is within them," Ginsberg said. "It's time to seize power in the Universe, that's what I say . . . not merely over Russia or America—seize power over the moon—take the sun over."

For Didion, who had never marched to the Beats—or the hippies, as the press tagged them, playing off Norman Mailer's term *hipster,* youngsters wearing flowers in their hair up and down the Haight—the Kingdom of Heaven was not nigh in psychedelic shenanigans. For her, this epic experiment, under no one's supervision, was closer to William Carlos Williams's warning in his introduction to *Howl:* "Hold back the edges of your gowns, Ladies, we are going through hell."

The essay "Slouching Towards Bethlehem" probably began as a series of discussions with Ted and Shirley Streshinsky. "After Delano, we saw Joan and John in the Bay Area," Shirley said. "I suppose the idea for a story on the subculture was talked about, because either Joan or Ted, or perhaps both of them, proposed the story to *The Saturday Evening Post.* Our friend Paul Hawken, who was very much part of the beginning of the hippie movement, had something to do with it. He was the son of one of Ted's good friends, and during that period spent a lot of time at our house and convinced Ted that the counterculture movement was worth a story."

Like Didion, Paul Hawken was a fifth-generation Californian. In time, he would become a wealthy entrepreneur, selling macrobiotics and "gentleperson" gardening supplies. He established the Erewhon Natural Foods store in Boston, helped Stewart Brand publish *The Whole Earth Catalog,* and became a political adviser to Jerry Brown and Gary Hart. In the mid-1960s, he was living in the Haight with his friend Bill Tara, promoting theater and rock concerts in an old firehouse on Sacramento Street, just north of the Haight, in the Sunset District. His specialty was light shows. He gave Janis Joplin and Big Brother and the Holding Company one of their first breaks, and he was an early supporter of Jerry Garcia and the Warlocks (later the Grateful Dead). At the time, he embraced the hippie "lifestyle," but he was by no means one of the "missing children" Didion would emphasize in her essay. Like Chet Helms and Bill Graham, better-known local rock promoters, he was a budding businessman. "When everybody else had long hair, I cut mine off," he said. "I've always been a contrarian."

Didion met him in the Streshinskys' kitchen. "I remember Paul not being sure how to handle a movie company who wanted to rent the warehouse space where Paul seemed to be in charge, and where Kesey's 'Electric Kool-Aid Acid Test' was performed," Shirley said. "Joan offered to handle the negotiation with the film company for Paul because she had some experience with movie producers."

Hawken became one of Didion's informal guides to the Haight. In her essay, the Warehouse, which she described as "total theater, a continual happening," and where she always felt "good," was probably the alley space at 65 Hariett Street, south of Market, where Hawken lived with Tara and Tara's sometime girlfriend, Jean Allison Young. "Somebody is usually doing something interesting, like working on a light show" in the Warehouse, Didion wrote, "and there are a lot of interesting things around, like an old Chevrolet touring car which is used as a bed and a vast American flag fluttering up in the shadows and an overstuffed chair suspended like a swing from the rafters, the point of that being that it gives you a sensory-deprivation high." She called the place "the garage of a condemned hotel." Young said it was "actually an old factory for making the pre-packaged small half-pies that you could buy at a convenience store. Initially, we had a wicked problem with rats and mice . . . and had so many cockroaches that we used to have a monthly 'cockroach killing party' with Raid and beer. Great fun."

Didion visited—"I just stayed around awhile, and made a few friends," she said—in the spring and early summer of 1967. She "stayed at a new (then) motel on University Avenue in Berkeley. Ted would pick her up and they spent the day, sometimes very long days, in the city," Shirley told me. "Sometimes Ted would get the film developed so we could project the pictures on the wall in our living room so Joan could see them. He was doing some really wild photojournalism for then. Even for now, I think." Most of the pictures were deliberately blurry and double-exposed, to simulate an LSD trip.

LSD had been declared illegal in California seven or eight months before. On that day, the hippie community had gathered in the Panhandle of Golden Gate Park to hear free music by Big Brother and the Holding Company, Wildflower, and the Dead, and to drop acid in unison in defiance of the new law. The Merry Pranksters pulled up in their Magic Bus, minus Ken Kesey, who'd fled the country on drug charges. Celebrants had been urged to bring to the park "photos of personal saints and gurus and heroes of the underground . . . children . . . flowers . . . drums . . . incense . . . symbols . . . [and] costumes." Organizer Allen Cohen said, "We wanted to create a celebration of innocence. We were not guilty of using illegal substances. We were celebrating transcendental consciousness. The beauty of the universe. The beauty of being."

This was the Haight at its peak—before reporters outnumbered residents, before grifters moved in for quick scores and easy lays, before STP and harder drugs flooded the back alleys (shipped, some thought, by the Mafia or the CIA; after all, the neighborhood was a ready-made market . . . *or* an enclosed clinic, perfect for experimenting).

On January 14, 1967, ten to twenty thousand people went to Golden Gate Park for "The Human Be-In, A Gathering of the Tribes," an attempt to unite the Haight community with Berkeley activists. Allen Ginsberg chanted. Timothy Leary spoke. The Hells Angels guarded power cables so rock bands could perform. ("We're in the same business," Kesey told the Angels. "You break people's bones, I break people's heads.") For the occasion, Owsley Stanley made enough acid to float the park. Linda Gravenites, a Dead hanger-on who lived with the band in their old Victorian at 710 Ashbury, recalled Owsley showing up with a "giant restaurant mayonnaise jar filled with teeny, tiny White Lightning pills. They were all gone by the end of the day."

And so was the Haight's ambience. "Up until then, people came because they were full to overflowing and were sharing their fullness," Gravenites told Alice Echols, Janis Joplin's biographer. "After that"—spurred by sensationalist sex and drug stories in the press—"it was the empties who came, wanting to be filled."

By the time Didion showed up, even the Haight's biggest believers realized the party was over. Posters began to appear on street corners: "Pretty little 16-year-old middle-class chick comes to the Haight to see what it's all about & gets picked up by a 17-year-old street dealer who spends all day shooting her full of speed again & again . . . Rape is as common as bullshit on Haight Street. . . . Minds and bodies are being maimed as we watch, a scale model of Vietnam." A mime troupe passed out flyers: "IF YOU DON'T KNOW, BY AUGUST HAIGHT STREET WILL BE A CEMETERY." That August, George Harrison dropped in to witness the love and spiritual fulfillment he'd been hearing about and left profoundly frightened, having been assaulted by addicts and drunks. On October 6, the Haight's residents held a mock funeral, hoisting a coffin through the neighborhoods amidst a psychedelic parade, declaring the "Death of Hippie."

The cover of the September 23, 1967, issue of *The Saturday Evening Post* featured a splashy Ted Streshinsky photo of a top-hatted hippie grinning through face paint, with the caption "The Hippie Cult: Who They Are, What They Want, Why They Act That Way"—topics Didion's essay failed to address, even remotely. Her real subject crawled into the piece about a quarter of the way through, in the form of a three-year-old named Michael, the child of a hippie girl. His mother got high every day and neglected him. Didion first met him in the Warehouse, "a very blond and pale and dirty child on a rocking horse with no paint." His presence pleased her, though she worried about his lack of supervision. While no one was playing with him, he tried to light a pair of joss sticks. Left alone, he crooned to himself, mesmerized by a blue theatrical spotlight. She recognized him in other children she encountered, children tangled accidentally in lamp cords, children fighting on the streets, children on acid— in "High Kindergarten." In the essay, Didion stressed that the parents of these children were also just kids, "pathetically unequipped."

One day, she watched some of her new "friends" drop acid—she wanted to observe what happened when the "flash" kicked in. "The only LSD we could get was the real Sandoz" stuff, Jean Young said. Taking it was a "spiritual experience." What Didion saw that day was petulance, impatience, narcissism. At the moment of the flash, she heard someone mutter a single, breathy "Wow."

These were adolescents "who were never taught and would never now learn the games that had held the society together," she wrote.

Significantly, the one major change she made in the essay from the magazine version to its appearance a year later in her book was the addition of a scene in which she tried to teach Michael the words to "Frère Jacques." The point of the scene was that no one else paid attention to the child. Only Didion seemed to care.

Rarely in the essay does Didion step forth to judge what she witnesses. But toward the end she cannot hold her tongue: these children are "less in rebellion against the society than ignorant of it, able only to feed back certain of its most publicized self-doubts, *Vietnam, Saran Wrap, diet pills, the Bomb*," she writes.

But that's not quite the point.

The point is, "These were children who grew up cut loose from the web of cousins and great-aunts and family doctors and lifelong neighbors who had traditionally suggested and enforced the society's values."

In retrospect, this reference to the severing of family ties clearly shows Didion in the Haight worrying about her adopted daughter back in the house on Franklin Avenue, the house cased all day by strangers driving unmarked panel trucks. And as in all her subsequent work, whenever she wrote about her daughter, she was also writing about herself.

In the essay, just before her lament about the torn family web, she quotes a San Francisco psychiatrist she'd interviewed:

> Anybody who thinks this is all about drugs has his head in a bag. It's a social movement, quintessentially romantic, the kind that recurs in times of real social crisis. The themes are always the same. A return to innocence. The invocation of an earlier authority and control. The mysteries of the blood. An itch for the transcendental, for purification. Right there you've got the ways that romanticism historically ends up in trouble, lends itself to authoritarianism. When the direction appears. How long do you think it'll take for that to happen?

Didion notes: "[T]he peculiar beauty of this [authoritarian] potential, as far as . . . activists were concerned, was that it remained not clear at all to most of the inhabitants of the District, perhaps because the few seventeen-year-olds who are political realists tend not to adopt romantic idealism as a life style."

Blind romanticism, political realism: two extremes in Didion's life, the arc (moving from one to the other) of her *personal* narrative, and of the career she was about to establish.

The *shape* of her writing—fragmented, jagged—suggested the chaos of contemporary circumstances. But the voice was icy with principled realism. One had to attend to both. Only with both could we begin to reconstruct the world.

Prior to visiting the Haight, Didion felt the act of writing *couldn't* contain the world any longer—the world had gotten out of hand; rendering it was irrelevant. Many more times, she'd be assailed by this doubt. But for now, she had rediscovered her center.

The children.

A child.

In just a few years, her child would describe for her a vivid recurring nightmare in which a "Broken Man" came to take her away. He always wore a blue work shirt. Lowering his eyes, he'd mutter, "*Hello, Quintana.*"

4

Didion still considered herself a novelist. Her nonfiction pieces for *The Saturday Evening Post* helped pay the bills, that's all. She would not have thought of collecting them into a book without the encouragement of Henry Robbins.

But "Slouching Towards Bethlehem" was different. It may have begun as just another magazine assignment with Ted Streshinsky; it became the first essay she felt she *had* to write—and the first piece she had no idea how to shape. Later, she would say it was "imperative" for her to deal "directly and flatly with the evidence of atomization, the proof that things fall apart." Doing the piece, she became increasingly dependent on Dexies and gin. "I was . . . as sick as I have ever been when I was writing [it]," she said. It "was a very odd piece to do, because I was in [San Francisco] for quite a long time, longer than I'd ever spent before on a piece . . . and I kept staying because I kept having the sense that I wasn't getting it. I did not understand what was going on, and I finally came home, and I still didn't think I had it . . . Usually on a piece, there comes a day when you know you never have to do another interview. You can go home, you've gotten it. Well, that day never came on that piece. The piece had to be written right away. So I wrote it right away. But I wrote it in just a series of scenes, exactly how it happened to me, and that was the only way I could write it because I had no conclusions at all." She was aware that at the center of the essay was a frightened concern for children. She'd been feeling "cut off" from Quintana while researching it, and that was why the Michael scenes were "very real" to her. Otherwise, "[t]hat piece is a blank for me still," she said. "I have no idea whether it was good or bad, you know . . ."

She remembered "running so close to deadline with 'Slouching Towards Bethlehem' which [was] already on the cover of *The Saturday Evening Post* that, in order to get it to New York by closing, I had to drive it to an air freight hangar at LAX one Sunday morning . . . Before I left that morning, I happened to buy *The New York Times*. That was the upside of needing to go to LAX. LAX and the Beverly Hills Hotel were the only places in 1967 where you could buy *The New York Times*.

"And I spent the rest of that Sunday [at] my brother-in-law's . . . pretending to read the paper while I fought against the overwhelming impulse that I needed to go back to the airport, go to San Francisco, and re-check the piece."

Reactions to the article, once it appeared in *The Saturday Evening Post*, left her "despondent." Friends congratulated her on having "finished the piece 'just in time,' because 'the whole fad's dead now, *fini, kaput.*'" She said, "I suppose almost everyone who writes is afflicted some of the time by the suspicion that nobody out there is listening, but it seemed to me then (perhaps because the piece was important to me) that I had never gotten a feedback so universally beside the point."

She also received a letter from one of the people she'd profiled—a girl she'd met through Paul Hawken—accusing Didion of being "unfair" to her and her friends and to the hippie scene in general.

It helped that Henry Robbins got what she was doing—so much so that he hoped she'd consider expanding the essay to book length. He had convinced her to sign with FSG despite her doubts (her agent had extricated her from her remaining contractual obligations to Obolensky). She'd told Robbins she'd been fiddling with an L.A. novel, tentatively titled *Maria Talking*. At this point, she had little more to work with than Lillian Hellman's line "What makes Iago evil?" and a scattered set of freeway scenes, but that was enough for Robbins. He felt her nonfiction was special, and if it took a novel contract to lure her into the fold, so be it. On July 12, 1967, he offered a six-thousand-dollar advance on the unfinished novel. He also said, "I want to include a special option clause *in addition* to the usual option, specifying an option on a particular book. This option will be a nonfiction book, tentatively titled *Slouching Towards Bethlehem* and dealing with the LSD life in California." The total advance, then, payable in installments, was twelve thousand dollars.

She worried she'd let him down. The "Slouching" piece, she said, couldn't possibly be made into a book, as its style was "mindless." And any *collection* of her articles "would either prove that I contradicted myself every month or that I always said the same thing every month, and I didn't know which would be worse."

Meanwhile, Dunne's "Strike!" article had appeared in the May 6 issue of *The Saturday Evening Post* and immediately drew the threat of a lawsuit from lawyers representing the Di Giorgio Corporation. They objected to "inaccuracies" in the piece and said they would "protect" the company if these statements reappeared in book form. Dunne's reporting was airtight. Robbins responded that any "alleged errors" Dunne may have made were "matters of interpretation rather than fact," and this ended the legal harrumphing.

Certain *Saturday Evening Post* readers were less easy to appease. Some canceled their subscriptions to the magazine. A typical letter went like this:

"The author has clearly conveyed the impression that the Valley is a backward, illiterate section populated by slow-thinking, tight-fisted, provincial-minded farmers. We have lived in the Valley 46 years. We do not think the one month Mr. Dunne spent in Delano qualified him to make the vast generalizations about the weather, the people, and the situation." One grower wrote, "The sweet and gentle Chavez [Dunne portrayed] was well-trained in the ultra-liberal school for Radicals headed by Alinsky!"

These responses were only the first signs of trouble for *Delano*. In August, salesmen on the road, pitching the volume to store owners in advance of publication, reported resistance: "I've tried several approaches on the DELANO with pathetic success," one publisher's representative wrote to Roger Straus. "[T]he customer . . . read[s] that it's about a grape strike in California, and take[s] a . . . 'So who the hell cares. Next' attitude."

Spooked by these reports, Dunne kept revising the manuscript, right up to the galley stage. He hoped his brother Stephen, now working as a graphic designer in Michigan, might design the cover. The FSG Art Department did not warm to this idea, and Stephen felt slighted (Dunne conceded that his brother could be "a very difficult young man").

Robbins tried to solicit blurbs from John Steinbeck and Bobby Kennedy. Neither man responded.

While Dunne prepared to launch *Delano*, Didion was bundling up her nonfiction pieces for Robbins and her new literary agent, Lois Wallace, at William Morris. Wallace was a tough-talking, chain-smoking woman of independent means who worked with literature for the sheer love of it.

Didion began to see the possibilities of a book divided into reportage, essays, reviews, and travel pieces. Robbins didn't want reviews. Concentrate on thematic links, he said. Initially, Didion thought to include her short story "The Welfare Island Ferry." Whether she intended to rewrite it as nonfiction, retaining the New York atmosphere and its focus on desperate young professionals, isn't clear. Perhaps this was her first move toward writing "Goodbye to All That," which she eventually composed for a specially themed issue of *The Saturday Evening Post* on the topic of "Love."

"The [thematic] combinations are endless," Wallace wrote Henry Robbins, tongue in cheek. "On Keeping John Wayne: Notes from an Enchanted Home. The Seacoast of Pearl Harbor. Emotional Blackmail: How Can I Tell Them There's Nothing Left?"

On August 1, buoyed by Robbins's support, Didion reported she'd made real headway on the novel. She had a new title for it, a crapshooter's phrase, *Play It As It Lays*. She admitted her husband didn't much care for the title. Robbins wasn't sure, either: The "'as it lays' part . . . somehow sounds awkward," he said, "and that last word always causes a certain amount of trouble."

More bad news from the road: Store owners on the Great Plains didn't want to stock Dunne's book. *Delano* was going to be a tougher sell than anyone had realized. Before it even appeared, Dunne sensed a waning of enthusiasm in-house. Simultaneously, excitement increased for Didion's projects. On August 24, Dunne received a note from Roger Straus wishing him luck on publication day. Straus added, "Will you tell Joan, please, that a night or two ago I read 'Slouching Towards Bethlehem' and thought it simply marvelous."

On September 27, Robbins sent Dunne the first advance review, a snippy little item from *Kirkus* "confus[ing] objectivity with neutrality," Robbins said. He then spent the rest of the letter on a "postscript to Joan—How are you feeling about the title [of your collection] at this point . . . [I] have wondered a bit if it doesn't throw too much weight on the hippie piece . . . when the book as a whole"—as *he* had finally conceived it—"is more about, well, the confrontation between you and 'the golden land.'"

Dunne handed the letter to his wife and brooded over the clipping from *Kirkus*.

If Dunne had learned anything useful as a journeyman reporter, it was not to sit still. Rather than wait for *Delano* to sail or fail, he would move on with a fresh project.

He approached Richard D. Zanuck, vice president in charge of production at Twentieth Century–Fox, to ask if he could trace the making of a motion picture from beginning to end, from boardrooms, screening rooms, and back lots to gala premiere. To his surprise, Zanuck said yes. "There was no reason for him to give [access] to me, and . . . I don't know why he did; the nature of reporting is such that it certainly was not to his advantage to let me, or any reporter, see the inner workings of his studio," Dunne said. But Zanuck gave him a parking space and an office and a secretary to type his notes, if he wanted. At the Fox studio, he "became as anonymous as a piece of furniture," Dunne said. "My notebook was always out and visible, but I rarely took notes. After a meeting, I would race back to my office and transcribe the scene I had just witnessed . . . [or] duck into the men's room and jot down the things I wished to remember."

The movie whose troubled history he would chronicle was *Dr. Dolittle*, starring Rex Harrison and a cast of mammals. It was a major undertaking for Fox. Prior to the movie's release, the studio negotiated with more than fifty companies for tie-in advertising; together, these companies planned to spend over twelve million dollars on retail displays, cereal boxes, dolls, clocks and watches, T-shirts, and fast food wrapped in cute *Dolittle* packaging. The studio felt it couldn't miss—hence, perhaps, Zanuck's confidence in allowing a reporter on his lot. Music and animals: Who could resist?

For Dunne, a side benefit of the project would be his personal education, an intimate glimpse into the system's culture, which might lead to screenwriting work. His experiences in Delano—showing up, hanging out, waiting for the story to come to him—made him think he should adopt a more deliberative stance this time. It didn't do to get *too* attached to a piece (he was preparing himself for disappointment with the book). He decided he knew the voice he desired this time: "[T]he omniscient cool narrator. I knew the style I wanted: short takes, shifting among a whole range of onstage and offstage characters. I knew where I wanted to start . . . and I knew where I wanted it to end." No saints or tyrants, no big issues. "As a story it was reasonable enough to pass, and I sometimes believed what I said," Norman Mailer wrote in his Hollywood novel, *The Deer Park*. This was Dunne's attitude toward the Fox story, and along the way—because the studios were being challenged by independent talents with more and more cash (much of it washing in on the tide of rock 'n' roll)—he would detail significant changes in the entertainment industry, the clash of old and new.

5

That clash of old and new occurred in the Dunnes' living room on any given weekend. "There was a jasmine vine grown over the verandah of the big house on Franklin Avenue, and in the evenings the smell of jasmine came in through all the open doors and windows. I made bouillabaisse for people," Didion said.

"She cooked nonstop. She made stuff like beef Wellington—for a sit-down dinner for thirty-five people—with a side dish, Cobb salad or something, for those who didn't eat meat," said Eve Babitz. "It's the first time I ever saw Spode china. She seemed to be the only sensible person in the world in those days. She could make dinner for forty people with one hand tied around her back while everybody else was passed out on the floor."

These were not the traditional Hollywood parties Nick Dunne so adored, or the rigid affairs Didion had first attended upon moving to Los Angeles, where ladies took their coffee upstairs after dessert. By now, she knew many of the old-timers: Connie Wald, Natalie Wood, Sara Mankiewicz, Diana Lynn, Sandy Sturges. She knew their rebellious children: Jill Schary Robinson, Ann Marshall. Didion had also met the upstarts: Warren Beatty, Julie Christie, Teri Garr. And now she lived down the street from the Mamas and the Papas. "The two worlds met. Hollywood went rock 'n' roll and rock 'n' roll went Hollywood," said Barney Hoskyns, veteran observer of the L.A. music scene. Producer Lou Adler, fresh from pulling off the Monterey Pop Festival (which had introduced Jimi Hendrix and his flaming guitar to the world), palled around with Jack Nicholson and the Monkees in Laurel Canyon. At the Chateau Marmont, John Phillips, Papa John, partied with—and later swapped partners with—Roman Polanski.

Initially, Didion watched, amused, as rock became a novelty among the children of movie stars in West Hollywood. They cased pawnshops for cheap guitars, taught themselves a handful of chords, and grew their hair like the Beatles. But in the fall of 1966, just as the Dunnes were moving into the Franklin Avenue house, Pandora's Box, a popular coffeehouse on Sunset, a few blocks away, drew the attention of the LAPD and the Los Angeles County Sheriff's Department. There were numerous complaints about loud music, drug use, and underage drinking on the Strip. Pandora's Box did not, in fact, serve alcohol, but its manager, Al Mitchell, acted as a sponsor of sorts to high school students and teenage runaways in the area, so residents and local property owners viewed the coffeehouse as a trouble spot. (Veteran Strip watchers saw the heavy hand of mob-controlled business owners, in league with corrupt cops, clearing the street for *their* clientele—somewhere in the background lurked Sidney Korshak.)

The authorities enforced a curfew requiring everyone under eighteen to be off the Strip by ten P.M. Pandora's Box would be closed. This news sparked an impromptu riot outside the coffeehouse one night, which trickled up into the Dunnes' neighborhood. Watts it wasn't—these were middle-class kids raising a little hell because they wanted to stay out late. They pushed a city bus on its side and a few heads got billy-clubbed. But Stephen Stills and the Buffalo Springfield captured the moment in a song called "For What It's Worth": "There's a man with a gun over there. . . . Stop, children, what's that sound?"

Basically, Stills was demanding to be served a drink after hours, but never mind—the song got taken up as an antiestablishment anthem. When the Lou Adler–produced antiwar chant "Eve of Destruction" by Barry Mc-Guire hit number one, *Billboard* reported cynically, but accurately, "Folk + Rock + Protest = Dollars."

At the parties in her house, "We put 'Lay Lady Lay' on the record player or 'Suzanne,'" Didion said. They also played "Visions of Johanna" and "Midnight Confessions." Many of the L.A. session musicians were Okie transplants, and Didion caught their Dust Bowl rhythms in many of the tunes, the accents she'd heard in the speech of her middle-school classmates, and the country lilt of the broadcasts out of Tulsa that she listened to as a teenager on the car radio. The music was a cushion. She cooked to it. This was her special performance, a soothing role while grab-ass chaos rolled around the twenty-eight rooms above, about, and below her. Meanwhile, "John was in charge," Babitz said. "He was the talker," serving drinks, seeing to everyone's needs.

Babitz noticed perceptual differences between the Dunnes' generation, whose preferred relaxant was alcohol, and younger people at the parties, who liked pills and synthetic stimulants. But really, "no one cared," she said. "By then, *everyone* was smoking pot." "Joan and I connected," she told *Vanity Fair.* "The drugs she was on, I was on. She looks like she'd take downers, but really she's a Hell's Angels girl, white trash." As her date, Babitz often brought Peter Pilafian, an Armenian roadie with the Mamas and the Papas, and she talked about her cover art for Buffalo Springfield's second album, a Joseph Cornell–inspired collage. Later, she would print, on special paper called Delmarva Text, a limited edition of psychedelic posters featuring the British band Cream. "Joan bought the Ginger Baker poster and put it in her house. She was, like, the only one who liked it," Babitz said.

Her remarks remind us how traditionally underappreciated the visual arts had been in L.A.—their influence on Didion, through figures like Babitz, has rarely been mentioned. At the time, "Los Angeles had no modern art museum and few galleries, which was exactly what renegade artists liked about it: Ed Ruscha, David Hockney, Robert Irwin, Ed Kienholz, Bruce Nauman . . . Judy Chicago . . . ," wrote Hunter Drohojowska-Philp. "[A] prevailing permissiveness in Los Angeles in the 1960s brought about countless innovations: Andy Warhol's first show, Marcel Duchamp's first retrospective, Frank Gehry's unique architecture, Rudi Gernreich's topless bathing suit, Dennis Hopper's *Easy Rider,* the Beach Boys, the Byrds, and the Doors. In the 1960s, Los Angeles was the epicenter of cool."

Didion's friend Earl McGrath opened a small art gallery on North Robertson Boulevard, on the edge of Beverly Hills. "He never made any money because he didn't try very hard to sell the art," Babitz said. "It's a miracle he survived—but he had the best parties in the world." At these parties, and at her own—through Babitz, Ann Marshall, and Teri Garr—Didion met the "Lumberjacks," macho male painters associated with Walter Hopps's Ferus Gallery, L.A.'s first Pop Art center. The best known of these artists was Ed Ruscha (another Okie). In the early sixties, driving from Oklahoma City to Los Angeles on Route 66, he fell in love with the simple geometric architecture of filling stations. In 1963 he self-published a paperback book entitled *Twentysix Gasoline Stations,* featuring straightforward black-and-white photographs of the generally unremarkable structures. *Artforum* sneered: "[T]he book is so curious, and so doomed to oblivion that there is an obligation, of sorts, to document its existence." In fact, in the years since, *Twentysix Gasoline Stations* has been celebrated as a milestone in modern American art: It announced a distinctly Western sensibility based on close observation of (often manufactured) objects, suspending all judgment of them. "I want absolutely neutral material," Ruscha said. "My pictures are not that interesting, nor the subject matter. They are simply a collection of 'facts.'" His words might describe the literary style of *Play It As It Lays,* published a few years later by a woman who shared his fondness for gas stations.

In this context, we see that Didion's obsession with biker films was not just a guilty pleasure, but a recognition of a developing artistic style rooted in the raw, rough textures and materialistic culture of the American West.

Like Ruscha, Dennis Hopper was an acquaintance of hers. His photographic skills may well have exceeded his talents as an actor. He took Ruscha's cue, snapping pictures of the vernacular on L.A. street corners (including a famous gas station shot, *Double Standard*), and making the quintessential biker film—short on story and character but blazing with style—*Easy Rider* (1969).

What really distinguished this West Coast style from the New York art world was its "direct response to life rather than to [aesthetic] 'problems,'" said art critic John Coplans. Its blunt representational approach revealed a "deep understanding of the lie of the evolution of [artistic] progress" and an affirmation that "art springs directly from life, with all its anguish." (His words may give us a clue as to why Didion was so perplexed by the hippies in the Haight, who, as novelist C. D. B. Bryan said, had embraced a "contemporary morality . . . based upon aesthetic rather than social values." Didion did not share the hippies' escapist, "It's all too beautiful" impulse; however, what remained fundamentally Western about San Francisco's LSD culture, and *did* attract her, was the value it placed on the "immediate, direct experience.")

Immediacy and directness were essential to the new Western art. "There is a very thin line as to whether this book [*Twentysix Gasoline Stations*] is worthless or has any value—to most people it is probably worthless," Ruscha said. This mixing of high and low would become a Pop Art principle; given the astonishing work of Robert Rauschenberg and Jasper Johns, it would come to be associated mostly with New York. But arguably its origins were in L.A. (the Ferus Gallery mounted the first American Pop Art show).

Didion's version of the Pop Art credo? "I never ask."

Often, on party nights, she asked Sandy Sturges if her boys would baby-sit Quintana. (The first time Didion went to Sturges's door, Sturges thought she was a little girl.) On evenings when the jasmine drifted through her open windows and people began to gather in her living room, "I imagined that my . . . life was simple and sweet," Didion wrote. "[S]ometimes it was, but there were odd things going around town. There were rumors . . . nothing was unimaginable. The mystical flirtation with the idea of 'sin'—this sense that it was possible to go 'too far,' and that many people were doing it—was very much with us."

The person closest to her who had gone too far was her brother-in-law. In late 1967 and early 1968, the drugs on the streets, and eventually in the upscale homes, got harder. Heroin and coke shoved aside hallucinogens . . . and then people jumped back into their old paraphernalia, to play again among cellophane flowers.

Nick leaped. Over and over. Whenever he could. He remained charming and gregarious. He had never lacked friends who could supply him with the latest thrills. One of his budding pals was a hairdresser to the stars, Jay Sebring. "The first time I dropped acid, I dropped it with Jay," Nick recalled. "He brought it over to my house on Walden Drive one time when Lenny and the kids were at her mother's ranch." Sebring loved to wear leather jackets and ride motorcycles with Paul Newman and Steve McQueen.

"Jay had a private room for his steady clients so that they wouldn't have to be seen by the other customers," Nick said. "I had a regular appointment every third week, and it was in that room that I met Sharon Tate. She would often be sitting there in a chair, just to be with Jay as he worked. She looked so young that I thought at first she was coming there after school."

Tate was an aspiring actress who had just appeared as a character named

Malibu in a picture that had nothing much going for it except a Byrds soundtrack and lots of shots of swimming pools.

"She wore her blonde hair straight and long," Nick said of Tate. "She was quiet and friendly and smiled a lot at our conversations. Jay . . . couldn't stop looking at her." On the day before she traveled to England to shoot a movie called *Eye of the Devil*, Nick and Sebring toasted her with champagne. While overseas, she would meet Roman Polanski.

Nick recalled feeling uneasy that day, sipping champagne in Sebring's private room.

It was a time for the "jitters," Didion wrote. The jitters were "setting in."

The demonstrations on Sunset continued, but in the meantime the clubs had gotten louder, raunchier, rougher. "You could smell the semen on the street in front of the Troubadour," Eve Babitz said.

In the evenings, Didion would check to see that Quintana was safely tucked into her bed, her moon-shaped night-light glowing ("my moon lamp," Quintana called it), and then she would make dinner for her visitors.

One night, a baby-sitter Didion had hired told her that death floated in Didion's aura.

She had her Dexies and gin. Compazine for anxiety. Still, she mustered the energy to cook for dozens. She put MoMA place cards, with the guests' names on them, at each place setting on tables around the rooms. It was an incredible performance. "She was drunk and on drugs—no wonder she was miserable. So how come she held it together so much better than all the rest of us?" Eve Babitz wondered.

In the summer of 1968, the Dunnes threw a party for Tom Wolfe to celebrate the publication of *The Electric Kool-Aid Acid Test*. "We invited one hundred people," Dunne said. "[A]fter the first 250 showed up, we stopped counting." Describing the party to one interviewer, he said, "It was a fucking zoo."

Nick's thirteen-year-old boy, Griffin, had heard Janis Joplin was going to make an appearance at the party, so he talked Lenny into letting him go. At some point in the evening, a bald German man who seemed to be experiencing a bad acid trip latched onto the boy, asking his help getting settled somewhere. "I thought it was Colonel Klink" from the television show *Hogan's Heroes*, Griffin said. It was the film director Otto Preminger.

Joplin arrived at around ten-thirty, while Dunne was eating in the kitchen: "Chicken salad. Glasses of dry sherry," he said. She asked him to get her a little brandy. "[W]hen I gave it to her in a snifter, she said, 'What're you doing? Saving it?'" "She had just done a concert," Didion recalled. She wanted the brandy in a water tumbler, with a shot of Bénédictine in it. Tom Wolfe remembered that, just before Joplin "passed out on the divan, she said, 'I paid my dues. I paid my dues.'" Two years later, she'd die on Franklin Avenue, in room 109 of the Landmark Motel, a Polynesian-themed monstrosity—a favorite of rock stars, said the the Byrds' David Crosby, because of the "convenience of being close to street dealers." She shot a balloon of smack. It was unusually potent; this same supply killed eight other people that weekend. Days later, the word on Franklin Avenue was that this was the best dope going: "It's so strong it OD'd Janis."

If Didion had been given to metaphor, her house was the perfect emblem of dread: a huge, unmanageable space where, at any moment, the pipes might burst. Slush, rushing above and below you. She stuck to her role in the kitchen, stirring simmering pots, staring at a line from the Karl Shapiro poem: "It is raining in California." She thought of the Hoover Dam, which she had visited not long ago for a possible *Saturday Evening Post* column: all that surging energy held in check. She remembered the cranes and the generators and the transformers, the hundred-ton steel shaft piercing the glassy surface. Organization. Control. She remembered one of the workers telling her the dam's marble star map fixed forever the dam's dedication date. He said it was for when they were all gone and the dam was left. She thought of the wind and the setting sun. She pictured torrents of water crashing through an empty world. And then she made an elaborate meal for her guests, many of whom (some of them strangers) were still in the house, asleep, when she awoke the following morning, padding barefoot over worn hardwood floors, past the brittle and crumbling window shades.

Chapter Sixteen

---�֍---

1

The year was 1968. In the late afternoons, in the slanting light, on the clay tennis court behind the house on Franklin Avenue, Quintana sat alone, pulling weeds.

On Zuma Beach in Malibu, where the Dunnes would live in just a few years, *The Planet of the Apes* crew shot a seminal scene ("We've got entertainment *and* a message in this picture," said the movie's star). Charlton Heston, one of the last humans on Earth, discovered, half buried in sand, a broken Statue of Liberty and screamed in rage at the realization that America had destroyed itself.

On March 31, 1968, aware of Gallup Polls suggesting that only 23 percent of the American people approved of his handling of the Vietnam War, Lyndon Johnson announced on television that he would not seek nor "accept the nomination of my party as your president."

On April 4, Martin Luther King Jr. was shot to death in Memphis. The following week, rioting flared in Harlem, Washington, D.C., Boston, Chicago, Newark, and Detroit.

On April 23, student protesters at Columbia University occupied the lobby of Hamilton Hall and prevented the dean from leaving his office.

On June 3, a woman claiming she was on a mission to destroy all men shot Andy Warhol.

On June 6, Robert Kennedy was assassinated in the Ambassador Hotel in Los Angeles while on his way to visit Cesar Chavez, and thank him and the farmworkers who had helped him win the California Democratic primary.

2

The underground press was poor, in every sense of the word, but it was doing a finer job than the corporate media of documenting why most Americans thought the country was self-destructing.

While Didion hit the Haight, *Time* ran a cover story on "The Hippies: Philosophy of a Subculture." The magazine's insights into the hippie philosophy went like this: "They find an almost childlike fascination in beads, blossoms, and bells"; "[i]ndoors or outdoors, any place can provide a dance floor for hippies, who think that they are undulating in motion with the universe, experiencing joy and well-being."

The papers were even worse than the magazines.

"The only American newspapers that do not leave me in the grip of a profound physical conviction that the oxygen has been cut off from my brain tissue, very probably by an Associated Press wire, are *The Wall Street Journal* . . . [though] I have a minimal interest in much of what it tells me . . . the Los Angeles *Free Press,* the Los Angeles *Open City* and the *East Village Other,*" Didion said in *The Saturday Evening Post* (whose rush toward bankruptcy gave it a certain healthy recklessness where its editorial policies were concerned). These papers spoke to her straightforwardly, though they were "amateurish and badly written," "silly," and "not sufficiently inhibited by information." All other American newspapers reeked of "mendacity" by pretending to be objective. "Do not misread me: I admire objectivity very much indeed, but I fail to see how it can be achieved if the reader does not understand the writer's particular bias . . . It is the genius of these [underground] papers that they talk directly to their readers. They assume that the reader is a friend, that he is disturbed about something, and that he will understand if they talk to him straight; the assumption of a shared language and a common ethic lends their reports a considerable cogency of style," Didion said—and here we see precisely why "Slouching Towards Bethlehem" succeeded while "The Hippies: Philosophy of a Subculture" did not.

Toward the end of her piece, she listed a central reason for the failures of the mainstream press: The papers do not tell the "real story"; rather, they speak in insider "code" and "reflect the official ethic." Over thirty years later, in *Political Fictions,* she would echo and amplify this theme.

The papers were one problem. Readers were another. *Delano* attracted little notice. Henry Robbins groused, "I find that most people east of Nevada haven't the slightest knowledge of the strike and its significance."

The book's best review appeared in *The Kansas City Star,* Dunne wrote a friend—a University of Missouri English professor said *Delano* restored one's faith in nonfiction. "A lot of shit," Dunne said, but it was good for the ego. "All I can say is, *Nosotros Venceremos.*"

Years later, once Didion and Dunne became established, he would tell interviewers they never competed. But he was clearly distressed at *Delano*'s small ripples while his publisher and editor evinced mounting excitement over *Slouching Towards Bethlehem.* He chided Robbins over talk of a book party for Joan in New York—had *Delano* not deserved a bash? Only kidding, he said, but it was a joke he would not let go.

He couldn't help but feel his *Dolittle* project was slight, though probably it would enjoy greater public interest than the grape strikes, and he discovered he didn't much care for the studio men he met. The Fox atmosphere was toxic. The sums involved in making movies, he learned, often resembled the national debts of emerging nations. And there was no shortage of self-importance.

In the Haight, Dunne's wife had grabbed the sixties by its lanky purple hair.

What did *he* have? Rex Harrison on a giraffe.

Around the house, his temper slipped over little things.

Fox pissed him off, but he liked making connections. And his foggy brother Nick was still working successfully as a film producer—Nick would soon bankroll for the screen Mart Crowley's hit play, *The Boys in the Band.* The Dunnes had begun to consider screenplays again, especially since the *The Saturday Evening Post* might blow away. A producer friend had pitched them an idea—a heart-transplant thriller featuring an ailing Howard Hughes character whose thugs kill a former Olympic athlete for his heart. They'd done a treatment. The picture never got made, but CBS bought the treatment for fifty thousand dollars, allowing the Dunnes to join the Writers Guild for health insurance.

Soon after returning from the Haight, Didion read James Mills's novel of heroin addiction in New York City, *The Panic in Needle Park.* It was a powerful love story with a driving narrative, ready-made for the movies, she believed. Her husband and her brother-in-law agreed.

Dunne thought of Jim Morrison for the lead role of the street hustler Bobby. Nick knew Morrison. So did Eve Babitz and her sister Mirandi, who designed many of Morrison's outfits, including his signature leather pants. At the beginning of 1968, the Doors were at the peak of their popularity. The New Hollywood renegades—Peter Fonda, Dennis Hopper, Terry Southern, now haunting the Magic Castle hotel just up the road from the Dunnes, writing their bike opera, *Easy Rider*—dismissed the Doors as poseurs, but the teenage children of studio executives had fallen for the pants; the band was getting movie offers and stirring the interest of avant-garde filmmakers such as Jacques Demy and Agnès Varda.

One evening in early spring, Didion and Dunne sat in on a Doors recording session. She hoped to get an article for *The Saturday Evening Post* (she captured the narcoleptic scene in her essay "The White Album"). Dunne wanted to check Morrison's suitability for *Panic*. The band was making its third album, *Waiting for the Sun*, in the Two Terrible Guys Studio near Sunset and Highland.

Two things were working against the Doors in March 1968: First, Morrison saw himself as a rock poet, but the band's growing popularity meant their producer, Paul Rothchild, saw them as a hit machine. He had rejected Morrison's more ambitious music, such as "Celebration of the Lizard," for poppier tunes like "Hello, I Love You." Morrison was unhappy and losing interest in recording. Also, by this time, on a daily basis he was regularly putting away two shots of whiskey and a six-pack of beer.

These facts meant the Doors were no longer "the Norman Mailers of the Top Forty," as Didion called them. Nor was rock music, in general, the force it had been. "Protest songs are dead," Roger McGuinn, the Byrds' head songwriter, had declared. "I don't see anything is to be gained by marching around with a sign or anything."

Didion's essay "The White Album" offers the Doors' session as an example of the anomie freezing the culture in the late 1960s. At first, Morrison is not in the studio; everyone is waiting for him so that they can get on with their work; when he actually arrives, no one notices. The musicians speak as if "from behind some disabling aphasia." Didion says, "There was a sense that no one was going to leave the room, ever." Unforgettably, she presents an image of Morrison lighting a match and deliberately lowering it "to the fly of his black vinyl pants."

In fact, Eve Babitz told me, Morrison burst into the studio, drunk, towing a couple of blitzed young girls. He *did* light matches, but he tossed them at Didion, flirting and laughing.

She did not get her interview for *The Saturday Evening Post*.

Dunne did not get a star, that night, for *The Panic in Needle Park*.

His temper did not abate and the couple's tensions escalated.

"Each of us was mad at the other half the time," Didion recalled of this period. Describing young couples, she said, "You fight because you don't understand each other."

Stoned guests filled the house (a friend of Bud Trillin's had come and stayed the night and gotten profoundly drunk; she threw up, and the stain matched the pattern in the carpet, maybe even improving it a little, which told Dunne something about the house he occupied). Sometimes strangers followed Dunne home from the market, veering off in the direction of the Landmark Motel when they realized he had noticed them. The jitters were increasing. And Joan Didion was about to become Joan Didion.

At Christmas, the couple enjoyed a brief trip on a cruise ship skirting the coast of Mexico. And in the spring of 1968, they shared a splendid time on Mount Shasta, camping in a tent in a wilderness a quarter mile from a hippie farmhouse. *Esquire* had asked Dunne to write a piece on communal life in California. It seemed Easterners couldn't get their fill of macrobiotniks and goat-milk drinkers. Quintana stayed with her grandparents in Sacramento. Didion had bought a large white dog and named it Prince Albert. Albert ran through sunny meadows while Didion sat naked at her husband's typewriter by the bank of a noisy creek.

Thank God for magazine work. It made them flush. It kept them engaged.

It's worth recounting a few of the assignments they accepted during this period, to illustrate how busy they were (and how often Quintana remained apart from them). Prior to *this* assignment, Dunne had gone to Death Valley to write about car wrecks on empty blacktops; he'd gone to the Owens Valley to learn firsthand that "Manifest Destiny" was nothing more than a journey from "waterhole to waterhole." For *The Saturday Evening Post*, Didion had visited Alcatraz's empty cells, finding crumpled on the floor an old Easter service program: *"Why seek ye the living among the dead?"*; she had taken a brief trip east, to see the "lawns of the men" who had built the great railroads, leaving nothing behind "but the shadows of migrainous women, and the pony carts waiting for the long-dead children."

Most disturbingly, Dunne had spent a couple days at Montana's Malmstrom Air Force Base, headquarters of the Strategic Air Command's 341st Strategic Missile Wing. He flew over stiff fields glazed with ice to see the fruit of the Bevatron: the nuclear missile silos piercing the ground, and the young soldiers in charge of the birds, each armed with a snub-nosed .38 in case a colleague went berserk.

As the Dunnes' friend Jane Howard, a *Life* correspondent, once put it, magazines—bad as they were—served as "my arena, my stage, the channel for most of my energies." To work for magazines was "to possess a dizzying degree of what [the poet] Marianne Moore [called] accessibility of experience."

Plus, in 1968 you could fly from L.A. to San Francisco for twelve dollars a pop. You could run off to do a story and be home by midnight. Or your husband could fly up for dinner with you at Ernie's if you were stuck in the Bay Area on a lengthy piece.

Together, now, the couple shared a column in *The Saturday Evening Post*, "Points West," trading the writing chores every other month. This was far more satisfying to Didion than trying to publish fiction regularly, in spite of thinking of herself as a novelist. Her short story "When Did Music Come This Way? Children Dear, Was It Yesterday?," written three years earlier, had been rejected by more than two dozen magazines ("so depressing that I'm going to sit under a cloud of angst and gloom all afternoon . . . I'm sorry we are seldom inclined to give our readers this bad a time," said an editor at *Good Housekeeping*). Finally, Didion dumped the story into an obscure literary journal, *The Denver Quarterly*, for fifty bucks.

So she welcomed her magazine work. She taped inside her closet door a packing list so she could head out on a story without stopping to think: "*2 skirts / 2 jerseys or leotards / 1 pullover sweater / 2 pair shoes / stockings / bra . . . cigarettes / bourbon . . . aspirin, prescriptions, Tampax.*" She never took a watch, she tells us in "The White Album." She'd always have to call Los Angeles and ask Dunne what time it was. If it was early evening, she knew her baby girl would be out picking weeds on the tennis court.

3

"Pretty Nancy" didn't know who'd arrived at her door. If she'd understood how this demure young reporter felt about her, she'd never have let her in.

In the spring of 1968, Governor and Nancy Reagan were living in a rented white brick house with steep Tudor peaks, at 1341 45th Street in Sacramento, in a neighborhood known as the "Fab 40s." The intersection of Forty-sixth and J had once been a streetcar turnaround for the J Street line, so it was unusually wide; the neighborhood's lots were excessive, the homes lavish.

The Reagans had occupied the Governor's Mansion at Sixteenth and H—the old Steffens place beloved of Didion—for only four months before Mrs. Reagan declared it a fire trap, not to her taste. Now, for twelve hundred dollars a month, "payable by the state to a group of Reagan's friends," Didion wrote, the governor and his wife enjoyed a more modern space, with six bedrooms and a pool.

On the sunny spring morning when Mrs. Reagan opened her door to greet Joan Didion, with whom she'd agreed to talk for *The Saturday Evening Post,* she smiled. "That, apparently, was my big mistake," she would write in her memoir, *My Turn,* the title of which revealed her lifelong bitterness at the press.

"I . . . enjoyed the time we spent together," Mrs. Reagan wrote. The formal interview was civil and pleasant. She'd thought they were getting along fine. Some weeks later, on a plane trip to Chicago, she happened to notice a copy of *The Saturday Evening Post* and thumbed through it eagerly. She was appalled to find Didion's piece "dripping with sarcasm," beginning with the title, "Pretty Nancy." "[M]y smile was described as 'a study in frozen insincerity,'" Mrs. Reagan wrote. "Well, I wasn't insincere. And I smile, I'm afraid, the way I smile. I couldn't help but wonder: Would she have liked it better if I had snarled? She had obviously written the story in her mind before she ever met me."

"It was kind of a mean piece. Even those of us who weren't Nancy fans thought this . . . was over the top," said Lou Cannon, then bureau chief for the *San Jose Mercury News.*

Mrs. Reagan never recovered from the insult. From then on, wary of all reporters, she was especially suspicious of females. "My biggest fault, it seems, was that I was too polite, too much a lady," she wrote (Old Hollywood in a sadly debauched world). She came to believe that one reason female reporters went after her was that "some women aren't all that crazy about a woman who wears size fours, and . . . seems to have no trouble staying slim." This would hardly account for Didion's reaction to her.

To avoid further betrayals, Mrs. Reagan tightly choreographed all her future interviews. This had been Didion's point: A former actress, Nancy Reagan represented the formal entrance into politics of the studio mind-set, where all actions, on and off the screen, are scripted in advance, taken care of by ad executives. That day on Forty-fifth Street, Didion had been flabbergasted by the arrival of a television crew who considered "watch[ing] Nancy Reagan being watched by me, or I could watch Nancy Reagan being watched by the three of them, or one of the cameramen could step back and do a *cinéma vérité* study of the rest of us watching and being watched by one another." The news people set up a scene in Mrs. Reagan's garden where she would fake the nipping of a flower bud for the cameras. "Fake the nip, yeah," said one of the cameramen. "Fake the nip."

Didion never changed her mind about "Pretty Nancy." In 1987, following press reports that Mrs. Reagan was an "aggressive manipulator of the affairs of state, who, after three months of acrimonious trying, had succeeded in ousting . . . [the] White House chief of staff," Didion reiterated that she was "not one of Nancy Reagan's greatest admirers": "Her only interest is protecting her and his face to the world. She has no intrinsic interest in politics."

Just two ladies chatting in the garden, that's all. But while Nancy faked the nip, elsewhere in Ronald Reagan's California, hidden from the hippies in the Haight, out of sight of the investors who'd bought the governor a house, 75 percent of the ammunition used in Vietnam was being shipped from Port Chicago, on a spit in the San Francisco Bay: 100,000 tons of shells and rockets a month, moved from the magazine at the U.S. Naval Weapons Station in the hills above the port to the loading piers less than a mile from the city proper. On assignment for *The Saturday Evening Post,* Dunne drove out there one day. "It has the feeling of the dust bowl," he wrote. "A windmill flopped aimlessly in the breeze. Cattle grazed, and bales of hay punctuated the sunburnt hills that contain hundreds of thousands of tons of death." No one working at the port seemed to know or remember that one night, in the summer of 1944, two munitions ships exploded, killing 322 stevedores and shattering windows throughout the city, sending shock waves fifty miles distant.

Dunne visited an army induction center in Oakland, where Berkeley students arrived early in the mornings to yell at recruiters, then shouldered their book bags and hurried off to their eight o'clock classes. He was allowed to tour Building 590 at the Oakland Army Base, "hot and close and smell[ing] of sweat." This was where enlisted soldiers spent their last twenty-four hours before boarding buses to Travis Air Force Base, halfway between Oakland and Sacramento, to be lifted on a World Airways Boeing 707 to Anchorage and then to Japan's Yokota Air Base and then to Bien Hoa, South Vietnam. Building 590 housed two thousand men. "Dozens of vending machines disgorge an endless variety of coffee, milk, soft drinks, ice cream, sandwiches, pastry, Nalley's Hot Tamales, Nalley's Hot Enchiladas, Nalley's Chili Con Carne," Dunne wrote. "In the latrine, men have written all over the walls the date of their departure." Above a phone booth, a sign read YOUR LAST CHANCE.

He dropped in one day on a Quaker meeting hall in a tumble-down section of Pasadena "where the rich used to live, second- and third-generation money from the East in an atmosphere so sedate . . . the only sound was the hardening of arteries," he said. Now it was a neighborhood of crumbling garden apartments. There, members of the Resistance, a New Left group, offered sanctuary to draft resisters and boys who'd gone AWOL. These were not conscientious objectors, despite the activists' attempt to make them over into rebels. They were lost kids, Dunne thought, boys who'd enlisted because their parents wanted them to and who found they couldn't cut it. They could go to Canada, but the group wanted them to stay, take a public stand, risk court-martial and prison to draw attention to the system's evils. More to the point, said one of the boys, "If Canada is a bummer, you're stuck there for the rest of your life."

These were fissures in the land of Reagan, and they needed close study. Nearly half a million American troops had been deployed overseas. Now, even *Time* magazine, which had once censored Dunne's attempts to tell the truth about the war, was asking, "How many men must the U.S. send?" Reagan was being coy about his plans. At a GOP governor's meeting in Grand Teton, he had recently told the press he had no intention of ever running for president, but "if the Republican Party comes beating at my door, I wouldn't say, 'Get lost, fellows.'" This was why it mattered if "Pretty Nancy" faked the nip.

4

Didion's profile of the governor's wife appeared in the June 1, 1968, issue of *The Saturday Evening Post*, days after FSG's official release date for *Slouching Towards Bethlehem*. Perhaps to avoid the possible surge of attention (*might* there be attention?), Didion took herself and her family to Hawaii.

The first inkling she'd had that her book might get noticed came at a signing at L.A.'s Pickwick Bookstore in mid-May. She sold thirty copies and felt overwhelmed that the store stocked as many of her books as it did of Arthur Hailey's ready-for-the-box-office *Airport*.

Heady but nerve-racking. There were other reasons for escaping the mainland. *The Saturday Evening Post,* continuing to bleed cash, had just undergone a personnel shuffle; no one knew what this meant for the future, but the Dunnes were worried. And then in March, Robert Giroux, a quiet, genial man, had come to Los Angeles for a visit. Didion had been dismayed to learn how poor the lines of communication were at her new publisher. The Dunnes took their guest to the Bistro. Halfway through dinner, Giroux told Didion he had just finished *Slouching Towards Bethlehem,* liked it, and wondered if she would ever consider turning her hand to fiction. After an awkward pause, Didion told him she'd published a novel. "I hope we get a look at your next one," Giroux said. While Didion's eyes darted, Dunne changed the subject.

So Hawaii was just the ticket. On the beach, Didion was simply "Quintana's mommy." The hotel desk clerk remembered Quintana's name and said hello to her every morning. Didion could be "mindlessly happy" in Honolulu, she said, "good-natured to an extent that would surprise my acquaintances on the mainland. The place is manageable. I know what I will find" on the beach, among the life-insurance salesmen on incentive trips, the San Francisco divorcées, and the NBC television executives. A new TV drama, *Hawaii Five-O,* started filming that year, and the series' star, Jack Lord, booked rooms at the Kahala for all the guest stars. The sixties seemed not to have happened here. All the women dressed like Pat Nixon, in turquoise and yellow, waiting for cars under pink porte cocheres.

Outside the cordoned-off sections of sand, reserved for the patrons of the large luxury hotels, one might occasionally find a roll of barbed wire left over from the war, or overhear old-timers talking about the fires at Pearl Harbor—how, after the Japanese attack, older children from the public schools were given unloaded guns and told to go guard the reservoirs. Or one might hear an argument about how the war had been a good thing; at least it had modernized the islands and broken the hold of the colonial families who'd controlled all the sugar.

On the hotels' private beaches, one could ignore the fragile tourism and defense economy on which this spun-sugar paradise had been built. One could pretend it wasn't an armed camp. At the Kahala or the Royal Hawaiian, Didion could imagine young matrons in print dresses and tight little hats stepping off the *Lurline,* trailing valets and nurses and steamer trunks. She could believe she heard on the wind someone performing "My Little Grass Shack in Kealakekua Hawaii" the way a distant aunt used to sing it back in Sacramento.

Looking across a golf course, she could see a vast walled house, its blue-tiled roof reflecting sun diamonds back at the sea. Each day she watched the maid unlock the house's front gate and rouse the English sheepdog there. She wanted that house.

Papers came a day or two late from the mainland. On the morning after the California primary, people stood around the newsstand at the Royal Hawaiian reading about the heavy voter turnout. None of them knew that at that very moment Bobby Kennedy lay dying in L.A.'s Good Samaritan Hospital.

During the afternoons, Dunne left Didion alone with Quintana to visit the Armed Forces Recreation Center at Fort DeRussy in Honolulu. Troops from Saigon, Danang, and Bien Hoa came for five-day leaves to meet their wives and mothers. Maybe he'd get a story. One day he heard an orientation officer warn the troops, "You are at all times prey to subversive elements. These subversives will try to induce you to desert. If you become suspicious of any subversive elements, contact the proper military authorities and safeguard your country."

Late one afternoon, Dunne agreed to watch Quintana, and Didion got a chance to wander off alone. She dropped by the Punchbowl again. Banyan trees and rain trees waved in the center of the crater, over the fresh, moist graves. Mothers and fathers wept in curling mist.

She went to Schofield Barracks, where James Jones had set his mighty novel *From Here to Eternity*. The base was located near the Wahiawa Reservoir, in a scrabbly part of the island, a mix of red dirt and crushed white coral, smoky with cane fires, plagued with signs for massage parlors and collard greens. Jones's book made *Slouching Towards Bethlehem* seem paltry. And yet no one here seemed to have read it. The bookstores didn't stock it.

Diesel slicked the air.

She remembered afternoons she'd spent as a girl on army posts, wearing a red poppy on her dress, following her father around the country. She remembered playing with dogs on the lawns of lieutenant colonels, sitting in clear sunshine and reading books that seemed to matter. These days, the national press was reporting that residents of Bikini Atoll, living in intolerable slums on a place called Kill Island, were still unable to return to their home, twenty-two years after the atomic tests.

As it was in the beginning, is now and ever shall be, world without end.

The ashy yellow light, slanting now through the canebrakes, appeared to burden the limbs of the palms.

5

Didion had a busy June. In addition to visiting Hawaii, while *Slouching To-wards Bethlehem* made its way to reviewers' desks, she was diagnosed in the outpatient psychiatric clinic at St. John's Hospital in Santa Monica with severe alienation and "reality contact" impairment. The Rorschach, The-matic Apperception, and Sentence Completion tests, as well as the Minne-sota Multiphasic Personality Inventory suggested "a personality in process of deterioration"; "the content of patient's responses is highly unconventional and frequently bizarre, filled with sexual and anatomical preoccupations"; she has a "fundamentally pessimistic, fatalistic, and depressive view of the world around her. It is as though she feels deeply that all human effort is fore-doomed to failure, a conviction which seems to push her further into a de-pendent, passive withdrawal."

That she submitted to these tests as her book materialized suggests the overwhelming levels of anxiety, anticipation, and pressure caused by publi-cation, a common circumstance for authors. To some degree, her profile fits *any* "creative personality," particularly in the letdown after an especially fer-tile span, when a project is done, one relinquishes control of it and can only await the reactions of strangers.

She wrote that her breakdown did not seem to her "an inappropriate response to the summer of 1968"—a thematic aperçu within "The White Album"'s tour of social disintegration, but a swift elision of her personal trou-bles. Certainly, in the wake of the spring's political assassinations and campus upsets, no one felt sanguine. "Many saw the unleashing of a dark, latent psy-chosis in the national character, a stain that had its start with the first settlement of a hostile continent," *Time* reported. Recently, in New Orleans, District Attorney Jim Garrison, in a high-profile trial, had raised the possi-bility of conspiracy in the killing of JFK, lifting the lid on Miami's Cuban exile community and certain connections in that city with the mob, rekin-dling public doubts about the veracity of the Warren Report; Didion was not alone in believing she shared, in the words of her doctors, "a world of people moved by strange, conflicted, poorly comprehended, and, above all, devious motivations." She lived in the very neighborhood of cultural meltdown, glamour gone groovy gone gritty, with weekly demonstrations and threats of violence just blocks away on the Strip; she lived in the Hollywood rumor mill, steeped in stories of bigger and bigger parties, harder and harder drugs. Tales of orgies fluttered like scented envelopes up and down the hills. It had become chic to keep a pair of handcuffs in the bedroom. "[L]ibidinal preoc-cupations . . . distorted and bizarre" (a concern for Didion's analysts) would have appeared in the psychiatric profiles of anyone north of La Brea.

Could Didion really have been surprised by the results of her tests? As the young California poet Robert Hass had written, "It became clear to me that alienation was a state approaching sanity, a way of being human in a mon-strously inhuman world, and that feeling human was a useful form of politi-cal subversion."

In fact, Didion's push to finish her essay collection, the pressure of the looming contract for an uncompleted novel, her husband's unhappiness with the reception of *his* book, as well as the rigorous travel schedule they main-tained as reporters for *The Saturday Evening Post*, was reason enough for "an attack of vertigo, nausea, and a feeling that she was going to pass out."

A psychosis in the national character was never the point. And Elavil would not be the answer.

In roughly the same period, personally and professionally, Didion responded to a *Harper's Bazaar* questionnaire, "Singular Voices: 100 Women in Touch with Our Times." Aside from asserting that the most significant change in our society was its "total breakdown," her answers sketched a woman gener-ally at peace with herself, insofar as peace was possible on a daily basis in a tumultuous time, in the midst of a hectic career. She seemed satisfied with her work—it was as "vital" to her as anything else in her life, and she would be "bereft" without it; she did not feel stifled in a male-dominated world—she could not imagine accomplishing anything without the encouragement of men; she cooked for relaxation and avoided all housework and laundry, leav-ing those chores to the maid, unless there was an emergency; she did not feel she had ever made a "significant choice"—"One day and one thing led to an-other and pretty soon a pattern was set, irreversible."

How do you feel when you consider that you will probably live longer than most men?

"It never occurs to me," she said.

6

In publishing circles, summer is generally considered a slow time for serious books: It's beach-read season. But in the spring and summer of 1968, while the president was reading about the decline of the King of Beasts in *Aesop's*

Fables, Farrar, Straus and Giroux released three volumes the critics called essential to understanding the culture. The books were all associated with Henry Robbins.

They were Donald Barthelme's groundbreaking short story collection, *Unspeakable Practices, Unnatural Acts,* Tom Wolfe's *The Electric Kool-Aid Acid Test,* and Didion's *Slouching Towards Bethlehem.*

Of Barthelme, William Gass wrote in *The New York Review of Books,* "[He offers] a dizzying series of swift, smooth modulations, a harmony of discords"—the new national speech. He chronicles our use of "love, wine, cigarettes, and hobbies, in our barricades, to shore against our ruin," and he reports that it "is not going well."

In *The New York Times,* C. D. B. Bryan said Wolfe's "enthusiasm and literary fireworks . . . make it difficult for the reader to remain detached" while trying to determine if the counterculture is dangerous to, or prophetic about, America's future.

And Didion's old friend Dan Wakefield said flatly in *The New York Times Book Review* that *Slouching Towards Bethlehem* brought together "some of the finest magazine pieces published by anyone in this country in recent years. Now that Truman Capote has pronounced that such work may achieve the stature of 'art,' perhaps it is possible for this collection to be recognized as it should be: not as a better or worse example of what some people call 'mere journalism,' but as a rich display of some of the best prose written today in this country."

Wakefield's review made an issue of disagreements in the press about a new form of journalism, debates increasing in frequency and vehemence since the 1965 appearance of Capote's *In Cold Blood* and Jimmy Breslin's columns in the *New York Herald Tribune.* In the weeks before *Slouching Towards Bethlehem's* rollout, the publication of Norman Mailer's *The Armies of the Night,* about the march on the Pentagon in October 1967, intensified the arguments.

Alfred Kazin nicely framed the stakes Mailer had raised: "Mailer presents this book as [a] nonfiction novel," he said. Like many contemporary American writers, he has been living the "'crisis of the novel.' He . . . [has been] so sensitive to politics, power and society in America, so engrossed in the search for solutions and revelations that the moralist . . . left little time to the novelist." Now, it was the "coalescence of American disorder (always an obsession of Mailer's) with all the self-confidence he feels as a novelist . . . that has produced 'Armies of the Night' . . . [I]t is a fact that only a born novelist could have written a piece of history so intelligent, mischievous, penetrating and alive."

Said Gay Talese, Mailer's fellow traveler, "The new journalism, though often reading like fiction, is not fiction. It is, or should be, as reliable as the most reliable reportage although it seeks a larger truth than is possible through the mere compilation of verifiable facts, the use of direct quotations, and adherence to the rigid organizational style of the older form. The new journalism allows, demands in fact, a more imaginative approach to reporting, and it permits the writer to inject himself into the narrative if he wishes."

This is a variation of Didion's admiration of the reporting available in the underground press. Traditionalists were disturbed by what they perceived to be a reckless disregard for objectivity and a narcissistic insistence on placing the writer front and center. It's also true that many of the attacks on the New Journalism were personal responses to Tom Wolfe's abrasive personality (in print). He deliberately irritated literary purists. In 1972, writing with typical insouciance in *New York* magazine, he'd summarize his view of the skirmish: The New Journalists "never dreamed that anything they were going to write for newspapers or magazines would wreak such evil havoc in the literary world . . . causing panic, dethroning the novel as the number one literary genre, starting the first new direction in American literature in half a century . . ."

It was this sort of braggadocio in his attack on *The New Yorker* in the *Herald Tribune* ("Tiny Mummies! The True Story of the Ruler of 43rd Street's Land of the Walking Dead!") that raised Dwight Macdonald's hackles. He published a two-part piece in *The New York Review of Books* entitled "Parajournalism, or Tom Wolfe and His Magic Writing Machine" (August 26, 1965, and February 3, 1966). "A new kind of journalism is being born," he wrote. "It might be called 'parajournalism' from the Greek *para,* 'beside' . . . 'against': something similar in form but different in function . . . It is a bastard form, having it both ways, exploiting the factual authority of journalism, and the atmospheric license of fiction. Entertainment rather than information is the aim of its producers . . ."

This literary infighting held little interest for readers—or for most writers, who just went about their business—but a few points emerged from the battle that shed light on the changing nature of American literature, and suggested why, taken together, Barthelme, Wolfe, and Didion were essential to understanding the current state of the culture. It was precisely the "crisis of the novel" that birthed Donald Barthelme: Fearful that traditional literary forms could not adequately present the realities of our monstrously inhuman world, he had created a language for fiction embodying, like a trash compactor, our wasteful, contradictory speech, and, by extension, our mixed self-perceptions. From the opposite direction, traditional journalistic forms proved inadequate to contain the nation's growing appetite for extravagant experiences, many of them made possible by new drugs and new technologies that no one, it seemed, could control.

Like Mailer, Didion revered the novel's lyricism and interiority, but she, too, felt the genre's crisis: Story premises no longer held for her. Plot and character had gone spongy, soaked through with predictability. Like Wolfe, she wanted to report the essentials of our national life, but who knew what they were now—certainly the *Los Angeles Times* hadn't a clue, speaking, as it did, in a journalistic code chiseled decades earlier.

New language and new forms were necessary, but they would not be easily achieved. Even Wolfe stumbled along the way. In his first pass at Ken Kesey, he wrote, "So far nobody in or out of the medical profession knows exactly what LSD does to the body, chiefly because so little is known about the workings of the central nervous system as a whole." This was as stuffy as *anything* in the *Times*. For Wolfe, it took plunging into the experience to get the essence of the story. One night, he dropped 125 micrograms of acid. Instead of reporting on the drug, he found language to convey it (channeling himself through *Kesey's* trips—this was journalism, not autobiography): "The ceiling is moving—not in a crazed swirl but along its own planes its own planes of light and shadow and surface . . ."

Later, Wolfe would say, "Despite the skepticism I brought [to the story] I [was] suddenly experiencing *their* feeling. . . . If I could stop what I was doing, I would be one of the Pranksters."

Didion never went that far in the Haight. Still, as Wakefield wrote, "though her own personality does not self-indulgently intrude itself upon her subjects, it informs and illuminates them." This is what made her journalism so unique: "The reader comes to admire what can only be called the *character* of this observer at work."

In preparing the collection for publication, Didion labored hard to *shape* her character, in the way the essays appeared together as a package. It was Robbins's idea to lead with "Some Dreamers of the Golden Dream," a brilliant choice, Didion thought, as she had come to accept his view that the book reflected a native daughter's confrontation with California: her reevaluation of youthful romance, her wonder and dismay at the changes time had forced.

At the last minute, she inserted into her preface the paragraph explaining her paralysis over writing's irrelevancy, and her need to confront disorder. This sewed a thematic thread through pieces written, initially, far apart and for different reasons.

The final essay she wrote for the book, her profile of the hopeless revolutionary Michael Laski, whom she'd thought was the "cat's ass," according to Dunne, anchored another theme central to the volume: "I am comfortable with the Michael Laskis of the world, with those who live outside rather than in, those in whom the sense of dread is so acute that they turn to extreme and doomed commitments; I know something about dread myself, and appreciate the elaborate systems with which some people manage to fill the void, appreciate all the opiates of the people, whether they are as accessible as alcohol and heroin and promiscuity or as hard to come by as faith in God or History." In this seamless melding of her personality with that of her subject; the fluidity of style, combining confession with political cant, all in the same smooth rhythm; and in the sweeping, if ironic, statement about behaviors and beliefs (ending with an implicit assertion of principles), she demonstrated the advantages of the New Journalism.

It was a book of outsiders and extremists. It was a book of geographical and spiritual improbabilities. The essays, both empathetic and restrained, assumed the reader was a friend—a friend who listened to rock 'n' roll and who'd voted for Barry Goldwater. "I had a strong feeling that it was necessary, that there was no reason to trust the reporter unless you knew where the reporter was. And if you didn't know where the reporter was standing, then I really objected to the notion of objectivity . . . because it didn't seem to me very real," she said.

As for voice: *Run River* had taught her one kind of rhythm. "The fiction voice is like a liturgy, there's a lot of repetition," she said. In her nonfiction, she discovered that in addition to repetition, there were a "lot of clauses. It gets denser and denser. I'm not going to make it simple. It seems to me you can get a lot more thought in. You can make it come alive."

Nonfiction, then, could be as challenging to compose as fiction. And she had become a different writer since publishing her novel. *Run River* was the work of someone longing to live outside the bonds of history, in a lazy, unchanging current of nostalgia smelling of rice and hops. *Slouching Towards Bethlehem* was a frightened, reckless embrace of what was and what could never be, of what would flourish only briefly and then die.

On the cover, Robbins wanted a Ted Streshinsky photo of her, capturing her "beauty," her "hunted look." She was dead set against a bright "hippie" jacket (FSG *did* splash a small rainbow over the title). She preferred a jacket based around a stark black-and-white photographic image, for two reasons: This was a book of fact, and a photo would suggest that; but also, in our time, everyone knows photos can be manipulated, *blurring* fact and fiction. This would give the cover a great feeling of *now*, of *what's happening*. As for the author photo, maybe Ted's pose of her eating an apple during a hippie demonstration, she said, or a shot of her in a cell at Alcatraz: something grainy, perhaps even washed-out, something "pretty shocking," to the point of "downright mystery."

In the end, Robbins got the "hunted" look he wanted—Didion in Golden Gate Park, standing troubled, gazing into the distance, while the missing children huddle nearby. But her cover suggestions show how intensely involved she was in manufacturing her public image, off the page and on.

The attention to detail paid off. Generally, the reviews were laudatory. *Time* chided her for being "bleak and joyless"; her tone was "somewhere between Despond and Nostalgia." But the book "approaches art," the reviewer said. "What most captivates the reader is the fascination of discovering how her brittle sensibilities and flamboyant neuroses react to events . . . Didion suffers constantly, but compellingly and magically."

Gender was a major issue for reviewers. "Journalism by women is the price the man's world pays for having disappointed them. Here at their best are the unforgiving eye, the unforgiving ear, the concealed hat-pin style," wrote Melvin Maddocks in *The Christian Science Monitor*.

And *Time*'s review concluded with Didion's wish in "John Wayne: A Love Song" for a man who would take her "to that bend in the river where the cottonwoods grow." "Many young men (and older ones, too), reading her sentimental, compassionate, and appealing passages would be willing to do just that," said the magazine.

7

Tom Wolfe was a lightning rod and his exuberant style, stippled with typographical play, was rigged to pop like a can of snakes, but after the appearance of *The Armies of the Night* and *Slouching Towards Bethlehem*, no one could doubt the seriousness and power of the New Journalism, however broad the label may have been (and wildly *inaccurate*—as Jack Newfield said, "Defoe, Addison and Steele, Stephen Crane, and Mark Twain were all new journalists according to most definitions").

"In the Sixties you kept hearing that reporting was the new art form. While that was beguiling, I felt that not enough was said about how complex it had become," said Nora Sayre, one of the best journalists of the period (she was the New York correspondent for *The New Statesman*). "First, you struggled with the facts you knew and couldn't print—since you didn't want to send certain people to jail or to be subpoenaed for your confidential sources. Second, many were afraid to talk to you, fearing that they would be quoted accurately—just as much as they feared misquotation. (Valid fears.) Third, although you deplored the traditional media's distortions and felt you must correct the straight press, honesty often demanded that you report bad news from your own side."

She agreed with Robert Scholes: Ours was a hysterical age. This fact placed special burdens on storytellers. Scholes coined another new term, *Hystorians*. "The so-called stylistic excesses of such men as Norman Mailer and Tom Wolfe are in my view no more than the indispensable equipment they must employ in doing justice to our times," he said. "[H]ysteria cannot be assimilated and conveyed by one totally aloof." He joined the chorus decrying the faded formulas of old-fashioned journalism, which merely supported a given paper's editorial policies. "The hystorian fights this tendency toward formula with his own personality," Scholes said.

In the simplest, gravest terms, this meant being a witness to your time. A solemn responsibility. "I am not the society in microcosm. I am a thirty-four-year-old woman with long straight hair and an old bikini bathing suit and bad nerves," Didion would assert in one of her essays. And yet she protested too much. She ended this same piece by tracking the "movements of the Army day" at Schofield Barracks and concluded, "James Jones had known a simple truth." "[T]he Army was nothing more or less than life itself." If the whole is the sum of its parts, then the life of our times rests in each of us, particularly in those devoted to the act, and the art, of witnessing. A dedicated hystorian (in an "old bikini bathing suit"), Didion felt this in her bones.

In the late summer of 1968, after her return from Hawaii, after the flurry of reviews for *Slouching Towards Bethlehem*, and her visit to St. John's Hospital, she and her fellow reporters would need to strain their witnessing powers to the limit to keep pace with what appeared to be the rapid disintegration of America's democratic process.

With LBJ's weary admission of failure and the murder of Bobby Kennedy, the choosing of the new president was cast in an elegiac light. The Mass mourning for Kennedy would be the last image of unity—of diversity *truly* coalescing—in this troubled political season.

In August, during the Republican and Democratic National Conventions, and particularly during the violence in Chicago, it was as if the war in Vietnam had spread across the globe, to be fought in front of Macy's.

REACH OUT AND GRAB THE GREATEST SUMMER EVER, said banners on the sides of Chicago police trucks.

"Chicago is a police state," Paul Krassner, editor of the underground magazine *The Realist*, warned his readers. "The cops want to turn our parks into graveyards."

"We will try to develop a Community of Consciousness," Abbie Hoffman said.

And in an example of what Norman Mailer called "hippie prose," Ed Sanders of the rock band the Fugs expressed many young people's expectations of their week in the Windy City: "[J]oy, nooky, circle groups, laughing, dancing, sharing, grass, magic, meditation, music, theatre, and weirdo mutant-jissomed chromosome-damaged ape-chortles."

The stage was rigged to explode.

While convention chair Carl Albert tried to keep order in the hall, wheezing his pinched Okie vowels at the cameras, and Hawaii senator Daniel Inouye broke protocol, standing at the podium and reciting the country's perils rather than cheering his candidate, kids on the streets greased their faces with Vaseline, anticipating tear gas. Tear gas set your breath on fire. In Lincoln Park, Allen Ginsberg's Hindu chanting sounded like a death rattle, ravaged by the poison. Behind him, William Burroughs stood like a ghost, wearing a gray fedora.

In McCarthy headquarters inside the Hilton Hotel, people tore up sheets to make bandages for victims of police clubs. The city sealed its manhole covers with hot tar so that no one could hide below street level.

Stop, children, look around.

There's a man with a gun over there.

For most observers, the debacle at the Democratic Convention was the summer's main political news. Didion saw it differently. In a city run by a thuggish mayor, a place where money moved on rivers of blood, where the smell of watery shit seeping from slaughterhouses still hung like prophecy in the air, the horror in the streets was not surprising.

The real story had taken place weeks earlier in Miami, a city Lyndon Johnson had once described as "not American."

It was a city of old Cubans seething with resentment, armed with packets of plastique; of late-night deals at the edges of airport runways; and the story was, the Republicans had come to town. The country's deep pockets had gathered for cocktails in the lobby of the Fontainebleau Hotel. The most ambitious men in the nation were there: John Wayne. Barry Goldwater. Ronald Reagan. Billy Graham. Richard Nixon arrived to the fanfare of two marching bands playing "Nixon's the One," while blond cheerleaders danced beneath floating red balloons and Graham proclaimed him more realistic than Jesus. It was *his* time—the "time, I think, when the man and the moment in history come together," Nixon said.

While Nixon stood in the convention hall, weaving a sweet narrative of his journey to success from the bosom of a peace-loving, football-playing family, from nights as a boy listening to distant train whistles and dreaming of "faraway places where he'd like to go," the real story found its syntax in the daily numbers of war dead in Vietnam, the bodies flown to the Punchbowl Crater—for in defeat, four years earlier, Barry Goldwater had managed to stamp his policies on the political Right. His passions guided the party now (the party's other venerable leader, the more temperate Dwight Eisenhower, languished that summer in Walter Reed Hospital following a series of heart attacks). The war had become America's major global initiative.

But here was the other part of the story. The "country had learned an almost unendurable lesson—its history in Asia was next to done," Mailer reported from Miami. Goldwater's vision "depressed some part of America's optimism . . . the country had begun to wear away inside."

And now, riding these vast crosscurrents, California was about to seize the White House.

Nixon's California was the Golden Land of Golf, of Puritanism and austerity.

Didion had traveled sun-hardened stretches in the center of the state, where these concepts failed to stick, as did the idea of America as a cultural or economic force. In *that* California, people spoke in tongues and played with rattlesnakes in defiance of Satan or Uncle Sam. They'd put a gun in your face if you came anywhere near them. They'd pick up young hitchhikers off the sides of the roads and vanish with them, fates unknown, in the hypnotic memory wipe of ceaselessly moving metal. That California, too, would accompany Tricky Dick to the banks of the Potomac, whether he knew it or not.

It was his time. But his time was beyond him. Beyond us all. That was the story told in Miami in the summer of 1968.

8

All fall, at Hollywood parties, presidential politics topped the talk. Only here, it seemed, could the result be uncertain.

The liberal hopefuls reminded Didion of Las Vegas wedding couples she'd witnessed outside the twenty-four-hour chapels, stumbling, drunk and impulsive, into a dream of happily ever after. The A-listers would gather in the hills above the Strip, past the old Mocambo, at Sammy Davis Jr.'s house for Hollywood "political action" parties, where, Didion said, "political ideas are reduced to choices between the good (equality is good) and the bad (genocide is bad)." While Hollywood gentry debated the finer points of the war or expressed continuing support for the grape strikes or discussed whether or not William Styron's *The Confessions of Nat Turner* promoted racism, the disaffected children of the people who used to sip the Mocambo's vodka tonics and dance to Old Blue Eyes were throwing bottles at cops in front of Ciro's while the Byrds floated eight miles high.

One night, at a party in Bel-Air, Didion met Nora Ephron, a fine young journalist (she was ever sharp, and yet the *Newsweek* staff put her to work in its *mailroom*!). They'd become great friends—they agreed that writing never helped them understand a damn thing. Didion was also introduced to Roman Polanski and Sharon Tate. That night, Didion wore the dress in which she'd married, the backless silk dress she'd bought the day JFK was shot. Polanski spilled a glass of wine on it. The red stain seemed portentous, and would come to seem more so; only half kidding, one of Didion's friends began to call the area around Franklin Avenue the "senseless-killing neighborhood." Even in a year of chaos—perhaps *especially* in a year of chaos—people sought symbols and narrative links, though Ephron and Didion could have told them not to bother.

Just that October, a few miles from Didion's house, in Laurel Canyon, a former silent movie actor, Ramon Novarro, had been murdered in his home by a pair of self-described hustlers looking for stardom or cash or *something* they felt Novarro had promised them. (A hustler, said one of the killers, is "someone who can talk—not just to men, to women, too . . . There are a lot of lonely people in this town, man.")

Two blocks from the Dunnes' home stood the Black Dahlia house, resembling a Mayan temple. The couple had heard rumors that, in the forties, in the basement of the house, a prominent L.A. physician had tortured and sliced in half an aspiring actress, Elizabeth Short (aka the Black Dahlia, presumably because of the color of her hair). The doctor's son, Steve Hodel, suspected his father of the murder, and suggested a connection between the Hollywood killing and the dismemberment, years ago, of Suzanne Degnan in Chicago. Dunne would base some of his novel *True Confessions* on details from the Black Dahlia case.

Crazy violence was becoming a way to reckon time in California—normally difficult, said Eve Babitz, "since there [were] no winters." There were just "earthquakes, parties, and certain people. And songs." But the best-by date had passed. Most of the songs, overproduced, too smooth, had started to blur: "The Byrds and the Beach Boys and the Mamas and the Papas . . . sounded as though they came out of a Frostie Freeze machine pipe organ."

This was also true of the prose in the corporate press. Politics. Crime. All part of the Great American Muzak.

Late in 1968, the *Los Angeles Times* named Didion one of its Women of the Year, along with Greer Garson and Nancy Reagan. Didion was celebrated for her achievement as the author of *Slouching Towards Bethlehem*—for becoming Joan Didion. As she would later write in her essay "The White Album," she was performing, day by day, barely up to the task. She was just like her mother, improvising, wearing her red suede sandals, her cashmere leggings, hoop earrings, and big enameled beads.

The newspaper editors placed her among Leaders, Pillars of the Community, Centers of the American Family.

"We hear sirens in the night," Richard Nixon had said back in August, asserting *his* vision of leadership. "We see Americans hating each other, fighting each other, killing each other." No matter. "Tonight I see the face of a child. . . . [H]e's an American child. . . . He is a poet. . . . He is everything we ever hoped to be and everything we dare to dream to be."

American children, raised by Women of the Year.

Because of them, Nixon said, "I believe that historians will recall that 1968 marked the beginning of the American generation in world history."

In the crash pad next to the house, a couple had taken to making love on the lawn, in full view of Quintana's bedroom window.

"Where you was?" Quintana, wearing fuzzy pink slippers, asked her mother whenever Didion returned home from a party or a shopping trip.

In the evenings, Quintana bounce-stepped onto the tennis court. "I remember watching her weed it, kneeling on fat baby knees, the ragged stuffed animal she addressed as 'Bunny Rabbit' at her side," Didion wrote, heartbroken, a few years after her daughter had died.

Chapter Seventeen

———— ❈ ————

1

The "snake book."

Blood and champagne.

This is how the era would end.

Nora Sayre reports that, during the Nixon presidency, Air Force One was stocked with "an adequate supply" of the president's blood type "in the likelihood of attempted assassination," and "cases of American champagne for toasting his hosts at a reciprocal banquet." "That vast jet, pounding through the skies full of blood and bubbly, stayed with me as a symbol for peacekeeping" during this period, Sayre wrote.

"Mommy's snake book" was Quintana's name for Didion's second novel, *Play It As It Lays.* When the novel appeared in 1970, it came in a bold jacket designed by the distinctive book artist Janet Halverson. A rattler's silhouette curled across the stark white cover, its forked tongue flicking a small setting sun. Didion worked hard on the book throughout 1968 (making extensive notes) and 1969 (composing the chapters). Quintana's earliest memories of her mother's industry nestled in the reptile's coils. The creature charmed her mom, dragged her away in the drafty old house. Didion would sit on the sun porch—the smell of aloe wafting through the windows—and say she needed to work. In the evenings, when there wasn't a party, she'd light votive candles and set them on the living room windowsills. She'd sip bourbon and reread the pages she'd written that day.

Quintana danced to the eight-track player: the Mamas and the Papas, "Do You Want to Dance?" "I wanna dance," Quintana shouted. Years later, in *Blue*

Nights, to convey an ache of innocence, Didion would sketch scenes of her daughter talking back to the song, but she didn't note that the Mamas and the Papas were sometimes guests in her daughter's house.

"Turn! Turn! Turn!" Quintana sang with the Byrds. To everything there is a season. This was the season of Mommy's snake book. Her mother would say she needed to work. Quintana would say the same about herself when Didion asked her to do something.

It was also election season. You couldn't go to a restaurant without hearing Nixon's name.

One night, the Dunnes had dinner with Jim Mills, author of *The Panic in Needle Park.* He was an associate editor at *Life. The Panic in Needle Park* had begun years earlier as an article and photo essay for the magazine. But when the Dunnes met him, hoping to option his book for a picture, he wanted to talk politics.

LBJ had just gone on television to announce a temporary bombing halt in Vietnam. Mills insisted that the American people were overly sensitive to the word *nuclear.* Many lives could have been saved in Southeast Asia if the United States had nuked it, he said. Didion had once considered this position, but her time with Dunne had tempered her views, and the couple thought Mills slightly cracked. Didion had decided not to vote in this election— the thought of choosing the lesser of two evils appalled her.

But the movie looked like a go. Mills was receptive. Along with Nick, the Dunnes agreed to put up $1,000 for a year's option against $17,500 and 5 percent of net profits. Didion would write a film treatment. Nick thought he could find further financing, maybe at Fox (Dunne's time there had taught him that the studios were down, not out; you needed a studio to get *anything* done, and they operated with brute efficiency—around town, people called Disney "Duckau").

Mills's story line was relentlessly grim, but Didion had learned the art of the pitch. What's the picture about? "Romeo and Juliet on junk," she said.

Dunne was eager to finish his *Dolittle* project. Nothing about it surprised him. "Writing is essentially donkey work, manual labor of the mind," he'd say later. "What makes it bearable are those moments . . . when the book takes over, takes on a life of its own, goes off in unexpected directions. There were no detours like that in *The Studio*. My notes were like plans for a bridge. Writing the book was like building that bridge."

He could barely lug his carcass to another studio meeting. He couldn't stomach another working dinner at the Daisy, glancing at the glazed wall mirrors (strategically placed so everybody could stare at fellow diners without appearing to strain), listening to the studio heads discuss dubbing a picture in Israel:

"What do they speak there? Yiddish?"

"I don't know. Hebrew maybe."

"What's 'pussy' in Hebrew?"

He groaned at the mountains of caviar honoring *Hello, Dolly!* now that the Wardrobe Department had determined Babs's dress was sufficiently functional.

He'd had enough of the studio's divine eminence. All he wanted now was a book party in New York. (Presumably, FSG had thrown the promised bash for *Slouching Towards Bethlehem*.) Dunne told Henry Robbins he wasn't really pressing for a party, but just for kicks, he wondered, How many people might I invite?

What *really* nagged him was fear that *The Studio* was not a worthy follow-up to *Delano*, and *Delano* had vanished with little notice. Meanwhile, his wife had become the muse of the sixties. Even so, critical acclaim for *Slouching Towards Bethlehem* had not translated into robust sales. New American Library refused to make a public offer for the paperback rights (eventually, Dell would extend a $1,250 advance). Literary success could be as gloomy as failure.

2

"It is the season . . . of divorce," Didion had written of the cheating couples in "Some Dreamers of the Golden Dream." At the end of 1969, shortly after discussing in print the possibility that she and her husband might separate, she would refer to her own "season of doubt."

"We communicated in nuance," Dunne wrote.

Let's take a look.

At the end of "Los Angeles Notebook," in the final section of *Slouching Towards Bethlehem*, Didion sits in a piano bar in Encino. Piano bars in Encino, she writes, are where people "tell each other about their first wives and last husbands." She does not say what she was doing there alone. She *does* say she went to a pay phone and called a friend in New York. He asked her why she was there. She replied, "Why not?"

In *Play It As It Lays*, Encino is the faceless part of L.A. where Maria's domestic dreams die in a bloody pail. ("Didion's description of Maria's abortion and her subsequent horror at the waste, the fetus in the pail . . . is all too true," wrote the critic Barbara Harrison.) "You familiar with this area, Maria?" asks a doctor's go-between in the novel. "Nice homes here. Nice for kids."

Adding his own nuance to the mix, Dunne often told friends at parties during this period—sometimes joking, sometimes not—that his marriage was a week-to-week affair.

Contributing to their difficulties at this time were the stresses of writing, money, lots of drinking, Dunne's quickness to anger, and Didion's "theatrical temperament"—especially, it seems, in 1969, and again three years later, when, Didion wrote, "John and I were having a fight [and] he took it out on Quintana. She cried. I told her she and I were leaving, she and I were going to LAX, she and I were flying away from him."

Without placing blame on either party, one of the couple's old friends said Didion should have taken Quintana and gone to live with Frank and Eduene. Didion's sufferings, whatever their causes, were as intense as Maria's tensions with her husband in the novel.

"Did they have trouble? Oh, yes. And all those stories you read in the paper about Joan's reclusiveness? I don't understand why you'd think they're true," Eve Babitz told me. "Maybe it was John shouting over her. And she preferred it. John could be the idiot and she didn't have to be. He pounded down doors, and that's why Quintana hated him. Joan would never leave him—*he* got to be the obnoxious one. She thought staying with him proved she had character."

In November 1969, after a particularly cloudy period, Didion wrote of an attempt at reconciliation: "We . . . refrain from mentioning the kicked-down doors, the hospitalized psychotics [presumably, when she was diagnosed at St. John's] and the packed suitcases."

"Why do you always have to be right. Why do you always have to have the last word. For once in your life, just let it go," Didion wrote years later, invoking the echo of Dunne's voice.

When *Play It As It Lays* was published, Didion acknowledged suffering severe marital setbacks. "Anyway, John and I stayed together," she told an interviewer. "A lot of marriages are surviving infidelity around the country . . . [it] isn't really that important except as a betrayal."

"Betrayal," Dunne wrote in *Vegas*, "never worked for us" as a major reason to fight.

"If you can make the promise over again, then the marriage should survive," Didion said. "I don't really think infidelity is that important."

Vegas recounts a phone call on this very topic, illustrating the couple's highly nuanced communication. (Remember: Dunne called *Vegas* a "fictionalized memoir"—about as nuanced as you can get.) He had gone to Nevada, partly to work, partly to escape home, and he was interviewing various residents of the underbelly. He called his wife one evening. "What's new with you?" she said. He said he had a date "with a nineteen-year-old tonight. She's supposed to suck me and fuck me." "It's research," Didion said. "It's a type, the girl who's always available . . . You're missing the story if you don't meet her." "But I don't *want* to fuck her," Dunne said.

"There was a long silence at the other end of the telephone," Dunne wrote. "'Well, that can be part of the story, too,' she said.

"There seemed to be nothing more to say. I was the one who was supposed to be detached."

Dunne writes of buying Quintana a baseball mitt the spring she turned three and throwing a ball with her to fill his anguished days. He writes of a growing restlessness, of going to movies alone, driving the freeways for hours, and dreaming of escape. He writes of the "familiar season of discontent" at home, of moving from "crisis to crisis like old repertory actors going from town to town, every crisis an opening night with new depths to plumb in the performance." He writes that his wife had "too high a trouble quotient." She often slept with a leaky ice bag on her head, to ward off "PMT, the Santa Ana and all forms of bad karma."

She fell into the lassitude she'd witnessed in her mother: Nothing made any difference. She promised him "she'd try harder to make things matter." He told her he'd heard that before. Eventually, he spent eighteen months, off and on, in a residential motel just off the Strip in Las Vegas among hookers, cardsharps, and comedians, drafting a book.

Whatever else led to this "season of doubt," writing played its part. Though neither could imagine *not* being married to a writer, though they counted on each other for editorial and professional support, an edginess grew between them—not *competition* so much as *sadness* that things could not always be equal. And in *this* particular space, this constant struggle to right the balance, there was little, if any, room for Quintana, who would parrot back at them their daily withdrawals.

Many years later, Didion would say she heard her daughter's comments as "precocious"; now, she realized, they "could be construed in retrospect as pleas for help." She "was already more aware of what was going on around her than I had any idea."

Among other things, what was going on around Quintana, early in 1969, was her father's increasing worry about the worth of his current project—perhaps one reason so much was riding, for him, on a book party in New York. Didion wanted to fix things. "She claimed that [in my writing] I vandalized other people's lives instead of coming to grips with my own," Dunne wrote. "It was an argument without a rebuttal, which is what made it particularly infuriating."

It was also an argument about traditional reporting (Dunne's special gift) versus the trendy, more personal style of nonfiction.

Coming to grips with her own life—for which she'd been praised in reviews of *Slouching Towards Bethlehem*—was dangerously self-absorbing, making it hard for Didion to make things matter. In *Life* magazine, she wrote that lately she felt herself "a sleepwalker, moving through the world unconscious . . . alert only to the stuff of bad dreams, the children burning in the locked car in the supermarket parking lot, the bike boys stripping down stolen cars on the captive cripple's ranch, the freeway sniper . . . the cunning Okie faces that turn up in military investigations . . ."

Each of these grisly topics appears in newspaper clippings among the rough drafts of *Play It As It Lays* in Berkeley's Bancroft Library. Didion saved them while working on the novel. Across the top of each column, she scrawled "Maria"—in the book, Maria obsesses over violent newspaper stories. Didion's comments in *Life* indicate a scary blurring between author and character.

At one point, Didion made a note about "voice"—how she would like to disguise her tone and speak like a teenager, though she was *not* a teenager anymore. It is unclear whether she was speaking of her own voice or Maria's—or perhaps she was speaking *as* Maria.

Anyway, the couple stayed together : "I am reminded that we laugh at the same things."

And then there was Quintana, weeding the tennis court.

Quintana, strolling with them around the lake in MacArthur Park. She was accosted one evening by an old man suddenly lurching at her out of the dark from a bench: "That child is the picture of Ginger Rogers," he said.

One night, in the garden out back, where the rats ate the avocados, she put a seedpod up her nose. Didion drove her to Children's Hospital. The attending pediatrician had been called away from a lavish party and wore a dinner jacket to the clinic. Quintana found this interesting. The following night, she sniffed up another seedpod so that she could meet the handsome doctor again.

3

The atmosphere in the neighborhood remained the same: Still the outlandish parties. Still the whispered talk. Satanic rituals. Filmed orgies. Public humiliations (whippings, sodomy) in retaliation for bad dope deals.

"There were simply too many drugs in that community," said Noel Parmentel. "Hooch I understand. But not the other." He had become a Hollywood fixture, dropping in on the Dunnes, staying at the Chateau Marmont. He was trying to produce a film of Walker Percy's *The Moviegoer*. His drinking buddies included Robert Mitchum and Amanda Blake, *Gunsmoke*'s Miss Kitty. He'd hang with Cass Elliot, from whom he heard the dark rumors. "Cass used to send a limo to the airport for me, you know, with someone holding a sign: MR. PARMENTEL. She was great—a musical genius but all she wanted to do was look like Michelle [Phillips]. I did her a big favor once, stupidly. Through a congressman I knew, I got her scumbag boyfriend bailed out of jail."

The man's name, he couldn't recall, but Cass's drug-dealing beaux would fill Laurel Canyon. Maybe it was Pic Dawson, who came and went, like so many, from Cass's house, or maybe it was William Doyle, whom she introduced at parties in the spring of 1969 as her fiancé. By summer's end, the LAPD had taken a special interest in Doyle. He admitted selling MDA to Voytek Frykowski, Cass's neighbor. Allegedly, Frykowski sold these same pills to Tex Watson and Linda Kasabian, who said the drugs were worthless. Watson would be convicted of killing Frykowski in Sharon Tate's house.

Cass couldn't stop talking that spring about the murder of Bobby Kennedy. The assassination and the turmoil at the Democratic National Convention the previous August had piqued her interest in politics. She thought maybe she'd run for the Senate someday. The night Bobby was shot, she'd been having dinner with Sharon and Roman in Malibu, and she couldn't believe how shattered she felt, as if the whole country were bleeding out in that darkened hotel kitchen.

One night at a party, Michelle Phillips told Didion a stunning story, emblematic of the times: A version of it would appear as the penultimate chapter of *Play It As It Lays*. When Phillips was seventeen, she said, her best friend, a woman named Tamar Hodel, decided to kill herself. Hodel had introduced Phillips to folk music. Listen to Peter, Paul and Mary, she'd say—two rabbis and a hooker. She had been jilted by the singer Scott McKenzie ("If you're going to San Francisco"). She asked Phillips to help her gobble forty-eight Seconal.

After Hodel had swallowed the pills, Phillips dragged her, comatose, to an unmade bed and lay there watching her. Finally, she fell asleep. John Phillips arrived and discovered the women in time to drive Hodel to a hospital and get her stomach pumped. Michelle had been scared, but—passive, young—she never questioned whether she should honor her friend's request.

Didion took this story and gave it to Maria. As her friend BZ sinks into a Seconal haze, Maria holds his hand: "She closed her eyes against the light . . . and her mind against what was going to happen . . ."

Phillips told other stories that spring. Through Dennis Wilson, the Beach Boys' drummer, her husband, John, had met this fellow Charlie Manson. Manson was a songwriter, convinced that Terry Melcher, the Byrds' producer, would get him a contract (Melcher was Doris Day's son, a child of Old Hollywood). Manson was going to be a rock star. John didn't think much of his talent, but he was an entertaining talker and he was always surrounded by pretty girls. Fun to be around. He and the girls lived occasionally on a former ranch—the backdrop for a lot of old Westerns, Manson said, Tom Mix, Howard Hughes.

Lately, though, John didn't like to party with people. For some reason, he had grown "quite paranoid," Phillips said.

What Phillips didn't know, when she related this story, was that Manson had begun to instruct his followers to sneak onto peoples' lawns and break into their houses—particularly places they'd been to, at flings and things—just to see if they could get away with it. Manson called this activity "creepy crawling."

John "heard sounds one night and went downstairs carrying a shotgun," Phillips said. "I waited, without much anxiety, for him to come back. 'I saw six people,' he said when he returned, 'all dressed in black, in tights and leotards, men and women, and they were in the Rolls-Royce, out in the garage, and when I went to the door, they all tiptoed away like penguins.'"

Phillips didn't believe him. She took the gun, gave him a Valium, and told him to come to bed.

Months later, she knew. They'd been "creepy crawled."

4

For Dunne's New York book party, on May 14, 1969, Farrar, Straus and Giroux reserved the Gauguin Room in the Gallery of Modern Art, complete with cocktails, hors d'oeuvres, and a piano player. Until the moment he left California, Dunne waffled in letters to Robbins. He said he didn't like going to New York (not true), that he wasn't looking forward to the party (not true), that he was pathologically paranoid about the "lit biz" (true of everyone). He said he had turned down three motion pictures in the past three weeks, costing him $175,000, and he didn't know if New York was worth it. The movie offers may or may not have been genuine; the only obvious game in play was Didion's unfinished treatment of *The Panic in Needle Park* and Nick's inability, so far, to interest studios in the "downbeat" material.

FSG planned a full-page ad for *The Studio* in *The New York Times,* which pleased Dunne but made him skittish. The rollout was smooth and highly supportive of Dunne but didn't quell his fears. He didn't want his bio to mention *Delano*—the distance between farmworkers and studio executives was so great, even *he* wondered what kind of résumé he was building.

Most tellingly, he had dropped his longtime agent, Carl Brandt, for Lynn Nesbit, who was shepherding the careers of Tom Wolfe and Donald Barthelme.

Dunne was not going through the motions of a breakdown, as his wife had, on the eve of his all-important second book, but his inner pitchings were no less turbulent. Whereas Didion acted out, to steel herself for the long run, Dunne bit back on his tensions—perhaps straining his heart (he'd wonder about this later). This was a difference between them, based in a shared understanding, and it was a way of balancing the scales.

As the guests wandered from the Gauguin Room to the penthouse lounge, sipping Singapore slings, picking at small plates of satay chicken or spiced apples, Didion realized she had missed New York men. They *looked* at women; you could catch their eye. They actually wanted to talk to you, instead of just probing to see what you could do for them, like the men in L.A. On the other hand, she *hadn't* missed that overbearing East Coast chauvinism toward the

West. New Yorkers had no idea what an apocalyptic romance California was having with itself. Didion had not realized, until leaving L.A., quite how *dark* that city had gotten, "much darker than it was anyplace else," she said.

The ambivalence Dunne had felt *before* the celebration must have intensified during the evening. It was the same doubt characterizing his book: an insider's account written from the perspective of an outsider who very much wanted *in*. "Although it is not necessary for a writer to be a prick, neither does it hurt," Dunne would say. "A writer is an eternal outsider, his nose pressed against whatever window on the other side of which he sees his material." And yet he always wanted to *smash* that window, and then be magnanimous enough to pay the damages.

On top of everything, he hadn't anticipated that the affair would turn into a wake for *The Saturday Evening Post.* The magazine had finally drowned in debt, losing a defamation suit to University of Alabama football coach Bear Bryant. In a pair of articles, the magazine had accused Bryant of encouraging violence on the field and of fixing a game. The magazine was ordered to pay over three million dollars in damages; in January, it had published an excerpt from *The Studio;* by February, it was gone. Dunne invited all the editors to his party. By now, they were "scattered to the four winds, [but] to my surprise they all came, inconvenient though it must have been," he said. "We fell upon each other, sharers of a unique experience."

He and Didion would move on to write a regular column for *Esquire* and they would enjoy many years of association with *The New York Review of Books,* but never again would they experience the freedom to *indulge* stories quite the way they had at *The Saturday Evening Post* . . . in the Haight or in the Valley's poisoned fields.

A certain expansive spirit vanished with *The Saturday Evening Post:* a foretaste of the blight that would kill American magazines over the next three decades.

"May all the one-eyed critics lose their other eye," said William Emerson, the magazine's old editor in chief.

Dunne raised a glass to that.

5

Months later, Didion would be startled to learn directly from Linda Kasabian that the night the Manson Family "did the LaBianca murder, they were driving along Franklin Avenue looking for a place to hit . . . and we had French windows open, lights blazing all along on the street." The votives perked on the windowsills. Maybe Quintana was dancing to "Turn! Turn! Turn!" Champagne flowed at parties up and down the block.

Franklin Avenue—the "senseless-killing neighborhood"—was one of Charlie Manson's playgrounds. In the late 1950s, he had lived in an apartment a block from the Dunnes' house, running a bogus talent agency, 3-Star Enterprises, as a front for a prostitution ring. His buddy Tex Watson had a girlfriend living on Franklin. In the months before the Tate-LaBianca murders, he said, he sometimes sunbathed on his girlfriend's deck, "drinking beer and smoking grass while we watched all the big limousines drive up for the parties, dumping out beautiful people whom we never could quite recognize." Allegedly, Manson shot to death a dope dealer in the Franklin Garden Apartments, in the shadow of the Magic Castle hotel.

On the afternoon of August 9, 1969, while *Easy Rider* played on area movie screens, while *Portnoy's Complaint, Slaughterhouse-Five,* and *The God-father* brought an unusually high volume of readers into bookstores, word spread from Sunset up into the hills about the slayings at 10050 Cielo Drive. Didion was swimming in the pool at her sister-in-law Lenny's house in Beverly Hills when Natalie Wood phoned with the news. "I can remember we had a baby-sitter from Nayarit then, and she was very frightened . . . when we heard about the murders," Didion said. "I assured her, 'Don't worry. It has nothing to do with us,' but it did. It had to do with everyone."

It seemed everybody knew somebody who had slept with, sold drugs to, or partied with the victims; in days to come, the people claiming to have been invited to the Cielo house that night exhausted the Hollywood A-list. Actor Steve McQueen said the L.A. sewer system was full of expensive drugs the day the news broke, as everyone, fearing visits from the cops, flushed their stuff.

Roman Polanski accused John Phillips of being the killer.

Michelle Phillips slipped a pistol into her purse. "Darling, put the gun away," a friend had to tell her one night at the Daisy.

Suspicion spread like the tear gas on Sunset.

"It was the most bizarre period of my life," Michelle Phillips said. "It could have been anyone, as far as I was concerned. The last conversation I ever had with Sharon was about wallpaper for her nursery." Tate was eight months pregnant the night she was killed.

Didion was not alone in harboring "a kind of conflicting sense that . . .

they [the victims] had somehow done it to themselves, that it had to do with too much sex, drugs, and rock and roll."

"[This] investigation has caused a lot of people a lot of pain, because a lot of people feel they're guilty or they have something to hide about something, and go through enormous emotional wringers. This is what Cass is hysterical about," William Doyle told LAPD lieutenant Earl Deemer on August 30.

Early reports about the crime "were garbled and contradictory," Didion wrote in her essay "The White Album." "One caller would say hoods, the next would say chains. There were twenty dead, no, twelve, ten, eighteen. Black masses were imagined, and bad trips blamed. I remember all of the day's misinformation very clearly, and I also remember this, and wish I did not: *I remember that no one was surprised.*"

Nick Dunne was surprised. He had last seen Sharon Tate at a party at Tony Curtis's house. "His rose garden was lovely," Nick said. "As I remember it all these years later, there were gravel pathways between the beds of roses and boxwood borders. At one point that night, I went out into the garden and there was Sharon, all alone, walking on a path by the white roses in full bloom. She was pregnant, and dressed in something white and billowing. It was like a scene in a movie watching her. She made me think of Daisy Buchanan in *The Great Gatsby*. . . . We talked about old times at [Jay Sebring's] barbershop, and the marvelous turns her life had taken. I was smoking a joint, and she took a few tokes. . . . She was joyous about having the baby, and she had never looked more beautiful."

Nick had been in New York, producing *The Boys in the Band,* when Lenny called to tell him about the killings. He flew home immediately. "People were sending their children out of town for safety, and ours were going to my mother-in-law's ranch outside San Diego," he said. He remembered that "Steve McQueen packed a gun at Jay Sebring's funeral, where he gave one of the eulogies."

"Many people I know in Los Angeles believe that the Sixties ended on August 9, 1969," Didion wrote, adding to the press's overheated valedictions. It was really only the crowd at the Daisy whose sixties had come to an end, but this fact slipped at a certain point; the media managed to superimpose Manson's face, with his crude swastika etched between his eyes, over psychedelic images of flowers and peace signs. Manson became a cult doll for the press, a penny-ante pimp inflated into a symbol for the national psychosis. But at ground level, in the community most directly affected, Didion's reporting got right to the point: "The tension broke that day. The paranoia was fulfilled."

If the California narrative was an apocalyptic romance, the East maintained its sentimentality. A week after the Tate-LaBianca murders, on August 15, 16, and 17, the Woodstock Festival—officially, the Woodstock Music and Art Fair—in Bethel, New York, took place; it was valorized by *Time* magazine as the "greatest peaceful event in history," a fulfillment of the sixties' loftiest ideals.

Expectations for peaceful assembly were admittedly low after the previous year's Democratic National Convention, and there was delicious irony in watching the antiwar crowd raise its arms toward food and medical supplies airlifted onto mud-soaked fields by the U.S. Army.

But for the purposes of *our* narrative, we need to look past the Peace and Love, past Janis and Jimi, and the naked bodies packed like rabbits in a box, to a five-piece rock band from Woodstock, who often played with a larger musical collective called the Bummers, a "Commedia dell'Arte style group of cowboys and Indians." The Bummers performed folk rock at the Provincetown Playhouse in Greenwich Village, produced an Off-Off-Broadway musical called *The Golden Screw*, and regularly appeared at the Woodstock Sound-Outs, annual mini-festivals held just south of Route 212 on the Glasco Turnpike. The Sound-Outs began in 1967 and became, according to Woodstock promoter Michael Lang, "kind of the spark for the Festival." The Bummer's drummer was a young man named Gerry Michael. He played a variety of styles, backing performers such as Bonnie Raitt, Paul Butterfield, and Juma Sultan, who accompanied Hendrix's band at the '69 event.

Gerry Michael was not a symbol of anything, neither apocalypse nor hope. He deserves quick note, at this point, only because he figures prominently in a later part of Didion's story. In 2003, Gerry Michael, then a widower in his fifties, would marry Quintana Roo Dunne, whom Michael's son said he met in a bar, and who would die just over two years later (the official cause would be "acute pancreatitis").

"I wanna dance."

The rock poet Ed Sanders covered the first Manson trial for the *Freep* (as everyone called the *Los Angeles Free Press*), straining to grant Manson a presumption of innocence: Like Sanders, Manson had long hair. Sanders's attitude countered that of the mainstream press, which had already convicted Manson because he had long hair.

Dozens of reporters (and prosecutors) hoped to advance their careers with this story; among the many journalists given access to members of the Family in prison rooms, the Los Angeles County Courthouse, or the offices of the *Freep* (recently bombproofed after a series of threats from right-wing, anti-Castro partisans) was Joan Didion. She spent several evenings interviewing Linda Kasabian at the Sybil Brand Institute for Women. Kasabian had been the "wheel person" for the killers on the two-night murder run. At the time, she was the mother of an infant. How could the mother of an infant involve herself in the senseless killing of a woman who was eight months pregnant? If any writer could have understood Linda Kasabian, it was probably Joan Didion, who had spent the past year clipping from newspapers stories of children burning to death in supermarket parking lots and who was writing a novel ending with a woman passively watching a friend commit suicide.

"In fact we never talked about 'the case,'" Didion wrote. "We talked instead about Linda's childhood pastimes and disappointments, her high-school romances and her concern for her children."

6

Two of Nick's children, Alex and Dominique, stood frightened and confused next to their grim-faced uncle and aunt the night their father got arrested at LAX. Nick had arrived from a vacation in Mexico. Didion and Dunne had agreed to pick him up, and took his kids along to greet him. Someone tipped the airport police that he was carrying a "lid" of grass. They strip-searched and handcuffed him in front of his family in the Western Airlines waiting room. "I was at the time the vice president of a studio [Four Star, a television company owned by David Niven, Dick Powell, and Charles Boyer] and possessed the haughty attitude that came with the job, an attitude that did not endear me to the arresting officers," Nick said. "Outside, there was a police car with a screaming siren and flashing red lights, waiting for me. . . . Manson himself couldn't have drawn a bigger crowd than I did that Sunday night at LAX. There was a very tall cop on either side of me, each with a hand in my armpit, and they lifted me off the floor with my feet dangling." He seemed a sad clown in his Brooks Brothers blazer and Gucci loafers. "The cops insisted on calling me Mr. Vice President in mocking voices."

He stayed overnight in a Venice jail. The following day, Didion and Dunne bailed him out, saying nothing. He had endangered the *Needle Park* project. It was a hard-enough sell without being wrapped in the trade papers' gossip columns. Worse, he had humiliated them—and his kids—in public.

For several months, in the midst of the Manson craziness, his slippage had exceeded everyone's darkest fears. Most mornings he ate alone in a coffee shop called Nibblers, on the corner of Spalding and Wilshire. Sometimes the faded old movie queen Norma Shearer came in for breakfast, and without acknowledging he knew who she was, he'd talk with her about good Old Hollywood, when MGM ruled the world and kept us all safe.

One day, when his pot bust was about to come to trial, he got a call from Sid Korshak's buddy Beldon Katleman. "He said he wanted to see me right away. It was an order, not a request," Nick said. Katleman owned Gary Cooper's old house in Holmby Hills. He was wearing a terry-cloth robe when Nick arrived. He told Nick to join him in the steam room. There, he said, no one could hear them. "What kind of trouble are you in?" he asked. "Who's the judge?"

Weeks later, all of Nick's charges were dropped. "Who the hell do you know?" asked one of the arresting cops, outside the courtroom. "Why don't you assholes *drink* instead of using dope?"

Later, Katleman explained his generosity to Nick: "When I first came to this town from Vegas, nobody ever spoke to me at parties, but you did."

7

On November 14, 1969, Didion finished drafting *Play It As It Lays.* The following day, she and her husband and their daughter flew to Honolulu.

George Hunt, the managing editor of *Life,* had recently offered her a regular column—perhaps at the prompting of Jim Mills—and she thought she might start by writing something about Hawaii. Shortly after she accepted the offer, Ralph Graves replaced Hunt. Graves had decided to shake up the staid old magazine. He hired Norman Mailer to cover the moon landing. On the cover of the June 27, 1969, issue, he had run a picture of a young man in military uniform, with the caption "The Faces of the American Dead in Vietnam: One Week's Toll." Inside were photographs of 242 soldiers killed the previous week, and the quietly devastating statement "The numbers of the dead are average for every seven-day period during this stage of the war."

This was new territory for a publication associated with unquestioning patriotism.

Dunne warned his wife that working for the editors of a Luce outfit would be like getting "nibbled to death by ducks," but they had, she said, promised "to put me out in a world of revolution, which sounded really attractive."

Two days before the couple's departure for the islands, Seymour Hersh released an article through the Dispatch News Service, picked up by thirty-five American newspapers, including the *Chicago Sun-Times*, the *St. Louis Post-Dispatch*, and *The Milwaukee Journal*. The article began, "William L. Calley, Jr., 26 years old, is a mild-mannered, boyish-looking Vietnam combat veteran with the nickname 'Rusty.' The Army is completing an investigation of charges that he deliberately murdered at least 109 Vietnamese civilians in a search-and-destroy mission in March 1968 in a Viet Cong stronghold known as 'Pinkville.'"

Hersh had tried to interest *Life* and *Look* in the story, but he failed. Previously, *The New York Times* had buried deep inside the paper a two-paragraph AP piece based on a press release from Georgia's Fort Benning mentioning, almost in passing, the charges against Calley. It had taken the military establishment almost a year to acknowledge that the massacre in My Lai was not precisely the "outstanding action" Gen. William C. Westmoreland had called it.

Pressure on the army to investigate the incident grew after a former door gunner from the Eleventh Infantry Brigade, who had flown over My Lai and witnessed the carnage, sent a letter to thirty congressmen imploring them to look into the matter. Most legislators ignored him, but Barry Goldwater and a pair of others urged the House Armed Services Committee to strong-arm the Pentagon.

"These factors are not in dispute," Hersh wrote. "There are always some civilian casualties in a combat operation . . . You can't afford to guess whether a civilian is a Viet Cong or not. Either you shoot them or they shoot you . . . Calley's friends in the Officer's Corps at Fort Benning, many of them West Point graduates, are indignant. 'They're using this as a Goddamned example,' one officer complained. 'He's a good soldier. He followed orders.'"

When she learned these facts, Didion phoned her editor at *Life*, Loudon Wainright. His wife said he'd have to call her back.

It was a Sunday afternoon. "He's watching the NFL game," Dunne told her. "He'll call you at halftime."

When he *did* phone, she said she wanted to do her first column from

Saigon. He said no. "Some of the guys are going out," he told her, then suggested she stay put and just introduce herself.

Seething, she went for a walk on the sand, but it didn't calm her down. Each afternoon, the talk on the Kahala beach was all about Ted Kennedy and that girl who'd drowned in his car. Nationwide, the adults were misbehaving. As a result, the children, mostly young women, were dying.

"Where did the morning went?" Quintana asked Didion one day, still on mainland time, expecting the sun.

Day by day, Hersh's reports, picked up now by all the major papers, detailed the event at My Lai. He quoted Sgt. Michael Bernhardt: "It was point-blank murder and I was standing there watching it. . . . They were setting fire to the hootches and huts and waiting for people to come out and then shooting them up. They were going into the hootches and shooting them up. They were gathering people in groups and shooting them. As I walked in, you could see piles of people, all through the village."

In an interview *Didion* could have gotten, Gen. Fred C. Weyand said, "The American way of war is particularly violent, deadly and dreadful. We believe in using 'things'—artillery, bombs, massive firepower—in order to conserve our soldiers' lives . . . [W]e should have made the realities of war obvious to the American people before they witnessed it on their television screens."

For Didion, My Lai was another case of betrayal by romance. Before leaving for Quang Ngai Province, Calley and Charlie Company had joined the First Battalion, Twentieth Infantry for training at Schofield. James Jones had endeared the base to her. She always visited it whenever she flew to Hawaii. Now it was poisoned ground.

"There was a lot of illusion in our national history," Reinhold Niebuhr said, around this time. "[I]t is about to be shattered."

Didion was the chronicler of shattered romance. She needed to be in Saigon. Loudon Wainwright had suggested she introduce herself. Well, okay. She'd give *Life*'s readers one *hell* of an introduction.

Betrayal was very much on her mind.

"I had better tell you where I am, and why," she wrote. "I am sitting in a high-ceilinged room in the Royal Hawaiian Hotel in Honolulu watching the long translucent curtains billow in the winds . . . My husband switches off the TV set and stares out the window. I avoid his eyes and brush the baby's hair . . . We are here on this island in the middle of the Pacific in lieu of filing for divorce."

"Maybe it can be all right," she says she said to him.

"Maybe," he replied.

Dunne took Quintana to the Honolulu Zoo to give Didion time to finish the piece. Then he edited it and went with her to file it at the Western Union office. "At the Western Union office he wrote REGARDS, DIDION at the end of it," Didion wrote later. "That was what you always put at the end of a cable, he said. Why, I said. Because you do, he said."

Life's readers did not know what to make of such an apparently candid piece. Many of them wrote to complain that the magazine's new columnist was no Little Miss Sunshine. The editors began to wonder if they'd made a mistake. They "didn't get it. [Didion's] pieces [in *Life*] made such an impact— not just on people who were literary. . . . I know housewives who had [her column] over the sink," Dan Wakefield said later: *You mean it's okay to admit you think about divorce? To think of yourself, when the world's grappling with so many crises?*

"I am not the society in microcosm," she had said. And yet . . .

Even more than with *Slouching Towards Bethlehem*, Joan Didion was about to become Joan Didion, the woman who wrote the books, the woman *in* the books, in narratives of fact and fiction.

She had introduced herself properly.

"It was a big shock to find myself in a certain kind of limited public eye" because of that divorce column, she claimed. "I thought I was always going to be writing these books that I would finance somehow, that no one would ever review or read."

On December 31, Henry Robbins wrote to Jane Fonda: "We saw you on the David Frost Show last week and were terribly pleased to hear you speak so excitedly about Joan Didion's piece in *Life* magazine . . . Joan has just completed a new novel, *Play It As It Lays,* which Farrar, Straus and Giroux will be publishing in the spring. If you were impressed and touched by her *Life* article, you'll be positively overwhelmed by this forthcoming book. We were."

Chapter Eighteen

———— ❧ ————

1

Quintana had no coat. She wore a bright frangipani lei in the cold Connecticut air. Shivering on the runway at Hartford's Bradley Field, she told her mother it was okay, that children with leis don't wear coats. She was glad to be staying with her dad's mom for a while. Her last few days in Hawaii had been cooped up and crazy, first because an earthquake had struck the Aleutians, threatening tsunamis in Honolulu, and second because the tsunamis didn't come, leaving the family to suffer its tensions with no hope of distraction. She couldn't go to the beach. Her parents were awfully careful with each other, and quiet.

They dropped her in West Hartford because of their movie project. Nick had cut a production deal with Joseph E. Levine at Avco-Embassy, an independent studio responsible for *The Graduate* and *Carnal Knowledge*. The Dunnes intended to go to New York to see Needle Park.

Friends in the city were stunned to run into them at a party. People made embarrassed allusions to the *Life* piece. "In lieu of divorce. In lieu of!" Didion told them, and laughed.

The couple stayed at the Hotel Alamac at Seventy-first and Broadway, near Sherman and Verdi squares; together, these were known as Needle Park. The Alamac, nineteen stories high, topped with large decorative concrete urns, was a luxury hotel when it opened in the 1920s, featuring orchestras in its Congo Room and hosting international chess tournaments, but by 1969 it was a run-down residential establishment housing mostly the elderly unemployed. The City University of New York leased three floors there, offering remedial classes to high school kids, but the program was troubled: The black and Puerto Rican students demanded nonwhite teachers and the administration despised its radical young faculty, assigning Che Guevara and Mao Tse-tung. Violence hung in the air. On the residential floors, drug use and prostitution passed the hours. Didion kept her eyes down in the jerky old elevators.

She didn't last long at the Alamac. She wanted to leave the moment she discovered the management wouldn't bring her clean white sheets every day (she went to Bloomingdale's and bought her own fresh towels). For a while, though, she got to play Hard-Boiled Reporter (*to pack: bras and bourbon*). Observing the bloody needles discarded in the halls, watching the bartender at P&J Café drag overdosed patrons from his bathroom to the curb at Verdi Square, meeting recovering addicts from Phoenix House nearby, she gathered telling details for the screenplay. Blissfully, Dunne indulged his voyeuristic tendencies.

The intersection of Amsterdam, Seventy-first, and Broadway was an urban pressure point, a tumor of traffic swelling around a jam in the city's nerve system. The pressure was heightened by Robert Moses's slum-clearance campaign and by the destructive wave rolling through neighborhoods here following the ground-breaking ceremony at Lincoln Center. Veteran residents fled; absentee landlords took over; city services declined; fewer cops patrolled the streets; conditions decayed; drug dealers claimed their spots.

It was the perfect setting for a New Hollywood love story.

With *Bonnie and Clyde, Easy Rider,* and *Midnight Cowboy,* the studios had encountered both a threat to their operation and a new formula that, if successfully absorbed, would reinvent them: the studio picture as "indie," often shot on location with nonunion crews, featuring gritty subject matter wrapped around traditional narrative elements, the love story, the buddy flick, the road movie, the updated Western. In committing to *The Panic in Needle Park,* Avco was just like every other studio in 1969—"narcotized," Didion said, "by *Easy Rider*'s grosses" and convinced that "all that was needed to get a picture off the ground was the suggestion of a $750,000 budget, a low-cost . . . crew, and this terrific 22-year-old kid director." In fact, to direct the picture, Nick had lined up Jerry Schatzberg, a fashion photographer best known for snapping the cover of Bob Dylan's *Blonde on Blonde.* Nick had also tapped *Midnight Cowboy*'s director of photography, Adam Holender. Didion may have been miserable at the Alamac, but in terms of the project, she couldn't have had happier timing. At no other point in cinematic history could the movie she was writing get made.

"Miss Didion, do you have any luggage?" asked the Alamac night clerk when the couple checked in. He seemed mildly surprised when she said yes. Jazz players smoked in the lobby, milling quietly between sets at a nearby nightclub. Toothless old men clutching tubs of cottage cheese shuffled into the elevators, smelling of days-old cough syrup and unwashed clothes.

In the room—tiled floors, yellow walls—Dunne phoned to make an appointment to interview a drug dealer in a Blimpy Burger down the block (a friend had put him in touch with a fellow who supplied movie people, filming in New York, with all the goodies they'd need). "I'll be there around noon," the dealer said. "Or anyway between noon and four."

Didion called Quintana. She had a new dress, she told her mother. Didion asked what kind of dress it was. Quintana said she had to go, she had to work.

Didion phoned her mother in California. Here, in this bleak hotel, away from her daughter, she longed to be ten again, or sixteen, enjoying Christmas at home while a soft winter rain pattered the windows. Her mother agreed with her: In the old days, Christmas used to be better, before the family drank too much and gave one another too many presents.

"I had wanted to make this Christmas a 'nice' Christmas, for my husband and for our baby," Didion wrote in one of her *Life* columns. She had wanted to perceive herself "in a new and flattering light," she said, to get past marital squabbles and create an atmosphere at home where "no harsh words" would be spoken. She had wanted to "imprint indelibly upon her [daughter's] memory some trace of the rituals of family love."

Instead, she was sitting in the near dark on a hard bed, listening to the raised voices of Puerto Rican call girls in the hallway.

The next day, "[m]y husband and I see our lawyer, who tells us that because of a movie in which we are involved, he has incorporated us in the state of Delaware. I abandon the attempt to understand why," she wrote.

The dealer in the Blimpy Burger turned out to be a sixteen-year-old high school student wearing braces on his front teeth. His mother was an addict and his brother also sold drugs. He peddled pot and heroin on the Upper West Side on his bicycle. He wasn't, himself, currently "shooting." Could he have a small role in the movie? Sure, Didion said.

He put the Dunnes in touch with some of his clients, who went to the couple's room at the Alamac. Dunne gave them Hostess Twinkies and pocket change, and the addicts shot up, a real-life performance for the writers.

To file her *Life* drafts, Didion walked to a nearby press office, which had an AP wire. In California, the big story was the Rolling Stones' disastrous concert at Altamont, at which the Hells Angels had murdered a boy. Instantly, the press labeled the event the anti-Woodstock and claimed it was the *next* thing—after Manson—tolling the death of 1960s idealism.

Didion stood one night in the nearly deserted press office, listening to the clatter of the AP wire, thinking about Christmas wreaths. She started to cry. "I tell myself that I am crying because the baby told me in November that she wanted a necklace for Christmas, and instead of stringing beads by firelight I am watching an AP wire in an empty office," she wrote later. "But of course that is not why I am crying at all. Watching an AP wire in an empty office is precisely what I want to be doing: women do not end up in empty offices and Blimpy Burgers by accident." She was tired and feeling sorry for herself. And despite doing what she wanted to be doing, she couldn't help but wonder, she wrote, "if indeed we have been doing anything right."

2

Just over six months later, her former *National Review* colleague John Leonard would write in *The New York Times*, in a review of *Play It As It Lays*, "There hasn't been another American writer of Joan Didion's quality since Nathaniel West. She writes with a razor, carving her characters out of her perceptions with strokes so swift and economical that each scene ends almost before the reader is aware of it; and yet the characters go on bleeding afterwards."

On the front page of the Sunday *New York Times Book Review*, novelist Lore Segal wrote, "A new novel by Joan Didion is something of an event." This was true, Segal said, not because of Didion's previous novel, but because "she has gathered quite a following with her nonfiction pieces." It was "interesting to wonder what sort of fiction Miss Didion's beautiful writerly skills would now make of her clear-eyed and anguished perception of our time."

The rough drafts and notes for the novel archived in the Bancroft Library suggest word music and silence were at stake in composing the book as much as an accurate "perception of our time." As Didion said later, "I just wanted to write a fast novel. . . . [I]t was going to exist in a white space. It was going to exist between the paragraphs." She was harking back to the mysteries in pioneer tales and family histories. Who was telling this story? From what angle? And why? How would our understanding be affected?

She made elaborate notes to herself concerning narrative distance and the flexibility of point of view. Originally, "I wanted to make it all first person," she said, "but I wasn't good enough to maintain [it] at first. . . . [O]ne night I realized that I had some first person and some third person and that I was going to have to go with both, or just not write a book at all. I was scared."

Finally, she understood that, for the reader to *feel* Maria's dislocations, it would be necessary to alienate Maria not only from the other characters but also from the novel's controlling voice. Thus, the "pull-back third person" narrator (the novel's omniscient consciousness) never acknowledges Maria's abortion. It's only in "close third," when the voice creeps nearer Maria's perceptions, that trouble can be traced. Of course, the "pull-back" voice and the "close" voice are the same—like a camera zooming in and out. The deliberate blurriness made it difficult for many readers to distinguish Maria, the narrator, and the author. This difficulty was compounded, Segal said in her review, by the fact that "in her essays [Didion] chooses to speak in her own person. . . . [S]he has given herself the task of interpreting and coming to terms with the period of time which has produced Maria," and therefore "it is less impertinent than usual for the critic to deduce the writer from her creature."

Yes and no. We mustn't dismiss the artist's craft. A consistent pattern emerged in Didion's revisions of *Play It As It Lays*. This pattern zeroed in on adverbs. Initially, her habit was to place adverbs *after* the verbs in every sentence. Often in revision, she would reverse this order. Thus "The water in the pool was always 85 degrees" became "The water in the pool always was 85 degrees." The latter forced greater distance between subject and verb, a gap, a jump in a film reel—further fracturing Maria's perceptions of the world, and our view of her. Finally, Didion was *not* "her creature," in spite of their many similarities. She was standing back, observing, shading.

"Grammar is a piano I play by ear," she said. Like a series of musical staves, grammar became a set of bars between author and character, clarifying the substance and nature of the novel's performance.

Aesthetic considerations so dominated Didion's approach to the writing, they threatened to undermine the story structure. At first, the novel was set in New York. Maria was a model. Then she became an actress in California. In interviews, and in the essay "How I Write," Didion said the novel's genesis had nothing to do with "'character' or 'plot' or even 'incident.'" It began with "something actually witnessed," she said. "A young woman with long hair and a short white halter walks through the casino at the Riviera in Las Vegas at one in the morning. She crosses the casino alone and picks up a house telephone. I watch her because I have heard her paged, and recognize her name: she is a minor actress I see around Los Angeles from time to time, in places like Jax and once in a gynecologist's office in the Beverly Hills Clinic, but have never met. I know nothing about her. Who is paging her? Why is she here to be paged? How exactly did she come to this? It was precisely this moment in Las Vegas that made *Play It As It Lays* begin to tell itself to me.'"

It was also true that she'd collected notes, clippings, and scattered observations for quite some time, including her early *Vogue* piece on Ingrid Bergman's "withdrawal" in front of the camera and an intriguing quote from a newspaper about "Bond Girl" Jill St. John, whom Didion had seen around Hollywood on the arm of Henry Kissinger. In the quote, which Didion jotted down among her notes for the novel, St. John complained that, as a minor celebrity and sex object, she was exposed to "all eyes," but "no one talks to me."

In November 1969, "I showed [the novel] to John and then I sent it to Henry Robbins," Didion said. "It was quite rough, with places marked 'chapters to come.'"

Many of the rough draft pages start with weather reports, as if a running climate record might impose order on the material.

The holes were enormous. What was certain was a sense of rhythm.

"Henry . . . and John and I sat down one night in New York and talked, for about an hour before dinner, about what needed doing," Didion said. "We all knew what it needed. We all agreed. After that I took a couple of weeks and ran it through. It was just typing and pulling the line through. For example, I didn't know that BZ was an important character in *Play It As It Lays* until the last few weeks I was working on it. So those places I marked 'chapter to come' were largely places where I was going to go back and pull BZ through, hit him harder, prepare for the way it finally went" (that is, BZ's overdose in front of Maria, from Michelle Phillips's story about her friend Tamar Hodel). "I didn't realize until after I'd written it that it was essentially the same ending as *Run River*. The women let the men commit suicide."

For many readers, Maria's abortion is the centerpiece of the book—it is Maria's lowest point, physically and psychologically, and she never recovers from it. It is related, in her mind, to leaky pipes and crumbling houses. "I try not to think of dead things and plumbing," she says.

When asked if the abortion was simply "a narrative strategy," Didion said it "didn't occur to me until I'd written quite a bit of the book." The book needed an active moment, a moment which changed things for Maria. . . ."

In fact, her notes indicate that the abortion scene was central all along to her conception of the story. Yet, in an interview in *The Paris Review* in 1978, she insisted plot devices in her novels were generally "very arbitrary." For example, "I remember writing a passage in which Kate [Maria's emotionally impaired daughter] came home from school and showed Maria a lot of drawings, orange and blue crayon drawings, and when Maria asked what they were, Kate said, 'Pools on fire.' You can see I wasn't having too much success writing this child. So I put her in a hospital. You never meet her. Now, it turned out to have a great deal of importance—Kate's being in the hospital is a very large element in *Play It As It Lays*—but it began because I couldn't write a child, no other reason."

Perhaps, but it's essential to note that Didion later told radio host Michael Silverblatt that Quintana *was* the girl in *Play It As It Lays*: "By the time I finished it, she [Quintana] was clearly talking"; and Didion would continue to encounter trouble "writing a child," even when, as in *Blue Nights,* her child was the ostensible subject of the book.

She told Henry Robbins she didn't want a novel in which a series of events *happened* to a character; the character's fall should be experienced imperceptibly by the reader—an enactment of fatalism.

Maria, she said, has no will. She is incapable of love. She cannot take positive action. She isn't brave enough to gamble.

"This isn't going to—you're never going to—you're never going to—this book isn't going to make it," Dunne told her one night.

"And I didn't think it was going to make it, either," Didion said. "[I]t was my third book and I had not made it until then. . . . You think you have some stable talent which will show no matter what you're writing, and if it doesn't seem to be getting across to the audience once, you can't imagine the moment when it suddenly will."

Still, Dunne tried to help her as professionally as he could. In a long typed note, dated November 18, 1969 (written, therefore, in Hawaii), he said cautiously that he liked the novel but he had several reservations. The most serious of these concerned the character Ivan Morell (the name was later changed to Ivan Costello). Costello appears to be based on Noel Parmentel—Parmentel certainly thought so. "I told them both I wished to God they'd meet some new people," he said. Didion's notes identify Costello as the other man Maria loved once, and by whom she had an aborted child. Originally, he was never to be seen in the novel, but he does make a cameo appearance.

Morell/Costello, Dunne wrote, needs to be firmly cast in Maria's New York past, with no continuing role to play in her life except as a destructive force against which her other loves are measured. Carter, Maria's husband, is a more stable version of Morell, Dunne said. This distinction should be clear.

In his view, Maria loved to cause trouble. Daily life she couldn't handle. Tragedy was a navigable sea.

Play It As It Lays, published seven years after *Run River*, indicates a growing crisis of faith in narrative. Maria Wyeth, a disintegrating movie actress, no longer desires to close her eyes and make a wish, as Lily McClellan does at the end of the first novel. Instead, Maria defines herself by what she *doesn't* want: "She would never: *walk through the Sands or Caesar's alone after midnight*. She would never: *ball at a party, do S-M unless she wanted to, borrow furs from Abe Lipsey, deal*. She would never: *carry a Yorkshire in Beverly Hills*."

As in *Run River*, snakes in a garden open the book—pygmy rattlers and corals with "two glands of neurotoxic poison"—but archetypes, myths, and story logic fall away sharply thereafter. "To look for 'reasons' is beside the point," Maria says, one of her few confident statements. And: "I might as well lay it on the line, I have trouble with *as it was*."

Even her name is problematic. She needs to inform the reader that "[my name] is pronounced Mar-*eye*-ah, to get it straight at the outset." On even the simplest level, language wobbles.

"We had a lot of things and places that came and went," Maria says, "a cattle ranch with no cattle and a ski resort picked up on somebody's second mortgage and a motel that would have been advantageously situated at a freeway exit had the freeway been built." The consumer binge tearing apart the McClellans has left behind a hollow world for people like Maria. Even the old fairy tales (*"Ain't she the prettiest little bride?"*) are unavailable; in this sexual free market, relationships come and go like parcels of real estate.

Promise doesn't merely disappoint. It either fails to materialize—the freeway doesn't get built—or it fosters unprecedented tragedy. Domestic safety has been forfeited for a fragile public space: a badly planned for, poorly located motel.

As the novel begins, Maria tries, wanly, to orient herself. She cites an old narrative: "What makes Iago evil? some people ask. I never ask."

The reader wonders, Who are "some people"? Aside from literature professors and theater directors, who ever asks, "What makes Iago evil?" Maria is an actress, apparently with *some* classical training, but a Shakespearean she's not. As we learn more about her, we wonder where a perpetually stoned film player could encounter people who talk this way?

The movies Maria's friends make are hardly John Wayne Westerns. They are trifles, forgettable narratives, illusions of fear or pleasure, promoting no code other than instant self-gratification. In one film, made by her husband, bikers gang-rape Maria.

Snippets of film dialogue filter into the real lives of the movie people as nuggets of fake cleverness. A man to whom Maria confesses her emptiness dismisses her desperation. Then he says, apropos of nothing, "You got a map of Peru?" When Maria doesn't respond, he snaps, "That's funny, Maria. That's a line from *Dark Passage*."

In this lost paradise, language has become completely unmoored, no longer serviceable.

And the reliable old road story? It offers only speed.

The novel is related through various points of view, starting with Maria, shifting to her husband, then to a friend. After these initial first-person sections, the book is divided into eighty-four fragmented, omnisciently narrated segments. The quick, vivid fragments and the fluid points of view give the novel a restless urgency—a set of flimsy binoculars in the hands of a witnessing intelligence always on the move, chasing after Maria, focusing and refocusing, zooming in on the run. What holds the novel together, even as Maria splinters before our eyes, is this relentless pursuit of an elusive quarry.

What holds it together is the longing for story.

3

"In the preface to her essays [Miss Didion] says that she has sometimes been 'paralyzed by the conviction that writing is an irrelevant act.' Her new book feels as if it were written out of an insufficient impulse by a writer who doesn't know what else to do with all that talent and skill," Lore Segal concluded in her front-page review. "It is . . . Joan Didion's own lack of faith in what she is writing [that] puts her book in that heartbreaking category—a bad novel by a very good writer."

Kirkus concurred, calling the book "an ephemeral form of survival kitsch."

Many more critics agreed with John Leonard's assessment that Didion had placed herself in the forefront of American novelists. In some ways the critical reception wasn't crucial. On the heels of *Slouching Towards Bethlehem* and the famous divorce piece in *Life*, *Play It As It Lays* stirred already-intense reader interest in Didion. An excerpt appeared in *Cosmopolitan* magazine. FSG pounded the advertising, with "teaser ads" three days a week in *The New York Times*, the *San Francisco Chronicle*, *The Boston Globe*, and *Book World*. On August 9, the publisher bought a full-page ad in the *Los Angeles Times Book Review*. The result was on-average national sales of a thousand copies a week in the first few weeks after publication. Following the novel's appearance in *Publishers Weekly*'s bestseller rankings, sales topped five thousand a week in September. Bantam paid a $55,000 advance for paperback rights. The novel would be nominated for a National Book Award.

Much of this interest stemmed from readers' identification of Didion with "her creature." The esteemed translator Herman Briffault wrote Henry Robbins a long, admiring letter on the book, insisting that any reader could discern its autobiographical core. The novelist was clearly "hurt" in a "shattering" world where sex, divorce, and abortion were treated as trivial matters. Robbins replied, yes, "the heroine, like the author herself, is a tortured soul. . . . Didion is exploring the 'nothingness' after one has been used as an object."

Even Lore Segal, for whom the novel didn't work, found it most convincing when the author's "high intelligence" cut through pale literary gestures. Didion thought she didn't "write the child" well, but Segal disagreed: "When Maria speaks of her little daughter with an unspecified mental imbalance . . . what might have been sentimental is moving and true." It's just that Didion didn't want to go there. Her reluctance only added to the mystery and provoked further speculation about the author.

Didion always claimed she expected the novel to fail. Dan Wakefield doesn't buy this. "I can't believe when she was writing *Play It As It Lays* she didn't think she would be a star. Because she *was* a star. She deserved to be," he said. "I remember staying with [the Dunnes] in Hollywood in '68. [I went] up to Joan's office to look at her typewriter. In it was the first paragraph of *Play It [A]s It Lays*, and I remember thinking, 'Wow!' "

Didion's subsequent protests that her fame was unwelcome also ring false. "There was a certain tendency to read *Play It As It Lays* as an autobiographical novel, I suppose because I lived out here and looked skinny in photographs and nobody knew anything else about me," she said in a *Paris Review* interview. What she didn't say was that those photographs were very carefully arranged and disseminated in the press.

Julian Wasser, who had snapped Eve Babitz playing chess with Marcel Duchamp, who had caught Bobby Kennedy in the Ambassador Hotel moments before he was shot, who had captured Vietnam's Madame Nhu right after her husband was assassinated, posed Didion in front of her yellow Corvette Stingray behind the Franklin Avenue house. Didion wore a pale, thick caftan and sandals. She held a cigarette, the smoke, in one pose, wreathing her face and her shoulder-length hair. She leaned on the car, disaffected and bored (it seemed), and at one point danced casually around it. The pictures were teasing and sexy, the contour of a leg just visible beneath the caftan, and no reader of *Play It As It Lays* would fail to imagine Maria cruising the freeways in *her* Corvette, cracking a hard-boiled egg on the steering wheel. Didion knew she was forging the connection—or at the very least, acquiescing to the photographer's desire to do so.

The images became part of the narrative. Readers thought they *knew* this woman.

PART SIX

Didion and Dunne in their Malibu home, December 1977, shortly after the publication of *A Book of Common Prayer*. (AP Photo)

Didion in Malibu, June 1979, having just published *The White Album*. (AP Photo)

Left: Didion in her New York apartment, in front of a portrait of Dunne, September 2005, upon publication of *The Year of Magical Thinking.* (AP Photo/Kathy Willens)

Right: Didion in Dunne's office in their New York apartment, following his death, September 2005. (AP Photo/Kathy Willens)

Left: Didion in front of a painting of Quintana in her New York apartment, September 2007. (AP Photo/Kathy Willens)

Above: Didion, Dunne, and Quintana on the deck of their Malibu home, October 1976. (© John Bryson/Sygma/CORBIS)

Left: Didion in 1981, just prior to the publication of *Salvador*. (© John Bryson/Sygma/CORBIS)

Below: Didion in Haight-Ashbury, April 1967. (© Ted Streshinsky/CORBIS)

Left: Didion in Haight-Ashbury, April 1967. (© Ted Streshinsky/ CORBIS)

Below: Didion in Alcatraz prison, March 1967. (© Ted Streshinsky/ CORBIS)

Didion and Dunne in their New York apartment, 2000. (© Richard Schulman/CORBIS)

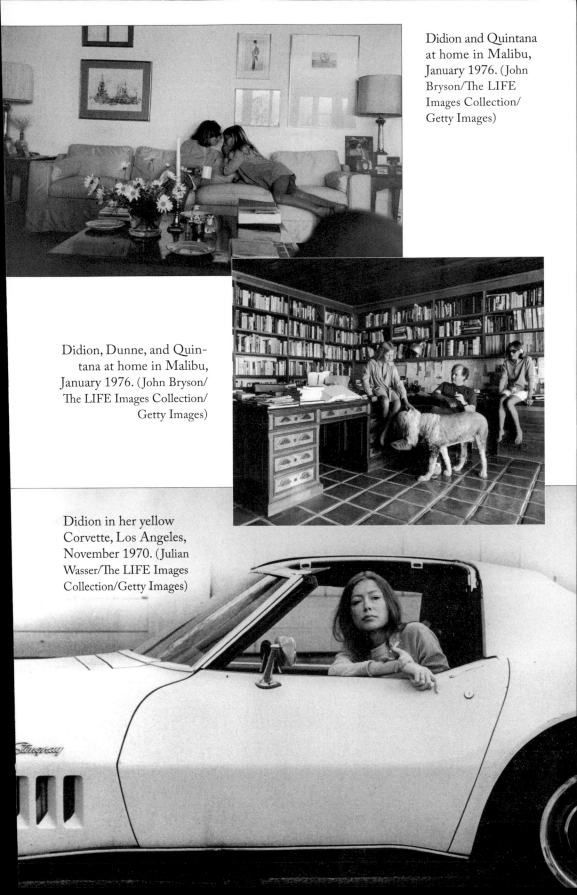

Didion and Quintana at home in Malibu, January 1976. (John Bryson/The LIFE Images Collection/Getty Images)

Didion, Dunne, and Quintana at home in Malibu, January 1976. (John Bryson/The LIFE Images Collection/Getty Images)

Didion in her yellow Corvette, Los Angeles, November 1970. (Julian Wasser/The LIFE Images Collection/Getty Images)

Didion and Dunne, October 1972. (Frank Edwards/Archive Photos/ Getty Images)

Above: Didion at home in Malibu, 1977. (CSU Archives/Everett Collection/Newscom)

Left: Didion on the street in New York, March 2009. (Nancy Kaszerman/ZUMAPRESS/Newscom)

President Obama presents Didion with a National Humanities Medal at the White House, July 2013. (Polaris)

Didion next to her typewriter in Brentwood, 1988. (Nancy Ellison/Polaris)

Didion with Vanessa Redgrave in Didion's New York apartment, discussing the stage production of *The Year of Magical Thinking*, May 2006. (Chester Higgins/*The New York Times*/Redux)

Above: Dominick Dunne, Didion, and Quintana at John Gregory Dunne's memorial service at Saint John the Divine. (Don Hogan/*The New York Times/*Redux)

Above: Didion, Quintana, and Abigail McCarthy, New York, September 1977. (Don Hogan/*The New York Times/*Redux)

Left: Didion in New York, September 2012. (Teresa Zabala/*The New York Times/*Redux)

Chapter Nineteen

———— ❧ ————

1

The Dunnes' move to Malibu in January 1971 was an attempt to heal following the previous years' excesses—or so Didion presented it in her essay "The White Album." "This . . . house on the sea had itself been very much a part of the Sixties, and for some months after we took possession I would come across souvenirs of that period in its history—a piece of Scientology literature beneath a drawer lining, a copy of *Stranger in a Strange Land* stuck deep on a closet shelf—but after a while we did some construction, and between the power saws and the sea wind the place got exorcised," she wrote.

"She still had parties nonstop, so the move to Malibu wasn't as antisocial as I first thought it was," Eve Babitz told me. "But driving out there was horrible." (Even though, in those days, it was only twenty minutes from Sunset to the Pacific Coast Highway.) The Dunnes' new place, a spacious ocean-facing house with a wide terrace over the water, wall-size windows, a white brick fireplace (used year-round to dispel the chill in the air), and redwood ceilings, was located above the beach at 33428 Pacific Coast Highway, just beyond Decker Canyon at the west end of Malibu, some distance from the pastel swarms of B-list actors swelling the Colony. Interest rates were high and the housing market was slightly depressed, yet the area, formerly a private ranch, was becoming more accessible with the opening of the Kanan-Dume Road, near the school Quintana would attend. Late in the afternoon, on the beautifully clear day the family moved into the house, Didion made a run in her Corvette to the Trancas Market, three and a half miles down the highway, cranking up KRLA, "the heart of rock and roll!" By the time she got home, the fog was so thick that she couldn't find her driveway. She held her breath, tried to forget the cliff's edge, two hundred feet above the slamming waves, inched her way forward, and finally made a slow left turn.

Soon, she learned not to keep the Corvette's top down in the drive: Occasionally, king snakes fell from the trees or the eaves of the garage into the backseat.

"The hills are scrubby and barren, infested with bikers and rattlesnakes, scarred with cuts and old burns and new R.V. parks," Didion said of Trancas and Zuma canyons (*Zuma* is a Chumash word suggesting "abundance"). In truth, between wildfires, the hills splay out in patches of parsley-green as one travels north and west from Los Angeles, enveloped by a sudden sense of isolation. Crows drift over ice plants and agave, the rainy yellow shimmer of mustard seeding the slopes as after-burn, draping low, reddish brown outcrops lined with scrappy eucalyptus. Pelicans dodge warm drafts of frying oil from the fish markets, salt and gasoline rising from the tides and from the buses and lettuce trucks ratcheting into low gear on their way to Oregon from Tijuana.

The Dunnes' house was secluded on a small road just off the highway, with only three year-round neighbors in close proximity (though gradually the area filled with picture people, first the carpenters and cinematographers— like the Dunnes' neighbor Dick Moore—who were not required on movie sets every day, freelancers with plenty of time to sit around beach fires smoking the very good dope cultivated in Big Sur, and then more and more A-listers, as the canyons slicked up and the village expanded, with Cross Creek Plaza, lots of new bars, gun shops proudly flying California Bear flags, and a Swenson's ice-cream parlor).

"There are not only no blacks in Malibu," Josie Mankiewicz told Dunne when she heard where he was going, "there are no brunettes."

"On this littoral there seemed to be no cellulite, either," he wrote.

Off and on, for over six months, the Dunnes engaged a construction crew to expand the waterside deck, install waxed pine bookshelves, and lay terracotta floor tiles. The men tore out prefabricated plywood walls and pulled up "icky green" flooring. Harrison Ford headed the crew. "They were the most sophisticated people I knew," Ford said. "I was the first thing they saw in the morning and the last thing they saw before cocktails."

In *Vegas,* Dunne wrote, "[W]hat had started as a two-month job . . . [stretched] into its sixth month and the construction account was four thousand dollars overdrawn. . . . I fired the contractor. 'Jesus, man, I understand,' he said. He was an out-of-work actor and his crew sniffed a lot of cocaine and when he left he unexpectedly gave me a soul-brother handshake, grabbing my thumb while I was left with an unimportant part of his little finger." The next day, Dunne realized the only thing separating him and his family from the Pacific Ocean was a clear sheet of Pliofilm where the French doors were supposed to go. "I rehired the contractor," he wrote. "'Jesus, man, I understand,' the contractor said."

Didion was enamored not of the ocean but of the "look of the horizon . . . It is always there, flat." If she was no longer *physically comfortable* in the Central Valley, she needed the solacing *feel* of her childhood geography. Each day ended fast, no muss—a snuffing of the sun in the sea, a healthy glass of bourbon. She felt Malibu was "a new kind of life. We were living on the frontier, as it were." She had her husband and her sheepdog and her barefoot child getting splinters in her heels on the redwood deck. She had hurricane lamps, her family's rosewood piano (it had sailed around the Cape in 1848), her grandmother's hanging quilts sewn on a covered wagon, and a Federal table once owned by her husband's great-great-grandmother. She had her mother's Craftsman dinner knives. She had straight-backed wooden chairs hand-painted by her mother-in-law, shipped from Connecticut. She had, on her wall, a large black-and-white photo of a stark valley roadside with a sign pointing to Sacramento, and she had Eve Babitz's Ginger Baker poster above the tub in the bathroom.

Tucked into the frame, behind another picture, she found a note to her in Noel's handwriting—the one he'd left on his earlier visit: "You were wrong." What about? Everything, no doubt. She burned the note and didn't tell her husband about it.

Just outside the window of the room she used as her office, she hung the family's clothes on a line to dry in the salt wind: her comfy old fisherman's sweater, her husband's blue extra-large bathrobe, her daughter's black wool challis dress. She liked a small, enclosed space in which to write—surrounding herself with talismans of the latest project: postcards, maps, trinkets, and shells. (Her husband spread his books around a fourteen-foot table in a large library opening onto the ocean.) She liked the clothes outside, warm sleeves flapping—gentle puffs of breath—curtaining her view. She liked it that she could barely hear her own voice, sometimes, over the crashing of water on the boulders below.

Often at dinner she'd place a white orchid in her hair—her hair lightly reddened, lightly blonded by the sun.

She felt comforted by the crystalline stars appearing one by one over kelp-cluttered sea foam.

Her daughter went to sleep to the sound of the waves and awoke whenever the surf went silent at the tide's lowest ebb.

The elements aligned for happiness.

Maybe the sixties really *were* over. The riots on Sunset Strip had petered out soon after Huey Newton went to prison: "Free the Strip! Free Huey!" Peace, then. It all seemed so distant. Miles down the road.

Cielo Drive. The Landmark Motel. Such an evil time. In the rearview mirror.

Now: the straight road ahead. Her husband had taken a full physical (for his insurance policy). Everything normal: prostate, EKG, EEG. The doctor had told him, in passing, he had "soft shoulders," but that wasn't a medical condition, and if this was the worst he could say, well then . . . bring on the breakers!

And she . . . "I was so unhappy" writing *Play It As It Lays*, she admitted now to friends. "I didn't realize until I finished it how depressed it had made me to write it. Then I finished it and suddenly it was like having something lifted from the top of my head, you know? Suddenly I was a happy person." People "were talking about this book. Not in a huge way, but in a way I hadn't experienced before. It made me feel good. It made me feel closer to it. . . . [F]rom that time on I had more confidence."

And why not?

James Dickey had called her, in print, "the finest woman prose stylist writing in English today."

Her old teacher Mark Schorer had said, "One thinks of the great *performers*—in ballet, opera, circuses. Miss Didion, it seems to me, is blessed with everything."

Alfred Kazin flew from New York to interview her for *Harper's* magazine. The day he arrived, a small wildfire flared in the canyon hills, but this didn't stop surfers from lugging their boards to the ocean and riding the swells under an angry canopy of red-black ash. Kazin invited Didion to lunch at Scandia on the Strip, annoyed when Dunne came along. The couple seemed inseparable—in his journal, Kazin noted an almost constant electric "ripple" between them.

Dunne dominated the conversation, telling Kazin that California was the best place a writer could be to chronicle the American scene. He said Nixon was the "most interesting personality in the White House since FDR," and he told Kazin he thought "one of these days the President will crack in public."

After eating, they all drove back to Malibu. "People who live in a beach house don't know how wary it makes them," Kazin wrote. Didion's decision to move here, to keep an eye *on the edge*, told him she was a "very vulnerable, very defensive young woman whose style in all things is somehow to keep the world off, to keep it from eating her up, and so"—casting protective spells—"[she] describes Southern California in terms of fire, rattlesnakes, cave-ins, earthquakes, the indifference to other people's disasters, and the terrible wind called the Santa Ana."

In the magazine piece, he characterized Didion as "subtle," as possessing an "alarmed fragility," and falling into "many silences." In his private journal, he said she was "full of body language. . . . Her face runs the gamut from poor old Sookie to the temptress with long blonde-red locks. She can look at you and past you without the slightest hint of a concession. The unspoken is a most important part of her presence in the world."

She was trying to tell him, This is what a happy woman looks like.

2

The determined insistence on happiness arose in part because, in spite of her new confidence as a writer, the previous year had been hectic and disturbing on many levels. She had left the Alamac Hotel in late December 1969 and only a short while later found herself in eastern Oregon, doing a column for *Life* on the nerve gas storage mounds at the army depot in Umatilla County. On arriving in the town of Hermiston, she felt at home initially, listening to locals in the Caravan Broiler talk about wheat shares and Shell Oil and high-moisture grain, but she was there to interview a funeral director who had been a strong booster of President Nixon's plan to store VX and GB nerve gas on twenty-thousand acres just outside of town, for the employment it would stimulate. The people protesting the gas shipments were college kids in the liberal cushion of Eugene and big-city wine drinkers over in Portland, he said—"the academic-community-Moratorium-and-other-mothers-for-peace-or-whatever." "They talk about a few drops of it killing thousands of people. Well, really, you'd need pretty ideal conditions for that," he said. "And if you give yourself an injection within thirty seconds, there's no effect whatsoever."

She drove into the hardscrabble area. The flat horizon here wasn't so flat anymore. Over a thousand mounds—reinforced concrete under sod and sagebrush—"mutilated the land," Didion wrote. She stood one day among the staggered rows of humps, interlaced with fifty miles of railroad track, and realized she was "not in a frontier town at all but in a post-frontier town." All over the West, in places like this, settlers felt "cut free from the ambiguities of history. They could afford their innocent blend of self-interest and optimism. They still had a big country and a big sky and cheap expendable land, and they could still tap the Columbia for all the water and power they needed and the best was still to come, or so they thought."

These ruminations helped seed *Where I Was From* (initially called *Fairy Tales*), a book she would not be able to write for another thirty years; for now, she still believed that the "ambiguities of history" would prevent mutilations of the land if the present generation became aware of them. In fact, the West's history was *always* one of self-corrosion. In time, her perceptions would shift.

For the moment, she was acutely aware that there were no Woody Guthrie tunes riding the prairie wind and that she should be home helping her daughter arrange a tea party for her stuffed bunny, planning a celebration for her fourth birthday. Instead, she was standing in an empty mound examining protective clothing and petting a white rabbit used to indicate gas leakage. "Pretty healthy rabbit," an army colonel told her. "We've never lost a rabbit in the line of duty."

Perhaps farther east, out in the desert near Pendleton, the environment would relax her. But her sense of desolation only deepened. The manager of the motel she checked into was a Mormon. The day she left, he asked her, "If you can't believe you're going to heaven in your own body and on a first-name basis with all the members of your family, then what's the point of dying?"

Months later, Quintana lost Bunny Rabbit. No more tea parties. She left him in a suite at the Royal Hawaiian Hotel and remembered him only on the evening Pan Am flight back to LAX. In *Blue Nights*, Didion wrote, "[M]y child mourned Bunny Rabbit's cruel fate: Bunny Rabbit was lost, Bunny Rabbit was left behind, Bunny Rabbit had been abandoned."

By the time they landed in Los Angeles, Quintana had consoled herself: Bunny Rabbit would be enjoying the room service at the Royal Hawaiian, swimming, rafting to the reef.

While Didion paced underground in Oregon, plans were proceeding for *The Panic in Needle Park*.

Dunne had taken her film treatment, stitched in dialogue, and finished a full draft, but the final version of the screenplay would owe its power to Didion's sensibility.

It begins with the aftermath of a back-alley abortion; Helen, the hapless girl who tumbles into addiction in a pathetic attempt to keep her boyfriend, resembles a lost kid from Haight-Ashbury; she sums up her middle-class childhood in Fort Wayne, Indiana, speaking like a Sacramento housewife: "We had a lawn."

Every scene in the film bristles with the sordid details of the bloody drug use Didion had witnessed on Broadway or in the darkened rooms at the Alamac. "Basically, we just reported," she said. "We were reporters, John and I."

"We rehearsed it as though it were a stage play," said Kitty Winn, the actress who played Helen. "No improvisation. It's all the script. And it spoiled me forever. I don't think I ever enjoyed doing another film as much again."

"It was a fantastic script," Jerry Schatzberg said. Years later, re-screening the film, he'd think certain scenes must have been spontaneously captured on-camera, but then he'd check the screenplay and *always* the action or dialogue "was in the original script."

Avco dropped the film—possibly frightened by the writing. "I didn't see it as a happy ending," Didion said. "At the time we wrote the script . . . it wasn't a time in the history of the world when stories like this . . . [well,] they didn't end in rehab."

Fox picked up the option. Dick Zanuck, whom Dunne had shadowed for a year to write *The Studio,* suggested Henry Fonda for the lead. Politely, Dunne hinted that Fonda might be forty years too old for the part. *Peter* Fonda, maybe? The studio wanted nothing to do with Peter Fonda.

Nick Dunne had seen Kitty Winn, a classically trained actress, perform a stage version of George Bernard Shaw's *Saint Joan* in San Francisco. He sent a copy of the *Needle Park* script to her. "I never found out what [he] saw in my . . . performance that screamed 'drug addict,' but whatever. I stayed up all night reading it," Winn said. "So extraordinary: two people locked in a co-dependent relationship, a battleground."

Schatzberg came fully on board when his business manager told him Al Pacino, a dynamic young actor who'd never had a lead movie role, was interested in playing the part of Bobby. "I'd seen Al four years earlier onstage," Schatzberg said. "He was so different . . . I related to him. You know, we come from different parts of the Bronx, but there's still Bronx in both of us. And I thought, 'Boy, if I ever did a film, that's the guy.'"

Meanwhile, Schatzberg had met Adam Holender, a Polish immigrant, through Roman Polanski. "When you come from a gray, grimy Communist country, you notice things," urban details, lights, shadows, angles that American cinematographers overlook, he said. His extraordinary work in *Midnight*

Cowboy, a combination of psychedelia and rat-infested realism, convinced Schatzberg no other director of photography would do on *Needle Park*.

"[We were] a group of improbables," Schatzberg said—a pair of literary writers, a fashion photographer, an Eastern European émigré, two unknown stage actors, and a perpetually stoned producer, on a budget of just over a million dollars ('We didn't have money for heroin,' Winn quipped) but we pulled it off."

For six weeks, Schatzberg rehearsed his actors on-site, copping gestures from the recovering addicts at Phoenix House, working with Holender on the documentary feel he wanted for the film. "The thoroughness" of preparation and attention to detail "was fantastic," Didion said. She couldn't have gotten luckier her first time out with a script, though the New York location and the tedious production process did not always lead to happy times. Filming began in mid-October and wrapped on December 22. Fox photo stills show Didion and the Dunne brothers shivering in Needle Park or posed in front of the Alamac. Didion's long, straight hair, parted in the middle, looks unwashed, as if she were channeling the lives of her subjects. The braces-wearing drug dealer, whom she had promised a part in the film, was nowhere to be found—though she thought she glimpsed him one day in the crowds ringing the filming perimeter. She worried he was using again and felt too ashamed to approach them.

In the publicity shots, Nick, wearing a fleece-lined jacket, standing with his hands in his pockets on the corner of Broadway and Seventy-first, has the unmistakably fierce, wide-eyed look of a man flying on coke. Didion huddles close to her husband.

Besides coke, Nick was inhaling amyl nitrate back in his room at the Volney Hotel. One night, "drunk and stoned," he "knocked over a lit candle onto the curtains, which went up in flame," he wrote in his memoir, *The Way We Lived Then*.

The Fox publicity materials praised Nick as an experienced producer who "knew exactly how to launch a production in New York"; he was doing "valiant and invaluable" work in bringing to the screen a cautionary tale about the dangers of drugs. But his behavior threatened to scuttle the project.

Meanwhile, his brother Greg was not endearing himself to local reporters milling around the sets. "Neither of us likes to come back here to New York," he said of himself and Joan. "It seems banal to us. Los Angeles is such a trip. It's like having a grandstand seat on the birth of the future. But New York, well, it's like having a grandstand seat on the death of the past."

Didion attempted a softer tone. In spite of the wretchedness of this part of the Upper West Side, she said, "writing the film was great fun for us—and we learned a lot along the way."

Filming was a different story. "When a picture is shooting, a lot of things seem arbitrary, or you might've done them differently if you thought twice about it. When we were shooting, I was overcome with what I had failed to do," she said later. "[Y]ou're hypersensitive to everything that might be wrong."

The day Kitty Winn prepared to play the postabortion scene, she recalled every tragedy she'd ever experienced in order to assume the proper mindset. "All loss is loss," she figured. "I don't know that [Joan and I] ever talked about it." She decided the abortion was included in the film to indicate a "relationship gone wrong."

"I never thought this was a picture about drugs," Didion said. "It was a picture about betrayal. Love."

While elements were locking in place for the filming and the eventual release of the movie in time for the May 1971 Cannes Film Festival, jury selection was beginning for the Manson trial. Manson had assaulted a bailiff; he had screamed at the judge that he couldn't get a fair hearing. "You can kill me now!" he shouted in the courtroom, spreading his arms like Jesus on the cross. His lawyer admitted "there is a minimum of client control in this case."

A young man in Berkeley, identifying himself as Rabbit, called Ed Sanders at the *Los Angeles Free Press* and said he was organizing a giant benefit rock concert to raise legal funds for the Manson Family. Not surprisingly, he had so far secured zero commitments from big-name bands, but Squeaky Fromme, one of Charlie's girls, had given him home movies from Spahn Ranch to screen onstage.

Linda Kasabian, nine months pregnant with her second child, had agreed to offer prosecutors full cooperation and to testify against Manson in exchange for a request for immunity. This news got lost in the press beneath coverage of the Weathermen who had blown up a ten-room town house in Greenwich Village while bungling the making of a bomb, and again weeks later by reports on the shootings at Kent State. Manson, apparently concerned that *his* brand of violence might seem tame in Nitro-America (*were* the sixties over?) carved a swastika into his forehead and issued pronouncements:

"Death is psychosomatic," he said, and "You have created the monster. I am not of you, from you . . . I have Xed myself from your world."

On August 3, 1970, Kasabian was again eclipsed in the media. On that day, President Nixon, speaking in Denver, mentioned off the cuff that he had noted the "coverage of the Charles Manson case. Front page every day in the papers . . . Here is a man who was guilty, directly or indirectly, of eight murders without reason. Here is a man yet who, as far as the coverage was concerned, appeared to be a rather glamorous figure . . ."

Immediately, Manson assailed the judge: "Your Honor, the President said we are guilty, so why go on with the trial?" He smuggled into the courtroom a hand-printed sign: NIXON GUILTY.

What nearly got missed in all this was Kasabian's third day of testimony at the Santa Monica Courthouse. Between admitting she'd taken fifty LSD trips and had sex with every man at the ranch, between agreeing she'd slept just fine following the Tate murders, and confessing she'd willingly driven the car for the second killing spree, Linda Kasabian, "demure" and "pigtailed," according to the *Los Angeles Times,* said "author Joan Didion" was writing a book about her. She had been promised 25 percent of any profits from the book, she testified. She was not interested in becoming famous. She hoped the book would influence young people to remain "straight."

A week earlier, before her first day on the witness stand, prosecutor Vincent Bugliosi convinced her not to wear a long dress because "long is for evening." She needed to make a favorable impression on the jury. Didion, by now a confidante of sorts after several interviews at the Sybil Brand Institute for Women, offered, maternally, to go to I. Magnin in Beverly Hills and buy Kasabian the dress of her choice—"Size 9 Petite." Kasabian had recently given birth to her baby. "Mini but not extremely mini," she said. "In velvet if possible. Emerald green or gold." Either that, or a "Mexican peasant dress, smocked or embroidered."

Didion delivered the dress to Kasabian and her attorney, Gary Fleischman, at Fleischman's office on Rodeo Drive. Kasabian's husband, Bob, was there, wearing a long white robe. Didion watched them climb into Fleischman's Cadillac convertible and drive off to Santa Monica, cheerily waving goodbye. She was grateful to be done with Sybil Brand. There, walking down antiseptic institutional hallways to meet with Kasabian, she would pass through half a dozen doors. They locked behind her, each a "little death," she said. She remembered a white rabbit grazing on the grass beside the prison gate as Fleischman signed them in one day. After each interview, she would return to Franklin Avenue, "have two drinks and make . . . a hamburger and eat it ravenously."

The day Kasabian wore the I. Magnin dress, she hoped to sneak into the courtroom unseen by gawkers or reporters, but Family hangers-on discovered her arrival and screamed at her, "You'll kill us all, you'll kill us all!"

Ed Sanders said Squeaky Fromme showed up at the *Freep*'s offices one day during the trial, vaguely warning the paper not to print negative stories about Charlie. Eventually, Manson groupies would wonder if Didion failed to complete her book on Linda Kasabian because she feared retaliation by Family members. Actually, other factors scotched the project, not the least of which was Didion's frenetic schedule.

In order to convict Manson, Susan Atkins, Patricia Krenwinkel, and Leslie Van Houten, Bugliosi had deemed it best to deemphasize the drug deals and petty thievery and build a prosecution around a vast conspiracy. Manson, he said, had masterminded a plot called Helter Skelter (based on subliminal messages from the Beatles song), an attempt to start a race war—from which the Family would emerge as world rulers—by committing a series of murders and blaming the violence on the Black Panthers. The success of Bugliosi's trial strategy would depend on Linda Kasabian's performance, her "demure" and "pigtailed" appearance, her I. Magnin dress.

Despite a few faltering moments, despite throat-cutting gestures directed her way by Manson as she testified, she did her job. By the end of the year, the jury had found Manson and the three women guilty. The women didn't appear to be concerned. They had taken heart, in September, when the Weathermen broke Timothy Leary out of the San Luis Obispo federal prison, where he was serving a ten-year drug sentence. Maybe Charlie could escape, too! As for Manson, he maintained his innocence, and cleverly played on the media's desire to make him a symbol. "In the name of Christian justice, someone should cut your head off!" he told the judge at one point. "I am only what you made me. I am only a reflection of you . . . You made your children what they are . . . these children that come at you with their knives, they are your children. You taught them. I didn't teach them . . . As for Helter Skelter. Helter Skelter is confusion. Confusion is coming down fast . . . it is not my conspiracy. . . . Why blame it on me? I didn't write the music."

"On August 13 [1970], all charges were dropped against Linda Kasabian, and she was set free. For a while thereafter she was a minor media celebrity,"

Ed Sanders reported. Kasabian flew to New Hampshire to be with her mother and two children. "A few weeks after Kasabian had returned to the East Coast, Didion wanted to visit her and work on the book," Sanders said. "Kasabian wouldn't oblige because she was going to be spending the weekend at Yale, watching the football game."

Eventually, Didion *did* travel to New Hampshire, and on one occasion Kasabian went to see her in New York. Didion and Quintana went with her and her kids on the Staten Island Ferry to see the Statue of Liberty. One of these kids, Tanya, two and a half, Kasabian had left behind at Spahn Ranch two days after the LaBianca killings. "You abandoned your child with the very people you considered to be a band of murderers?" a defense attorney asked her during the trial. "Yes," she replied. "Just something inside me told me she would be all right."

Henry Robbins was terribly excited by the prospect of a Didion book on Linda Kasabian. It was the perfect confluence of author and subject, he thought. He spoke to her about it eagerly on Halloween night, 1970, when the Dunnes went to visit him and his wife at their apartment on West Eighty-sixth Street. Quintana went trick-or-treating on every floor of the building with Robbins's two kids while Robbins told Didion what a damned good book he thought this would make. She'd already expended considerable energy on the interviews. Magazines were clamoring for serial rights. Now all she had to do was write it.

Kasabian seemed confused: Would this be a book *about* her—or *by* her, written with Didion's help? The situation knotted when Didion and FSG received letters from an attorney representing Bartyk Frykowski, in the matter of the wrongful death of his father at the hands of the defendants, including one Linda Kasabian. The defendants should not profit from their actions, the letters said. Any moneys accruing to Kasabian would be treated as a fraud against creditors.

Robbins replied, saying Didion had no contract with Kasabian, and no intention of securing one. He *didn't* say FSG had drawn up a draft agreement with Didion for the book, or that Kasabian (whom he referred to, privately, as "Pussy") might *expect* money from it.

In the meantime, Kasabian had bought a camping trailer with her husband and hit the road, leaving no forwarding address. Didion didn't know how to reach her.

Periodically, Robbins checked with his author, hoping her interest in the

Kasabian project hadn't flagged. She said nothing to him about it. She'd decided to make a Southern pilgrimage, on *Life*'s dime, to gather material for columns and to start a novel. (All those reviewers who'd called *Run River* a Southern novel? Well, maybe this time she'd damn well *give* them a Southern novel!)

Dunne was in hunter-gatherer mode as well, so he went along (Quintana stayed in Sacramento). "The idea was . . . to drink Dr. Pepper at the general store and do the underwear and the dirty shirts at the crossroads coin laundry, to go to Little League games and get my hair cut while my wife got a manicure or a pedicure in the local beauty parlor—in other words, to take the pulse of the white South," he said, revealing how firmly he'd determined already what the South had to offer. Here was a difference between him and his wife: Though she pitched a similarly clichéd idea to the *Life* editors, telling them she'd offer something like "The Mind of the South," she carried no preconceptions into the bayous; more impressively, she aimed herself in whatever direction turned up, even when she didn't understand it, when it appeared to make no connection to anything she might do, when it couldn't be disseminated, much less *paragraphed*, for years. She would not produce "The Mind of the South." She would not produce a Southern novel. But New Orleans and the Mississippi Gulf Coast were the "most interesting place[s] I had been in a long time," she said. "[E]verything everybody said was astonishing to me." Insights from the trip would enrich several future books, in surprising and unpredictable ways.

For example, she didn't expect to find in New Orleans "a strong sense of the Caribbean." In this slumgullion atmosphere, she realized she'd been hearing, for years now, "weird stories . . . coming out about that part of the world," and she wondered if a new cultural narrative was forming. "This was a time when people"—like her husband—"kept saying California was the face of America's future," but she wasn't sure that was true anymore—another manifestation, perhaps, of her wish for the sixties, the *California* sixties, to be dead. The history of the United States had always been linked to Latin America—she knew this from her grandfather's writings, from the illegals working in her house, caring for Quintana—but new currents seemed to be blowing along the borders. Though her awareness of this was only shadows, "what I was actually interested in was the South as a gateway to the Caribbean," she said.

She remembered Jim Garrison, the New Orleans district attorney who'd opened an investigation into the John Kennedy assassination (and provided the first public viewing of the Zapruder film). Though his prosecution of Clay

Shaw, the New Orleans businessman he accused of conspiring with Oswald and a man named David Ferrie to murder the president in a "triangulation of crossfire" was ludicrously unfounded, the names Garrison exposed, rightly or wrongly, kept pointing to Miami, to Cuba, and to a "whole underbelly I'd never seen before," Didion said. "It was just real news to me. I started thinking about that part of the world, from the Gulf Coast to down around Miami. The whole Caribbean connection. There was something going on in the Caribbean that I didn't understand."

Not until 1988, on a return trip to the Crescent City, would she try to locate 544 Camp Street, where, reportedly, Oswald had rented an office in 1963 to distribute "Fair Play for Cuba" leaflets, either as a Castro supporter or as someone posing as a Castro supporter while joining the opposition, or, more sinisterly, while leaving false trails as part of an assassination conspiracy.

In 1988 the small Newman Building no longer stood; even in 1970, Didion would have found no trace of Oswald, but she was well aware of the Camp Street address. People, she said, "had taken the American political narrative seriously at 544 Camp."

In 1979 the House Select Committee on Assassinations, convened by the U.S. House of Representatives with Gerald Ford's approval, would say "the testimony of a number of witnesses . . . placing Oswald and Ferrie together in early September 1963" in and around Camp Street "may be credible." Furthermore, "Ferrie's experience with the underground activities of the Cuban exile movement and as a private investigator for [gangster] Carlos Marcello . . . might have made him a good candidate to participate in a conspiracy plot."

Didion would seize these details, citing the House Committee document in her notes for *Miami* (1987). She would not forget her trip to New Orleans in the summer of 1970, or her first inkling that the corner of Camp Street might be "one of those occasional accidental intersections where the remote narrative"—tucked into the underbelly, hidden from public view—"had collided with the actual life of the country."

For Dunne, the South's great revelation that summer was the "road glass." "Whenever some member of the local gentry would pick us up to take us out to dinner, there would be a 'road glass' on the dashboard, some spirits to fortify us for the ride to the local country club or the Holiday Inn dining room, martinis or a little straight whiskey with ice to tide us over," he wrote. "The ubiquitous road glass was the perfect pagan icon of the secular South."

Sitting beside him, or sipping Scotch on Walker Percy's rainy wooden porch in Covington, Louisiana, his wife brooded on her growing insight that "in the South they remained convinced that they had bloodied their land with history." What a difference from the West. In California, she was only just beginning to grasp, "we did not believe that history could bloody the land, or even touch it."

When finally, without fanfare or warning, Didion told Henry Robbins the Kasabian project had died in her mind of natural causes, he was exasperated, even a little furious, though he kept it from her. In a letter to Marc Joffe of Bantam Books, with whom he'd coordinated publication arrangements, Robbins said he didn't understand why Didion couldn't have made her decision six months ago or at least let them know what she was thinking. This was in line with her refusal to acknowledge Roger Straus's attempts to nominate her for Rockefeller Foundation grants and other prizes. Was it simply negligence? Sometimes she didn't seem to grasp, even minimally, what it meant to be a citizen of the profession.

So now there would be no damned good Joan Didion book about the end of the 1960s. What a shame, Robbins thought. She had been poised to do it, and she had flinched.

Marc Joffe asked for Didion's research notes and her transcripts of the interviews with Kasabian so that Bantam could pursue its own Manson project. There is no record of Didion's response.

She had already moved on, months earlier telling her editors at *Life* she was dissatisfied with their tepid support. "I had a year's contract and I let them off at the end of six months, because they simply weren't running me," she said. "I mean, I would file every week, and the pieces wouldn't run. I could have actually just made them pay me for the year . . . but that seemed too dispiriting to even contemplate." The editors found her far too dark. She had never forgiven them for denying her Vietnam. "Some of the guys are going out," Loudon Wainright had told her. The guys! For God's sakes, Mary McCarthy had slipped in-country and done *exactly* what Didion hoped to do—that is, parse the military language ("Napalm has become 'Incinder-Jell,' which makes it sound like Jell-O," McCarthy had written). The Calley trial was scheduled to start soon; the casualty figures weren't even *close* to adding up.

Saint Mary had found her angel in Robert Silvers at *The New York Review of Books*. Didion needed a champion. To spur herself, she framed and hung on her wall a telex she'd managed to acquire concerning the death tolls in Vietnam.

By now, she'd moved on, as well, to tackle a screenplay based on Lois Gould's novel *Such Good Friends*. Otto Preminger, "the all-time top-seeded Hollywood bully boy," according to Dunne, had hired the two of them to rewrite a script drafted three times by others. One night in early August of 1970, the Dunnes joined Preminger at the Bistro to toast the deal. With them was a young man named David Patrick Columbia, a friend of Preminger's son; later, Columbia would establish the New York Social Diary online. He recalled Didion as "the antithesis of the smooth and creamy tinsel and glitz that was . . . *haute* Hollywood, and which filled the room that night. She looked like a super-cool, best-selling author" in her blue-and-white cotton dress. "Her 'importance' in the room that night [had been] palpable from the moment she and her husband entered. Otto, no doubt, was aware beforehand that it would be. He too was drawn to 'names' and hot talent and always hired them for his projects."

After dinner, the group drove to Paramount Studios for a private screening of *The Diary of a Mad Housewife*, then walked across the lot to Preminger's offices to discuss the Gould project. Columbia said he was impressed with Dunne's ability to command the conversation with Preminger, as the men sat across a desk from one another. Didion sat silently, listening, as Dunne cajoled Preminger "with all the required subtle (and not so) deferences." Already, Dunne sensed that "if Otto thought he could beat up on you, then he would beat up on you without mercy." His "rage was never far beneath the surface." So Dunne charmed the great man with a combination of "business and celebrity gossip," Columbia said—it was a chat "between two pros" in "thrall" to the glamour of Hollywood.

Preminger pressed the Dunnes (whom he, like most people, thought of as the Didions) to go to New York for the fall and work with him every day in his offices on the script. They were going east, anyway, for the filming of *The Panic in Needle Park*. Before decamping, though, the couple had occasion to house-sit for a few days for a friend in Malibu. Didion stared at the comforting flat horizon and felt—not for the first time—she could be happy at the ocean. Happy? Miss Leaky Ice Pack? With that on the table, it took little to convince Dunne they should look seriously at the first available house on the coast.

Then they left for New York, subletting a "grimy, roach-infested" apartment, Dunne said. For fourteen weeks—between visits to the movie set— they met Preminger for five hours every day in his Fifth Avenue offices, trying to finalize the script. Dunne had learned a few tricks. "Studio executives are notoriously literal-minded, and the easiest way to soothe them when they complain about the mood of a scene is simply to add stage direction," he said. "Thus, if they maintain that, 'BOBBY: *You dumb bitch*' is too grim, you change the line to: 'BOBBY (*Engagingly*): *You dumb bitch.*'"

Preminger wanted to add a "nice lesbian relationship, the most common thing in the world" to the story. Didion didn't think so. Oh yes, he said. "Very easy to arrange, does not threaten the marriage."

"If he got angry with us, the top of his bald head would turn bright red," Dunne said. At least he had finally gotten their names straight: "[W]ith elaborate politeness he would refer to Joan in his Teutonic accent as, 'Misss-isss Dunne.'"

For lunch each day, they'd walk to La Côte Basque on West Fifty-fifth Street. There, among rich bouquets of roses and French village murals, they'd continue discussing the script unless they were interrupted by a showbiz manager. To Preminger's delight, these managers would invariably introduce him to "Miss Universe contestants they had signed to personal services contracts." Dunne recalled meeting "Miss Philippines and Miss Ceylon."

Back in Malibu, a twenty-year-old one-story house in need of work had come on the market. It had once belonged to Michelle Phillips. Flush with movie money, the Dunnes decided to fly back at Christmas to close the sale, though they figured they were offering fifteen thousand dollars too much. "I forbid you to go," Preminger said. Didion's silence told him she didn't care. His pate turned red. "If you worked for a studio, Misss-isss Dunne, this behavior would not be tolerated," he said. When the couple left New York, Preminger yanked them off the script, threatened a two-million-dollar lawsuit, and put a lien against their remaining fee. They settled for forty cents on the dollar, and made for the sea.

3

The happiest woman Didion had ever seen was dying of breast cancer. "My blessed cancer," Trudy Dixon would say, and she genuinely meant it.

Trudy and her husband, Mike, came to dinner at the Franklin Street house one night, a couple of years before the Dunnes moved to Malibu. Trudy had been a philosophy student at Wellesley and was now working as an editor at the Zen Center in San Francisco, transcribing the teachings of Shunryu

Suzuki for a regular newsletter called *Wind Bell,* and collecting his lectures for the book that became *Zen Mind, Beginner's Mind,* arguably the most important reason for Buddhism's spread in the United States in the 1970s. Didion knew the place from her time in the Haight. She dismissed what she'd heard of its teachings. Zen, Krishna, acid—so much purple haze.

But Trudy Dixon impressed her. Didion had met Trudy and Mike, an artist who painted under the name Willard Dixon, through Earl McGrath. "Trudy had been struggling with breast cancer for some time and I had to carry her from place to place," Mike told me. Despite her illness, she devoted herself to organizing, into simple and comprehensible English, the often obscure and culturally specific koans central to Buddhist practice. Didion was fascinated by the project's linguistic challenge, but even more, she witnessed in Trudy an embodiment of the teachings' aims to lead the mind toward "letting go . . . [of] what doesn't matter."

"She was totally inspiring in her ability to deal with the fact that she'd be dead in a short time," Didion said. "She was on final morphine, and she'd made arrangements for her small children . . . She spoke about it with equanimity, which would have been impossible for me."

When Trudy died in 1969, Suzuki wailed like a wounded animal. He had never known such a perfect disciple.

In 1970, *Zen Mind, Beginner's Mind* appeared in a limited edition. For a while, in Malibu, Didion read the book "every night to relax when I went to bed," she said. "It was very soothing to me."

She had no intention of becoming a Buddhist: "I didn't like [meditation] at all. But the book is wonderful." It was suffused with her memories of Trudy Dixon. The woman's calm dictated the very syntax of the sentences.

For Didion, then, this was a personal, rather than a religious, exploration. Her embrace of *Zen Mind, Beginner's Mind* also indicates her self-correcting ability, a quality that would characterize much of her later writing. She moved from ignoring Zen to reconsidering it, rethinking her initial reaction to it, and then—unlike a zealous convert—quietly appreciating aspects of it that she found useful in her daily life.

Primarily, the book provided a pleasurable reading experience.

Beyond that, she recognized commonsense truths in its insistence on careful daily practice. "[W]e should not do [something] as if it were preparing for something else," Suzuki said (in Trudy's transcription). "This should be true in your everyday life. To cook, or to fix some food, is not preparation . . . it is practice . . . it is to express your sincerity. So when you cook you should express yourself in your activity in the kitchen. You should allow yourself plenty of time; you should work on it with nothing in your mind, and without expecting anything. You should just cook!"

Cooking *had* become a contemplative, ritualistic act for Didion: Suzuki's words made sense to her. She could see the benefits of extending his approach not only to commonplace acts but also to writing. Practicing without expectation, remaining alert to permutations, resisting expertise and habits of thought: "In the beginner's mind there are many possibilities, but in the expert's there are few," Suzuki said.

Above all, rigid attachment to *anything* brings sorrow and dissatisfaction, he taught: Change is the essence of existence. This thought reminded Didion of the line from the Episcopal liturgy: "As it was in the beginning, is now and ever shall be, world without end." "'As it was in the beginning' . . . means ever-changing, in my interpretation. Which may not be the orthodox interpretation," Didion said.

She could not believe now, any more than she could accept when she was a girl, the orthodox notion of a "personal God, a God that is personally interested in me . . . And as far as the soul [goes] . . . I have understood the entire thing symbolically. I mean, it makes a lot of sense to me symbolically. But it doesn't if it's supposed to be real."

She could much more readily entertain the Buddhist concepts of "impermanence, nonself, and suffering."

In Trudy Dixon, she'd seen a tangible example of accepting *change* and *suffering;* just so, she had, in the waves below her Malibu house, a daily reminder of the paradoxical relationship between permanence and change: the ever-abiding sea and its constantly shifting nature, moment to moment, breaker to breaker.

Through all this contemplation, her grandfather's love of the "vast indifference" of geology returned to her in a powerful new context, enfolded in the rhythms of the Episcopal liturgy and *Zen Mind*'s weave of voices.

Constant land movement.

"I found earthquakes, even when I was in them, deeply satisfying . . . reveal[ing] evidence of the scheme in action," she said. "I learned to find equal meaning in the repeated rituals of domestic life. Setting the table. Lighting the candles. Building the fire. Cooking. All those soufflés, all that crème caramel, all those daubes and albondigas and gumbos. Clean sheets, stacks of clean towels, hurricane lamps for storms, enough water and food to see us through whatever geological event came our way."

Meaning, Didion said now. Not *happiness.* A distinction began to appear to her.

"What I have made for myself is personal, but is not exactly peace," she would write.

For one thing, peace was impossible with such a restless husband.

In the stage version of *The Year of Magical Thinking,* she would mention the fight one morning in Malibu that ended with her threat to take Quintana to LAX and fly away from Dunne. Quintana settled the standoff, insisting they "couldn't do that to him." ("[D]id she think herself safer with him than with me?" Didion asked.)

Dunne's version of the same incident read differently. In *Vegas,* he said a member of the construction crew he'd hired "lit a joint [one day] and began to scar the concrete block on which the tile was being laid with a jackhammer. The noise from the jackhammer made my daughter cry and my wife said she would take her to Sacramento that morning and I said I would go back to Vegas the next day."

In Sacramento, Didion, hoping to calm her nerves, took Quintana to Old Sac, a redeveloped area of town featuring restored saloons and wooden sidewalks from the city's pioneer-boom days. She was about to tell her daughter how generations of her cousins had walked these alleys, how her great-grandfather had owned a tavern on Front Street, but then "I stopped. Quintana was adopted. Any ghosts on this wooden sidewalk were not in fact Quintana's responsibility," Didion wrote. "This wooden sidewalk did not in fact represent anywhere Quintana was from."

So they flew back home on a Pacific Southwest Airlines plane. Painted on its nose was a big, silly smile. Quintana loved flying "The Smile."

Meanwhile, in Vegas (or wherever he'd travel to get away from his wife), Dunne would sit alone, usually in a motel room, and imagine being interviewed on *The Dick Cavett Show,* the Famous Author discussing weighty subjects from "the weather . . . [to] my Nobel Prize." But then he'd remember: "[My] voice on the air gets high and squeaky and my stammer prevents me from indulging in articulate patter." He'd start to feel sorry for himself. He *had* written two good books, hadn't he? Why hadn't they earned more notice? He was pushing forty—my God. In the past, when his friends turned thirty-five, he'd send them notes: "Halfway home." Now the joke didn't seem so funny.

Once, plagued with the jits, he took the red-eye to New York and stayed in the apartment of a friend. He listened to the World Series on the radio, and in the evenings he went to the "Frank E. Campbell funeral home on Madison Avenue at 81st to see if I knew anyone who had died." This was voyeurism keyed to his mortality. He'd return to the apartment and gobble Heath bars and Oreos—the old cures for the blues he'd shared with his brother Stephen.

Then he flew back to Vegas.

He missed his wife and child. But if he called home, he knew what he'd get—silence or recriminations: "[S]he was lonely and depressed . . . the wind was blowing and there were fires at Point Dume. The maid had quit, the fire insurance had been canceled and the engine in the Corvette had seized on the Ventura Freeway . . . [S]he had called Detroit and told the head of public relations at General Motors that if the warranty was not honored she was going to drive the car to Detroit and burn the motherfucker on the lawn of John Z. DeLorean . . . The head of public relations had suggested she see a psychiatrist."

Sometimes living with her was like "living with [a] piranha," he told her.

One night he went alone to a party in Venice. "It was like all those terrible parties in the Village in the fifties . . . Cinder-block bookcases full of Hesse and Tolkien. Gallon jugs of Almaden Mountain Red, plastic cups and no ice." People wearing batik shirts were rolling joints and insisting that Walt Disney had been frozen.

A girl asked him to take her home, and he sat around with her and her ex-husband, a wraith in tie-dyed jeans, watching the boy clean a "kilo of marijuana."

What the hell was he doing?

Sometimes, at his most depressed, he would imagine writing suicide notes, but "[w]hatever minimal impulse I had for suicide was negated by the craft of writing the suicide note. It became a technical problem." He could not stop revising.

"When are you coming home?" his wife asked when she called.

One day, for no particular reason, the "bad season . . . was over," he said. If they couldn't fire the contractor, they couldn't get a divorce, he reasoned. They were stuck with each other, at least until they got the house in order.

Chronologically, the Dunnes' uneasy peace—individually and together—appeared to coincide with the beginning of Quintana's nightmares about the Broken Man. "He has on a blue work shirt, like a repair man," Quintana told her mother. "Short sleeves. He has his name on his shirt. On the right-hand side. His name is David, Bill, Steve, one of those common names. I would guess this man is maybe age fifty to fifty-nine. Brown belt, navy-blue pants, black really shiny shoes. And he talks to me in a really deep voice: *Hello, Quintana. I'm going to lock you here in the garage.*"

One good thing: She had learned from her mother contempt for abstractions.

On some occasions, she said the Broken Man wore a cap with the word GULF on it.

The Point Dume Gulf Station was just down the road from their house. Some of the guys in Harrison Ford's crew wore blue work shirts.

But Didion did not waste energy searching for the sources of her child's mental jigsaw. The details, and Quintana's certainty about this figure, were too vivid. "Don't let the Broken Man catch me," she would say. "If the Broken Man comes, I'll hang onto the fence and won't let him take me."

In *Blue Nights*, Didion wrote, "I realized my fear of The Broken Man to be as unquestioning as her own."

4

In the spring of 1971, *The Panic in Needle Park* was chosen to be an official entry at the Cannes Film Festival. The festival was celebrating its twenty-fifth anniversary by giving Charlie Chaplin the Légion d'honneur. Twentieth Century–Fox paid the Dunnes' way to France. Didion had never been to Europe, and she was so excited (traveling first-class, no less!), she boarded the airplane barefoot.

Quintana remained behind with family. As a gift, Didion would bring her a cashmere turtleneck sweater from London.

The Dunnes stayed at the Carlton on the Promenade de la Croisette, overlooking the Mediterranean. Every day, "the hall porter brought endless bottles of chateau d'Yquem, a studio publicity man handed out crisp, new hundred-franc notes as petty cash, every night there was dinner for six, eight, twelve at La Reserve: it all went on the budget of the picture," Dunne said.

Nick loved being a big-time producer on the world stage, and he kept his behavior in check. What most annoyed his brother and sister-in-law was the credit he took for every aspect of the film. *He* claimed to have discovered the James Mills novel; *he* claimed to have spotted the potential for a love story in the midst of junkie angst. "To me, it's a strong anti-drug film," he said sanctimoniously, and Didion could hear the resentment in his voice when he told a reporter, "You know, Joan has become a great sort of best seller and everything with her book, *Play It As It Lays.*" He only mentioned this because Didion and Dunne were now writing a screenplay from the novel and Nick was set to produce it. The "three of us" cooked it up, he told the press. "Frank Perry is going to direct that."

The initial reaction to *The Panic in Needle Park* at Cannes was underwhelming. *Women's Wear Daily* called the movie "disappointing." "There was great anticipation for this film," the reviewer said. "[O]ne expects . . . stinging cynicism" from "Miss Didion," but the film is "full of misery for so long . . . it is simply too much to sit through."

Jerry Schatzberg had gotten the reaction *he'd* wanted. Keith Richards, at Cannes to promote the Stones' concert film, *Gimme Shelter,* was so impressed by *Panic*'s authenticity, he asked Schatzberg, "Are you doing the hard stuff?"

Subsequent reviewers praised the movie's realism and lack of sentimentality—the *New York Post* said, "[I]t must be considered one of the year's top films both in [the] timeliness of its material and the skill of presentation. Like it or loathe it, you have to believe it."

Kitty Winn, walking the beach wearing jeans, profoundly uncomfortable with so much glamour and celebrity hoopla, won the judges over. They gave her the Best Actress Award. "When a reporter who had interviewed me came to the door [with the news], it blew my mind," she said. But on the whole, the experience traumatized her.

Like Didion, she was the daughter of an army colonel; she approached her work with discipline and seriousness.

Acting was one thing. The movie business was another.

While Didion enjoyed the luxury of Cannes—and Dunne ate it up—Winn recoiled. She would soon leave the profession, and live a quiet life as a wife and mother. "The idea of stardom I find frightening," she said. "When I think of a star I think of a monster taking over someone's personality, obliterating them."

Chapter Twenty

———— ❖ ————

1

By the mid-1970s, embedded on the coast, Didion and Dunne were stars. Producers came to *them*, from L.A., for business or story-conference lunches. Didion had little time to practice Zen, but she made a ritual of arranging the picture people in her living room, facing the ocean, and serving them "a cold leek soup, antipasto, baguettes of French bread, fruit, Brie, and white wine," Dunne said. These lunches were "programmed to reinforce the notion that the turf [was] ours, and that it would be bad form for a guest to push aberrant ideas; we [were] no longer employees, but host and hostess."

Actress Leslie Caron remembered driving to Trancas to "listen to Joan Didion and John Gregory Dunne," who had been described to her as "the new voices of California literature." The combination of their books, magazine articles, and screenplays made them triple threats: a two-headed juggernaut. They stood at the center of a growing community of film people, musicians, and writers in Malibu: Steven Spielberg, Lee Grant, Katharine Ross, Brian Moore, Peter Boyle, Julia and Michael Phillips, Martin Scorsese, and Paul Newman and Joanne Woodward. It was "very heady," said Paul Schrader. Every weekend "[we] would have a barbecue, swim, lie in the sun, listen to music, and talk about movies. A lot of these writers and directors helped each other . . . Even though we were relatively unknown, there was a real feeling that the world was our oyster."

Naturally, Didion saw her new life in darker terms: "[T]he spirit of the place [was] one of shared isolation and adversity," she wrote. "I never loved the house on the Pacific Coast Highway more than on those many days when it was impossible to leave it, when fire or flood had in fact closed the highway."

At least they'd buried the sixties. The casualties from that period lay all along the trail. Morrison, Joplin, Hendrix, Mama Cass. The national conscience. William Calley had been convicted of mass murder, but Nixon made sure his house arrest at Fort Benning was more party than pain.

Cocaine was ravaging the entertainment industry; big money warped the studios' product; but Didion, perched on an ancient landslide, overlooking tidal swells and the "acid yellow" of mustard glazing the hills, rode a different crest.

For her, Hollywood was the "last stable society."

The late 1960s had been a "hangover" from the *Easy Rider* orgy, before the studios figured out how to reinvent themselves, take power back from the young upstarts, reassert control of distribution and development money. But they'd done it—"all the terrific 22-year-old directors went back to shooting television commercials and all the creative 24-year-old producers used up the leases on their office space at Warner Brothers by sitting out there in the dull Burbank sunlight smoking dope before lunch and running one another's unreleased pictures after lunch," Didion wrote in a 1973 essay entitled "In Hollywood."

The fact that she and Dunne could publish coruscating pieces on Hollywood and remain players in town only added to their luster. Picture people loved to read about themselves: *Hey, you know, what the hell, as long as folks are talking . . .*

So she could get her hair done at Gene Shacove's and rest assured that even the hairdressers were "looking for the action," trying to pull together a "beautiful story" and all the "elements" (writers, stars), to scare up studio interest. She could be certain most people would practice discretion at parties because discretion was not only good taste, it was "good business." Bottom line: Everyone wanted to be "bankable." This was a clear form of right and wrong—a great comfort to Didion—and she was relieved to learn that she had not arrived in Hollywood *too late* (as she had feared in the lost domain of Franklin Avenue).

Of course she saw the irony: The "last stable society" existed to generate texts, images, and songs whose sole purpose was to disseminate restlessness. Fear, titillation, subversion, promises of freedom and release—massive *instability*—were Hollywood's métier. It was no surprise that one screen-bedazzled group after another rose to demand its rights, just as poor Lucille Miller had, seeking noir thrills in San Berdoo.

You laughed and cried with La Raza! Cheered the Panthers!

And now—grab the edges of your gowns—get ready for the women's movement!

Here was a prime target for Didion. Squatting in her "stable" nest, she had already ridiculed some of the movement's heroines (Joan Baez was "a personality before she was entirely a person," she'd declared). In another essay, while praising Hollywood's social hierarchy, Didion disparaged feminism's "invention of women as a 'class.'" "To make an omelette you need not only those broken eggs but someone 'oppressed' to break them," she'd scoffed.

Her omelette sparked a skirmish with the editors of *Ms.* magazine. They published a response to Didion written by Catharine Stimpson. "Her attitudes pose a problem for us all," Stimpson said. "[She] insists that grief, which is enduring, can only be endured . . . [and] if women resist suffering, they must be perpetual children."

Didion's critique of the movement was slyer than Stimpson allowed. For instance, she'd objected to feminist crusaders scorching Western novels for their patriarchal structures and calling for celebrations of the feminine. "The idea that fiction has certain irreducible ambiguities seemed never to occur to these women"; the truth is, "fiction is in most ways hostile to ideology," she wrote. Besides, Joseph Conrad grasped far more about birth and blood than George Eliot ever did.

As for the glories of female orgasm: "I think sex is a lot darker than Kate Millet does," Didion said. "It seems to me a fairly right fantasy . . . that men want to ravage and women want to be ravaged." She provoked her readers further: "I agree with every single thing that Norman Mailer puts down on paper . . . [H]e is one of the few people who can write about sex without embarrassing me." That man's unspeakable name was guaranteed to rile the sisters.

Beneath the wit and intelligence of Didion's attack lay painful memories of her independence in New York.

In her essay, in a tone of sustained mockery, she wrote of the oppressed "Everywoman" who needed "contraceptives because she was raped on every date . . . and raped finally on the abortionist's table. During the fashion for shoes with pointed toes, she . . . had her toes amputated." Didion's point—"why did [this Everywoman] not get herself another gynecologist, another job, why did she not get out of bed and turn the television off"—did not cancel the fact that she had just described the lives of many of the young women she had known at *Vogue,* including—on some days—herself.

It was better, she thought, to operate in a stable society where serving the antipasto and the white wine meant good business as well as being the good little woman.

A lot of good business came her way.

The early to mid-1970s was a "fine time for writers in Hollywood," said Tim Steele. "The studios had begun to squeeze out the independents. They'd front money to the creative people and keep them on staff. The studios took all the risk out of it for writers. By '71, '72, in addition to movies, the studios dominated everything made for TV. Then they began to be purchased by conglomerates such as Gulf & Western. A writer could get $100,000 for doing a rewrite—and not a lot of people were doing it back then. It was a small world, really."

In an essay called "Tinsel" (1974), Dunne listed a handful of screen projects offered him and his wife. While at Cannes, he said, they had reread *Tender Is the Night*; back in Los Angeles, they'd learned that Fox held the remake rights to the novel, which reduced the book to a five-page single-spaced synopsis. They declined to draft a treatment. They were asked to do "an extension of *The Graduate*" and "*Rebel Without a Cause* in the west Valley, with a girl in the James Dean part." They were pitched an early version of the Serpico story, for a movie reprising the winning formula of *Butch Cassidy and the Sundance Kid*. "Write me a Western," said Sam Peckinpah, the prospective director. "Jesus, Sam, it's about two cops in New York City," Dunne said. "Every story is a Western," Peckinpah insisted.

On another occasion, a producer gave them a "hot idea": "World War II." "What do you want us to do with it?" Dunne asked. "You're the writers," he said.

All of the producers said, "What if?" Again and again: "What if?" That was their contribution to story outlines. What if *this* happened? Or *that*?

A major part of each deal was the travel budget—the Dunnes needed time and distance from daily events (and child rearing) to work on a script. A thousand dollars a week and a chauffeured limousine at their beck and call, at the St. Francis in San Francisco, the Regency in New York, the Ambassador East in Chicago, and, most regularly, the Royal Hawaiian: This was the "attraction of borrowed luxury," Dunne said—what it meant to be a star, if you were a writer.

They had become a team, equal partners, and in the process they had stopped fighting so much. Dunne still carried the disappointment of a literary reputation incommensurate with his hopes, but the respect he'd earned was not inconsiderable, and he had discovered in himself an innate facility for Hollywood deal making. In meetings, he was usually forced to take the lead because "Hollywood is largely a boy's club," he said. "[F]or years Joan was tolerated only as an 'honorary guy' or perhaps an 'associate guy,' whose primary function was to take notes," Dunne said. "'Is John there?' an executive's assistant [would] say over the telephone when calling for his master. 'This is Joan.' 'Tell John to call when he gets home.'"

Thus it was in the "last stable society."

If Didion would not accept women as an oppressed class within the industry, she had to admit that writers—for all the perks and steady work—straddled the lowest rungs. With his class sensitivities, festering since childhood, Dunne was especially vulnerable to social slights. "You're a Mel," a producer joked with a friend of his one day. "Screenwriters are all named Mel. Producers are named Marty. In this town, the Martys hire the Mels."

At least this was an injustice Dunne could share with his wife. It strengthened their teamwork.

As for sexism—well, even *women* were capable of oppressing women.

Enter Pauline Kael.

The Dunnes met her one night in New York at an Academy Awards party thrown by Lynn Nesbit. "She was perched in front of the television set, a tiny, birdlike woman in a Pucci knockdown and orthopedic shoes, giving the raspberry to each award," Dunne said. He hesitated to introduce her to his wife. "She had despised . . . *Play It As It Lays* (Wilfrid Sheed had reported her reading it aloud derisively on the beaches of Long Island) . . . and Joan in turn had hammered Kael over the years [in print], suggesting among other things 'vocational guidance.'" When the women met, they "circled each other warily," Dunne said, these two Central Californians, "and they hit upon their rhythm—Valley talk. They talked about ranches and pickups and whiskey on the floorboards and the Silverado Trail, two tough little numbers, each with the instincts of a mongoose and an amiable contempt for the other's work, putting on a good old girl number. It was a funny act to watch."

During the course of the evening, Dunne mentioned to Kael that Frank Perry would be directing the movie version of *Play It As It Lays*. Nick had made a distribution deal with Universal-Paramount, which had done quite well with Perry's *Diary of a Mad Housewife*. Kael thought Perry ham-handed and self-important; she asked Dunne why in the world they'd tapped *him*? Dunne said they'd really wanted Sam Peckinpah but the "studios reacted to Sam's doing a picture about a woman as if . . . Hitler [were to] do a film about the Jewish question." Perry was a self-proclaimed "Didion freak." She's the "most important voice writing in English today. She's past Mailer, Styron, Jones, the war guys," he'd said. He'd put up his own money to direct her novel.

None of this pleased Kael, a Peckinpah admirer. She sniffed an inside job.

Several months later, in her review of *Play It As It Lays* in *The New Yorker*, Kael accused Didion of bringing to the screen the "ultimate princess fantasy," which is "to be so glamorously sensitive and beautiful that you have to be taken care of; you are simply too sensitive for this world—you see the truth, and so you suffer more than ordinary people, and can't function." She admitted she found Didion's novel laughable—"I know I have a lower tolerance for this sort of thing than many people, but should it be tolerated?"—and more than that, she found *Didion* ridiculous. She implied that Didion, the sensitive martyr, had seduced the men closest to her, her husband, her brother-in-law, and now Perry, into making her movie. It was a "novelist's wish fulfillment: narration that retains the most 'eloquent' passages in the book, dialogue virtually intact." "Perry hasn't found a 'visual equivalent' for [Didion's] famished prose, but maybe this high-class-whorehouse style of moviemaking is the *true* equivalent."

To date, this was the roughest mauling Didion had endured in print. It was personal and it was mean—on a par with Didion's treatment of Nancy Reagan. But because it involved professional matters—one writer, one movie insider to another—it contained a curious subtext. Against the odds, and in spite of continuing slights, Didion had become a powerful presence in a mostly male industry. Now here was an equally formidable woman pulling her down, publicly, personally, over traditionally "female" issues—sensitivity, silent suffering, suspicions of sleeping her way to the top.

You can *have* your damn solidarity, your movement, Didion must have thought. You old mongoose.

As for Dunne, he chivalrously defended his wife, as a knight of the stable society was required to do. Kael, he wrote, was "ludicrous . . . less a critic than a den mother" (*two* could sling this gender crap) "swatting her favorites gently when they get out of line, lavishing them with attention, smothering them with superlatives for their successes."

If Didion was a Whore, Kael was an Overbearing Mom. Apparently, there was no room in this discussion for appraising solid professionals, doing their jobs.

Play It As It Lays was certainly not a Joan Didion vanity project. It was a complex collaboration. "The four of us"—Didion, Dunne, Nick, and Perry—"locked ourselves into a hotel suite," said the director. "We had this enormous bulletin board and all these stick-pins and colored file cards. It's the old writer's trick: To avoid writing, you go to the stationery store and freak out. Anyway, we broke the novel down into every one of its fragments and arranged them in order, and then rearranged them into our order and kept a master key so we knew how every shot was related and when every pay-off came. Then Joan and John wrote the screenplay."

Didion was fascinated with film editing—"cutting," she called it. The white spaces, the gaps, in the novel became quick cuts in the film, fragments of Maria's life repeated out of sequence. In particular, her abortion haunts her: Bloody images, memories of the doctor's gloved hand—these flit through her mind and across the screen when she and the viewer least expect them.

The editing alone took seven weeks and cost over a million dollars. Perry wanted a visual "mosaic" rather than a series of "definite statements," in keeping with "the one-dimensional concern with the surface as employed in the book." He was trying for a "radical departure" in texture. "I don't really know of any other screen stories that have been told in this fragmented form, which is the representation of [Maria's] chaotic thought processes. I believe this sort of subjective storytelling is a major new direction for film. And a most important one."

Roy Lichtenstein joined the team as a visual consultant—the reason, Vincent Canby wrote, that the "dreadful Los Angeles freeway becomes, on the screen . . . a magnificent op art design—graceful gray loops on which tiny spots of red, yellow and aquamarine zoom in mindless motion." Mental disintegration never looked so good.

"I wanted Lichtenstein because of his fascination with the visually banal," Perry said. "It's so much part of the landscape here . . . [and] it's important because it represents the future of the country. It's the bellwether of the United States. Each day New England grows more like California. California does not grow like New England. It's plastic. It's artificial. It's also dynamic."

Cost overruns mounted, including helicopter rentals for the freeway shots and lost camera equipment. Behind the scenes, Nick tussled with the studio. "[W]e had a studio chief who hated the movie, just hated it, and he would say this to anybody," Nick said. "Ned Tanen, the head of Universal at the time, hated the book and called [the script] a piece of shit on our first meeting . . . [He] hated every single day's dailies, and he was the most awful person. It was so bitter."

The filming was bitter for Didion, as well, but for entirely personal reasons. Her friend Diana Lynn had been scheduled to play a role in the movie, making a career comeback, but she suffered a stroke following a wardrobe fitting a few days before shooting began. She died a few days later, at the age of forty-five, in the ICU at Cedars-Sinai. Lynn had changed Didion's life, urging her to call Blake Watson and arrange Quintana's adoption. Now Quintana's Broken Man had taken Lynn away.

At the end of the movie, Maria says, "I know what nothing is, and keep on playing . . . Why not?"

Observers on the sets witnessed a similar grim stoicism hardening Didion's features.

The movie was not a hit, but Weld's performance ("a lot of puckers" conveying "cotton-candy misery," according to Kael) earned her a Best Actress Award at the 1972 Venice Film Festival, and a Golden Globe nomination. Perry and Didion felt they'd achieved what they set out to do. The director believed that, together, the book and film made "incredibly essential statement[s] about where we're going in this country." The critics were split. Though some, like Stanley Kauffmann, dismissed it as "pretentious, posturing, [and] empty," based on the work of a "phony serious novelist," others readily accepted the premise of Hollywood decadence as a harbinger of national destiny. Charles Champlin said it was "the year's most effective capturing of women's dissatisfaction," and Rex Reed called it "profound," the "first truly existential film ever made in this country."

The Dunnes had now successfully released two unusual, uncompromising movies.

Their partnership earned them mentor status among a group of young writers. Jon Carroll, Dunne's cousin—"his mother and my grandmother were sisters," he said—was living in San Francisco, writing for *Rolling Stone*. "I was intimidated by John. We were in the same field and he'd had success I hadn't had yet. He was large and gruff and knew everyone," Carroll told me. "The temptation to treat him as a father figure was great. And he welcomed that. He enjoyed being my spirit guide, showing me around L.A."

Carroll's connection to the Dunnes stood him well in the *Rolling Stone* offices. Founded with table scraps in 1967 by Jann Wenner, a Berkeley dropout galvanized by the Free Speech Movement, and Ralph Gleason, a former *Ramparts* editor and music critic for the *San Francisco Chronicle*, *Rolling Stone* revered Didion. Cameron Crowe, then a young writer struggling to find his style, remembered that "Jann Wenner gave me a copy of *Slouching Towards Bethlehem* . . . He said, 'This is the future of what you're doing now if you can hook into a more thoughtful, more soulful place.' I read one of her profiles on Jim Morrison and saw that it was about so much more than just Morrison. . . . [It] ended up being about life in California, the weather, and existence. I thought, 'I get it! This is big picture stuff!'"

In the end, though, Wenner was just another businessman who wanted to do coke "with rock stars," Carroll lamented. "[He] broke our hearts." "I left *Rolling Stone* not on the best of terms," he told me delicately. He went on to edit *New West*, Clay Felker's magazine, which Felker "meant to be a clone of *New York*." In just a few years, *New West* would become an important outlet for the Dunnes' work.

Sara Davidson, a neophyte journalist, was another young writer making frequent pilgrimages to the Dunnes for lunch and advice, dazzled and amused by the way they'd "finish each other's sentences, batting the narrative back and forth as in a badminton game."

One day, Eve Babitz surprised Didion with a piece she'd written about Hollywood High School. It was called "The Sheik," a witty portrait of movie-star kids who know they own the world. Didion was charmed by it and she championed it with Grover Lewis, a *Rolling Stone* editor. On her advice, he bought "The Sheik," and from there Babitz developed a series of incisive vignettes for her first book, *Eve's Hollywood* (1974), dedicated, in part, to "the Didion-Dunnes, for having to be what I'm not."

Another young writer, Susanna Moore, had appeared at the Dunnes' parties (introduced to them by Connie Wald), though she would not publish her first novel until the early 1980s. Eventually, she would become one of Didion's closest friends. A tall, dark-haired former model, she had worked for a while as a script reader for Jack Nicholson and as Warren Beatty's personal assistant. She was nineteen when she applied for the job with Beatty. Just two years before that, she'd left Hawaii, where she'd lived since she was a girl. Her island background intrigued the Dunnes. Shortly after meeting them, she married production designer Richard Sylbert (*Shampoo, Chinatown, Catch-22*). Didion and Roman Polanski agreed to become godparents to her daughter, Lulu.

2

Meanwhile, the Dunnes had difficulty managing their own daughter. "Before Quintana was born, before she came to live with me . . . I assumed that I was mother material," Didion said years later. "It was only when I had to face the reality of actually having the perfect baby in my arms that I kind of felt not, not up to it . . . I didn't have a clue what was involved."

"I wish I could have stopped Quintana at age two," she said.

On the day Leslie Caron came to listen to the "new voices of California literature," she recognized that Quintana was "already a health worry" for the Dunnes. She was a "remarkably precocious baby," she said, but something was *off* in her affect. It was simply odd to see a child talking and behaving so much like a grown-up.

In *Blue Nights,* Didion speaks, as well, of her daughter's "dizzying alterations of infancy and sophistication," the "strenuousness with which she tried to present the face of a convincing adult." For instance, Quintana called her toys "sundries," apparently because of the sundry shops "in the many hotels to which she had already been taken." She made a dollhouse featuring a central "projection room" with "Dolby Sound." One night, she told her parents nonchalantly, "I just noticed I have cancer." (It was chicken pox.)

Didion speaks obliquely of her daughter's "quicksilver changes of mood," and of her own failure to seek treatment for Quintana because that wasn't the kind of thing people did in her family—though, in fact, it was; perhaps memories of her father's stay in Letterman continued to haunt her. One day, while the Dunnes were out, Quintana placed a call to a state psychiatric facility named Camarillo ("the hospital in which Charlie Parker once detoxed," Didion felt obliged to report). Quintana "had called Camarillo, she advised us, to find out what she needed to do if she was going crazy. She was five years old."

On the *Blue Nights* promotional tour, when interviewers asked Didion how in the world a five-year-old could have known about Camarillo, she waved the question away. It was just a place people talked about sometimes. Actually, it was a place her friend Josh Greenfeld talked about. His son Noah had been born with severe brain damage. On occasion, Greenfeld threatened to take his boy to Camarillo. The name awakened Quintana's abandonment fears. Quintana "was always very sweet, very solicitous of Noah," Greenfeld told me. "There was something special . . . something she identified with in him."

Her closest friend was Susan Traylor, daughter of the acting teachers William Traylor and Peggy Feury. Their students included Sean Penn, Meg Ryan, Michelle Pfeiffer, and Anjelica Huston. "[We] would sit on the couch in the kitchen and all of these people would come to be around my parents for inspiration," Traylor said. "And these people would talk about their relationships and all of their hard times, right in front of us. We were kids!"

At Point Dume Marine Science Elementary School, Quintana and Traylor met Bob Dylan's son, Jesse. Dylan had bought a large Spanish-style house in Malibu following his 1975 Rolling Thunder Revue tour. The kids flirted together on the beach, mimicking behaviors learned from the adults. (Eventually, Traylor and Jesse Dylan would marry.)

Quintana developed romantic notions of her own. "I've loved Donny Osmond for six months," she told Sara Davidson matter-of-factly one night. They were sitting in Quintana's bedroom: white walls painted with trees and flowers, blue-and-white gingham curtains. "I want to marry him when I'm twenty. I think he's a sweet person and I like his records. I want to live with him in a big white house with a swimming pool and have lots of babies. But I don't want all the babies to come at once!"

She wrote Osmond a letter: "We have a lot to talk about. Can I come to Las Vegas?"

She had learned that people were always available to you if you got a budget, made a deal.

Around this time, possibly on a screenplay junket, Didion happened to take Quintana to the Chicago Museum of Art, where a Georgia O'Keeffe exhibit stunned her daughter. Quintana ran to a stair landing and stared at the abstract shapes on a *Sky Above Clouds* canvas. "Who drew it?" she whispered to her mother. Didion told her. "I need to talk to her," Quintana said.

Didion bought a reproduction of the painting, framed it, and hung it on the wall in Malibu, next to the photo of the open road leading to Sacramento. Sky and earth. Whether or not the combination grounded Quintana, it seemed to soothe Didion as she padded in her sandals to her study.

"*Brush your teeth, brush your hair, shush I'm working,*" Quintana scribbled on a piece of paper under the heading "Mom's Sayings." She posted it on the garage wall, like a little Martin Luther.

She left a crayoned note one day: "*Dear Mom, when you opened the door it was me who ran away XXXXX—Q.*"

When her cousin Dominique came to baby-sit her one afternoon, Quintana left a card for her mother on the kitchen table: "*Roses are red, violets are blue. I wish you weren't home and Dominique does too. Love, Happy Mother's Day, D & Q.*"

In school, she wrote a poem called "The World": "The world / Has nothing / But morning / And night / It has no / Day or lunch / So this world / Is poor and desertid [*sic*]."

On most days, the world certainly looked fragile on the Pacific Coast Highway between the house and the classroom buildings. School officials felt obligated to send notes home to parents advising them of contingency plans when fires came roaring down the hills. "Dry winds and dust, hair full of knots. Gardens are dead, animals not fed," Quintana wrote when asked by her teacher for an "autumn" poem.

Didion couldn't keep from critiquing her daughter's jottings and correcting her grammar—unlike Eduene, who, when Didion was a girl, urged a notebook on her child to make her go away. Under scrutiny, Quintana became self-conscious about her prose. In time, she'd view writing the way her father did: as a way of settling scores.

One day, Susan Traylor rode in the car to school with Dunne and his daughter. Quintana showed him a paper she'd written. He asked her if she'd let her mother proof it, and when she said no, Traylor was shocked to see Dunne toss the paper out the window.

In the mornings, Dunne generally got up early, fetched wood for the living room fireplace, woke Quintana, and made her breakfast. "Joan was trying to finish a book" during this period "and she would work until two or three in the morning, then have a drink and read some poetry before she came to bed," he said. "She always made Q's lunch the night before, and put it in this little blue lunchbox. . . . [Not] your basic peanut butter and jelly schoolbox lunch. Thin little sandwiches with their crusts cut off, cut into four triangular pieces . . . Or else there would be homemade fried chicken, with little salt and pepper shakers. And for dessert, stemmed strawberries, with sour cream and brown sugar." Quintana had to wear a plaid jumper and white sweater as a school uniform. She'd pull her hair back in a ponytail. "So I'd take Q to school, and she'd walk down this steep hill," Dunne said. "I would watch her disappear down that hill, the Pacific a great big blue background, and I thought it was as beautiful as anything I'd ever seen. So I said to Joan, 'You got to see this, babe.' The next morning Joan came with us, and when she saw Q disappear down that hill she began to cry."

In *Blue Nights*, Didion flagellates herself for being a bad mother. Quintana "was already a person. I could never afford to see that," she writes, suggesting, in hindsight, a refusal to countenance time, change, aging; a denial of the troubles she witnessed in her daughter. At the time, though, in a 1972 radio interview, she was *quite* aware of being "apprehensive about everything and anxious so I have to try not to lay [my neuroses] on her, and anyways, she wouldn't have any of it if I did try. I mean, she's very, very . . ." She didn't seem to know what else to say about Quintana. "She's very competent, I mean, she's, ahhh . . ."

Here was the thing: One of the young Mexican girls who'd worked for the Dunnes as a nanny since Quintana was born had left her husband around the time the family moved to Malibu. "She was pregnant, and she stayed with us until the baby was born," Didion said. "Then she and the baby lived with us. When the baby was six months old, the girl went on vacation, took the baby home to Mexico. The baby, who had never been fed on anything but American formula, never eaten off anything but sterile dishes, became ill in Mazatlan, dehydrated, and was dead in twenty-four hours. It was a terrible thing. But we didn't know how bad it was for Quintana until we went to visit a friend who had a baby. Quintana looked at the baby, smiled at his grandmother, and said politely, 'When is he going to die?'"

3

Nick's Hollywood career was about to come to an end.

"I was not one who learned my lesson after my first mistake," he admitted. "The humiliating experience of my arrest [at LAX] was merely the first in a series of public shames that followed on the way to the bottom. I did not value my life highly at that point and did dangerous things with dangerous people."

He recalled one night being in some "stranger's closet with people I didn't know, using Turnbull & Asser ties to find a vein to shoot cocaine. One of the strangers overdosed and died, but I had already run and was never questioned. Then, [when I was] stoned again, a crazed psychopath I'd invited over for some cocaine beat me up, tied me up, put a brown bag over my face, and dropped lighted matches on the bag. God came back to me, posthaste. So did my Catholicism. 'God, help this man who is killing me,' I said over and over and over. He left, quietly. I lived."

Between these escapades, he continued to work as a film producer, efficient and competent except for occasional tardiness at a meeting while nursing a terrible hangover. Just as he had believed his father's poor opinion of him as a child, he now believed Sinatra's view of him as a phony. I "rose too high," he said. "I didn't deserve to be where I was. My credits weren't good enough for the world I moved in."

He made a deal with Bob Evans at Paramount to produce an Elizabeth Taylor–Henry Fonda picture called *Ash Wednesday,* to be filmed in Rome. The screenplay had been written by a man named Jean-Claude Tramont, the story of a beautiful woman, anxious about getting older, who tries to rekindle her husband's lust by submitting to plastic surgery. The wisdom of asking audiences to accept Elizabeth Taylor as a candidate for beauty treatments involving sheep-gland injections should have been questioned by everyone involved in the production. The real problem was the quality of the script, "written . . . with all the fearlessness and perception demanded in the boiling of an egg," Vincent Canby said in his review. Nick knew he had a turkey here, but he couldn't pass up the chance to meet Liz Taylor and Richard Burton—who, boozing and fighting steadily, snubbed him anyway.

The worst moment came in the middle of shooting, in the Café de Flore in Paris, when he met his screenwriter for the first time. Tramont, Belgian-born and raised in France, according to his official biographies, was the fiancé of Sue Mengers, Barbra Streisand's agent and "the most powerful woman in Hollywood at the time," Nick said. In his memoir, *The Way We Lived Then,* he claimed Tramont was actually a fellow named Jack Schwartz, whom Nick had known twenty years earlier when he worked as a stage manager for NBC. Schwartz was a page boy then. When Mengers introduced them in Paris, Nick was stunned but said nothing. Immediately, he assumed this stinker of a screenplay had surfaced only through Mengers's pull. She was a heavyset woman, not particularly attractive to Nick—she was always wearing dumpy caftans—and he further assumed that Schwartz/Tramont was exploiting her affections to get ahead (in fact, he and Mengers remained married until his death from cancer in 1996).

Ash Wednesday premiered in New York in November 1973. Exhausted, ignored by the star of his movie, nervous and more self-destructive than ever, Nick didn't wait for the critics to trash it. To the studio's dismay, he declared publicly, "It's a minor film. It's not like *A Place in the Sun* . . . It's the end of Elizabeth Taylor's career. There's nothing riveting about *Ash Wednesday.*"

A couple weeks later, drunk at a dinner party in Los Angeles, he told several of the guests his Jack Schwartz story. "If the history of this movie ever gets written," he quipped, "it should be called 'When a Fat Girl Falls in Love.'"

Somehow, *Hollywood Reporter* columnist Marvene Jones learned of Nick's remark and printed it in the paper. Nick claimed he got a call from Bob Evans, a great friend of Mengers. "He just said to me, 'You're through. You are over in Hollywood,' and I was, and I knew it," Nick said.

This was confirmed for him when Ahmet Ertegün introduced him to Mick Jagger one day as "Joan Didion's brother-in-law."

Later, Evans demurred, "I don't remember" telling Nick he was through. "I may have said that. I could have."

"I was flattered that Nick Dunne would identify me as the person who ended his career in Hollywood because of my power. I wish it were true," Mengers said.

In any case, Nick had committed a far worse blunder than insulting a beloved agent. It was the one unforgivable sin in Hollywood.

He had made a movie that bombed.

Didion met Sue Mengers and Barbra Streisand one night at a party. Mengers's house was like "a John Woolf jewel, with great, tall, Hollywood Regency doors and a living room that looked over a largely unused, egg-shaped pool," Graydon Carter recalled.

Against this lavish backdrop, Streisand approached Didion and Dunne. With no introduction, she asked, "What do you think of fidelity in marriage?"

Apparently, she didn't stick around for the answer.

Didion was now throwing regular parties of her own—exclusive affairs, like Mengers's, but with a literary twist—"sort of new for the movie world," Nick said (though *he'd* invited Christopher Isherwood and Mart Crowley to *his* soirees). Gore Vidal, in love with Didion's prose, appeared at her door, and so did Truman Capote. Barry Farrell, whom Dunne had known at *Time,* became such a close friend, he and his wife named their adopted daughter

Joan. He'd written for *Life* magazine—covering the Manson trial—and took freelance assignments on the Hollywood crime beat. Dunne used to call him every night to "natter" about underworld gossip, slightly jealous of his seamy, hard-boiled existence. "In the background I could hear the noises from the mean streets outside his Hollywood office, the wailing sirens and the voices of the dispossessed floating up through the open window," Dunne said. For his part, Farrell admired Dunne's panache, both as a journalist and as a husband. He had watched the Dunnes in restaurants—when people stared at Didion, Dunne would lean back in his chair ever so slightly so that the gawkers could get a better view. Farrell had never seen anything so romantic.

Josh Greenfeld and his wife, Foumi, attended Didion's fetes whenever they could find a sitter for their troubled son. "Someday I'm going to kill that kid," Greenfeld said with a sigh. One night, he told Dunne he had driven up the coast to inspect Camarillo. Flies pestered helpless children in the wards while the staff read magazines in air-conditioned cubicles. He heard horrible rumors about patients raping one another.

Quintana probably heard his stories. She was often at the parties, said Eve Babitz: "When John got too loud, she'd move to the sober side of the table."

What Greenfeld appreciated about Didion's parties was this: No one ever tried to make him feel small. That was the *nice* thing about literary affairs. "Writers don't compete with each other," he said. "We compete with the fucking dead."

The man of whom this was truest was the Dunnes' neighbor, the Irish novelist Brian Moore. He and his wife, Jean, had moved into a $75,000 "shack on the Pacific," just up the coast. The frequent floodwaters "intermixed with good red mud" reminded him of damp, foggy Belfast days. He'd sit in his kitchen, watching pelicans soar past the windows, and turn his thoughts to stories. Though he'd done his share of screenplay work, for Alfred Hitchcock among others, he was, first and last, a determined novelist. He rarely let himself be distracted from his literary tasks. Though he enjoyed the Dunnes' parties, he liked to joke that he was the Count Dracula of the group, needing to return to his coffin while the others ushered in the dawn. But then Earl McGrath would burst through the door, along with David Hockney and Bianca Jagger, all wearing circus clothes, and he'd be persuaded to stay a little longer.

His temper could be as hair-trigger as Dunne's. Sometimes they got into drunken verbal jousts—just a couple of salty micks having it out. Moore took literature *very* seriously. He had no patience for writers like Capote and Mailer, he said, "show-business people" who were "shameless little puffers-up of their talents and muggers-in-public for anyone who would write them up." Dunne would tell him to lay off his pals; sometimes their voices rose and their bodies got a little too close, warm Scotches sloshing over the backs of their thumbs. Didion recalled one night, *not* in her house but at a dinner in Beverly Hills, when the evening "abruptly became a shambles" following a shouting match between the two men. Dunne "walked out and I fled," she said.

They all made up, and a week or so later, they'd gather by the fire over bourbons and mole, having a fine old time.

"I remember the first time I had dinner at [the Dunnes'] house. I'd let John . . . mix my drinks. By the time the main course was served I was on my knees in the bathroom throwing up into the toilet," wrote producer Julia Phillips in her memoir, *You'll Never Eat Lunch in This Town Again.* The Dunnes courted her assiduously after her success with *The Sting*—another rare woman with clout in the industry (until she went lights-out on coke). For a while, she considered making a movie of *Vegas*, which pleased Dunne no end. "Since I was in their bathroom anyway, I checked out their medicine cabinet," Phillips said. "Outside of my mother's, it was the most thrilling medicine cabinet I had ever seen. Ritalin, Librium, Miltown, Fioranol, Percodan . . . every upper, downer, and in-betweener of interest . . . circa 1973."

"All prescribed (in vain) for the migraine headaches with which my wife and I were both afflicted," Dunne responded later in print. "But to a junkie it is comforting to think everyone else is a junkie too."

And by the way, he said, he'd served her only "one Bloody Mary" that night.

The medicine cabinet needed a serious upgrade, with vast infusions of azithromycin, after a trip to the Cartagena Film Festival in the summer of 1973. The Dunnes had been invited as part of a contingent representing U.S. filmmakers. ("I recall invoking the name 'Jack Valenti' a lot," Didion said.)

"Why had the American film industry not made films about the Vietnam War?" people at parties wanted to know.

"What would be the point?" others argued. "They run that war on television."

Feverish, exhausted from travel, Didion preferred to flee the festival and walk the narrow cobblestone lanes, past the staggered stone steps of the San

Felipe fort and the old city walls, the yellowed rooftops visible from certain angles, and the Palace of the Inquisition, with its massive oak doors. Street markets sold high-quality leather goods, the deep, earthy smells of shoes and belts as rich as cured bacon in the hot, tented alleys, and old men played accordions, songs about war, in shadowed doorways. Everywhere, mountains, shot through with depleted silver mines. She had slipped into Conrad territory.

On the street corners, tabloid headlines read JACKIE Y ARI. "[I] bought a paper" to read about "how the princess *de los norteamericanos* ruled the king of the Greek sea by demanding of him pink champagne every night and *medialunas* every morning, a story a child might invent," she said. She made a note about a North American princess marrying a man of power, living in exile.

Fairy tales filled the air, as if the "whole history of the place" were a "mirage, a delusion on the high savannah, its gold and its emeralds unattainable, inaccessible, its isolation . . . splendid and unthinkable," Didion said. It occurred to her, especially when she considered visions of shimmering gold, that California's history was every bit as ephemeral—childlike in retellings—as South America's.

These thoughts roiled feverishly in her brain, along with the strange tales she'd heard in New Orleans about the Caribbean and its political ties to Latin American exiles up and down the Gulf Coast.

She'd lie in her hotel bed, trying to sort out these stories, while Dunne went to the festival's evening events and apologized for his wife's absence. The hotel's generator blinkered to a stop. No lights, no phone. Her fever, quite real, rose to 103.

She and Dunne flew to Bogotá—after waiting four days to book seats on the once-a-morning Avianca flight. She could no longer stand the blinding coastal dawns and the dusty winds. She thought she might die.

Waiting for her in the city, at the Hotel Tequendama, were "room service and Xerox *rápido* and long-distance operators who could get Los Angeles in ten minutes. . . . Hot water. Madeira consommé in cool dining rooms."

One day, in the sixteenth-century Church of San Francisco, she collapsed gratefully into a pew, and lit a candle for her daughter back home.

Even here, in what passed for urban modernity, a "dislocation of time fixed on the mind the awesome isolation of the place," she said. In the city's major movie theaters, the fare consisted of bad American films ten years old.

She admitted her discomfort: "I was aware of being an American in Colombia in a way I had not been in other places." Like a hasty travel writer, she fixed on "local color," on "a shantytown of packing-crate and tin-can shacks where a small boy, his body hideously scarred and his face obscured by a knitted mask, played listlessly with a yo-yo."

Always, Didion's literary approach had been to describe the *surface* of a place so thoroughly that its *depths* were exposed, like polishing wood until its grain came through. Her essay "In Bogotá" revealed the limitations of this strategy when the writer stepped outside her habitat: The details, culturally uninformed, risked superficiality and condescension. The outsider *did not know* what depths the surface might reveal.

Didion's essay did not bode well for her future observations of El Salvador, which she would turn to in the 1980s.

At parties in the city, she met officials from the American embassy, USIS men, information officers—all CIA, the Colombians believed. She met filmmakers who had worked with Norman Mailer, Rip Torn, and Richard Leacock on Mailer's movie *Maidstone*. It seemed Noel Parmentel had also joined the set, playing a small role in the film. Hearing his name in this faraway place forged another link for Didion between her visit to New Orleans and her South American trip. That night, she made a few more random notes.

On the way back to Los Angeles, the plane stopped to refuel at the Panama airport. It was six A.M. Heat rose off the tarmac and pasted her skirt to her legs. Her sandals stuck to the asphalt. Her fever had remained steady and imbued the colors she saw—on the airport's stucco walls, on the shiny Pan Am tail—with an astonishing aura, as if they had absorbed all the light in the world. She stepped inside a waiting lounge, assaulted by the blips and bloops of a slot machine.

The passengers waited for an hour, the smell of gas infusing the stench of tar and dust. In a newspaper she saw a photograph of a hijacked 707 burning at night in a Middle Eastern desert. The blue of the airport walls reminded her of the Bevatron in Berkeley. She thought of Henry Adams, the Dynamo, coal, Conrad's tales of mining in the tropics, politics.

She thought of Jackie and Ari, princesses and powerful men, moving around the world, transit lounges, transitional spaces. She saw herself sitting here—for decades, it seemed—en route, in limbo. Feverish. Waiting. Waiting. Waiting for what?

New Orleans.

Noel.

The Caribbean.

She made more notes. Without quite knowing it, she had begun what would become her third novel, *A Book of Common Prayer*—the template for all her remaining fiction.

Back home, abdominal pains accompanied the fever. She couldn't eat. Her weight dropped to seventy pounds. Doctors diagnosed her with paratyphoid. In Cartagena, she'd ingested tainted food or water—perhaps at a restaurant along the Bocagrande, the vast urban beach, from which she kept a receipt one night when she and her husband had three whiskies and a coco martinique; langoustines and steak pimiento; a *plato frío*. She'd kept the receipt to write off expenses, but also because the words *Boca Grande* ("Big Mouth") intrigued her; this would become the name of the fictional Latin American country in *A Book of Common Prayer*.

As her weight fluctuated dangerously, her mother arrived in Malibu to care for her and Quintana.

Didion would sit outside on the deck and watch the wind stir ashes from the chimney, dusting the house's smooth white bricks. She'd sit beside a neighbor's pool, watching Katharine Ross teach her daughter to swim by tossing a Tahitian shell into the water and telling Quintana the shell was hers if she could retrieve it.

One night, sometime during this period, Didion found Quintana under her bedcovers with a flashlight, gaping at Margaret Bourke-White's pictures of Buchenwald in an old *Life* magazine she'd found on the shelves. "That was what she *had to know*," Didion wrote.

Quintana's blue-and-white gingham curtains rustled in the breeze.

Politics. What on earth could you tell a child?

Friends brought her soufflés, soups, and desserts, and eventually Didion regained a little strength—enough to start worrying about cash again. Often, there was a considerable lag between the couples' script doctoring and the cutting of checks. They were making money, but not always fast enough. "I [made] graphs. If we only spent X dollars for the next nine months we could survive, but it didn't seem likely that we could only spend X dollars because we'd spent twice X dollars every month for the past year," she said.

The charges stacked up from their trips to Hawaii, where they usually *did* their rewrites. It was the perfect place to cogitate, undisturbed, because people in L.A. could never figure out the time difference.

To relax and plan—now that her strength was coming back—she and Dunne would take long walks on the beach—in Malibu, in Hawaii. Much more comfortable now in his skin, Dunne joked with Josh Greenfeld that one night on a beautiful beach they'd run into Jesus, and Jesus said, "I love Joan's work!"

It may have been on a beach in Honolulu, or it may have been in a car on the way to the Honolulu airport one day, that Dunne suggested a project to his wife, "sixteen words I would often later regret," he said.

She'd been telling him she might like to buy a house in Hawaii. What would he think of that?

What would *she* think of this? he said: "James Taylor and Carly Simon in a rock-and-roll version of *A Star Is Born*."

Chapter Twenty-one

———————— ✤ ————————

1

James Taylor and Carly Simon had nothing on Patty Hearst. Patty Hearst was America's biggest rock star. *Rolling Stone* said so. And who was Patty Hearst? Joan Didion with a carbine.

Of course, Didion saw in the Hearst misadventure "a parable for the period," but more than that, she saw a sister: another descendant of Western pioneers, a woman with a predilection for reinventing herself at every turn and leaving the past behind.

The facts were improbable and bizarre: On February 4, 1974, Patricia Campbell Hearst, a nineteen-year-old art history major at Berkeley, had made chicken noodle soup and tuna fish sandwiches in her duplex apartment at 2603 Benvenue Avenue. She had put on a blue bathrobe and watched a television program called *The Magician* with her twenty-six-year-old fiancé, a math instructor and her personal tutor, Steven Weed. At around nine P.M., a woman knocked on the door and told Hearst she'd hit a car. She asked to use the phone. Then two men, one black, one white, rushed into the apartment, beat Weed unconscious with a wine bottle, and bound and blindfolded Hearst. In the first of many details offering some credence later to conspiracy theories, the official FBI report on the kidnapping stated unequivocally that two black males hauled Hearst away; in fact, among her captors, there was only one African-American, Donald DeFreeze. Was the report mistaken? Who was this second black male? He is not mentioned again in documents outlining the case.

Before she was gagged and forced into a stolen 1964 Chevrolet Impala convertible, Hearst screamed, "Please no, not me!"

Patty Hearst was the mildly rebellious daughter of the vastly wealthy Randolph Hearst, heir to the Hearst Corporation, which owned the *San Francisco Examiner* as well as a chain of newspapers and magazines. Orson Welles had based the character Charles Kane on Patty's grandfather. No reminders of the family's Missouri heritage, its overland crossing in covered wagons, its Gold Rush and ranching successes decorated her apartment. She liked to play down her wealth with friends, talk back to her parents' praise of free-market capitalism. She had upset her family when, unmarried, she moved in with Weed. She smoked dope recreationally and dropped acid a few times just for the hell of it. But on balance, she appeared little different from most Berkeley coeds, a slightly rougher incarnation of the girl Didion had been, of the girls Didion had interviewed for her portrait of the campus in *Mademoiselle* over ten years earlier: a privileged young woman who had gone off to college and found a potential husband. Since the days of the Free Speech Movement, and the national trauma of the shootings at Kent State, Berkeley had mellowed. The kiosks just outside Sather Gate advertised acupuncture and meditation rather than sit-ins and revolution, sex therapy and psychic healing rather than marches and political action. Instead of *armed struggle, progressive legislation* was the new catchphrase, except among certain individuals and splinter groups farther off campus; indirectly, these outliers fueled the Hearst saga—embittered Vietnam vets, drifters who had come too late to the Golden Land's party or the anarchist rallies (all infiltrated now by police informers), escapees from the Haight, now a blasted waste, symbol of the sixties' ruin.

Human detritus from the hippie fallout fled into Bay Area neighborhoods and crossed the rest of the state. Groups calling themselves the Revolutionary Army and the New World Liberation Front planned bombings at the Berkeley Naval Architecture Building (this one didn't come off) and at electrical plants and neighborhood police stations (some of these schemes *did* work—spectacularly). A box of See's candy, rigged with explosives and left on Mayor Alioto's front porch, blew part of his house away.

When apprehended, most of these "groups" turned out to be one or two addled individuals seeking publicity.

Farther south, in and around L.A., "an unusually high number of savage murders, murders no one quite understood, and the likes of which few had seen before" were taking place, wrote Didion's friend Barry Farrell. "[D]ecapitations, dismemberments, eviscerations, and, occasionally, instances of cannibalism" were all too common. The LAPD called these incidents "overkills" and joked about the "curse of the Donner Party." Was there something in California geography—the rumbling ground, the vast horizon, the veering hot winds—fostering madness, or was this surge of violence the predictable aftermath of too many drugs, too many destabilization attempts by police of already unstable "revolutionary" groups, too many instances of government corruption (Hearst's papers were full of disturbing stories about the state's grandest son, Richard Nixon, denying wrongdoing regarding a break-in at a D.C. hotel called the Watergate, rejecting duplicity in the administration's Vietnam policy, despite mounds of evidence in the leaked Pentagon Papers).

Whatever the cause of the problem, state authorities decided the solution was crackdown and control. But here's where the *real* trouble started, in the California penal empire—the "nation's most dysfunctional prison system," said David Talbot, a San Francisco journalist.

On March 5, 1973, the Symbionese Liberation Army, in the person of Donald DeFreeze, walked right out of Soledad Prison, an escapee in no visible hurry, undeterred by any guards, having been counseled inside on "black power" by a man with apparent ties to the CIA. Less than a year later, the SLA would pull up to Patty Hearst's door on Benvenue Avenue.

It was a pioneer tale for the new era, and Didion was hooked.

Donald DeFreeze, she learned, was reliably reported to have been recruited by Detective Sergeant R. G. Farwell in 1967 to be an informant for the LAPD's Criminal Conspiracy Section, later the Public Disorder Intelligence Unit. The PDIU had been established to monitor groups posing potential public danger; it would be disbanded in 1983, after more than a decade of allegedly "spying on law-abiding individuals and groups," including the state's attorney general, John Van de Kamp, and Jerry Brown, and engaging in "incidents of conspiracy to commit murder, kidnapping, false arrest, burglary and theft." DeFreeze was well treated by this unit. He lived high, until he allegedly robbed a prostitute and was sentenced, in December 1969, to five to fifteen years in the prison at Vacaville.

There, he joined an officially sanctioned prisoner-education group, the Black Cultural Association, run by a linguistics instructor at Berkeley, Colston Westbrook, whose goal, he said, was to instill racial pride and strategies for self-help among the prisoners. Association meetings generally began with the unveiling of the tricolored Republic of New Afrika flag and black-power salutes. To outsiders, it looked suspiciously like Westbrook was training the prisoners to be revolutionaries. Later, DeFreeze denounced him, on a tape sent to San Francisco radio station KSAN, as a "government agent now working for Military Intelligence while giving assistance to the FBI."

Though Westbrook "tried to keep his military and intelligence backgrounds hidden" while running meetings of the Black Cultural Association, wrote David Talbot, "stories circulated about the brainwashing techniques he had learned in Asia" while working for a "CIA-controlled firm," and "how he was applying them at Vacaville."

Westbrook was especially close to Donald DeFreeze. He helped DeFreeze establish his own prison course, teaching the seven principles of Kwanzaa: self-determination, production, cooperation, collective work and responsibility, faith, unity, and creativity. DeFreeze renamed himself Cinque, after Sengbe Pieh, later known as Joseph Cinqué, an African slave who had led the rebellion, in 1839, on the *Amistad.*

Didion was fascinated to discover that a number of white students at Berkeley with leftist political passions or a desire to play radical signed up as tutors with the Black Cultural Association. In this way, Cinque met William Wolfe, who would become Patty Hearst's lover ("the gentlest, most beautiful man I've ever known," she said) *or* her serial rapist, depending on who's telling the story; he was the son of a wealthy anesthesiologist who, like Hearst, had rebelled against his family's conservative values. He lived in a Maoist commune in Berkeley called Peking House.

A private investigator named Lake Headley, trying to piece together the SLA story, claimed that among Cinque's visitor-tutors at Vacaville were Patricia Soltysik, a former student-body treasurer at Dos Pueblos High School in Goleta, California; Nancy Ling Perry, a former Goldwater supporter disillusioned by the JFK assassination, Vietnam, and the killing of Martin Luther King Jr.; and Patty Hearst, using a fake ID with the name Mary Alice Siems.

What *is* certain is that Hearst made at least passing contact with Nancy Ling Perry. Perry sold fruit juice every day at the Fruity Rudy stand on Telegraph Avenue. Hearst bought from her. So did Sara Davidson. The whole community knew her, Didion learned from Davidson: She was a "kind, honest person with strong humanist convictions."

In December 1972, Cinque was abruptly transferred to Soledad Prison in the Central California coastal farming country. Westbrook followed him there, teaching community relations to the prison guards. Cinque's fellow prisoners didn't trust him; he seemed strangely cozy with the prison officials, and they all assumed he was a snitch. Unconfirmed reports said Hearst visited him. Cinque's Kwanzaa-based principles had now become the revolutionary platform of what he called the Symbionese Liberation Army: "[T]he name 'symbionese' is taken from the word symbiosis and we define its meaning as a body of dissimilar bodies and organisms living in deep and loving harmony," he wrote in a dense manifesto.

According to Lake Headley's report on the group, while Cinque was in Soledad, "[d]iscussions were held between Patricia Campbell Hearst and the Symbionese Liberation Army concerning a kidnapping—not her own."

This allegation encouraged conspiracy theorists to interpret Hearst's cry at the moment of her abduction—"Please no, not me!"—as an expression of irritated surprise, as in, *It's supposed to be* someone else*! What are you doing?*

In March 1973, Cinque was made late-night boiler attendant at a remote section of the prison grounds near the area where Colston Westbrook always taught his class. One night, a guard dropped Cinque off at the boiler and drove away. Cinque scaled a small, unguarded fence and made his way up Highway 101. Prison officials were slow to respond, and in the coming days they did little to track him down. Cinque sought refuge with William Wolfe and his cohorts in Peking House. There, he brought his army of white radicals together in preparation for the "Declaration of Revolutionary War & The Symbionese Program." He fashioned a flag featuring a seven-headed cobra, an ancient symbol signifying "God and life" and representing the seven Kwanzaa principles, he said—though it actually appears to have been lifted from the cover of a Jimi Hendrix album.

Cinque approached most of the radical groups in the Bay Area, offering himself as a revolutionary "hit man." No one trusted him. The Black Panthers accused Cinque of secretly working for the government, stirring up "hatred, fear and disunity in the black community."

The Reverend Jim Jones of the San Francisco's Peoples Temple, a fast-talking figure of great interest to Didion, was caught on tape by an FBI bug saying he had it on good authority that Cinque "was palsy-walsy with everybody in the glass house"—that is, he was inside the Establishment. (Eventually, some journalists suspected Jones, too, of being a government informant.)

Soon after the SLA had run off with Patty Hearst, with or without her cooperation, Cinque issued a public demand: Randolph Hearst must sponsor a massive food giveaway to the city's poor, he said—his daughter's "health" depended on it. Hastily, Colston Westbrook arranged a press conference on the Berkeley campus to read an open letter to Cinque, complimenting him on his "brilliant" political strategy but urging him not to harm Hearst in any way. At one point, he made a reference to Cinque's "leader," as if he and Cinque both followed orders from some other superior. Later, he shrugged this off, but he never really explained it. The radical community assumed Westbrook was sending his protégé a coded message.

If this was the case, then Cinque chose this moment to break publicly with his mentor. He warned Westbrook he'd be "shot on sight."

Didion followed the inside story intensely through the reporting of Sara Davidson, Barry Farrell, and other journalist friends. The food giveaway further revealed to them all the SLA's divisive effect. Leftist groups suspicious of Cinque, refusing to sanction the effort, could be accused of turning their backs on the poor, the very people they claimed to fight for; extremists who *did* support the program might gain some official respectability, and move closer to the political mainstream.

Jim Jones seized the moment to curry favor with the San Francisco community and its political leaders. Just ten days after Hearst's abduction, he went on a local radio station to say the Peoples Temple would offer two thousand dollars to help free her—and then he offered himself and other Peoples Temple members as hostages in exchange for Hearst. The Hearst family and the SLA rejected his gesture.

California welfare officials estimated that a food distribution effort matching the SLA's vision would cost around $400 million. Randolph Hearst pulled together two million dollars from the Hearst Foundation and his private coffers—after being snubbed by the city's business leaders, the Red Cross, the United Way, and the Bank of America, which offered a loan even Hearst could not repay.

Distribution centers were established, including a former Del Monte banana-processing plant on Mission Creek. The SLA asked the Black Panthers and the United Farm Workers to help move the food, but both refused, the Panthers claiming they wouldn't support the SLA's "extortion," and the farmworkers puzzled that Cinque had also asked the Safeway food chain to participate in the scheme. The farmworkers were leading a boycott against Safeway as part of the ongoing grape strikes.

On February 22, near riots occurred at the churches and distribution centers offering food. Hundreds of people, mostly black women, many with babies in their arms (reinforcing entrenched stereotypes of the poor), lined up and were jostled by gangs openly stealing the crates. Workers, panicked among shoving crowds, tossed boxes off the backs of moving trucks, injuring several people. High-end grocery chains had sold Hearst tainted food—"75% slop"—at inflated prices. The crowds claimed it was inedible; angry young men hurled frozen turkey legs through plate-glass windows. The SLA issued a statement calling the food "hog feed."

Governor Reagan, observing the long lines of poor women on television, said, "It's just too bad we can't have an epidemic of botulism." He said those who took the food were in danger of having their welfare checks cut off.

The SLA released a tape of Patty Hearst expressing disappointment in her father, saying she didn't believe he was making a good-faith effort to get her back.

Just two months later, on April 3, the SLA distributed a photograph of Hearst with her hair cropped short, wearing a beret, and standing, legs spread, holding an M1 carbine in her hands, in front of a banner with a seven-headed cobra. The image was powerful and stylish: Irving Penn on an acid-laced martini.

Her taped message said she had joined the SLA: "I have been given the name Tania after a comrade who fought alongside Che in Bolivia . . ." She also stated, "One thing I learned is that the corporate ruling class will do anything in their power in order to maintain their position of control over the masses, even if this means the sacrifice of one of their own."

The Hearst family claimed she had been brainwashed.

Photos of the gun-toting girl appeared all over the Berkeley campus, saying "We love you Tania."

At first, sorting through the images, suspicions, and contradictory reports regarding Patty Hearst, Didion saw it all as evidence of "one California busy being born and another busy dying."

She saw in the young woman a fellow beneficiary (or romantic victim) of a family always "looking for a stake" in the Golden Land, claiming and then radically abandoning one perceived treasure after another.

Seven-headed cobra.

Mommy's snake book.

On October 20, 1975, Jann Wenner, the editor of *Rolling Stone*—who had asked both Didion and Dunne to cover the Patty Hearst trial for the magazine—received what surely must have been one of the strangest proposals he had ever seen from an author. In the course of two single-spaced typed pages, Didion listed for him, in a long vertical column, all the things that interested her about Hearst's capture and trial, none of which, at first blush, seemed to have anything to do with Patricia Campbell Hearst. These included Grace Cathedral, Francis Ford Coppola, the opening of the opera, the great fire and earthquake, the tea garden in Golden Gate Park, the I. Magnin children's department, the Spinsters, the Bachelors (philanthropic organizations in San Francisco), and the "weddings of my cousins."

Didion remembered being blindfolded during her induction into the Mañana Club as an adolescent, and being harangued by the governor's daughter. Was Patty Hearst's experience, her fear, her social terror, in any way similar to hers?

She conceded that Wenner would probably want a more investigative and fast-breaking report on the Hearst story, but her interest was in California life as revealed and exposed by the events. She said she and her husband would probably do the reporting together but that she would write the piece because he was working on a book (*True Confessions*—also based on a legendary California crime saga).

On the same day Didion sent this letter to Wenner, her agent, Lois Wallace, wrote James Silberman at Random House, pitching a nonfiction book by Didion on the "California experience," based on the notes she would make for *Rolling Stone* on the Patty Hearst trial. Wallace said Didion had long wanted to write a history of California; she had proposed a book called *Fairy Tales* to FSG on the subject, but she had abandoned it because she didn't want it to be "autobiographical" and she couldn't find the proper frame.

Tania was now her way in.

"The Patty Hearst trial is one in which the history of California is called as a character witness," Wallace wrote. The Western "mentality" is "what has produced Joan's family, the Huntingtons, the Nolans, and the Hearsts."

The "events of [the] trial [will] bring the forces about which Joan has wanted to write into dramatic play."

How could a daughter of luxury turn into a bank-robbing guerilla doll?

What makes Iago evil?

Narratives emerged, on air and in print, to try to explain this latest California quake. Since the JFK killing, conspiracy theories had become a dominant narrative mode in America, and gained particular traction in the West, in the wave of mass slaughters à la Manson, the revolutionary bombings, the savage murders in the canyons and the hills, the incidents of cannibalism.

One of the most popular radio shows in San Francisco during this period was *Dialogue Conspiracy* on KLRB-FM, hosted by Mae Brussell, the daughter of a Beverly Hills rabbi and the granddaughter of the founder of the I. Magnin department stores (among Didion's favorite spots to shop). Profoundly disturbed by the Kennedy assassination, Brussell read all twenty-six volumes of the Warren Report, concluded it was a government whitewash of a widespread high-level plot, and became a dedicated conspiracy researcher. What made her so compelling, and her theories hard to dismiss, was her thoroughness, her reasonable tone, and her close reading skills, certainly on a par with anyone who had come out of the Berkeley English Department.

When asked, "Who is the SLA and why did they kidnap Patty Hearst?," Brussell replied that Cinque was the nation's first black Lee Harvey Oswald, a patsy trained and motivated by the government to stir up radical groups, giving authorities an excuse to (at the very least) expand domestic spying and (at most) impose martial law. This view was shared, of course, by most of California's radical groups, and by Lake Headley, whose private investigations into the SLA led him to conclude that Cinque had turned against his government trainers, signing his death warrant. "He'll be killed, probably in a shootout," Headley said: They can't allow him to talk. Of course, this is precisely what happened.

Credible reports in mainstream newspapers, including Hearst's, listing activities of the CIA's Operation CHAOS (illegal covert actions aimed at neutralizing groups and individuals deemed a threat to national security), lent credence to Brussell's suspicions, even the most outlandish, as when, for example, she claimed that the death of every major rock star—Jim, Jimi, Janis, Cass—could be traced to the CIA's determination to eradicate "an art form that has been . . . one of the most important cultural revolutions in history."

In the end, Didion, tracing her own distant connections, attended the Patty Hearst trial for only a few days.

Yet again she postponed her book on the "California experience"; finally, it would take the death of her parents, her freedom from *their* views of the state, to give her the confidence she needed to approach the material properly.

But she *did* write an essay on Hearst, "Girl of the Golden West." The title was an obvious play on her earlier Lucille Miller piece about Western romance and the violence it can spawn. It was not an attempt to answer the "Why" of Patricia Hearst; instead, it said the "Here and Now" of her was inevitable: her "abrupt sloughing of the past has, to the California ear, a distant echo, and the echo is of emigrant diaries. 'Don't let this letter dishearten anybody, never take no cutoffs and hurry along as fast as you can,' one of the surviving children of the Donner Party concluded her account of that crossing." Didion would repeat this quote in *Where I Was From*. For her, Hearst's statements—"Don't examine your feelings. Never examine your feelings—they're no help at all"—proved that "Patricia Campbell Hearst had cut her losses and headed west, as her great-grandfather had before her."

At her trial, where she was convicted of bank robbery and sentenced to seven years in prison, Hearst "seemed to project an emotional distance, a peculiar combination of passivity and pragmatic restlessness," Didion said. (Hearst's prison term was commuted by Jimmy Carter; years later, she was pardoned by Bill Clinton.) Didion knew *she* exhibited Hearst's qualities, just as she shared the young woman's family background. Perhaps the similarities were *so* close, she could penetrate no further beyond stitching general connections.

"Girl of the Golden West" is not one of Didion's finest performances. It concludes with a shrug ("This was a California girl, and she was raised on a history that placed not much emphasis on *why*"). The essay expresses an uncharacteristic faith in coincidence: Didion "happened" to keep an issue of *The San Francisco Bay Guardian* recounting the end of the trial, she said; one day, many years later, she thumbed through the paper to find, as well, an article on a "minister . . . compared at one point to Cesar Chavez, [who] was responsible, according to the writer, for a 'mind-boggling' range of social service programs . . . [T]he minister of course was the Reverend Jim Jones."

Didion makes nothing of this coincidence. She mentions it only to illustrate the insanity of San Francisco in the mid-1970s. If the Mae Brussells were suspicious of the world, and constructed narratives to explain it, Didion was suspicious of the narratives we use to explain the world. In her writings of the 1980s, on Miami and El Salvador, she would walk a little closer to Brussell's side of the street (by then, she would see, for example, that Operation CHAOS began with CIA debriefings of disgruntled refugees from Castro's Cuba who were seeking revenge and perhaps retribution from an American president they perceived as a traitor) but for now, "I never ask" would be Didion's pat answer.

2

In considering—and not quite hitting—the *real* story of Patty Hearst, Didion felt sure the periphery was the key. She looked for an out-of-the-way anecdote, seemingly insignificant, channeling all of California; the pioneer experience in its modern manifestations; the historical imperative; the chain of forces shaping Tania: a verbal image as immediately impactful as the spread legs, the carbine, and the cobra.

She was after this same effect in *Play It As It Lays,* a "fast novel," a method of presentation allowing us to perceive Maria in a flash.

A snake book.

A poetic impulse, surpassing narrative.

Somewhere on the edge of the story.

She remembered an anecdote that Lewis Lapham of *Harper's* magazine told her. He'd heard that Abigail Folger had been called home by her family to attend a wedding rehearsal dinner a year before she became one of the victims in the house on Cielo Drive. She was twenty-one at the time. She showed up late at the rehearsal, stoned and wearing an inappropriate dress, trying to remember what she had to do to be a daughter.

Didion thought this the best story she'd heard about the Manson case—perhaps the very best story about the 1960s.

Not quite hitting it.

Along with the usual challenges of thinking straight, composing carefully and well, she faced certain off-the-page impediments to her writing during this period. In the summer of 1973, Henry Robbins had a heart attack. At forty-five, his life had started to unravel. In the spring of that year, FSG had made him editor in chief. One of his first acts was to sign Didion for a nonfiction book, with an advance of sixty thousand dollars, payable in two installments. Presumably, this was the ill-fated *Fairy Tales,* which not even Patty Hearst could save.

From the stress or the headiness of his new position, Robbins had more arguments with his colleagues. He began an affair with a publicist in the office. He told friends his wife had been diagnosed with schizophrenia and was difficult to live with. By this point, his two children were attending private schools; his $25,000-a-year salary wouldn't stretch. As an independent—and during a publishing downturn—FSG was strapped. In fact, Roger Straus ordered a salary freeze and threatened pay cuts for the company's top officers. He pressured his editors to drop their "marginal titles" and pursue "Godfather type-book[s]." This raised Robbins's hackles even further.

As he lay in the hospital following his heart attack, doctors told his girlfriend he was "touch and go." Once he recovered, he told buddies his illness had "frightened the whiskers" off him. He "had to try a new life."

Dick Snyder, the head of Simon & Schuster, got wind of Robbins's restlessness and made him an offer. S&S was still retooling after the departure of Robert Gottlieb, who'd taken Joseph Heller and his best literary authors to Knopf. Snyder said he'd make Robbins an executive editor and vice president, and he'd almost double his salary. Robbins knew Snyder cared little for literature; he was a far more commercial and unabashedly crass businessman than Roger Straus, but in the end, Robbins said, "[f]inancial considerations are very important." With a bottle of champagne delivered to his house, wrapped in best wishes from S&S, the deal was settled.

What this meant for Robbins's authors was unclear. Didion felt extremely anxious. She had not published a book since 1970, and *Fairy Tales* was not snapping into focus. To make matters worse, before she could work things out, Robbins's defection became public. A reporter named Sarah Gallick published a short column in *Harper's* magazine saying "such major writers as Joan Didion and Donald Barthelme . . . wanted to follow [Robbins] to S&S, [but] Roger Straus was refusing to release them from their contract option clauses." So "here is Henry Robbins at S&S, receiving a high salary, and he has no big authors." Nevertheless, Gallick said, "Didion, with the help of her agent, Lois Wallace, has managed to 'leap over the wall.'"

Straus, fearing serious damage to FSG's reputation, swore to his colleagues, "None of [my] authors"—Didion, Donald Barthelme, Tom Wolfe, Grace Paley, Walker Percy—"are leaving Farrar, Straus. Over my dead body."

He did manage to wheedle most of the writers into staying, but Didion proved to be a tougher bird than he was. Through Lois Wallace, she told Straus she had come to see Robbins as a "surrogate father" and couldn't possibly separate from him. She offered to repay the thirty-thousand-dollar first installment on her nonfiction book. She invited Robbins to be a guest in her house for an extended period, a clear signal to Straus where her loyalties lay.

By now, she had begun the novel that would eventually become *A Book of Common Prayer*. Straus invited Wallace to his office, "to our part of town where the rents are low and the literary aromas are vintage," to discuss the possibility of buying the novel in lieu of the nonfiction book. Straus said the novel would satisfy the existing contract. Wallace knew Didion still wished to go with Henry Robbins. She set up an auction for the book among five publishers, clearly designed to give the edge to S&S and to knock FSG out of the bidding. To no one's surprise, Robbins got the novel as well as a contract for a nonfiction collection tentatively titled *Dream Time Magic*. The combined advance equaled $210,000.

Straus felt betrayed. He threatened legal action. But then he backed off, fearing the financial risks. At no point was he ever ugly with Didion. In fact, a year after the dust had settled, he wrote her a lovely letter, expressing his hope that "the new novel is going well," reiterating that "we are very big admirers of Didion at Union Square West, and if the time came when you would like to discuss publication of a book with us, we should like to have that happen."

He was savvy enough to realize Didion was "not the kind of writer that should be put on the block." He told Wallace's business partner "there was no way she'd earn back her S & S advance: Not good agenting!"

He was right. Eventually, S&S proved to be a snake pit for both Robbins and Didion. Though there was never any question she would follow her editor wherever he went, this was a move she'd often regret.

3

How did Edith Wharton do it?

Her summer house was always full of guests.

She wrote a novel a year, working every morning.

Didion read a biography of her, and came away "terribly impressed." "I just couldn't see how it could be," she said. Wharton's guests "would be served breakfasts in their rooms, then work on their letters or whatever until noon, and then everyone would gather in the garden and Wharton would appear and an excursion would be planned for the afternoon . . . The degree of order she must have had! I've thought about it a lot. For one thing, the telephone didn't ring, but still, the degree of organization required to live that kind of life . . ."

Didion could only dream of it. The guests in her Malibu house took no excursions except down to the beach, where they drank and wondered who would make a movie of the Patty Hearst story, and who would play Patty. It was like the fevered speculation, a few years earlier, about Roman Polanski: To which high-flying bidder would he sell the rights to his murdered wife?

It turned out, in a few years the Dunnes' friend Paul Schrader would make the Patty Hearst movie, and Natasha Richardson would play the lead role. Around the time of Hearst's trial, the Dunnes got to know Tasha, "an uncertain but determined adolescent with a little too much makeup and star-tlingly white stockings," Didion said. Tasha's father, Tony, the distinguished theater and film director, was renting the former home of *Deep Throat* star Linda Lovelace on Kings Road in Hollywood. He had become a good friend of the Dunnes, so when Tasha came to visit from London, where she lived with her mother, Vanessa Redgrave, he introduced her to Quintana and her parents. Instantly, Quintana saw Tasha as a role model. She began experimenting with makeup—something it took Didion a while to notice.

The Wharton summer-house effect was impossible to achieve on warm, lazy evenings when actors, producers, and directors circled one another, working the room. One night, Didion threw a party for around sixty people. She made Mexican chicken; the house smelled of onions and peppers. She hired bartenders and caterers to set up the buffet. She wore a batiste dress, bought in the children's department at Bonwit Teller (her weight was still down, ever since her visit to Cartagena). According to Sara Davidson, a guest at the party that night, Warren Beatty prowled the house, telling people he wanted to do "some gynecological detective work. I'm a combination gynecologist and detective." At one point, Davidson said, he pulled up a rattan chair, facing Didion on the couch, "opened his knees and pressed her knees between his. 'This is it for me,' he said. 'This is all I want, right here. I'm happy.'" Didion fidgeted. Beatty looked at his watch and said, "I don't have to be on the set until ten Monday morning."

Didion said, "This is not . . . feasible."

Did Wharton have to put up with such nonsense?

One thing she *might* have envied was the long, slow drive, much of it skirting the coast, into Los Angeles and back—about forty miles each way. On these journeys, with Dunne at the wheel, Didion spun ideas for her novel, speaking into the wind, testing her husband's reactions. The Southern novel she had once envisioned had given way—but not completely!—to the hallucinatory setting of the Panama airport, which would not leave her mind. But now she also wanted to write about San Francisco—the SLA shenanigans had tugged her attention back to the Bay Area. Novels would be so much easier to write if she started with plot instead of setting, but apparently this was never going to work for her.

So one night in the car, she just decided "to make it all one book"—New Orleans, San Francisco, Central America—she'd "fold in all the various elements so that it would be like seeing more colors than you can possibly take in with one look."

Offhandedly, Dunne suggested the title *A Book of Common Prayer.* "Maybe because he thought it would take a lot of prayer to get such a project off the ground," Didion said.

Off the ground they went, taking Quintana, to Chicago, Cleveland, Johnstown, Pennsylvania, and Buffalo. Chasing rock stars.

John Foreman, whom Dunne had met his sophomore year at Princeton, when Nick took him with Grace Kelly to a party, was a producer now, and he loved the rock 'n' roll movie idea. The Dunnes had worked with him on a number of aborted "deals," including a thriller set in an oil field, an idea hatched one day when Dunne thumbed through the annual report of a defunct oil-drilling outfit in which he'd invested. He was in over his head on that one, never even wrote a treatment, but the beauty of *A Star Is Born* was that the picture could be the vehicle for a sound-track album. The right package, here, needed only a slender thread to hold it together, and the Warner Bros. music people could do the rest. It was rumored that Carly Simon said no to the project because the story of a self-destructive rock singer and his beautiful partner was too close to the life she actually lived with James Taylor; certainly, Warner Bros. liked Simon, whose career was soaring, but they wanted nothing to do with Taylor, whose trajectory had veered into a ditch following constant drug abuse. No matter. They could get Elvis. They could get Liza Minnelli. Whoever.

To prepare for writing the screenplay, the Dunnes hit the road to learn about the rock 'n' roll business: "[T]hree weeks of one-night stands in the armpit auditoria and cities of the land," Dunne said.

"You'd find yourself in . . . Pennsylvania on a summer's night with a really bad English metal band—you know, I mean just hopeless—and being really thrilled," Didion said.

In Johnstown, Dunne spent "the better part of an afternoon listening to Uriah Heep's bass player debate the pros and cons of a fretless neck on a Gibson."

In Cleveland, he watched a member of Led Zeppelin scrawl on a dressing room wall "Call KL 5-2033 for good head." Dunne said he phoned. "KL 5-2033 asked my room number at the Hollenden House, any friend of the Zeppelin was a friend of hers."

In Chicago, "a groupie talked about mainlining adrenaline. 'It only makes you scared,' she said, 'for twenty minutes.'"

Robert Lamm, the keyboardist for the band Chicago, recalled staying in a "roomy suite" at the Ambassador East in the Windy City. "Led Zeppelin had just left . . . leaving the management in shock, having swung on the large chandelier in the lobby, pulling it down," he said. "Mid-afternoon [one day] there was a knock at the door. I opened it to see [bandmate] James Guercio standing with a man and woman I did not recognize. Ushered in, introduced, they then took a short tour of the suite. The couple was soon questioning me about all manner of 'rock band' routine: travel modes, wardrobe, luggage, sleep schedule, sound checks, food intake, drug intake, and what-all."

This was one instance when the Dunnes' usually sure instincts, their combined ear for the culture's noise, failed them—one story they didn't *get right.* Too much focus on the riffs and fills. They missed the solos and the bridge.

They were working on an assumption about rock "authenticity" no longer current by the early 1970s. With Dylan, the Beatles, and the Stones, theatricality had been tailored to suit what appeared to be "genuine" stage personae (however mercurial, in Dylan's case). The rock star was either a prophet or a garage-band-mutt like the rest of us; either way, he didn't traffic in bullshit or pretend to be anything other than what he was ("It's only rock 'n' roll, but I like it").

By 1973 most arena-size rock audiences were hooting "authenticity" off the stage. Glam had kicked down the stadium doors, wearing Elton John's platform shoes. David Bowie coiffed and colored his hair, smudged his gender out of all recognition, and performed as a futuristic messenger for an alien entity that was either a collective consciousness or a giant black hole—it wasn't clear.

In the sixties, sincerity and authenticity had led us all to walk, naively, into the flaming eyes of the National Guardsmen's bayonetted rifles, into stinging clouds of tear gas, into Nixon's not being a crook.

So now we wanted to forget. We wanted a show. We wanted our nightly six grams of coke. We wanted velour bomber jackets and Stirling Cooper trousers. We wanted to see blood on the stage and heads bitten off of bats.

This was a sea change in the culture of rock 'n' roll that Dunne failed to register as he dialed KL 5-2033. Not that it would matter in the end. Eventually, Barbra Streisand seized control of the *Star Is Born* project, and exhibited even less understanding of rock than the Dunnes did.

At the Ambassador Hotel in Chicago, in the Pump Room at midnight, Quintana "ate caviar for the first time," Didion said. This was a "mixed success since she wanted it again at every meal thereafter and did not yet entirely understand the difference between 'on expenses' and 'not on expenses.'" Earlier that evening, she had sat through a Chicago concert "onstage, on one of the amps. The band had played 'Does Anybody Really Know What Time It Is?' and '25 or 6 to 4.' She had referred to the band as 'the boys.'"

The Dunnes left the stadium with the musicians, and "the crowd had rocked the car," delighting Quintana.

These "three weeks of one-night stands" thrilled and energized her. It was so much better than being at home. On the road, wrapped in the pounding music, she was beyond the Broken Man's reach.

The next day, after the midnight caviar, she "did not want to go to her grandmother's in West Hartford," Didion wrote. "[S]he had advised me . . . she wanted to go to Detroit with the boys."

4

For Cinque, as for the wanna-be rock star Charles Manson, it had always been the girls. "I crave the power Charlie Manson had," Cinque said.

Whether Cinque had Manson's alleged ability to inhabit his girls' heads and make them do his bidding was the central issue in Patty Hearst's trial—a strategy devised by Hearst's lawyer, F. Lee Bailey, who had recently defended one of the soldiers involved in the My Lai massacre.

The SLA saga had begun with stories of CIA mind-control techniques, in the person of Colston Westbrook, Cinque's prison mentor, and ended on the same note, with the court testimony of Louis Jolyon "Jolly" West, a psychiatrist who argued that Hearst had been "brainwashed" through drug and sensory-deprivation methods. West, whose research had been heavily funded by the CIA, was an early experimenter with LSD. In the early 1960s, he'd set himself up in a safe house in the Haight where, he later reported, "an ongoing program of intensive interdisciplinary study into the life and times of hippies was undertaken . . . The Haight-Ashbury district proved to be an interesting laboratory for observations concerning a wide variety of phenomena."

What these "phenomena" were, and how much he provoked them using government resources, is unclear, but his place was said to have been filled with young people "blasting off" on various drugs.

In any case, the Hearst jury did not swallow his testimony, and Patty went to prison. A short time later, in the aftermath of the Jonestown tragedy in Guyana, no less an eminence than John Wayne called for her release. "If everybody is willing to accept the fact that one man can brainwash nine hundred people into committing suicide"—in a compound adjacent to a former CIA training facility, as it happened—"why can't they believe a treacherous bunch like the Symbionese Army could brainwash one little girl? She was one little girl tortured and confined and threatened with her life."

The brave protector of little girls was still promising a safe haven at the bend in the river. At least a few of the little girls had different ideas, gleaned, it seemed, from the rough justice stylized in Hollywood Westerns. On September 5, 1975, just a few months after desperately attempting to contact Led Zeppelin's guitarist, Jimmy Page, to warn him of "bad energy," Squeaky Fromme, one of Manson's girls, pointed a Colt .45 at Gerald Ford in Sacramento's Capitol Park. Seventeen days later, Sara Jane Moore, an FBI informant under the supervision of Special Agent Charles Bates, who had initially headed the FBI's investigation of the Watergate break-in, and who had most recently advised Randolph Hearst during the kidnapping ordeal, fired a .38-caliber revolver at Ford across the street from San Francisco's St. Francis Hotel.

Conspiracy theorists delighted in pointing out that, at the time of these attempts on his life, Ford, a former member of the Warren Commission, had appointed a House committee to investigate U.S. intelligence activities, including assassinations.

The sixties kept ending and not ending. But as images of finality go, it was hard to beat the inferno at Fifty-fourth and Compton on May 17, 1974, the ramshackle roof exploding and igniting the palm tree above it as hundreds of policemen and FBI agents ringed the neighborhood, scattering mothers and kids crouched behind eroding cinder-block walls—all of it broadcast live on television, with the audience believing Patty Hearst was burning alive inside. In fact, she sat watching the spectacle on television, too, in a motel room near Disneyland.

It was the "greatest domestic firefight in the history of mobile television news coverage," said Didion's friend Barry Farrell. As he put it, "[I]t was clear that the miniscule army [the SLA] had touched upon the sorest of American vulnerabilities, the temptation to see in new calamities the appearance of new entertainments."

This wasn't a "police shoot-out, it was a police shoot-in," said one neighborhood resident. Someone scrawled a message on a charred wall in front of the house: "It Took 500 Cops" to kill six people, including Cinque and William Wolfe (though later reports claimed that only nineteen SWAT team members participated in the gunfire). It went without saying that if the outlaws had holed up in Beverly Hills or Brentwood, the situation would have been handled quite differently. When the flames erupted, police did not allow firefighters anywhere near the neighborhood to put them out. It seemed no one wanted Cinque to stand before a multiheaded, cobralike bank of microphones to say what he knew. "The LAPD was making a statement to revolutionaries to stay out of the city," said a witness. They were saying, *Once and for all, this is the end of the sixties.*

Except, as Barry Farrell wrote, in paying the SLA the "homage of a coast-to-coast auto-da-fe," the authorities legitimized the paranoia of antigovernment forces, Left *and* Right (in what would become a repeated pattern at Ruby Ridge, Idaho, and Waco, Texas); "to die in a flaming house with a flaming palm above you and something resembling the American Division crouched in the street outside is not exactly what it means to be defeated," Farrell wrote, "not when it happens in plain sight of millions of viewers, among whom an unhealthy number may be presumed to have been inspired by the show . . . the six inside the house had died the only death that could give full meaning to the idea of being a 'terrorist.'"

Without knowing it, the nation had witnessed, in this California drama, the *Coming Soon* of the MOVE fire in Philadelphia, of Oklahoma City and 9/11—terrorism as showbiz extravaganza. In retrospect, the moment was made all the more indelible by the resignation, in disgrace, of Yorba Linda's Richard Nixon from the presidency just three months after the embers had settled in South-Central L.A. (Quintana called him "President Nixon Vietnam Watergate, almost as if he had a three-tiered name like John Quincy Adams," Dunne said.)

The Watergate affair had a long, shadowy history, many layers and complications, but in Nixon's mind it boiled down to a shoot-out with his perceived domestic enemies: protest marchers, hippies, rock stars, and his fellow politicians.

I don't know what happened to this country.

Busy being born, busy dying.

Not much emphasis on *why.*

Chapter Twenty-two

————— ❖ —————

1

Nineteen seventy-five: "[T]here was a sense that something was happening that spring in Berkeley, something important and memorable that you didn't want to miss out on," wrote Caitlin Flanagan, referring to what she called "Didion-mania." Flanagan was fourteen in 1975. Her father, chair of the Berkeley English Department, was hosting Didion as a Regents' Lecturer, a position established with the aid of Didion's old teachers Mark Schorer and James Hart to bring to campus, for a monthlong teaching appointment and culminating public address, a scholar or artist who worked outside academia. Though Didion had published only two novels and a book of essays at that point, she had achieved a higher profile than most of her former classmates, and there was "the impression that she had returned to Berkeley a prodigal, but ready at last to put herself on the right path," Flanagan said. Schorer had never relinquished his hope that she would come back to him from the crass magazine world, "put her nose to the grindstone of Henry James criticism," earn her Ph.D. (better late than never), and take her proper place in front of a classroom. "Who can blame those two old teachers for wanting to bring their bright-eyed girl back to Berkeley, who can blame them for wanting to keep her forever in Wheeler Hall with the transom windows and the parquet floors and the Beaux Arts balconies and the perfect bay views?" Flanagan wrote. "They had a fondness for her that was the old man's fondness for a very young woman he has helped along the way, something far past lust, something that was instead the deepest kind of affection."

Toward securing establishment recognition, Didion's major cachet was her inclusion in Tom Wolfe's 1973 anthology, *The New Journalism*. She didn't know why she'd appeared in such company—"Certainly I have nothing in common with Hunter [Thompson]," she had said—but her name in the table of contents, as only one of two women (Barbara Goldsmith was the other), among such notables as Truman Capote, Norman Mailer, Michael Herr, Gay Talese, Terry Southern, and George Plimpton, began a process of canonization, planting Didion as a geodetic mark in the American literary landscape. In his introductory manifesto, Wolfe made his now-familiar argument that the New Journalism was an exciting new prose form, more with-it than the novel. But what really made the anthology a benchmark, and its writers a posse to be reckoned with, was the growing recognition that this exciting new form championed more or less traditional American values. Its radical practitioners only *pretended* to rock the yacht.

At heart, Didion was still a Goldwater girl (though she had just registered as a Democrat in order to vote for Jerry Brown as governor of California in the 1974 primary). Barbara Goldsmith's profile of the actress Viva, her contribution to Wolfe's anthology, was a rather scolding exposé of the seamy side of Andy Warhol's Factory. And Hunter Thompson had revealed himself as an old curmudgeon, writing, on the occasion of Richard Nixon's reelection in 1972, "This may be the year when we finally come face to face with ourselves; finally just lay back and say it—that we are really just a nation of 220 million used car salesmen with all the money we need to buy guns, and no qualms at all about killing anybody else in the world who tries to make us uncomfortable." His subversive rant was really a nostalgic longing for a lost domain.

Establishment king- and queen-makers could reward such work, knowing they'd be hailed as adventurers while championing standard beliefs.

But it wasn't Didion's Establishment mantle that created the fervor at Berkeley in the spring of 1975. It was the harder-to-see resonance she had with certain readers, mostly women at this point, and mostly through her essays—it was the passion of the housewife who had taped Didion's *Life* columns above her kitchen sink, who felt she was being spoken to by a friend. The nature and depth of this passion may have surprised Didion as much as it shocked her former professors, but there it was.

In Establishment terms, on the local scene that April and May, she was very nearly a bust. She took a single room in the Faculty Club, in the center of campus, and quickly isolated herself. Later she claimed she spent most of her free time writing *A Book of Common Prayer;* more than a third of the novel had already been drafted by this point. Dunne had praised it, to Lois Wallace, as the best thing Joan had ever done. "At night I would be the only person on the campus," Didion said. "After the library closed, there I'd be. It was so extraordinary. I slipped right back into a sort of student depression. You know, I started wearing a dirty raincoat again and I walked around . . . I had nuts in my pocket. I mean, it was really odd. And very gratifying, in a way, to close a circle . . . this extraordinary experience of going back to someplace that was a very emotional period of your life. Walking back into that life nineteen years later, or whatever it was . . ."

She hoarded bits of chocolate in her tiny desk drawer. She ate tacos for dinner. "[I] wrapped myself in my bedspread and read until two a.m., smoked too many cigarettes, and regretted, like a student, only their cost," she said. "I fell not only into the habits but into the moods of the student day. Every morning I was hopeful, determined, energized by the campanile bells and by the smell of eucalyptus and by the day's projected accomplishments. . . . I would write five pages, return all calls, lunch on raisins and answer ten letters. I would at last read E. H. Gombrich. . . . And yet every afternoon by four o'clock, I was once again dulled, glazed, sunk in an excess of carbohydrates and in my own mediocrity, in my failure—still, after twenty years!—to 'live up to' the day's possibilities."

Her routine contrasted starkly with her role as inspirational teacher. She thought she had prepared well to assume a sage aura; that same spring, she had been asked to give a commencement address at UC Riverside—academia was tugging fiercely at her raincoat!—and she had written a talk projecting the persona she hoped would carry her through her collegiate commitments. "I'm not telling you to make the world better, because I don't think that progress is necessarily part of the package," she planned to tell the Riverside kids (the Kimberlys and Sherrys and Debbis she had mocked in "Some Dreamers of the Golden Dream"). "I'm just telling you to live in it. Not just to endure it, not just to suffer it, not just to pass through it, but to live in it. To try to get the picture. To live recklessly. To take chances. To make your own work and take pride in it. To seize the moment. And if you ask me why you should bother to do that, I could tell you that the grave's a fine and private place, but none I think there do embrace. Nor do they sing there, or write, or argue, or see the tidal bore on the Amazon, or touch their children. And that's what there is to do and get it while you can and good luck with it."

Now here she was at Berkeley, wrapped in a bedspread, nibbling chocolate in the dark in the middle of the night.

A previous year's tenure at Yale had not steeled her, as she had hoped it would, for academic rigor. In New Haven, she had been asked to conduct a seminar on American literature, have tea with a group of nonfiction students, and meet with a film class—but this last she could do with her husband, and none of the events required a formal talk. More pressing that fall was the swift illness and death, in December, of Dunne's mother. From the cancer diagnosis to the funeral was a mere four months. Always a secretive woman, she was only slightly more accommodating, Dunne found, when faced with her final end. One night he asked for her wisdom in coping with marital tensions. "Drink," she said drily. "Drugs." There was one good thing about dying, she told him: "I won't have to read about Richard Nixon or Patty Hearst anymore." Dunne's grief during this period was balanced by intense curiosity: When he saw the funeral attendants carrying his mother from the house in a gray body bag, he was surprised. "I had always thought body bags were black," he said. He "was already making notes" for *True Confessions,* and this was a useful detail.

For Didion, mother loss, followed by a return to a college campus, was disorienting, almost as if there had been a glitch in time and she was young and old all at once.

So it was that in Berkeley she barely felt adult enough to fulfill one of her official duties as Regents' Lecturer: being guest of honor at a formal dinner in the home of the English Department's chair. According to Caitlin Flanagan, the evening was a disaster. "The immediate impression she gave, patently obvious even to a 14-year-old, was one of a person in misery," Flanagan wrote. "I can tell you this for certain: anything you have ever read by Didion about the shyness that plagued her in her youth, and about her inarticulateness in those days, in the face of even the most banal questions, was not a writer's exaggeration of a minor character trait for literary effect. The contemporary diagnosis for the young woman at our dinner table would be profound—crippling—social-anxiety disorder."

"She never took her purse off her lap!" Flanagan's mother exclaimed afterward. "She took it to the dinner table!"

The entire time, Didion had an "anxious expression" on her face. After dinner, clutching her purse, she couldn't wait to leave as the faculty men drank gallons of Irish coffee. Once she'd gone, the "consensus was that the little lady had her work cut out for her," Flanagan said. Maybe she wasn't classroom material after all.

One student said the class was terribly awkward and tense. Didion would read to them in a barely audible voice or stare at them in silence, drumming her fingers on the desk.

We get a clear view of what she *tried* to teach from her novel *Democracy*

(1984). In a wholly autobiographical passage, she says she met "a dozen or so students in the English Department to discuss the idea of democracy in the work of certain post-industrial writers. I spent my classroom time pointing out similarities in style and presumably in ideas of democracy (the hypothesis being that the way a writer constructed a sentence reflected the way that writer thought), between George Orwell and Ernest Hemingway, Henry Adams and Norman Mailer." She asked her students to "[c]onsider the role of the writer in a post-industrial society" (recently, she had decided that the nation's inability to come to terms with the loss of its manufacturing-based economy accounted, in large measure, for the social unrest of the 1960s). "Consider the political implications of both the reliance on and the distrust of abstract words."

Twenty years earlier, she said, "I had considered the same questions or ones like them. In 1955 on this campus I had first noticed the quickening of time. In 1975 time was no longer just quickening but collapsing, falling in on itself, the way a disintegrating star contracts into a black hole."

This image may have occurred to her because she remembered her student days, when she would glance up the hill at the blue lights of the Bevatron, and absorb, like radiation, the early Cold War expectation that her adult life would be lived "in the face of definite annihilation." She remembered reading Henry Adams on the Dynamo and the Virgin. She imagined the "blue in the glass at Chartres" as the same blue surrounding the fuel rods inside the TRIGA Mark III, the nuclear reactor pool in Etcheverry Hall, "the blue that is actually a shock wave in the water"—the same blue as the medicine bottles tossed from covered wagons by her pioneer ancestors. She recalled Adams saying that, in developing massive machinery and fresh forms of energy, Western civilization had moved from thirteenth-century unity to nineteenth-century multiplicity, from belief in the moral force of the Holy Virgin to the anxiety of fragmentation. And now, in 1975, as she stood staring at the bland brick facade of Etcheverry Hall, the fragments of the Industrial Age were themselves fading under still more powerful bundles of energy and their increasingly abstract economies—all an indeterminate blue, the color of very late evening.

2

That spring, in Berkeley, the "question of whether one spoke of Saigon 'falling' or of Saigon's 'liberation'" was the major preoccupation of the students, if not the English Department faculty (the faculty was busy discussing the "plotting of *Vanity Fair, Middlemarch,* and *Bleak House*"). In her old raincoat—her regressive lassitude—she could do little between classes other than walk down to Telegraph Avenue and buy the latest *San Francisco Chronicle, San Francisco Examiner, Oakland Tribune, Los Angeles Times, Berkeley Gazette,* and *New York Times.* "Tank battalions vanished between editions," she wrote. "Three hundred fixed-wing aircraft disappeared in the new lead on a story about the president playing golf at the El Dorado Country Club in Palm Desert, California." Code names for the American evacuations of Phnom Penh and Saigon puffed up the headlines: EAGLE PULL, FREQUENT WIND. She learned that the "colors of the landing lights for the helicopters on the roof of the American Embassy in Saigon were red, white and blue." She learned that the "amount of cash burned in the courtyard of the DAO in Saigon before the last helicopter left was three-and-a-half million dollars American and eighty-five million piastres." Each new detail added to the "black hole effect."

She would sit on a bench on Telegraph Avenue, considering the chaotic and incomplete dispatches out of Vietnam, considering the clamoring local disorder—the drug buys up and down the street, the cheap, bad food and the tepid coffee for sale, the stand where Nancy Ling Perry had sold fruit juice to Patty Hearst; she considered the shadow cast by Etcheverry Hall, and she concluded, intuitively, that the Berkeley-aided nuclear bomb tests in the Pacific, in the 1940s and 1950s, with their raze-it-and-leave-it results, "formed a straight line to pushing the helicopters off the aircraft carriers when we were abandoning Saigon. It was a very clear progression in my mind."

It was hard, then, for her to trundle back to campus and concentrate on teaching "ideas of democracy" in American literature. The images broadcast from Southeast Asia clashed with words issued from Washington ("peace with honor," an "orderly end to the assistance effort") and seemed absolutely to deride the language of democracy—perhaps the concept itself.

Here again "the hypothesis being that the way a writer constructed a sentence reflected the way that writer thought."

"I'm a writer," a stranger told her one day, standing in the doorway of her temporary office.

"What have you written?" she asked him.

"Nothing you'll ever dare to read," he snapped. He smirked at her. He said he admired only Céline and Djuna Barnes. Barnes was the only woman who'd ever written anything worth a damn. He sat threateningly on the edge of Didion's desk and said, "Your time's gone, your fever's over."

"It had probably been a couple of decades, English 106A, since I had last heard about Céline and Djuna Barnes and how women could not write, since I had last encountered this particular brand of extraliterary machismo," Didion commented later. She said she locked her office door after the man left and sat silently for a long while in the afternoon light. "At nineteen I had wanted to write," she said. "At forty I still wanted to write, and nothing that had happened in the years between made me any more certain that I could."

At the beginning of March 1975, fixed-wing aircraft began evacuating American civilians and "at risk" South Vietnamese (those who had worked for, or with, the Americans) from Tan Son Nhat Airport. On April 3, President Ford announced Operation Babylift, an initiative to evacuate two thousand Vietnamese orphans, many of them fathered by U.S. servicemen. One of the operation's Lockheed C-5A Galaxy planes crashed in a muddy rice paddy, killing 138 passengers, including 78 children. Within days of this tragedy, North Vietnamese forces began a final push toward Saigon, attacking Tan Son Nhat and killing the last two American soldiers to "officially" die in the Vietnam conflict. The fixed-wing evacuations were suspended, and Operation Frequent Wind began, a planned series of helicopter convoys leaving from the Defense Attaché Office at the airport, the American embassy in Saigon, and other rendezvous spots in the city. The American radio network was scheduled to play Irving Berlin's "White Christmas" as a signal to U.S. personnel that the final evacuation had begun. CH-53 and CH-46 choppers as well as UH-1 Hueys would ferry civilians to the carrier ships of the Seventh Fleet waiting in the South China Sea.

On April 30, according to a *New York Times* article Didion read in her room at the Berkeley Faculty Club, "large numbers of . . . Vietnamese clawed their way up the 10-foot wall of the [American] embassy compound in desperate attempts" to be taken aboard the choppers landing on the small, flat roof and "escape approaching Communist troops. United States marines and civilians used pistol and rifle butts to dislodge them." Several men and women got snagged on the wall's barbed wire and hung helplessly, bleeding over the courtyard stones as ashes from destroyed top-secret intelligence reports spat from incinerator pipes, coating the compound. "People held up their children, asking Americans to take them over the fence."

So many helicopters—eighty-one that final day—crowded the TF-76 carrier ships, some of the choppers were shoved off the decks to make room for others. Pilots were ordered to ditch into the sea, and wait to be rescued, since the USS *Okinawa* and others had no landing room. One Huey pilot, told there was no space for him aboard the USS *Blue Ridge*, leaped from his helicopter as it circled forty feet over the sea. The chopper crashed into the side of the ship; its rotor blade sheared off, grinding into an American Bell 205 that was refueling on deck. Moments later, another helicopter tried to land and crashed into the disabled Bell.

In the days ahead, while President Ford insisted that "Americans can [now] regain the sense of pride that existed before Vietnam," and as Didion prepared for her final lecture at Berkeley, she learned from newspaper accounts that the "number of Vietnamese soldiers who managed to get aboard the last American 727 to leave Da Nang was three hundred and thirty. The number of Vietnamese soldiers to drop from the wheel wells of the 727 was one." In a speech at Tulane University, President Ford reiterated that America was a "good neighbor to all people and the enemy of none."

Consider the political implications of both the reliance on and the distrust of abstract words.

3

"There's something *weird* going on with Joan Didion and women," Caitlin Flanagan said her father remarked one night.

"Apparently, vast numbers of women—students, staff members, faculty, Berkeley people—were thronging to her office hours, hanging around the door of her classroom, arranging their schedules so that they could bump into her, or at least catch a glimpse of her, as she walked from the Faculty Club to Wheeler Hall," Flanagan said. "It was becoming clear that she didn't have just readers; she had fans—not the way writers have fans, but the way musicians and actors have fans—and that almost all of them were female." The English Department faculty had pretty much written her off. She could never be embraced by the Establishment; she just wasn't cut out for it. Said Flanagan: They "hadn't simply underestimated" her "huge, mesmerizing power" over certain readers. They had been "almost entirely unaware of it."

A reporter named Susan Braudy arrived to interview Didion for *Ms.* Apparently, the magazine had forgiven Didion for her attack on the women's movement, and decided a successful female writer was a feminist icon, regardless of her politics.

Braudy's approach to writing her article was to tell Didion she had spoken to a friend of hers—usually someone Didion didn't know very well—and that the person in question had said this or that. Then she'd ask Didion what she thought. What Didion thought was that this reporter was terribly annoying. The process reenforced her belief that interviewing people for biographical profiles was generally a waste of time. When Greg Dunne heard that Braudy had asked his wife why she wrote about such emotionally crippled women, instead of strong women like herself, he exploded, saying this reporter knew nothing about literature.

Dunne had gone to Berkeley at his wife's insistence. She had gotten nervous, anticipating the public talk capping her stay here. Further, she had dragooned Henry Robbins into flying from New York for moral support. She wanted to hand him personally the manuscript of *A Book of Common Prayer*. She needed his immediate encouragement and enthusiasm—plus, she distrusted Susan Braudy. Didion planned to read from the novel as part of her talk, and she didn't want to see it quoted in *Ms*. Somehow, the pages would be safe in Henry's hands. If *Ms*. tried any funny business, he would know what to do. "[E]ditors do not, in the real world, get on the night TWA to California to soothe a jumpy midlist writer," she wrote later. But that's precisely what Robbins did.

The English Department secretary had booked a room for Didion's lecture. One afternoon, she and Flanagan's father took the Dunnes to check it out. Heidi, the secretary, asked Didion if the room suited her.

Later, in a letter to Lois Wallace, Didion said she had worked up the nerve to say the room was too tiny for the audience she'd attract. The chair, impatient and disbelieving, gave her a thin smile but agreed to indulge her and book another space.

Flanagan told a different story. "Didion said nothing" to Heidi, she wrote. "[She] just looked up at her husband. He remarked coldly, 'It's too small,' and Joan nodded fiercely, as though this were obvious.

"Never antagonize a secretary. Heidi marched back to her desk and scheduled Didion's talk in the biggest hall she could book. Let her see how she liked lecturing to a half-filled room!"

When Didion saw the new lecture hall, she panicked. The first one had been too small, but this was a monster—she didn't believe she could fill it. Heidi had set her up.

In fact, on the night of the lecture, "tearful women . . . were turned away at the door, others [were] grateful to stand in the back or to sit on the floor . . .

[It was] a huge, rapt crowd of the type that doesn't feature in even the wildest dreams of most writers," Flanagan wrote. "It was a madhouse."

Before she was introduced onstage, Didion hid in a bathroom, convinced she was going to vomit.

Trembling in front of the microphone, she cleared her throat and said, "I've been sitting here trying to get used to the idea that I'm here and you're there, but it may take me a little while. So if I look at my feet and don't talk very loud, I hope you'll bear with me until I get used to the idea."

Her lecture was entitled "Why I Write." She told her adoring audience, "[T]here's no getting around the fact that setting words on paper is the tactic of a secret bully, an invasion, an imposition of the writer's sensibility on the reader's most private space."

She said—in front of the English Department faculty, many of whom had stopped taking her seriously until this stunning crowd showed up—she could no longer remember most of what she'd learned as a Berkeley undergraduate. Really, what she'd learned was that she was not an intellectual but a writer: "By which I mean not a 'good' writer or a 'bad' writer but simply a writer, a person whose most absorbed and passionate hours are spent arranging words on pieces of paper. Had my credentials been in order I would never have become a writer." So much for Schorer's dream of getting her back.

How does one write? Not by revisiting the dusty tomes of Henry James criticism. Not by swaggering into a teacher's office, arrogantly announcing oneself as a writer and declaring the teacher's time was done.

No.

One becomes a writer by being the inappropriate and dismissible creature the faculty had laughed about after the formal dinner. "You just lie low . . . You stay quiet," Didion said. "You don't talk to many people and you keep your nervous system from shorting out . . ."

The standing-room-only crowd pressed forward.

This was one mouse who damn well knew how to roar.

Chapter Twenty-three

❧

1

If Didion became a girl again on the Berkeley campus, nibbling nuts from her raincoat pocket, she aged rapidly while writing *A Book of Common Prayer.* "I don't mean physically. I mean that in adopting [the main character's] point of view, I felt much sharper, harsher," she said. "I adopted a lot of the mannerisms and attitudes of an impatient, sixty-year-old dying woman. I would cut people off in the middle of conversations. I fell into Grace because I was trying to maintain her tone."

It was the tone, of course, of Dunne's dying mother, just as the girl in the book, on the lam from the FBI, is, in some measure, Patty Hearst. These recent events made their way into the novel the way radiation from the TRIGA Mark III bathed anything straying unprotected into its radius; Didion began to see the novelist's job as wandering, vulnerable, into the culture's red zones, setting off the alarms.

But in speaking, in the novel, as an older woman *about* a younger one with a misguided daughter she's never understood, Didion was—more crucially—speaking to herself, observing her life from the wide end of the telescope, returning with warnings from the future, a form of magical thinking available only in fiction. "*A Book of Common Prayer* to some extent has to do with my own daughter's growing up," she admitted to Susan Stamberg on National Public Radio. "My child is nowhere near the age of Marin, the girl in the novel, but she's no longer a baby. I think that part of this book came out of the apprehension that we are going to both be adults pretty soon . . . And [the daughter] has been misperceived by her mother most of her life."

Didion was quick to distinguish her biography from her artistry. "What I work out in a book isn't what the book is about. I mean, this book isn't about mothers and daughters. That's part of what it was for me, but I don't think it's what it is for a reader."

For the reader, it was a rare artifact: an American political novel. Since her trips to the Gulf Coast states and to Colombia, since her research on the Southern hemisphere and its economic ties to the Northern one, her notion of what a contemporary American novel needed to be had changed.

The fractured style of *all* her late novels (*A Book of Common Prayer, Democracy, The Last Thing He Wanted*) is qualitatively different from the fragmentations in her earlier work. It conveys not a broken sensibility so much as the shattered texture of American public life. More pointedly than before, she assumes, in these books, a communal rather than an individual voice.

Behind this new emphasis was a firm conviction, though at the time of *A Book of Common Prayer*, it was inchoate in her mind. She would not articulate it directly until the essays in *After Henry* and *Political Fictions*, starting in the 1990s. But already she was feeling the *rhythm*, the *structure*, of her conviction, and here is what she knew: The people inside America's governing process, including the journalists who report on officials' behavior, have "congealed into a permanent political class, the defining characteristic of which [is] its readiness to abandon those not inside the process."

These insiders use fables and romances (*we favor the freedom fighters; that's what this party is all about; strong bipartisan support; putting the American people first*) to obscure the ruthless, exclusive nature of the process.

This is how the world is, the powerful swear from on high. This is the way it has always been. Self-evidently, their claims are not true. What *is* true is harder to find these days. It was easy to see the squalor of a squatters' camp in a California fruit field in the 1930s. It's much harder to see the link between a civil war in Central America and a drug blight in Compton (a subject Didion would track in the 1980s).

Instead of clear connections, we have—on the news, on the Internet, in videos—flash pictures in variable sequence.

Or to put it another way: In the kind of domestic narrative Didion once followed (in *Run River* and even in *Play It As It Lays*) the house in which the couple will or will not live happily ever after is a given. The later Didion, intent upon cracking official fables, insists the *real* narratives are these: who owns the land on which the house was built; who built the house and when; who sold the house to whom; when, why, and for how much; who, ultimately,

benefited from the sale; where did the proceeds actually go; for what purposes was the house actually used?

This is no longer a world aspiring to happily ever after. It is a world of
transactions ever more complex, leading to mass movements of money and
consolidations of power. And it requires a new kind of storytelling.

In Berkeley, Didion had put a Xeroxed manuscript of the unfinished novel
into Henry Robbins's hands. She continued to tinker with the story and add
to it, using her husband's notes. He read as she worked and offered handwritten suggestions on yellow legal sheets, which she typed up and studied
during revisions. Mostly, his comments had to do with clarifying details and
keeping the point of view straight: Like a narrator in a Conrad novel, Grace
tells stories about others, and it is not always clear how she knows what she
knows.

Dunne worried about the book's bleak vision: In Didion's view, politics
was essentially a planet-wide arms deal.

The novel offered a dark picture of North American power moves from a
fresh angle. "In North America, social tensions that arise tend to be undercut and co-opted quite soon, but in Latin America there does not seem to be
any political machinery for delaying the revolution. Everything is thrown
into bold relief. There is a collapsing of time. Everything is both older than
you could ever know, and it started this morning," Didion said.

She had hired a personal secretary and researcher, a young woman named
Tina Moore, to help her with business correspondence as well as materials
for the novel. She was a "fantastic researcher," Didion said. "She would go
to the UCLA library, and I would say, 'Bring me back anything on plantation life in Central America.' And she would come back and say, 'This is really what you're looking for—you'll love this.' And it would not be plantation
life in Latin America. It would be Ceylon, but it would be fantastic. She had
an instinct for what was the same story, and what I was looking for. What I
was looking for were rules for living in the tropics. I didn't know that, but
that's what I found."

Her screenplay work had given her confidence in "intercutting" dialogue
among several characters at once, and she enjoyed trying her hand at "big
set-piece scenes with a lot of different speakers—when you've got twelve people around a dinner table talking at cross purposes." She realized when she
got within twenty pages of the end that she "still hadn't delivered [the] revolution" she'd promised earlier in the book. The novel "had a lot of threads,

and I'd overlooked this one. So then I had to go back and lay in the preparation for the revolution." It was like sewing, "setting in a sleeve . . . I mean I had to work that revolution in on the bias, had to ease out the wrinkles with my fingers."

She freely embraced the fact that she was writing a "romance," that her women were "romantic heroines rather than actual women in actual situations." She had constructed a brooding allegory of the life of our times.

On March 24, 1976, Henry Robbins wrote Didion to say *A Book of Common Prayer* was a novel of great "power and beauty." He said, "I see what John means about . . . perhaps laying on the ambience of rot and death too heavily, but it didn't and doesn't bother me . . . The novel *is* about death (just as *Play It As It Lays* was in its different way), and I don't find these thematic signals intrusive." He concluded, "It's a wonderful book, and I know it will be recognized as such—even by those who were frightened of *Play It As It Lays*. You're not going to have to wait for the appreciation this time."

She retreated into her study, surrounded by the magic objects easing her into her dream world and getting her past the "low dread" she felt each morning before beginning to write: postcards from Cartagena, a volume entitled *Inside South America*, a book of useful phrases (*Quiere ser mi testiga*, "Do you want to be my witness?"), a newspaper photograph of a man washing blood off the floor of a bombed Caribbean hotel lobby, lists of arms (M2, AR-15, Kalashnikov), lists of names (Graciela, Grace) written on sheets of onionskin paper stapled together, books of botany and medicines (*Tropical Nature, An Epilome of the Laboratory Diagnosis and Treatment of Tropical Diseases*—"For persistent vomiting: A few drops of 1:1000 solution of adrenalin in a little water, taken by mouth with sips of iced champagne").

Scattered across her desk were several forty-nine-cent Wire-In-Dex pads of ruled index cards containing images or lines of dialogue: "The oil rainbow slick on the water." "He runs guns. I wish they had caviar." Of these last two sentences, Didion said later, "When I heard Charlotte say this [in my mind], I had a very clear fix on who she was."

She saved newspaper articles on matters that would not make it into the novel, but they indicate how political her thinking had become, and they anticipate future projects: profiles of Vietnamese orphans, of Nicaraguan rebel groups, of money deals in and out of Miami.

There was a Pablo Neruda poem, "A Certain Weariness," clipped from *The New Yorker*: "I don't want to be tired alone. / I want you to grow tired along with me."

"As a child of comfortable family in the temperate zone she had been as a matter of course provided with clean sheets, orthodontia, lamb chops, living grandparents . . . ballet lessons, and casual timely information about menstruation and the care of flat silver," says Grace Strasser-Mendana, the narrator of *A Book of Common Prayer*. She is speaking about a woman named Charlotte Douglas.

Grace, in her sixties and dying of cancer, remains, like Conrad's Marlow, largely in the story's background, infusing every image in the book with her sensibility—but obliquely. Public, rather than private, incidents dominate the action. "I tell you . . . about myself only to legitimize my voice," Grace says.

Charlotte, a "child of the western United States," had been provided with "faith in the values of certain frontiers on which her family had lived, in the virtues of clean and irrigated land, of high-yield crops, of thrift, industry and the judicial system, of prayers and education, and in the generally upward spiral of history." In other words, she was a member of the Blue Sky Tribe, and John Wayne rode through her dreams.

But these details are merely introductory, the last remnants of a novel like *Run River*. "Some women . . . marry or do not marry with equanimity," Grace says. "They divorce or do not. They can leave a bed and forget it. They . . . get up and scramble eggs."

"So you know the story," she says dismissively at the start of the novel, preparing us for something else entirely. Though we do not know it yet, the domestic has been swamped by America's "underwater narrative," which is powered by nothing that cozy families, in their mortgaged homes, can possibly perceive. Behind the nice houses and the slick new shopping malls, the political class is busy making deals and counterdeals in anonymous rooms in remote terrains that the average citizen cannot find on any map.

Charlotte's daughter, Marin, a Patty Hearst–type radicalized by the 1960s, goes underground. Charlotte, unhinged by her daughter's disappearance, and harassed by the FBI in its efforts to find the girl, retreats to a small Latin American country, a place resembling Costaguana in Conrad's *Nostromo*. It seems to have "no history"—or maybe *too many* parallel pasts. It is called Boca Grande: Big Mouth, a vacant maw spewing disputatious language designed to preserve the "deniability" of anyone who passes through the region, since the only visitors here are the "occasional mineral geologist or CIA man traveling on one or another incorporeal AID mission."

Along the way, Charlotte gives birth to a hydrocephalic baby. It dies a few weeks later: the third dead infant we've met (so to speak) in as many Didion novels.

Charlotte waits, in vain, at the Boca Grande airport—as Didion once waited in Panama—for a plane that might connect her, somehow, to her daughter, Marin.

Grace, the widow of a wealthy man with financial stakes in Boca Grande, takes an interest in her fellow exile. Grace was raised in the American West, among transients in a hotel. She feels a kinship, a "common prayer," with Charlotte (though the childlike Charlotte is far more naive): They're shaped by the same Blue Sky values, disappointed by greedy, ambitious husbands, adrift now in an unchartable world, their hopes blasted by forces they cannot see, much less confront.

Each night, as Grace rinses her hair, she is aware of Liberian tankers in the bay outside her window, shadows on "incorporeal" missions (Liberian registration is usually a false cover for clandestine ships—slipping the narrative as easily as they slip in and out of foreign harbors).

In *A Book of Common Prayer,* Didion has cast off the social satire of Edith Wharton with its love of surface contours—a residue of which remained in *Play It As It Lays*; she has moved beyond the Gothic insularity of Poe, beyond the arbitrary postmodern collages of many of her contemporaries, and into a Melvillean world of confidence men and shifting sight (early on, Charlotte writes a paper on Melville for a college professor who later becomes her husband; he gives her an F).

One night, at the Hotel del Caribe, where Charlotte lives on Boca Grande, the generator flickers out, and she sits "alone in the dark at the ballroom piano until three A.M. picking out with one hand, over and over again and in every possible tempo, the melodic line of a single song." (The scene recalls Didion's essay "On the Morning After the Sixties," where the melancholy father of a Berkeley frat boy tweaked a tune, hoping to find the happy chords of his past—the essay itself an echo of Didion's dad trying, throughout her childhood, to cheer himself up by playing ragtime piano.) The dance floor, site of so many fairy-tale triumphs, has gone black; still, the abandoned princess keeps trying to find the right structural rhythm, the one continuous line getting her to the end of the only song she was ever taught to play.

But the melody won't carry on the island of Boca Grande.

None of the usual rituals or forms, nothing on which Charlotte has depended in her temperate life, will suffice now. As Grace says, words—accepted definitions, explanations, points of contact—don't work here.

At the end of the novel, once Charlotte has died brutally as a result of her refusal to acknowledge the realities of political violence, Grace locates Marin "in a dirty room in Buffalo" to bear final witness, to tell the girl her mother "always kept [her] in her mind." Marin, hardened by her radicalism, doesn't care—or pretends not to. In the end, she *does* break down.

The scene is a mirror image of the final section of Conrad's *Heart of Darkness,* when Marlow cannot tell Kurtz's intended the truth of what happened to her beloved in the wilderness. In Conrad, women, cosseted by strict social expectations, unaware of the world's primal darkness, must be lied to for their own protection. In Didion, women are exposed to the horror just as much as the men are; if they remain deluded, it's not because they haven't *tried* to see the truth. It's because, since Conrad's day, the truth has become a seven-headed cobra (Kalashnikovs, the TRIGA Mark III).

Says Grace, "I have not been the witness I wanted to be."

No one could.

On August 7, 1976, Didion wrote Lois Wallace, detailing her expectations for a sales strategy in marketing the novel. She trusted Henry Robbins, but perhaps she had already seen that he would hit a wall at Simon & Schuster in attemps to promote literary fiction. Another editor at the house remarked that a novel called *A Book of Common Prayer* might well end up on the religion shelf. The comment upset Didion, not because she feared she'd have to change her title (she was not about to), but because it suggested a less than wholehearted approach to selling the book. There was no point in pushing a literary novel as a rousing good adventure yarn—futzing with the title made no difference. No. The way to sell a literary novel, Didion said, was to make it An Event. She believed the book had commercial potential if the reading public could be persuaded *hers* was the novel to buy this year, whether or not they read it: Its appearance was a Major Literary Milestone. Therefore, the sales possibilities lay entirely in S&S promoting the book as A Novel by Joan Didion, with her name in larger letters on the cover than the title. Sell the author and the author's importance more than the book itself.

The novel's rollout had to be handled with a kind of arrogant certainty, she said, and she expected Wallace to inject a shot of testosterone into the S&S sales staff.

Whether the letter was prompted by pure anxiety over Simon & Schuster, or genuine confidence after her successful lecture at Berkeley, Didion was sincere in her plan for selling the book. (And she seems to have gotten her way: On the cover of the first-edition hardback, her name, printed in all caps at the top, is bolder than the title.)

She closed her letter by announcing to Wallace that she'd just bought a red fox coat.

S&S's Dick Snyder *did* have a blockbuster mentality and little patience for the placid backwater of literary fiction. In 1974, after a few weak years, he'd resuscitated the company financially with a deal he'd very nearly declined: *All the President's Men*, by Bob Woodward and Carl Bernstein, the story of their reporting trail in the Watergate affair.

All the President's Men became the *definition* of "blockbuster." Now, just weeks before the official publication date of *A Book of Common Prayer*, the movie of the Woodward-Bernstein story, starring Robert Redford and Dustin Hoffman, was gobbling up review space, pumping new life into the paperback, and generating buzz for this year's sequel, *The Final Days*, charting the end of the Nixon presidency. For the foreseeable future, Simon & Schuster would devote its best resources to selling *this* book. Tricky Dick had screwed Didion.

She bore no animosity toward Carl Bernstein, who had married her friend Nora Ephron in April. A charming rogue, he entertained Didion; she recognized he was probably the sort of man "capable of having sex with a venetian blind" (the reputation preceding, and surviving, his union with Ephron), but he never troubled her with his randiness or his gossip, and they got along fine. He admired her writing. The only potential awkwardness in their friendship occurred around certain others: Ben Stein, another new Didion pal, a former Nixon speechwriter (once rumored to have been Deep Throat), now trying to break into the movie business. Didion and Dunne were enormously helpful to him, introducing him to their picture agents. They were amused by his continuing support for Nixon. "I just think he was a saint!" he'd say. "[So] he was a politician who lied. How remarkable!" Probably not a good idea to herd him into the same room with Bernstein.

The other difficulty was Bernstein's partner. Woodward didn't particularly care for Nora Ephron or her social circle. "I just didn't have the natural connection with Nora," he admitted. "I remember I heard Nora talk about some dinner and holding a discourse on the kind of lettuce that had been served. 'Can you believe they served that kind of lettuce?' There was just this sense that she had been offended . . . it just wasn't the way I lived." He'd never have made it in Old Sac. And—grateful as Didion was for his exposure of the used-car salesman muttering to himself in the White House at night—he didn't endear himself to her.

2

"I remember going to a party at Joan's house in Trancas. I did not like the party, but Joan was so incredibly nice. Couldn't have been more hospitable," Ben Stein told me. "The people at the party were just uninteresting. I remember sitting at a table with John's brother Nick, and he was particularly uninteresting."

"I wasn't invited [anywhere] much anymore," Nick said. "In my journal of that period I recorded with names every snub, every slight. Already I had almost jumped in front of a train in Santa Barbara. At the last second I let it pass me. Already I'd had a major flirtation with a kitchen knife that I took to bed with me, as if I could make it happen in my sleep, thereby absolving me of any responsibility in the eyes of God, or so I thought. The love that I felt for Los Angeles turned to hate." He knew it wouldn't be long before he'd have to abandon the community altogether. He was no longer a deal maker. That distinction belonged to his brother now.

Working the room, chatting people up, refilling their drinks, Dunne loved to pique his guests' curiosity, remarking coyly about his efforts on *A Star Is Born*, "Put it this way, it's our beads, but it's not our necklace."

Didion would just smile, cook, arrange bowls of chicken salad on a table, and replenish the hors d'ouvres trays.

Sometimes, late in the evenings when the parties were winding down, when the chairs had been shoved aside to make space and it seemed that the largest piece of furniture in the room was the ocean outside, Nick's daughter Dominique and Quintana would walk through the house, grazing on leftovers, Quintana wearing a too-big sweatshirt, her skin lightly reddened from days in the sun. When asked what they'd been doing, the girls said they'd been working.

It was through her parents' work, before and during the long negotiations over *A Star Is Born*, that Quintana met Barbra Streisand's son, Jason. "I wasn't crazy about their playing in the cage with the pet lion cub, but I figured what the hell, this was Hollywood," Dunne said.

In the latter half of 1975, Quintana spent a lot of time alone, or with Dominique and Susan Traylor, as her folks fiddled with the script for *A Star Is Born*.

Their original screenplay was entitled *Rainbow Road*. "It should make us a lot of money," Didion said at the outset. "In fact, we saw it basically as a picture about money."

John Foreman took it to Jerry Schatzberg; the Dunnes were delighted to work with him again. Richard Perry, the music producer recruited by Warner Bros., found the screenplay unrealistic and trite. These people didn't know their rock 'n' roll. The Dunnes reworked the story (after screening *Seven Days in May* and *The Third Man* to remind themselves of scene composition and pacing; *The Third Man*, they thought, was the perfect movie).

Meanwhile, Sue Mengers took the screenplay to Streisand, who had an outstanding four- to six-million-dollar contract for a musical in which she would perform six songs. The contract called for the movie to be delivered by December 1976. Streisand detested the script. The man's part was bigger than the female lead's. This picture had no romance.

Streisand's latest boyfriend, Jon Peters, an illiterate hairdresser with dreams of producing movies, saw the script and asked Streisand to reconsider the part. "I had seen Barbra at the Cocoanut Grove . . . [W]hen [she] sang . . . the power she had—the magic in her fingers and face—controlled the entire room," he said. He wanted to reproduce that experience on-screen, and he convinced Streisand he could do it. "Jon has a way of seeing me, he knows me as a woman, as a sexual being, and I'm tired of being just Funny Girl, a self-deprecating waif," she said now. Peters bumped aside John Foreman as executive producer; Schatzberg fled the project.

Years later, in a book proposal distilling his life story, Peters (working with the writer William Stadiem) took complete credit for *A Star Is Born*. Speaking of himself in the third person, he said:

> Jon's brainstorm was to do a rock 'n' roll version of *A Star Is Born* . . . Los Angeles had replaced London as the center of the rock universe, a universe in which Jon fancied himself a player who wanted to become a master. He also wanted to make Barbra over to be cool and hip, not just a Broadway icon. Here was his chance to have it all . . . Jon even found a script of the remake called "Rainbow Road," by Hollywood's then most powerful and prestigious screenwriting couple, Joan Didion and John Gregory Dunne. The only problem was that Jon could not read it. His illiteracy was his darkest, most shameful secret . . . The

showdown script meetings between the reformatory dropout [Peters] and the snobby intellectual Dunnes was the stuff of farce. The dropout won. He fired the Dunnes and went through draft after draft with the biggest scribes in the business.

Peters's memoir was never published. His assertions that the Dunnes were cowed by him and that he fired them do not square with the couple's recollections. Already, prior to Streisand's commitment, the Dunnes worried that "*A Star Is Born* was becoming a career" and they wanted to abandon it, Dunne said. Then, when Streisand came aboard, "[v]enality forced us to reconsider . . . with Barbra Streisand involved, we knew we weren't going to get poor."

Soon Peters was referring to the project as "my film" and "my concept." The Dunnes looked for a way out. He just wanted to shoot his girlfriend's ass. "We couldn't . . . quit, because then we would have been in breach of contract and lost our 'points,' or percentage of the profits," Dunne wrote. "Nor could we be fired, because then we would have left with our points intact, and the business people would have none of that. They wanted to give us some of our points back, which we refused to do until it was stipulated that we could leave without being in breach. It took eight weeks to negotiate this point."

Meanwhile, Peters said he could direct. He said he could star in the movie. He said he could sing—"Put a band behind me, and I can sing. If not, shout around me." Finally, the studio convinced him to let the veteran Frank Pierson direct the film. "The Didion/Dunne third draft script [was] by far the best—sharp and tough-minded," Pierson said. But by now, Peters was adamant: The movie should be a thinly disguised version of his love affair with Streisand. She agreed. "People are curious: they want to know about us," she said. "That's what they come to see."

Pierson asked the studio heads why they'd allowed a callow egotist like Jon Peters to take control of a six-million-dollar musical. "It doesn't matter," he was told. "It would be nice if the picture was good, but the bottom line is to get [Streisand] to the studio. Shoot her singing six numbers and we'll make sixty million."

3

Throughout the months of writing both *A Book of Common Prayer* and the screenplay for *A Star Is Born*, Didion found Zen-like relief from the pressures of her work in the mundane rituals of shopping, cooking, controlling what went into her refrigerator (though it's also true that, as she worked on her novel and Dunne worked on his, days would pass when no one spoke to anyone else in the house, no one made meals or opened the mail). More than anything else, she took pleasure in meditative retreats to certain locations along the coast and in activities she shared with her daughter.

For company and moral support, she hoped to take Quintana on the road with her during the tour S&S was busy arranging for *A Book of Common Prayer* (the publisher's attempt to create an event; at least it was *something*).

"We are going to miss planes, we are going to miss meals, we are going to lose luggage," Didion warned Quintana.

"And . . . and then what?" Quintana asked.

"No matter what happens, we'll be fine."

In the meantime, Quintana volunteered a few hours a month as a nurse's aide at St. John's Hospital in Santa Monica, where she had been born. Didion always made sure her blue-and-white pinafore was clean. Quintana swam regular laps back to shore from beyond the Zuma Beach breakers (having been dropped off by a boat) as part of her training in the Junior Lifeguards program. One day, when Didion went there to pick her up, she found her daughter huddled, all alone, in a towel behind a dune. The beach was deserted. The lifeguards had insisted on taking everyone home—"for absolutely no reason," Quintana told her mother. There must be a reason, Didion said. "Only the sharks," Quintana said. "They were just blues."

The lifeguards' lookout, a pale blue wooden structure in the center of Zuma Beach (near the spot where Charlton Heston had discovered the shattered Statue of Liberty in *Planet of the Apes*), was a cozy enclave to which Didion would love to have retreated. "I would drive past Zuma some late foggy nights and see [men] moving around behind the lookout's lighted windows, the only other souls awake in all of northern Malibu," she said. "It seemed to me a curious, almost beatified career choice, electing to save those in peril upon the sea." Once, after a Santa Ana wind off the Mojave Desert had set ablaze 69,000 acres of Los Angeles County, with soot blighting the beaches, clouding the high tide, making it look like tinfoil burned in an oven, the lifeguards' bunker seemed to her even more essentially safe, a squat, solid hut in the midst of "some grave solar dislocation."

But her absolute favorite retreat, where she went to eat lunch by herself, was Arthur Freed Orchids. She'd drive past cheap new motels and condominiums, past rolling straw-colored hills smelling like mud-caked wooden trowels, and pull into a tucked-away complex of greenhouses full of the "most aqueous filtered light, the softest tropical air, the most silent clouds of flowers." They reminded her of the greenhouse she used to haunt, walking home from school when she was nine—where she "used up" the air, according to the owner. Here, the keeper of the plants, an Jalisco-born middle-aged man named Amado Vazquez, left her alone in the perfect atmosphere (seventy-two degrees, 60 percent humidity), among the phalaenopsis (most fertile "at full moon because in nature it must be pollinated by a night-flying moth," he told her). "He seemed to assume that I had my own reasons for being there," Didion said. "He would speak only to offer a nut he had just cracked, or a flower cut from a plant he was pruning."

Eventually, Vazquez bought out Arthur Freed and opened his own place, Zuma Canyon Orchids—it stands today, among tall Monterey pines and dusty agave plants, cactus gardens and herb gardens, off a winding road pocked with flood-warning signs.

To Didion, Vazquez was the embodiment of Zen, an expression of the deepest caring in each delicate touch of a petal—of a Leopard Prince, a Walnut Valley Halo, purple, white, and orange—in each gentle tug of the pulleys and chains releasing cascades of water among the swaying leaves in row after row along the greenhouse walls.

"I had never talked to anyone so direct and unembarrassed about the things he loved," Didion said, and she never wanted to leave.

"You want to know how I feel about the plants?" he confided in her one day. "I'll tell you. I will die in orchids."

Of course, Sacramento was Didion's oldest, surest retreat. As with her previous three books, she had gone there to finish *A Book of Common Prayer*, undisturbed by visitors, her daughter, or ringing telephones. When she'd reached the last chapters, she felt she had become impossible to live with, fighting over everything, unable to cope with Quintana's need for help on her homework. "I'm like a child in my parents' house," she said.

Eduene, silent, left her alone.

4

A Book of Common Prayer was an evil impulse," Noel Parmentel told me in the summer of 2013. "A hostile act against a close friend."

He remains convinced that a character in the novel, Warren Bogart, Charlotte Douglas's drunk and abusive ex-husband, the estranged father of her child, was based on him. He feels the portrait was defamatory.

"Lewis Lapham called me and said, 'It's all about you!' Part of it was published in *Harper's*. I thought, My God, look at this. Sidney Zion, a lawyer for writers [best known for outing Daniel Ellsberg as the one who leaked the Pentagon Papers] said I should threaten a lawsuit against Joan and the publisher. He thought they'd settle."

On January 28, 1977, Parmentel wrote Dick Snyder at S&S, Cc-ing Didion and Lois Wallace, warning him not to publish this "calumny." He said the characterization was malicious, a serious invasion of his privacy, and extremely damaging to him personally.

Wallace called him. "Noel, it's not about you," she said.

"Come on. Get serious," he replied.

He wouldn't talk to Didion. "She tried to get in touch with me. I wouldn't," he said. "The deed had been done. Lawyers were advising her. I don't know why she did it. I suspect it was Greg. I have a hunch he told Joan, 'Noel won't get mad. He's seen it before.'"

A suggestive line in the novel, describing Charlotte, may indicate how Didion had often felt when caught between her husband's affections and a lingering regard for her former lover: "[S]he was incapable of walking normally across the room in the presence of two men with whom she had slept. Her legs seemed to lock unnaturally into her pelvic bones. Her body went stiff, as if convulsed by the question of who had access to it and who did not." On some level, as well as being a story about mothers and daughters, *A Book of Common Prayer* may also have been a book of demarcations.

Simon & Schuster responded to Parmentel's threat with a curt letter denying his charge, but adding, in any case, that "it would [not] be legally improper" for Didion to have based a character on him in a work of fiction. "Were we or any other publisher to accede to this kind of unjustified complaint, it would give a power of censorship over every book . . . to every person who believes they can show a resemblance to themselves in the text," the letter said.

"The problem was, I couldn't prove 'malice,'" Parmentel said. Nor could he afford a protracted lawsuit. It saddened him to see his long friendship with Didion end in such a fashion, but he never spoke to her again. "What got me mad was I didn't spend time with Quintana anymore," he told me. "I used to see her as a child in Hartford. I was her godfather. I didn't get to see her grow up."

5

Quintana's math book and her unsolved equations sprawled across the hotel desk, among scattered pages of the Boston Ritz-Carlton's stationery. Quintana was napping in the next room, in a giant bed covered with Judy Blume books.

Didion ordered iced drinks from room service and sat answering a reporter's questions. She and her daughter had been on the road now for over a week, on the *Common Prayer* book tour. Radio stations and television stations in New York, Hartford, Washington, D.C., Boston, Chicago, Los Angeles, San Francisco, Dallas, Houston—they were all the same cramped space: wicker settees and camera cables and Styrofoam cups half filled with cold coffee. Always the same uninflected questions were posed: "Where are we heading . . . [and where were they heading] 'as Americans' . . . or 'as American women'"? It didn't matter what she said; the shows' hosts were only looking for her to fill three or four minutes of airtime until the next hair spray commercial. Most of them had no idea what her book was about and some of them never got its name right—or hers, either, for that matter.

Hotel rooms: the St. Regis, the Ritz-Carlton, the Jefferson. Quintana became deft and efficient at ringing up room service: lamb chops, consommé, oatmeal, crab salad. She ordered bourbon on the rocks for her mother and signed for her Shirley Temples. She learned to call for the car whenever her mother had an appointment with an interviewer, and if the car failed to show up on time, she knew to check the itinerary and phone the Simon & Schuster publicity director. Her mother had always hated talking on the telephone, and Quintana was happy to make the arrangements.

Of course, this wasn't Quintana's first experience with extended hotel stays and her mother's on-the-go work schedule. ("She's remarkably well-adjusted," Nick once observed. "Considering that every time I see her she's in a different city.") There were the frequent trips to Hawaii. There were the three weeks of rock gigs. And once, when she was five or six, her parents had taken her to Tucson, where they huddled with a script producer on a picture called *The Life and Times of Judge Roy Bean*, starring Paul Newman.

It took Didion many years to admit these business trips might have had a powerful, and not purely positive, effect on her daughter.

For example, in 1973, in an essay later published in *The White Album*, Didion mentioned Quintana only in passing in her haste to tell a funny anecdote: "We go out to dinner in Tucson: the sitter tells me that she has obtained for her crippled son an autographed picture of Paul Newman. I ask how old her son is. 'Thirty-four,' she says."

In 2011, in *Blue Nights,* Didion expanded this story, admitting more agency: "The Hilton Inn, where the production was based during its Tucson location, sent a babysitter to stay with [Quintana] while we watched the dailies. The babysitter asked her to get Paul Newman's autograph. A crippled son was mentioned. Quintana got the autograph, delivered it to the babysitter, then burst into tears. It was never clear to me whether she was crying about the crippled son or about feeling played by the babysitter."

As a consequence of her mother's job. At five or six years old.

"[S]he had no business in these hotels," Didion finally conceded.

She also said she found the name of Quintana's birth mother in the Tucson telephone directory. She said she took the directory to her husband and they told the producer there should be no media reports about the Dunnes' presence in Arizona: "[U]nder no condition should Quintana's name appear in connection with the picture." Didion didn't want to risk meeting the mother on the set one day, asking to see her daughter.

Most likely, as in the incident of the lecture hall at Berkeley, she put her husband up to talking to the film's producer. "I believed as I did so that I was protecting both Quintana and her mother," she wrote.

Now, on the S&S book tour, Quintana was out and about each day, highly public and active, in many ways her mother's best representative. In D.C., *The Washington Post*'s Katharine Graham asked her, "How do you like our monuments?" "What monuments?" Quintana said. She'd not had time for the Lincoln or Washington Memorials. She'd been too busy learning her way around newsrooms and the National Public Radio broadcast booths. "Had an interesting talk with Carl Bernstein," she wrote in the journal her fifth-grade teacher had asked her to keep on the tour as part of an English assignment. She chatted with Peggy Noonan, soon to be one of Ronald Reagan's speechwriters—Noonan was then working at WEEI radio in Boston. Quintana got to hear the latest Steely Dan and Fleetwood Mac records before anyone else in the country. She made sure her mother didn't forget to pack her thousand-watt hair blower whenever they left a hotel.

Quintana's favorite city was Dallas. She liked its flat horizon. Boston made the bottom of her list: It was "all white," she said. "You mean you didn't see many black people in Boston?" Susan Traylor's mother asked her once she got home. "No," Quintana said. "I mean it's not in color."

In the air, Didion and her daughter traveled first-class—S&S was no longer an old-fashioned gentlemen's publisher. Stamped across Didion's itinerary was the bland phrase "A Division of Gulf & Western Corporation." She was now part of a loose conglomeration of companies, none of them having anything to do with one another except being owned by the same giant and owing that giant a profit. Books were an afterthought in the giant's global transactions.

What's that title again?

She traveled the way her brother, a corporate real-estate broker, traveled—in style, regretting that most Americans were too soft these days to make it cross-country by wagon: "[W]e were often, my child and I, the only female passengers, and I apprehended for the first time those particular illusions of mobility which power American business"—*and* the political class. "Time was money. Motion was progress. Decisions were snap." She perceived that the planet's economics, trade deals, and wars, all indistinguishable, were driven mostly by men sipping gin and tonics in climate-controlled cabins above the clouds, keeping tenuous ties to people and places on the ground's shaky crust.

6

An Event? *A Book of Common Prayer* sold moderately well, even made the bestseller lists in certain local markets. It earned over $100,000 in paperback sales. But the publishing experience dismayed Didion. She and her agent wrangled with S&S and Pocket Books (the paperback publisher) over royalty statements, which they considered consistently inaccurate and far too low; eventually, Simon & Schuster remaindered hundreds of hardback copies.

Predictably, *Kirkus* gave Didion a hard time, proclaiming, in its review, that she offered readers "more sad songs," in a "glossy, synthetic" novel whose characters were not "really alive." Russell Davies, writing in *The Times Literary Supplement,* said the novel seemed more European than American in expressing doubt about "its own capacity to come up with the truth" about anything: "This is a manner and stance much favored by German writers today, but whereas the contemporary Germans seem to have . . . moral relativity on the brain chiefly because they are embarrassed to have at the backs of their minds moral certainties about the German past, Ms. Didion's obliqueness is more a matter of temperamental dread . . . [stemming from the] rhythmic, natural chaos of womanhood," he wrote. His assessment reveals how difficult it has always been for even sophisticated readers to accept American political novels—as though, relative to Europe, America's past was not bloody enough to warrant uncertainty and "moral relativity": these states of mind, then, must be factors of gender.

On the other hand, Joyce Carol Oates, writing in *The New York Times*, recognized Didion's heroine as "a not untypical North American who simply revises history, personal and collective, as she goes along . . . a martyr, perhaps, to our 'generally upward spiral of history.'" Oates said Didion was "an articulate witness to the most stubborn and intractable truths of our time, a memorable voice, partly eulogistic, partly despairing; always in control."

"The oft-rewritten script, attributed in its final version to John Gregory Dunne, Joan Didion, and Frank Pierson . . . cannot even begin to convey why the highly successful rock star John Norman Howard . . . is going to pot . . . beyond ascribing it all to some undefined death wish we are meant to take for granted in these post-Joplin-Hendrix-Morrison days," said John Simon in his review of *A Star Is Born.*

In *Newsweek,* Jay Cocks noted, "A concert sequence, where the debuting Barbra brings a hostile rocker audience to their feet with the wonder of her funkiness, is a milestone of piquant absurdity, equivalent, perhaps, to having Kate Smith conquer Woodstock."

"During the filming, [Streisand] claimed that there weren't enough close-ups of her," Simon said. "[S]he re-edited the film to suit her enormous ego . . . [It] makes me marvel at the megalomania of the whole undertaking. And then I realize . . . that this hyperbolic ego and bloated countenance are things people shell out money for as for no other actress; that this progressively more belligerent caterwauling can sell anything—concerts, records, movies. And I feel as if our entire society were ready to flush itself down in something even worse than a collective death wish—a collective will to live in ugliness and self-debasement."

The Dunnes weren't worried. Their lawyer, Morton Leavy, got them $175,000 up front for their work on the script, plus a "windfall" settlement, "including a stipulation that we share in the music and record royalties, a clause not previously included in our contract," Dunne said. The movie went on to earn over $66 million, a percentage of which made a nice payday for the snobby intellectuals.

On March 28, 1977, while Didion and Quintana were staying at the St. Regis Hotel in New York, finishing up their tour for *A Book of Common Prayer*, Streisand took the stage at the Academy Awards ceremony in Los Angeles to perform "Evergreen," the love theme from *A Star Is Born*. Two months earlier, on the Dunnes' thirteenth wedding anniversary, Quintana had watched the Golden Globes at home on television with her father. Didion had had a migraine that night and had gone to bed early. Streisand won several awards, including Best Actress in a Musical or Comedy, for *A Star Is Born*. At one point, Dunne went into the bedroom to tell his wife happy anniversary. To cheer her up, he said, "Quintana just said, 'Barbra went up there three times, and she never once thanked us.'"

Chapter Twenty-four

1

"I knew doom when I saw it." So wrote Lawrence Clark Powell, an early Malibu settler, of the Christmas 1956 fire that burned from the canyons and hills all the way down to the sea, destroying the houses of picture people who'd moved to the Colony to escape the madness of McCarthyism. Hell had followed them there.

Fires were, and always would be, a given of the place, pumped by the wind as if by a bellows through the tunnel of the San Fernando Valley. Didion knew this. As the granddaughter of a geologist, she knew wildfires could crack the very structure of the soil, reaching temperatures of over two thousand degrees and creating a water-repellent layer of ground, hastening erosion and flooding. Life on the coast could only and ever be a temporary affair.

At first, and for several years now, Didion had been willing to live with the risk. The Didions were gamblers, after all. But by 1978, there were other reasons to consider a move.

Los Angeles County went to war with home owners in Trancas, commissioning plans to open a public beach. Already, the state owned the forests across the Pacific Coast Highway, and it aggressively pursued strategies for expropriating private homes or forcing the owners to sell. (Ever since the original coastal ranch had been subdivided in the 1940s, the general public had very little access to the glories of Malibu. "The seven million people within an hour's drive" of the area "got Beach Boys music and surfer movies, but the 20,000 residents kept the beach," said one historian.) The Dunnes wearied of land-use battles.

Also, Quintana would soon reach middle-school age and needed a more stable environment. She was such a paradox. On the one hand, she was very much the young adult. One day, Didion remembered, Quintana accompanied her to a meeting with her motion picture agent at the William Morris office in Beverly Hills. Quintana listened attentively to the business negotiations, drinking water from a heavy Baccarat glass, and at the end, she asked the pertinent question, "But when do you give her the money?"

On the other hand, she was still, of course, a child. At her eighth birthday party, she sat in the house with twenty-five other girls after the gifts had been opened. "[A]s little girls do, they were discussing things gynecological," Dunne said, "specifically the orifice in their mothers' bodies from which they had emerged at birth." Quintana announced, "I didn't. I was adopted." She delivered this statement so matter-of-factly, her friends wanted special status, too. "Well, I was *almost* adopted," one said.

Quintana had begun to ask questions about her "other mother." One night at dinner, she said she'd like to meet her someday, but it would be difficult, since she didn't know her name. "There finally was the moment," Dunne said. "We took a deep breath." He and his wife decided to tell Quintana all they knew about the woman in Tucson. Didion felt extremely anxious, but, as if to reassure her, Quintana said if she ever met her natural mother, "I'd put one arm around Mom and one arm around my other mommy, and I'd say, 'Hello, Mommies.'"

A girl this bright, this vulnerable, was bound to suffer plenty through puberty. Like all teens, she'd step into scary temptations, as if slogging through grainy beach tar. But perhaps Malibu was *too* scary—or seductively easy; recently, one of her young friends had overdosed on Quaaludes and drowned off Zuma Beach.

"What do you think? Shall we buy a house today?" Dunne would joke whenever he had occasion to drive into Los Angeles.

The couple agreed a move was in the cards. On top of everything else, the Trancas house had begun to feel too small. It wasn't the Zen haven Didion had hoped it would be. Quintana walked in on them one day when they were making love. No one said a word about this later. Last December's leftover ribbons, wrapping paper, and tissues cluttered Didion's study floor— she had no place to put them. And she didn't have room in her kitchen for her marble pastry slab. She placed it in the bathroom, but there was just "something obscene about rolling pastry in the bathroom."

She was tired of staring at the scorched fireplace bricks; tired of cleaning up, even with hired help, the same chairs and tables after late-night parties.

The parties themselves—their own and their neighbors'—had become predictable and dull. They'd always viewed parties as sources of "combat intelligence from the social battlefield," Dunne said, but these days, what were they learning? "She fucked her way to the middle," an agent would say of a female studio executive.

Please. They'd heard it a hundred times.

2

Dunne had tried to grow a beard. *That* was novel. Unfortunately, the experiment sprang from a familiar source: his restlessness, which always triggered his temper. He'd walk around the too-small house, grousing about the "Saturday jits." "I got anxiety crawling all over me," he'd say.

Still, with the warm critical reception for *True Confessions,* Dunne had emerged in the literary world as more than Mr. Joan Didion, and he felt pleased about that. For years, he had been the "ideal writer's wife," said Josh Greenfeld, protecting Didion from outside intrusions, running interference for her, answering the telephone, encouraging her during public appearances. Now, without abandoning these responsibilities, he felt lighter, more confident.

Didion and Dunne became better writers because of their mutual support—the association especially benefited Dunne. Their marriage had not just endured; it had strengthened. "They were like one person," his brother said—despite the occasional jits.

So when Didion finally met Mary McCarthy's angel, Robert Silvers of *The New York Review of Books,* and he asked her to write for him, Dunne (clean-shaven once more) would not be far behind. In time, *he* would be the one to oil the social machinery, deepening the relationships all around.

Didion's attachment to *The New York Review of Books* sparked perhaps the most productive phase of her career. As an editor, Robert Silvers intuitively grasped her literary gifts and untapped potential. Like Didion, he exhibited a socially awkward streak, preferring his editorial work to most other activities. Food, for example—expensive dinners in garrulous company—didn't much interest him. "[F]rankly, I'm in the office most of the time, and people tend to bring me one thing or another [to eat]," he said.

From 1975 to 1982—during Didion's apprenticeship with Silvers— Shelley Wanger worked as Silvers's assistant in the Fisk Building. The Fisk was a bland brick structure in Manhattan's West Fifties "whose lobby smelled of the Chinese food from the Yangtze River Restaurant that opened onto it," Wanger wrote. (Soon, the magazine would move into more spacious offices on the thirteenth floor, nevertheless keeping "a comforting air of disheveled, bohemian mess," reflecting Silvers's personality.)

He chain-smoked Nat Sherman cigarettes and worked round the clock, jotting ideas onto matchbook covers and various slivers of paper he'd slip into his suit coat pockets. "In the evening, if Bob did not go to dinner or the opera, around 8:30 he might go for some quick laps at the Henry Hudson Hotel on nearby 57th Street, return to have a dinner of soup delivered from the Carnegie Deli, and settle in, sometimes until after midnight," Wanger wrote. "Who could match his stamina?"

He always attributed the *Review*'s success to its habit of skeptical inquiry (with an unapologetic liberal bias), and he chalked up his skill as an editor to his capacity for admiring the genius of certain writers. The *Review* was cliquish. It betrayed no elitist qualms. If readers weren't up to its offerings, well then, they could always go back to *The New York Times Book Review*. As one reporter put it, in a profile of the magazine's ethos, "Even the telephone sex for sale [in the ads in the back] is cultured: 'All fetishes, domination/submission fantasies explored by Ivy-League-educated Goddess.'"

Silvers discovered Didion's writing in the early 1970s. "I just thought she was a marvelous observer of American life," he said. "In my ignorance, I had missed her work in *National Review* . . ." He told another reporter that she is "by no means predictable, by no means an easily classifiable liberal or conservative, she is interested in whether or not people are morally evasive, smug, manipulative, or cruel—those qualities of moral action are very central to all her political work."

Her first piece for him was an exposé of the film industry, similar to her husband's reporting in *The Studio*. Eventually, Dunne became a regular contributor, as well, coaxing both his editor and his wife to combine their work with at least *some* attempts at pleasure. He said his pieces for the magazine usually began "with lunch at Patsy's, a nondescript Italian restaurant on the West Side of Manhattan . . . On the second floor, at the top of the stairs, Bob drinks Pellegrino and eats only the inside of the bread, all the while neatly brushing the crust crumbs with his knife into his left hand, and from there onto the butter plate, and sometimes the floor, with not a break in the conversation."

And the *range* of conversation! It was always astonishing. "If he doesn't know [something], he will learn it," Dunne said. "And if he knows it, and you're writing about it, you're going to get it. Books, clips, press releases. *The Wall Street Journal*, *The Washington Post*, the *Times*, magazines, desktop publishing."

Truly: a print-world angel.

3

From the vantage point of the heavens—if not quite from the windows of Didion's house—Trancas Canyon narrowed from mountainous parklands to gentle slopes to grassy tableland at its mouth. The creek, draining a vast watershed, once ran the length of the canyon but now funneled into a concrete flood-control channel, culminating in a disturbed coastal lagoon near a shopping center. A garden-supply outfit occupied one of the few discernible mounds in the flatlands, the hump the last remnant of a Chumash burial site. Most striking, from an aerial view, was the small number of roads for such a densely developed region, restricting evacuation routes and fire department access. Commercial and political interests seemed to have combined to enforce the coast's permanent "disaster area" status, guaranteeing periodic infusions of government money.

On October 23, 1978, the face of doom belonged to a fifteen-year-old boy from Agoura. That day, just for the hell of it (spurred by Lord knows what scary temptation), he took a lit cigarette and wrapped it inside a matchbook until the matchbook began to burn. Then he tossed the matches into clumps of mountain chaparral and coastal sage scrub.

At 12:11 P.M., the Agoura fire alarms rang. Just over two hours later—faster than anyone had ever seen—flames jumped the Pacific Coast Highway, melting a stretch of its asphalt, and reached the sea, powered by fifty-mile-an-hour winds. Six engine companies, twenty-eight camp crews, eight bulldozers, six five-hundred-gallon-capacity helicopters, and six fixed-wing tankers with a two-thousand-gallon capacity finally brought the fires under control, but not before they had destroyed 25,000 acres of watershed, 230 homes, and over 250 other structures.

Just three months earlier, the Dunnes had finally left their house by the sea and moved to Brentwood Park, where they had purchased a two-story Colonial resembling "a house in West Hartford," Didion said, "a house [John's] mother might have lived in."

Quintana, who had fiercely resisted the move, referred to it as her parents' "suburbia house."

Early one October morning, Didion stood at an upstairs window of her new home, overlooking her swimming pool, watching the not-so-distant smoke in the hills. Either as a gesture of irony or California stoicism, the radio played James Taylor singing "Fire and Rain." Announcers warned listeners that the fire's final stand might be made at Sunset Boulevard. Didion startled, as a "house on a hill above Sunset implode[d]" in front of her eyes, "its oxygen sucked out by the force of the fire." Palm fronds ignited—an eerie echo of the SLA shoot-out.

Throughout the day, radio reports said cedar houses snapped like popcorn and fireballs rained upon tidal pools. Intrepid surfers rode the waves in defiance of the ashen skies. Power lines tangled by the winds broke and sent forth bolts of lightning. Wild rabbits sparked into flame, starting hundreds of brush fires wherever they hopped. Several area families raised Arabian horses; mares turned to char in the fields. Some of the animals had to be shot on the beach.

There were reports of wealthy matrons loading boxes of jewels into kayaks and paddling out to the breakers. When rescued by lifeguards, they admitted they had left their maids behind.

A few days later, around the first of November, the Pacific Coast Highway reopened. Grieving in advance, Didion drove out to Arthur Freed Orchids. She found Amado Vazquez standing amid cracked glass and melted metal in what had been the main greenhouse. "I lost three years," he said softly, indicating shards of beakers that had once held seedlings.

"I thought we both would cry," Didion said.

The good news was, Vazquez was on the verge of opening his new nursery, Zuma Canyon Orchids. That acreage had survived. "You want today to see flowers, we go down to the other place," he told Didion.

She thanked him and said she did not need to see the flowers. She wished him good luck and went to observe the spot where she had lived only three months ago. "The fire had come to within 125 feet of the property, then stopped or turned or been beaten back, it was hard to tell which," she said. "In any case it was no longer our house."

She stared out over the sea to her beloved flat horizon and then turned to survey the hills where, days earlier, as winds teased the flames into grotesque, writhing arms, a hawk had flown over the highway and exploded in midair.

PART SEVEN

Chapter Twenty-five

———— ❊ ————

1

"Poor dope. He always wanted a pool . . . in the end he got himself a pool: only the price turned out to be a little high," says the two-bit screenwriter Joe Gillis, speaking from beyond his watery grave. As his voice addresses us (really, it's William Holden's), we witness his fully clothed body floating facedown in a silent-film star's deep end.

The famous opening of Billy Wilder's *Sunset Boulevard* portrays L.A. swimming pools as traps—deadly pits hollowed out by 1950s decadence. Between the movie and the news of Rodney King's death in a backyard pool, in 2012, lies a series of images defining California through its best-known private luxury: Dustin Hoffman in *The Graduate* as an alienated sixties kid pulling on scuba gear and hiding from his parents at the bottom of their pool; punked-out skateboarders swarming concrete canyons emptied of water by drought and the escalating housing prices of the 1970s.

In 1978, the year Didion and Dunne moved to Brentwood Park and Didion owned, for the first time, a backyard swimming pool, her friend the painter David Hockney created twenty-nine images out of pressed paper pulp, freezing the movement of light on chlorinated water and blue rain needles pattering placid surfaces. Previously, Hockney had painted the violence of a splash; bodies elongated by the aquatic refraction of light. He had rendered swimmers in an atmosphere so thick, they may as well have been torn from their earthly companions—those left grieving, searching for their lost ones in a cloudless crystal ball.

"Water in a swimming pool is different from, say, water in a river, which is mostly reflection because the water isn't clear," Hockney said. "A swimming pool has clarity. The water is transparent, and drawing transparency is an interesting problem."

Of course, Hockney's transparency was unnatural, formed by chemicals, maintenance, and what Didion called "control of the uncontrollable." A "pool is, for many of us in the West, a symbol not of affluence but of order," she once wrote. "[W]ater . . . made available and useful . . . infinitely soothing to the western eye." But this was peace bought by a terrible knowledge: our estrangement from the land.

We inhabit a desert. Yet on lot after densely packed lot, we form artificial oases, kidney-shaped and heated. We suffer through drought. Yet annually over twenty thousand gallons of water evaporate from an uncovered pool. An unholy accommodation, with alienation the only possible result.

Thus, Didion's certainty that the "apparent ease of California life is an illusion," even for those who can afford a backyard pool. Thus, the "interesting problem" of drawing, or freezing in writing, this particular "transparency," which, like the California sunlight, conveys a certain pitilessness in its vibrancy.

The Dunnes lived in the "apparent ease" of Brentwood for ten years, from June 1978 to the summer of 1988, at 202 Chadbourne Avenue, on the corner of Chadbourne and Marlboro. In the midafternoons one summer, just after four o'clock, Dunne liked to wade out into the shallow water, rereading William Styron's novel *Sophie's Choice* to study its structure. Didion would work in the garden, tending her roses, thyme, santolina, and feverfew—for which she had convinced Dunne to pay landscapers to tear out the back lawn—and then together they would retire into their library, wrapped in towels, make drinks, and watch a BBC television series called *Tenko,* about several English women imprisoned in Malaya during World War II. In *The Year of Magical Thinking,* Didion says they would work for a couple hours after the show ended each night, "John in his office at the top of the stairs, me in the glassed-in porch across the hall that had become my office." Afterward, at around seven-thirty, they'd go out for dinner—often chicken or shrimp quesadillas at Morton's, where the "room was cool and polished and dark inside but you could see the twilight outside."

For a while, they may have believed—certainly, they *wanted* to believe—that their rituals and daily cleansings enclosed them, like orchids in a greenhouse, protected from change and disturbance, as they'd tried to be in Malibu. Here in Brentwood—where "we'll have a better life," Didion assured Sara Davidson—the community felt just as insulated as Trancas had on its very best days. All the neighbors knew one another and recognized one another's illegal Mexican help. Few African-Americans lived in the area, the most prominent being O. J. Simpson, about whom "white Americans could congratulate themselves with the spurious notion that they were colorblind, a conclusion made possible by Simpson's conversion of himself into a white man's idea of an acceptable black man," Dunne wrote. Simpson was the "quintessential intimate stranger, the person we think we know because of his celebrity" (a condition the Dunnes knew something about). The retired football player, "famous for formerly being famous," lived about a minute, by car, from Chadbourne Avenue, near the mayor, Richard Riordan, and the president of Creative Artists Agency, Michael Ovitz, in those days enjoying his fifteen minutes as "the most powerful man in Hollywood." Dunne often saw Simpson at the Brentwood Mart, a series of one-story boutique stores where Dunne bought his books, newspapers, and magazines, got his hair cut, and sometimes ate ribs at the drugstore. Simpson's appearance here—always wearing tennis outfits, always browsing *USA Today*—seemed an indicator of the transparency of affluence in L.A. society. But perhaps, like an artificial pool in the desert, it reflected a forced accommodation, an exception casting into greater relief the illusion of racial mobility.

Rodney King, who had learned to swim as a child in the irrigation canals near his grandmother's house in Sacramento, and who bought a house with a pool after receiving $3.8 million from the city of Los Angeles in a civil suit following his beating at the hands of five cops near the Children's Museum, once said, "If you don't know Los Angeles, it's hard to explain how different it is from the pictures you see on television and in movies. No pretty palm trees and manicured lawns or any of that. No fancy boutiques or pretty buildings with shiny windows. All the big houses and Beverly Hills"—and Brentwood—"may only be about ten miles north, and the beautiful beach houses on the ocean in Malibu only about ten miles to the west, but those places may as well be a million miles away."

2

It was a tough year to try to give up smoking.

The house needed plenty of work: potting the orchids on the mantelpiece, placing the porcelain end tables and the lavender love seats just so in the den, angling the small wooden breakfast table exactly right, next to the Chickering piano. Above the piano Didion hung a framed aerial photo of Delano Vineyards. (Poor Cesar! Workers' wages had dipped, and reports said he'd become quite paranoid, looking for scapegoats in his ranks.) She draped chintz over the black leather sofa her husband loved so much, an old gift from his mother; he felt almost mystical about it because one night, at a party in Malibu, a pair of guests, a man and a woman, former AP reporters who'd covered Vietnam in its worst period, and who hadn't run into each other since their days together in Southeast Asia, sat on that sofa, staring into each other's eyes and saying nothing all evening.

The dining room curtains had to go: such strict, regular pleats! Didion was certain this geometric pattern set off migraines, the way the monotony of cookbook recipes could mess with her alpha waves. If only she'd been big-boned and five ten, she could have stopped the pains in her body and strong-armed the furniture until she felt more at ease in her surroundings. "All the time we were living at the beach I wanted a house like this," she admitted to Michiko Kakutani. "I wanted a house with a center-hall plan with the living room on your right and the dining hall on your left when you come in. I imagined if I had this house, a piece of order and peace would fall into my life, but order and peace did not fall into my life. Living in a two-story house doesn't take away the risks."

On the other hand, she liked the sloppy and even slightly dangerous placement of the child's chair in the den, out in the middle of everything, covered with Quintana's cheery old sun hats.

She stuck her tennis racket in a closet: The lessons hadn't taken.

She scrambled through boxes to find the snapshot of Donner Pass she simply *had* to see on her study desk. While Dunne paneled his larger room with wood, she neatened her work space (so many books!—she couldn't stand the *weight* of other people's opinions staring down at her from the shelves).

She arranged cut-glass bowls in the kitchen (where she *did* have a marble slab for rolling pastry dough), vases, settings of china and silver, reserving a special place for the Craftsman dinner knife she'd found among ice plants below her Malibu deck when county officials had come to conduct a geological inspection. The inspection was required before the Dunnes could sell the house and move to Brentwood. Apparently, the knife had slipped through the deck's redwood slats one night. It was dull and scratched, its wooden handle pitted. Didion thought she might give it to Quintana when her daughter was older, a memento of her childhood at the beach—along with her baby teeth, saved in a satin jeweler's box.

Didion lined a room with her hurricane lamps, as though expecting domestic storms.

A pest-control man told her she'd probably have a rat problem in her avocado trees out back. She deadheaded and groomed her lilies of the Nile, her agapanthus and blue starbursts. She spray-washed the balcony trellises, hosed off the brick patio. She paid arborists to trim the deciduous trees; Dunne said the trees seemed "to shed their leaves not seasonally but whenever they got nervous."

The neighborhood took lots of getting to know: its pacing, the timing of its lawn waterings, its morning and afternoon schedules. Recently, a woman across the street had backed into Dunne's pearl-gray Jag, denting its side, as she'd pulled out of her driveway. (And now the damn Corvette needed a new transmission!)

At a party one night, John Cheever told Dunne he loved visiting this part of town. Tudor homes, Colonial homes, white New England trim—the neighborhood reminded him of Connecticut.

On the weekends, Didion mapped out her shopping routes—this area, west and sloping all the way down to the sea, was blessed with the best supermarkets in the world. Sometimes she drove out to El Mercado de Los Angeles, in the shadow of ratty billboards announcing daily flights to San Salvador. There, she'd pick up cheeses, chicken, and salsa. She was in the mood for chili these days.

Among the market stalls, she moved past elderly men who wore only undershirts, past children tugging silver Mylar balloons on kid-sticky nylon strings. Brass bands blew competing tunes from the beer joints. Her neighbors had told her the "newly arrived" tended to gather at the market—undocumented families looking for work. If she needed extra house help, this was the place to come. Reliable help was hard to get.

Sara Davidson reported visiting the Dunnes one day at their Brentwood home to introduce them to her new baby. She took along her nanny, a young woman named Mary, the daughter of a truck driver. Mary said "cain't" and "youse," visibly discomfiting Dunne. Later, when Davidson learned that Mary had been stealing from her, Dunne said he wasn't surprised: "You don't know White Trash."

Protection, insulation, control. "I'm going to have a 'me' decade," Didion said. She'd hired a new housekeeper. Her personal secretaries and her niece Dominique, now twenty, were available for baby-sitting Quintana. Dominique liked to swim in the pool.

One night, Didion thought it would be lovely to float candles and gardenias in the pool's deep end for an outdoor party. She lit the candles and used a pool skimmer to arrange the flowers in pleasing patterns, but they all got sucked into the filter intake, and she drenched herself trying to pluck the soggy stems from the water. Through her clinging dress, her ribs in the mirror looked like the slender slats of a deck chair. Control was not so easy to establish.

So why did she think she could handle tossing away her cigarettes? The conviction had struck her one day; by happenstance, she'd run into an old teacher of hers from Berkeley, Jim Hart. He told her his wife had just died of lung cancer. He said he missed taking walks with her. Right then, Didion decided to stop smoking. She told Dunne she was doing this so he wouldn't pine for her on evening strolls around the neighborhood.

Then she read about the Italian political leader Aldo Moro: When he was kidnapped by terrorists, press profiles of him stressed that he'd been a man of moderate habits, smoking only five cigarettes a day. Didion figured since the cigarettes didn't kill him (his kidnappers shot him to death), she could afford to be moderate, too. From then on, five a day was her bargain with herself.

3

Quintana's unhappiness caused the family's greatest adjustment problems. Her laid-back life at the beach had not prepared her for the rigors of classes at the Westlake School for Girls or the rigid social order she had to plow her way into as an outsider. Westlake, enrolling about seven hundred students, many of them from Hollywood's business and entertainment elite, occupied its current buildings at North Faring Road because the Janns Investment Company decided it would make a solid anchor for the Holmby Hills development. This pragmatic, profit-oriented ethos set the tone for all work and activity at the school. The kids wore conforming blue uniforms and hauled their parents' attitudes into the crowded hallways. "Kids grow up and become aware of what their parents do, and they can be tough, Hollywood kids," said Tim Steele. "They learn their parents' ruthless business techniques and they learn about power, but they only know it as habit." (Didion agreed: "Writers do not get gross from dollar one, nor do they get the Thalberg Award, nor do they even determine when and where a meeting will take place: these are facts of local life known even to children," she said.)

"In those days, public schools weren't shunned they way they are now; it didn't really matter where a kid went to school—public or private. All their parents were in the business, so the kids would meet and mingle," Steele said. "I heard of schoolteachers teaching the sons and daughters of television producers and studio heads. If a kid was in danger of flunking, she'd threaten to have the teacher fired. That's the way things got done in Hollywood. The whole damn business was like high school. And vice versa."

Didion rather enjoyed her vicarious return to school, reading *Moby-Dick* along with her daughter—she relished the assignments more than Quintana did: For the first time, she *got* what Melville was doing. Quintana wrote papers on Angel Clare's role in *Tess of the d'Urbervilles* and on the nervous system's responses to stress—often while eating alone off a TV tray in her bedroom.

Meanwhile, her parents would be out at Ma Maison, dining with the "same old faces": George Cukor, Jacqueline Bisset, Dustin Hoffman, Carl Bernstein. For Didion, the move to Brentwood was one more step toward securing the "last stable society." "This place never changes," Carl Bernstein told her approvingly one night at the restaurant. "No," Didion said. "Time stands still here."

For her daughter, the "suburbia house" meant a terrible upheaval. Like Didion, Quintana was always haunted by the thought of a lost domain: the family she believed she would never know. Now the beach became a vanished world to which she could not quite return. Naturally, she visited Malibu friends and sometimes stayed overnight at Susan Traylor's house; still, everything had changed in spite of her efforts to hold them steady, despite her mother's denial of time.

"[W]e encourage them to remain children . . . our investments in each other remain too freighted ever to see the other clear," Didion would write in *Blue Nights*.

Quintana tried to tell her who she was, indirectly, obliquely, with a dollop of irony—the family style.

"It bothered her father: [Quintana] didn't seem to want to read anything he'd written, or that I'd written," Didion said. "When I asked her about it, she said, 'When you read something, you form an opinion about it, right? I don't want to form an opinion about my mother and father.'"

But this was a mask, like saying, with a smirk, "suburbia house," instead of shouting, *I hate these little sitting rooms off each of our bedrooms. I can't stand being so far from my friends. How could you bring me to a place like this?*

Of course she'd dipped into her parents' writing—seen her mother's fascination with trauma and terror, winced at her father's knowledge of anal and oral sex. He was more clued in than his wife to the "person" developing under their roof, just as Quintana saw *Dunne* more clearly (shocked that he'd hidden so many "adult" subjects from her). As a result, they fought more bitterly than ever—over space, chores, schoolwork. After arguing with her father, she'd imagine her birth parents. In her mind, they were always young and smiling. She'd think maybe they'd be more gently understanding of her.

She told her folks she'd decided to write a novel "just to show you." In the prologue she wrote, "Some of the events are based on the truth and others are fictitious. The names have not yet been definitively changed." The main character, Quintana, suspects she's pregnant. She informs her parents. "They said that they would provide the abortion but after that they did not even care about her any more. She could live in their suburbia house in Brentwood, but they didn't even care what she did any more. That was fine in her book. Her father had a bad temper, but it showed that they cared very much about their only child. Now, they didn't even care any more. Quintana would lead her life any way she wanted."

"Just to show you": Not only can I write, as you do—and about the very same subjects—but *I* can get pregnant. Or my character can. Take that.

"[T]hey would provide the abortion." Who or what is aborted? Afterward, the character Quintana becomes a ghost in the house.

The novel ended with a fragment: "On the next pages you will find out why and how Quintana died and her friends became complete burnouts at the age of eighteen."

Quintana wasn't the only member of the extended family worrying about early burnout or trying to write fiction.

Nick had finally hit bottom. "Day-to-day living became unbearable," he said. He'd blown most of his money on his drug habits. "I sold my West Highland terrier named Alfie to Connie Wald for $300. . . . What kind of a man would *sell* his dog?"

"Desperate to save myself, I went through a spiritual stage. I started attending the Church of Self-Realization at the end of Sunset Boulevard just before the beach. It was a beautiful and tranquil place. A friend and I meditated there, but we always smoked a joint first, which wasn't really the point," he said. "Then I went into the hospital overnight to have a cyst removed. In the recovery room, still under anesthesia, I suffered cardiac arrest and nearly checked out."

Shortly afterward, in September 1978, he got into his two-door Ford Granada—by now, he'd lost his Mercedes—and drove to Oregon. Retrospectively, he framed the story this way: "I had heard the word[s] *Cascade Mountains,* and I was attracted to the peacefulness of the sound of 'cascade.' In a hamlet called Camp Sherman, on the Metolius River, I had a flat tire. I didn't have any idea how to change a tire, and I was too weary to learn. The nearest garage was closed[, so] I rented a one-room cabin, with kitchenette and bath."

In fact, he'd had some foreknowledge of Camp Sherman, according to Joyce Osika, the woman who rented him the cabin at Twin View Resort. "He did tell me that a lady in his apartment [in Beverly Hills] had suggested to him, 'If you want quiet and solitude, go to Camp Sherman,'" Osika said. Nick moved his typewriter into cabin number 5, and stayed for six months.

"There were 150-foot-high pine trees outside it and views of Black Butte and snow-capped Mount Jefferson," Nick said. "I was like a whipped dog when I came . . . but there was something about this place that had an incredible effect on me."

In the afternoons he walked to the mouth of the Metolius, fed by numerous springs, flowing north and east toward Lake Billy Chinook and the Deschutes River. At the Camp Sherman Store, just across a little footbridge, a fly fisherman told him (though he had no intention of fishing) that the best flies to try in the fall were the blue-winged olives or the no. 8 Dirty Bird. He didn't believe a word. He could tell a good storyteller when he saw one.

He was trying to write a story. Later, he'd say he just gave fiction a what-the-hell whirl. But in truth, he had an agent in Hollywood, Arnold Stiefel. Stiefel had taken Nick to the Polo Lounge right before Nick drove north. "You're dead meat in the picture business," he said. Nick said he already knew that. So Stiefel suggested he ghost-write a sequel to Joyce Haber's novel, *The Users.* Nick had produced a television movie of *The Users,* and he knew enough Hollywood gossip to write a rousing tale. In cabin 5 each day, he plotted chapters.

But mostly he "licked [his] wounds" and tried to shed his Tinseled skin. "I had no telephone and no television, and I literally lived in silence," he said. He sat for hours, not moving, in an orange Naugahyde chair. He stopped drinking and drugging. "All that bullshit ended in the cabin. I used to think it was 'this person's fault' that I didn't get that movie, or 'that person' did this or that. I came to realize that the fault was always mine."

He was surprised one day to find in his mailbox a letter from Truman Capote. They'd never been close, but Capote could sympathize with Nick:

He'd had his own problems with chemical dependencies, and recently he'd been shunned by Hollywood society after publishing excerpts of his nasty roman à clef, *Answered Prayers,* in *Esquire.* On ecru-colored Tiffany paper, Capote said he admired Nick for trying to straighten himself out: "But remember this, that is not where you belong, and when you get out of it what you went there to get, you have to return to your own life."

Capote died two years later. "I felt sure that if he had done what I had done, he wouldn't have been dead so early," Nick said.

He also received in the mail one afternoon a pair of L. L. Bean rubber boots. They came from his brother Stephen, who hoped he'd spend many happy hours walking in the woods.

Nick's daughter Dominique and his eldest son, Griffin, had decided to try acting. Dominique earned small roles in televisions shows, *Family, CHiPs,* and *Fame.* Quintana was thrilled to see her cousin on the screen. Griffin skipped college and entered showbiz by running the popcorn stand at Radio City Music Hall. He became buddies with the camels in the annual Christmas nativity scene. "I fed them a lot of popcorn," he said. Soon, he was appearing in obscure movies, but then he followed his father's old example and, with a couple partners, bought the film rights to Ann Beattie's novel *Chilly Scenes of Winter.* He and his partners drove to Boston to seal the deal with Beattie. "It was like seeing three of my characters walk through the door," she said—hapless, post-sixties types, wondering what's next. (Beattie had been praised by reviewers as Joan Didion for a new generation, minimalist and melancholy.) Joan Micklin Silver directed the movie, originally titled *Head Over Heels.* It premiered in New York while Nick was busy pursuing asceticism in Oregon. Griffin pleaded with his father to come celebrate his success, but Nick refused. He was doing important work, he said, reassessing his past. Besides, money was a problem.

Didion and Dunne had lent Nick ten thousand dollars, and he was careful how he spent it. Accepting the loan (it was more like a gift) also fueled his shame when he was around the family. "A terrible resentment builds when you've borrowed money and can't pay it back, although they never once reminded me of my obligation," Nick said. His "important work" consisted of more than just sitting in penitential solitude, which is how he presented the period later. In his search for an "epiphany," he sent "long, artful" letters to his brother in Brentwood. They were "full of character evaluation and private secrets and revisionist family history," Dunne wrote in his memoir, *Harp.*

"[B]lame was sprinkled like holy water; the archbishop of this schismatic church was careful to douse himself as well as his . . . family." (Dunne's language is enlightening here; at the time, he had recently finished *True Confessions*, about a pair of quarreling brothers, one a volatile, tough-talking cop, the other a self-righteous priest.)

"I had the uneasy feeling that there was an audience for this exchange of letters to which I was not privy, with the result that my answers became at best perfunctory," Dunne said.

On one occasion, Nick's rakings through family foibles so enraged Dunne, he threw the letter in the fire. In a terse note he told his brother he had done so. Nick wrote back, "Fuck you!" "[M]y note, he said, had been much discussed at his support group, which at least confirmed my suspicion that ours had not been a private correspondence," Dunne said.

4

I wake and feel the fell of dark, not day . . .

Gerard Manley Hopkins.

Hopkins's poetry solaced Dunne in the months ahead.

He and Nick later disagreed about the timing of the calls. Dunne said he got the news at four-thirty in the morning and immediately phoned Nick. Nick remembered that Joyce Osika knocked on his cabin door at about three A.M., saying he had a call down at the lodge from his brother.

What is not in dispute: Nick gave a cry of extraordinary "bleakness." Then he told Dunne that "he had been contemplating suicide himself, perhaps at the exact same moment as Stephen."

Their little brother. The one who had always "played life on the dark keys." Who had always cried, in place of his brothers, whenever their father got mad. Who had never outgrown the stigma of his childhood stutter, according to an old friend, Lem Bainton. Who had been told by FSG he couldn't design the cover of his brother's first book. Who apparently felt he'd never been *wanted* enough. In his garage in New Canaan, Connecticut, he had carefully taped shut the windows and doors of his car, started the engine, and asphyxiated himself.

Dunne was still angry at Nick for the letters, the loan. On the phone, he said there was no need for Nick to fly back east for the funeral; after all, he was so much older than Stephen and never really knew him that well. Nick was offended. Of course he'd go to the funeral. Then Dunne said he would not give Nick any more money. Nick erupted, calling his brother "wanton and insensitive."

At the funeral in Connecticut—one of the last times they'd see their sisters, Harriet and Virginia, both of whom would die of breast cancer—the brothers, one a prince of Hollywood, the other in exile, barely spoke.

Before flying to New Canaan, Dunne had changed his will. Originally, Stephen had been named Quintana's guardian in the event that "mutual disaster" befell her mother and father.

O the mind, mind has mountains, cliffs of fall, Frightful, sheer . . .

Another unbearable loss.

One morning, in the Fourteenth Street subway station near Union Square in Manhattan, Henry Robbins dropped dead of a heart attack. He was fifty-one years old. His old coworkers at Farrar, Straus and Giroux noted the irony: He had crumpled near the FSG offices—"under Roger's gaze," as one colleague put it. "To the end, Roger was looking down on Henry."

The two of them had never reconciled after Robbins's departure from FSG to Simon & Schuster, though Robbins would surely have agreed with Straus's recent declaration, in *The New York Times,* that a "lot of publishing houses are being run by accountants, businessmen and lawyers with very little concern for books. They could just as well be selling spaghetti or rugs."

Dick Snyder, at S&S, assumed Straus was needling him personally with these remarks, and he responded publicly: "I think his opinion is not only groundless, but opportunistic." He accused Straus of using corporations as whipping boys, to dupe writers into staying with a penny-pinching independent.

Despite Robbins's ire at Straus's persnickety business practices, he had always been happier at FSG than he would ever be with Snyder, for precisely the reasons Straus had indicated in the *Times*: He was shoveling pasta. Shortly before his death, he had left S&S to become editor in chief at Dutton, where he had published John Irving's enormously successful *The World According to Garp.*

This time, when he made a move, he didn't take Didion with him—the contractual bonds were far too complicated.

And then he was gone altogether.

"[W]e are all terminal cases," Irving had written in *Garp*—a line he repeated at Robbins's memorial service at the Society for Ethical Culture at Sixty-fourth Street and Central Park West. Doris Grumbach said, "Because of [Henry's] importance to us, we must have thought him exempt. Tragically, we were wrong."

Didion was too upset to speak at the service, but she later called herself, in print, "Henry's orphan sister." Robbins's real sister did not appreciate these words. Margi Fox, Robbins's niece, said that, of all the speakers at the service—a bunch of egotistical writers, who could only talk about what Henry had done for *them*—John Gregory Dunne was the one person courteous enough to mention the family's loss.

Straus seized the sad occasion to woo Didion one more time: "I would be less than honest with you if I didn't say that would you wish to 'come home again,' the door would be open," he wrote her on August 8, 1979. "It may be premature of me to state the blunt fact . . . over and under the heads of whoever the agents are these days . . ."

There is no record of a reply.

5

London. Paris. Honolulu. New York.

Kuala Lumpur.

The Sherry-Netherland. The Dorchester. The Plaza Athénée.

The Peninsula Hotel in the heart of Hong Kong.

In spite of recent moves, adjustments, and funerals, the Dunnes never slowed their travels, nor would they in the decade ahead. "Vacations" weren't part of the plan. A writer is working, wherever she goes—whether or not she's got a specific assignment or interest in a project. Dunne's idea of a relaxing afternoon in Honolulu was to go to the courthouse and watch a trial, as he often did in Santa Monica.

Didion was still trying to convince him they should buy a house in Hawaii. It was the only "benign climate" she had ever known, she said. The air smelled of flowers. The place was *pink*. It made her feel good.

Maybe, he said. Maybe.

They each kept travel notebooks. And they were competitive. Whoever used a detail first in a novel or an essay—well, fair enough. One night in Jakarta, while having drinks with the American ambassador, Dunne ordered a Scotch on the rocks. He got a Scotch and soda instead. The ambassador waved over the servant and asked him to change the order. "It's part of the exaggerated politeness of the Indonesians," he explained to the Dunnes. "They would never ask you to repeat your order. That would imply you were not speaking clearly and would be impolite." Dunne noticed his wife sketching the scene and figured she'd beat him to the punch on this one.

At their request, one afternoon the Dunnes were given a tour of Kai Tak East, a transit camp for Vietnamese refugees near Kai Tak Airport, in Kowloon, Hong Kong. Refugees were big business in this part of the world. A writer could exploit them as easily as a Vietnamese official, a Hong Kong policeman, or a Chinese syndicate trading ID cards for blocks of gold.

As she had in Bogotá, Didion scratched in her notebook several scenes of local color: an old woman bleeding out a live chicken with a paring knife as "children with bright scarlet rashes on their cheeks giggled and staggered, mimicking the chicken"; women cooking, warming their hands over woks; cast-off clothing piled in a sweltering room smelling of jasmine, shit, and sesame oil.

Didion learned that of the "11,573 Vietnamese who had passed through Kai Tak East since the camp opened, in June 1979, only some 2,000 had been, by December, relocated, the largest number of them to the United States and Canada. The rest waited, filled out forms, pretended fluency in languages they had barely heard spoken."

This sad knowledge would inform her novel *Democracy*.

She was most struck by the abandoned children, the children without parents, the parents who had lost their kids, slumped in the dirt in the cold winter sunlight. "*Mes filles, mes filles!*" someone was always crying.

Dominique had her hands full, staying with Quintana while the Dunnes traveled the world. She was also helping her father.

She had spent an evening with him and her brother in New York, following her uncle's funeral in Connecticut. Griffin made them all laugh, telling stories about the movie he'd produced and a play he was in. Nick assured his children he was no longer tempted by suicide—not after staring at his brother's casket.

Still, he was far from fine. When he arrived back at the Portland airport, he broke down. "[The] events of the last few years caught up with me, and I totally fell apart in a fit of weeping and keening," he said. "I didn't care that people were staring at me. I had never cried like that before."

He took a Greyhound bus to Camp Sherman and stayed in the cabin a few more weeks. Then, with Dominique's help, he returned to L.A. "I had no money, but I had a beautiful apartment that somebody sublet when I was away, and beautiful things, and I sold every single thing I owned," he said (an exaggeration). "Every stick of furniture, every piece of porcelain, crystal, and silver, every book, every Porthault sheet and towel, all the things I always thought I couldn't live without. I even sold my monogrammed Turnbull & Asser shirts and all the ashtrays I'd stolen from Claridge's in London, the Ritz in Paris, and the Palace Hotel in St. Moritz, when the going was good."

Dominique gave him a thousand dollars so he could pay the last month's rent on his apartment. "She stayed by my side during the entire three-day sale, tagging, wrapping, carrying, keeping up my spirits," he said. "I'll never forget that. She was divine."

Soon thereafter, turning to Griffin for help, he took a room on West Ninth Street, in New York's Greenwich Village. "It was smaller than the cabin in Oregon," he said. "I didn't know then that I would write my first bestseller in that room, but I was filled with hope again."

6

"Simon & Schuster [has] published Joan's last two books, both of which were on the NYTimes Bestseller list for a long time. However, the novel, *A Book of Common Prayer*, sold only about 50,000 copies in hardcover (maybe 5,000 less) and it hasn't set the world on paperback fire . . . *The White Album* has done much, much better with 90,000 sold in hardcover and another printing just ordered," Lois Wallace reported to her business partner, Anthony Sheil, on November 30, 1979.

In August, while Roger Straus was courting Didion, Wallace had conducted an auction for the paperback rights to *The White Album*, upping the price, through five rounds of bidding among seven publishers, from $65,000 to $247,500, the amount paid by Pocket Books.

The White Album, Didion's second collection of essays, was welcomed by reviewers as a sequel to *Slouching Towards Bethlehem*: Didion's final word on the American 1960s. In particular, critics lauded the title piece as a masterpiece of "montage, a style that best suits the spirit of the age she is describing." A scrapbook of terror, from the Black Panthers to the nihilism of the Doors to the Manson murders, it is a fractured document of writing's failure to truly grasp anything.

Girding the central essay's denial of meaning—especially of any cultural, social, or political hope of salvation—Didion constructs a series of short pieces portraying California as the pinnacle of American infrastructure. It is not a happy picture. One by one, she examines the bureaucracies overseeing water supply, traffic patterns, museum acquisitions, official properties, and artistic aspirations—not to mention the West's unique spirituality.

She writes about James Pike, an old Okie, who became the bishop of California and served at Grace Episcopal Cathedral after being dean of Saint John the Divine in New York. She traces his restless movement through one holy passion after another until he dies in a Jordanian desert, hoping to experience the wilderness as Jesus had, carrying only a little extra equipment: a cheap map from Avis and a bottle of Coke. For Didion, Pike's need for constant reinvention "smells of the Sixties in this country, those years when no one at all seemed to have any memory or mooring."

This uncharacteristically broad statement, placed among the gridlock of *official* "moorings" (that is, government control of water and cars), suggests the sixties' rot lay in a flawed liberal vision adamant about regulating individual rights. In Didion's mind, the liberal paradox guarantees insanity. Thus, we get James Pike instead of John Wayne or even Howard Hughes.

But Didion is not always easy to read, ideologically. She begins her essay "The Getty" by saying, "Something [about the new Getty Museum] embarrasses people." The staid collection of antiquities smacks of "learning"; the place is "unremittingly reproachful . . . to generations trained in the conviction that a museum is meant to be fun, with Calder mobiles and Barcelona chairs." What people want in a museum is a space that will "set the natural child in each of us free."

At first, then, the essay appears to mock the museumgoing public, too ignorant to know what's good for it. But then Didion quotes the Getty's founder: In his design dream, he refused to "pay for any 'tinted-glass-and-stainless-steel monstrosity'"; in gathering his antiquities, with the aim of pleasing visitors, he knew he was "flouting the 'doctrinaire and elitist' views . . . endemic in [the] Art World."

Didion's essay is a bait and switch. The people who don't have any idea what's good for them aren't the slow-witted members of the museumgoing public. In fact, the museumgoing public visits the Getty in "large numbers": they find the spot as awesome "as its founder knew they would."

No, the people who don't have any idea what's good for them are the cutting-edge art world insiders, supporters of the International Style of architecture ("tinted-glass-and-stainless-steel"), and abstract art ("Calder mobiles"). Take *that*, MoMA!

In one sense, Didion's social vision remains unchanged here from earlier essays: She disapproves of regulation in art as in any other sphere; her sympathies lie with a populist view of the "people," who may not understand fine art but know what they like. However, class and wealth—and their impacts on our individual views of what it means to be human—are complex affairs, as Didion's conclusion makes clear: "On the whole, 'the critics' distrust great wealth, but 'the public' does not," she writes. "On the whole, 'the critics' subscribe to the romantic view of man's possibilities, but 'the public' does not. In the end the Getty stands above the Pacific Coast Highway as one of those odd monuments, a palpable contract between the very rich and the people who distrust them least."

Trickle-down aesthetics? A privileged view? Perhaps. But Didion's vantage point here is neither at the top of the hill nor on the road's rugged shoulder. She inhabits the interstices of language, drifting back and forth.

The section on California is followed in *The White Album* by Didion's attack on the women's movement, a dour assessment of Doris Lessing, and a portrait of a feminist icon (before there *was* a movement) Georgia O'Keeffe. O'Keeffe, "equipped early with an immutable sense of who she was," shuns social constructions of identity. It is the natural landscape of the West, embodied in the figure of a sister with a gun, that firmly roots the painter. Here, Didion reveals her sentimentality (normally, she distrusts the word *immutable;* it doesn't fit her geologic perspective).

The White Album ends with evocations of American spaces, followed by "On the Morning After the Sixties" and "Quiet Days in Malibu," unconvincing paeans to survival. Once again, Didion rejects any march toward the future requiring a social commitment: "If I could believe that going to a barricade would affect man's fate in the slightest I would go to that barricade, and quite often I wish that I could, but it would be less than honest to say that I expect to happen upon such a happy ending."

Of course, there are lots of barricades. A swimming pool can be a barricade.

Didion had made her choices.

"Her nervous system is a San Andreas Fault. Language is her seismograph and style her sanity. Nobody writes better English prose than Joan Didion.

Try to rearrange one of her sentences, and you've realized that the sentence was inevitable, a hologram," John Leonard wrote in his review of *The White Album* in *The New York Times*. He said the book was full of the "stuff of the bad dreams of the 1960s" but its real genius was to leave unsaid the nightmares' cause—like an odor pervading everything, so thick that we barely register it: "Vietnam [goes] unmentioned."

If *The White Album* was a sequel to *Slouching Towards Bethlehem*, it did not represent an advance to Martin Amis. In *The London Review of Books*, he said, "In her relatively self-effacing preface to *Slouching Towards Bethlehem*, Miss Didion admitted, 'Whatever I write reflects, somewhat gratuitously, how I feel.' Ten years on, the emphasis has changed; you might even say . . . that whatever Miss Didion feels reflects how she writes. 'Gratuitous' hardly comes into it anymore." Amis did not buy her frail persona: "Only someone fairly assured about certain of her bearings would presume to address her readers in this (in fact) markedly high-handed style. The style bespeaks celebrity, a concerned and captive following."

In her Georgia O'Keeffe essay, Didion had declared, *"Style is character,"* speaking of the time Quintana stood dazzled in front of the canvases and asked to speak to the painter. Amis objected: "The extent to which style isn't character can be gauged by . . . reading a literary biography, or by trying to imagine a genuinely forthright discussion between Georgia O'Keeffe and Miss Didion's seven-year-old daughter."

7

Even more than *The White Album*, a piece she wrote for *The New York Review of Books* on the movies of Woody Allen prompted passionate letters of response, most of them angry. In recent years, Allen had made *Annie Hall*, *Interiors*, and *Manhattan*, films most critics considered proof of mature artistry. Didion called them "adolescent" fantasies whose "social reality" was "dim in the extreme," deriving "more from show business than from anywhere else." Notable in her critique was her strict defense of realism in art, her use of the phrase "the large coastal cities of the United States" to describe Allen's fan base (in conservative circles, "the large coastal cities of the United States" was code for "liberal"—Didion used this trigger language with ease a full twenty years before the general public learned its subtext), and her disgust with Allen for displaying the same sort of elitism she was often accused of flouting. She dismissed his characters for having dinner at Elaine's and talking showbiz—while, in any given week, she could be found having dinner at Ma Maison and talking showbiz. She complained of a teenage character in *Manhattan* whose parents were never on-screen: The character, she said, "put me in mind of an American International Pictures executive who once advised me, by way of pointing out the absence of adult characters in AIP beach movies, that nobody ever paid $3 to see a parent." To slam Allen for being a pure creature of the entertainment business by invoking *her* insider status seemed a questionable strategy.

Just two months after her piece on Allen appeared, Didion endured a harsh attack by Barbara Grizzuti Harrison, a regular reviewer for *The Nation* and many other publications. "When I am asked why I do not find Joan Didion appealing, I am tempted to answer—not entirely facetiously—that my charity does not naturally extend itself to someone . . . who has chosen to burden her daughter with the name Quintana Roo," Harrison began.

"I knew I wasn't going to get a break if my daughter's name was fair game in the first line," Didion said later.

The piece was a catalog listing of the major faults Didion's critics had charged her with over the years. Harrison called her a "neurasthenic Cher" whose prose style was a "bag of tricks." Her style depended mainly on juxtapositions of "nihilism" with "ripeness and plenitude," as in the line, "In the years after Luis was shot water hyacinths clogged the culverts at Progresso" (from *A Book of Common Prayer*).

Harrison seemed to miss the fact that Didion's "bag of tricks" was the essence of literary art: *plot* (the nihilistic movement of time toward inevitable death) balanced against *lyricism* (those blissful moments of clarity—"ripeness" of imagery—in which time seems to stop, and, just for an instant, the world reveals itself to us).

Harrison bristled at Didion's politics ("Ayn Rand's . . . rugged individualists whose religion is laissez-faire capitalism . . . would find themselves at home" in her work), her removal from the world (her "observations about the self-serving 'children' of the 1960s are dead accurate; but that doesn't give her the right to fiddle while Watts burns"), and, most of all, her class superiority (to Didion, "[Lucille] Maxwell Miller's real sin . . . was to live in a subdivision house in the San Bernardino Valley and to hope to find 'the good life' there, instead of in Brentwood Park or Malibu").

Generally, in the past, Didion had accepted public criticism better than her husband—Dunne wanted to throttle this woman (and it was too bad Henry Robbins wasn't around to go after her). "I was sorry [Harrison] felt so strongly about me," Didion said. "But you couldn't get too worked up about it since it was so over the top."

Perhaps the most jarring aspect of the piece was its timing—at least as far as Didion was concerned. Harrison had accused her of reporting only on her own sensibility and preferring to love her own pain. Yet, writing about Woody Allen, Didion had declared, "Most of us remember very well [the] secret signals and sighs of adolescence, remember the dramatic apprehension of our own mortality and other 'more terrifying unsolvable problems about the universe,' but eventually we realize we are not the first to notice that people die." Her irritation with Allen signaled a shift in her thinking, which her work would reflect over the next ten years. Essentially, she was telling Woody to grow up, to get over himself. The reason her critique seemed so misplaced was *precisely* because she was talking to herself. Woody Allen's failings—his self-absorption, his privileged perspective—were her own. She knew it. It was easier for her to see how these weaknesses softened Allen's work than it was for her to locate the problems in her own writing. But then Harrison came along to remind her. Didion wanted a way out. She was tired of being Miss Lonelyhearts. And the world was demanding more of us *all*.

Chapter Twenty-six

─────── ❧ ───────

1

Ronald Reagan's election to the presidency of the United States galvanized Didion as a writer in ways she had not been motivated before.
Her books of the 1980s were extremely political, icily angry, and all
of a piece. They are best understood in concert.

The easy rap against Reagan has always been that he was a movie actor,
following the scripts of his advisers, more interested in performance than in
the substance of governing. Didion saw him more as a studio head or producer, asking his cabinet, *What if* this *happened, or that?*—as if world events
did not spring from history or facts on the ground, but could be fashioned
from whole cloth. For example, in 1967, he'd told the *Los Angeles Times* he
had a "feeling" about Vietnam (not that he'd been there, or read the intelligence reports). "I have a feeling that we are doing better in the war than the
people have been told."

Just change the script.

What if *this* happened?

Trust me. "The people" will line up—around the block, around the country—to purchase tickets. They *want* to believe our magic. ("The gruesome
quiet of an entirely imaginary world," said Hannah Arendt, of propaganda.)

For Didion, the bigger problem with the Reagan presidency was his kitchen
cabinet, the California cronies who had bankrolled him, shaped his image,
got him elected governor, and now pushed him onto the national stage. It
was bad enough that these men—media CEOs, attorneys, oil-field brats,
beer distributors—were calling the shots (what business did a restauranteur

have being the president's foreign intelligence adviser?), but it was their wives who were *really* in control, arranging the parties in Brentwood where incentives got launched (while the Secret Service boys bolted food in the laundry rooms).

In charge of all *this* was "Pretty Nancy," for whom Didion had had an immediate and persistent antipathy.

"Get him off his feet!" she'd say, sweeping into a room, hovering around her husband.

Didion could just picture it.

Among Nancy's friends was Lee Annenberg, niece of Columbia Pictures' Harry Cohn, once married to Beldon Katleman, the Las Vegas casino owner who'd bailed Nick out of his pot scrape. Lee had also been married, for a while, to Lewis Rosenstiel, king of the Schenley liquor empire, for whom Anthony Kennedy had lobbied before setting off to the Supreme Court. Nancy and Lee were pals of Betsy Bloomingdale, who had worked with Lenny as a member of the Colleagues, raising money for unwed mothers. Betsy got Nancy into the Colleagues in 1962, and boy, could Pretty *work* a charity! She'd pop around from the Colleagues to the Foster Grandparents to the Vietnam Veterans' groups in the hospitals, making friends with the women who ran the boards; then she'd call their rich husbands and say, "You know, we need more money for the campaign, or what are we going to do about this, or why is Ronnie getting bad press on that? How can you help?"

Didion understood how it worked: the phone calls, the cocktails, schmoozing on the green-and-red linen sofas. All the Hollywood players were making their way to Washington—people, some would say, who, in smarts and taste, had fucked their way to the middle and who were bound to pull the country down to their level.

"There was a lot of ideological fervor in Washington" at the time of the first Reagan administration. "And all those people there turned up in think tanks. Well, Dinesh D'Souza [who'd become a Reagan policy adviser] writes a book. It's going to be bought by all those people in think tanks, right? At the American Enterprise Institute, the Heritage Foundation [funded by the president's beer-making buddy, Joseph Coors]. There's a certain built-in sale on those books," Didion said.

Didion: A reporter in Washington "is not going to have sources unless [he] write[s] the kinds of stories [the sources] want to see written." (Of Bob Woodward's books, in which he merely repeated the stories insiders wanted public in order to advance their agendas, Didion said that "these are books in which measurable cerebral activity is virtually absent.")

Didion: The "critical reading faculty" in this country "atrophied" around the time Reagan took office. She said this was not a coincidence.

2

In *Salvador*, and even more forcefully in *Miami*, published thirteen and seventeen years, respectively, after *Play It As It Lays*, Didion reconsidered the intelligibility of narrative.

Salvador opens with an image of abandoned American-owned hotels—"ghost resorts"—on El Salvador's Pacific beaches. To land at the airport built to service these shells, she says, "is to plunge directly into a state where no ground is solid, no depth of field reliable, no perception so definite that it might not dissolve into its reverse. The only logic is that of acquiescence."

So much for narrative, we think.

As she has done so often, Didion foregrounds her nervous personality in the book, her ache for solidity and depth in a place where nothing fits. She has left her California valley, entered the chaos of civil war in a brutal foreign land. Why? As her grandfather taught her, California has long historical ties to Latin America; it emerged from, and much of its vitality still depends on, Latin cultures. A fifth-generation Californian still trying to write a definitive history of the West, Didion hopes to cast back beyond childhood stories and uncover the actual nature of her soil.

Ultimately, then, the subject of her reporting in El Salvador is the United States—once upon a time and now under Reagan, as it settles more deeply into what she perceives to be unjustifiable belligerence around the globe.

With the publication of *Salvador* in 1983, Didion insisted the surest way to understand this country was to leave it—to adopt, toward it, a different point of view. America's affairs around the world caged the nation's domestic politics. The confusions she experienced at home might be at least partially relieved by a broader perspective. In the end, her frustration with a national story that never seemed clear—a frustration painstakingly expressed in earlier books—did not force her to reject narrative; it led her to believe that *how we live* could not be described in the usual manner, or discovered in the usual places. But that didn't mean the story didn't exist.

How could it be tracked? The princess needed to escape the trap of her castle, her ranch house, her nice new shopping mall. She had to visit the consulate, the foreign hotel (where other traps awaited, no doubt). The story would no longer be found, or at least it would not be completed, in a domestic setting. *That* vision was too narrow.

The narrative shards of the tale—the madness of contemporary American life, both at home and abroad—lay strewn across public squares: archives, libraries, battle sites, forgotten museums. The princess had to camp in the Hall of Records, and study every paper trail she could find.

Before sinking fully into *Salvador,* let's dolly back for a moment.

Typically, we speak of "scenes" in a narrative. Increasingly, in the 1980s, Didion's writing discovered the *real* American stories not *in* the scenes, but *behind* them, in obscure rooms in queer places with unpronounceable names, where our government's military and economic interests coiled in dank corners. The scenes were all surface, illusion, advertising and propaganda, impenetrable jargon: an apparently arbitrary mix where nothing fit; a glut of information so loud and rapid-fire, we ceased to believe in any coherent story.

Behind the scenes, in the outposts and archives, in the safe houses and bunkers, a logical, continuous, and traceable—if findable—narrative was unfolding all along.

Who would have imagined that, after the American hostages were freed in Tehran, when President Reagan inscribed a Bible to an Iranian official, it might have some connection to TOW missiles, half a world away, sold to the Nicaraguan Contras? Who would have suspected that the Nicaraguan rebels might have something to do with a rash of cocaine deaths on the streets of Los Angeles?

As it turned out, the narrative ties were there. It wasn't that the premises of our national story weren't valid, as Didion had once feared; it was that the premises were different from what we'd been led to expect.

"I'm not sure that I have a social conscience," she averred at the time. "It's more an insistence that people tell the truth. The decision to go to El Salvador came one morning at the breakfast table. I was reading the newspaper and it just didn't make sense."

In fact, Robert Silvers had "expressed interest in having one or both of us [she or Dunne] write something about it," she told Hilton Als in 2004. For several months, they'd considered a Latin American trip: The newsman Tom Brokaw had made them "desperate to go." One night at a dinner, he'd told them "he'd been in Beirut, but El Salvador was the only place where he'd

ever been scared." Sent in March 1982 to cover the "elections"—a performance staged to suggest that the Salvadoran government was "making a concerted and significant effort to comply with internationally recognized human
rights," giving Reagan cover for military aid—he "woke up in the middle of
the night and the fear came over him." He took his mattress off his bed and
put it in the window, he said, afraid of getting shot.

Could be a hell of a story, the couple agreed. Besides, Didion was wrestling with the early drafts of a novel (the manuscripts that would eventually
coalesce into *Democracy*). She worried she'd never finish. She needed a break.

"What's *she* doing here? Wearing those big dark sunglasses," Paul Van-
Develder remembered thinking on June 15, 1982, the day Didion stepped
off a LACSA flight from LAX and walked across the patio of the Sheraton
Hotel in San Salvador, chaperoned by Christopher Dickey, the Central American bureau chief for *The Washington Post*. VanDevelder was a photojournal-
ist working for United Press International. John Newhagen, UPI's bureau
chief, was also struck by Didion's "large sunglasses and sun hat": The press
corps knew who she was and she had not arrived unnoticed. Many of the
veteran journalists considered her an "effete literati" who'd hang around for
two weeks, make notes for a book on the war, and "split" (which is pretty
much what she did). They were wary of her because they spent much of their
time drinking beer around the pool at the Sheraton or the Camino Real,
recounting how they'd broken this story or that and some *other* writer had
seized their reporting to become famous. The more sauced they got, the more
the journalists fired one another's distrust. So Didion and Dunne—who
tended to keep their distance—were sources of bitter bemusement. Van-
Develder: "I remember over drinks one night at the Camino Real, someone
looking at John Gregory Dunne across the room and saying, 'What a bummer to be John Gregory Dunne, the second-best writer married to the first-
best writer.'"

"We all wore T-shirts that said across the back '*Periodiste! No disparate!*'
('Journalist! Don't shoot')," VanDevelder explained. "It was a scary time. Four
Dutch journalists had just been killed—one of them was the boyfriend of
Sue Meiselas," the well-known Magnum photographer.

A year and six months before Didion went to El Salvador, four American Maryknoll nuns had been murdered on the road to the San Salvador airport. Not quite a year before that, Archbishop Oscar Romero had been shot
to death while preaching a sermon. And then in December 1981, evidence
surfaced—including several photographs taken by Susan Meiselas—suggesting
that a massacre of mostly children, adolescents, and pregnant women had

occurred at the hands of government troops in a village called El Mozote. The Salvadoran leadership's "concerted and significant effort to comply with internationally recognized human rights" appeared meager at best, but this did not deter the Reagan administration, which was determined to fund the troops in order to beat back Communism (Reagan's bugaboo since his days as president of the Screen Actors Guild) and to "revise" America's failed counter-insurgency efforts in Vietnam.

In response to what had occurred at El Mozote, American embassy offi-cials worried only about crafting a report that would "have credibility among people" in Washington "whose priorities were definitely not necessarily about getting at exactly what happened."

"Consider the political implications of both the reliance on and the dis-trust of abstract words." . . . "The consciousness of the human organism is carried in its grammar."

In spite of Susan Meiselas's photographs of mass burials, charred skulls, and children's decomposing bodies in the mud, in spite of detailed accounts of El Mozote by Raymond Bonner in *The New York Times* and Alma Guillermo-prieto in *The Washington Post*, the Reagan administration insisted there was no credible evidence of a massacre; no credible evidence that the Salvadoran ar-my's Atlacatl Battalion, trained by U.S. Special Forces and armed with M16s firing ammunition manufactured at Lake City, Missouri, had committed any such atrocity.

The facts on the ground disappeared. Didion wrote, "El Mozote entered the thin air of policy."

Just change the script.

Trust me.

Didion was uncomfortably aware that these events were occurring "only six years" after Gerald Ford had cheered America's renewed pride, and "most of us [had] watched the helicopters lift off the roof of the Saigon embassy and get pushed off the flight decks of the U.S. fleet into the South China Sea."

On their first day in El Salvador, the Dunnes rented a car. "I was just pan-icked about driving," Didion recalled. "There were a lot of roadblocks, and if it got difficult, if it got beyond the range of my rather limited Spanish, it could have been really unpleasant."

"But it's the only way you can really see a country," Dunne insisted.

Back home in Brentwood, they had recently hired a housekeeper from

El Salvador, a woman named Maria Ynez Camacho. Before the Dunnes boarded the plane in Los Angeles, Camacho had given Didion "repeated instructions about what we must and must not do," Didion said. But on the ground, amid pervasive threats of violence, one's choices were severely confined—if they were really choices at all.

"[W]e went out to the body dump," Dunne said: Puerto del Diablo, craggy slabs of moss-covered stone, just south of San Salvador.

"It was like throwing a child in a swimming pool. The idea of getting over my fear by going to a body dump!" Didion said. Standing on the edge of a large open pit, sweating, aware of the silence, hearing only the shriek of cicadas, she experienced a "cumulative impact" as she viewed the "pecked and maggoty masses of flesh, bone, hair." "You just switch into another gear," she recalled. "You don't remain yourself, quite. You perform."

"Nothing fresh, I hear?" an embassy officer said to her when she returned to the city. It took her a moment to realize he meant that there were no new bodies on the pile.

Dunne tried to keep her spirits high, to distract her, telling her funny stories and pointing out odd details wherever they went. One day, in the military zone in San Miguel, he called Didion's attention to a young soldier wearing fatigues and a baseball cap, standing against a chain link fence surrounding an army base, his AR-16 slung upside down on his shoulder; through the fence, he was getting a blow job from a woman on her knees on the other side of the perimeter.

Didion's pocket notebook from the trip, housed now in the Bancroft Library at Berkeley, is marked "Restricted," but the day I visited the archives, I discovered a broken seal. A previous researcher must have cut it. I opened the notebook's blue cardboard cover and saw Didion's precise, tiny handwriting pinning quick impressions to the page.

Guards everywhere.

Translucent corrugated plastic windows.

An embassy officer at a party one night saying there was no more *bang bang* in the Falklands now, so the journalists would probably all come scurrying back.

Little blond children in the streets.

Where were the birds? (Circling the dumps, plucking the eyes of the corpses?)

A taxi driver crossing himself as he passed through an intersection.

The Restaurant Gran Bonanza.

What of the future?

On certain pages of the notebook, the handwriting began calmly, legibly, and then devolved into large, hurried loops, as if Didion were sprinting for her life.

She chose several lines from Conrad's *Heart of Darkness* as an epigraph to *Salvador*. Across the pages of Kurtz's report on the "Suppression of Savage Customs"—a compendium of "noble words" expressing "civilization's" work in underdeveloped countries—the *real* story explodes in a fevered hand: "Exterminate all the brutes!"

Time and again, in her published reflections on El Salvador, Didion portrays herself venturing from her hotel room into gruesome sites of murder, rape, and other violations of the human. In a world under siege, a person learns to focus only on what's in front of her—a strategy for steadying herself, of calling no attention her way—"the models and colors of armored vehicles, the makes and calibers of weapons, the particular methods of dismemberment and decapitation used in particular instances." These are the details "on which the visitor to Salvador learns immediately to concentrate, to the exclusion of past or future concerns"—that is, to the exclusion of narrative— "as in a prolonged amnesiac fugue."

But after a while, once she gets used to the fact that terror "is the given of the place," she discovers links among accumulated details. However unfathomable war may seem on the ground, in the nitrate fog of gunfire, threats, and disappearances, it does not erupt without reason. Its causes may be complex and hidden, but they are also specific. Step by step, Didion begins to understand the "mechanism[s] of terror."

For example, she learns that "names are understood locally to have only a situational meaning, and the change of name is meant to be accepted as a change in the nature of the thing named." If a government organization is reported to have committed human rights abuses, it simply changes its name as a means of escaping the charges. The Didion who wrote *Play It As It Lays* and the essay "The White Album," suffering severe narrative doubt, would have been content to note her inability to keep a grip on the facts in the white noise of El Salvador's linguistic madness. But now she understands that *renaming* is a deliberate government "tactic," an attempt to "solv[e] a problem" by obfuscation. She connects the dots between the ill-constructed surface and the narrative reasoning behind the scene. She starts to grasp that many, if not most, of the confusions of contemporary life are purposeful, serving particular political ends.

On June 28, 1982, after twelve days touring El Salvador, the Dunnes caught a TACA flight to Miami, transferred to Eastern Airlines, and spent the night in the Hotel Carlyle in New York. Sitting in the restaurant, staring at her blue pocket notebook, Didion felt as great a disorientation as she had ever known. It was accompanied by a sense of urgency. Almost immediately, she began to translate her notes into a narrative, working faster than she ever had. Maybe she was experiencing the magic realism of the astonishing Colombian novelist, Gabriel García Márquez: a sense of existing simultaneously in two different worlds, the El Salvador of the U.S. press, holding free elections and observing human rights, and the El Salvador of the maggoty Puerto del Diablo.

Quintana flew from Los Angeles to join her parents at the Carlyle on June 29. On July 1, they all drove to Hartford in a rented car to visit Dunne's aunt Harriet. The following day, the Dunnes dropped Quintana at Bennington. She was sixteen now and had started to think about college. Bennington offered a monthlong summer program for high school students that provided the experience of living on a college campus along with opportunities for "refining . . . artistic expression, combining hands-on work with independent study and research."

Quintana's parents had told her she had a "great ability to sense things that are going on, like observing other people the way a writer does." She'd also developed an interest in photography. Recently, Kurt Vonnegut's wife, Jill Krementz, had interviewed and photographed her for a book called *How It Feels to Be Adopted*, featuring the stories of nineteen teenagers. Quintana was getting used to being a literary character, appearing in people's pages. Maybe it was time she *really* tried a book of her own—perhaps Bennington could help her decide.

In the meantime, her parents flew to Paris and London, Didion writing all the while. In New York, she'd received all sorts of material from Robert Silvers, news clippings and statistics, to help her with her story. She worked throughout the summer, having returned to Los Angeles in mid-July. Finally, she sent a draft manuscript to Christopher Dickey. He fact-checked it for her, corrected some of her spelling of Latin American place names and organizations, and declared it "terrific."

Robert Silvers ran Didion's entire account of her trip in three installments in *The New York Review of Books*—on November 4, November 18, and December 2, 1982. Simon & Schuster offered her a $35,000 advance for the book, to be published the following March.

Michael Korda, Didion's editor at S&S, thought she had done for El Salvador what Graham Greene had done for Panama in his famous writings about Gen. Omar Torrijos Herrera.

Didion was disappointed in the end. Though it had been "gratifying to write something so topical . . . and to produce it fast," the book "had no impact," she said. "Zero. None. It was discouraging."

(In 1983 the State Department invited Didion to join a cultural exchange tour in Buenos Aires, apparently unaware of, or indifferent to, her take on its Latin American policies. She accepted the invitation.)

A number of reviewers and scholars—among them, Ken Smith and Georgia Johnston—scorned Didion's lack of objective reporting in *Salvador,* and the paucity of her historical and political knowledge. They complained that, as she had done in her writings about Bogotá and Hong Kong, she depended on local color and sensationalistic detail to jar the reader's emotions (though, in the book, Didion claimed she was not at all interested in achieving easy irony through "color"). She substituted particular anecdotes for more general ideological observations.

These criticisms stirred the debate, once more, between mainstream journalism and the New Journalism. In a useful overview, Sandra Braman, a teacher of mass communications at the University of Wisconsin–Milwaukee, compared Raymond Bonner's reporting for *The New York Times* from June 1982 to Didion's coverage of the events in El Salvador during the same narrow period. Bonner filed thirteen stories, on deadline, in June. "According to the text," Braman writes, "Bonner collected facts by attending public ceremonies and press conferences, reading newspapers and magazines, listening to the radio (or reading CIA-supplied transcripts of broadcasts, per a description of the process provided by Didion), and then making phone calls or seeking personal interviews with officials to get their responses to statements made by other officials." By contrast, Didion kept a running list of random notes and personal observations throughout the month. "She attended to information from her own senses of sight, smell, hearing, and touch," Braman says. "Her written and aural sources were extremely diverse."

The "geographic source of news" for most of Bonner's dispatches was San Salvador and Washington, D.C., political capitals in the business of dispensing official information. By contrast, Didion "participated in informal and formal social gatherings, and absorbed facts during daily transactions such as at the drugstore or in a restaurant . . . quasi-official sites such as the morgue, and unofficial sites like a number of neighborhoods."

Braman concludes, "Bonner and *The New York Times* rely almost exclusively upon facts that list numbers—of dead, of disappeared, of land titles, of votes—and names—the Land for the Tillers program, the election, the president. Didion, on the other hand, specifically notes the uselessness of this kind of fact in El Salvador: 'All numbers in El Salvador tended to materialize and vanish and rematerialize in a different form, as if numbers denoted only the "use" of numbers, an intention, a wish, a recognition that someone, somewhere, for whatever reason, needed to hear the ineffable expressed as a number.'" Bonner's accounts were "disjointed." "Two kinds of stories appeared: Ray Bonner reported on the violence, and the next day there was an anonymous story repeating a State Department statement that the killing had declined." For Didion, "[c]ollecting facts was a 24-hour job and occurred whether a situation was explicitly reportorial or not."

As Braman says, whatever one thinks of the virtues of traditional reporting versus the techniques of the New Journalism—or even if one acknowledges the benefits of both—it's impossible to ignore the fact that corporate news outlets exist primarily to disseminate "the passage of bureaucratically recognized events through administrative procedures." For better or worse, subjective accounts remind us that human life is a "perpetual frontier."

Either way, the problem remains: finding a "diction that won't be outflanked by events," in the words of Terrence Des Pres.

During the war in El Salvador—perhaps as in any war—imagination may have been scarcer, and more necessary, than objectivity.

In a remarkable book entitled *The Body in Pain*, Elaine Scarry writes that "what is quite literally at stake in the body in pain is the making and unmaking of the world." Torture, she says, "not only deconstructs the 'products' of the imagination, but deconstructs the act of imagining itself." This is true in the case of an individual body and it is true in the case of a country, especially when tortured, dismembered bodies are left as messages to survivors that they are not allowed to imagine an alternative to oppression: "If you bury this body, the same will happen to you," the Salvadoran death squads warned intimidated citizens.

Scarry claims that imagination's "labor" is "centrally bound up with the elementary moral distinction between hurting and not hurting." Imagination is "simply, centrally, and indefatigably at work on behalf of sentience."

So when Joan Didion arrives in El Salvador wearing monster glasses and a floppy sun hat, it is easy to distrust her motives; easy, later, to find instances of political and cultural naïveté in her account of what she saw; but in her act of witnessing and imagining (with unrelenting intelligence), she counters the forces of hurting and the void. She reconstructs a dismembered world, a severed narrative, the way the priests and nuns at the Maryknoll mission would reassemble the hacked-apart victims of the death squads, tenderly placing the bloody stumps in proper order on the ground.

3

Didion was adamant that she not be confused with an investigative reporter. On the verge of publishing *Miami*, in August 1987, she wrote an angry letter to Michael Korda and Lois Wallace, saying she had just received three copies of the bound galleys from Simon & Schuster and found the back copy inaccurate and damaging to the book: a publicist had declared *Miami* a work of investigative journalism liable to make headline news. Didion objected: She had written a book of observation and reflection, and to mischaracterize her in this fashion, or to suggest *Miami* was filled with breaking stories (her whole point was that people failed to acknowledge what they already knew), was to toss her to hostile reviewers who would scream they had been duped. From now on, she said, Simon & Schuster should talk about the book it *had*, not the book it might have wanted. If the final jacket copy said anything about headline news, she was going to insist it be reprinted. (The final copy mentioned only "masterful reporting.")

Didion granted James Atlas an interview at her house in Brentwood for a *Vanity Fair* profile timed to coincide with the book's appearance. With Atlas, too, she took great pains not to be misunderstood. "I'm crazy about Miami," she told him. "I like the weather, the light, the warm soft rain on Biscayne Bay; I like the Cubans, the liveliness of the scene."

None of this made it into the book. Still, hers was a *personal* take on the city: That's what she had to make clear.

What *was* in the book? Well, for one thing, Atlas said, "I came away from [it] with the distinct suspicion that [John] Kennedy's assassination was set in motion by members of the Cuban community operating out of Miami."

"I think there *was* a conspiracy," she admitted. As she spoke, she leafed through *The Report of the Select Committee on Assassinations* on her coffee table.

"I don't have any idea who instigated it, but the way people were thinking encouraged whatever did happen. There's a kind of collective amnesia about the whole thing. The Warren Commission constructed its mission to be restoring equilibrium. No one really wanted to know."

Now we have intimations of connections between Colombian cocaine cartels and the funding of the Nicaraguan Contras, she said. All part of the same political culture.

Perhaps. Still, "I find the incongruity hard to ignore," Atlas said to her. What does any of this have to do with *you?* Why leave your "orderly world," with its "fresh-cut flowers on the piano," to chase down these phantoms in their military fatigues?

She became quite exercised:

> "I was irritated that so many people have found it easy to overlook what's going on, to live in the comfort zone," she ventures, clasping her hands and gazing down at the floor. Clearly agitated, she gets up and goes over to sit in a chair by the fireplace. "I suppose I'm interested in . . . Washington . . . um . . . Casey . . . It's quite inchoate, as you can guess." She subsides in her chair and cries, "John!"
>
> Her husband, John Gregory Dunne, appears. "Help me," she implores him. "What is the interest here?"
>
> Large, genial, enthusiastic, Dunne settles down on a sofa and considers. "I think it began with an interest in tropical climates. That soft underbelly that runs from Brownsville, Texas, to Miami. Here." He shows me on a map.

Inchoate or not, Didion's vision had already convinced Atlas. "Ever since she made her reputation in the late sixties . . . Didion has been on the hot trail of the *Zeitgeist,*" he wrote. "In a way, she's defined it . . . [I]n *Salvador* (1983), she foresaw where the U.S. government would next commit itself to a disastrous foreign policy in the name of anti-Communism . . . it's turned out to be prophetic. What was happening in El Salvador then is happening in Nicaragua now."

In *Miami*, Didion asserts that an "underwater narrative" drives the shattered surface of life in South Florida, in a city neither here nor there (geographically, Miami belongs to the United States, but culturally, spiritually—even in the "hips and décolletage" of the women—it feels like Latin America). In its earliest passages, the book evokes the "liquidity" and "cognitive dissonance" of the place, establishing the difficulty of locating a coherent story.

She conveys Miami's disjunctions through juxtapositions. "[I]n 1959 when Fulgencio Batista" and his friends flew out of Havana "on an Aerovias DC-4," she says, "the women still wore the evening dresses in which they had gone to dinner." She parses the clashing national rhetoric: What Washington calls the "disposal problem" (that is, how to manage so many furious Cuban exiles), "Miami calls *la lucha*," or the struggle for a liberated Cuba.

As the book proceeds, Didion dwells on causes more than perplexities. As it turns out, the place's bafflements are willful, born of prejudice or arrogant disinterest: Though Cubans constitute 56 percent of Miami's population, the Anglo press gives them scant coverage. A *Miami Herald* reporter calls the Hispanic population a "teeming, incomprehensible presence" without even trying to gauge its rhythms.

The city's bewilderments spring, as well, from public leaders' desire to avoid discussion of certain subjects: the Bay of Pigs fiasco, John F. Kennedy's assassination; according to officials, even to broach these topics is to blunt the crucial "healing process" necessary for communal health.

And in part, puzzlement results from dirty little secrets (note how Didion ends the following sentence in the passive voice, nailing language's complicity in the crimes):

> That *la lucha* had become, during the years since the Bay of Pigs, a matter of assassinations and bombings on the streets of American cities, of plots and counterplots and covert dealings involving American citizens and American institutions, of attitudes and actions which had shadowed the abrupt termination of two American presidencies and would eventually shadow the immobilization of a third, was a peculiarity left . . . officially unexplored.

Didion's longing for story leaves nothing unturned. Predictably, at this point in her career, images start to fit for her in the interiors of a hotel. In the Omni, downtown, she sees Miami's "social dynamic" revealed "in a single tableau."

At night, unemployed black teenagers gaze up from the streets outside the Omni at the hotel's out-of-reach windows, while Cuban men wearing black tie tango with "women in Chanel and Valentino evening dresses on the ballroom level." These Cubans have gained entry into America's elite spaces because their fathers, fleeing the island in the 1950s and early 1960s, were given Miami's service jobs, leading eventually to more gainful employment. Otherwise, these jobs might have gone to local blacks—the fathers of the aimless boys on the streets. For Didion, the hotel is the "most theatrical possible illustration of how a native proletariat can be left behind in a city open to the convulsions of the Third World, something which had happened . . . first and most dramatically in Miami but had been happening since in other parts" of the United States.

The more she delves beneath Miami's "provisional" surface, discovering narrative strands, the more she recovers a belief in cause and effect, consequences, and narrative itself, asserting the capacity of "individuals" to "affect events directly."

She begins to hear similarities in the way elderly Cuban exiles talk about the Kennedy administration's covert activities against Castro in the early 1960s and the way young people speak of the Reagan administration's illegal war in Nicaragua. An old and disastrous story in American politics appears to be playing out again.

Even more startling, the more she sees and hears, the more it becomes apparent that the same *players* are driving events. The story is coherent, continuous, and understandable, after all, despite the U.S. government's attempts to preserve deniability.

She learns about a man named Theodore Shackley, chief of station at a Central Intelligence Agency facility on the University of Miami campus in 1962, then the "largest CIA installation, outside Langley, in the world." There, nearly four hundred CIA case officers trained and coordinated thousands of Cuban agents. This is the same man, Shackley, "who left Miami in 1965, spent from 1966 until 1972 as political officer and chief of station in Vientiane and Saigon, and turned up in 1987 in the Tower Commission report"—on the Iran-Contra scandal—"meeting . . . in Hamburg with [arms dealer] Manucher Ghorbanifar and with the former head of SAVAK counterespionage."

Shackley is one of dozens of men Didion discovers, loses, and finds again, through obscure public records and newspaper archives, overheard rumors and conversations, men who are playing hide-and-seek, popping up at opportune moments in odd, out-of-the way places. By bringing their movements to light, she sketches possible connections between seemingly disparate events: the Bay of Pigs, the Kennedy assassination, the coup in Chile, the Vietnam War, the worldwide heroin trade, the Watergate break-in, the Nixon resignation, the Iran-Contra affair, the cocaine blight in L.A., the rise of global terrorism.

We are a long way from the princess in her castle, but perhaps, Didion hints, we are on our way to understanding why the castle came to be such a trap, why the princess had to leave it, drifting, confused, through an ever more cryptic nation. Perhaps we are on our way to understanding that narrative didn't fail after all; it simply had to expand and refocus to encompass more complex realities. We are on our way to grasping why the princess might find comfort as a literary critic, a parser of language—and why she might find the *real* story in the Hall of Records.

The problem with conspiracy theories is threefold: They are impossible to prove; they attract extremists stoked by paranoia; and they have become so popularized in movies, TV dramas, and on the Internet, their claims are easily dismissed as entertainment. "The truth is out there" was just another advertising slogan.

What distinguishes Joan Didion from an exploitative figure like, say, Oliver Stone, and the rabble of Web voices, is her disciplined thinking, her organization in the midst of fragmentation. In an early essay titled "On Morality" she wrote:

> As it happens I am in Death Valley, in a room at the Enterprise Motel and Trailer Park, and it is July, and it is hot. In fact it is 119 degrees. I cannot seem to make the air conditioner work, but there is a small refrigerator, and I can wrap ice cubes in a towel and hold them against the small of my back. With the help of the ice cubes I have been trying to think, because *The American Scholar* asked me to, in some abstract way about "morality," a word I distrust more every day, but my mind veers inflexibly toward the particular.

A devotion to the particular (it is not just hot; it is, in fact, 119 degrees), an admission of frailty, and a distrust of whatever she has been told to think about make Didion a more trustworthy witness than run-of-the-mill conspiracists.

In her room at the Enterprise Motel and Trailer Park, she thinks about a car wreck she has read about in the paper, and a nurse who said, "You can't just leave a body on the highway. It's immoral." "It was one instance when I did not distrust the word," Didion says, "because [the nurse] meant something quite specific. She meant that if a body is left alone for even a few minutes on the desert, the coyotes close in and eat the flesh."

In the final analysis, Didion's attraction to conspiracy tales, particularly in the 1980s, has less to do with the intrigues themselves than with her persistent longing for a narrative, *any* narrative, to alleviate the pain of confusion.

"We tell ourselves stories in order to live"—and if the story is not readily apparent, we will weave one out of whatever scraps are at hand; we will use our puzzlement as a motivating factor; we will tell our way out of any trap, or goddamn seedy motel.

4

Between *Salvador* and *Miami*, Didion published her fourth novel, *Democracy* (1984), inspired, in part, by her travels to Singapore, Hong Kong, and Malaysia—but chiefly by her love of Hawaii. *Democracy* looked back to the fall of Saigon. It placed that moment—in Didion's canon—in the midst of Reagan's Central America shenanigans. Indirectly, she suggested a connection, and forced a reexamination of the recent past in light of the present.

As the book opens, Didion's oldest fears seem to have recurred. One by one, narrative verities fail.

Setting? Don't count on it.

As the "granddaughter of a geologist, I learned early to anticipate the absolute mutability of hills and waterfalls and even islands," declares the narrator, a woman named Joan Didion.

History? Backstory? Sorry.

In this humid, mutable world, no one can "write anything down, the point of the pen would go right through the paper."

Emotion, psychological motivation, depth of character? Try again.

Didion can find no human feeling or satisfactory explanations for why people do what they do. She has only "[c]olors, moisture, heat . . . blue in the air."

Fables and romance won't do, either. No "dawn's early light." Instead, we hear a government man reminisce: "The light at dawn during those Pacific tests was something to see." It's nuclear winter rather than Reagan's "Morning in America."

"Call me the author," Didion says, plunging us into mealy Melvillean fog. She says, "I began thinking about Inez Victor and Jack Lovett"—the novel's protagonists—"at a point in my life when I lacked certainty, lacked even that minimum level of ego which all writers recognize as essential to the writing of novels, lacked conviction."

She continues: "When novelists speak of the unpredictability of human behavior they usually mean not unpredictability at all but a higher predictability, a more complex pattern discernible only after the fact." But she won't play even *this* narrative bait and switch, because she recognizes its foolishness, and she wants to find a deeper, truer story.

She has come to these dire straits because she views American democracy now as a poisonous language game:

> In the spring of 1975, during the closing days of what [the government] called "the assistance effort" in Vietnam, I happened to be teaching at Berkeley [she says, the Joan Didion of the novel blurring into the woman we think we know] . . . I spent my classroom time pointing out similarities in style, and presumably in ideas of democracy . . . between George Orwell and Ernest Hemingway, Henry Adams and Norman Mailer.

The passage implies *some* faith in narrative, as practiced by Orwell, Hemingway, and the rest. But official language—"assistance effort," masking, among other things, the napalming of Vietnamese villagers—mocks any effort now to teach the value of sentences, style, or thought. Language no longer describes the problems of democracy. It is *part* of the problem. (*Paraleipsis*: the rhetorical strategy of emphasizing a point by appearing to gloss over it—this is the new American speech, and it becomes the speech of Didion's novel.)

For a committed writer, the only moral recourse, at this point in American history, is to strip away whatever might be contaminated by the bad politics of our time: setting, history, backstory, psychological motivation, romance, fable. We begin with whatever's left—"colors, moisture, heat, blue in the air." From there, we build our story (the very opposite of the "generalizing impulse").

In this way, grasping not at abstractions or received forms, but at strict particulars, Didion recovers some measure of trust in words. Ironically, she winds up telling an old-fashioned love story—about Inez, who comes from a "family in which the colonial impulse had marked every member," and Jack, a player like the men on the government's "secret team," a fellow whose name eventually leaks out of "various investigations into arms and currency and technology dealings on the part of certain former or perhaps even current overt and covert agents of the United States government."

Like Charlotte Douglas, Inez had learned the princess song, but the tune goes sour. This is, after all, 1975—one of the lowest points in American democracy. Its "assistance effort" has become a cesspool.

Inez loses her husband, a U.S. senator, to praetorian ambitions; like

Charlotte, she loses her daughter—and her son—to all-consuming capitalism, which is loosed like anarchy upon the world. The only possible hero for her is a man in the thick of the hidden narrative, a man who speaks nostalgically of the beauty of nuclear tests. Inez steps out of the fairy tale and into the secret story. Because "nothing in this situation encourages the basic narrative assumption, which is that the past is prologue to the present, the options remain open here," Didion says. "Anything could happen."

In the end, Inez winds up teaching American literature in Kuala Lumpur. One day, Didion reads about her in the London *Guardian*, and the words bring back to her a "sudden sense of Inez." So, as it turns out, language has not been ruined beyond all use, nor has it lost its power to plumb the truth. It simply must not be invoked to cover the "flotsam of some territorial imperative" left behind by the venalities of democracy.

"When I started thinking about the novel . . . I called it *Angel Visits*," Didion said. "All the early notes were marked *AV*. An 'angel visit,' I had read somewhere, was a nineteenth-century usage for a 'pleasant interlude of a short duration,' and this was to be a novel that took place entirely in the rather somnolent life of American Hawaii. It was to be, as the narrator of *Democracy* eventually notes, 'a study in provincial manners, in the acute tyrannies of class and privilege by which people assert themselves against the tropics' [a thematic link between *Democracy* and *Salvador* and *Miami*] . . . This was actually the novel I set out to write."

The rough drafts of the book in the Bancroft Library confirm this: They start and restart with various narrators describing the social life of a colonial family living in Honolulu during World War II. Eventually, it became "clear that this was not the direction the novel was taking," Didion said. The book proved recalcitrant. Just three days before finishing it, she was "weeping" over its pages.

Why did the novel go awry?

Henry Adams: "[I]f man should continue to set free the infinite forces of nature, and attain the control of cosmic forces on a cosmic scale"—as "man" had done in the Pacific, with nuclear testing—then "the consequences may be as surprising as the change of water to vapor, of the worm to butterfly, or radium to electrons." "What Adams really meant was that in the physics-driven machine age, traditional historical narrative was losing its force—except perhaps in its conventional role to describe 'the decline and fall' of any age," says critic Timothy Parrish.

Didion felt this historical decline in her bones. Any novel she wrote would need to reflect it, or the novel would be false. Her original subject, "provincial manners," was merely the fairy tale designed to disguise cracks in the national story. As a form, history, Adams said, "must submit to the final and fundamental necessity of Degradation."

So in degradation—of political culture, morality, social ties, language, and provincial manners—Didion found the proper subject and style of her novel.

Not that it ceased to be a novel of manners, entirely. Michael Szalay, another perceptive critic, said Didion was writing about the social tensions "within the Democratic Party between the party's liberal wing and . . . 'the American business elite.'" These tensions offered numerous "opportunities for high romance . . . on the periphery of a crumbling empire."

Szalay saw a "thinly veiled Jackie Kennedy" in the portrait of Inez Christian (though Inez's drinking brings her closer to Teddy's wife, Joan) and claimed that her husband, Harry Victor, was "a left-leaning liberal transparently modeled after the Kennedys"—"less a character than an *ad hominem* attack on sixties liberalism."

Whether or not Didion had the Kennedys in mind, the novel proved prophetic in tracing the decline of New Deal liberalism, embodied in the sixties by the youthful, grinning face of JFK, and the rise of the Democratic Party's more pragmatic clan, reflected in the Democratic Leadership Council, formed just one year after the publication of *Democracy*. The council set out to weaken the party's traditional ties to minority groups and to court the private sector more assiduously—all in an effort to counter the conservative ideologies spawned by Ronald Reagan's popularity. The council's vision would pave the way for a more centrist Democratic leader, Bill Clinton, in the 1990s—prefigured in the novel by Harry Victor's son, Adlai(!), who claims it is time for *his* generation to enter the dialgoue, and who is referred to by his sister Jessie, a budding novelist, as an "asshole."

Didion claimed that her husband came up with the title *Democracy,* but it seems likely she had Henry Adams's 1879 novel of the same name in mind. As we've seen, Adams had always been a touchstone for Didion; *his* heroine, like Inez, becomes disillusioned with the experience of American democracy, and flees to an "older" world.

It seems not only likely but undeniable that Jessie, the troubled young girl in the Victor family, struggling with drug addiction, is another projection—like Marin in *A Book of Common Prayer*—of Didion's fears for Quintana. At one point, Jessie says to her mother, "Let me die and get it over with. Let me be in the ground and go to sleep." In *Blue Nights*, Didion quotes Quintana as saying, "*Let me just be in the ground. Let me just be in the ground and go to sleep.*"

Quintana was roughly thirteen to seventeen years old when Didion wrote *Democracy*. The book is dedicated to her and her cousin Dominique. By the time the novel appeared, one of them was dead and the other had predicted her early burnout and demise in a fragment of a novel written "just to show you."

Democracy's leading man, the shadowy Jack Lovett, moving in and out of Saigon, is clearly another projection of the rugged individual, the man of action, to whom Didion had always been drawn. The "Joan Didion" narrating the novel says, "After I finished my first novel and left *Vogue* and started reporting I actually ran into [Jack] quite a bit . . . he seemed to exempt me from his instinctive distrust of reporters." Later, quite indirectly, the novel suggests that Jack has had an ongoing affair with an American reporter, a woman who "kept a copy of *Modern English Usage* on the kitchen table, and a paperback copy of *Homage to Catalonia* in the drawer of the bed table" (Orwell, we recall, being one of the writers "Joan Didion" taught while Saigon fell).

John Wayne was still the love of her life.

Mary McCarthy did not know what to make of *Democracy*. In an extensive discussion of it in *The New York Times Book Review*, she wrote, "[D]espite an appearance of factuality achieved by the author's total recall of names, middle names, [and] dates . . . 'Democracy' is deeply mysterious, cryptic, enigmatic, like a tarot pack or most of Joan Didion's work. One way of looking at that work is to decide that it has been influenced by movies . . . Like the camera, [Didion's] mental apparatus does not think but projects images, very haunting and troubling ones for the most part, precisely because they are mute."

Like a freshman English major, McCarthy went symbol hunting, hoping to find the key to unlock the book. She was deeply irritated by Didion's throwaway mention of the Tropical Belt Coal Company. McCarthy was convinced this was a literary reference, but she could not track it down. Conrad, Kipling; Graham Greene, Waugh? In a rather schoolmarmish letter, published in the *Times* two weeks later, John Gregory Dunne informed "Miss McCarthy" that the Tropical Belt Coal Company appeared on the first page of Conrad's *Victory*. Left unsaid was the fact that knowing this reference did not unlock the novel. Didion's whole point was that the modern American novelist can no longer depend on traditional references or methods to be keys of any sort: Our national politics have compromised language too thoroughly.

In stressing this point—a point McCarthy apparently missed—Didion unveiled a major contemporary influence on her work: V. S. Naipaul. "[J]argon ends by competing with jargon," he had written. This insight is a better key to understanding *Democracy* than anything McCarthy scrabbled for in her review.

In a discussion of Naipaul's work in *The New York Review of Books,* Didion argued that Conrad's *Nostromo* predicted Naipaul's wish for himself as a writer: "The wisdom of the heart [has] no concern with the erection or demolition of theories," Conrad wrote. "[It] has no random words at its command. The words it pronounces"—the words a writer should write—"have the value of acts of integrity, tolerance and compassion."

This is precisely what Didion wished for herself.

Democracy frets about words, their ubiquitous misuse in our public discourse. The novel is an intense, fractured, and groping attempt to rescue words and restore to them their "integrity."

It is an ambitious project, probably doomed to failure—but in the land of paraleipsis, its intent is essential. *Democracy* is one of the finest achievements of twentieth-century American fiction.

5

At two o'clock in the morning, John Gregory Dunne circled a chilly room, glancing furtively at cold, dead bodies. With him was the Belgian-born film director Ulu Grosbard, who would bring Dunne's novel *True Confessions* to the screen. The novel included a morgue scene, so the men had asked a homicide detective to sneak them into the L.A. morgue—"absolutely against regulations," Dunne said—to witness an autopsy and to see the "decomp room," where the medical examiner stored rotting corpses. To counter the smell, Dunne smoked a cigar.

The homicide detective wanted to be a technical adviser on the film, in return for touring the men through the underworld.

It wasn't crime or L.A. noir that attracted Grosbard to Dunne's novel; it was the story of the brothers, the conflict between the cop and the priest, the ambitious ascetic and the softhearted cynic.

Jealous of his brother's social standing, enraged by his self-righteousness, the cop commits an act of betrayal. It results in his brother's banishment and exile to a lonely desert church, ending his hopes of becoming a bishop. Toward the close of his life—"the arteries to the pump are shot," he says—the priest forgives his brother: "In a way you were my salvation . . . You made me remember something I forgot." He has become a simple man, embracing everyday rituals—like Nick in his Oregon cabin.

The movie was released in 1981, a year before Dunne found himself on the edge of a body dump in El Salvador. It received mixed reviews—and a public slap from William F. Buckley Jr., who complained about Hollywood's pleasure in presenting corrupt priests on the screen—but its ambitious story line restored some credibility to the Didion-Dunne screenwriting team after the lucrative embarrassment of *A Star Is Born*. (Though it was Grosbard who persuaded the couple to draft a less plot-driven script. "Oddly enough, they had thrown out a lot of stuff from the book that I thought was important to the story," he said—primarily the complexity of the sibling rivalry.)

At a studio-sponsored preview in Boston, the Dunnes received a dispiriting evaluation of the movie from the marketing team: The film would appeal best to people with sixteen or more years of education. In any case, they were guaranteed $150,000 up front, in addition to the purchase price, and a production bonus of $100,000.

In 1982, Dunne published his second novel, *Dutch Shea, Jr.*, to generally good reviews. Michiko Kakutani ran a lengthy profile of him in *The New York Times*, pulling him further out of Didion's shadow. "[He] has established a distinctive voice, at once colloquial and knowing, street-smart and darkly comic," she wrote.

Dutch Shea, Jr., was about a sad-sack defense attorney haunted by the death of his daughter. In the end, while declaring a steady belief in God, he commits suicide. The story's details were drawn from Dunne's reporting on trials at the Santa Monica courthouse. Fears for Quintana and grief over his younger brother's final act gave the book its emotional depth.

"I've always thought a novelist only has one character, and that is himself," Dunne said. His protagonists were his "mouthpieces": "What I mean is, I have one character or sensibility which I project into situations"—situations gleaned on the beat while talking to other people about their professions.

At first blush, little seemed to link his genre novels to his wife's edgy, self-reflexive fictions, but the couple's friend Paul Schrader once argued that detective noir concerns the disillusionment and moral uncertainty of postwar American culture, "the loss of public honor, heroic conventions, personal integrity and finally, psychic stability." Here, husband and wife found grim common ground.

The commercial successes of *Dutch Shea, Jr.*, and the movie of *True Confessions* (defying the marketing research) boosted Dunne's already considerable confidence. He seemed to occupy more *space* than before: To a colleague, Lois Wallace complained she couldn't conduct any business for his wife without having him poke his nose into every detail.

Around this time, Didion took a high-handed tone in several letters to her agent, regarding her displeasure over *Democracy*'s foreign rights: She wanted a deal different from the one the agency had negotiated. She didn't like being condescended to (as she perceived it) by young publisher's representatives who showed no regard for the many years she'd spent in the writing business. Wallace and the publisher's reps were stunned by her vehemence. Didion announced that she would not be available for an interview with *Time* magazine; she felt *Time* had quoted her out of context on a previous occasion, so she didn't feel like talking to them. She continued to believe Simon & Schuster was cheating her on royalties. Dunne's love of a good verbal fight seemed to be hardening his wife's already firm attitudes toward business.

In a letter one day, Dunne chastised Christopher Lehmann-Haupt for mentioning, in print, that "Miss Didion's dust-jacket image" on *Democracy* "was thought to be in questionable taste by a number of fastidious observers" (who these observers were, he never made clear). The picture, "credited to Miss Didion's daughter, Quintana Roo Dunne, presents the author wading in a skirt and sweater that cling sufficiently to reveal somewhat more of the anatomy than one is accustomed to seeing in a dust-jacket portrait," Lehmann-Haupt wrote. Didion's response to the controversy? "It just shows somebody standing in the water," she told Lehmann-Haupt. "It has terrific water and it has terrific clouds, and it makes me look relaxed and pleasant, as opposed to the intense or worried way I usually look in photographs. It's hard for me to say what message it gives because I'm just not in the habit of analyzing myself a lot." She said she had hung an enlargement of the photograph on the wall of her living room, next to other pictures taken by Quintana.

In his letter, Dunne wondered when the Nipple Comintern had become so almighty powerful—and when had Lehmann-Haupt joined the Legion of Decency? He explained that, as it happened, his wife had not worn underwear since college for reasons gynecological (and certainly not since her recent hysterectomy). For that matter, neither did his daughter wear underwear. He said he did not mention this to titillate, but to suggest that questions of taste should not be asked if the standards were those of "fastidious observers" twitching at the sight of a nipple through a sweater while ignoring (or buying the official propaganda about) mass murders and suicides.

The power of photography—and the nature of pornography—was much on his mind at the moment, because ever since his night in the L.A. morgue, he'd possessed a photocopied "Murder Book," an official "history of an investigation, containing police reports, forensic photographs, [and] autopsies." The homicide detective who guided him through the morgue gave him the original book and said he could keep it for twenty-four hours. Dunne photocopied it, thinking it might provide useful details for some future writing project.

The book covered an unsolved murder from 1944. It contained a forensic photograph of a naked girl on a gurney in the morgue. Her body had been battered. Someone had draped a doily over her pubic area—"an absurd daintiness," Dunne said, almost the most horrific thing in the picture. He kept returning to the photo: The girl was only seventeen, just a little older than Quintana, and she had gone to the same school Quintana now attended.

Chapter Twenty-seven

———————— ❧ ————————

1

Quintana had added no new chapters to her novel, but she *had* hung a second Jim Morrison poster on her bedroom wall. The first, a shot of him bare-chested, his arms spread, and brooding under all that gorgeous hair, proclaimed him "An American Poet." You could count his ribs in the light of the desk lamp, perched just below the poster, right above her bulky electric typewriter. In the second poster, Jim looked less like a rock god, more approachable, just an everyday sort of guy, sweet-faced, someone your mom might have talked to (Quintana's had!).

Now he was dead.

These days, she was taking tons of pictures—of friends, of Malibu, where she still would have preferred to live—tacking them to felt boards on her desk. The desk was her neatest spot. Sometimes, after school, she could walk into her room, sit in her desk chair, wearing the white pullover blouse and the sleeveless sweater she'd worn to classes that day, her hair still nicely combed, straight down over her shoulders, stare at her pens and pencils all perfectly arranged in little metal containers, and imagine herself a young professional, a person with possibilities and places to go.

Otherwise, and elsewhere, things were a mess, but it was important not to show it. Anna Connolly, who'd known Quintana since seventh grade, said, "In truth, she and I were not behaving in ways appropriate to our age—but she was always dignified." They'd retreat to Quintana's sitting room, where she kept her stereo and books and her *Panic in Needle Park* poster, and they'd play Led Zeppelin records. "Directly across the hall, facing her door, was the door to Joan's office, which I recall as being closed most of the time. Whether Joan was in there or not, I can't say," Connolly told me. In most of her memories of the Chadbourne house, Quintana's parents are absent. "It's likely they were there (or one was), but I also feel they left us to enjoy ourselves on our own. The flowers, the pool, the kitchen . . . I do remember going with her parents to Trader Vic's at least once, and I was impressed by her father, as he seemed important to me."

Generally, Connolly and Quintana "spent a lot of time at the Beach Club, on PCH near the Santa Monica Canyon," Connolly said. "I was not a member, and I'm not sure if she was, but we were there a lot."

Everyone knew how easy it was for underage kids to get drinks in most of the exclusive clubs along Palisades Beach. This was a strip where no one over twenty-two ever seemed to go. Even the bouncers in the bars appeared too young to drive.

Quintana was marvelous company in places like the Beach Club: She had a jolly laugh, a generous smile, and big blue eyes. She charmed everybody. And she was a good, loyal friend. Connolly would never forget Quintana's inspiring support of her when they first met and the "mean" girls in seventh grade were tormenting Connolly. Quintana "would not speak to any of them anymore," even though they had been friends of hers; she "showed real character," Connolly thought.

Jerry's was a well-known liquor store in Brentwood where the skate rats liked to chill after dark. Teens would gather in front of the store and ask young customers to buy them sixers of Mickey's Big Mouth.

But this was child's stuff. "There were always open bars at Hollywood parties where the kids of parents in the business could get drinks," said Tim Steele.

"I knew a lot of privileged kids in L.A. with problems—obviously, I *was* such a kid," said Matthew Specktor, a young Los Angeles novelist and a good friend of Anna Connolly's. "As for Quintana . . ." He's careful, as are so many of Quintana's old friends and acquaintances when discussing her. "I think our upbringings were pretty similar—we ate with similar cutlery, so to speak." (He remembered well the Dunnes' Salvadoran housekeeper.) "I don't know what Quintana's problems were, but I've heard tell there were some real drug issues, right?" The important point, he told me, was that "the problems of that era, the problems *I* had, regardless of their relative intensity, were inseparable from the city's atmosphere, which is what Didion is in large part describing" in her work. He recalled a holiday party he attended when he was fifteen, where a screenwriter cut lines of coke on a table directly in front of him and his mother, and no one thought anything of it. The screenwriter was "agitated because he owed the studio a draft on Monday morning and just then—Thursday night—he hadn't written a single word. It was all part of the same picture: the drugs, the movies, the horror—whatever not-quite-nameable thing Didion was pointing at." This was Quintana's world.

And then she'd visit Malibu—reminded of the world she'd lost. The stark white light. The smell of hibiscus. She'd stroll happily along the beach, near a bluff leading up to the Pacific Coast Highway; she'd run her fingers across a thin branch of oak leaves or roses, and her fingertips came away gray, covered with thick, rich pollen. *This* was her home.

It's not that the social scene here was necessarily easier to negotiate than the one in Brentwood; it's just that she'd been better prepared for it before being plucked away to suburbia. In fact, Malibu could be "socially vicious," said Karl Greenfeld. A "surfers-rule, no-fat-chix ethic" was "strictly enforced." Those who weren't "blond, strong, handsome, fast, and harsh enough turn[ed] invisible" or became "victims of that gang of surfers and skateboarders who rule[d] our teenage wasteland. Brewing just out of sight [was] a subculture of fear and kid-on-kid violence."

"Karl knew some of the same people Quintana did—those beach community people," said his father, Josh. "It's astonishing how fast kids grow up on the coast."

Karl recalled his adolescence as a "haze of marijuana smoke," Cheap Trick records, and a lot of "crappy, low-grade THC." He recalled the students' cars in the school parking lots as finer than those of the teachers (Quintana drove to Malibu now in her own car, shiny red, with a vanity license plate, QROO). He recalled a lot of single-parent households and absentee moms and dads—yet it was *those* parents who passed Proposition 13, "lowering property taxes and gutting California's public schools." He also recalled a lot of family cats being locked out of empty houses during the day, eaten by coyotes.

Then there were the parties in the houses of people whose parents were away—stereos cranked to the max, playing the Sex Pistols, Triumph, the Dead Kennedys. Kids pumped fists in the air and chanted along with the Clash: "I'm so bored with the U . . . S . . . A!" The children of celebrities pretended to *disparage* fame, or rather, "mainstream popularity," said Matthew Specktor. "De Niro was cool, or Kubrick—you know, it was about a certain art house credibility." The backroom dope deals, the backroom sex.

Josh Greenfeld said he heard a persistent rumor that a well-known movie star, a star about whom "everyone had stories—and they were probably all true," had "deflowered" Quintana. Just another Hollywood rumor, but it wouldn't go away. In any case, what was certain, he said, was that "Quintana had a hard time of it. Everyone knew that."

It's not precisely clear when Didion began to take her daughter to specialists, but at a certain point, she saw Quintana "wishing for death as she lay on the floor of her sitting room in Brentwood Park, the sitting room from which she had been able to look into the pink magnolia. *Let me just be in the ground,* she had kept sobbing." In *Blue Nights,* Didion writes, "She was depressed. She was anxious. Because she was depressed and because she was anxious she drank too much. This was called medicating herself."

The specialists diagnosed Quintana's "depths, shallows, [and] quicksilver changes" as manic depression or OCD, and finally as "borderline personality disorder," often a medical catchall for people whose moods lurch unpredictably from sadness to hostility without visible provocation. "Borderline individuals are the psychological equivalent of third-degree-burn patients," clinical psychologist Marsha Linehan once said. "They simply have, so to speak, no emotional skin."

Doctors could not advise Didion whether the core of Quintana's problems was genetic or environmental, a result of family dynamics, or a combination of all three, but in any event, Didion did not trust what they were telling her. "I have not yet seen that case in which a 'diagnosis' led to a 'cure,' or in fact to any outcome other than a confirmed, and therefore an enforced, debility," she wrote. The wallpaper in Quintana's sitting room may as well have been malarial yellow, straight out of a Charlotte Perkins Gilman story.

"Let me just be in the ground. . . . Let me just be in the ground and go to sleep."

2

On November 17, 1982, Susanna Moore wrote Quintana a condolence note. She said she understood sudden, crushing loss—her mother had died when she was very young. This had not granted her any particular wisdom. No one could say anything to ease the pain. But she wanted Quintana to know that she had been thinking of her.

What is heartbreaking about Quintana's response—a rather perfunctory thank-you note—is the paper on which it's written. Like her mother,

Quintana had ordered personalized letterhead stationery—but underneath her name, in bold Colonna MT script, the paper was ruled like a grade-school notebook, and Quintana's handwriting, in pencil, wavered from dark to light.

The occasion for this exchange was the murder of Quintana's twenty-two-year-old cousin, Dominique. On the evening of October 30, Dominique's former boyfriend, John Thomas Sweeney, a chef at Ma Maison, strangled her for nearly three and a half minutes in what he later claimed was a black-out fit of rage. Dominique, who had just appeared in her first feature-length motion picture, Steven Spielberg's *Poltergeist,* had lived with Sweeney for several months in a one-bedroom house in West Hollywood, but then she began to fear his temper, his nasty jealousy of her friends, whom he considered snobs (he had been born to a poor family in Pennsylvania's coal country). She broke up with him. On the night police arrived at her residence and found Sweeney hunched over her unmoving body in the driveway, he said, according to a police department spokesperson, "I killed my girlfriend."

Nick got a call at five in the morning, in his tiny Manhattan apartment, from Detective Harold Johnston of the Los Angeles Homicide Bureau. The detective told him his daughter was near death at Cedars-Sinai Medical Center. Lenny came on the phone. "I need you," she said.

"What happened?" Nick asked.

"Sweeney."

"I'll be on the first plane."

Nick had met Sweeney some months earlier at a lunch with his daughter and her boyfriend; he had sensed the man's simmering tension and Dominique's unhappiness. Later, on the telephone, she told her father, "He's not in love with me, Dad. He's obsessed with me. It's driving me crazy." Her brother, Alex, couldn't stand the guy, and Lenny knew Dominique feared him. Dominique had told her this in tears one night, after she'd fled to the house of a friend of hers, an artist named Norman Carby, to hide from Sweeney.

Nick and Griffin caught a TWA flight to LAX and drove straight to Lenny's house on Crescent Avenue in Beverly Hills. She had moved from the residence on Walden, the place she'd shared with Nick when they were married, because she needed a smaller, more negotiable space. She had been diagnosed with multiple sclerosis. She was confined now to a wheelchair.

"The news is not good," she told Nick. The doctors had mentioned "brain damage." The hospital phoned to ask "permission to insert a bolt into Dominique's skull to relieve the pressure on her brain."

Sometime over the next couple days, Didion accompanied Lenny to the ICU. Dominique lay still, encoiled in tubes, her eyes, enlarged, staring at nothing, her hair shaved off. Didion had known Sweeney a little. He had gone to her house with Dominique to stay with Quintana on a couple occasions when the Dunnes were away.

It was like giving the Broken Man the key to your front door.

"She looks even worse than Diana did," Lenny said, holding her daughter's limp hand. She was remembering Diana Lynn Hall, who had died in this ICU following a stroke—Diana, who had encouraged Didion to phone Blake Watson, setting in motion the adoption process leading her to Quintana.

When Lenny mentioned Diana, Didion understood what she meant. She was saying that Dominique was going to die.

If the girl was being kept alive by machines, did this mean she was already technically dead? As opposed to what—*really* dead?

Technical life?

"It's not black and white," one of the residents told them.

This exchange, slightly shaded, made it into *Democracy:* "It's not necessarily an either-or situation." "Life and death? Are not necessarily either-or?"

In fact, Dominique never regained consciousness and was pronounced dead less than a week after entering the ICU.

Nick kissed her good-bye on his final day with her, pressing his lips to her bald head and whispering, "Give me your talent."

The press referred to her as the niece of John Gregory Dunne and Joan Didion. This enraged him. "Oh, what difference does it make?" Lenny said—with "such despair in her voice, I felt ashamed to be concerned with such a trivial matter at such a crucial time," Nick said. But he couldn't let it go. His ex-mother-in-law agreed with him. "Listen to what he's saying to you," she told Lenny. "It sounds as if Dominique was an orphan raised by her aunt and uncle." Lenny instructed Nick, miserably, "You handle it." So he called a publicist. The cabin in Oregon hadn't *entirely* flushed Hollywood from his system.

Later, Nick published a lengthy account of his daughter's murder. In it, he mentioned, in passing, that on the eve of the funeral, he didn't have the heart to watch the "two television programs" featuring Dominique, playing that evening on the networks. "Also on television that night was a film I had produced, never before seen on television, and another film my brother had written, also being shown for the first time," he wrote. The real point of the story seemed to be that his publicist was working overtime.

Quintana had been staying overnight with Susan Traylor in Malibu when news came that Dominique had been found strangled in her driveway. Quintana's parents called her at six in the morning.

After the funeral, she told her mother and father, "Most people I know at Westlake don't even know anyone who died, and just since I've been there I've had a murder and a suicide in my family."

As if it were the school's fault. The curse of the suburbia house.

Her father told her, "It all evens out in the end."

Didion assumed he meant good news eventually balances the bad.

Quintana understood him to mean that she shouldn't worry, that sooner or later, everyone *else* will get bad news, too.

"I have watched too many murder trials, known too many lawyers and too many judges and too many prosecutors, to have many illusions about the criminal-justice system," Dunne wrote later. "Any trial is a ritual complete with its own totems. Calumny is the language spoken, the lie accepted, the half-truth chiseled on stone." Before John Sweeney's first preliminary hearing on first-degree-murder charges, Dunne said, "I could predict that the counsel for the accused would present the standard defense strategy in cases of this sort: the victim, unable to speak for herself, would be put on trial, and presented, in effect, as a co-conspirator in her own murder."

"John, who knew his way around the Santa Monica courthouse, thought that we should accept a plea bargain, and emissaries from the defense were sent to us to effect one," Nick said.

Reasons for *not* going to trial were: Lenny's frail health would be further endangered by the drawn-out ordeal; the event would be a media storm, given Dominique's youth and relative celebrity; Dominique would be presented as a participant in her demise—neighbors would be called to the stand to testify that she'd had frequent fights with Sweeney, that she and her friends had condescended to him; the judge, Burton S. Katz, a theatrical man who had once prosecuted several members of the Manson Family, loved to play to the press. The defense attorney knew how to flatter him, and apparently the judge held the district attorney in ill favor.

"Lenny, Griffin, Alex and I felt pushed, as if we didn't matter," Nick said.

"The district attorney wanted a trial, and so did we. So we went to trial. John and Joan went to Paris."

The brothers did not speak again, substantively, for a very long time.

Sweeney appeared in the courtroom each day clutching a white Bible.

"When Miss Dunne got in from the bars, how drunk was she?" Sweeney's defense attorney asked one of the witnesses again and again.

The judge would not allow testimony from one of Sweeney's previous girlfriends that he had regularly abused her, on the grounds that it would be "prejudicial."

On the day the judge announced the jury's verdict, he "opened first one envelope and then the other, milking his moment before the television camera like a starlet at the Golden Globes," Nick said. Sweeney was convicted of voluntary manslaughter, maximum sentence six and a half years, with possible parole in two and half. In fact, Sweeney served very little jail time and was soon working again as a chef at the Chronicle, a trendy Santa Monica restaurant. From there, he moved to Seattle and changed his name. The Dunnes finally lost track of him (but not before Nick toyed with the idea of hiring Anthony Pellicano, a private detective, to kill him. "Dominick, you don't want to do this," Pellicano told him, and Nick's rage crumbled into helpless grief).

On the day the judge announced the verdict in the courtroom, Sweeney's attorney, realizing he'd gotten his client's charges drastically reduced, shouted, "I am ecstatic!"

The judge said justice had been served, and he thanked the jury on behalf of the lawyers and the families involved in the case. Trembling, Nick yelled at the bench, "Not for our family, Judge Katz!"

"You will have your chance to speak at the time of the sentencing, Mr. Dunne," said the judge.

"It's too late then."

"I will have to ask the bailiff to remove you from the courtroom."

"No. I'm leaving the courtroom. It's all over here."

He pushed Lenny's wheelchair up the aisle ("Lenny—sick, devastated, and the bravest of all of us," he said). At the double doors at the rear, he turned again toward the judge and shouted, "You have withheld important evidence from this jury about this man's history of violence against women."

Later, after the press had criticized the judge's handling of the trial, Katz expressed outrage at the jury's lenient verdict. "It was as if he had suddenly become a different human being," Nick said. Shortly afterward, Sweeney was freed.

Ultimately, the trial became a source of redemption for Nick. He told the story this way: Two days before the trial was scheduled to begin, he was introduced to Tina Brown, then in talks to assume the editorship of *Vanity Fair*. She suggested he keep a journal throughout the proceedings and afterward come see her in New York.

"If I hadn't kept that journal . . . I would have gone mad. What I saw in the courtroom filled me with the kind of rage that only writing about it could quell," Nick said. And "Tina . . . saw something in me I didn't know I possessed." Under her guidance, and with the help of Wayne Lawson, *Vanity Fair*'s new literary editor, he edited and shaped the journal entries into an article for the magazine, "Justice: A Father's Account of the Trial of His Daughter's Killer." It ran in the March 1984 issue and established a fresh career for him. "For the first time in my life, I felt I was in step with my destiny," he said. Tina Brown's *Vanity Fair* became a "great, highbrow, bling-bling icon about tony influentials," said one media critic—and Nick's was *the* new voice of the magazine. For the next two decades, he would cover one celebrity murder trial after another, pretending no lack of prejudice, always championing the victims and their families. He had found his way back to Hollywood, discovered new outlets for his star worshiping, name-dropping, partygoing—girded now by a moral crusade. As *Vanity Fair*'s Graydon Carter once said, "Wealthy people aren't quite shooting themselves at the rate we'd like them to, for Dominick's purposes." In addition to his reporting for the magazine, Nick wrote bestselling novels based on his trial notes and his proximity to the upper crust. He had moved to colonize the territory once ruled exclusively by his brother and sister-in-law. As a result, their war got colder.

And still, Quintana added no new pages to *her* novel. She had written just enough to "show you," and then she'd stopped.

Shortly after losing Dominique, however, she had written in a school journal, "I had an exciting revelation while studying a poem by John Keats. In the poem, 'Endymion,' there is a line that seems to tell my present fear of life: *Pass into nothingness.*"

3

In the mid-1980s, as the publicity surrounding Dominique's murder ebbed, Didion and Dunne held court regularly in the art gallery of their friend Earl McGrath on North Robertson Boulevard. In a profile for *The New York Times Magazine,* Leslie Garis set the scene:

"The guests, gathered on a terrace beneath hibiscus trees, are more interested in each other than the show . . . The women are thin and tanned and wear very high heels. . . . Didion sits at a table quietly. She is peaceful. An endless stream of people comes to her, bending down to kiss her. She asks after their children, remembering personal details about everyone. Anjelica Huston, all legs in a little black dress, Teri Garr, George Stevens Jr., Tony Richardson, Michelle Phillips, Jean Vanderbilt and George Segal come to pay respects to the tiny woman with a gardenia in her hair." (Painfully missing was Natalie Wood, who had drowned off Catalina Island—apparently after a tense, drunken evening with her husband and Christopher Walken, just another one of those nights; Didion could still remember wearing Natalie's dress to functions like this, Natalie checking her teeth in the reflection of her dinner knife.)

Meanwhile, Dunne roamed the terrace with a Scotch in his hand, chatting with frowning, sinewy men about the weekend's box-office grosses.

With the deaths of Truman Capote and Christopher Isherwood, the Dunnes were L.A.'s uncontested lit royalty (even to her face, people called Didion the "Kafka of Brentwood Park"). At Capote's funeral in the Westwood Mortuary, she was appalled at the litany of star-fucker tributes. Is *this* what she could expect when *her* time came?

"The last time I saw Joan was at the Beach Café. There was a party for her on the outdoor terrace," said Don Bachardy. Isherwood had died and Didion was quite aware of her new queenly status. "At the time I was with a man who was about the same age in relation to me as I was with Isherwood when Isherwood and I first got together," Bachardy told me. "Joan immediately expressed her disapproval with facial expressions and words to the effect of 'I expected better of you.' I think she thought I should be a kind of literary widow devoted to the memory of Isherwood."

Stardom had its drawbacks. "Wacko" letters came to the Chadbourne house: "You still have not taken my advice and dumped that miserable piece of

Jewish dreck you are married to," a man wrote Dunne. "I know, I know, you are going to tell me she is a WASP from Sacramento. B. S. She went to New York City anxious to break into publishing and came upon the idea that if she put on the Jewish Whining Act she could get published. Well, she succeeded all too well. Now her whole thing is permeated with the Jewish whine."

One day, an ad appeared in the "Classified" section of the *Los Angeles Times*, announcing "BRENTWOOD PARK STEAL! Famous writers' loss is your gain." Whether as a joke or as a genuinely hostile gesture, some anonymous person had created the appearance of scandal or misfortune in the Dunne household, purportedly forcing them to sell off their property. The Dunnes never learned who placed the ad. In an outraged letter to the newspaper, Dunne's greatest pique seemed reserved for the suggestion that his house was worth only $995,000.

The couple received endless requests for favors. A small press in Mississippi wondered if Didion would contribute a favorite recipe to a venture called *The Great American Writers' Cookbook*. The next thing she knew, the editors were selling first serial rights to magazines. She told her lawyers to sue the press if *Playboy* printed her recipe for Mexican chicken.

Worst were the missed opportunities—they came her way in the first place because of who she was, but who she was could turn around and bite her. Britain's *Sunday Times* magazine contacted Lois Wallace about the possibility of sending Didion to South Africa to expose that society's underbelly as she'd done in El Salvador. Didion expressed her keen interest in going, but then the magazine withdrew its offer, citing the new editor's change of heart. "That's Rupert Murdoch for you," Dunne said.

Sometimes she just wanted to disappear into the daily routine of a typical wife and mom. "At some point . . . I think I twigged to the fact that I was no longer the woman in the yellow Corvette," she said. "I needed a new car because with the Corvette there was always something wrong . . . [and] maybe it was the idea of [living in] Brentwood . . . when I gave up the yellow Corvette—and I literally gave up on it, I turned it in on a Volvo station wagon—the dealer was baffled."

And Quintana was appalled. She wanted the objects in her life to stay the same—without fail. She liked predictable rituals. For a luncheon around the swimming pool on her sixteenth birthday, she wanted cucumber and watercress sandwiches because her mother had always served cucumber and watercress sandwiches at parties.

For a while, she'd had a sort of boyfriend whose very nice mother had given Quintana a suede coat. She wondered about the etiquette of wearing the coat when she'd dumped the boy. Rituals were important.

Her new rituals included counseling for "a stressful time," or for "adolescent substance abuse." (In *Democracy*, Didion appears to draw upon certain exchanges she and Quintana might have experienced in therapists' offices: "It might be useful to talk about you. Your own life. How you perceive it" [a doctor says to the mother]. "My life isn't really the problem at hand. Is it?" "The 'problem at hand,' as you put it, is substance habituation. I notice you smoke." "I do, yes. I also drink coffee. What I don't do is shoot heroin.")

For Quintana, some of the best times were those spent traveling, with or without her parents: Hawaii, always Hawaii, where her father would take her and Susan Traylor to watch a trial at the Honolulu courthouse for an afternoon's entertainment; Paris, where she'd almost had a play date, once, with Princess Stephanie; Barbados (her mother *did* love the tropics); Saint-Tropez, the summer after she'd turned fifteen, traveling with Tasha Richardson and her dad, swimming topless and teasing the Italian boys on the beach, pretending to be a college girl from UCLA.

At a nearby bookstore in Saint-Tropez, she'd found a book in English called *Baby Animals and Their Mothers* and mailed it to her mom. She included a postcard, saying the book "reminded me of you." The postcard featured an infant polar bear with its mother, and the caption "Cuddling on the ice floe."

Better to remain on the move instead of lying on the sitting room floor, thinking about suicide and murder, wishing to be in the ground. "*Like when someone dies, don't dwell on it*," she'd told her mother.

If only she could take her own advice.

The quiet "suburbia" life—and the Volvo station wagon—required steady support, so the Dunnes reentered the screenwriting fray. They took early cracks at scripts for *The Old Gringo*, a vehicle for Jane Fonda and Gregory Peck, and *The Little Drummer Girl*, a John le Carré spy story. Eventually, *The Old Gringo*'s producers turned to other writers, and *Drummer Girl* "foundered on the twin rocks of Hollywood deal-making—hubris and ego," according to Dunne.

For a while, Didion hoped *A Book of Common Prayer* would be made into a picture (Joseph Losey showed some interest, with a possible script by Harold Pinter; Didion could just *see* Vanessa Redgrave as Charlotte), but nothing came of the plans.

In the late 1970s, Lawrence Schiller, a former *Life* and *Look* photographer, now a producer, and a one-man blizzard of publishing deals, had obtained the rights to the Gary Gilmore story (Utah had sentenced Gilmore to die by firing squad for murdering two young Mormons). Schiller approached several people, including Barry Farrell and Didion, about collaborating on a Gilmore project. Eventually, Norman Mailer took the assignment and produced his magnificent *The Executioner's Song*. Didion read an early draft of the novel and suggested several cuts, which Mailer accepted. In the mid-1980s, she crossed paths with Mailer again: She and her husband wrote a screenplay based on his early novel *The Deer Park*. This was another project—centered on Hollywood's cynical deals—that failed to make it to the screen. Amid several scenes of cruelty in the script, one touching moment stands out: The daughter of a producer plucks at her father's sleeve "to get his attention, which she has never enjoyed."

Perhaps the antic screenplay work, as well as the experience of rereading Mailer's Hollywood novel, led Dunne to create Jack Broderick, the screenwriting protagonist of *his* next novel, *The Red White and Blue* (1987). Broderick, another "mouthpiece" for Dunne, writes movie scripts because "the pay is good, the responsibility small, the emotional stake minimal." Like Mailer's hero, he inhabits a world where "celebrity and political action make common cause"; a world as an enormous courthouse where *everyone* is "not guilty by reason of insanity." As in *True Confessions*, a self-righteous brother appears in this book, celibate and severely deficient in humanity. Dunne dedicated the novel to Earl McGrath, and he used the occasion of its writing to empty his reporter's notebooks of leftover details from Vietnam, Delano, and El Salvador.

4

Didion wrote, "There is in the development of every motion picture a process known as 'licking the script,' that period during which the 'story' is shaped and altered to fit the idealized character who must be at its center."

For her, the 1980s—her Brentwood years, the years when her writing first became overtly political—were notable for mistaking *rhetoric* and *action*. In this, the culture followed the mind-set of its actor president, who understood "licking the script," who grasped the storytelling value of symbolism. For example, Didion noted that, after the Grenada invasion in 1983—"a lovely little war," according to one correspondent, ostensibly mounted to counter

Soviet and Cuban influence on the island—"the number of medals awarded eventually exceeded the number of actual combatants."

And still the books kept coming from the corridors of the think tanks. *Ronald Reagan: How an Ordinary Man Became an Extraordinary Leader* (an "idealized character"), by Dinesh D'Souza, written for a "new generation with no alternative source of information." And whose reading skills had badly eroded.

Looking back on this exhausted decade, Didion understood that the last real moment, before the script's illusions locked into place, was the Christmas season of the Iranian hostage crisis—*before* Reagan's inauguration. She remembered, in Hawaii, following the events on hotel televisions; she recalled running into her old friend Nancy Kennedy in Honolulu's Outrigger Canoe Club; they'd kissed and shared a drink; Didion had smiled, watching Nancy laugh and argue with her children at the table, the way she had laughed and argued with Didion when they were kids at her parents' table in Sacramento—another world altogether.

That day in the Outrigger, Nancy promised they'd get together again soon. A few months later, she was dead of cancer in New York's Lenox Hill Hospital.

In the mid to late 1980s, whenever Didion returned to Sacramento for a visit, she thought of Nancy and those sweet, laughing fights. *Like when someone dies, don't dwell on it.*

Sometimes, between screenwriting assignments or her husband's work on *The Red White and Blue,* she convinced Dunne to travel with her. In Sactown, at dinners with her brother and old family friends—CEOs, federal judges—they'd reminisce about their childhoods or they'd discuss the unreality of the national script: the Reagan Doctrine, Jessie Jackson's threat to the stability of the old Democratic Party, Nancy Reagan's astrologer.

Words, words, words.

Well. It's *easy* to mock public figures, one or another dinner guest said.

Yes, but words matter, Dunne argued genially over drinks one night. For instance, it genuinely hurts when a reviewer calls you "slime" in a newspaper.

Still, they're only words, said his brother-in-law. They had no substantial effect on Dunne's ability to make a living. On the other hand, a CEO could be fired by his board after one bad quarter. The Ninth Circuit or the Supreme Court could come along and reverse every decision a federal judge made.

Writers took words too seriously. They should join the rest of us here in the real world. Where it's "Morning in America."

More and more, Dunne used words Didion hadn't heard him utter before. Old, he said. He felt old (he was in his mid-fifties). He said he'd like to be alone with her in front of the fireplace instead of going out to a party. He said he didn't like to drive so much after dark.

He groaned when he bent to feed Casey, their little black Bouvier des Flandres.

He groaned at the clutter of female *stuff* all around him: Quintana's plastic pink razors, Fiorinal for migraine, Naturetin-K for bloat, HydroDiuril for premenstrual symptoms, all those damn Compazine suppositories. It was like a fucking pharmacy, he thought.

He said he felt restless (*that* she *had* heard before).

He said they weren't having any fun. He talked about an older couple they'd met once in Indonesia, people who seemed to *embrace* life following their retirement, traveling, teaching, learning all they could. He wanted to *be* that older couple.

He wondered about moving to New York. Since 1984 they'd kept a pied-à-terre on West Fifty-eighth Street in Manhattan for their frequent trips to meet with editors or to do media gigs for their books. Maybe they should just settle there (as they'd done in the past, they could ask their secretary to FedEx Meyer lemons and fresh tortillas to them whenever they got homesick for California).

He thought maybe he'd written all he could about Los Angeles.

He was overweight and not feeling well.

Didion tried to dismiss this talk as his usual "jits" whenever he'd finished a major project, or as his typical Irish gloom ("Two things the Irish would think are wonderful are, one, kissing the Blarney Stone and, two, slipping and falling when you're kissing the Blarney Stone and cracking your head open," he liked to say).

But then his doctor diagnosed him as borderline diabetic and told him to go on the wagon. In the evenings, he mixed various healthy concoctions— "odd waters," Didion called them. She found it "very tedious" drinking alone.

He'd wade out silently into the center of the pool, reading. She'd pull on a pair of sweatpants and go into the garden, snipping stalks for brewing lemongrass tea. She'd sit and thumb through Penelope Hobhouse's *Color in Your Garden* and contemplate changes she might make. After a while, Dunne seemed to settle (his glucose levels reached an acceptable plateau) and the nights were usually pleasant.

Of course, his abstinence didn't last.

Late in 1987, he consented to a series of medical checkups for insurance purposes—if doctors declared him generally fit, his policy value would increase by 50 percent "in light of the many changes in interest rates and product design," said an official letter he'd received. He got an EKG and did a treadmill test. "You've got a glitch," his internist said.

"What kind of glitch?"

"An abnormality. I want you to see a cardiologist."

A short while later, a friend of the Dunnes died in a waterskiing accident—a man they didn't know well but whom they'd always liked, one of those charming Hollywood characters you'd see everywhere. He had played tennis part-time for a living and worked as a restaurant greeter. His memorial service was scheduled one afternoon on a private tennis court in Beverly Hills. Didion arrived on her own. Dunne planned to meet her there following an appointment with a cardiologist in Santa Monica.

The day was bad enough already: The tennis player had known John Sweeney—they'd met in the restaurant business. Sweeney was now out of jail. Dunne feared running into him at the service and having to restrain himself. Maybe it was just as well he'd be late.

In his account of these matters in *Harp*, a "more or less" true rendering of the day, he wrote, Sweeney did not show. There "had not been an appropriate moment" during the memorial to tell his wife about the doctor visit. When the service ended, she asked him what the cardiologist had said. Later, she would claim to have no clear memory of the exchange. She had simply not taken it in. "He said I was a candidate for a catastrophic cardiovascular event," Dunne said. "He scared the shit out of me, babe." Then, he said, he started to cry.

PART EIGHT

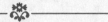

Chapter Twenty-eight

———— ✿ ————

1

I now know how I'm going to die," Dunne said.

"*You no more know how you're going to die than I do or anyone else does,*" Didion replied.

Doctors informed him he had a "hemodynamically significant lesion" in his left anterior descending artery (LAD) as well as a 90 percent narrowing in the circumflex marginal artery. An internist he knew in New York told him cardiologists called the LAD the "widowmaker."

He sought advice from specialists. One day, sitting with his shirt unbuttoned in an examining room, he noticed a Jim Dine print on the wall. "I know Jim," he told a nurse, but his jauntiness faded; he realized the insider connections he'd worked hard all his life to arrange didn't help him one whit now. Now he wondered what sort of "pretentious asshole" would hang a Jim Dine print in his examining room.

"Milk it, but no excessive melodramatics," he wrote one afternoon in a notebook. After all, he was a writer and this was great material. But the melodramatics were hard to avoid, both on the page and off. He began to compose his obituary in his head. "I was ever aware of mundane last times," he wrote in *Harp*. "[T]his was the last time I would have dinner at Morton's, the last time I would have a lube job on the Volvo, the last time I would have kung pao shrimp, the last time I would go to Dodger Stadium, the last time I would see a perfect pair of tits. Ah, sex, the last time this, the last time that, the last fucking hard-on."

Eventually, his doctors concurred: An angiogram was in order, followed possibly by an angioplasty (if the angiogram confirmed the EKG results). Without medical intervention, he had a high likelihood of a major heart attack, or even a *massive* attack. Not even prayer would help with that.

He made plans in case the worst occurred. Calvin Trillin would break the news to Quintana, now attending college in New York. He updated his financial records for "the little widow." He worried that Didion wouldn't be able to take care of herself. Who was he kidding? She was as tough as a little machine, with a much better head than he for business.

He hoped there'd be time for a priest to arrive to administer the sacrament, whatever the circumstances. He'd lost his faith long ago, but confronted now with *last times,* he had to admit he was Catholic to the core. The old rituals still moved him. Gregorian chants made him cry.

He scheduled the angiogram at St. John's Hospital in Santa Monica, where his greatest blessing, Quintana, had come wriggling into the world. Friends told him to forget his genetic history—these modern life-saving techniques hadn't existed when his father died. A literary agent he knew told him about someone who'd sailed through his angioplasty with nary a hitch: "He's too terrible to die. Not that you have to be a terrible person to come through this thing; you're not a terrible person at all."

On the day of the procedure, in late September 1987, the admitting nurse insisted that he watch television soap operas in his room while he waited, because that's what *all* the patients did. She couldn't fathom anyone reading a book—besides, no one would keep track of the book once he was wheeled down to the cath lab. Repeatedly, the TV networks played clips of Bob Fosse's movie *All That Jazz,* because Fosse had died that day. "Bye, bye, life," Roy Scheider, as Fosse, said again and again as he slipped away following open-heart surgery.

The angiogram confirmed the EKG: 90 percent blockage. An angioplasty was scheduled for a week later. Doctors would make an incision in his left groin and snake a balloon into his artery to dilate the LAD.

When the day came, the OR seemed as cold as the L.A. morgue. The anesthesiologist inserted an IV of Valium into his arm. "I don't think I've been this stoned since 1968," Dunne joked with the efficient young fellow.

"Few of us have, Mr. Dunne. Few of us have."

Bach and Mozart piped through the OR speakers. Dunne focused as well as he could on the TV monitors above his head, which showed the various pathways in his chest. It was like looking at a map of the Los Angeles freeway system.

Poof, poof, poof went his heart.

He tried to imagine cruising Sunset to the Malibu beach, but mostly what he thought of (to the extent he thought of *anything*) was that this whole ordeal was going to cost somewhere in the neighborhood of forty grand. He'd have to keep rewriting scripts just to maintain his Guild insurance.

Two days later, as he lay recovering in his fourth-floor hospital room, his bed began to shake. "Sister," he said to the floor nun puttering around the room, straightening pill bottles, "I think this is a fucking earthquake." "I think you're right, Mr. Dunne." She grabbed the bed and held on tight. He was hooked to an IV and couldn't do anything. He was still bleeding from his groin incision. He knew this wing was in an older part of the hospital and hoped it was built to code. More than that, he worried about the fact that he'd just said "fuck" in front of a nun.

"Spectacular," his cardiologist pronounced ten days later, examining the latest EKG results. Six months after this, Dunne's LAD remained dilated. His cholesterol was down and he'd lost twenty-five pounds. "You've bought yourself a new life," the internist said.

Dunne's first thought: *What the fuck do I do with it?*

2

This was much worse than the jits. For months he'd concentrated so intensely on his heart, on learning the parameters of the problem, the alternative solutions, the risks, the chances of recovery. The news was good now, and he felt physically fit, but a sense of anticlimax hovered around him, similar to finishing a book, of being deep inside the dream, then coming out of it, having no idea what to do next.

Add to that the knowledge that his body had been invaded—the uneasy sensation that he was not quite the same, that he would never again be the man he had been.

And who had he been?

He totted it all up.

"Twenty-four years, nearly a quarter of a century, five houses, seven books published, four film scripts produced, a million or two words pounded out on typewriter and computer; a marriage that survived, a daughter born and raised to her majority, three siblings dead, plus a mother and an aunt, a suicide in the family and a murder . . ."

The doctors had given his heart a jump start. Now, he figured, the rest of his life needed a "goose."

"I don't know why we moved back to New York," Didion would say years later, recalling this chapter of her life. "It was not a very thought-out decision."

Dunne presented a different story, claiming they'd both contemplated a move for quite some time; they were weary of the "hetero-coastal" travel (Dunne refused to be "bi-anything")—though the travel never stopped, so *that* was hardly a reason to move. At most, he said, the decision to return permanently to New York was only slightly "accelerated" by his cardiac episode.

He craved the change more than she did. "I don't know. John was between books. He was sort of restless. Our daughter was at Barnard . . . Suddenly it seemed as if there was no particular reason to stay," Didion said.

"[We've] stayed too long at the fair. I [feel] tapped out," he insisted. And in response, Didion heard her mother's voice in her ear: *What difference does it make?*

In their conflicting accounts of reaching the final decision, they agreed on one detail: One night, on one of their many back-and-forths between the coasts, probably early in 1988, their plane to Los Angeles got stuck for several hours on a runway in Newark. It was there, while sitting tired and disgruntled on the airplane that they admitted aloud to each other, *This just isn't adding up*.

Let's do it, Dunne said.

Why not, Didion replied.

3

Quintana had not started her college career at Barnard. Impressed by the summer program she'd attended years earlier, she enrolled, as a freshman, at Bennington, in Vermont—at the time, the most expensive private liberal arts college in the country.

Jonathan Lethem, Quintana's classmate, called the mid-eighties at Bennington, simply, "cocaine days," an era of "scandal-plagued faculty." The campus was a minor literary salon: In addition to Lethem, Donna Tartt, Jill Eisenstadt, Lawrence David, Reginald Shepherd, Joseph Clarke, and Bret Easton Ellis enrolled. Ellis had secured an agent already through the help of one of his teachers, Joe McGinniss, who admired Ellis's stories "about youth culture in L.A." They were "very much in the style of Joan Didion," Ellis admitted. "It was inconvenient that I liked him," Lethem wrote later. "Bret stood perfectly for what outraged me at that school, and terrified me, too, the blithe conversion of privilege into artistic fame."

Ellis befriended Quintana and told her how much he loved her mother's writing. ("I would rewrite paragraphs of hers just to see how she would do it," he'd say later.) Quintana seemed genuinely shocked at the level of celebrity her parents enjoyed among her peers; she'd always known they were public figures, but this was par for the course in West Hollywood. Here, among youthful scribes on the make, her mom and dad were *heroes*. Why hadn't they told her?

"Quintana seemed spooky to me, or perhaps I mean spooked," Lethem told me. "It's too easy to project a profound sadness back onto those very scarce encounters we had, but there's certainly nothing about the way she moved through that campus world that would contradict an impression of profound sadness. My impression of her inaccessibility is strong. She seemed bound up in something impenetrable with the small number of others she was available to, and very likely was charismatic within that circuit—what was conveyed to me was a blank surface onto which I, for various reasons that are probably typical of me, projected the sadness."

Yet Lethem was not the only one who felt a force field of melancholy enveloping Quintana, especially on early-autumn nights with the smell of rotting apples in the air. She was pushing the limits and her unhappiness showed. The hermetic atmosphere, the frequent cold and snow, the competitive artistic striving, the social hierarchies (those with or without financial aid, and those, like Lethem, who had to work to pay for their classes), the easy availability of chemical stimulants—they all combined to make Quintana a desperate creature during her first year away from home. She lived in one of the newer suites of dorms. In her whitewashed room she hung various hats on the walls and kimonos next to colorful lacy blouses. One fellow resident swore she displayed a collection of whips, but she may have mistaken Quintana's exotic belts for more outré objects. Quintana had turned her standard-issue college desk into a cosmetics counter—eyeliners, flaming fingernail polish, compacts—and its drawers into a pharmaceutical dispensary, everything from Anacin to Demerol.

"Wet Wednesdays" and "Thirsty Thursdays" at the local bars lured her out of her room, and visits to the Laundromat or fast-food joints at one A.M.; film screenings at Tishman Hall (where, Lethem wrote, the campus sophisticates hooted at the likes of John Wayne), or a house party where everyone tanked up on grain-alcohol punch under the limbs of the yew trees and tried to rhyme like rappers while dancing to Talking Heads or Siouxsie and the Banshees. Quintana was gritty, showy, and tough; she talked fast and loud, and her voice, when she chattered about the boys she was dating or wanted to date (she shared her father's fondness for the word *fuck*), or when she recounted volcanic nausea after a day of drinking or getting high, could rise to the level of a shriek.

The students at Bennington who didn't like Quintana, or those who didn't really know her, could cite her loudness, her hectoring tone, her theatrical and melodramatic public presence (all that California *enthusiasm,* so different from Eastern reserve) as character flaws; those closer to her saw how instantly empathetic she became when a friend of hers experienced grief or family sorrows. She was compassionate, pragmatic, and wholly present in such moments, offering genuine sympathy and plenty of drink and drugs to ease the pain.

4

With renewed physical vigor, Dunne made arrangements to put the Brentwood house on the market. It sold immediately. If it hadn't, Didion said later, they probably would have changed their minds about moving.

By this time, Didion was well acquainted with her daughter's frailties and propensities, and she suspected Quintana was struggling, living on her own in the East, trying to establish an identity and a direction. Didion knew "it was upsetting to her" at Bennington when she "found that one or both of her parents had names that were known to her teachers." In an interview with radio host Don Swaim during this period, Didion said, "I have a child in college now . . . I think being in college is the hardest time for children. It's really scary." Yet the notion of settling nearer a troubled child never arose in Didion's conversations about reasons to move.

"I have a highly developed capacity for denial," she'd say years later.

Ron and Carol Herman, who bought the house from the Dunnes, found the property slightly run-down. "The 'bones' of the house were good but we needed to change the floor plan to fill the needs of our growing family," Carol Herman told me. Didion had loved this house; if she had fantasized it would still be hers, in some magical way, even though she'd agreed to leave it, the

Hermans' plans destroyed that illusion. Ron Herman said he imagined his daughter getting married in the backyard garden someday.

There was now no available switchback for Didion.

(In *Blue Nights,* she complained that the "man who was buying the house" had insisted they kill the termites by "tenting it and pumping in Vikane and chloropicirin," wiping out the mint and the pink magnolia and the stephanotis in the garden. She said she could smell Vikane weeks later in New York as she opened boxes.)

Meanwhile, the Dunnes had decided their pied-à-terre on West Fifty-eighth Street was too small to accommodate them full-time. Whenever they arrived, they'd "have to arrange to get the windows washed and get food in," Didion said, so now they packed up the furniture, the Rauschenberg and Richard Serra prints. Natasha Richardson, fresh from playing Patty Hearst in Paul Schrader's film, bought the place from them. They located an available co-op apartment on the fifth floor of an eleven-story 1920s-era building at 30 East 71st, on the corner of Madison, across the street from St. James's Episcopal Church. It was steps away from Central Park.

The apartment needed painting; it also needed some new flooring and more stylish lighting fixtures. The Dunnes wanted built-in bookcases. "Oh no," friends told them. "You don't know New York contractors. They'll lie about their bids. They'll lie about the amount of time the job will take." These people made Manhattan sound like a vast criminal enterprise. In time, Didion would agree with them, but initially the warnings had no effect. The Dunnes wanted the apartment. "There weren't too many ways I was going to do it if it wasn't *right,*" Didion said.

In Brentwood, they rented an industrial-size Dumpster and planted it in their driveway. Twenty-four years, 26,000 pounds of *stuff,* about 18,000 pounds of which would have to go. There were old tax returns, newspaper clippings, college yearbooks, high school literary magazines, clothes, and shoes, shoes, shoes. They also unearthed an invitation from Princeton, asking Dunne to return and deliver a public lecture as a distinguished alumnus; reviews of his books, her books, accusing them, each in their turn, of being entrepreneurs of angst; a letter to Dunne from a fellow screenwriter: "[Y]ou took all those years to write what—that it's all shit? For Christ sake, don't you think we know that?"

Some of their old friends chided them for leaving. Dunne's cousin Jon

Carroll called from San Francisco to say, "I hope you're not going to move back east and then tell the world how terrible California is, a perfect place . . . if you're an orange."

"When they left, Joan gave her housekeeper the Volvo," Josh Greenfeld said. "She was a very compassionate person, Joan—always good to her Latino help." He and his wife, Foumi, spent a final evening reminiscing with the Dunnes. "I knew how much I'd miss John. A lot of people counted on him here. He was always the first guy to call if you had car trouble. He'd do anything for you. And Joan—she was the best person to compare writing stories with. I remember one day she said to me, 'What are you writing?' I said, 'College entrance essays for my kid.' 'Me, too!' she said. 'It's the hardest writing I've ever done!' With Joan, everything was an exaggeration—oh, I was going to miss that, too. The *drama* she created. What an entertainment! If they had a small leak in the roof, she'd say, 'I had to set out buckets and buckets!'"

There was no exaggerating the domestic mess crushing them now. When the Vikane sprayers came, the Dunnes moved into the Bel-Air Sands Motel, beside the San Diego Freeway, to make their final arrangements. Dunne would fly to New York and open up the new apartment. Didion would spend some time with her parents first. Frank and Eduene had moved to Carmel. (Sacramento had gotten too big, Eduene complained. Too much traffic. Fast food everywhere.)

Early one morning, before taking their separate flights, Didion and Dunne stopped by the empty Chadbourne house one last time. Silently, like ghosts of their former selves, they moved through the hallways, opening each door, running their hands through the cupboards, peering into every closet. They remembered the endless flat horizons at Malibu; the wisteria perfume pervading the vast back patio on Franklin Boulevard; the sea caves at Portuguese Bend and Dunne's shouted advice to his wife to ride the waves, just go with the change. They knew they'd visit Los Angeles many times, but they also understood it was unlikely they'd ever again live in California.

They circled the kitchen, stepped out into the garden. Like figures in a Hockney painting, they stood at the lip of the pool, staring into the shifting patterns of a strange other world. "You ready?" Dunne asked.

"Yes," Didion said. She placed her head on his shoulder, and they wept.

Somehow, in scoping out the new place, she'd missed the fact that the morning sunlight didn't go all the way through the apartment. But she was pleased with the shade of the new wall paint she'd chosen—a combination of pale green and yellow, an "underwater color," she said, "very restful." It contrasted nicely with the white wooden trim and the white high-beamed ceilings.

All day, on moving day, the van clogged traffic on the street out front. "I just tried to ignore [the honking horns]," Didion said. "I tried to think, now what kind of people would do such a thing, not that we were the instigators."

The first thing she did was unpack her hurricane lamps. "All ready in case of a storm," she joked with her husband. She spread seashells on her fireplace mantel, hovered over the glass-topped coffee table, imagining it adorned with purple orchids. She placed the wicker-backed chair first here, then there. It took four men to haul Dunne's mother's old couch up the service stairwell. Didion arranged various pairs of sunglasses across a large pewter platter—what to do with them all? Framed pictures, posters, photos—if she didn't have a flat horizon to stare at on the wall, she knew she'd get really anxious.

St. James's bells reverberated through the open windows, sonorous and comforting. Reflections of the evening sun lifted off the tip of its spire like light from a star.

She set to work fixing up a bedroom for Quintana, who had asked if she could still be a "Californian." Dunne said Quintana was too old now—she'd never again live at home.

Didion paused and said a girl couldn't *not* keep a room in her mother's house, even if she didn't sleep in it.

In the mornings, they walked through Central Park, sometimes in tandem with their dog, Casey (a "pain in the ass," Dunne said), sometimes separately while the other was writing. In the evenings, they had their two drinks before dinner, then went to Elio's at Second and Eighty-fourth, where the waiters reserved a special table for them, brought Dunne a Scotch, Didion a bourbon, and an extra bucket of ice for both. They talked about what a good move this had been—in the past, on separate assignments, they'd not spent enough time together. Now, centrally located in New York, they could do more joint reporting. The movie business had gotten too bloated—so much cash, so much risk. It took a lifetime to get a picture made these days. Best to step away for a while. Besides: no brush fires here, no snakes in a pool.

After the vitello Milanese, they'd stroll up Madison, past some of the most expensive real estate on the planet, and the best shopping in the world:

Tiffany, Prada, Ralph Lauren. Still, Didion could spot the aftershocks of the 1987 stock market crash. At Seventy-second Street, a building sat empty; eventually, Ralph Lauren would occupy that space as well, but for now, it was padlocked and dark. Rats scurried through it. Homeless men spread sleeping bags up and down the block.

Even in *this* neighborhood, Didion felt the "city's rage at being broke and being in another recession and not having a general comfort level." This awareness slowly opened her to the "stories the city [told] itself to rationalize its class contradictions" and its byzantine economic networks, "the distortion and flattening of character," reducing events to simple narratives: "Lady Liberty, huddled masses, ticker-tape parades, heroes, gutters, bright lights, broken hearts, eight million stories in the naked city." All of this, she figured— watching, reading, piecing it together—disguised the fact that New York did not exactly operate on a "market economy but on little deals, payoffs, accommodations, *baksheesh*, arrangements that circumvent the direct exchange of goods and services." Hence, the self-congratulatory boast, "If you can make it here, you can make it anywhere." 'Cause ain't no one gettin' a fair shake on *this* corner, sister.

At street level, on the docks and in the warehouses, small-potatoes jefes hustled to protect what turf they could. The jewelry. The fish. The garments. You got garbage? Want it gone? Let's powwow.

Didion's *oh-no*-ing friends had it right. Manhattan *was* a vast criminal enterprise, wrapped in an ink-colored cloak of sentimental stories. *Small Town Girl Chases Lifelong Dream in the Heart of the Big Apple. The Lights of Broadway!*

Meanwhile, and don't forget it, pal, all the produce lands in *my* pockets, got it?

How different the city looked to her now from the way it had when she'd last lived here, nearly a quarter of a century ago—then it was a dazzling procession of headlights reflecting off wet gray pavement, bare branches at dawn waving gently over the benches in Washington Square Park, billowing yellow curtains blowing through open windows, twining the rusty railings of the fire escapes.

How different from the City of Angels—there, it wasn't the media's job to mask existing crime, but to create the foundational narratives institutionalizing graft. Harrison Gray Otis wanted water in L.A., so the *Los Angeles Times* presented the Owens River swindle as manifest destiny. Anyone who opposed it was an "enemy of the city." In New York, narratives were damage control. In Los Angeles, they were opportunistic slogans, the war cries of unchecked capital formation.

The criminalization of sentiment: the basis of all American politics.

This wasn't just an abstraction to Didion. In time, and for about ten years, she served as the president of her co-op board. She wrestled with the fine print of leases, of hiring and replacing supers, of contractual bids for repairing water damage in the elevator shafts. She was sued by a neighbor who felt she did not do enough, as board president, to settle a dispute between the neighbor and supermodel Cindy Crawford, who lived in the apartment upstairs, and who, the neighbor contended, made ungodly amounts of noise, subjecting her to "telephones ringing, closet doors opening and closing, toilets flushing and baths running"—all the "intimate sounds of daily life."

But these were examples of the big and obvious politics of binding arbitration, sad human nature.

From her service on the board, Didion understood the more nefarious consequences of fantasy politics when they expanded, more generally, into the nation's complex business. When "social and economic phenomena" got "personalized," they came to seem intractable, impervious to legislative solutions. They were *our* problems, *our* fault. Poverty, racism, infanticide? Mea culpa. Moreover, these character failings kept us blaming *one another* rather than officials.

Meanwhile, the political process—stumping, campaigns and balloons—was packaged as purely "electoral": the coronation of leaders "who could in turn inspire the individual citizen to 'participate,' or 'make a difference.' 'Will you help?'" Votes and money were what our leaders had in mind—not direct involvement: God knows you've got your *own* problems to work out; leave it to *me* to speak for the American people.

5

One Sunday morning in February 1989, Dunne pulled on a pair of black sweatpants—*Princeton* stitched across the left side—laced up his tennis shoes, and set off for a morning walk across the park. Traffic was light; he headed up Cedar Hill adjacent to the Met. His knees stiffened. His breath came hard. Sweat stung his eyes. He stopped and bent double, gasping. Joggers raced past him.

The next thing he was aware of, inches from his face, was the asphalt road.

Chapter Twenty-nine

———— ❖ ————

1

In *Harp,* Dunne reported that as soon as he came to himself with the help of a Good Samaritan offering to call a cab to take him to the emergency room, he decided not to tell his wife he had passed out. He thanked the good man for his concern. He was fine now. He sat on a bench and focused on the back wall of the museum until his breathing returned to normal. Didion had made dinner plans for that night. It would be a shame to cancel . . . no need to worry anyone.

He got up to walk home and spied his wife with Casey on a leash. Right away, he softened and told her everything: "[W]e had not stayed married for twenty-five years by keeping secrets, however unpleasant, from one another." In crisis times, he tended to fold, while she turned fierce.

The following day, a cardiologist informed him he had symptoms of aortic stenosis. Open-heart surgery would probably be necessary to replace the aortic valve—and while they were in there, they would do a bypass to finesse the job of the angioplasty.

The surgery was scheduled. At the last minute, it was scrubbed: An angiogram showed no aortic stenosis after all. Perhaps, doctors said, it was just a vasovagal response.

"I was quite desolate for about a year" in New York, Didion said. Worries about her husband's health, his undiminished restlessness; worries about her daughter, who had transferred in a haze of unhappiness to Barnard, where at least she had found a more welcoming community; worries about lost knickknacks or books (several boxes remained to be unpacked)—it all hampered her writing.

Not that she didn't have plenty of work. Almost as soon as they'd moved, she agreed to do "Letter from Los Angeles" pieces for Robert Gottlieb at *The New Yorker*, and she'd flown to California several times. Bob Silvers wondered if she might like to cover domestic political campaigns for *The New York Review of Books*. The idea would never have occurred to her. "Bob kept pushing me in that direction," she said. It was his "trust. Nothing else. . . . He recognized it was a learning experience for me. Domestic politics . . . was something I simply knew nothing about. And I had no interest . . . [but he] is really good at ascertaining what might interest you at any given moment and then throwing a bunch of stuff at you that might or might not be related, and letting you go with it."

Silvers arranged press credentials for her and so, one summer day in 1988, she arrived at the Butler Aviation terminal at Newark airport and awaited the contact from the Jesse Jackson campaign she'd been instructed to meet. The contact didn't show. Apparently, the woman was already in California, preparing her candidate for the primary. Didion was sent to Hangar 14 and then to Post J, an unmarked gate to the tarmac. At Post J, Secret Service agents kept asking members of the Jackson campaign, "Who's she? She hasn't been cleared . . . what's she doing here?" "All I know is, she's got the right names in Chicago," said a campaign staffer, checking her papers. Her bags were swept for weapons. She was allowed to get on the plane. For a while, she sat alone in the cabin. The pilot poked his head out the cockpit door. "Give me a guesstimate how many people are flying," he said to her, as if she should know. "None of this seemed promising," Didion remarked in a journal she was keeping.

At LAX, she got on a bus for a Jackson rally in South Central. The afternoon sunlight was gorgeous. The freeway looked stunning. "I was just in tears the whole way," Didion said. "I couldn't even deal with the rally because it was so beautiful. Los Angeles was so beautiful, and I had given it up. It took me a while to get sorted out," which she needed to do in order to concentrate on the campaign.

She told her husband all this on the phone. Since she was going to be away, he had decided to fly to Ireland to investigate his family heritage for *Harp*, the memoir he was trying to figure out how to write. *Was* it a memoir? Or fiction? Or a reporter's notebook? He wasn't sure, a symptom of his restlessness. He'd forgotten how much he hated traveling alone. The *idea* of it appealed to him, but the reality was something else. Didion mentioned a speechwriter she had met at the rally. "He's a fucking snake," Dunne warned her. *All* speechwriters were snakes. She knew this. Their mutual wariness—their protection against being surprised—was a bond they missed whenever they were apart. She mentioned an actress of their acquaintance, a "political groupie" who'd been tagging along on the campaign bus. "She still has that insane glitter in her eye," Didion said. "It comes from trying to remember who she hasn't fucked," Dunne quipped.

About this snake—Didion wondered how to *get him right* in her notes. "An artful presentation of a coherent untruth," she said. *That's* the speechwriter's job. "Not bad," Dunne told her. "How's it going?" she asked him. "What the fuck am I doing here?" he said.

Alone in the Irish town of Roscommon, he felt dull, noticing nothing. If only his wife were here! He got drunk by himself in the bars. He tried to revive his old snooping habits. Randomly, he dropped in on a stranger's funeral Mass, just to see what was up. "Pat Curtin's ma," a priest told him. "I see." "The whole town was pulling for her to make a hundred years young." "Of course." "Tough as an old boot, she was. And just as mean, if truth be told."

What the fuck am I—?

If Didion was slightly more focused and vigilant—once she'd recovered from her homesickness—it was because she had a specific assignment, though the story was depressing. Listening, observing, she came to think of her fellow reporters as part of a "small but highly visible group of people who, day by day and through administration after administration, relay Washington to the world, tell its story, agree among themselves upon and then disseminate its narrative."

She wrote, "They report the stories. They write the op-ed pieces. They appear on the talk shows. They consult, they advise, they swap jobs, they travel with unmarked passports between the public and the private, the West Wing and the green room. They make up the nation's permanent professional political class." They also moved through restricted landscapes, speaking obscure languages the rest of the country couldn't even begin to access.

While her mother ordered room service at the Hyatt Wilshire and her father sat in a Roscommon pub, Quintana flew to Guatemala and Nicaragua. Between her classes at Barnard, she had worked as a freelancer in the photo department at *Newsweek*. An editor there arranged for her to travel with the photographer Bill Gentile and other journalists covering Nicaragua's civil war and America's involvement in it. When she returned, she published pictures and an account of her experiences in the *Columbia Spectator*.

She arrived first in Antigua, for a crash course in Spanish. While there, she stayed with a host family. "I don't know how good an idea it really is," she wrote. "I can't stand living with a family . . . I don't know if it's this particular family or the whole idea of it. There's something about going into people's family in general. No matter what, it's always an invasion. You always feel like an imposition and an intrusion."

She was "scared out of [her] mind" in the city. She'd never witnessed poverty up close, and her memories of New York now—"bankers and artists walk[ing] the streets with a specific intent, looking toward the next deal or lucky break"—seemed like mirages. She took discreet photographs of women carrying knapsacks of corn or wood, or women cooking and sewing by a fire. She "imagined these beautiful people being wiped out in an ambush."

In Nicaragua, she was wary of eating the red beans, rice, and tough meats sold on the streets. To her fellow travelers, she explained her lack of appetite as a manifestation of dengue fever. "I was afraid and ashamed to tell my secret," she wrote. "[A] little later, out came the Campbell's, bought at the Diplomat Store"—cream of mushroom, cream of asparagus. She hid chocolate in the drawer with her underwear in her hotel room. "Often, I found myself in the bathroom with the wood roaches and whatever else, just munching away on the creamy, delectable substance. I knew that if someone saw me they would either think I was crazy or just a pig."

Her irregular eating and sleeping, her inexperience with the language, and her fear wore her down. "Everybody talks so loud," she wrote at one point. They "scream . . . in Spanish, while you lay [*sic*] there in total nausea not knowing when next you're going to blow chow." The vocabulary may not have been her mother's, but otherwise this was pure Didion. "I'm going out of my mind."

One afternoon, she sat in the bed of a pickup truck with several sweating men, listening to a speech by Daniel Ortega. She was sunburned, exhausted, and hungry. "Tears streamed from beneath my sunglasses," she said.

Also like her mother, she had a keen eye for striking details: the "dark brown feet in sandals" of a woman lying without a casket in an open grave, "the bottoms of the feet appearing much lighter than the rest: the wrinkles, the dirt, and the hardship." In Managua, "everything was orange, yellow, dry, and cold," she said. At a bullfight, when the "bull was lying worn out in the dirt . . . a man lean[ed] down and [bit] the bull's testicles off, screaming in celebration. He then proceeded to eat the testicles."

Her photographs of mothers of the missing and dead in front of a Nicaraguan government office were sensitive and telling. On the women's faces, dignity, tough as tree bark, chipped away around the eyes, revealing a soft skin of pain underneath.

Near the end of her stay, she spoke to a boy named Danilo, the son of the woman who "developed and supervised the manufacture of all the uniforms for the Sandinista army." He had been injured in battle, and still carried shrapnel in his brain. He sat and stared at the sky all day, smoking cigarettes. He told Quintana he could remember pleasant, peaceful years with his family—he "knew there was a time when he was healthy," but that time belonged to a lost domain. He said, "Everything is different now, and I don't know why."

Back in New York, she'd gone to work for Sipa USA, the U.S. bureau for Paris-based Sipa Press, a photo agency founded by a Turkish journalist in 1973. The agency distributed thousands of photographs per day to publications and media outlets in dozens of countries. In 1987 it opened its U.S. branch on Seventh Avenue in Manhattan. It specialized in editorial news and entertainment content. Quintana was a talented, energetic photographer with field experience, and she had access to people in the entertainment business. While at Barnard, she had served as the photo editor for the *Spectator*, and this made her attractive to Sipa, as well. It had been unusual for a transfer student to enjoy such swift acceptance on the *Spectator* staff (though some of Quintana's classmates thought having famous writer parents didn't hurt); she did solid work. Overall, she was happier at Barnard than she had been at Bennington. During the day, she settled into productive routines, academically and professionally, but she remained intense—*too* intense for many of her acquaintances—and excessive in her partygoing.

She lived in an apartment on 116th Street but rarely stayed home in the evenings. She'd been coming to New York since she was a child: The city was *hers*. Sometimes she'd rent a limo with friends and drive around Manhattan all night, hoisting cocktails in the backseat. She could outdrink most of her peers, female and male, and she was impatient with people who couldn't keep up with her. For a while, she'd heap attention on someone and then drop them without warning.

MTV was just getting started in those days, shooting segments in New York studios. Quintana, who'd been hanging around rock stars since she was a kid, felt right at home with the hip young crowd.

Funny, pretty, and charismatic, she possessed her father's volubility and gregariousness, and her mother's bladelike wit, with no stammering shyness to keep it in check. She was deeply loyal to her family and quick to hold a grudge if she felt any of them had been slighted. All her life, she'd been exposed to heavy drinking and lavish parties, but whether these examples drove her to self-destructive behavior, whether she was truly trying to counter suicidal impulses (*Let me just be in the ground*) or whether she had inherited a tendency toward alcoholism from her birth family were questions Didion never could answer.

At Christmas 1989, once her mother had returned from her California sojourns and her father had finished with Ireland, Quintana joined her parents for a family trip to Barbados. In *Blue Nights*, Didion reported that her daughter "had gone immediately to bed" when they arrived, perhaps a way of saying she'd been drinking on the plane. Throughout *Blue Nights*, Didion remains adamantly indirect, yet nuanced, about Quintana. Didion sat up outside their rented house, listening to a radio, she says; she learned the United States had just invaded Panama. Early the next morning, she woke Quintana to tell her the news—Barbados might be threatened—and Quintana covered her head with the sheet. She didn't care. She said she knew "exactly yesterday" that the United States was going to invade. All the Sipa photographers had been stopping by the office to pick up their press credentials for the Panama story. Quintana burrowed deep into her bed. "I did not ask her why she had not thought the invasion of Panama worth a mention on the five-hour fight down," Didion wrote.

Later Quintana snapped a photo of the ocean and gave the picture to her parents, with an inscription on the back: *"For Mom and Dad. Try to imagine the seductive sea if you can, love XX, Q."*

2

All the travel, the family worries, and the chaos of resettling kept Didion off her feed for several months. She felt she just wasn't *getting* New York this time around.

She'd identified its self-congratulatory sentimentality, but how to talk about it? What to say? Then an incident occurred to sharpen her thinking.

On April 19, 1989, between 8:30 and 9:30 P.M., Trisha Meili, a twenty-eight-year-old white employee of the Wall Street investment bank Salomon

Brothers, went for her regular evening jog through Central Park. She was discovered four hours later, stripped of her clothing, beaten so badly that her left eye had dislodged from its socket. She had lost 75 percent of her blood, she was suffering from severe hypothermia, and, Didion wrote, "the characteristic surface wrinkles of her brain" were "flattened." Dirt and twigs "found in her vagina" suggested rape.

In 1989, 3,254 rapes were reported in New York City, but *this* was the one singled out by Governor Mario Cuomo as "the ultimate shriek of alarm."

This was the one with all the requisite elements to fulfill New York's sentimental self-portrait.

"Teen Wolfpack Beats and Rapes Wall Street Exec on Jogging Path," read one headline.

"One [assailant] shouted 'hit the beat' and they all started rapping to 'Wild Thing.'"

"[C]rimes are universally understood to be news to the extent that they offer, however erroneously, a story, a lesson, a high concept," Didion wrote. The lesson here was that the city's recent economic downturn had nothing to do with the stock market or financial regulation or globalization, but with teen "wolves" (read: nonwhites) infiltrating "our" (read: whites) Edenic park, ruining everything, spreading crime and garbage, and attacking our dynamic young leaders (the victim was "probably one of the top four or five students of the decade"; "fun-loving," though only "when time permitted"). Furthermore, she was a "Bacharach bride," Didion said: hardworking, middle-class, and ethical—that is, virginal (metaphorically speaking) in contrast to the dark beasts who went after her on the path that night.

Most of the establishment press refused to announce her name, in order to "protect" her (a "magical" assumption, Didion wrote), while the names of the five boys arrested—one Latino, four African-American—remained on full and constant display, despite the fact that all were minors and they had not yet been arraigned. The journalistic convention of not naming a rape victim, as though rape were a violation of a "nature best kept secret," Didion saw as further sentimentality—a refusal to acknowledge what had really happened, how *often* it happened in American culture and *why*, or to discuss the matter seriously.

DNA and other physical evidence indicated that none of the five boys was guilty of the rape. There was "no matching semen, no matching fingernail scrapings, no matching blood." The boys claimed the cops had coerced them into confessing (denying them, in some instances, the presence of their parents or of lawyers)—and, in fact, as the office of the New York district attorney admitted, in retrospect, "The accounts given by the five defendants differed from one another on the specific details on virtually every major aspect of the crime . . . [and] some of what they said was simply contrary to established fact." Nevertheless, all five were convicted and served significant jail time. Putting them away was an important step in "taking back" the city, in the city's self-fulfilling narrative.

Meanwhile, Meili, given scant odds of surviving, began to recover. The *New York Post* called her "Lady Courage." The New York *Daily News* and *New York Newsday* made her "A Profile in Courage." *The New York Times* said she was a symbol of "New York rising above the dirt."

Didion bucked the mainstream trend in questioning the fairness of the criminal justice system and in wondering, in print, if the boys were really guilty. In part, she developed her contrariness by turning a disadvantage into a plus. She couldn't get a police pass into the courtroom, so she analyzed the trial *coverage,* the language of the headlines, the strategies of the legal teams *planting* rumors through the very act of denying them. She explained her methods later: "You're going to get it right if you tell yourself a story about it. If you go below the surface, you get it wrong. If you get the surface right, it will tell you the rest." Once again, she learned it was the edges of a piece where she belonged.

In this case, the edges led her to *The City Sun* and the *Amsterdam News,* papers distributed in African-American neighborhoods. These outlets regularly named the victim, described the assault and its aftermath in detail, and openly questioned what they perceived to be a rush to judgment. As she had done in the 1960s, trolling the underground press for news she'd otherwise miss, Didion turned to alternative sources for narratives countering the dominant sentiment. For example, she heard a statement by the Reverend Calvin O. Butts of Harlem's Abyssinian Baptist Church: "What you do in the United States of America when a white woman is raped is round up a bunch of black youths, and I think that's what happened here." Of course, this was a familiar narrative, too, steeped in its own sentimentality, but like a tributary to a much larger river, it needed to be marked on the map.

Didion published "Sentimental Journeys," her account of the Central Park Jogger case, in the January 17, 1991, issue of *The New York Review of Books* (it was one of the first pieces she composed on a computer, which made its through line more "logical," she said). The essay gave the lie to former *Wall Street Journal* reporter David Blum's judgment of the *Review* a few years before. Writing in *New York,* Blum claimed the *Review* had lost its urgency after the turbulent 1960s, that it had "grown steadily less inflammatory and controversial." Didion's piece condemned not only the courts but also the press and the unquestioned cultural assumptions structuring the stories most Americans told themselves.

In 2002 the New York State Supreme Court would vacate the convictions of the so-called Central Park Five when DNA evidence, revisited, and an accurate confession by a serial rapist named Matias Reyes proved the five men innocent.

Getting the city right. Money and fashion, New York's hemoglobin—*that* she'd discovered long ago as a *Vogue* girl, and she didn't mind a little transfusion now and then. On September 22, 1991, *Businessweek* announced that the Gap clothing line had increased its recent monthly sales by 21 percent—it now owned 2 percent of the nation's one-hundred-billion-dollar-a-year apparel market—by conducting a "savvy ad campaign featuring such celebrities as Spike Lee and Joan Didion." These celebrities had helped the Gap turn "plain clothing such as jeans and T-shirts into fashion statements." In one ad, Didion posed with Quintana for photographer Annie Leibovitz. Mother and daughter both wore black turtleneck sweaters; Didion nestled her left cheek against her daughter's temple and stared wistfully into the lens, as if this moment meant everything to her and she'd never let this little girl go.

The Gap wasn't the only company seeking her endorsement. Gulf & Western, owner of Simon & Schuster, asked her one year to make a "contribution" to its annual shareholders' report, to be distributed to 55,000 shareholders as well as to the "financial community, bankers, press contacts, [and] public relations sources." Didion wrote a puff piece, professing a faith she didn't possess: "Some years back it became a kind of tic to assume that we trembled on the threshold of a world in which the written word would vanish, in which the occasional book might survive, an example of craft from the past . . . What we are seeing in fact is one aspect of a great social revolution in the United States, in which people in even the most unlikely social and economic circumstances have come to treat books not as exotic objects of reverence on someone else's shelf but as the essential tools and pastimes of daily life." The director of S&S's Corporate Communications "anticipate[d] a terrifically positive response" to her words; not only would the piece provide "useful promotion" for her books, but Gulf & Western had just been crowned a guardian of literature and civilization.

In reality, Didion felt S&S didn't give a damn about literature, authors, or books qua books; Dick Snyder was pushing a product for profit, and he wasn't doing a particularly good job of it in her case. When Henry Robbins left, the last friend of letters had passed. Furthermore, reading skills were eroding and bookstores were running just ahead of the wrecking ball: After twenty-one years, the venerable Rizzoli, with its beautiful handwrought chandeliers, cherrywood paneling, and hand-carved marble doorframe, had been forced out of its Fifth Avenue home by a real-estate developer. Somehow the store had managed to relocate, but still, it wasn't the same, and in general the book business seemed fragile.

Real estate was the business to be in. Didion had always known this; her family had thrived on the knowledge. Recently, she'd formed, with her brother, a limited liability company, JJD Carmel Investments, registered in California and Nevada, to consolidate and protect the family's property holdings and her brother's commercial brokerage operations. James had become one of the leading real-estate executives in the nation. He was the CEO of Coldwell Banker and had purchased the company, along with an investment group, for $300 million. He was also the CEO of CB Commercial and headed up a nonprofit group, Roundtable, frequently briefing the White House and the U.S. Congress on the needs and positions of the nation's real-estate community. As his partner in the LLC and as one of its officers, Didion had gone from fashion writer to sixties icon to Hollywood player to Joan Didion, Incorporated.

Along with Dunne, Elaine May, and novelist Peter Feibleman, she centralized her business activities still further, establishing the DBA Company (Doing Business As), to channel her screenplay work into a more manageable niche. In a book called *Monster: Living Off the Big Screen* (1997), Dunne lists a dizzying number of scripts that he and Didion simultaneously wrote or rewrote, at various stages, in the late 1980s and early 1990s. They sincerely wanted to step away from the greater part of what he termed the "Hollywood ratfuck," but the money was good and they figured if they accepted only rewrites on films already in production, with detailed budgets, definite start dates, and all the elements locked into place, they could avoid risks and wasted time. DBA was designed to keep them out of Hollywood meetings and to set up a fee structure like that of a law firm—"so much to read a script . . . so much per hour (including telephone conferences), so much per day, so much per week, so much for a production draft, so much for a polish, so much for looping dialogue."

The company sputtered. "[A]fter each of us [Didion, May, Feibleman, and Dunne] had exempted those picture-makers with whom we had long-term professional and personal relationships, there were very few people left to share," Dunne said. And it was hard to abandon "back-burner projects" good for quick bursts of cash. The move to New York had been more expensive than they'd anticipated; medical charges had piled up; and as the result of a "venomous" five-month writers' strike in 1988, several contracts they'd counted on had been canceled, including an adaptation of Dunne's novel *Dutch Shea, Jr.*, and a Western about the California water wars.

"[I]t was a class issue," Didion wrote of the strike—"about whether the people who made the biggest money were or were not going to give a little to the people who made the less big money."

"Fuck 'em, they're weaklings," one director said of the Writers Guild in the middle of the strike, and, in fact, the Guild wound up accepting terms it had initially rejected, which kept the picture-making machine more or less at status quo.

"Not until July of 1988, at the Democratic National Convention in Atlanta, did the emotional core of the strike come clear to me," Didion wrote. On assignment for *The New York Review of Books*, she had gone to the Omni, but the credentials Bob Silvers had secured for her did not give her immediate access to the convention floor. She ran into the director Paul Mazursky, who, "like all the other industry people I saw in Atlanta, had a top pass, one of the several all-access passes," she said. Since she was working as a reporter and he only seemed to be schmoozing, she asked if she could borrow his pass for half an hour. He said he'd "really like" to do this for her, but he thought not. "He seemed surprised that I had asked, and uncomfortable that I had breached the natural order of the community as we both knew it," Didion wrote. "[D]irectors and actors and producers, I should have understood, have floor passes. Writers do not, which is why they strike."

As a consequence of the canceled contracts, Didion and Dunne continued to accept whatever screenplay work they could get. Dunne labored away on a script for Lorimar called *Playland*, about the gangster Bugsy Siegel, but then Warner Bros. bought Lorimar and killed most of its outstanding commitments. "We feel this project has a lot of potential," a Warner's vice president told Dunne about the Siegel story, and he knew the script was dead. (Eventually, he'd fold some of the material into his fourth novel.)

The dreaded Hollywood meetings went on, made even worse by the long flights out from New York. One meeting was so disastrous, "full of so many silences we could not decode that we wondered why we had been summoned," Dunne said. After that, he and Didion worked up a signal. If they were sitting in a meeting together and it started to go sour, or if one of them wanted to bail, one would look at the other and say, "White Christmas." This was, of course, the U.S. military's trigger for evacuation during the fall of Saigon, the last song played: "[I]t's time to cut our losses and split."

3

On Christmas Day 1990, the Dunnes flew to Honolulu with Quintana. While running for a cab in the Honolulu airport, Dunne fainted. He was out for only a few seconds, and he managed to convince Didion not to call a doctor unless it happened again.

They had come for a quiet, sunny getaway to work on a rewrite for Disney, a "whammy picture" (a thriller) called *Ultimatum*, whose "concept line" read this way: "When terrorists threaten to set off a nuclear weapon on the eve of a presidential election, a top aide must find it." As President Bush had just given Iraq a deadline of January 15 to pull out of Kuwait or face the consequences, it "did not seem the most fortuitous moment for an Arab terrorist story," Dunne thought, but the script was money in the bank, and after this most recent blackout, he was more convinced than ever they might need it. They asked the Kahala Hilton to place a laser printer in their room, and each day they swam, worked, lunched, swam, and worked some more, and then met Quintana for dinner. Dunne did not faint again. The screenplay they produced read like a "'Saturday Night Live' skit," said one Disney-Touchstone source (one problem the Dunnes faced was trying to "visualize what you see on the screen when you look at a generic terrorist"). After several more rewrites, and a raft of other writers, Disney abandoned the project, having spent around three million dollars on its development.

The day he returned to New York, Dunne saw his cardiologist and described the fainting spell. After an echocardiogram and an angiogram, the doctor determined that Dunne was suffering from a congenital defect of the aortic valve—his father's killer. "You have open-heart surgery [now] or you die," the doctor said bluntly.

A week later, after a five-and-a-half-hour operation, he had a brand-new plastic valve in his heart. In the McKeen Pavilion at Columbia-Presbyterian Hospital, near Saint John the Divine (where, coincidentally, the Dunnes had tucked the nuclear device in their *Ultimatum* scenario), he was wheeled into a recovery room. In the next room, the heiress Sunny von Bülow lay in a coma, watched by private security guards, though she'd been in this comatose state for nearly ten years. Her husband, Claus, had twice been accused of attempting to murder her. Dunne's brother Nick had written about the von Bulöws for *Vanity Fair* ("The children talked, the servants talked, mistresses talked, duchesses talked")—it was one of the celebrity crime tales on which he'd made his name since Dominique's killing. Now Nick's brother considered the guards, and the heiress's private nurses, with increasing irritation.

Each day, nurses wheeled him into the McKeen atrium for high tea while a pianist played "Send in the Clowns."

His new plastic valve made an audible *click.*

Quintana called him the "Tin Man."

Chapter Thirty

1

"Hi, this is Bill Clinton. Is Governor Brown there?"

Most days, Dunne replied that the governor had just stepped out. It was July 1992, the eve of the Democratic National Convention, and the candidates were not playing nice. Brown refused to endorse the Clinton-Gore ticket, and he was running around New York calling Clinton a "bobbing, weaving target that has no moral compass." Didion had noted Clinton's "reservoir of self-pity, the quickness to blame, the narrowing of the eyes, as in a wildlife documentary, when things did not go his way." She said this was a response "so reliable that the aides on Jerry Brown's . . . campaign looked for situations in which it could be provoked." Clinton's people wanted to muzzle Brown, rein him in before the convention—they called this "unifying the party." They refused to give the former California governor a prime speaking slot at the big balloon-dropping extravaganza.

Throughout the primaries, the Dunnes had offered Brown a room in their apartment as a resting spot and base of operations. Neither of them had registered to vote, but they supported Brown's "guerrilla" campaign—his staff of grassroots volunteers, his refusal to accept individual contributions of over one hundred dollars, his calls for congressional term limits and a flat tax. As one reporter said, "He seemed to be the most left-wing and right-wing man in the field," unpredictable in his policies, bipartisan in his condemnation of political corruption, and almost proud of his derisive nickname in the press, "Governor Moonbeam," affixed to him because of rapturous remarks he'd made about the environment, his former Zen practices, Ronald Reagan's ostentatious governor's mansion, and his fascination with new technologies (which were science fiction to the press).

Didion had known Brown ever since she'd gone to Berkeley with his sister Barbara.

Dunne loved the fact that "Jerry rubs people the wrong way. He drives them truly around the bend. They get rabid, and it tickles me."

Few observers gave Brown a chance at the presidential nomination. Besides making people crazy, he faced a primary process designed by the Democratic Leadership Council to position the party more centrally. The DLC had invented Super Tuesday, packing primaries in the Southern states in order to front-load the voting against candidates perceived to be too liberal. The council felt it imperative to shake off the Vietnam-era image of the party—certainly, it wanted no replay of Chicago.

Which is why the Clinton team was tying up the Dunnes' telephones and fax machine, trying desperately to "reason" with Governor Brown.

That he had the Clintons so exercised as late as July was testament to his passion and the passion of his volunteers. In December 1991, the Dunnes had arranged a luncheon for Brown, inviting all the publishers, editors, and writers they could get—Carl Bernstein, Calvin Trillin, Barbara Epstein, editors from *Esquire, Foreign Affairs, The Nation,* and *The Village Voice.* Didion did not consider it a conflict of interest to host a candidate while covering the presidential race for *The New York Review of Books.* Dunne said most of the guests patronized Brown, writing him off in advance. Then he won Maine and Colorado, and beat Clinton in the Connecticut primary. "What did you know?" Dunne's friends began to ask.

"If he gets New York, he gets the nomination," Brown's staffers said.

Right before the New York primary, in April, Brown named Jesse Jackson as his running mate—a mistake, said many of his aides, especially considering the large number of Jewish voters in New York. Jackson had enraged the Jewish community, broad-brushing Manhattan as "Hymietown."

"He's apologized [for that]. He feels terrible," Brown said. He's a "powerful leader who inspires and draws people to vote who've never been involved." He stuck by his choice.

On the day of the primary, he and his supporters watched returns at the Drug, Hospital, and Health Care Employees Union, Local 1199, which had endorsed him. Once the television networks declared Clinton the winner, Didion extended her arms to Governor Brown, who tried to remain upbeat. He squeezed her hands.

Dunne told him that most of the Irish help in their building had supported him. Small consolation.

Later, at a disconsolate reception at the Royalton Hotel, staffers generally agreed: The Jackson deal sank their man. "There's an old saying in the Talmud," said one of Brown's old friends. "A person can acquire the world in one moment, and can lose the world in one moment."

This whole venture has been "an experiment," another man countered. "No one's run a campaign before on a hundred bucks a person. The other candidates have all dropped out and we're still here. That's the bottom line."

By May, Clinton had clinched the party's nomination, and in July, when Brown rode into Penn Station on a train, a rather sparse crowd greeted him. He would not be president, but he was still competing to be heard. Clinton and Gore, he said, must do more than simply claim, "We're change agents, we're a new generation." The Democratic Party platform was "full of gooey and imprecise language."

2

The building's doormen were used to escorting celebrities to apartment 5A. In December 1990, the Dunnes had hosted Natasha Richardson's wedding to producer Robert Fox. Fifty guests attended, including Tasha's mother, Vanessa Redgrave, fresh off the *Concorde* from London after performing the previous night in a production of *Three Sisters*. The actor Rupert Everett heard the couple had had a "blinding fight" two days before and nearly called the whole thing off. But on the eve of the wedding, when Tasha, Quintana, and their girlfriends drank with Everett and Fox at the Wyndham Hotel "before leaving for their hen night," all seemed well again. Still, Tasha's father, Tony, appeared to anticipate disappointment for his daughter. At breakfast before the wedding, he joked that as part of his toast later he would recite from *Romeo and Juliet*: "A gloomy peace this morning with it brings, the sun for sorrow will not show his head." He seemed melancholy, Everett said, "slightly breathless and utterly compelling."

Richardson was also ill. Within a year, he'd be dead of a neurological infection resulting from the AIDS virus.

"I never knew anyone who so loved to make things, or anyone who had such limited interest in what he'd already made. What Tony loved was the sheer act of doing it," Didion said, and she admired him for it immensely. The previous fall, in Spain, he had directed a twenty-one-minute adaptation by Didion and Dunne of Ernest Hemingway's "Hills Like White Elephants" for an HBO film project entitled *Women and Men: Stories of Seduction*. The short starred James Woods and Melanie Griffith as the American and the girl. In the Dunnes' version of the story—unlike Hemingway's—the man is a writer and he asks the woman, explicitly, to get an abortion: "As far as I know I only have one life to live, and by God, I'm going to live it where it interests me. I have no romantic feelings about home or family or any other baggage," he says (in what is plainly Dunne's syntax). It's clear the woman believes she's being asked to sacrifice her child for the sake of literary ambition. She can't stand knowing that the man will turn all of *this* into a story someday. But that's what writers do.

The adaptation of "Hills Like White Elephants" was one of several screenwriting jobs the Dunnes kept their hand in during this period, for infusions of cash and for the purpose of protecting their health insurance.

Dunne's old friend John Foreman brought him a script idea: a picture based on the life of the late television correspondent and anchorwoman Jessica Savitch. One afternoon, Didion met with a Disney producer who'd expressed interest in the project. She came away despondent—not because she was hurting, having recently dropped a heavy tabletop on her leg, shearing off most of her skin from her right knee to her ankle; not because she couldn't get a cab and had to walk fourteen blocks in the snow; but because, this being Disney, the producer wanted to know "what is going to happen in this picture that will make the audience walk out feeling uplifted, good about something and good about themselves."

Savitch had been "a small-town girl with more ambition than brains," said Dunne, "an overactive libido, a sexual ambivalence, a tenuous hold on the truth, a taste for controlled substances . . . [and] a certain mental instability." She died at thirty-six in a freak drowning accident.

It did not seem likely that Disney would make this movie. The days of *Easy Rider* and *Midnight Cowboy* were over.

Didion had other reasons for despondency: Tony Richardson had not looked good to her. She did not want to think about her motivation for tackling further screenplays. And her father, in his mid-eighties, was failing. His sadness had turned largely to silence. Between script rewrites and frequent discussions with Bob Silvers over possible angles in her coverage of the presidential primaries, she spoke often to her mother and brother on the phone. Occasionally, Frank would get on the line. She never knew what he'd talk about—or why. Once, he told her California had gotten too cold ever since the state had built all those dams.

"This calls for a drink," he used to say on almost every occasion, good or bad.

It certainly did.

On top of everything else, Didion remained convinced that Simon & Schuster had never been on the up-and-up when reporting her royalties. And they obviously didn't know how to sell her. Only *Salvador* and *The White Album* had earned back their advances. Some of her books had gone out of print. They weren't available in paperback. Her foreign sales had declined. She was locked into contracts now for a new essay collection and a novel; these contracts bore an extra forty-thousand-dollar burden, in addition to the advances, for the canceled *Fairy Tales* agreement. She felt she was being punished. She wanted to leave S&S.

In January 1991, she had offered to return the money advanced to her and to terminate the outstanding contracts. Her editor, Michael Korda, said a compromise might be possible. Perhaps she could deliver the essays and they could cancel the fiction. But then nothing happened and she believed the company was stalling.

On March 26, 1991, she wrote Dick Snyder a chilly letter suggesting that he did not respect her, that he only wanted to wield power over his authors— and besides, her husband had just had a piece of his heart replaced. She'd endured enough.

Snyder responded with an equally frosty note. He said they'd been friends for many years, so they could be frank with each other. There was no possibility of releasing her from her contracts. He looked forward to publishing her next book. He'd heard John was feeling much better, and that made him happy.

Didion turned her anger on her agent. Wallace, she thought, should have been able to handle this situation. Maybe her husband's agent, Lynn Nesbit, could do a better job. She phoned Wallace to tell her so.

Another Didion drama—Wallace had seen plenty of them. But this one was serious, and she was hurt by it. She had represented Didion for twenty-four years, and brilliantly, and this was her reward.

In the event, the contract for the essay collection proved impervious. Didion gathered pieces she had written for *The New Yorker*, *The New York Review of*

Books, and *New West,* and in the spring of 1992, Simon & Schuster published her third collection, *After Henry.* The title, the introduction in praise of Henry Robbins, and the book's dedication were slaps at S&S. "This book is dedicated to Henry Robbins and to Bret Easton Ellis, each of whom did time with its publisher," she wrote.

The previous fall, S&S had canceled its contract to publish Ellis's novel *American Psycho*—which was on the verge of being shipped to stores—when *Time* and *Spy* magazines revealed the novel's gleefully sadistic contents. Dick Snyder and Martin Davis, the chair of Paramount Communications (Paramount was S&S's new owner), tried to position themselves as moral arbiters; in fact, their last-minute actions made it appear they had no idea what was in this book they were supposed to publish. They had failed to communicate with their editors and were now afraid of the book's reception. The Authors Guild accused Paramount of censorship (Alfred A. Knopf wound up publishing Ellis's novel). Snyder's decision, during the period he was refusing to renegotiate Didion's contracts, further convinced her that she and her publisher "were on different channels and have different ideas about what and how to publish." She told *The New York Times,* "The dedication speaks for itself." "I don't think there's anything in that dedication that Simon and Schuster doesn't already know."

After Henry was a less personal collection than *Slouching Towards Bethlehem* or *The White Album.* Didion's prose style and sensibility remained powerful and distinct, but taken together, the essays proved how thoroughly, in recent years, she had evolved into an accurate analyst of cultural pathologies rather than a mere stunned witness to them. Narrative continued to be her central obsession. She read the wordings of politics, the legal system, and the media as closely as she'd read the paragraphs of Henry James or Joseph Conrad. If there was a weakness to her approach, it lay in her emphasis on public figures' deceptions without fully exploring the social realities these figures addressed. Still, Constance Casey, reviewing the book for the *Los Angeles Times,* was moved to say, "I'd never thought of Joan Didion as dependable before. But after reading these 11 pieces of superior reporting and criticism, I now think of her as a writer who can be relied on to get the story straight." Even *Kirkus,* so often critical of Didion in the past, applauded: "[S]he's truly one of the premier essayists of our time," its reviewer said.

The America profiled in *After Henry* was a country of stupid moments staged by its leaders for public consumption (Michael Dukakis tossing a baseball with staffers on an airport tarmac to prove he was a "regular guy" deserving of the presidency), a media machine in thrall to the celebrity subjects it covered and susceptible to bottom-line thinking poisonous to investigative reporting (the content of the *Los Angeles Times* was now mostly determined by "marketing people," a "deliberate dumb-down" of the paper), and major cities whose citizens were convinced they were being "systematically ruined, violated, raped by [their] underclass."

The common denominator in all areas of American public life was the angry craving in everyone to find, wherever they looked, "an exact representation of their own victimization."

3

The presidential primaries had made one thing clear: The cultural conversation in 1992 was all about the 1960s. "Governor Moonbeam" was cast as a California hippie whose radical ideas couldn't possibly be taken seriously. Bill Clinton exhibited the narcissism of the Free Love generation—and he played rock 'n' roll saxophone, for God's sakes!

More seriously, political figures on the Right, such as Robert Bork and Marvin Olasky (who would become an unofficial adviser to George W. Bush), were presenting, as a given, America's Gomorrah-like fall from God's grace as a consequence of rock music's "subversion of authority" and of 1960s immorality in general, including equal rights for women (a view "not far from that of the Taliban," Didion wrote).

Sixties condemnations came wrapped in religious rhetoric, hopelessly smudging political and spiritual practices. In response to the Republican Party's efforts to tie New Deal liberalism to Sodom, the Democratic Party decided, in the words of one of its strategists, that "the old-time religion just won't work any more," meaning the party had failed to win five of the last six national elections because of its commitments to the working class, immigrants, minority communities, reproductive rights, and income equality. Time for a change. Party leaders must not speak of "entitlement" now, but of "empowerment": Like the Republicans, the Democrats shifted their rhetoric to the right. The result would be new policy approaches—for example, the end of "welfare as we know it."

Clinton's people wanted him to move away from the Democratic Party's "Vietnam base" and position himself as a "Reagan Democrat." Clinton announced, "The choice we offer is not conservative or liberal, in many ways it is not even Republican or Democratic. It is different. It is new. . . . I call it a

New Covenant." (This phrase was considerably better than his earlier try, "The Third Way," which, Didion noted, "sounded infelicitously Peruvian.") The New Covenant was a plan to "reinvent government"—in other words, a management reorganization, in which old bureaucrats would be eliminated at the hands of new bureaucrats brought in explicitly to eliminate the old bureaucrats. Lest anyone be confused as to what this meant for the American people, the Covenant was a "new choice based on old values."

Its implementation (that is, raising enough money from a wealthier donor base than the party had usually attracted) meant reducing political language to coded messages aimed specifically at this shiny new donor type. So, as per guidelines to party officials from Democratic pollsters: "Instead of talking about Democrats lifting someone out of poverty, describe the party's goal as helping average Americans live the good life; [instead] of saying Democrats want to eliminate homelessness and educate the underclass, talk about finding a way for young couples to buy their first home."

Just change the language—as the government in El Salvador had done to cover its bloody tracks.

Meanwhile, rather than pointing out the emptiness of this linguistic shell game, and breaking down the policy ramifications, the media were busy dreaming up dramatic narratives to entrance readers and viewers. The presidential election was a horse race. Who's ahead? Who's falling behind this week?

A "crisis" was more heart-pounding, therefore easier to pitch to an audience, than a complex "structural malfunction," the probing of which would require intelligence and patience by both commentators and listeners (as in the Savings and Loan debacle). A program featuring two relatively uninformed people yelling at each other, purportedly from the Left and the Right, but really from within the financial package offered to them by the television network, was cheaper to produce than a program *about* something, based on committed investigative reporting.

"At Madison Square Garden in New York from July 13, 1992, until the balloons fell on the evening of July 16, four days and nights devoted to heralding the perfected 'centrism' of the Democratic Party, no hint of what had once been that party's nominal constituency was allowed to penetrate prime time, nor was any suggestion of what had once been that party's tacit role, that of assimilating immigration and franchising the economically disenfranchised, or what used to be called 'co-opting' discontent," Didion wrote. "Jesse Jackson and Jimmy Carter got slotted in during the All-Star Game. Jerry Brown spoke of 'the people who fight our wars but never come to our receptions' mainly on C-SPAN."

On December 22, Lois Wallace wrote Didion to say how sorry she was to have heard of Frank Didion's death, after a short stint in a nursing home. The loss of a parent is never easy, she said, even if that parent was old or unwell.

The business between Wallace and Didion was done.

Three months after her father died, Didion flew to California to speak at a University of California's Charter Day ceremony. She picked up her mother in Monterey and drove to Berkeley with her. The plan was to spend a relaxing few days at the Claremont Hotel following Didion's talk.

In *Where I Was From*, Didion writes that her mother seemed confused as they motored up 101. "Are we on the right road?" she asked. Didion assured her they were. "Then where did it all go?" Eduene replied.

"She meant where did Gilroy go, where was the Milias Hotel, where could my father eat short ribs now. She meant where did San Juan Bautista go, why was it no longer so sweetly remote as it had been on the day of my wedding there in 1964," Didion wrote. The "familiar open vista[s] had been relentlessly replaced" by "mile after mile of pastel subdivisions and labyrinthine exits and entrances to freeways that had not previously existed."

California had become "all San Jose," Eduene said.

When they checked into the Claremont, Didion glanced into the bar. She recalled she had last been there in 1955 "with the son of a rancher from Mendocino County . . . I had my roommate's driver's license and a crème de menthe frappe."

On the day of the ceremony, Didion gave her talk. Then the academic procession began. Afterward, her mother told her she had nearly cried "in front of everybody" when she saw a small group of fellows shuffling along behind a banner, "Class of 1931."

"They were all old men," said Eduene.

The Class of 1931 had been Frank Didion's class.

"They were just like your father."

"There was no believable comfort I could offer my mother: she was right," Didion wrote. "They were all old men and it was all San Jose."

Chapter Thirty-one

———— ❧ ————

1

The Dunne brothers' estrangement deepened in the late 1980s and early 1990s as Nick became the voice of *Vanity Fair*. In Los Angeles, his coverage of the trial of Erik Menendez—one of a pair of boys accused of shotgunning their wealthy parents—put him at odds with Menendez's defense attorney, Leslie Abramson. He couldn't abide the fact that she found Erik "adorable" or that she reportedly got $700,000 to try to free a murderer (Nick had already convicted the boy). She, in turn, couldn't stand Nick's prosecution bias—didn't he *know* lying was "endemic" among cops, and that an astonishing number of judges were "remarkably stupid, totally crazy or deplorably lazy"?—nor did she appreciate his condescending descriptions of her in his articles ("Leslie Abramson's curly blond hair bounces, Orphan Annie style, when she walks and talks"). She called his *Vanity Fair* work a series of "venomous little pieces." He was "Judith Krantz in pants."

Her greatest transgression, from Nick's point of view, was her friendship with his brother. Dunne "admired her, and she doted on him," Nick said. A tough-talking character named Leah Kaye in Dunne's *The Red White and Blue*, "a believer in the value of effect," a brilliant, ruthless woman who wears white silk blouses and Italian suede skirts, was clearly based on Abramson (and salt-and-peppered with Didion).

Nick found his brother's admiration for her courtroom work "curious . . . in light of what's happened to a murdered child in our family," he said. "If that's what he thinks is right, that's fine for him. But not for me. It's not right for me to remain friendly with him."

Publicly, Dunne would only acknowledge his relationship with Nick as "complicated."

Griffin Dunne urged his father and uncle to patch things up, but then in 1994, Dunne dedicated his Hollywood novel *Playland* to Abramson, "at the very time she and I were in public conflict," Nick said. "After that my brother and I did not speak for more than six years."

They clashed, as well, over the O. J. Simpson trial. They both covered it, Nick for *Vanity Fair*, Dunne for *The New York Review of Books*. Dunne assumed a snide stance toward the legal proceedings; for Nick, equally enthralled and horrified by the testimony, it was "All O.J., all the time!"

Simpson's alleged butchery of his ex-wife, Nicole Brown, and her friend Ronald Goldman, a waiter at Mezzaluna, "a second-rate Brentwood restaurant" in Dunne's opinion, wrenched open L.A.'s racial divide—just like the Rodney King beating—while TV's blow-by-blow presentation of the trial polarized the rest of the country.

Dunne's coverage of the case tended to linger on the media spectacle. Of the Bronco incident (when Simpson apparently tried to flee from police in a friend's white van), he wrote, "Ninety-five million Americans in two-thirds of the nation's households tuned in on the longest, slowest chase in television history, a chase that no film director would dare stage."

By contrast, Nick relied on innuendo to convict Simpson in his own private court: "On a wet Sunday morning in February, I met with a man I know in West Los Angeles who told me an extraordinary story about a plastic surgeon he is acquainted with in Beverly Hills whose name I cannot reveal. On two occasions during Simpson's glory days as a University of Southern California football star, the plastic surgeon claims, he was hired to repair the faces of two young women Simpson had allegedly beaten up."

When Simpson was acquitted in the criminal trial, Nick assured his readers the *real* punishment would materialize later. At dinner at Le Colonial, Tina Sinatra had told him, "O.J. will never be accepted back into the world he so desperately wants to be a part of. Never. They will never take him back."

2

The brothers' kerfuffle continued to knock about in the press and later escalated in a hail of books. Playwright and novelist Gary Indiana published a novel entitled *Resentment: A Comedy*, a reimagining of the Menendez trials, featuring a character obviously modeled on Nick, Fawbus Kennedy, "a third-rate middlebrow Depends ad." Indiana sketched Kennedy as sexually ambiguous.

He took on Dunne and Didion as well, casting them as Sean Kennedy and Cora Winchell:

> Can you imagine . . . what a family dinner with the three of them must be like, Fawbus Kennedy imploding with rage that he'll never get notices as serious as Sean's notices, and Sean pretending to himself that his last book was just as good as Cora's, and Cora meanwhile thinking that she's the golden canary of American letters, and of course . . . the joke is that all three of them can't get through a paragraph without telling you which famous people they know . . . Fawbus is blatant and vulgar about it and Sean tries to give it a little ironic twist, whereas Cora has perfected the art of making her snobbery and name-dropping read like world-weary deprecation.

This might have been the final dustup—how embarrassing it was that the family rivalry had become a target for parody!—but then Nick published a "novel in the form of a memoir" about the O. J. Simpson trial, *Another City, Not My Own,* a lightly altered fictionalization of his *Vanity Fair* articles. "The litany of show-business and upper-crust names in the book is staggering," wrote Alex Ross; Nick's admission that he's a "terrible name-dropper" was like "O.J. admitting he had his problems with Nicole."

Yet again that might have been the end of it—until the *Los Angeles Times* asked Gary Indiana to review Nick's book. "I am not aware of any animus toward Dunne on the part of Indiana . . . that would get in the way of a judicious and fair review," said Steve Wasserman, the paper's book review editor.

"Wasserman is a fucking liar," Nick said. He accused the editor of setting him up: "As you know, Indiana, whom I have never met, has previously attacked me in the most mocking manner in his book called *Resentment: A Comedy,* a book I understand . . . you greatly admire . . . You set me up to be demolished."

Worse, Nick strongly suspected that Wasserman had been persuaded to tap Indiana by his colleague Tim Rutten, who happened to be Leslie Abramson's husband, a friend of the Dunnes, and the ghostwriter of Simpson's lawyer's account of the trial. It was a plot, and somewhere near its center sat Nick's brother and sister-in-law. He was sure of it. He wasn't keeping quiet. *The New York Observer* got wind of his allegations and remarked, "It seems that [Dominick] Dunne's conversion to the more commercial side of the literary business, and his embrace of the glitzier manifestations of fame, strained his relationship with his brother, Ms. Didion and their intellectual circle."

The year ended with all this terrible animosity.

It began with Lenny's death.

Seven years earlier, she had left Los Angeles to return to her family's ranch, Yerba Buena, in Nogales, Arizona. There she built a house and tucked herself in with round-the-clock nursing to tend to the worsening symptoms of her multiple sclerosis. She had never really recovered from Dominique's death—nor had her younger son, Alex, whom Nick once described as "sensitive and shy and incredibly spiritual." He never seemed to get rooted; for a while, he did social work in San Francisco. In the summer of 1995, while visiting his mother, he disappeared for three days in the scorching desert around the Santa Rita Mountains. Authorities swore he couldn't survive. Lenny called Nick, who was staying in L.A., covering the Simpson trial, and Griffin flew in from New York. In Arizona, Nick spent his time going to McDonald's, buying cheeseburgers for the search crews—horseback, helicopter, and foot patrols, combing an eight-square-mile wilderness. "I thought he was dead," Nick said. "I was thinking, 'Where will we bury him? Will we bury him with Dominique?'" Then Alex reemerged from the canyons as swiftly as he had vanished, whereupon he related a story of hunger and disorientation and remarkable recovery, a "transcendental experience." His tale baffled law enforcement. "It's a little less than plausible," said Capt. Mark Pettit, grousing about the $26,000 bill for the search—passed on to taxpayers. "He's suddenly able to walk out . . . I think that's nothing short of divine intervention."

Whatever happened, wherever Alex had gone, he did not repent and keep his family informed of his whereabouts. A few years later, Nick told a friend, "We've lost Alex in our lives. He has left us. I think the trouble started at the time of the murder. I think [Alex and Dominique] were the closest brother and sister I ever saw. He has just left us . . . I have not heard from Alex."

Worries about her son, coupled with the ongoing grief for her daughter, had sapped Lenny's strength, and in January 1997, at the age of sixty-four, she died. Nick asked that "in lieu of flowers, donations be sent to Justice for Homicide Victims," an advocacy group Lenny had founded. The Dunne clan did not agree on much these days, but they all acknowledged that Lenny had been the one member of the family beyond reproach.

3

In *The Last Thing He Wanted,* a novel published in 1996, Didion included the following exchange between a troubled daughter and her mother:

> *We had a real life and now we don't and just because I'm your daughter I'm supposed to like it and I don't.*
> What exactly did you have in Malibu that you don't have now . . .
> You could open the door in Malibu and be at the beach . . . Or the Jacuzzi. Or the pool . . .

About the time Didion's novel appeared, Quintana checked into the Hazelden rehabilitation center in Minnesota. "She was twenty-nine or thirty," Didion recalled. She had finally admitted her daughter's addiction: "She drank too much. She was an alcoholic. People would call her an alcoholic."

Hazelden, located on five hundred wooded acres north of St. Paul, had been established in 1949 as a male-only facility in a tiny farmhouse. By the time Quintana arrived, a complex of buildings served nearly two thousand addicts, hewing closely to the twelve-step program of Alcoholics Anonymous. "It's like a Big Ten campus though without the frat parties and football," said one former resident. Quintana's room resembled that of a generic hotel, and the starchy food—breaded pork chops and spaghetti—put pounds on her. The rules were strict: no immodest clothing, no talking to members of the opposite sex, no missing daily seminars. The standard treatment lasted twenty-eight days.

Didion told Susanna Moore the hallways reeked of cigarette smoke.

The time was structured around counseling, yoga, meditation, and motivational speeches. Group activities were encouraged.

During this period, while hoping against hope for her daughter's recovery, and while writing and promoting her new novel, Didion drafted, with Dunne, fifteen iterations of the former Jessica Savitch story. Producers had come and gone (Dunne's old friend John Foreman had died of a heart attack); Disney was in play, then wasn't, then was again; and the story had morphed into a more wholesome tale about heroic, ambitious newscasters searching for truth. What's it *really* about? Dunne asked Scott Rudin, one of the new producers on board. "It's about two movie stars," Rudin said. Robert Redford and Michelle Pfeiffer had committed to the project.

Didion and Dunne had stuck with the screenwriting, it seemed, to stay just one step ahead of trouble. Even in the abstract, Didion liked *momentum* and *schedules*, something to distract her, keep her mind Off *What difference does it make?* And always, always, there was the need for medical insurance. Dunne had been bitten on the ankle by an insect in an Off-Broadway theater one night while watching Quintana perform in a drama by a playwright friend of hers; from the bite, he'd contracted bacterial cellulitis, a grave risk to someone with a plastic aortic valve. He spent seven days in the hospital. Then Didion suffered a detached retina and underwent laser surgery.

So when Quintana emerged from Hazelden, she wasn't the only one in the family courting rebirth. For her, it was like learning to walk again. Susanna Moore invited her to a party one night honoring a young novelist. Quintana accepted the invitation but did not show up. Later, she wrote Moore a note. She apologized for being a jerk. Booze had always been her public screen; it was difficult to get through an affair without a drink. It wouldn't always be this way—someday she'd go out again with confidence. But for now, she was keeping her social life quiet.

One night, out to dinner in Santa Monica with Leslie Abramson and her husband, the Dunnes ran into Disney's Michael Eisner. They talked about the Dunnes' rewrites of the Jessica Savitch story and about how the movie was finally under way. Recently, Eisner had survived a heart bypass. Dunne mentioned he'd had the same procedure. Eisner replied, "Of course, mine was more serious." Stunned into silence by what was, after all, a fairly typical example of crass Hollywood boasting, Dunne heard his wife "exclaim in outrage, '*It was not!*'"

Up Close & Personal, starring Robert Redford and Michelle Pfeiffer, was released in March 1996. Viewers could be forgiven for thinking they were rewatching *A Star Is Born:* Once more (this time under pressure from Disney), Didion and Dunne had told the story of a jaded, self-destructive professional meeting a tragic end while his beautiful female companion rose to glory.

Reviewer Michael Medved seems to have seen a different movie. The film, he said, presents an "uncritical endorsement of . . . advocacy journalism . . . in which a reporter injects his own opinions into a story and takes off to humiliate or destroy some powerful public figure."

If one didn't know better, it sounded as though Dunne had made a picture in praise of his brother.

Chapter Thirty-two

———— ✣ ————

1

"Some real things have happened lately." So begins *The Last Thing He Wanted*, Didion's fifth novel.

The opening sentence evokes artificiality as well as reality: The "real things" are anomalies. This is language cancerous with its own negation. It is the language of contemporary American democracy, employed to muddle operations on the ground.

At present, our society is experiencing something "interestingly described on page 1513 of the *Merck Manual* (Fifteenth Edition) as a sustained reactive depression, a bereavement reaction to the leaving of familiar environments," Didion says.

In a secretive, strange, jargon-laden environment, riddled with competing texts, each with its own vocabulary and agendas, its own obscurities and selective details, the writer finds herself in a prickly situation: Words, the tools of her trade, are worn and compromised by the abusive public uses to which they're turned; as a result, her position as storyteller, witness, and sage has become utterly suspect. "You know me, or think you do. The not quite omniscient author," Didion says. She has abandoned her plans to adopt a fictional persona. "I wanted to come at this straight. I wanted to bring my own baggage and unpack it in front of you." Echoing her essay "The White Album" nearly thirty years earlier, she attempts to fix authority through weakness, confessing her limitations. And she wishes to eliminate all extraneous fictions.

Every assertion, she qualifies. Sometimes this rhetorical movement reveals her uncertainty: "History's rough draft. We used to say. When we still believed that history merited a second look."

Though blithely denying it, she is, of course, intensely engaged in taking second looks. Her uncertainty becomes a management strategy.

At other points, her qualifications puncture official pretenses: "You may recall the rhetoric of the time in question. . . . *This wasn't a zero-sum deal. . . . Elements beyond our control. . . . And yet. Still.*"

Elsewhere, the narrator seizes particulars in a world of "weightless" definitions. Like Charlotte Douglas "picking out with one hand, over and over again and in every possible tempo, the melodic line of a single song," the "not quite omniscient author" worries the few useful notes she can find. Out of jargon, misinformation, and obsessive repetitions, she forms a weirdly beautiful music: "I still believe in history. Let me amend that. I still believe in history to the extent that I believe history to be made exclusively and at random by people . . . doing a little business, keeping a hand in, an oar in the water, the wolf from the door . . . They may not remember all the names they used but they remember the names they did not use. They may have trouble sorting out the details of all they knew but they remember having known it. They remember they had some moves. They remember they had personal knowledge of certain actions."

The story's time frame is sharply specific: Like the fall of Saigon, it's another vast crater in American democracy. "If you remember 1984, which I notice fewer and fewer of us care to do, you already know some of what happened to Elena McMahon that summer," Didion writes:

> You know the context, you remember the names, *Theodore Shackley Clair George Dewey Clarridge Richard Secord Alan Fiers Felix Rodriguez aka "Max Gomez" John Hull Southern Air Lake Resources Stanford Technology Donald Gregg Aguacate Elliott Abrams Robert Owen aka "T. C." Ilopango aka "Cincinnati,"* all swimming together in the glare off the C-123 that fell from the sky into Nicaragua. Not many women got caught in this glare.

Elena McMahon gets caught because her father, Dick, is one of those men, like Jack Lovett in *Democracy,* who has an oar in the water. When he falls ill, and is subsequently murdered in Miami, Elena—a now-familiar Didion princess, her royal hopes dashed—walks out of the story scripted for her, and into a narrative whose outlines can only be glimpsed among the mutable hills. Her father's last wish—the last thing he wanted—is for her to complete his final arms deal in an obscure Latin American location. The deal gets muddied in a messy assassination plot, Americans killing Americans to advance American interests. "You know the context, you remember the names."

Unable to *read* the real story, Elena becomes its casualty. The Marlow-like narrator attempts to connect variable images in flash sequences but winds up wishing only that Elena could have been saved. Her potential hero, a government official named Treat Morrison, who has worked on special assignment at various American consulates, is the intended target of an assassination scheme. Though he survives, he is unable to rescue his princess. She is shot to death for murky reasons in a soon-forgotten place. "I want[ed] those two"—Elena and Treat—"to have been together all their lives," the narrator says. Like Lily at the end of *Run River,* she craves one final fairy-tale wish.

The wish fails. John Wayne has gone the way of the cottonwoods; the stars' orbits are deteriorating. But in her late fiction, Didion has returned to the *possibility* of wishing.

Toward the end of the book, the narrator reads about a conference at an old resort hotel in the Florida Keys. Eight former members of the Kennedy administration had gathered to reassess the 1962 Cuban missile crisis. "The hotel was pink. There was a winter storm off the Caribbean." She imagines the storm continuing indefinitely, the "[p]ower failing . . . the candles blowing out at the table in the main dining room . . . the pale linen curtains in the main dining room blowing out, the rain on the parquet floor, the isolation, the excitement, the tropical storm. Imperfect memories. *Time yet for a hundred indecisions. A hundred visions and revisions.*"

This scene reverberates with Robert Kennedy's funeral, watched on the verandah of the Royal Hawaiian Hotel; with the ballroom in the Hotel del Caribe, where Charlotte picks out a single tune in the dark; with the crumbling hotel where Elena lives, trying to complete her father's arms deal.

American outposts, American dreams. Public, private. The ruins of colonialism. Kennedy, Cuba . . . the buried story eroding so many fairy-tale premises—like "democracy"—withering so many of our hopes.

And yet, in the narrator's imagination, in this decrepit old resort, there is time yet for visions and revisions, time to find value in ambiguity and indecision. Time to script a new story.

"I wanted to do a very, very tight plot, just a single thread—you wouldn't even see the thread and then when you pulled it at the end [of the novel] everything would fall into place," Didion explained in an interview. "So essentially what you have to do, I found, is you have to make it up every day as you go along. And then you have to play the cards you already have on the table—you have to deal with what you've already said. Quite often, you've got yourself into things that seem to lead nowhere, but if you force yourself to deal with them, that was the discipline of it." Every now and then, she said, you have to "step back from it a little bit. Otherwise it's going to get linear, 'and then she said, and then she did . . .' It doesn't keep you awake to write it."

As with *Play It As It Lays*, she proceeded by "sketching in a rhythm and letting that rhythm tell me what it was I was saying." Her rough draft paragraphs were stippled with "x," "xx," or "xxxx," indicating words to come—syllabics more crucial than content, at first. "The arrangement was the meaning," Didion said. It was akin to scoring music.

Which is not to say she had no story in mind. "I knew the end required a double set-up [the plot to kill Treat Morrison, the killing of Elena, the official blame placed on her posthumously for all the nefarious doings] but I didn't know what the set-up would be until I got there," she said. "I had to write it in about three months in order to keep the plot in my mind." She made good use of newspaper databases, stories from the Iran-Contra years—not the lead stories or the headlines (which typically obscured the *real* news), but two-inch wire stories that "tended to appear just under the page-fourteen continuation of the page-one story," two-inch wire stories that "had to do with chartered aircraft of uncertain ownership that did or did not leave one or another southern airport loaded with one or another kind of cargo."

In a review of the novel, Michiko Kakutani wrote in *The New York Times* that Didion's "conspiratorial view of history" was rife with "self-delusion" and "paranoia"; Kakutani seemed not to have read "history's rough draft" in her own paper, from which Didion drew heavily. The thriller plot in *The Last Thing He Wanted* bore strong similarities to an actual reported assassination scheme against the American ambassador to El Salvador, Thomas R. Pickering, in 1984, a scheme very close to being a case of Americans killing other Americans through their Salvadoran proxies, in a nation whose government, and its death squads, was supported by U.S. resources and personnel. (In the summer of that year, the summer of Didion's novel, Senator Jesse Helms of North Carolina accused Pickering of trying to "strangle liberty in the night," and gave a lavish welcome, in Washington, to Roberto d'Aubuisson, the man allegedly behind the plan to murder the ambassador, a man convinced that he had the unwavering support of the U.S. government.)

"You know the context, you remember the names."

Didion certainly did.

Kakutani said it was "hard to buy" the sort of "history she believes in," but Didion's experience with literary plotting had equipped her with insight into the kinds of affairs appearing, in outline, in the two-inch wire stories below the fold on page fourteen. Just as a writer must use the cards on the table and deal with what she's already said, so, too, "[i]f you put an assassination plot into play you follow it with an assassination attempt. If you stage an assassination attempt you put somebody out front. A front, an assassin. A front with a suitable background. A front who can be silenced in the assassination attempt."

Cause and effect. Narrative. Playing out the hand.

Every gambler knows the game.

"I'm not sure I know what business [he's] in," Didion's heroine says to her father about some shadowy character she's just met while traveling cross-country.

"Christ, what business are they all in," the old arms dealer says.

2

Figuratively speaking, *Americans killing Americans to advance American interests* summed up the play during the years Didion reassessed Iran-Contra and covered political campaigns.

Of the Clinton impeachment proceedings, she wrote, "What . . . occurred was . . . a covert effort to advance a particular agenda by bringing down a president," and to set up a patsy by naming "the citizens themselves as co-conspirators in the nation's moral degradation."

The American people, acting as Lee Harvey Oswald, moved into the line of fire when the permanent political class in Hollywood, New York, and Washington decided it wanted Clinton gone and needed cover.

("He came in here and he trashed the place, and it's not his place," said journalist and Washington insider David Broder, unintentionally giving the game away.)

"The question of 'impeachment' . . . had come up practically from the inauguration," Didion said: the "idea of using the legal system to basically entrap" this outsider. When an investigation into Clinton's real-estate dealings came up empty, the impeachment plotters turned to the president's affair with White House intern Monica Lewinsky to plant a smoking gun (or to finger a suspicious stain on a dress). And who was to blame for the country's "quandary"? "No analysis can absolve the [American] people themselves of responsibility," said Don Eberly of the Civil Society Project (a nonprofit dedicated to "non-governmental institutions of American society as the indispensable foundation of public virtue").

In fact, according to polls, most citizens—while not all enamored of Clinton—had sniffed out the foul scheming of the president's sanctimonious opponents. "He's the luckiest man alive," Didion said. He was blessed with odious enemies.

She was not the only one to point out that the *Referral to the United States House of Representatives,* a tome listing Clinton's sexual transgressions by Independent Counsel Kenneth Starr, read like a soft-porn novel with "an unreliable first person narrator."

It was hard to buy the masturbatory but holier-than-thou history promoted by the permanent political class. These were people "who don't have a very deep commitment to the rest of the country; in fact, none," Didion said.

And any English major will tell you: You can't bring down a president, making "basic craft error[s]."

True to her contrary nature, she registered to vote so she could support Clinton during his second campaign in the face of what she saw as ongoing coup attempts by the Children of Reagan, California Dreamers who'd marched into the East demanding low taxes and real estate zoned for business.

Her voter ID, however, did not mean that she embraced "voting as a consumer transaction (the voter 'pays' with his or her vote to obtain the ear of his or her professional politician, or his or her 'leader,' or by logical extension, his or her 'superior')." Given both major parties' crass appeals to the rabid fringes of their bases, their attempts to limit the actual number of voters in play and to corral them in gerrymandered districts, "choice" was a political fable: Only "sentimentally does 'the vote' give 'the voter' an empathetic listener in the political class, let alone any leverage on the workings of that class," dominated as it is by vast wealth and armies of lobbyists.

Didion's view seemed validated in Florida in 2000 during the Bush-Gore recount. "It was a perfect thing from the parties' point of view," she said, referring to "reducing the electorate to a few hundred voters and then fighting over them for 35 days." She went on to say, "I don't think it had anything to do with the democratic process or with anything in our politics that came before." The "fact that the 2000 presidential election in Florida could come down to only a handful of votes [was] still popularly presented as evidence that 'every vote counts,' conclusive proof of the absolute power of the American voter." Yet "what those days actually demonstrated, from the morning on Day One when the candidate whose brother happened to be governor of Florida lined up the critical Tallahassee law firms until the evening on Day Thirty-Five when the Supreme Court decided *Bush v. Gore* for the same candidate, was the immateriality of the voter against the raw power of being inside the process."

She chafed at Cokie Roberts, a television pundit who'd stated, "I think people do think [what's happening is] political but they think that's okay. They expect the court to be political and—they wanted this election to be over." What Roberts had done, Didion said, was make the case "of the permanent political class for order, for continuity, for the perpetuation of the contract that delivered only to itself"—precisely what it had been seeking to do during the Clinton impeachment proceedings. And if citizens complained about the way the election was being decided, once again they were morally deficient. The "'rule of law' was repeatedly invoked" during the ordeal, Didion noticed, "although how a matter as demonstrably lawyered up as the Florida recount could . . . threaten the rule of law was unclear."

Earlier that year, another Florida drama had riveted Didion's attention. In April, armed agents of the U.S. Border Patrol conducted a predawn raid on a small house in Miami to snatch a six-year-old boy named Elián González from his uncle. Protesters surrounded the home, screaming, "Assassins!" They threw bottles and rocks and were met with Mace and pepper spray.

Months before this, the boy had been found floating in the ocean by two fishermen, who turned him over to the Coast Guard. His mother had drowned in an attempt to escape from Cuba and come to the United States. Elián's father, in Havana, wanted him back, against the wishes of his brother. Finally, Attorney General Janet Reno ordered Elián's uncle to give him up. He did so only at gunpoint.

The episode reminded Didion of the Cuban exiles she'd spoken to in Miami while researching her book on that city. Many of them had come to the United States as part of Operación Pedro Pan (Operation Peter Pan) in the early 1960s, a series of airlifts, over a period of twenty-two months, evacuating more than fourteen thousand children from Cuba, under the auspices of the Archdiocese of Miami, to shield them from Castro's revolution amid rumors of indoctrination and deportation to Russia. Parents willingly relinquished their kids to the Land of Freedom. "Many underground operatives" in Cuba "made their participation" in U.S.-sponsored anti-Castro activities "contingent upon the safety of their children," said historian Victor Triay. "For CIA strategists, then, the children's exodus was a preparatory gesture for what became the Bay of Pigs invasion." In the decades of recrimination following the Bay of Pigs, the children of Pedro Pan wondered if they'd been tokens in some larger game. As Didion had written, "If you stage an . . . attempt you put somebody out front." A cover. A chit. "A front who can be silenced . . ." Or who'll remain silent out of ignorance.

In the years since, presidents from Kennedy to Clinton had visited Florida, promising these displaced children a true and liberated home.

And now here was the latest leader, George W. Bush, appointed by his Supreme Court (with the support of Didion's old friend Anthony Kennedy). "He's a very mysterious figure to me," Didion said of Bush. "[H]e operates a lot of the time behind the screen of everyone around him"—for example, the fleet of lawyers in Miami. "The extent to which he's operating at all we have no idea."

On the campaign trail, he'd talked less about domestic goals or global vision than he did about supporting "faith-based" groups (nongovernmental institutions indispensable to public virtue), promoting "redemption" rather than "reform" in new urban policies, and his "personal transformation" at the hands of his Lord and Savior Jesus Christ, who had weaned him from his addiction to alcohol. From the White House, this teetotaler would work to change people's "hearts," he told the children of Pedro Pan.

The president of Neverland.

Chapter Thirty-three

This calls for a drink, her grandfather might have said.

But Quintana was either not drinking or trying hard not to drink during this period.

"It's been very up and down emotionally," she told reporter Celia McGee, who wrote a Society column for the New York *Daily News.* On October 22, 1998, McGee inserted this item into her column: "At *Elle Décor* magazine . . . photography editor Quintana Roo Dunne, the adopted daughter of writers Joan Didion and John Gregory Dunne, was recently traced by one of her biological sisters. In contact with her birth family for the first time in more than 30 years, Dunne said, 'It's quite a drama.'"

Here's how Didion recounted the drama in *Blue Nights*: "[O]n a Saturday morning when she was alone in her apartment and vulnerable to whatever bad or good news arrived at her door, the perfect child [Quintana] received a Federal Express letter from a young woman who convincingly identified herself as her sister, her full sister, one of two younger children later born, although we had not before known this, to Quintana's natural mother and father." It seemed Quintana's birth parents had decided to stay together after they'd given her up for adoption. Now they were divorced. The mother lived in Dallas, the father somewhere in Florida. Quintana's younger brother, estranged from his mother, lived in Texas. Quintana's sister, against her mother's advice, turned to the Internet to try to locate her lost sibling. She contacted a private detective, who said that for two hundred dollars he could find Quintana by accessing her Con Ed account. "The sister had agreed to the deal," Didion wrote. "I cannot easily express what I thought about this. On the one hand, I told myself, it could hardly be a surprise. We had spent thirty-two years considering just such a possibility. . . . On the other hand, I told myself, it now seemed too late, not the right time. . . . There comes a point, I told myself, at which a family is, for better or worse, finished."

"Saturday delivery," Quintana said when she showed Didion and Dunne her sister's FedEx note. She repeated this over and over, Didion wrote, "as if maintaining focus on this one point could put her world back together."

Quintana had moved into a spacious apartment at 14 Sutton Place South. Nora Sheehan, a well-known publication designer (creative director and art designer for several magazines, including *Architectural Digest, WSJ Magazine, Travel & Leisure*), had hired her at *Elle Décor*. Quintana had become a regular in the "12-step recovery community on the Upper East Side," according to Sue Kaufman, another member of that community at the time. "She was very, very class conscious," Kaufman recalled. "Quintana could be an extremely gracious, kind and open person *unless* she felt that a person were one millimeter beneath her on the social ladder. In those cases, she was at best distant, and more regularly aggressively hostile." She had gained weight and apparently still struggled with the quicksilver mood changes doctors had diagnosed as borderline personality disorder. "The scary thing about Quintana was that she could unpredictably go into a rage that always suggested the possibility of violence," Kaufman said.

On her best days, "she was so excited to see you or talk to you every time you met or called," said Amy Cooper, Quintana's intern at *Elle Décor*. "She had a big voice. I can still hear it: 'Oh HI!' It was never Hey or Hi or Hello, it was always this really big, 'Oh HI!' She was so nice. She had a big personality and was always friendly to everyone but didn't take any shit, either. We would sneak off a few times a day together and take smoke breaks in one of the magazine closets on our floor. I had only been living in NYC for a few months when I started there. I had no idea who her parents were until she told me and probably didn't realize until much later that they were such a big deal. Quintana was pretty humble about it. I think she wanted to make a name for herself on her own, not on her family name. She once had a party at her apartment where I met Joan, but I don't remember too much except how the hell could anyone afford an apartment with multiple bedrooms in New York!"

Quintana told Cooper she'd developed a "new thing" to keep herself occupied during her leisure hours: She'd buy blank journals and "paste a bunch of random funny magazine photos to the front and back." Cooper shared with me one of Quintana's collages: On a journal's small front page, a tiny nude woman dangles from a tree limb above an outsized ape; the word *Bombay* and a lemon twist adorn the ape's head; in the sky float a pair of male and female lips. It's a hasty creation, just for fun, but it's visually dazzling, ample proof that Quintana had earned her place at *Elle Décor* with a unique and genuine talent.

"I remember Quintana talking about meeting her biological family and being nervous about it," Cooper said. "I seem to recall her saying that they were very nice."

Didion reported in *Blue Nights* that Quintana met her sister, first in New York and then in Dallas, a few months after receiving her letter. Griffin met the sister in Quintana's apartment and mistook her for Quintana, they looked so much alike. Didion said "[m]argaritas were mixed" on this occasion, but she did not say whether Quintana was drinking. Didion and Dunne met the young woman at dinner at a restaurant. Strained smiles were the order of the evening.

A month later, Quintana called Didion from Dallas, where she had gone to meet her natural mother and other members of the extended family. On the phone "she had seemed distraught, on the edge of tears," Didion wrote. Quintana's cousins had shared family snapshots with her and remarked on her close resemblance to grandmothers and aunts; they assumed she was ready to be fully embraced by them, when, after all, they were strangers to her.

Shortly after this, her birth father wrote to her from Florida. "What a long strange journey this has been," said the letter with the postmark from Neverland.

Didion said her daughter began to cry as she read the letter aloud to her.

Whatever genetic dispositions Quintana had inherited from her natural parents, her wit had been fired in her adopted mother's crucible. "On top of everything else," Quintana said, "my father has to be a Deadhead."

PART NINE

Chapter Thirty-four

———— ❦ ————

1

On September 11, 2001, Didion's *Political Fictions* appeared in bookstores. In it, she declared that "half the nation's citizens had only a vassal relationship to the government under which they lived, that the democracy we spoke of spreading throughout the world was now in our own country only an ideality" and that this had "come to be seen, against the higher priority of keeping the process in the hands of those who already held it, as facts without application."

That same morning, two hijacked American passenger jets slammed into the World Trade Center towers, and another one destroyed a portion of the Pentagon. Thousands of U.S. citizens lay dead in the smoking rubble.

In the days that followed, television and newspaper reporters claimed that among the attacks' casualties were humor and irony. No one felt like laughing or skewering political leaders. Dissent, critiques of the president, antiwar sentiments—these were widely discouraged. The political class seemed to say, We know what is just and unjust. Patriotism. Unity. We must speak with one voice. All happy families are alike. In this atmosphere, Didion's *Political Fictions*—her writing in general—was not openly embraced by the commentariat.

For example, in *The New York Times,* Edward Rothstein accused "postmodern" writers of fostering terrorism by spreading relativistic thought. What we needed instead was "moral clarity."

"One good thing could come from this horror: it could spell the end of the age of irony," said Roger Rosenblatt in *Time.*

Yet Michiko Kakutani admitted ours was a "frightened and fragmented world": Irony could be a "potent weapon" for dissecting our worries. Certainly, the disorientations Didion had dismantled in her writing remained viral across the globe, and they were hard to ignore. For example, rereading in *Miami* about John Singlaub's fund-raising events for the Nicaraguan Contras in the 1980s—five-hundred-dollar-a-plate dinners at which the "*mujaheddin* in Afghanistan . . . would [also] be among the freedom fighters to benefit." Or rereading in *Political Fictions* about Vice President George H. W. Bush in 1986 passing up a Jordanian photo op because there was "nothing to be gained from showing him schmoozing with Arabs." Or rereading in *After Henry* that a preference for "broad strokes" is "not new in New York . . . [it] has been for well over a hundred years the heart of the way the city presents itself . . . heroes . . . broken hearts . . . [obscuring] not only the city's actual tensions of race and class but also, more significantly, the civic and commercial arrangements that rendered those tensions irreconcilable."

And what of the conspiracy theories? The view of history Kakutani found so hard to "buy" in Didion's work? Was it paranoia or a glimpse of the *true* narrative of our times to note that in 1974 an out-of-work tire salesman named Samuel Byck, jittery with unspecified rage at Richard Nixon, wrote to Jack Anderson, a columnist for *The Washington Post,* "I will try to get [a] plane aloft and fly it toward the target area, which will be Washington, D.C. I will shoot the pilot and then in the last few minutes try to steer the plane into the target, which is the White House."

At the time, Nixon was grappling with the Watergate fallout.

And in fact, Byck *did* try to hijack a plane, on February 22, 1974, at the Baltimore/Washington International Airport, killing one pilot and wounding another before being corralled by police and shooting himself.

Was it paranoia or a glimpse of the *true* narrative of our times to note that one of the biggest investors in George W. Bush's first business venture, Arbusto Energy in Midland, Texas, was a man named James R. Bath, whom *Time* magazine described as a "deal broker"? Said *Time,* Bath's "alleged associations run from the CIA to a major shareholder and director of the Bank of Credit & Commerce," which eventually shut down amid allegations of drug-money laundering and arms dealing. Reports said Bath made his fortune investing money for a man named Sheikh Khalid bin Mahfouz and another Saudi linked to the Bank of Credit & Commerce, Sheikh Salem bin Laden, Osama's brother.

Was it paranoia or a glimpse of the *true* narrative of our times to note that President Bush, in the midst of ordering the bombing of Afghanistan, signed Executive Order 13223, placing severe restrictions on writers, scholars, journalists, and other citizens wishing to request presidential documents, past, present, and future—in effect, limiting access to archives and halls of records?

Was it paranoia or a glimpse of the *true* narrative of our times to note that among the largest beneficiaries of the 9/11 attacks were security-support service companies such as R. L. Oatman and Associates, "specializing in personal and corporation executive protection, training . . . consulting and investigation," and employing Mr. Theodore Shackley to speak on such topics as "Threat Assessment," "Domestic and International Travel," and "Choreography of Protection."

In *Why Buildings Fall Down*, the architects Matthys Levy and Mario Salvadori write, "Humanity learned how to destroy before it learned to build; to this day people often destroy what others have built. This paradoxical behavior can be historically followed along an exponentially increasing curve of violence and destruction, reaching its inconceivable climax in our own time."

Rising action: a linchpin of every successful narrative.

"Everyone's . . . talking about how" the terrorism story "plays," Didion told an *L.A. Weekly* interviewer a month after the events. "At one level, for the political class, it seemed not to have actually happened, or not to have penetrated. I was amazed by how rapidly everybody slipped this event into their previous agendas. . . . [P]eople seem to find lessons [in the attack] that have very much reflected their underlying preoccupations. I was unable to find any lessons in it."

She implied, though, that narrative's verities might provide some "useful context." It might be a good idea, she said, to "read Conrad's *The Secret Agent* again."

2

Four months before the towers toppled, Didion held her final conversation with her mother. From her apartment in New York, she spoke by telephone to Eduene, ninety now, in the care of nurses at her home in Monterey, who kept her on oxygen and administered morphine and Ativan as needed. Always frugal, Eduene had never liked lengthy long-distance phone calls, and she'd often get off the line so fast, she'd leave a discussion dangling. On this afternoon in May, she hung up on her daughter mid-sentence, but this seemed so typical of her, it was not until the following day, when Jim called with news of her death, that Didion realized Eduene "had been just too frail to keep the connection." Or maybe "not just too frail." Perhaps "too aware of what could be the import of this particular goodbye."

Didion's last physical encounter with her had occurred eight weeks earlier. Eduene had gone into the hospital due to congestive heart failure. Didion and Quintana flew to Monterey to help arrange home care and to oversee the transfer of equipment. Eduene told Didion she feared Jim wouldn't want to bother with family heirlooms, furniture, and other household items, and "when she died she wanted to make sure he didn't put everything into a dumpster and get rid of it. She wanted certain things to go to certain children, grandchildren, nephews," Didion said. "[S]he wanted me to take care of that." The only snag was, Didion was in denial about the state of her mother's health (after all, Eduene had survived chemotherapy twice in her seventies, when she'd been diagnosed with breast cancer). One morning, Eduene asked Quintana to bring her a small painted metal box from her bedroom table. Quintana set the box on the bed. Eduene took from it "two pieces of silver flatware," Didion said, "a small ladle and a small serving spoon, each wrapped in smoothed scraps of used tissue paper." She gave Quintana the spoon and Didion the ladle. She pointed out to Didion how satisfying the ladle's curved handle felt in the hand. That's why she'd set it aside. "I said that since it gave her pleasure she should continue to keep it," Didion wrote in *Where I Was From*. "'*Take it*,' she said, her voice urgent. 'I don't want it lost.' I was still pretending that she would get through the Sierra before the snows fell. She was not."

In the past, on flights back to California, following the setting sun, Didion had felt a "lightening of spirit as the land below opened up . . . *home, there, where I was from, me*, California," she wrote. This time, returning for her mother's memorial service, she said she wondered, *"who will look out for me now."*

She recalled the only two times she'd seen her mother cry: in wartime, outside a crowded military housing office, when she struggled to find space for her two small, uprooted children, and, years later, after her own mother's death, when she talked about stopping to eat someplace on a Good Friday; the restaurant had no fish on the menu, and she'd been taught that Fridays were not meat days. "I took one bite [of the meat] and I thought of Mother and I wanted to throw up," she told Didion. But then she said, "What difference does it make."

Didion recalled Eduene's delight the year Dunne gave her batches of John Birch "call-to-action" pamphlets for Christmas. It was clear where Didion's contrary nature was rooted.

She recalled her mother's growing irritation over tiny matters—her plain discomfort at dinners or family weddings, having to endure the loud conversations, her dizziness one day at the Monterey Bay Aquarium when the jellyfishes' dartings gave her vertigo.

She was detaching from the world. Didion saw that now.

"[W]ho will remember me as I was," Didion thought on the flight to California, on her way to what was once-upon-a-time her home, to say good-bye to her mother, *"who will know what happens to me now, where will I be from."*

Didion and her brother held their mother's memorial service at Saint John's Episcopal Chapel in Monterey, despite the fact that Eduene had rarely attended it, having declared some years before that she didn't really believe Christ was the son of God. ("[I]t's fine," her own mother had told her. "[N]obody has to believe all *that*.")

In general, the family was averse not to rituals but to the sentimentality at their core. Jim Didion was deeply offended by the undertaker, who had left a plastic rose on the bed where Eduene died.

In the chapel, Didion sat and listened to the litany from the Book of Common Prayer.

Eventually, she would take her mother's ashes back to New York and place them in a vault at Saint John the Divine (after all, the family cemetery in California had been sold, and the chapel in Monterey had failed to build a promised mausoleum).

After the service, she said, "I insisted to my brother . . . [that] we were going to divide up her furniture and so on, [and] he was so unwilling to do this that I ended up sending most of the stuff to [my] apartment." A small piecrust table, a teak chest, an angora cape. Quintana took a marble-topped Victorian table, oval in shape. Among Eduene's letters and clippings, Didion found a yellowed dance program from when she was a girl: *"Joan Didion and Nancy Kennedy,"* it read, *" 'Les Petites.' "*

In New York, in a locked sanctuary just off the main altar in Saint John the Divine, behind a black-and-ocher marble door—the swirls in the stone tracing time's steady geologic movements—Didion set her mother's urn. For weeks afterward, she dreamed that *she* had an apartment in Saint John the Divine. Each day, promptly at 6:00 P.M., the church's doors would be locked, so Didion needed to be snug inside by then.

3

"When my father died I kept moving. When my mother died I could not," she wrote.

She did follow through with a multi-city book tour, a week after 9/11, to promote *Political Fictions.* Her first stop was San Francisco, where she was glad not to be staying in the Mandarin, usually one of her favorite hotels; from the Mandarin, she would have been seeing the top of the Transamerica Building and probably couldn't have helped but imagine airplanes slamming into it.

Nor, being back now, could she forget her days in the Haight. For all the city's changes in three decades, it seemed to her that the political polarizations so apparent in the Vietnam era were still rippling just beneath the surface of American public life. In the wake of 9/11, the same old rhetoric—variations of "love it or leave it," "hawks and doves"—appeared to be hardening. In Berkeley, just days before she'd landed, an antiwar demonstration (students reacting to President Bush's vague bellicosity) had deteriorated into a flag-waving contest: "I dare you to spit on my flag!"

In her City Arts and Lectures appearance at the Herbst Theatre, Didion read, as a tribute to New York, a selection from "Goodbye to All That." When she got to the line describing the city as "an infinitely romantic notion, the mysterious nexus of all love and money and power—the shining and perishable dream itself," she paused.

"The last of the sentence nearly snagged inside her, then made its way out in a quaver," said a *Chronicle* reporter. "And then for just a few seconds Joan Didion wept."

On September 24, in Portland, Oregon, at the First Congregational Church, Didion, on the verge of tears again, seemed genuinely intrigued by what she would later call her "encounter with an America apparently immune to conventional wisdom." In San Francisco and now in Portland, the people she talked to recognized that a "good deal of opportunistic ground" had been seized by the Bush administration, using 9/11 as cover: As she would write later in *The New York Review of Books*, in an essay entitled "Fixed Ideas," "[T]he words 'bipartisanship' and 'national unity' had come to mean acquiescence to the administration's preexisting agenda—for example, the imperative for further tax cuts, the necessity for Arctic drilling, the systematic elimination of regulatory and union protections, even the funding for the missile shield—as if we had somehow missed noticing the recent demonstration of how limited, given a few box cutters and the willingness to die, superior technology can be."

Leave it to Westerners—here on the Left Coast, the people she met understood that "Washington was still talking about the protection and perpetuation of its own interests," proving more forcefully than ever the central thesis of *Political Fictions*. First the planes had been hijacked. Now the political class was hijacking the nation, veering it into policies, maybe even wars, most citizens didn't want. "These people got it," Didion said of her audiences. "They didn't like it. They stood up in public and they talked about it."

It happened again in Seattle, and in Los Angeles. Dear old L.A. . . . its long, beautiful, sweeping on-ramps where the San Diego intersected the Santa Monica, its searing sunsets glancing off the palm trees and the stark white wall of the Carnation Milk Building on Wilshire, its ocean breakers full of fluorescence . . .

The people got it in L.A.

"Bush says the country needs to be reborn," a journalist said to her, incredulously.

"They're all saying stuff like that."

"Do you think this event has sort of played right into—"

"Plays right into that, doesn't it? Yeah," Didion said. "That cleansing event that precedes the Rapture."

"Now I suppose we have to think about the Rapture."

"We kind of had the Rapture, didn't we?"

Occasionally, on the road, she had to defend herself against charges that she'd seen the light of the Left and been blinded by it, that her formerly conservative outlook, her contrarian spirit, had been replaced by liberal orthodoxies.

Thomas Mallon would write that her "view of our cold war victory [is] so blinkered that its chief consequence appears to have been not the liberation of Eastern Europe but economic downturn in Los Angeles County," making "Joan Didion much more typical of literary intellectuals than she used to be."

Joe Klein, hardly an impartial critic—Didion had *zinged* his reporting in a piece—called her political theories fantasies, and her "notion that non-voters are a seething, alienated mass who would turn every election into a Democratic Party landslide" a delusion. In fact, Didion had said no such thing.

She could be criticized fairly not from the Right or the Left, but from the red-hot center. She had become one of the people she disparaged, a reporter *inside the process.* "Remember Mencken?" said her friend Earl McGrath when asked about the ironies of her makeover. *"Don't get too close to the bastards; you might get to like them?* Well, I think Joan got to like them."

As for her personal politics: "My responses are pretty much the same as they were when I was voting for Goldwater. I don't see a whole lot of shift," she insisted. "[T]hey're pretty straightforward, stay-out-of-our-hair politics." It's the *parties* that changed, she argued: "I don't know who is represented by the current Democratic Party, or the current Republican Party." The Democrats had moved to the right and the Republicans were no longer averse to swollen bureaucracies. So where to turn?

Didion's "political trajectory" was based on an "unorthodox conservatism" serving as "the foundation for idiosyncratic critiques of power," Rachel Donadio observed accurately. In her maturity, Didion's self-correcting quality, her ability to be ruthlessly self-evaluative and change her mind when she saw she'd been wrong, trumped her contrarian streak. If she had a strong capacity for denial, she had an even stronger will to shuck her illusions once she'd exposed them.

"I think of political writing as in many ways a futile act," Didion said. But "you are obligated to do things you think are futile. It's like living. Life ends in death, but you live it, you know."

In New York, she dreamed of being locked inside her apartment in Saint John the Divine, next to her mother's ashes.

The city had changed in the short time she'd been gone. "[P]eople, if they got it, had stopped talking about it," she wrote. "I came in from Kennedy to find American flags flying all over the Upper East Side, at least as far north as 96th Street, flags that had not been there in the first week after the fact." The attack on the World Trade Center "was being processed, obscured, systematically leached of history and so of meaning," she observed. It was "finally rendered less readable than it had seemed on the morning it happened. As if overnight, the irreconcilable event had been made manageable, reduced to the sentimental . . . [to] repeated pieties that would come to seem in some ways as destructive as the event itself. We now had 'the loved ones,' we had 'the families,' we had 'the heroes.'"

President Bush, whose leadership the pundits sorely questioned before the attack, and who was conspicuously missing from view on the day itself, was trotted out by his handlers at flag-waving events, swearing to bring the world's "evildoers" to justice. In *The Washington Post*, David Broder praised the president's "moral clarity" and likened him to Lincoln. CNN said he was poised to lead us into "America's New War" (though the enemy and the proper battlefront had yet to be identified). "[T]his reinvention of Bush as a leader . . . was entirely required by the narrative of the moment," Didion said.

As for the coming battle: "You know that famous Vietnam thing—how do we get out of Vietnam? There's a sense in which we're not going to be able to say that we won this one and leave," Didion suggested. "I think there will probably be an unpredictable [political] shift of some kind. I don't mean a shift to the left or a shift to the right. I mean a shift I can't even imagine."

The beginnings of this shift, whatever it would be, were already apparent. "[W]e have been instructed at regular intervals since September 11, 2001, [that] 'they' attacked us because they hate everything we stand for, our freedom most of all," wrote *New York Times* columnist Frank Rich. "If that is the case, history will have to explain why post-9/11 America was so quick to rein in the freedom of debate even as we paid constant self-congratulatory lip service to this moral distinction between them and us. September was not over before Ari Fleischer, the President's press secretary, set the tone. 'There are reminders to all Americans they need to watch what they say, watch what they do,'" he said.

At first, Didion had noticed people thronging bookstores immediately after the attacks, buying volumes on Islam, on American foreign policy, on Iraq and Afghanistan. Like folks in Seattle and Portland and San Francisco, they *wanted* to "get it," to study, to learn. But then—as political scientist Steven Weber observed—the national "discussion got short-circuited." The "tone of the discussion switched, and it became: What's wrong with the Islamic world that it failed to produce democracy, science, education, its own enlightenment, and created societies that breed terror?" In Weber's estimation, it was a "long-term failure of the political leadership, the intelligentsia, and the media in this country that we didn't take the discussion that was forming in late September and try to move it forward in a constructive way."

Instead, Didion said, it became a "discussion with nowhere to go."

Predictably, the narrative settled on fantasies (nonexistent weapons of mass destruction) and familiar tropes (national security) to bolster the administration's previous priorities. "I made up my mind that Saddam needs to go," said President Bush, and so the invasion of Iraq, a country that had nothing directly to do with the 9/11 attacks, became a self-fulfilling prophecy—a Catch-22. "Given all we have said as a leading world power about the necessity for regime change in Iraq, our credibility would be badly damaged if that regime change did not take place," said James R. Schlesinger of the Defense Policy Board.

In the early days of the war stirrings, Didion would travel to the World Trade Center site. She didn't have a police pass, so she would stand at the nearest barricade, about a block away from the crater. "It draws you toward it," she said. "It has almost the impact of a great cathedral." The site's power lay "not exactly [in] the amount of the destruction," she thought. "Other things have been destroyed through our lifetime; a higher number of people have died in a lot of combat situations. This, you can't quite come to terms with it, you can't quite grapple with it. It's a really direct challenge to our idea of . . . modernity, to our idea of progress, to our idea of secular democracy. Someone said, 'You can't have that, we can take that away.' That is what everyone is trying to come to terms with."

The rush to war seemed to her an obvious warning that the harm we'd do ourselves in overreacting to the tragedy posed our gravest danger. "I think that democracy has shallow roots in America," she said. "Unless people take care of it, it is not assured."

Instead, over and over, our leaders loved to gamble with it—*this* impulse, Didion recognized all too well, especially in the recovered alcoholic George W. Bush.

In her own attempts to *get it,* she discovered enough to know that for decades, leading up to this moment, America's policies in the Middle East had been one shell game after another: "Stall. Keep the options open. Make certain promises in public, and conflicting ones in private. This was always a high-risk business," Didion said. Now our bluffs had been called.

To cite one important instance, in the 1980s we had armed the mujahideen in Afghanistan to fight the Russians, but we had lost control of them, just as the FBI lost control of the Symbionese Liberation Army in California in the 1970s, and now our training and weapons were turned against us.

In response, our leaders behaved like desperate addicts: double down, another try, come on—just this one last time. *What business are they* all *in.* It was like the portrait of the feeble old gambler in *The Last Thing He Wanted,* the father, slipping away, sipping a glass of bourbon-laced Ensure: "Jesus Christ," he says. "I needed this deal."

Chapter Thirty-five

※

1

The deaths of her parents freed Didion—indeed, filled her with urgency, especially in the wake of 9/11—to reexamine extensively the California myths she'd inherited from them, and finally, after decades, to complete the book she'd once wanted to call *Fairy Tales*. *Where I Was From*, published early in 2003 (a year that would end by taking her, tragically, to *where she would go*), was, as one critic has pointed out, an aria made for the concert stage, a muscular combination of essay, reporting, and memoir, a now-dissonant, now-harmonized amalgamation of American prose styles loosed upon the impossible subject of *whatever happened to this country*, a story beginning, for Didion, with the nation's westward expansion.

The book was a grand performance dedicated to Frank and Eduene, who would never see it. Twice in her lifetime, Didion had become so nervous before giving a reading that she had wanted to throw up, and on both occasions her parents had been sitting in the audience. Now their seats were empty. The show was for them (had *always* been for them), but their absence was required for it to work, a further complication in the writing, a parenthetical catch of the breath, a sob in the syntax: This was not a book about *dis*enchantment with her origins so much as *loss* of charm. She wrote, "There is no real way to deal with everything we lose."

Technically, the challenge was to find a proper form for American social history (in so many ways, the story of California was the story of America, just as an individual's life could illustrate the cultural life of an era). "All of the great English fiction was social history," Didion said, "but I came to feel that it was impossible to write social history in America because it didn't have a unified audience. There wasn't a universally accepted social norm, so it was much harder to write." She believed that fiction was no longer up to the task— or its *readers* weren't. "I think specifically novels [have been devalued now] because people don't understand unreliable narrators, for example; they believe that anything the narrator of a novel tells them is supposed to be the truth. They read a novel as if they were reading nonfiction. They literally do not seem to grasp the difference."

Some aspect of unreliability had always been essential to Didion's literary voice, even in nonfiction: The act of witnessing suggested the need to observe precisely because one did not know what was happening. And it was in the shivering core of this vulnerability, mixed with the loss of her parents' world, that the voice of *Where I Was From* began to emerge. Some of what she knew, she knew from history, she would say. Some of what she knew, she believed. Some of what she knew, she didn't know, because she had believed it once and now no longer did. It was a voice she had first tried with full confidence in fiction, in *A Book of Common Prayer,* following Conrad's example: "[T]he not quite omniscient author."

Take a deep breath. Read aloud the first sentence of *Where I Was From.* It announces the book's intentions; it offers a tone of elegy and remembrance as well as of historical accuracy, of intimacy and objectivity; it has the sweep of the continent: "My great-great-great-great-great-grandmother Elizabeth Scott was born in 1766, grew up on the Virginia and Carolina frontiers, at age sixteen married an eighteen-year-old veteran of the Revolution and the Cherokee expeditions named Benjamin Hardin IV, moved with him into Tennessee and Kentucky and died on still another frontier, the Oil Trough Bottom on the south bank of the White River in what is now Arkansas but was then Missouri Territory."

The voice's expansiveness enabled Didion to move fluidly from the diaries of the pioneers in her family to pioneer history in general; from the dreams of those who'd made the crossing to the disappointments of their ancestors; from California's intellectual traditions to her personal educational progress; from the state's self-delusions to the lies of its developers, and the fairy tales she'd been sold like so much hardscrabble.

"California likes to be fooled," said a character in Frank Norris's great American novel, *The Octopus.* This was Didion's conclusion, too, and the central point she wanted to make.

2

Throughout *Where I Was From*, Didion guards against nostalgia—the romantic yearning for a lost domain, which she felt had curdled *Run River*—but it was hard for her not to suspect that some fatal tipping point had now been reached, that at last what was good about California had been irretrievably trashed.

Her fear was most apparently realized in the state's latest trade-off: public schools for private prisons, another example of California's "willingness to abandon at a dizzying rate," Didion thought. "I mean, the notion of taking care of other people who might or might not be troubled, which people all over the world do, seems not to have entered into [the state's thinking]." And the legislature's reckless dismantling of the once "amazing" U.C. system of higher education: "Well, it is hard to know how you get out from under that," she said.

Toward the end of the book, she revisits "towns I knew, towns I thought of as my own interior landscape, towns I had thought I understood, towns in the Sacramento and San Joaquin Valleys"—towns now so "impoverished in spirit as well as in fact that the only way their citizens could think to reverse their fortune was by getting themselves a state prison," building and staffing it in lieu of adequately funding their schools.

On the one hand, "[w]e were seeing nothing 'new' here," she said. "We were seeing one more version of making our deal with the Southern Pacific. We were seeing one more version of making our bed with the federal government."

On the other hand, we might well be witnessing an irreparable tragedy. In Delano, where once the community had tussled over the picking of grapes, the fight was now over whether to build a second detention facility near the ten-year-old North Kern State Prison, contracting the work out to the Nashville-based Corrections Corporation of America, all for the sake of a few low-paying local hires. Cesar Chavez had died in his sleep in 1993, at the age of sixty-six, an embittered and increasingly marginalized icon of California's flickering promise in the 1960s. That promise seemed to have devolved into America's war on drugs, a desire to fill as many prison beds as possible, add more, and get communities like Delano to pass bond measures in the misguided hope that a new private jail would enrich the county.

"[W]hen the families of inmates move into a prison town, they not only strain the limited resources of local schools and social service agencies but bring emotionally stressed children into the community and school system," Didion wrote. "'The students are all very high risk,' a school official . . . told *The Los Angeles Times*. 'They come from single-parent homes. They're latchkey kids, often on AFDC. It's very obvious they're from a whole different area. It creates societal conflicts. The child does not fit in.'"

And here was the real heart of *Where I Was From*. Once again, Didion was writing about displaced children.

Motherless now, fatherless, she was the mother of an adopted girl with no attachments to her ancestors.

The long, rolling cadences of history and heritage in the book's overture vanish in the coda, in a single fierce line: "It was only Quintana who was real."

Quintana, living in a Golden State of Abandonment.

When critics accused Didion of "saying goodbye to California" with this book, of giving up on the place, she was astonished. They had mistaken her sorrow for anger. She said, "It's a love song, as I read it."

Now that she had written it, she might finally be at peace with laying her parents to rest; she might finally relinquish her California driver's license (with her New York address on it). In one sense, the book is "about being older," she said, and the knowledge accruing from that.

Which was what? an interviewer asked.

Didion's answer made her sound like a child once more, heeding her mother's warnings. "Be a better person," she said. And then, as if the weight of all her losses was borne in upon her—her father's false-cheery calls for a drink, her mother's sad indifference, the valleys' rage to incarcerate the state's kids: "[N]obody can ever be nice enough."

Chapter Thirty-six

1

Didion tried to be cordial to Nick if they happened to attend the same party somewhere. Dunne wouldn't talk to his brother at all, but Didion would pause to say hello before spending the rest of the evening clear across the room from him. She felt helplessly motherly toward these two misbehaving boys. Nick seemed to cultivate friends and enemies in distinct counterpoint to his brother and sister-in-law—snubbing Leslie Abramson and courting Nancy Reagan, whom he'd met when he was back in L.A. covering the O. J. Simpson trial. Certain occasions brought the family together, as when Dunne's nephew Tony, son of his older brother Richard, began dating and then married Jimmy Breslin's daughter Rosemary. At dinners and gatherings celebrating the young couple, the Dunne family put on its Irish, a clannish front in case these noisy outsiders, the Breslins, burst onto the scene with the slightest condescension. "My father likes nobody," Rosemary wrote in a memoir entitled *Not Exactly What I Had in Mind* (1997). From a distance, Breslin was wary of the Dunnes; he feared his daughter "was dating some anemic offspring of a famous parent." He disdained "children of successful parents who do nothing but live off their famous or rich names and associate with others of similar stature and discuss how difficult it is being who they are as a way of explaining why they can't get real jobs," Rosemary said. The fact that Tony designed movie sets and had spent time at Hazelden didn't help matters. Also, as journalists, Jimmy Breslin and Dominick Dunne couldn't have been more different. Nick, "the chronicler of the society set"—and Breslin, "who [said] in all his years as a newsman the people he need[ed] to talk to always live[d] on the sixth floor with a broken elevator." But Nick could be a charmer when he wanted to, and he hit it off with Rosemary's cantankerous dad. Both men loved a good story. Rosemary said her father admired Didion and Dunne, "an extremely rare occurrence."

The Dunnes embraced Rosemary. A journalist and a screenwriter, she was smart and funny, and Didion respected her stoicism. Since her early thirties, she had suffered a rare autoimmune blood disorder. She was constantly anemic, often crippled with headaches; the long-term prognosis was sketchy. Didion impressed Rosemary as "someone with a center made of steel"; she was "fiercely protective of those she loved." Dunne took a particular interest in Rosemary's writing. Eventually, he became her "number one fan," calling her early in the mornings to congratulate her on magazine columns she'd published or to encourage her as she polished a script for the TV series *NYPD Blue*. She felt "lucky" to have them in her life.

By the early 2000s, Nick, his luck on the skids, may have wished he could join Breslin on a busted elevator, stuck between floors somewhere. He had been diagnosed with prostate cancer in 2001; he was still fighting with his brother; he was engaged in a very public feud with Robert Kennedy Jr.; and former congressman Gary Condit was suing him for defamation, reportedly for eleven million dollars.

The trouble was, Nick could never resist a story about a young woman's tragic ending. Over and over, he tried to rewrite Dominique's narrative. Hence, his spat with the Kennedys. The tension between them spanned fifty years, of course—the Dunnes' "steerage" roots had planted in Nick a jealousy of the wealthier Irish family; the jealousy grew as he tried to work his way into the upper class, managing to attend Bobby's wedding to Ethel Skakel ("I remember being dazzled by the beauty of the Skakel estate," he said); the jealousy shaded into rage as Nick witnessed "Joe Kennedy be so fuckin' mean" to his Hollywood pal Peter Lawford; and the rage became vengeance when Nick saw an opportunity to pile his justice crusade on the back of Michael Skakel, a nephew of Ethel Kennedy's.

Here's how it happened. In 1975 in Greenwich, Connecticut, Martha Moxley, a fifteen-year-old neighbor of the Skakels, was bludgeoned to death by a golf club later traced to the Skakel home. For lack of further evidence, the murder went unsolved. Nick was convinced that either Michael or his brother, Tommy, both teenagers in the mid-1970s, both with a history of emotional problems, and both of whom had evinced sexual interest in Martha, had killed her. The case became even more personal for him when he learned that Martha and Dominique had each been murdered on October 30.

In 1993, Nick published a novel entitled *A Season in Purgatory,* an obvious retelling of the Moxley affair, switching the murder weapon to a baseball bat. *Purgatory* renewed public interest in the Moxley case. Nick took the further step of acquiring a private investigator's report in which Michael Skakel's alibis on the night of Martha's killing conflicted. Nick passed this report to former L.A. cop Mark Fuhrman, late of the O. J. Simpson trial. Fuhrman published his own book, *Murder in Greenwich,* in 1998, implicating Michael Skakel in the girl's death. Shortly thereafter, the Connecticut state's attorney brought Skakel to trial. He was convicted and sent to prison.

Robert Kennedy Jr. blamed Nick—a "pathetic creature"—for railroading his innocent cousin. "The formula that Dominick Dunne has employed to fulfill his dreams has done damage to a lot of people," Kennedy said. "Dunne wants to write about two things, both of which are easy to sell: high-profile crimes and famous people. So he's forced to try to make connections between his high-profile protagonists and the crimes. . . . If you look at how he couches his accusations, it's always 'Somebody told me this.' 'An anonymous source said this.' So he's not saying it's true, but the average reader misses that nuance."

"I don't give a fuck about what that little shit has to say," Nick remarked of Kennedy to Chris Smith, a reporter for *New York* magazine. "That fucking asshole. This pompous, *pompous*, POMPOUS man. I don't care what he has to say. He's not a person that I have any feeling or respect for."

Nor did he respect Congressman Gary Condit, whose young D.C. intern, Chandra Levy, disappeared in May 2001. Months later, her remains turned up in Washington's Rock Creek Park. Condit, married and much older than Levy, told police he'd had a "friendship" with the girl but refused to elaborate, publicly, on the nature of their relationship. Investigators did not tie the congressman to her death (he was later exonerated), but tabloids cast suspicion on him, and Nick took an interest in the case. It would embroil him in another byzantine affair. In December 2001, before Levy's body was found, Nick went on radio and television with a bizarre story about a lead he'd been given in the investigation. He claimed to have met a "horse whisperer" who once worked for a Dubai sheikh who, in turn, procured young prostitutes for Washington power brokers when they visited the Middle East. The horse whisperer said Condit was a frequent guest at Middle Eastern embassies in Washington and "let it be known that he was in a relationship with a woman that was over, but she was a clinger. He couldn't get rid of her." Nick said Condit "created the environment that led to [Levy's] disappearance. And she shortly thereafter vanished." Nick said he had it on good authority that she'd been thrown from an airplane over the Atlantic Ocean.

Condit sued him. Quickly, Nick backtracked, admitting he'd fallen for an outlandish hoax. He told Condit's lawyers he'd be willing to settle. "I've had prostate cancer," he said. "I still think I've got a great book in me. . . . I don't want to tie up my creative period; the days are getting thin. And I don't want to waste it . . . on Gary Condit."

He was chastened, afraid to gossip in his usual manner at dinner parties, worried that if Condit pursued the lawsuit, he'd have no money to leave to his children.

During this season of troubles, he ran into Dunne "by happenstance" at "eight o'clock in the morning in the Hematology Department of New York–Presbyterian Hospital," he said. Both brothers were there to give blood samples, Nick for a PSA test, Dunne for a heart checkup. "We spoke," Nick said. "And then John called me on the phone to wish me well. It was such a nice call, so heartfelt. All the hostility that had built up simply vanished."

Soon thereafter, Dunne suggested to Griffin that they "all go to Elio's and laugh [their] asses off." "Let me tell you about reconciliation. It's a glorious thing," Nick reflected. "The thing that made our reconciliation so successful was that we never tried to clear up what had gone so wrong. We just let it go. There was too much about each other to enjoy."

They talked about their grandfather, who'd passed along his love of reading to them when they were kids; they talked about their parents, their late sisters, their poor brother Stephen. They talked about Dominique.

They would even pose together for a *Vanity Fair* photo shoot, publicly ending their estrangement.

When Nick was "loath to go out in public" in the fallout with the congressman, Dunne insisted, "Be seen. Don't hide."

Dunne was looking very thin. "He had these big, arty glasses. He was extremely quiet," said Meghan Daum, who interviewed Didion in her apartment one afternoon for a magazine profile. The days were long past when Dunne would finish Didion's sentences for her.

Nick recalled that during this period "John was having problems with his heart," which might account for his thinness and muted demeanor. "He had several overnight stays at New York–Presbyterian for what he always re-

ferred to as 'procedures,'" Nick said. "He was dismissive about their seriousness, but Griffin . . . told me, 'He always thought he was going to keel over
in Central Park.'"

Nick's medical treatments seemed to have vanquished his prostate cancer, and he would eventually settle with Gary Condit—not for eleven million dollars, but for a hefty sum he never disclosed. The last year or so had
been trying, but once again, Nick had taken a hard look at himself, admitted his mistakes, and bounced back firmly.

2

Quintana's defenses seemed to be crumbling. She had begun to receive reg-
ular phone calls from her natural mother in Dallas, urging Quintana to visit.
The woman wanted to discuss the circumstances that had forced her to put
Quintana up for adoption. These calls came usually very early in the morn-
ing when Quintana was getting ready for work and during a period when
Elle Décor was realigning its staff. Quintana feared for her job.

She spoke with a psychiatrist, seeking strategies for coping with her tensions. These conversations resulted in a letter to her mother. She confessed
that "being found" was "too much to handle" right now. The invitations to
visit Dallas were "too much too soon"; she needed to "step back" and "catch up
for a while."

In response, her birth mother wrote to say she would not be a burden,
and then she disconnected her telephone.

The gesture seemed calculated to throw all the guilt of the intervening
years onto Quintana. Didion makes it very clear in *Blue Nights* that she blames
the mother for "shattering" Quintana's world.

At about this time, Quintana's old friend from Westlake, Anna Connolly,
moved to New York. "I phoned her once or twice and hung up when I got no
answer," Connolly said. "She then called me back. Soon after, I visited her at
her apartment in the Sutton Place neighborhood. . . . It was the last time I
saw her. . . . I remember high ceilings, large rooms (though not a sprawling
place). Quintana and I both smoked and smoked, and we drank gin and tonics. . . . She said many things about her struggles and issues—in college, with
men, with work, and with drinking. . . . She had just met a bartender at a
nearby bar—I'm not sure if that was the man she eventually married."

It was. The bar was called the Mayfair, and it was located on the southwest corner of First Avenue and Fifty-third Street, a short walk from Quintana's apartment. The bartender was named Gerry Michael. He lived four blocks from Quintana, at Fifty-sixth and Second. "It was a meeting by proximity," said Michael's son, Sean: "In 2002 . . . she was a regular in the bar." Quintana was thirty-six; Michael was in his fifties. Sean was twenty-seven and came to regard Quintana as a "sister." "Q and my dad seemed two peas in a pod," he said. They both "loved to celebrate . . . she was no stranger to alcohol and could hold her own." Michael had been widowed about a year before. He'd been dating a young model—they "found comfort in each other after my mother's death," Sean said, but soon "different lifestyles and age difference blew a hole" in any ongoing romance. Shortly afterward, when Quintana walked into the Mayfair, projecting cheeriness in spite of her depression, unattached, and bigger than life, Michael was smitten. "Some of my father's friends and my dad himself thought Quintana had similarities to . . . my mother," Sean told me. "I didn't see that at all. But the minute I met Joan, I was struck by my father's ability to attract someone with so many [of the] same qualities. It was not Quintana but her mother! Her hair, her glasses, and her sense of personal justice. Her seeking of truth through writing. And her steely intelligence. All qualities of my mother." To Sean, Joan was "a delicate sparrow with hawk's eyes. Those eyes burn, letting anyone know that the power [inside] outstrips her fragile form. [She's] designed perfectly to telegraph her message."

Quintana had "softer sides," he reflected. "She was [quicker] to laugh" than Joan, "more innately curious about simple things and simple pleasures. And more heart-centered." Quintana shared "joy" with her father—they were "truly connected." "With Joan, I saw a real love there, too. But it was over a fence," Sean said. "Both would reach over [it] successfully and truly be together—but it would be for a short time. The fence would remain."

Over nightly cocktails in the Mayfair, talking with Michael, Quintana felt more and more comfortable. "The best quality I think any couple can have is that both individuals feel lucky. Lucky to have the other. They had that," Sean said. "And Quintana was a curious, lovable little bear, always up for a celebration and hoping for excitement around the next corner. It was in her eyes. A hunger for fun and human connection."

Like three-year-old Michael crawling through the 1960s in the essay "Slouching Towards Bethlehem," Gerry Michael was a child of the "vacuum," the era, in Didion's view, in which we could "no longer pretend that the society's atomization could be reversed."

He came from Woodstock, one of the 1960s energy centers, home for a while of Dylan and the Band, including the latter's legendary drummer, Levon Helm. Michael himself was a creative and talented drummer, and he got an early career start playing with the Bummers, which featured his brother Kevin on lead guitar, Tom Sankey on tenor guitar, Sankey's wife, Janet, on autoharp, and Frank Thumbheart on bass. In 1967 reviewers noted of Sankey's Off-Off-Broadway folk rock musical, *The Golden Screw*, that its antiwar songs were effective, along with its lyric renditions of lost innocence. ATCO released the cast album, featuring Michael on drums; it was hailed as the first rock theatrical recording. Afterward, the Bummers staged a show at Group 212, a Woodstock arts collective mixing music, poetry, painting, sculpture, dance, and electronica. Michael played at several of the Sound-Outs, minifestivals inspiring the 1969 extravaganza.

The Bummers secured a recording contract with RCA, with an advance of twelve thousand dollars, but "smutty lyrics" scotched the album.

In 1970, Michael married Tom Sankey's ex-wife, Janet. In addition to playing music, Janet joined the Off-Off-Broadway theater ensemble Theatre Genesis, which held productions in St. Mark's Church-in-the-Bowery. There she worked with Sam Shepard. Soon she was writing about art and community events for the *Woodstock Times* under the pen name Arabella Faunstock. She met and interviewed Bob Dylan in Bearsville, and they became friends (Dylan was part of the connective tissue between Gerry Michael and Quintana). In 1975, Janet gave birth to Sean.

When Quintana and Gerry Michael got engaged, Sean asked Didion what he should call her. "Step-Gran? Joan? My dad's wife's mother?" He said "she was immediate and emphatic: 'Grandmother.'"

Chapter Thirty-seven

———————— ❁ ————————

1

In early July 2003, three weeks before Quintana's wedding to Gerry Michael, Didion collapsed on the street and spent several nights in Columbia-Presbyterian's intensive care unit while doctors searched for the cause of a gastrointestinal bleed. They did not succeed, despite the techies' obvious excitement over their medical equipment. Didion was discharged, improved but still shaky.

In June, Dunne had undergone a radio-frequency ablation of the atrial-ventricular node and surgeons had implanted a Medtronic Kappa 900 SR pacemaker in his chest. This had followed nearly a year of frequent slippages into atrial fibrillation. Regularly, doctors shocked his heart into rhythm—a short procedure, but one requiring sedation each time—and placed him on Coumadin, a blood thinner. He bruised easily. His skin was paper-thin. The slightest change in his physical circumstances—a plane flight, a minor cold— could send him back into A-fib.

Once the pacemaker was in place, doctors assured him he could hold a cell phone to his heart, punch in a number, and "get a reading" on the device. This gave him confidence that his cell phone worked, but it did not calm him about the state of his heart.

He thought he was dying. He expressed doubts about everything he had ever written, including his latest novel, *Nothing Lost*, whose publication he was awaiting. His handwriting was growing fainter, as though he no longer trusted the force of his ideas. *"When something happens to me . . ."* he would say. Didion would interrupt to insist nothing was going to happen to him.

"But if it does. If it does," he would say, talking over her objections. She was to keep the apartment. She was to marry again. *"You don't understand,"* she told him, and the conversation would end.

He even said he wondered what he was doing in New York now. He spoke often of the backyard pool in Brentwood, the summer he was rereading *Sophie's Choice* and they would go into the house together in the early evening, wearing their bath towels, to watch television.

Such talk reminded Didion of a night alone in Brentwood; Quintana was off at school and Dunne had gone to spend some time in their pied-à-terre in New York. This was during his restless period in L.A., when he spoke of moving to New York and she didn't really want to. She went into the kitchen to feed the dog, and a flashing red light cut through the twilight in the window. She looked out and saw an ambulance parked in front of a house across Marlboro Street. The next day, she learned that the woman who lived in that house had just become a widow. Didion called Dunne and said maybe he had been right. Maybe they *should* spend more time in New York.

This memory sent her spiraling into an even earlier time in California, when they all lived in Malibu and she still owned the yellow Corvette. One day she had driven with Quintana to a fish place to buy lobsters for a big dinner. While they sat in the car, half a dozen bikers surrounded them and began popping wheelies. "What exactly do those wit-nits think they're doing?" Quintana said.

And then Didion remembered how Quintana had burst into tears in the backseat of the Volvo when they'd returned one evening to the Chadbourne neighborhood after selling the house, only to see that the new owners had torn huge chunks of it apart during the remodeling.

Didion was surrounded now by ghosts, by her "friend[s] from the bridge."

"Not our friend from the bridge" had become a family saying after Dunne's aunt Harriet had used the phrase to describe running into the same strangers again and again, seeing the same car, for example, in a supermarket parking lot that she had spotted a short while earlier on a bridge.

Didion's sense of *a short while* seemed to be contracting. Strangers seemed more and more familiar. Or else everyone was becoming a stranger.

Strolling up Madison past the Ralph Lauren store, or the empty space where the Madison Avenue Bookshop used to be, she'd see a woman wearing a big silver ring, surely the spirit of Allene Talmey ("Action verbs! Run it through again, sweetie!"), and, simultaneously, the reincarnation of Didion's great-aunt Nell. Here they were again, in midtown, flouncing through the twenty-first century. Oh, but where could they go? The worlds they had known had vanished. The frumpy Miss Daves—there she was, turning the corner into the park! And was that a whiff of Arpège in the air? The smell of egg salad, scarfed on the run just ahead of the next deadline?

Not long ago, for a *New York* magazine profile ("[Didion's] place in American letters is secure, if not easily summarized"), she'd been asked to do a photo shoot in a West Nineteenth Street studio, quiet and dark, while a rainstorm roared outside. The spooky conditions seemed appropriate, for now *she* was being asked to reincarnate the poses of the fashion models she used to watch while sitting on Irving Penn's floor. A photographer told her to look pensive. She should place her fingertips on her forehead and gaze into the middle distance. She'd spent the day laughing at herself, feeling surrounded by shades.

Once, while walking along Fifty-seventh Street between Fifth and Sixth, she had noticed "quick sunlight dappling, yellow leaves falling (but from what? . . .) . . . a shower of gold, spangled, very fast, a falling of the bright." She never experienced this light effect again. She wondered if she'd suffered a small seizure or stroke. She became convinced that she'd been given an "apprehension of death."

Similarly, years earlier in California, she'd dreamed of an ice island, a jagged bluish white, glittering in sunlight. She awoke, certain she'd witnessed death. Neither of these visions frightened her. "[O]n the contrary," she wrote, they were "transcendent, more beautiful than I could say, yet there was no doubt in my mind that what I had seen was death."

Over there just now! By the entrance to the park, next to a horse-drawn carriage, a man with heavy, gray Polish features. A flash of her dead old life in Hollywood: Roman. Quintana had complained a few months earlier that they wouldn't let Polanski go to the Oscars.

Didion did not want to think about death or about the passing of time or about Roman, her co-godparent to Susanna Moore's daughter—Susanna, whose ex-husband, Dick, had died of cancer the year before, but not before giving a deathbed interview to Peter Biskind about Hollywood's glory days.

In Hollywood, an interview was as good as a confession. Last rites. Cut!

The bridge to the glory days had burned long ago—with a lot of dear old friends trapped on it.

Susanna's daughter, fatherless now. These fragile little girls.

Quintana had said blithely one night at dinner that if she died, she wanted her organs to be donated. Dunne said he wanted his to be, too. Didion could not abide this conversation. Her loved ones, packaged like cut-up fryers in a frozen-food section.

And now, in front of the Gap store, who was this? A wisp of a girl. Trembling, unsteady on her heels, big, thick sunglasses pinching the bridge of her nose . . . looking up and down the street, perhaps, for her errant Southern knight.

Fifty years ago. Say hello to your future.

What do Episcopalians always say at the graveside? "In the midst of life we are in death."

2

"Let's do it," Quintana whispered (Gary Gilmore's words in front of the firing squad, as Quintana must have learned from her mother).

For her wedding, on the afternoon of July 26, 2003, she had chosen a simple long white dress and veil; a frangipani blossom tattooed just below her left shoulder was visible through the tulle. She wore her hair braided thickly down her back, as she had as a child. Woven through the braid were waxy stephanotis flowers (Didion could not help but recall the poisoned vines in Brentwood, once the new owner of their house had sprayed the Vikane). When Quintana knelt at the altar, the red soles of her satin shoes flashed at the spectators.

The Cathedral of Saint John the Divine, where Didion had interred her mother's ashes, had had its cornerstone laid in 1892, the year Ellis Island opened. The church's founders built a section surrounding the high altar called the Seven Chapels of the Tongues to commemorate the city's immigrants.

A Poet's Corner, on the north side of the nave, celebrated American literature, with plaques honoring Emily Dickinson and Mark Twain, among many others. The space lifted the secular to the plane of the sacred. It was where Didion and Dunne wished to be placed at rest.

For their daughter's wedding, they stepped past the peacocks in the courtyard and through the great bronze doors cast by Barbedienne of Paris, the same metalworker who cast the Statue of Liberty. Just inside the entryway, facing the nave, they stood in the tessellated light of the great rose window.

"I remember how unhappy John was that day," Josh Greenfeld told me.

"He didn't want a formal wedding. I think Joan and John probably wanted better for Q, but Gerry was a nice guy."

The children of Gerry's stepdaughter wore leis, at Quintana's request. At the reception, she had wanted pink champagne, a peach-colored cake, cucumber and watercress sandwiches, like the ones her mother had served at her birthdays in Brentwood.

She and Gerry planned to fly to St. Barths for their honeymoon. Didion and Dunne, both aware that neither was terribly healthy, made arrangements to go to Honolulu. What Didion looked forward to the most was the takeoff and landing, when Dunne would hold her hand. He always held her hand.

That evening after the ceremony, Quintana phoned them. "Wasn't that just about perfect," she said.

3

In the early fall, Dunne insisted he wanted to go to Paris. Didion argued with him. They didn't have enough money for another trip right now. They had too much to do. She had just begun researching a proposed book about Kobe Bryant and the Los Angeles Lakers. Dunne said he had a feeling that if he didn't go to Paris in November, he'd never go again. It infuriated her to be blackmailed into indulging his moroseness. "That settles it then," she said, "we're going." They spent two nearly silent days, but in the end, they *did* go to Paris in November. He *did* seem cheered, somewhat. He decided their joint epitaph should be "They Had a Good Time." They stayed at the Bristol and walked through the Jardin du Luxembourg in the rain. At Saint-Sulpice, Dunne received Communion. (Episcopalians "took" Communion, he informed his wife, resurrecting an argument they'd had for forty years; Catholics "received" it. This was an essential difference in attitude.)

Back in New York, he was amused one night by a CBS television movie about the Reagans. It never aired; Reagan supporters claimed it was politically biased, and the network caved to their protests, but Dunne got to see an advance copy of the film. In one scene, Nancy Reagan, lounging in a bubble bath, complained about being interviewed by "Joan Didion," whom she called a "hack" and a "bitch."

His amusements didn't last long these days. He griped he was not having fun. He told his wife one night, "You were right about Hawaii." She didn't know what he meant by this; she assumed he was referring to her old desire to buy a house in Honolulu. All she could remember now were their fights at the north shore of the island, the Punaluu-Hauula side, where the traffic got heavy and they'd get irritable, knowing they'd never make it back to the Kahala for lunch. She'd suggest going over to the Pali and eating at the Mekong instead. At which point he'd burrow deeper into his grumpiness and declare he was absolutely disinclined to eat Thai.

Regularly, he chastised himself—and implicitly her—for not emulating that great old couple they'd met in Indonesia back in 1980. Joe and Gertrude Black were their names. He saw them as exemplars of service to their fellow Americans in far-off corners of the globe, giving lectures and teaching political science. Compared to Joe and Gertrude Black, perhaps they had "fritter[ed] away" their lives.

Didion felt particularly dismayed by his mood one day when he shrugged off a note she'd made for him the night before. They'd been out to dinner. Normally, he carried with him, wherever he went, three-by-six-inch note cards on which to jot down ideas as they occurred to him. He'd forgotten the cards that night and had asked her to record a detail. When she gave him the slip of paper the following day, he said, "You can use it if you want to." This sounded like surrender.

Just as, a few days earlier, on her sixty-ninth birthday, he gave her what sounded like encouragement to go on without him. It had snowed all day that day. Great white clumps cascaded off St. James's slate roof across the street. Dunne was sitting in front of the fire. He pulled from a shelf a copy of *A Book of Common Prayer*. He said he wanted to find a particular passage in the novel to see how she'd accomplished something technically. He read aloud to her. "Goddamn. Don't ever tell me again you can't write," he said, closing the book. "That's my birthday present to you."

She cried.

On December 24, Didion wrote a short Merry Christmas e-mail to Susanna Moore, who was traveling in Florence. Didion said she envied her friend. New York was quite dismal; everyone was down with a terrible flu. For instance, Quintana had a fever of 103 and was going to miss the big Christmas Eve dinner.

Chapter Thirty-eight

──────── ❖ ────────

1

Of the deaths of her husband and daughter, we have primarily Didion's accounts, in the bestselling books *The Year of Magical Thinking* (2005) and *Blue Nights* (2011). Characteristically, Didion stippled these volumes with vivid incidents and medical terminology, yet many readers came away not knowing precisely what happened to Quintana. Nora Ephron's sister, Amy, writing in *The Los Angeles Review of Books*, offered a typical response: Quintana "fell into a kind of semi-conscious state induced by an infection that turned into septicemia (I think—it's not really clear exactly what occurred)."

This confusion beset her parents, as well.

"How does 'flu' morph into whole-body infection?" Dunne was obsessed with this question. He could not grasp the possibility. (Much later, Didion thought Quintana had contracted a particularly malignant strain of a previously unidentified avian flu, which news sources claimed had reached North America in 2003, but this was merely a hunch. "There really was no explanation given . . . [but] I'm convinced that's what killed her," she said.)

By Christmas Day 2003, Quintana's fever had not dropped and she called her mother in the morning complaining of having difficulty breathing. Didion could hear her labored, shallow inhales over the phone. Gerry Michael took his wife to the emergency room at Beth Israel North, the old Doctors Hospital, where *Vogue* girls had gone to rid themselves of unwanted fetuses. Quintana was found to be dehydrated, and her pulse rate was over 150. Her white blood cell count had crashed. Doctors gave her Ativan and Demerol, said she was suffering from "walking pneumonia." It was "nothing serious," they said, but just to be on the safe side, they'd admit her to the sixth-floor ICU.

That evening, her temperature spiked to over 104 degrees. She became agitated. Doctors increased her sedation. Her breathing trouble had worsened and she was intubated. Soon it became clear that she was not capable of breathing on her own. She had first confessed to "feeling terrible" seven days earlier. "I was in town to take Quintana and my dad to my sister's in Canada for Christmas," Sean Day Michael recalls. "I remember her shuffling out of her bedroom into the living room and saying, 'I think I have pneumonia.' The first time she went to the doctor's they sent her home—it was just the flu." This was on Monday, December 22. She was told to drink liquids and stay in bed.

So, here is one clear instance of what happened to her: Initially, doctors misdiagnosed her.

In the sixth-floor ICU, on the morning of December 26, internists discovered pneumonia in both lungs. It was growing. Her blood pressure had dropped, indicating septic shock, a body-wide inflammation caused by infection (often from bacteria picked up in the hospital) and, in severe cases such as Quintana's, complicated by organ dysfunction.

In her books, Didion does not address the possibility that years of alcohol abuse may have compromised Quintana's ability to respond to disease. Following the publication of *Blue Nights,* plenty of innuendo on this topic infected the Internet. Vile rumors concerning Quintana's drinking went viral, mostly from people who knew nothing at all about Quintana and whose purpose seemed to be to condemn Didion for obscuring her daughter's behavior. Didion kept silent about all this, but her view is not hard to imagine. She might point out, quite rightly, that to discuss her daughter's hospitalization in light of her alcoholism would be to pass judgment on Quintana (much the way a defense lawyer, representing a murderer in court, blames the victim instead of the real killer) and that, in judging Quintana, we are deluding ourselves: *She's* responsible, we think; that could never happen to *me.*

Which is to miss the point entirely.

Doctors don't really know what causes such systemic infections, and yet they happen all the time.

On this issue of Quintana's culpability, perhaps Sean Michael offers the best perspective. "Do I think her lifestyle contributed to her death? Absolutely," he says. "I think a nun's lifestyle contributes to her death, even if it's only getting run over by a truck" in front of the convent.

"She's still beautiful," Gerry Michael said one night as he and Didion and Dunne were leaving the ICU.

They had held her swollen hands. They had wept silently as the tubes burbled. Didion had brushed back her daughter's sweat-soaked hair; looking out the window, she could see ice floes on the East River. Dunne leaned over to kiss his daughter's face, near the corner of her fever-cracked lips. "More than one more day," he whispered. In *The Year of Magical Thinking,* Didion explained that this was a reference to Richard Lester's film *Robin and Marian.* "I love you more than even one more day," Maid Marian says to Robin Hood after she has dosed them both fatally with poison, ensuring their eternal union.

In the cab back home, Dunne could barely speak.

A few nights later, after a visit to the ICU, he called Nick. He "sobbed about his daughter," Nick said. "I had never heard him cry. . . . 'It was like watching Dominique on life support,' he told me."

The following evening, December 30, Dunne pulled on a scarf and an old red Windbreaker from the *Up Close & Personal* movie shoot, and he and his wife took a taxi to the hospital. An ICU doctor told them they still didn't know *"which way this is going."*

Afterward, in the cab, the Dunnes considered going out to eat, but they decided to return to the apartment instead and have a salad by the fire. Dunne said everything he had ever done was worthless. The new novel was worthless. His new article for *The New York Review of Books*—on Gavin Lambert's biography of Natalie Wood—was worthless. "Why did I waste time on a piece about Natalie Wood?" he said. He said again, "You were right about Hawaii."

And then he said, *"I don't think I'm up for this."*

Didion knew he meant dealing with Quintana's illness. *"You don't get a choice,"* she told him.

It was after eight o'clock when they reached home. Dunne tossed his scarf and jacket on a chair. Didion laid a fire (all the fires they'd shared! especially on those cold, cozy nights on the coast at Malibu). She got him a Scotch. Fitfully, in the last few days, he'd been reading a bound galley of David Fromkin's *Europe's Last Summer: Who Started the Great War in 1914?* He pushed the book aside, along with a copy of *The New Yorker,* and set down his drink. Didion walked into the kitchen to start dinner. She set a table in the living room, near the fire, and lit some candles. Dunne asked for a second drink.

He was talking to her about World War I, how it had colored the entire twentieth century; he asked her if she'd used the same Scotch in his second drink, because he didn't think it was a good idea to mix two different kinds.

And then he wasn't talking anymore.

Didion looked up. He slumped, his left hand raised. She said, *"Don't do that."* He didn't respond. She walked over and tried to lift him in his chair, thinking perhaps he had choked on some food. He tumbled forward, hitting his head on the table, and dropped to the floor.

Later, Didion said she remembered Quintana's dreams about the Broken Man—how she'd cling to the fence if he came for her. Somehow he'd gotten in. Into the apartment. Into the ICU at Beth Israel North. So far, Quintana kept hold of the fence. Her father had let go of it.

2

In contrast to her account of that evening in *The Year of Magical Thinking*, in which she said she didn't fully grasp what had happened until after the EMTs arrived from New York–Presbyterian, until after they had worked Dunne over on the living room floor with defibrillating paddles, until after they had transferred him to the hospital and she had followed in a second ambulance, to be met by a social worker, Nick said she told him on the phone, later that night, "The minute I got to him, I knew he was dead. The medics worked on him for fifteen minutes, but it was over."

At the hospital, she had been escorted into a curtained cubicle, where Dunne lay on a gurney. His face was bruised and a tooth was chipped from when he'd hit the table. Someone asked her if she wanted a priest. She said yes. Someone else placed in her hand her husband's cell phone, watch, credit cards, and money clip.

The person who most needed to know what had happened lay intubated and unconscious in an intensive care unit several blocks away.

Didion took a taxi home and walked into the silent apartment. The fire's embers glowed. The dinner sat untouched. Syringes lay scattered on the floor, left by the EMTs. A little blood darkened the space beneath the table. Dunne's scarf and *Up Close & Personal* jacket still lay across the chair where he had tossed them. His blue terry-cloth robe lay across a sofa in the bedroom. She remembered she used to have, tacked to the bulletin board in her office, an index card listing, in connection with a movie she'd been working on, the amount of time the brain can be deprived of oxygen before damage or death results.

She stood absolutely still, wondering what to do.

She made calls to the family. Gerry offered to come right over, but she said there was no need. Her brother Jim would fly out from California the next day. Somehow, Lynn Nesbit got the news, apparently from someone Nick had called, and arrived to see what she could do. Didion was both rattled and relieved by her presence. Nesbit was swiftly competent and would know what matters needed tending. She said she would call Christopher Lehmann-Haupt about placing an obituary in the papers.

According to Didion, "magical thinking" is an elaborate form of denial, sometimes indistinguishable from dementia.

For example, to announce Dunne's death publicly in an obituary would be to officially sanction and ensure his death, thus barring him from returning.

In the year ahead, Didion would find numerous occasions on which to practice her magic.

Case in point: It was fine to okay an autopsy, because an autopsy would determine the cause of death, which could then be reversed.

She could not throw away his shoes, because he was going to need them when he came back.

Nesbit offered to stay the night, but Didion said she'd be all right alone. She wrote that, the following morning when she awoke, she wondered for a moment why the other half of the bed was empty, and she experienced the same sort of "leaden" feeling enveloping her as she had after she and Dunne had fought.

Nick, Tony Dunne, and Rosemary Breslin accompanied her to the Frank E. Campbell funeral home to identify the body. This was the funeral home Dunne used to pop by in the fifties to see if anybody famous had died, back in the days when he was first courting Didion. The bruises on his face were no longer apparent: the undertaker's form of magical thinking.

The obituary in *The New York Times* read: "Mr. Dunne and Ms. Didion were probably America's best known writing couple"—as though she had died with him. They "were anointed as the First Family of Angst by *The Saturday Review* in 1982 for their unflinching explorations of the national soul, or often, the glaring lack of one."

Of course, he had been felled by the massive coronary he had always expected.

"I knew he had heart trouble. It wasn't a secret. He was always having something done to his heart. Anyone else could have figured out in a flash that he'd die from it. But it came as a surprise to me. That was my fault," Didion said.

"I couldn't help drawing a line from Q's condition to John's heart attack," said Sean Michael. "The jeopardy relayed daily by doctors with different diagnoses and different prognoses of recovery . . . it was too stressful on John."

As Didion was leaving the funeral home that day, her nephew Tony remarked to the undertaker that a clock in the main office, where they'd had to sign some papers, wasn't running. The undertaker replied in a rather mysteriously self-satisfied way that the clock hadn't run in many years.

3

Nearly three weeks after she'd been admitted to the ICU, Quintana was able to breathe without the aid of the breathing tube. Doctors decided to reduce the sedation so she could gradually awake. They advised Didion not to overload her with information in the first few days, as she would be intermittently and partially conscious, capable of absorbing only so much. The plan was for Gerry to be present with her when she opened her eyes. If she saw her mother, she'd wonder where her father was.

Quintana had other plans. On January 15, 2004, when she awoke, she learned from a nurse that Didion was sitting in a hallway just outside the room. "Then when is she coming in?" Quintana asked.

Didion approached her bed. "Where's Dad?" Quintana asked, her voice a raw whisper.

As calmly as she could, Didion told her what had happened, composing a narrative with the magical implication that, given her father's medical history, this was the way it was supposed to go. Quintana cried. Didion and Gerry held her until she dropped off to sleep again.

That evening, Quintana opened her eyes. "How's Dad?" she whispered.

Once more, Didion described the heart attack.

Quintana strained to make her voice louder. "But how is he *now*?"

Chapter Thirty-nine

❖

1

Didion had been grieving, but she had not been able to mourn, to mark her husband's passing ceremonially so as to give it diurnal heft, the community's blessing. She'd had Dunne cremated, but she wanted to wait until Quintana had been released from the hospital before holding a memorial service. Closure was not the goal of the service. She did not believe in closure. The service was the celebration of a life. The lighting of a candle. One last chance, with some form of her husband's presence, to listen to Gregorian chant, a ritual he had always loved.

Grief was another matter entirely. Grief was a type of solitude. It was impolite to burden others with your grief too much or for too long. They expected you to "get over it in time"—for *their* sakes, if not for yours. She found herself standing alone in her kitchen, in the blue twilight, eating at the counter. At first, congee from Chinatown was all she could keep down. Calvin Trillin brought it to her; he seemed to be the one friend who knew how to help her grieve. He understood. He had lost his wife. She told him she wasn't hungry; he said he knew but that the body needed sustenance. He left the congee and withdrew.

Always go to the text. That had been her default position, but the books she glanced at now, from the cheesiest self-help manuals recommended by friends to more nuanced accounts of psychology to academic studies of behavior, struck her as hollow. They failed to help her cope with what she was feeling. Only a copy of Emily Post's 1922 book on etiquette—which her mother had first showed her when they were snowbound together near the army base in Colorado Springs—soothed her, with its matter-of-fact approach to social necessities and social decorum, and its straightforward practicality: A "sunny room," preferably next to a fire, is the ideal spot for the bereaved; "[c]old milk is bad for someone who is already over-chilled."

She'd discovered she'd stopped dreaming. "Don't tell me your dream," Dunne used to say to her in the mornings, but he'd always end up listening to her.

On January 22, 2004, Beth Israel North discharged Quintana. She was running a fever from an infection she'd acquired in the hospital and she was too weak to stand on her own. Didion and Gerry Michael took her to Didion's apartment. At one point, Quintana got out of bed to fetch an extra quilt and fell to the floor. Didion could not lift her and called for help from a member of the building's staff.

Three days later, Gerry rushed her to the Columbia-Presbyterian emergency room because she was suffering from chest pains and a rising fever.

Here is another clear instance of what happened to her: The doctors at Beth Israel North could have predicted that after her extended immobility she had a high chance of developing pulmonary emboli, but they failed to prepare adequately for this possibility before releasing her.

Columbia-Presbyterian gave "Q a very new-on-the-scene blood thinner" to prevent further clotting while the existing clots dissolved, Sean Michael recalls. "It was meant to create more unrestricted circulatory functions and increase the blood's abilities to fight toxins and win the battle against her system's weakened immune system. It was a super-blood."

On February 3, she went home again. Along with her mother, Nick, and Tony, she began to plan her father's memorial service, which was to be held at Saint John the Divine. Didion told her she was thinking of reading W. H. Auden's "Funeral Blues," because the poem so perfectly captured the anger and helplessness she'd felt: "For nothing now can ever come to any good."

Quintana begged her not to read the poem. Everything about it was "wrong," she said. Didion acquiesced to her daughter's "vehement" request.

The memorial was scheduled for March 23 at four o'clock in the afternoon (Liz Smith announced in her newspaper gossip column that it would be the "place to be" in New York that day). In the weeks prior, Didion became a fierce and no-nonsense organizer. She arranged to have the marble plate on which her mother's name was inscribed recut to include her husband's. His ashes would rest next to Eduene's. She checked with friends who planned to speak, discussed what they were going to say, and offered suggestions. Susanna Moore was staying at the American Academy in Rome, but she adjusted her schedule to attend the service. Initially, Didion asked Moore to read a passage from *Henry V* that Dunne had always loved—all about reaching home safely. Finally, she decided the last section of Eliot's "East Coker" would be best, the part about mastering language when one no longer has anything to say.

Between e-mail discussions of poetry and grief, the women shared the horrors of osteoporosis, of Fosomax and exercise, the disgusting spectacle of aging. Later, in interviews, Didion would insist she never saw herself as old: "When John was alive, I saw myself through his eyes, and he saw me as how old I was when we got married." Marriage, she would say, was a journey through time but it was also a denial of time.

She told Moore it was heartening to hear how much she'd fallen in love with the beauties of Rome (in contrast to dirty New York); Moore's Roman rhapsodies had helped Didion see the world's possibilities again.

Dunne's memorial was an afternoon of "literature, liturgy, and laughter," said a *New York Times* reporter. "He understood the disastrous cardiovascular hand he'd been dealt, so he wasted nothing," David Halberstam remarked in his eulogy. He talked about Dunne's final, unfinished project, a book on contemporary patriotism and the "ever-widening gap" between people in the Bush administration—like his old Princeton classmate Donald H. Rumsfeld—who'd managed to avoid military service but who were now making war decisions, and the young men and women on the ground in Iraq and Afghanistan.

Moore read the "East Coker" passage and Nick read Catullus's "On His Brother's Death." Calvin Trillin recalled Dunne's love of gossip. There were readings from Ogden Nash and Gerard Manley Hopkins. Quintana's old friend Susan Traylor shared memories of attending a prostitute's trial in Hawaii with Dunne—his idea of taking the girls on vacation—and of going to a party at Mick Jagger's with him (he thought it was okay for the girls to miss school the next day). Daniel Morrissey, a Roman Catholic priest, read from the Gospel of Luke and from Saint Thomas Aquinas. He spoke of the God Dunne "wrestled with." Quintana had asked that the Gregorian chant be in Latin.

Weak but firmly composed, she read a poem she had written for her dad. Just eight months earlier, she had worn white in this cathedral for her wedding. Now she was clad in lusterless black.

"For a thousand years in thy sight are but as yesterday when it is past," the crowd recited. *"In paradisum deducant angeli."*

Wearing her sunglasses, Didion read a passage from *Harp*, a wry discussion of failing health. She said Dunne saw plainly what was coming while she had steered clear of it. "I thought I got it," she said. "But I was afraid to look at it. He had a straighter view of his own mortality than I could afford to have."

Later, in her "magical" delirium, she couldn't comprehend, emotionally, how she could have gone through the ritual of memorializing her husband and saying good-bye, and still he didn't return to her.

2

Quintana had arranged to take Gerry to California a day and a half after the memorial service to walk the beaches of her beloved Malibu and show him where she had grown up. "I had encouraged this," Didion wrote. "I wanted to see Malibu color on her face and hair again." Quintana was eager but anxious—packing for a trip always made her nervous, as though she'd lost control of all her things. She asked her mother if she'd be all right in California. Of course she'd be okay, Didion told her. It was a new beginning. She'd see the orchids at Zuma Canyon. She'd see the lifeguards' cozy hut. The hills would be full of wild mustard.

For Didion, too, perhaps the season had turned. The ice floes had melted in the rivers.

Just after seven o'clock on the evening of March 25, Didion's phone rang. It was her nephew Tony, saying he'd be right over. According to *The Year of Magical Thinking*, Didion knew his wife, Rosemary, had been weakened recently by a new experimental treatment for her blood disorder. She wondered if something had happened.

It wasn't Rosemary, Tony told her. It was Quintana.

At that very moment, doctors were performing emergency neurosurgery on her at the UCLA Medical Center in Los Angeles.

After landing at LAX and retrieving her bag, Quintana had fallen and hit her head on her way out of the arrivals terminal. "[My dad] said she was fine walking one minute. And then fell the next," Sean Michael said. "It was a fall anyone could have and barely remember a month later. But the blood rushed to the site of the impact in her head."

Later, Internet gossipmongers spread reckless stories that Quintana had been drinking on the plane and that this was the cause of her fall. These rumors received some support from friends of Quintana's who spoke to a reporter I interviewed (he preferred to remain off the record), and from "reliable" folks who related the story to Claire Potter, a professor of history at the New School. These folks would not go public.

Sean Michael doesn't buy the stories. "Do I know if she was drinking on the airplane? No. No idea. Was not told that by my dad." Even in her compromised state, given her past experience with alcohol, "she would have had to have had about twelve double Scotches to fall down." She never got "stupid drunk." Sean says the simple fact is that she was "light-headed from the blood thinner, her weakened immune system, and the flight itself." And because of the experimental medication, her natural coagulants had "turned off." When her head hit the ground, the blood "kept coming like a garden hose attached to your ear, creating almost instant brain damage."

Forty-two minutes later, doctors drilled into her head "to give the blood an escape route," Sean said. "At this point, she was considered lucky, as she had only been paralyzed on one side of her body. Her face was a heavy mask on one side—and lit with life on the other."

The following day, Didion flew from Teterboro to Los Angeles on Harrison Ford's private plane, along with her friend Earl McGrath. Ford "happened to be in New York and heard about Q's condition . . . and called to offer to take Joan," said Sean Michael. "I find that to be a beautiful thing," he said. "A man you hire to build cabinets, thirty years later is flying you in his private jet to your daughter's hospital bedside."

"You're safe," Didion whispered to Quintana in the intensive care unit at UCLA. *"I'm here. You're going to be all right."*

Part of Quintana's hair had been shaved and her skull had been stapled. Once again, she could breathe only with the aid of a tube. Doctors were not sure to what extent she might have suffered brain damage.

On the day the tube was removed, Quintana asked her mother, "When do you have to leave?" Didion said she would not leave until they left together.

For the next five weeks, Didion spent nights at the Beverly Wilshire Hotel, reading medical texts, from which she would quote to Quintana's doctors, to keep them on track. Patiently, they tolerated her intrusions. Because she had left New York so quickly and had brought only heavy winter clothes, she bought several pairs of blue cotton medical scrubs to wear to the hospital. Only later did she realize that the doctors might view this as a "suspicious violation of boundaries."

On April 1, Quintana's physicians inserted a tracheotomy tube to lessen the risk of windpipe damage and pneumonia once the breathing tube was removed. She was transferred from the ICU to an observation room. From the windows at UCLA, Didion said, she could look down into a swimming pool. It was always empty. One day, she remembered the night she had clogged the filter intake of the Brentwood pool with gardenias and floating candles in her misguided attempt to fancy up a party. This memory led her to an image of Dunne wading in the pool, reading *Sophie's Choice*. The trick was to avoid spinning back and back and back in one's mind . . . a cascade of memories that Didion termed the "vortex effect." It was hard to stop during those weeks in L.A., driving from hotel to hospital. She wouldn't go near Brentwood. She mapped alternate routes so she wouldn't have to pass through the intersection at Sunset and Beverly Glen, where she used to drive Quintana to the Westlake School for Girls. She did not tune the car radio to her old standby, KRLA, or to the Christian talk station that used to amuse her.

In the evenings, old friends distracted her at dinner: Connie Wald, Susan Traylor and Jesse Dylan, Earl McGrath. They'd go to Orso or Morton's (an old favorite of Dunne's—the vortex whirled very near on those nights). Before going to bed, she'd phone room service and order the following morning's breakfast, always huevos rancheros, one scrambled egg. She kept a tight lid on her routines. Strict lines. A safe little box.

But then the jacaranda would bloom. The Santa Ana would blow. She found herself in tears.

What if she had refused to move to New York in 1988? Would Quintana have come back to California after graduating from Barnard? Could the narrative have been different? No pneumonia—just that healthy Malibu sunshine.

Was Didion responsible for all that had happened?

I'm here. Maybe that was the problem, she thought.

I'm ready to die, but you and Jim need me. Her mother had said this on her deathbed to her children, who had lived to be in their sixties.

You're safe. I'm here. How thoroughly we delude ourselves.

On April 30, 2004, the UCLA doctors determined that Quintana was strong enough to fly cross-country on a Cessna with two paramedics and her mother to be admitted into the Rusk Institute at New York University Hospital for neuro rehab. Didion described the trip in *The Year of Magical Thinking*: They left on a morning when medical helicopters circled the roof at UCLA, "suggesting trauma all over Southern California," remote scenes "of highway carnage, distant falling cranes, bad days ahead for the husband or wife or mother or father who had not yet . . . gotten the call." *A globalizing impulse,* a therapist might have told her of this morose passage: *every depressive's fall-back position.* It had always been a key component of Didion's literary sensibility.

But in fact, on this day, from the air, she appeared to be right. Semis were jackknifed and abandoned for miles up and down I-5. The whole state seemed to be in crisis. Truckers were protesting the price of gasoline and had deliberately blocked the freeway.

In the Cessna, Didion sat on a small bench over oxygen canisters while the paramedics tended to her daughter. In a Kansas "cornfield," where the plane stopped to refuel, the pilots asked a couple of teenagers who managed the airstrip to drive to a nearby McDonald's for hamburgers. Didion took some air on the tarmac. Back in the Cessna, she tore pieces of meat from one of the hamburgers to hand-feed to her daughter. Quintana shook her head after only a few bites. "Am I going to make it?" she asked her mother. Didion chose to hear the question in its most limited sense. *You mean New York? Are you going to make it to New York?* "Definitely," she said.

That night, when Gerry met them at Rusk and asked how the flight had been, Didion said they'd shared a Big Mac. Quintana corrected her: "It was a Quarter Pounder."

From the first of May to mid-July, 2004, Quintana remained in the Rusk Institute on East Thirty-fourth Street, doing physical therapy eight hours a day, regaining her appetite, strengthening her right leg and arm, retraining the muscles around her right eye. On the weekends, Gerry would take her to lunch and a movie. Didion watered the plants in her apartment and visited in the afternoons, watching the koi in the institute's lobby pond with her.

The progress was slow but appeared to be steady. Didion began to imagine recovering a saner daily life. She could not yet concentrate well enough to write. But she could sort through her unopened mail. She could straighten the apartment. She could read.

3

That spring, Seymour Hersh's coverage of the growing Abu Ghraib prison scandal in Iraq gave her something besides medical texts on which to concentrate. As he had done in the case of the My Lai massacre, years earlier, Hersh got hold of official army documents never intended for public consumption. In the May 10, 2004, issue of *The New Yorker*, he reported that U.S. Army reservists, CIA personnel, and private contractors working secretly in the name of the United States government had committed "systematic . . . sadistic, blatant, and wanton criminal abuses" on detainees at Abu Ghraib, many of whom were civilians held indefinitely on no specific charges. These abuses included

> [b]reaking chemical lights and pouring the phosphoric liquid on detainees; pouring cold water on naked detainees; beating detainees with a broom handle and a chair; threatening male detainees with rape; allowing a military police guard to stitch the wound of a detainee who was injured after being slammed against a wall in his cell; sodomizing a detainee with a chemical light and perhaps a broom stick, and using military working dogs to frighten and intimidate detainees with threats of attack, and in one instance actually biting a detainee.

One of the prisoners had been punched so hard in the chest, he "almost went into cardiac arrest."

Hersh's allegations were fully supported by graphic photographs of hooded prisoners manacled or standing spread-eagled with electrical wires attached to their genitals. These photographs had been broadcast on CBS's *60 Minutes II*. Didion had spent months among swollen, pallid faces in intensive care units, and now she wished for blessed relief, but such was the state of the nation in the spring of 2004 that citizens could not turn anywhere without being assaulted by images of American soldiers leering and grinning and flashing thumbs-up gestures behind human pyramids of beaten, naked Iraqis, Iraqi men forced to masturbate in front of American females, or made to simulate oral sex on one another. Newspapers printed a widely disseminated photograph of a dead, blood-soaked body packed in ice and wrapped in cellophane, and an empty room coated in blood.

The military chain of command had fingered a handful of individuals at Abu Ghraib as bad apples, among them Spec. Charles A. Graner and Pvt. Lynndie England. Hersh reported that "senior military officers, and President Bush, insisted that the actions of a few did not reflect the conduct of the military as a whole." Yet even this early in the investigation, before the public learned that the Bush administration had legally sanctioned (by questionable means) the use of "enhanced interrogation techniques," the evidence was clear that there had been "collective wrong-doing and [a] failure of Army leadership at the highest levels." The army's own internal probe into events at Abu Ghraib turned up the fact that "Army intelligence officers, CIA agents, and private contractors 'actively requested that MP guards set physical and mental conditions for favorable interrogation of witnesses'" (that is, that they create a dungeon).

Gary Myers, a civilian lawyer who had been active in the My Lai prosecutions in the 1970s, signed on to defend one of the soldiers. He told Hersh, "Do you really think a group of kids from rural Virginia decided to do this on their own?"

Later, U.S. citizens would hear stories of black sites—secret American prisons—established all over the world. An e-mail trail would reveal that torture continued at Abu Ghraib over a year after the abuse photos had been made public and the United States government swore the aberrations had been corrected.

From the outset, Hersh addressed what Vice President Dick Cheney would offer as justification for violating the Geneva Conventions and the U.S. Constitution, holding prisoners without charges or legal representation, and subjecting them to "enhanced interrogation techniques." Torture doesn't work, a thirty-six-year veteran of the intelligence community swore to Hersh. People will "tell you what you want to hear. You don't get righteous information."

Faced with this allegation, Cheney said simply he didn't believe waterboarding was torture.

A caller to Rush Limbaugh's radio talk show said, What the hell, stacking beaten, naked men in a pile was merely a fraternity prank. Harmless fun.

"The photographs are us," Susan Sontag wrote.

Said Elaine Scarry, who had spoken so eloquently against the torture practices in El Salvador in the 1980s, from now on history's picture of America's place in the world will be the "image of a frightened, naked man clutching his genitals to protect them from a lunging dog."

4

Bob Silvers had asked Didion if she'd like to get back on the reporting trail and cover the national political conventions that summer. With Quintana steadily improving at Rusk, she said she'd give it a try.

In June, Rosemary Breslin died at Columbia-Presbyterian of cardiac and renal failure associated with her blood disease. She was forty-seven years old.

Around the first of July, Gerry Michael's insurance stopped paying for Quintana's rehab. Rusk made plans to discharge her. Doctors said a change of scene at this point would probably do her a world of good anyway. Didion didn't believe that. Gerry's erratic work schedule at the bar troubled her, in terms of Quintana's care. Nevertheless, Quintana returned with Gerry to her apartment at Sutton Place.

At the end of the month, Didion flew to Boston for the Democratic National Convention. At the Fleet Center, waiting in the security line to pick up her press credentials, then buying a hamburger at a McDonald's, she found herself crying. It was July 26. Quintana's wedding had been on July 26, a year ago. She remembered that the last time she'd attended a convention had been in 1992, at Madison Square Garden. That summer, her husband had always waited to eat dinner with her, even as late as eleven o'clock, when she'd returned from the Garden.

She knew she had to get out of there, away from the Fleet Center. She could not do this. She was still too fragile to work. On her way out of the hall, she wrote later, she tried to pretend she was in a Hitchcock movie. It was all just a game. Her panic had been scripted—the "shadowy silhouettes moving on the high catwalks . . . the empty commuter trains frozen in place . . ."

She watched the convention on television from her cozy room in the Parker House.

Over the next couple months, Quintana seemed to get better, and by October 4, Didion was sufficiently focused to begin drafting *The Year of Magical Thinking*, her "attempt," she said, "to make sense of [a] period . . . that cut loose any fixed idea I had ever had about death, about illness, about probability and luck, about good fortune and bad, about marriage and children and memory, about grief, about the ways in which people do and do not deal with the fact that life ends, about the shallowness of sanity, about life itself."

If her husband had practiced magic in his writing by attempting to exorcise his health fears through direct address, Didion's literary magic lay in the amount of control she believed language gave her—command through a balance of specificity and elision, through chronological rearrangement. For all her doubt about narrative, she placed enormous faith in word choice and syntax. *"Life changes in the instant,"* she wrote at the beginning of her new book. Not "in *an* instant," the more natural way of phrasing this, but "*the* instant," as if she could pin the very moment and, once she had it, shape it to different ends.

The Year of Magical Thinking is not a confession or a memoir. It is not an expression of grief. It is an analysis of a particular period of grief in an individual's life. As the critic Jeffrey Berman points out, Didion is indebted here to Freud's *Totem and Taboo,* which says, "Primitive men and neurotics attach a high valuation . . . to psychical acts" and exhibit "unshakable confidence in the possibility of controlling the world." Narcissism, according to Freud, is a key component of such thinking.

And if Dunne remains a wispy figure in the book, almost a pretext for Didion's discussions of herself, perhaps the cause can be traced to another work of Freud's. Didion quotes "Mourning and Melancholia," Freud's assertion that grief is a "pathological condition" requiring "medical treatment." In lieu of such treatment (its unavailability is a major cultural failing in the West, said Freud), the bereft must relinquish all attachments to the dead.

"Let them become the photograph on the table," Didion wrote. "Let them become the name on the trust accounts."

As Quintana had told her mother, *"Like when someone dies, don't dwell on it."*

Move on. Leave the bodies behind on the trail.

She finished most of the work on *The Year of Magical Thinking* in December 2004, exactly a year after Dunne had slumped, head forward, at the dinner table. She did not want to complete the book because "as January becomes February and February becomes summer, certain things will happen," she wrote. "My image of John at the instant of his death will become less immediate, less raw. It will become something that happened in another year."

She knew this needed to occur. She *wanted* it to occur, so she could get on with her life. But still.

She had a seemingly unshakable cold. She told Susanna Moore she thought of it as a horseshoe crab lodged in her head. It would be such a relief to leave it somewhere—maybe Chinatown.

A fire had ignited one night in part of Manhattan's subway system, closing several stations. As she was wrapping up her book, she had an image of rats emerging from the underground entryways, taking over the city.

Chapter Forty

─────── ❦ ───────

1

The year began with hope and high spirits. *The Year of Magical Thinking* went into production, and a book tour was scheduled for the fall. Didion had asked Quintana to read the manuscript; after all, it concerned her father. Vaguely, Quintana said, "[V]ery good. Really interesting."

Didion started to venture out in public. Recently, she had attended a UN Association dinner honoring Oprah Winfrey (how's *that* for misguided, she told Susanna Moore) and now Ahmet and Mica Ertegün, along with the editors of *Alem,* a Turkish fashion magazine, were hosting a gala in the Temple of Dendur at the Metropolitan Museum to promote East-West relations—Turkey sits on the borders of Iraq, Ertegün reminded the audience, prompting a few seconds of sober silence before drinks were poured and the laughter started up.

A few days later, Didion walked through the snow in Central Park, gazing at Christo and Jeanne-Claude's *The Gates,* an art installation featuring over seven thousand passageways made of saffron-colored fabric, spaced throughout the park, fluttering in bright rivers through the bare limbs of the trees. Ultimately, Didion considered *The Gates* boring but thought she'd probably miss it when it was gone. She was intermittently teary these days, but getting outdoors felt good.

Quintana, too, worked hard to feel normal. According to Susanna Moore, she threw a cocktail party in late February. Among clouds of cigarette smoke, Quintana looked a little dazed. For her thirty-ninth birthday, she wanted a small dinner in the Chinese restaurant Pig Heaven, on Third Avenue.

All was not well despite these efforts at gaiety. While prepping for a routine colonoscopy, Didion nearly fainted at the funeral of Henry Grunwald, *Time*'s former editor in chief. And Quintana's progress was hard to measure—steady one week, less so the next.

Money became an increasing worry for Didion. Quintana and Gerry could not pay their bills. Quintana counted on her mother to cover the costs of doctors, therapists, day help, and living aides. Didion couldn't seem to make her understand: Yes, from the movies and real-estate investments, they were well off, but eventually, the money would run out. She couldn't get a job—that is, a screenwriting assignment. She complained to Susanna Moore that she'd spoiled Quintana. In trying to protect her, she'd really been protecting *herself* against Quintana's loss, and her daughter had intuited she'd always clean up the mess. Why couldn't children take care of their parents for a change? Didion wondered.

Didion admitted she always felt she was going to fall these days; she feared she was on the verge of a stroke. She suspected she was experiencing a kind of vertigo associated with realizing, finally, she was really alone in the apartment.

One day, Gerry irritated her by asking if she'd ever thought of writing and producing a movie on her own. She wanted to scream and cry, all at once.

For the June 9, 2005, issue of *The New York Review of Books,* she wrote a consideration of the Terri Schiavo case, a remarkable task, given what she'd endured in the past eighteen months. Schiavo, who had lain in an unresponsive state for fifteen years following cardiac arrest, had become an ideological flash point. Her husband, claiming she never would have wanted to be kept alive through artificial means, had, over her parents' objections, obtained a court order authorizing the removal of her feeding tube. Right-to-Lifers, catching an opportunity to promote their antiabortion agenda by declaring all life, including Schiavo's, sacred, argued against the husband's intervention; proponents of choice (abortion, assisted suicide) supported Mr. Schiavo's decision. People on both sides of the debate, as well as several prominent politicians, appeared on television talk shows, shouting about whether "anybody" was at "home" in Terri Schiavo's brain, and revealing the depths of their insensitivity to the family, as well as their medical ignorance. Drawing upon Quintana's recent ordeal, and the death of Dominique, Didion wrote, "No one who has had even a passing exposure to brain injury can think of neurology as a field in which all questions are answerable." She condemned the media fist wavers for pushing old, ill-considered polarizations at the expense of one family's personal tragedy; for turning a complex, intimate situation into a thumbs-up or thumbs-down proposal (as cable news shows did with *all* American "issues"). Her sympathies lay not with political posturing, but with the parents' "unassuageable grief," the "fierce parental need to construe any abandonment of hope as a betrayal . . . of their child."

At the end of April 2005, Didion had complained to Susanna Moore of feeling frail and of having stomach pains. Ten days later, she was diagnosed with pneumonia forty-eight hours after eating dinner with Quintana. She said she'd left her daughter's apartment feeling unbelievably exhausted.

It was only three or four weeks after she'd received her diagnosis that Quintana "entered the hospital" for the final time, in Didion's words. She did not say in *Blue Nights* why Quintana entered the ICU at the New York–Presbyterian/Weill Cornell Medical Center on this specific occasion. In the stage version of *The Year of Magical Thinking,* she said Quintana "had been at home with Gerry, Sunday lunch"—a "lazy afternoon," the *"Times* half read"—when she experienced "sudden nausea, probably a stomach bug, it's going around." In *Blue Nights,* Didion said a doctor told her, "Your daughter wasn't in great condition when she arrived here." She underwent "five surgical interventions" while remaining "ventilated and sedated throughout." She went into septic shock. She died on August 26, 2005, of acute pancreatitis, an inflammation and infection of the pancreas usually caused in young people by prolonged drug or alcohol abuse.

Quintana's friend Susan Traylor believed Quintana's depressions and drinking were "probably intertwined" with her final illnesses.

Of her daughter's drinking, Didion said only, "Alcohol has its well-known defects as a medication for depression but no one has suggested—ask any doctor—that it is not the most effective anti-anxiety agent yet known."

Didion left the hospital on the afternoon of August 26 with Gerry Michael. In *Blue Nights,* she wrote that she cried beneath an underpass in Central Park to the sound of a busker playing a "torchy" song on a saxophone. "The power of cheap music," she thought Gerry said. Sean Michael told me she continued to walk with his father that day all the way to a pier or a clearing by the Hudson River on the Upper West Side. It was "an important moment" for them, he said, involving a "ritual of letting go."

A few months before she died, Quintana commissioned a painting from Sean, who liked to make abstractions in the manner of Gerhard Richter. "She asked specifically for the word 'Ambivert'" to appear on the canvas, he said.

She "explained its meaning to me as one who is both and neither an extrovert nor an introvert. I knew or felt I knew where she was coming from and why she loved the word. It's because she knew some would see her as an extrovert, with her boisterous nature and her sparkle as well as her forceful opinions. And then—the polarity. The shy approach to all things [involving] love and true intimacy. The inward search for personal meaning as it applied to her place in the world beyond her family, friends, and career. To her, I believe, the interior was a whole galaxy under her skin . . . as she sat and talked and walked and laughed through the normal light of day."

At Quintana's memorial service, held six weeks later at New York's Dominican Church of St. Vincent Ferrer, Didion read the poems she had recited to her baby girl whenever Quintana would say, "Do the peacocks" or "Do the apple trees"—Wallace Stevens's "Domination of Black" and T. S. Eliot's "Landscapes." Gerry, Susan Traylor, Griffin Dunne, and Calvin Trillin spoke. Patti Smith sang. Gregorian chant echoed beneath the high ceilings. The next day, along with Nick and Griffin, Didion placed Quintana's ashes in the marble wall in Saint John the Divine, next to her mother and her husband. The last place reserved there is for her.

Gerry Michael eventually returned to Woodstock, where he took up house painting, giving drum lessons, and working with a group to develop a local bartering system involving community service and professional trade-offs—an alternative to traditional economics. "Woodstock wasn't in his plans," his son told me. "It was a gradual decision that came from needing a retreat from the city and a foundation for a quieter life without . . . reminders of tragedy."

Didion told a reporter from *New York* magazine that she didn't see any reason to stay in touch with Gerry now that Quintana was dead.

"My dad lost a wife, Joan lost a daughter, and I lost a sister and a grandmother," Sean Michael said. "My father—I won't speak for him. Griffin—I won't speak for him. But I believe each hug or even a 'hello' if [they] run into [each other] is an instant reminder of death. You can't help thinking how this relationship would be *if*. It splits you, death."

"I promised myself that I would maintain momentum," Didion wrote, ever the pioneer woman making the arduous crossing. She did not cancel her book tour that fall for *The Year of Magical Thinking*. "[I]t did not cross my mind to cancel it because I simply didn't know what I would do if—I mean, I was never in my whole life going to stop grieving for Quintana. . . . [I]t was a question of are you going to live for the rest of your life. Get on a plane and live." She flew to Boston, Dallas, and Minneapolis. She flew to Washington, San Francisco, Los Angeles, Denver, Seattle, Chicago, Toronto, and Palm Springs. Everywhere she went, she got a "very strong emotional response to *Magical Thinking*," she said. In the past, when people had pressed her for advice or commiseration because they felt they'd made a personal connection to her through her writing, she'd found the situation awkward, disagreeable. This time, it was "not a crazy response; it's not demanding," she said. "It's people trying to make sense of a fairly universal experience that most people don't talk about. So this is a case when I have found myself able to deal with the response directly." She said she could "just lie back." She was a "witness" to other people's stories. "It was a role I found very comforting."

For a reading on an outdoor stage in Central Park one night, more than seven hundred people, mostly young, mostly women, showed up. Didion joked that she might need a band to back her. As she started to read, rain fell lightly, but no one left. Then the skies opened and the organizers cut things short. Didion walked to a tent where she sat and signed books for more than two hundred people, who waited patiently in line, shivering and soaked. One teenaged girl told Didion, "You're the awesomest."

Despite nights like that, many members of her audiences, presumably unacquainted with her previous books, noted on blog sites and social media that they found her baffling, disappointing—she was not the warm grief counselor some of them expected. Often, she was quiet, tense, curt onstage. Mark Feeney, a reporter for *The Boston Globe*, learned that "she in no way ingratiates herself" with interviewers—unusual for someone promoting a book, he said, especially a book on such an intimate topic. "She has a job to do, to answer questions with forthrightness and civility. But she doesn't make small talk. . . . There's back and forth, but no around and about." As he spoke to her about the deaths of her husband and daughter, he noticed she kept a tissue in her hand but rarely used it. If tears came, they went quickly.

"I don't think she's changed much in the last year and a half," Robert Silvers admitted to Feeney. "She's very much the same person. She has a completely unsentimental distance from the experiences she's had."

Traveling (to some of the same cities she'd visited on her very first book tour, when Quintana had accompanied her) gave her this self-perspective: "I think my view of death didn't change so dramatically after John died as after Quintana died. Very little bad can happen to me [now]. So I don't antic-ipate anything—I mean, I've always been kind of apprehensive, but that's sort of left me over the course of the summer."

The Year of Magical Thinking went on to become Didion's bestselling book in hardcover; by the end of the year, more than 200,000 copies had sold. This number would triple before the book appeared in paperback, where its sales continued to outpace Didion's previous efforts.

On November 16, 2005, she was given the National Book Award (542 volumes had been nominated that year in the nonfiction category—the most ever). The judges' citation read, in part, "*The Year of Magical Thinking* is a mas-terpiece in two genres: memoir and investigative journalism. The subject of the memoir is the year after the sudden death of the writer's husband. The target of the investigation, though, is the nature of folly and time. . . . What [Did-ion] offers is an unflinching journey into intimacy and grief."

Her acceptance speech was as brief and as curt as her tour appearances: "There is hardly anything I can say about this except thank you, and thank you to everybody at Knopf who accepted my idea that I could sit down and write a book about something that was not exactly anything but personal and that it would work. Thank you all."

2

Alfred Lunt and Lynn Fontanne, *O Mistress Mine*—the first play Didion re-membered seeing. She was around twelve at the time. A Saturday matinee in Sacramento. She could even recall some of the credits on the playbill: "Hats by John Frederics, Parliament cigarettes by Benson & Hedges."

Oh, how she'd wanted to be an actress!

As a very young teenager, she'd walked one day to the Senator Hotel, across the street from the state capitol, to audition for a representative of the Pasadena Playhouse. Her *real* ambition was to get to the American National Theater Academy in New York, but that was beyond her reach right then, so Pasadena would have to do. She remembered skipping her homework in the weeks before the audition, listening to the Theatre Guild on the radio, going to the city library to check out *Death of a Salesman*, *The Member of the Wedding*, and *Strange Interlude*. For the man from Pasadena, she thought maybe she'd read a Blanche DuBois speech from *A Streetcar Named Desire*. He'd make her an offer, she'd drop out of high school, and she'd be on her way. In fact, the man did not want to hear the Blanche DuBois speech. He asked Didion how tall she was. Five foot two, she told him, exaggerating by a quarter of an inch. "Absolutely too short for the stage," the man told her. "Although possibly you could aim for the cinema." So much for her career in the footlights.

Fifty years later, while she was flying from city to city to promote *The Year of Magical Thinking,* the theatrical and film producer Scott Rudin called to offer her a chance to resurrect her girlhood dreams, indirectly, by writing a play for Broadway. In early October 2005, he asked her how she'd like to adapt *Magical Thinking* for the stage. At first, she said no. Too much to do; she knew nothing about playwriting. But as the book tour wound down and she faced losing her forward motion, she contacted Rudin. He had a director in mind, the veteran David Hare, and he had some thoughts about restructuring the book as a monologue. She made notes as she spoke with him:

> The movement . . . should build sequentially, repeated refrains taking on new meaning as they build. The speaker is urgent, driven to tell us something we don't want to know. She is reporting, bringing us a dispatch from a far country. At some point we notice a slippage in this. We begin to suspect that the delivery of this report is all that holds the speaker together. We begin to sense a tension between what we are being told and what we are not being told—What's going on here? Is she crazy? Or is she aware that we think she's crazy and doesn't care? Is that the risk she is taking? Why is she taking it? Think of the Greeks, how ragged they are, how apparently careless of logical transition. Is there a deeper logic?

Shortly after the first of the year, Didion met with Rudin and David Hare in New York. She committed to the project. By then, "I knew that the play would be about language—that if it was to exist at all, it would need to exist in this subtext, in the collision between different kinds of language, the tension between what is said and not said," she recalled. Adapting the book for performance forced her to articulate what had always powered her writing: "The speaker would be someone who uses language not to communicate but to distance, to obscure what she thinks even from herself."

While she worked on the play, she also tried to "maintain momentum" in more familiar ways, refusing to isolate herself in her apartment. She went to dinner with friends; she attended gallery openings. The painter Eric Fischl had mounted a new show. He'd become famous in the 1980s for what *The New York Times* called "sexually simmering suburban scenes" and for being an art-world "bad boy," engaging in high-profile feuds with Julian Schnabel and Jeff Koons. More recently, he'd become a noted celebrity portraitist. Paul Simon, Lorne Michaels, Steve Martin, Chuck Close, and E. L. Doctorow had sat for him. In 2002 he'd made a joint portrait of Didion and Dunne. In the painting, they both face the viewer, standing at a distance from each other. Dunne hides his hands in his pockets. He appears wary, exhausted. Didion wears a large pair of sunglasses and has placed her arms across her chest. She grips her own shoulders, as if cradling herself for comfort. The two could be strangers.

Didion spent time correcting the proofs of her husband's final novel, *Nothing Lost,* to be published posthumously. Some of the details in the book were based on trips Dunne had made to rural Nebraska in the late 1990s to cover the trial of Brandon Teena's murderers. The case had fascinated him. Brandon Teena was a transgender man who moved to Falls City, Nebraska, to begin a new life for himself. He dated several women, which enraged two locals. These men raped and later killed him in coordinated assaults resembling nothing so much as high school football scrimmages. Dunne's account of the story in *The New Yorker,* "The Humboldt Murders" (January 19, 1997), was arguably his last great masterstroke of reporting, as fine as any work he'd done since *Delano.* Expanded, it would have been an American aria on a par with Capote's *In Cold Blood* and Mailer's *The Executioner's Song.* It suggested the extraordinary talent Dunne might have become if he hadn't been so dazzled by Hollywood, if he had left Hollywood sooner to report on the heartland.

In early spring 2006, Didion, Scott Rudin, and David Hare sat in the almost-empty Lion Theatre on West Forty-second Street as an actress read through a draft of Didion's adaptation of *The Year of Magical Thinking.* As the actress began, Didion held her breath. "Only when I realized that David and Scott and I were responding as if the words were not familiar did I stop hyperventilating," she said. "[W]e were all laughing. This was new, a surprise. I was free. We were watching a play."

A month later, Vanessa Redgrave agreed to play the part of Joan Didion.

Didion would tweak the monologue; setting and costume designers would soon start to work; there would be rehearsals, previews, and then the opening. "I remember liking the entire process a good deal," Didion wrote later. "I liked the quiet afternoons backstage with the stage managers and the electricians." She also enjoyed the marketing people, the advertisers, the PR men.

Meanwhile, she had to have laser surgery to correct her cataracts. She had to shake off a nasty upper respiratory infection. And Ahmet Ertegün fell backstage at the Beacon Theatre one night as the Rolling Stones prepared to play a concert marking Bill Clinton's sixtieth birthday. Ertegün hit his head and suffered a brain injury. Weeks later, he died. The loss of a friend was sorrowful enough, but the incident's similarity to Quintana's tumble at LAX haunted Didion.

3

She used the publication of several books by and about members of the Bush administration to maintain momentum and to write a coruscating piece on Dick Cheney for *The New York Review of Books,* which was published October 5, 2006. As of this writing, it remains one of her last lengthy political essays.

"Cheney did not take the lesson he might have taken from being in the White House at the time Saigon fell, which was that an administration can be overtaken by events that defeat the ameliorative power of adroit detail management," she wrote. Instead, he "took a more narrow lesson, the one that had to do with the inability of the White House to pursue victory if Congress 'tied its hands.'"

Cheney regarded Congress as a "massive inconvenience to governing" and the "separation of powers as a historical misunderstanding," Didion said. On his watch as vice president, he took it upon himself to erase the bad memories of Vietnam, Watergate, Iran-Contra; he did so by advocating the invasion of Iraq on false pretenses (he himself had never served in the military—he claimed he'd had other "priorities"), by working to legalize torture, by farming out military operations to private enterprise. Didion saw what he was up to: No one knew better than a Californian with family ties to the real-estate market that war was an ongoing redevelopment project. Cheney insisted that anything the president wished to do, regardless of existing laws, was "by definition legal." In his view, Watergate and Iran-Contra were mistakes only because the executive branch had "allowed the illegal to become illegal in the first place." He thought he could substitute *himself* for the "entire government."

To Didion, Cheney was nothing more than a crude, self-serving "ninth-grade bully in [a] junior high lunchroom, the one sprawled in the letter jacket so the seventh-graders must step over his feet."

Like John Gregory Dunne, Cheney had long suffered from heart disease. Following one of his many surgeries, his doctor recalled seeing the vice president's heart "separated from [his] body . . . festooned with surgical clamps . . . [bearing] the scars of its four-decade battle." The doctor said, "I turned from the heart to look down into the chest . . . the surreal void was a vivid reminder that there was no turning back."

I don't know what happened to this country.

4

"Vanessa Redgrave is not playing me, Vanessa Redgrave is playing a character who, for the sake of clarity, is called Joan Didion," Didion wrote of her play. Granting that every autobiographical "I" in a literary work is a persona, presented selectively and therefore distanced from its creator, it was disingenuous of Didion to ask her audiences to distinguish the character in the spotlight from the author of the book, billed as a memoir, on which the play was based (and from which the character read directly onstage). During the writing, she may have been able to separate herself from her experiences and emotions in order to analyze them, but her viewers were understandably unable to make a similarly dispassionate break.

I attended one of the earliest performances of *The Year of Magical Thinking* at the Booth Theatre in New York in the spring of 2007 (it premiered on March 29), and, as keenly aware as I was of the gap between literature and life, I found it jarring to watch tall, big-boned Vanessa Redgrave tell Joan Didion's story *as* Joan Didion, the famously frail bird in a sweater.

The disparity was as great as that between dramatic form and the form of Didion's play—for the staging revealed starkly that *The Year of Magical Thinking,* even as a book, had never been a taut narrative, a meditation, or a diarist's account of sorrow. Instead, it was a seasoned journalist's report with *self* as subject, interrogated, challenged, questioned. On whether this made effective theater, the critics were divided.

Redgrave sat alone onstage in front of a gray curtain, insisting that variations of her personal tragedies would be experienced by everyone in the theater, despite our urgent desire to deny that fact: "You think I'm crazy. You think I'm crazy because otherwise I'm dangerous. Radioactive. If I'm sane, what happened to me could happen to you. You want me to give you a good prognosis. I can't. So it's safer to think I'm crazy."

"I liked watching the performance[s] from a balcony above the lights," Didion said. "I liked being up there alone with the lights and the play."

On some nights, the crew brought in fried chicken, potato salad, corn bread, and greens from Piece of Chicken on Ninth Avenue, or matzo ball soup from the Hotel Edison's coffee shop, and Didion would eat with the crew backstage after a show at a small table with a checkered tablecloth and an electric candle. Everyone called this darkened little space "Café Didion."

Redgrave gave 144 performances of *The Year of Magical Thinking* at the Booth Theatre (following twenty-three preview performances). She was nominated for a Tony.

On the final night, Didion stood in the wings and drank champagne with the crew. For her curtain calls, Redgrave was handed a spray of yellow roses. When she left the theater that night, she placed the roses on the stage. Someone asked Didion if she wanted to take the flowers home. "I did not want the yellow roses touched," she wrote, indicating that even for her, the gap between literature and life had vanished. "I wanted the yellow roses right there, where Vanessa had left them, with John and Quintana on the stage of the Booth, lying there on the stage all night, lit only by the ghost light . . ."

In early August, Didion developed shingles. She ran a fever of 103; she had a rash, an earache, and severe pain in the facial nerves. She lost several pounds she could not afford to lose, despite the chocolate-vanilla ice cream stocked in her freezer as a hedge against dropping weight. She found she could not grasp things tightly. She wondered if her old symptoms of multiple sclerosis were returning. Buttoning a sweater or tying her shoes presented enormous challenges.

For nearly a month, she was forced to stay indoors. At first this seemed a minor blessing. She'd been drifting at dinners with friends, impatient with chitchat. Isolated in the apartment—staring at a black-and-white blowup of five-year-old Quintana, which was propped against the living room window—she discovered she was generally not a lonely person but that she easily grew bored.

She busied herself with a screenplay about Tom Dooley, a Vietnam navy doctor and humanitarian. It was her first solo picture project. She would not complete it.

Eventually, physical therapy and antiviral tablets helped relieve her pain.

In November, at the Mariott Marquis Hotel in New York, while she was feeling better, she was awarded a medal for Distinguished Contribution to

American Letters by the National Book Foundation. Presenting the award, Michael Cunningham said, "There are a handful of writers whose work has been so seminal, so of its time and beyond its time, that their names have come to function as adjectives. . . . Didionesque means, to me at least, a fearless and almost frighteningly astute vision of a world blandly and even cheerfully collapsing under the weight of its own sorrows. It's a world entangled in consumerism, disastrous politics, pop culture, the slow-motion avalanche of history, the non-division of wealth . . . all of which rumbles along as we continue to cope as best we can with human conditions."

Didion, wearing a dark sweater and a long, flowing pale pink scarf, conversed with Cunningham as he placed the medal around her neck; then, impatiently, she urged the crowd to sit down and be quiet. In an edgy voice, she said, "I didn't start writing to get a lifetime achievement award. In fact, it was pretty much the last thing on my mind. . . . Writing seemed to me . . . a job . . . done under pressure, a craft, but a craft that gave me inexplicable pleasure." She noted that the "last time I was in this room, Norman Mailer was getting this award." Mailer had died just a week before this year's ceremony. Didion paused, collecting herself. "*There* was someone who really, truly knew what writing was for," she said.

In the spring of 2008, Vanessa Redgrave took *The Year of Magical Thinking* to the National Theatre in London. Didion flew over for a performance. Rushing to greet Redgrave backstage one evening, she fell, but she broke none of her brittle bones.

In March of the following year, Redgrave was set to reprise her role in a special performance at Saint John the Divine, to benefit UNICEF and the "children of Gaza and southern Israel," but her daughter Natasha Richardson, forty-five, suffered a head injury on a beginner's ski slope north of Montreal, and the show was postponed. Richardson was flown to Lenox Hill Hospital in New York, where Didion visited her in the ICU the day before she died.

Patty Hearst. Blanche DuBois. So many fine roles Tasha had played, so many compelling personalities gone along with her final flickering.

"This was never supposed to happen to her," Redgrave, playing Didion, had proclaimed night after night in the darkened auditorium, speaking for us all.

Richardson's death recalled and intensified Didion's grief over Quintana, and she spoke more freely of her daughter now. "[S]omebody failed Quintana," she told a reporter around this time. "And I'm the person in sight, you know?"

"Did I lie to you?" she had written.

"Did I lie to you all your life?" Redgrave asked onstage. "When I said you're safe, I'm here, was that a lie or did you believe it?"

Looking back, the best thing about the play, Didion mused, was that for "five evenings and two afternoons a week," for "ninety full minutes," her daughter "did not need to be dead."

Chapter Forty-one

———— ❧ ————

1

"Y ou kind of grow into the role you have made for yourself," Didion said. "The real person becomes the role."

Ideally, the role does not call for aging. Or grief.

But, in fact, the real person goes to bed earlier and earlier each night—usually around seven-thirty. "I can hardly stay awake," Didion said. "If I stay up any later, I'm ruined for the next day."

She continued to smoke just five cigarettes every twenty-four hours.

Her preferred evening drink tended now to be white wine.

The real person suffered neuropathy in her feet. The real person had to have half her thyroid removed. She taped aloe leaves to her throat to heal the scar.

Her brother-in-law, Nick, had been diagnosed with bladder cancer. He insisted he would beat it: a role he played to the hilt.

A pair of Australian filmmakers, Kirsty de Garis and Timothy Jolley, had made a documentary about Nick's career, from his failure in Hollywood to his success as a writer for *Vanity Fair*. Didion agreed to be interviewed for the film, discussing Nick's novels. On camera, she said his dissection of American culture, through the manners and morals of the upper class, made him a Trollope for our time. Then she laughed, suggesting she didn't really believe what she'd said.

In November 2008, in the Oak Room at the Plaza, a screening was held for the film, *Dominick Dunne: After the Party*. Nick couldn't attend because of a scheduled surgery for his cancer. Didion went, along with Nora Ephron,

Tina Brown, Harry Evans, and Ian McEwan. They all said they loved the movie—"It got closer to my brother-in-law than anybody I have seen," Didion said—but most of the reception conversation consisted of gloomy forecasts for journalism and cautious hope following the presidential election, in which an African-American, Barack Obama, was elected president.

About journalism: "Good social reportage is very, very hard to find, particularly social journalism that has a heart and a point of view. And I came across Nick and I knew this guy must be able to write because he has such a way of telling a story," Tina Brown told a reporter from *The New York Observer.* We might not see Nick's like again, though: This was "a very depressing time" for writers, said Brown, "a kind of industrial revolution in media" in the rubble of which who and what would survive was not at all clear.

On the other hand, Obama's election struck most of the writers in the room as what Ian McEwan called a "restoration of literacy as a value." "I read both of [Mr. Obama's] books and he actually turns a very good paragraph," said McEwan.

"He does, doesn't he!" said Evans. "I think it is a new era." Rationality. Unity. American pride. "I think the change in spirit will last."

Didion wasn't sure. A few days after the film screening, at a symposium on the election at the New York Public Library, sponsored by *The New York Review of Books,* she said, "I couldn't count the number of snapshots I got e-mailed" just prior to the vote "showing people's babies dressed in Obama gear." Partisanship "could now be appropriately expressed by consumerism."

"I couldn't count the number of times I heard the words 'transformational' or 'inspirational,' or heard the 1960s evoked by people with no apparent memory that what drove the social revolution of the 1960s was not babies in cute T-shirts but the kind of resistance to that decade's war that in the case of our current wars, unmotivated by a draft, we have yet to see."

Expectations for Obama's performance were far too high, she believed: "Irony was now out. Naiveté, translated into 'hope,' was now in."

She recalled hearing "breathlessly on one [television] channel that the United States, on the basis of having carried off this presidential election, now had 'the congratulations of all the nations.' 'They want to be with us,' another commentator said. Imagining in 2008 that all the world's people wanted to be with us did not seem entirely different in kind from imagining in 2003 that we would be greeted with flowers when we invaded Iraq."

Obama's acceptance speech seemed so melancholy, almost rueful, Susanna Moore told Didion. As if he knew, in advance, that his administration would be little more than an extended footnote to the Bush years, given the continuing legacies of war, torture, a shattered economy, and domestic spying. It made her worried for the future.

Didion agreed. The ignorance of the triumphalism in the streets dispirited her. It seemed to her—as she had said at the Brooklyn Book Fair, a few days before the election—that the country had slipped into a "national coma," a coma "we ourselves" induced by "indulging the government in its fantasy of absolute power wielded absolutely." Instead of working communally to solve our problems, or electing responsible leaders, she said, we reduced crises to simplistic stories in order to forget them: The war in Iraq had been reduced to the troop "surge," and "who had or had not exhibited belief in it. Belief in the surge was equated with [the] success of the surge and by extension our entire engagement in Iraq, as if that success was an achieved fact rather than a wish." In a similar sleight of hand, we "solved" the economic crisis by "de-linking" loans from "any imperative to get them paid off." We "solved" the health care crisis by politicizing medical conditions instead of talking about what *real* reform would mean—"taking on the insurance industry."

No, Obama's election did not particularly cheer her. By the end of the year, she was also feeling anxious about the prospect of returning to Hawaii for the first time since the deaths of her husband and daughter. Honolulu would be lovely, but lonely, too. (At least the new president would be there, vacationing in what newscasters insisted on calling "this exotic place"!)

In preparation for leaving, she straightened the apartment as best she could so that she wouldn't return to a mess. It was still hard for her to throw certain things away—like copies of Dunne's *Princeton Alumni Weekly*. The university hadn't removed him from its mailing list. She should have just tossed the newsletter, but the obituaries obsessed her: too many youngish men—like Dunne—and many men from her father's generation, the last of them, for whom national service had been a sacred obligation.

2

One of her doctors told her she had "made an inadequate adjustment to aging."

She told him he was wrong. She had in fact "made no adjustment whatsoever to aging." In the role she was playing, she had "lived [her] entire life to date without seriously believing that [she] would age."

Meanwhile, early in the summer of 2010, the real person fainted in her bedroom one night (she had no memory, later, of falling to the floor). She awoke hours later with both legs bleeding, with blood on her forehead and one of her arms. She could not get up and she could not reach any of the thirteen telephones in the apartment. She went to sleep in a puddle of blood, having pulled a quilt down from a wicker chest to fold beneath her head.

On waking, she managed to pull herself up and phone a friend, who took her to Lenox Hill Hospital. The only available bed there, once she left the emergency room, was in a cardiac unit, where nurses falsely assumed she must've had cardiac trouble. "Your cardiac problem isn't showing up on the monitor," one said, as if Didion were purposely bedeviling her. Didion said she did not have a cardiac problem. "Of course you have a cardiac problem. Because otherwise you wouldn't be in the cardiac unit," the nurse replied.

Finally, after many days of tests at Lenox Hill and then at the New York–Presbyterian/Weill Cornell Medical Center, "[e]veryone agreed . . . there were no abnormalities to explain why I felt as frail as I did," she said.

You kind of grow into the role.

3

"No good at human relationships. Just can't do it," Nick told the actor Frank Langella one day in the spring of 2008. They were lunching together at Michael's on West Fifty-fifth Street. For years they had known each other glancingly, had said hello at parties, but Langella had always been wary of Nick's "practiced reporter's skill at charming you, then trying to trip you up; getting you to reveal something you hadn't intended to." Mostly, he avoided the man. What prompted this lunch was Langella's recent movie, *Starting Out in the Evening*, based on the Brian Morton novel about a lonely old writer estranged from his child. It touched Nick. He phoned Langella and admitted he'd related to the character in the film. "It was heartbreaking how that man threw his life away," he said.

Because of his cancer, Nick had reached another crisis moment, a searching time of brutal self-honesty and reassessment. He eagerly accepted when Langella suggested lunch. He poured his worries out to the actor. Langella recounted the scene in his memoir, *Dropped Names*. Nick said he was sick, he was going to fight the disease, but he wanted to resolve all of his unfinished business: He was still feuding with Graydon Carter—he believed the editor had not fully supported him in his conflict with Gary Condit; he was having trouble finishing his latest novel, in which the character Gus Bailey, Nick's alter ego in previous autobiographical fiction, struggled to accept his sexuality.

"So, are you gay?" Langella asked him.

"I'm nothing now," Nick said. "I've been celibate for twenty years. It just got too difficult for me to deal with."

"What did?"

"Hiding it. Wanting it."

Langella wondered if Nick had ever talked to his sons about his feelings. Nick recoiled in horror: "God no!" he said. "I'm a coward." He said he was sure Griffin knew anyway. In any case, he no longer missed sex.

Lunch ended with Nick's resolve to patch things up with Graydon Carter and to finish his book.

Over the course of the next several months, Nick pursued various treatments for his disease. Twice he flew to the Dominican Republic for stem-cell therapy, and twice he went to a stem-cell clinic in Germany, the first time in March 2009, and the second time in August. On the second visit, he contracted a serious infection, and Griffin arrived to bring him back home. When he met his father, he saw that Nick had asked an old friend to accompany him to the clinic. This fellow had been "a great friend of my sister's," Griffin said. He "just sort of went from being my sister's best friend to my father's best friend."

"Dominick and I met late June of 1974, to set the record straight," the friend, Norman Carby, explained to me. "He told me to keep a journal, as I was going to have a very interesting life." Carby was a painter, mainly of pastel-hued Southern California landscapes. He also manufactured fine jewelry, did silkscreens and lithographs, and worked in TV and film as a photographer. Through Nick, he met Didion and Dunne and "spent weekends at John and Joan's beach house in their absence," he said. He helped Dominique arrange her acting portfolio soon after she arrived in the States after studying in Italy. She had "an audition for a movie within two weeks of her return to America. I believe that was 1979," he recalled.

Carby had been a key witness at John Sweeney's trial. In the early 1980s, he lived on Cahuenga Boulevard in Los Angeles. Three weeks before Sweeney murdered Dominique, "Sweeney attacked her; hands around her throat," Nick told one interviewer. "She got in her car and went to this painter's house.

Great guy. She had a friendship with him, and he hid her for several days. He photographed her neck, which was used during the trial. She had gone on *Hill Street Blues* and played a battered woman, and a lot of it was not makeup. A lot of it was what [Sweeney] had done to her. But I've always been grateful to this guy." Nick explained that the painter had since moved to Hawaii but that annually he came to Chicago to visit his family. "I see him once a year over the Memorial Day weekend," Nick said. "After all these years, this amazing thing has happened. I now read him my novels [as I write them]. It started with the articles . . . and we've established this thing now. It's unbelievable. I talk to him every day now, this guy in Hawaii, and I read it to him rough, and then I hear it, because you can't read out loud to yourself."

Jim Hyde, the interviewer, asked the painter's name. "Norman Carby," Nick said. He added, somewhat obliquely, "It's an accidental thing that happened. Let life happen and go with it. Just go with it."

In 2009, when Griffin arrived in Germany to take his father home on a chartered plane, he saw this man "looking after" Nick. "I don't think he'd mind me mentioning his name," Griffin said. "There was Norman. I'll just say his name. He'd be fine."

Griffin said, "I saw the . . . history" between the two men. It's "one of the real kind of touching, grateful memories I have of Dad's last months."

In Nick's final novel, *Too Much Money*, which he *did* manage to finish, his character Gus Bailey admits he's closeted and celibate. He says, "Can't die with a secret, you know. I'm nervous about the kids, even though they're middle-aged men now. Not that they don't already know, I just never talk about it." And in an interview for the *Times* of London, just months before his death, Nick said, "I call myself a closeted bisexual celibate."

He could never speak directly to his children. In the summer of 2009, in his apartment at Forty-ninth and Lexington, he submitted to hospice care. Langella arrived to say good-bye one day. "Frank. I did it. I finished my book," Nick said. "It's going to be a hit, I think, Frank." He showed Langella a cardboard image of the cover and discussed the planned marketing of the novel. Langella noticed Griffin sitting on a sunporch off the living room, his back toward the hospital bed, staring out the window. It saddened Langella that "even on his deathbed," Nick was "unable to speak truth to a son sitting some twenty feet away." Instead, Nick "preferred rather to look at a mock-up of [his] new book title, discuss possible profits he would never enjoy, and have his hand held by a formerly estranged colleague."

Didion kept vigil at Nick's bedside in a straw chair on the sunporch. From time to time, she'd say something to the other visitors gathered around the bed, but her voice was so soft, on many occasions no one knew what she'd uttered.

She said good-bye one August afternoon by gently placing her hand on Nick's foot.

A memorial service took place a few weeks later at St. Vincent Ferrer, on a slightly overcast day with just a touch of autumn on the breeze. The service, featuring a High Mass, was a celebrity affair, as Nick would have wished. Among those attending were Stephen Sondheim, Mart Crowley, Richard Gere, Julianna Margulies, Tina Brown, Liev Schreiber, Dana Delany, Diane von Furstenberg. Martha Moxley's mother came. The service opened with Nick's favorite Cole Porter song, "Anything Goes," followed by a reading from the Book of Daniel by Norman Carby and a homily from Nick's friend Father Daniel Morrisey, who said Nick had been planning the details of the service for at least nine years.

Griffin spoke of his father's early marriage to Lenny. Alex came out of the shadows to say good-bye and to speak of his father's bravery following his sister's murder. Didion praised Nick's devotion to family, in spite of his disagreements with her husband; in the cathedral's airy vastness, few could hear her words.

Afterward, people milled around, recalling Nick's career. The last trial he'd covered for *Vanity Fair* was that of Phil Spector, accused of the shooting death of B-movie actress Lana Clarkson. Spector, one of rock 'n' roll's finest record producers, creator of the 1960s "Wall of Sound" with girl groups such as the Ronettes, had been known for years to play around with firearms, even in the studio (he'd once put a bullet into the ceiling during a John Lennon recording session). Nick had met him through Ahmet Ertegün in the late 1980s. In condemning a rock impresario as one of his last public gestures, and in arranging to open his memorial service with a Cole Porter song, Nick seemed to hearken back to Old Hollywood, to deny, once and for all, that the 1960s had ever happened.

In the end, so little is left. About a year after Nick died, the family held an estate auction. On a bright second floor space at the Stair Galleries on Warren Street in Hudson, New York, Nick's furniture, clothes, jewelry, and books were hastily displayed. It was clear that his famous name, and the celebrity elbows he'd rubbed, were not going to be enough to jack up the prices. So what if Dominick Dunne had owned this copy of a John P. Marquand novel? No one had read Marquand for years. The hardcover first edition sold for twenty-five dollars. An old Mexican leather box filled with jeweled cuff links from Tiffany & Company went for seven hundred dollars, probably less than it was worth. The chintz club chairs and the furniture from Nick's mother's house in Hartford brought as little as fifty dollars. The stuff was all out of style—not antique, just old. And no one really cared about the ashtrays Nick had filched from the Ritz. The most valuable pieces—Chinese export porcelain and tall-case clocks—Nick had inherited from Lenny when she died. He was the first to admit she had always outclassed him.

In an earlier century, when Melville haunted these streets, the gallery space had served as a plant for processing whale oil. The whales were gone. "Nowadays," one observer remarked, "the substance rendered here is the material remnants of people's lives." And that usually came down to "so much sentimental dross," no matter who you'd been, or whom you had known.

Epilogue: Life Limits

———————— ❖ ————————

1

When Didion's *Blue Nights* came out in the late fall of 2011, the publisher hailed it as "a work of stunning frankness about losing a daughter." It was hardly that. It was an impressionistic collage of isolated memories, slant observations, lists of objects, and riffs on rhythm. Several times during the writing, Didion nearly abandoned the project, but Lynn Nesbit, her agent, talked her out of it. The book went from being a meditation on parenting to a love song for Quintana to a lengthy complaint about aging and mortality. It ended up as none of these, quite.

"[T]here's a discernible remoteness to the whole presentation," Meghan Daum said in the *Los Angeles Review of Books*, and a "commitment to keeping emotion at arm's length." She said, "[A]t the risk of sounding like a philistine, I wanted some straighter talk. Is that an unfair request? Does the desire to know exactly what happened to Quintana represent a failure to meet the book on its own terms?" Daum answered herself, noting the book's "preference for aesthetic details," a "series of effects," and a good deal of "imagery." Another way of saying this is that *Blue Nights* is a poem, and asks to be read as such.

The opening nocturne, a description of "twilights turn[ing] long and blue" in "certain latitudes," becoming "more intense" even as they darken and fade, warning of the light's last appearance, is a clear allegory for aging and death. There is no mistaking the latitude to which Didion has sailed, nor her approach to discussing it. She will not tell us straight out what happened to Quintana—she makes it very plain, throughout these pages, how much she struggles to speak directly of her daughter. What she *will* do is call our attention to the blue-and-white curtains in Quintana's childhood bedroom and the blue-and-white curtains in the intensive care unit in which Quintana was intubated near the end of her life. Blue nights. Birth and death linked through poetic imagery: "When we talk about mortality we are talking about our children."

Naturally, the lyrical impulse reaches its inevitable conclusion in the book's final lines, culminating in a tiny grammatical knot almost unnoticeable. "Fade as the blue nights fade," Didion says, "go as the brightness goes." And then, speaking of missing and remembering Quintana, she writes, "there is no day in her life on which I do not see her." Common sense—the need for clarity—suggests this sentence should read, "there is no day in *my* life in which I do not see her." Most readers' minds, correcting for meaning, will silently substitute *my* for *her*. But Didion wrote "her." She equated herself with Quintana. She made mother and daughter, life and death, indistinguishable, separated not even by a sheer blue-and-white curtain. Not for the first time, Didion was both the lost child abandoned on the trail and the survivor, looking back: "When we talk about [*our*] mortality we are talking about our children."

After *Blue Nights* was published, she said she wasn't sure she would write anymore. Writing about "morality and culture" was "like pushing the stone uphill again. You write about X political events and nothing happens. That doesn't push you to write again," she said.

As much as we might yearn for the Didion who once commented so perceptively on California, as valuable as it would be to receive a report from her on the West's latest water wars or the transformation of San Francisco by the techno-riche or the new nexus of California money, commerce, entertainment, and politics—say, in the salons of Arianna Huffington or Lynda Resnick—she is a New Yorker now, increasingly out of touch with California. As she once wrote, "It is often said that New York is a city only for the very rich and the very poor. It is less often said that New York is also . . . a city only for the very young." She was once very young in New York. Now she is relatively rich there.

Now and then a rumor will surface in the press or on the Internet that Didion is writing a screenplay, a thriller, with Todd Field, or that Campbell Scott plans to direct a movie of *A Book of Common Prayer* starring Christina Hendricks, or that Didion has abandoned her part in an HBO biopic of Katharine Graham; now and then, Didion will be sighted walking with a cane along Park Avenue, crossing Fifty-seventh Street in thirteen-degree weather wearing only a thin coat and white slippers, her bare ankles exposed to the wind, or she'll be seen in the Yossi Yossi salon on the Upper East Side dishing with her hairdresser about Nancy Reagan's remoteness; now and then, she'll buy snacks at the William Poll deli on Lex or she'll be spotted at an Ed Ruscha retrospective at the Whitney, looking like a teenager in Uggs; now and then, someone will recall having seen her once, in the old days, at Elaine's, watching Mick Jagger greet Yoko Ono ("Dahling!"), or patrons of Swifty's restaurant will whisper about the small party dining quietly in the back room—Didion, Earl McGrath, and Barry Humphries (Broadway's "Dame Edna"). "Earl's job these days is taking care of Joan," Eve Babitz told me.

Since *Blue Nights*, there have been more occasions to mourn: Connie Wald, who died in her Beverly Hills home, site of so many splendid dinners, at the age of ninety-six; Nora Ephron, dead at seventy-one of pneumonia brought on by myeloid leukemia; Christopher Hitchens, who died of cancer at the age of sixty-two.

There have been illnesses, minor injuries, neurological scares, brief hospitalizations, a broken collarbone, resulting in canceled appearances—in Boise, Idaho, Santa Fe, New Mexico, and at the twenty-third annual PEN Center USA Literary Awards Festival in Los Angeles in October 2013. Governor Jerry Brown and Harrison Ford presented Didion a Lifetime Achievement Award in her absence.

She *did* travel to Yale University in 2011 to receive an honorary Doctor of Letters for her "unflinching" exploration of "love and loss, politics and place, social disorder and the search for meaning."

And on July 10, 2013, at the White House, President Barack Obama placed a heavy National Humanities Medal around her neck—many at the affair thought it would pull her to the floor. "I'm surprised she hasn't already gotten this award," Obama said. "[D]ecades into her career, she remains one of our sharpest and most respected observers of American politics and culture." For the ceremony, she wore a blue shawl and a plain flowered-print dress. Her bare arms were bone-thin, and the president had to help her onto the stage. She frowned with the effort of movement, looking a little lost, and she received the loudest ovation of the day (other Arts and Humanities Medal recipients that afternoon included Robert Silvers, Marilynne Robinson, Ernest Gaines, Kay Ryan, Tony Kushner, Ellsworth Kelly, Jill Ker Conway, Elaine May, Renée Fleming, Allen Toussaint, Herb Alpert, Frank Deford, and George Lucas). Didion steadied herself against the president, spreading her long, pale fingers against his dark suit. It was a striking image: this frail figure, the descendant of Western pioneers, reaching for the nation's first African-American president, an image confounding attempts by the Twitter-verse and Beltway pundits to decipher the moment's meaning. Was Didion politically conservative or liberal? Why had the White House chosen *her*? Was Obama sending a message? Appeasing Hollywood donors? The old *National Review* crowd? What did Didion think of *him*? Did this award bridge a generation gap? In the end, there was only one person's hand grasping the shoulder of another.

2

To "really love Joan Didion—to have been blown over by things like the smell of jasmine and the packing list she kept by her suitcase—you have to be female," Caitlin Flanagan wrote.

Katie Roiphe agreed: "There are . . . male writers who imitate Didion, though more of them borrow from Tom Wolfe. Think of all those articles you've read in *GQ* and *Esquire* with such Wolfian sound effects as 'Splat!' and internal free associations and liberal spatterings of exclamation points."

Roiphe's example probably tells us more about the editors of *GQ* and *Esquire* than it does about male writers, just as her (and Flanagan's) broad strokes reveal more about her than the boys. Calls to gender wars over Didion blur the fact that her range has been vast and her style has become the music of our time. In spite of her sharp particularities, she is, finally, one of the most inclusive writers of the era: politics, history, war, the arts, popular culture, science and medicine, international relations, the passing of the years.

Certainly, any writer concerned with California or grappling with the heritage of the West (which Didion proved was a confrontation with America at its core) must come to terms with her work. Matthew Specktor, whose novel, *American Dream Machine*, memorializes Hollywood's recent history, calls her "absolutely essential."

Finally, in considering Didion's literary legacy, one can't ignore her silence on certain matters of class and ethnicity. It is made all the more obvious by the richness of these subjects in the work of such writers as Susan Straight, Al Young, Amy Tan, and Richard Rodriguez. Yet this gap indicates less that California is no longer *where she was from* than that her California was specific and personal, despite its broader applications. She told us this all along.

Richard Rodriguez grew up in a far different Sacramento than Didion did, culturally and economically, but he admired her immensely and found her work galvanizing. In labeling writers, slotting them into cultural categories or dismissing them for what they *fail* to explore, we run the risk of politicizing literature, reading it as sociology, Rodriguez says: "Sociology is not literature. Sociology is the attempt to render an experience of averages and to search for the typical case from the average. The experience of literature is exactly the opposite. It looks for the particular, and then it seeks the universal through the particular rather than the other way around. So if you are a sociologist looking for the Mexican American experience, what you do is interview two hundred students and find out what they think. . . . What you do as a writer is, you write about one particular Mexican American kid. . . . If the writer is true, then people who are not Mexican American can say, 'I don't know who this kid is, but this reminds me of something I felt growing up.'"

On those blue, blue nights, slouching toward a center that would not hold or the diminishing days of autumn, this writer was always true. If we pause and bother to listen, we remain dreamers of Didion's dream.

3

Within a few days of the one-year anniversary of her husband's death, Didion went to Saint John the Divine. A security guard let her into the small chapel off the main altar, underneath construction scaffolding, so she could hang a lei, sent by Susanna Moore from Honolulu, on a brass rod holding the marble plate to the vault containing her mother's and husband's ashes. As she left the nave and wandered up the main aisle, she stared at the magnificent rose window over the front entrance until, from a certain position, the sunlight through the stained-glass inserts flooded her vision with blue.

Back in her neighborhood, so many changes were occurring, as they always did in New York. She wished she could tell her husband about them. Ralph Lauren seemed to be taking over the entire block between Seventy-first and Seventy-second streets. More bookstores had closed, here and across the length and breadth of Manhattan. "Sometimes I feel as if I'm working in a field that's disappearing right under my feet," said the great biographer Robert Caro.

Empty windows. Lost histories. Distant memories.

"Memories are what you no longer want to remember," Didion had discovered, padding through her silent apartment. Memories were no solace at all. Now Didion wished she hadn't saved the silver from her mother's house, her daughter's old school uniforms, her husband's shoes, the CD featuring the Israeli jazz pianist playing "Someone to Watch Over Me," possibly the last song Dunne had listened to the night he died, old wedding invitations (some of the couples long divorced), funeral notices for people she could no longer picture.

Writing *The Year of Magical Thinking* had not been an act of remembrance so much as a continuing engagement with her husband so that she wouldn't yet have to consign him to her dusty old drawer of the past.

Composing that book had been "like sitting down at the typewriter and bleeding," she told her friend Sara Davidson. "Some days I'd sit with tears streaming down my face." But she'd done it, and for a long time afterward, she'd kept herself busy. "I don't call it strength. I call it pragmatism," she'd said. What choice did she have? "I can handle it. I can cross the plains. Bury the baby."

Asked by a young interviewer, shortly after the appearance of *The Year Magical Thinking*, whether she could imagine falling in love again, she said, "I wouldn't get married again, I don't think. But fall in love? Absolutely."

It took the stumble in her bedroom, the constant IV infusions of bone-loss medication, the skin cancer treatments (she'd been *warned* all her life about sunning on tropical beaches!), the broken collarbone, the fevers, the PET scans, the physical therapy sessions, and, most of all, the writing of *Blue Nights* to change her tune.

"I just jumped ship," she told Sara Davidson one day about finishing the book. "I couldn't live with it anymore." So she brought it to a close. She went to dinner at Elio's to celebrate her relief.

After years of pushing hard, harder, she felt weary, listless. Perhaps she'd overdone it. She no longer wanted to go out for breakfast at Three Guys or to dinner at Tamarind, because what if she fell in the restaurant? She no longer cared about events at the Council on Foreign Relations, or window-shopping at Armani. She noticed people considering her "frail in an entirely more serious way—taxi drivers jump out of the cab to help me get out. In New York, that's pretty scary," she said.

Alone in the apartment one day, she found a journal Quintana had kept. Middle school? High school? Didion turned the soft white pages. Quintana said she hated Jane Austen—*and* her parents. Why did they always have to treat her like a child? She was quite capable of taking care of herself.

Perhaps it was then, that quiet instant while thumbing through the journal, staring out over the roof of St. James's, that Didion admitted she could no longer bury the baby: "It's not my code anymore . . . I'm not self-reliant."

But no. This scene was too much like the forced epiphany of an awkward short story.

Still, in essence, it was true. Pioneer stoicism no longer enabled her "to get through the day."

One afternoon, Sara Davidson asked her if she wanted live-in help. No, Didion said. The "idea of someone living in my apartment is repellent." Besides, she could call on over twenty staff members in the building in an emergency. She rarely kept her door locked anymore.

What, then? What did she want? What could she say she needed?

"Acceptance," Didion said. "Surrender."

Recalling this moment later, Davidson said Didion seemed to have surprised herself.

"Surrender was never close to my code before. But I don't mean giving up. I mean . . . giving yourself to what is."

She said that lately she'd been rereading *Zen Mind, Beginner's Mind*, recalling Trudy Dixon and the woman's serenity in her dying days. The book was a reminder to "let things go . . . letting go. Of what doesn't matter . . . Not much [is] important, not in the way I once thought it was."

Abandonment. It lay at the heart of the crossing story, the story of the sweeping American continent.

Not much is important. "But," Didion said, "the feeling of connection is." And there it was—the worm in the story, the snake in the garden; the problem, all along, with where she was from, with where she found herself now, with where we all seemed to be going. "[I]t's an enterprise the whole point of which is survival," she said of the old myth. Survival of the fittest. Capitalist logic. She paused to consider. If you've left what you loved behind—your reason for *moving* in the first place, for dreaming, for working—can you really be called a survivor? Softly, Didion said, "There's something missing in survival as a reason for being, you know?"

Notes

PREFACE: NARRATIVE LIMITS

xi "I used to say I was a writer": Didion quoted in Carrie Tuhy, "Joan Didion: Stepping into the River Styx, Again," *Publishers Weekly,* September 30, 2011; available at www.publishersweekly.com/pw/by-topic/authors/profiles/article /48908-joan-didion-stepping-into-the-river-styx-again.html.

xii "This book is called *Slouching Towards Bethlehem*": Joan Didion, *Slouching Towards Bethlehem* (New York: Modern Library, 2000), xxv.

xii "This book is called *Blue Nights*": Joan Didion, *Blue Nights* (New York: Alfred A. Knopf, 2011), 4.

xiii "generalizing impulse": Susan Sontag, *Where the Stress Falls* (New York: Farrar, Straus and Giroux, 2001), 16.

xiii "It occurred to me": Joan Didion, *Political Fictions* (New York: Alfred A. Knopf, 2001), 19.

xiii "No one who ever passed through an American public high school": ibid., 215.

xiv "It is a truth universally acknowledged": Jane Austen, *Pride and Prejudice* (New York: W. W. Norton, 2001), 3.

xiv "All happy families": Leo Tolstoy, *Anna Karenina* (Oxford: Oxford University Press, 1995) translated by Louise Maude and Aylmer Maude, 1.

xiv "We tell ourselves stories in order to live" and "doubt the premises": Joan Didion, *The White Album* (New York: Simon & Schuster, 1979), 11.

xiv "was meant to know the plot": ibid., 13.

xiv "love was sex": ibid., 21.

xiv "believe in the narrative": ibid., 13.

xiv "I watched Robert Kennedy's funeral": ibid.

xvii "conservative California Republicans": Didion, *Political Fictions*, 7.

xvii "lucky star": David Beers, *Blue Sky Dream: A Memoir of America's Fall from Grace* (New York: Doubleday, 1996), 17.

xvii "John Wayne rode through my childhood": Didion, *Slouching Towards Bethlehem*, 27.

xviii "supposed to give the orders" and "I did not grow up": ibid.

xviii "shocked and to a curious extent personally offended": Didion, *Political Fictions*, 7.

xviii "characterized by venality and doubt": Didion, *Slouching Towards Bethlehem*, 27.

xviii "I think people who grew up in California": Barbara Isenberg, *State of the Arts: California Artists Talk About Their Work* (New York: William Morrow, 2001), 331–32.

xix "passive" and "strange, conflicted": quoted in Didion, *The White Album*, 14, 15.

xix "I want you to know, as you read me": ibid., 133–34.

xx "I belong on the edge of a story": Joan Didion in conversation with Michael Bernstein, the Revelle Forum at the Neurosciences Institute, University of California at San Diego, October 15, 2002.

xx She wrote to the magazine's editor: Joan Didion to Jann Wenner, January 7, 1976. Lois Wallace Literary Agency Records, Harry Ransom Center, University of Texas at Austin.

xxi In a letter: Maryanne Vollers to *Rolling Stone*, January 18, 1979.

xxi On another occasion: Lois Wallace to Morton Leavy, October 13, 1988. Lois Wallace Literary Agency Records, Harry Ransom Center, University of Texas at Austin.

xxii "pretty cool customer": Joan Didion, *The Year of Magical Thinking* (New York: Alfred A. Knopf, 2005), 15.

xxii "Clearly, I'd say anything!": Joan Didion in conversation with Sloane Crosley at the New York Public Library, November 21, 2011.

xxii "I am so physically small": Didion, *Slouching Towards Bethlehem*, xxvii–xxviii.

xxii "[W]riting . . . no longer comes easily to me": Didion, *Blue Nights*, 105.

xxii "[T]here is always a point in the writing": Didion, *Slouching Towards Bethlehem*, xxvii.

xxii "bound to be friction": Doug Munro, "Confessions of a Serial Biographer: An Interview with Carl Rollyson," *History Now* 9, no. 1 (February 2003): 2.

xxii "perceived," "accurately reported," and "get it right": Didion, *The Year of Magical Thinking*, 156.

xxiii "a drudge" and subsequent quotes from Mark Schorer: Mark Schorer, *The World We Imagine* (New York: Farrar, Straus and Giroux, 1968), 221, 224–26, 230, 231, 232–33.

xxiii "women we invent": Joan Didion, "Introduction" in Elizabeth Hardwick, *Seduction and Betrayal: Women and Literature* (New York: New York Review of Books, 2001), xiv.

xxiii "masterpieces": Joseph Frank, *Dostoevsky: The Miraculous Years, 1865–1871* (Princeton, N.J.: Princeton University Press, 1995), xi.

CHAPTER 1

4 learned of the Donner Party: Didion probably also knew George R. Stewart's classic account, *Ordeal by Hunger: The Story of the Donner Party*, published in 1936, two years after Didion's birth.

4 "hardened": George H. Hinkle and Bliss McGlashan Hinkle, "Editors' Foreword," in C. F. McGlashan, *History of the Donner Party: A Tragedy of the Sierra* (Stanford, Calif.: Stanford University Press, 1940), vii.

4 "I am haunted by the cannibalism of the Donner Party": Alfred Kazin, "Joan Didion: Portrait of a Professional," *Harper's* magazine, December 1971, 112.

4 "Its language": Hinkle and Hinkle, "Editors' Foreword," *History of the Donner Party*, viii–ix.

4 "too important a part of western American history" and "I have made every effort": Julia Cooley Altrocchi, *Snow Covered Wagons: A Pioneer Epic: The Donner Party Expedition 1846–1847* (New York: Macmillan, 1936), ix–x.

4 "Foster has eaten": ibid., 152.

5 "a problematic elision or inflation," 'Just ready to go,' and "[T]he actual observer": Joan Didion, *Where I Was From* (New York: Alfred A. Knopf, 2003), 30.

5 "*writers are always selling somebody out*": Joan Didion, *Slouching Towards Bethlehem* (New York: Modern Library, 2000), xxviii.

6 "their supply of food becoming exhausted" and "Indians would visit": Diana Smith, "Dr. William Geiger, Jr.," Oregon Biographies Project, coordinated by Jenny Tenlen; available at www.freepages.genealogy/rootsweb.ancestry.com /~jtenlen/ORBios/wgeiger2.txt.

7 "with the sensible suggestion": Didion, *Slouching Towards Bethlehem*, 118–19.

7 "a certain predilection for the extreme": ibid., 119.

7 "lonely and resistant rearrangers" and "she is a singularly blessed and accepting child": ibid., 118.

7 "What difference does it make" and "they just get slept in again": Didion, *Where I Was From*, 207.

8 "passionately opinionated": ibid., 205.

8 "The authentic Western voice" and subsequent quotes from Didion's review: Joan Didion, "I Want to Go Ahead and Do It," *New York Times,* October 7, 1979; available at www.nytimes.com/books/97/05/04/reviews/mailer-song.html.

8 "I have already lost touch": Didion, *Slouching Towards Bethlehem,* 124.

9 "code of the West": Didion, *Where I Was From,* 96.

10 "selling of what I had preferred to think of as heritage": Joan Didion in conversation with David Ulin in the Los Angeles Public Library's ALOUD series, November 24, 2011.

10 "in a minute": Didion, *Where I Was From,* 15.

11 "adult" books: "Telling Stories in Order to Live," Academy of Achievement interview with Joan Didion, June 3, 2006; available at www.achievement.org /autodoc/page/did0int-1.

11 "wasn't allowed to listen to the radio": Didion quoted in Karen R. Long, "The Uncompromising Joan Didion Speaks Up in Cleveland," *Cleveland Plain Dealer,* May 13, 2009; available at www.cleveland.com/books/index.ssf/2009/05 /writer_joan_didion_whose_spare.html.

11 "I think biographies are very urgent to children": "Telling Stories in Order to Live."

11 "In the late summer of *what* year": Joan Didion, "Last Words," *The New Yorker,* November 9, 1998, 74.

11 "I was always embarrassed": Ernest Hemingway, *A Farewell to Arms* (New York: Charles Scribner's Sons, 1957), 177–78.

11 "magnetic": Hilton Als, "Joan Didion, The Art of Nonfiction No. 1," *The Paris Review* 48, no. 176 (Spring 2006); available at www.theparisreview.org/inter views/5601/the-art-of-nonfiction-no-1-joan-didion.

11 "I have not wrote you half the trouble we've had": Quoted in Didion, *Where I Was From,* 75.

CHAPTER 2

13 "stock of every kind could be seen": Joseph A. McGowan, *The Sacramento Valley: A Students' Guide to Localized History* (New York: Teacher's College Press, Columbia University, 1967), 24.

14 viewed Sacramento as a "cold" place: Christian L. Larsen, *Growth and Government in Sacramento* (Bloomington: Indiana University Press, 1965), 161.

14 "when the miners paid for everything in dust": Mark A. Eifler, *Gold Rush Capitalists: Greed and Growth in Sacramento* (Albuquerque: University of New Mexico Press, 2001), 240.

15 "The area was a streetcar suburb": William Burg to the author, December 9, 2011.

16 "My father, when I was first born": Connie Brod, *In Depth* interview with Joan Didion, Book TV, C-SPAN 2, 1992.

16 "fuzzy" about finances: Didion quoted in Susanna Rustin, "Legends of the Fall," *The Guardian*, May 20, 2005; available at www.theguardian.com/books/2005/may/21/usnationalbookawards.society.

16 "full of dread": Joan Didion, *Where I Was From* (New York: Alfred A. Knopf, 2003), 213.

18 "nervous" and "different": ibid., 12.

18 "Childhood is the kingdom where nobody dies": Edna St. Vincent Millay quoted in Joan Didion, *After Henry* (New York: Simon & Schuster, 1992), 17.

19 "Class . . . is something that we, as Americans": Didion quoted in Kel Munger, "Where She Was From," *Sacramento News and Review*, October 16, 2003; available at www.newsreview.com/sacramento/where-she-was-from/content?oid=1640.

19 "They were part of Sacramento's landed gentry": William Burg to the author, March 25, 2013.

20 "whose favorite game as a child": Joan Didion, *Run River* (New York: Ivan Obolensky, 1963), 100.

21 "successful impersonation of a non-depressed person": Didion quoted in Rustin, "Legends of the Fall."

21 "I wanted to be an actress": Linda Kuehl, "Joan Didion, The Art of Fiction No. 71," *The Paris Review* 20, no. 74 (Fall-Winter 1978); available at www.theparisreview.org/interviews/3439/the-art-of-fiction-no-71-joan-didion.

21 her father's dad, "didn't talk": Didion quoted in Rustin, "Legends of the Fall."

21 "If you were born in Sacramento": William Burg to the author, December 9, 2011.

21 "There used to be a comic strip": Didion quoted in Leslie Garis, "Didion and Dunne: The Rewards of a Literary Marriage," *New York Times Magazine*, February 8, 1987; available at www.nytimes.com/1987/02/08/magazine/didion-dunne-the-rewards-of-a-literary-marriage.html.

21 "muted greens and ivories": Didion, *Where I Was From*, 65.

21 "my mother says": Didion quoted in Rustin, "Legends of the Fall."

21 "eyes that reddened": Didion, *Where I Was From*, 13.

22 "clean plate club" and "She's not a human garbage can": Joan Didion, *Blue Nights* (New York: Alfred A. Knopf, 2011), 113.

22 act of rebellion: ibid.

22 She admitted Eduene found her willful and difficult: interview with Didion on "Morning Joe," MSNBC, November 25, 2011; available at www.msnbc .com/morning-joe/45436046#4543.

22 "My mother 'gave teas'": Joan Didion, "In Sable and Dark Glasses," *Vogue Daily*, October 31, 2011; available at www.vogue.com/magazine/print/in-sable-and -dark-glasses-joan-didion/.

22 "going page by page through an issue of *Vogue*": ibid.

22 "perfect white sauce": ibid.

23 "line your garden walk" and "that will happen only when the angels sing": Didion, *Where I Was From*, 198.

23 One of her troop mates told me: Joan Haug-West to the author, January 16, 2012.

23 "lucky number": Didion, "In Sable and Dark Glasses."

23 "I kept playing around with writing": Don Swaim's audio interview with Joan Didion, October 29, 1987; available at www.wiredforbooks.org/joandidion.

24 "Let that be the greatest of your worries": Didion, "In Sable and Dark Glasses."

24 LONELY OCEAN STILL HOLDS SECRET OF AMELIA'S FATE: *San Francisco Chronicle*, July 11, 1937; available at www.sfmuseum.org/hist6/amelia.html.

25 "hated" and subsequent Steinbeck quotes: John Steinbeck, *Their Blood Is Strong* (San Francisco: Simon J. Lublin Society of California, 1938), 1, 6–7, 30. This material was originally published by Steinbeck as "The Harvest Gypsies" in a series of articles in *San Francisco News*, October 5–12, 1936.

CHAPTER 3

26 Military records: *Official National Guard Register for 1939* (Washington, D.C.: United States Government Printing Office, 1940), 218.

27 "I tended to perceive the world": Linda Kuehl, "Joan Didion, The Art of Fiction, No. 71." *The Paris Review* 20, no. 74 (Fall-Winter 1978); available at www .theparisreview.org/interviews/3439/the-art-of-fiction-no-71-joan-didion.

27 "Meanwhile, we were living in a hotel": "Telling Stories in Order to Live," Academy of Achievement interview with Joan Didion, June 3, 2006; available at www.achievement.org/autodoc/page/did0int-1.

27 "It's an adventure": Joan Didion, *Where I Was From* (New York: Alfred A. Knopf, 2003), 208.

28 "Poor children do it": ibid.

29 "pilots kept spiraling down": ibid., 209.

30 "I did not at the time think this an unreasonable alternative": Joan Didion, *Blue Nights* (New York: Alfred A. Knopf, 2011), 95.

30 did "not now seem . . . an inappropriate response": Joan Didion, *The White Album* (New York: Simon & Schuster, 1979), 15.

30 "scouted the neighborhood, and made friends": Didion, *Blue Nights*, 95.

30 "military trash": Didion, *Where I Was From*, 209.

31 "false bravery": Didion quoted in Susanna Rustin, "Legends of the Fall," *The Guardian*, May 20, 2005; available at www.theguardian.com/books/2005/may 21/usnationalbookawards.society.

31 "for some time now": Didion, *The White Album*, 134.

31 "As far as my sense of place": "Telling Stories in Order to Live."

31 "we were snowbound": ibid.

31 "my dear mother": Herman Daniel Jerrett, *California's El Dorado Yesterday and Today* (Sacramento: Press of Jo Anderson, 1915), v.

31 "historical questions": Herman Daniel Jerrett, *Hills of Gold* (Sacramento: Cal-Central Press, 1963), ix.

31 "innocent": Didion, *Where I Was From*, 10.

32 "enthusiasm and pride": Jerrett, *California's El Dorado Yesterday and Today*, 127.

32 "taken out of the middle" and all other discussion of migraines, except where otherwise noted: Suzanne Styron and Jacki Ochs, "The Migraine Project," Eleventh Hour Films; available at www.migraineproject.com/#section0. See also Didion, *The White Album*, 169.

32 "those sick headaches": Joan Didion, "Thinking About Western Thinking," *Esquire*, February 1976, 14.

33 "My sense was that we lived in the only possible place": Adair Lara, "You Can't Keep the California Out of Joan Didion," *San Francisco Chronicle*, January 6, 2004, D1.

33 "There was a certain way that possibilities": Didion quoted in Kel Munger, "Where She Was From," *Sacramento News and Review*, October 16, 2003; available at www.newsreviews.com/sacramento/where-she-was-from/content?oid=1640.

33 "I think Mother just couldn't face": "Telling Stories in Order to Live."

33 "When the school was first built": Kel Munger to the author, December 6, 2011.

34 "idea that I was smarter": "Telling Stories in Order to Live."

34 "didn't get socialised," Didion quoted in Rustin, "Legends of the Fall."

34 "If you never learn how": Joan Didion, "American Summer," *Vogue*, May 1963, 117.

34 "It was mystifying to my mother": "The Female Angst," Anaïs Nin, Joan Didion, and Dory Previn, interview by Sally Davis, Pacifica Radio Archives Preservation and Access Project, KPFK, February 1, 1972; available at www.pacificaradio archives.org/recordings/bc0611.

34 "We did not fight": Joan Didion, *Slouching Towards Bethlehem* (New York: Modern Library, 2000), 149.

34 Frank brought Didion: Didion recounts this episode in "Making Up Stories," her 1979 Hopwood Lecture at the University of Michigan. The lecture appears in Robert A. Martin, ed., *The Writing Craft: Hopwood Lectures, 1965–1981* (Ann Arbor: University of Michigan Press, 1981), 235–48. Didion says she is not entirely certain she and her father ate cracked crab at lunch.

35 "Tax Collector": Resolution Number GF, City of Sacramento Records Library, June 26, 1942; available at www.records.cityofsacramento.org/ViewDocaspx ?ID=s6tFBnt4w.

36 "We had an irrigation problem": Didion, *Where I Was From*, 17.

36 "a color that existed": ibid.

36 "There's a lot of mystery to me about writing and performing": Kuehl, "Joan Didion, The Art of Fiction, No. 71."

37 "The trouble with these *new* people": Didion, *Where I Was From*, 95.

37 "downright rural region": William Burg to the author, December 9, 2011.

37 "well-fed Lincoln-Mercury dealers": Didion, *Slouching Towards Bethlehem*, 171–72.

37 "wanted to know": Didion quoted in Jemima Hunt, "The Didion Bible," *The Guardian*, January 12, 2003; available at www.theguardian.com/books2003 /jan/12/fiction.society.

38 "have so much trouble getting through the afternoon": Joan Didion, *Telling Stories* (Berkeley:, Calif.: Friends of the Bancroft Library, 1978), 35.

38 "I would have to say the rivers": Didion quoted in Rob Turner, "Where She Was From," *Sactown*, December 2011, 83.

38 "caught, in a military-surplus life raft": Didion, *The White Album*, 60.

38 "The generation she was close to": Kel Munger to the author, December 6, 2011.

39 "She was in a higher social class" and all other quotes in this chapter from Joan Haug-West: Joan Haug-West to the author, January 16, 2012.

39 "We had a very vibrant, active household": "A Love for the Law," Academy of Achievement interview with Anthony Kennedy, June 3, 2005; available at www.achievement.org/autodoc/page/ken0int-1.

39 "process of selection" and all other quotes in this chapter regarding the Mañana Club: *Judy Robinson v. Sacramento City etc. School District 245, California Appellate 2d 278*, September 29, 1966; available at www.law.justia.com /cases/california/calapp2d/245/278.html.

40 "one [could] imagine reading": Didion, *The White Album*, 71.

40 "a very tedious time in my life": Connie Brod, *In Depth* interview with Joan Didion, Book TV, C-SPAN 2, 1992.

40 "I tell myself that we are a long time underground": Joan Didion, *The Year of Magical Thinking* (New York: Alfred A. Knopf, 2005), 150.

40 "indiscriminately": Joan Didion, "I'll Take Romance," *National Review*, September 24, 1963, 246.

40 "pain seemed a shameful secret": Didion, *The White Album*, 169–70.

41 "I was struck by the sheer theatricality of his plays": Hilton Als, "Joan Didion, The Art of Nonfiction No. 1," *The Paris Review* 48, no. 176 (Spring 2006); available at www.theparisreview.org/interviews/560/the-art-of-nonfiction-no-1-joan-didion.

41 "missed that wild control of language": ibid.

41 "[He] made me afraid to put words down": Kuehl, "Joan Didion, The Art of Fiction No. 71."

42 "a great house": Didion quoted in Turner, "Where She Was From."

43 "They had knocked up girls and married them": Joan Didion, *Political Fictions* (New York: Alfred A. Knopf, 2001), 19–20.

43 "In a gentle sleep Sacramento dreamed": Didion, *Slouching Towards Bethlehem*, 157.

43 "That's a false portrayal of the city": Rob Turner to the author, December 7, 2011.

43 "I don't see any loss of character": Mel Lawson quoted in Lloyd Bruno, "Looking Backward with Lloyd Bruno" in *Suttertown News* (May 24–31, 1984), 12.

44 "I wouldn't call [it] reporting": Didion quoted in Turner, "Where She Was From."

44 "We were talking about some people that we knew": Didion quoted in Munger, "Where She Was From."

45 "Dear Joan" and subsequent quotes regarding this incident: Joan Didion, "On Being Unchosen by the College of One's Choice" in the "Points West" column, *The Saturday Evening Post*, April 6, 1968, 18–19.

CHAPTER 4

49 "manifestations of . . . tension": Joan Didion, *Where I Was From* (New York: Alfred A. Knopf, 2003), 213.

49 "some weeks or months": ibid., 214.

49 "responsibility for hospitalization": Lt. Col. Myra L. McDaniel, "Professional Services and Activities of Occupational Therapists, April 1947 to January 1961," in *Army Specialist Medical Corps*, gen. ed. Col. Colonel Robert S. Anderson, (Washington, D.C.: Office of the Surgeon General, 1968), 570.

49 "modern concept of personality development": Col. Albert J. Glass, "Army Psychiatry Before World War II," in *Neuropsychiatry in World War II*, vol. 1, gen. ed. Col. Robert S. Anderson, (Washington, D.C.: Office of the Surgeon General, 1966), 8.

50 "species of melancholy": ibid., 3.

50 "mind guys": Didion, *Where I Was From*, 214.

50 "scientific manner" and "most satisfactory results": Glass, "Army Psychiatry Before World War II," 11.

50 ADL, "Reality Testing Situations," and "Total Push Program": McDaniel, "Professional Services and Activities of Occupational Therapists, April 1947 to January 1961," 573, 577, 582.

50 "woman doctor": Didion, *Where I Was From*, 214.

51 "given pretty much a free hand": R. U. Sirius, "Hallucinogenic Weapons: The Other Chemical Warfare," interview with Dr. James S. Ketchum, January 10, 2007; available at www.10zenmonkeys.com/2007/01/10/hallucinogenic-weapons-the-other-chemical-warfare/.

51 "permission" and "test doses": Advisory Committee on Human Radiation Experiments Report (Washington, D.C.: U.S. Government Printing Office, 1995): Chapter 1, "The Department of Defense: Consent Is Formalized"; available at www.hss.doe.gov/healthsafety/ohre/roadmap.achre.chap1_3.html.

51 "Army and the CIA had conducted LSD experiments": ibid.

51 "In Bed": Joan Didion, *The White Album* (New York: Simon & Schuster, 1979), 170.

52 "*frisson* of one another": Joan Didion, *After Henry* (New York: Simon & Schuster, 1992), 97–98.

52 "MK-ULTRA Subproject 140": Advisory Committee on Human Radiation Experiments, "Memorandum for Discussion Purposes Only," February 8, 1995 (Washington, D.C.: U.S. Government Printing Office, 1995); available at www.gwu.edu/~nsarchive/radiation/dir/mstrat/intret.txt.

53 "climate, habits, and modes of life": quoted in Didion, *Where I Was From*, 196.

53 "[M]y aversion to outdoor games" and other details regarding Didion's golfer: Joan Didion, "Take No for an Answer," *Vogue*, October 1961, 133.

53 "All I want to do is preach" and all other quotes concerning Billy James Hargis: Adam Bernstein, "Evangelist Billy James Hargis Dies: Spread Anti-Communist Message," *Washington Post*, November 30, 2004.

54 "on almost every level": Hilton Als, "Joan Didion, The Art of Nonfiction No. 1," *The Paris Review* 48, no. 176 (Spring 2006); available at www.theparisreview.org/interviews/560/the-art-of-nonfiction-no-1-joan-didion.

54 wanted to "heave": Joan Didion letter to Peggy La Violette, August 9, 1955, Bancroft Library, University of California, Berkeley.

54 "social tradition," "Hard drinkers," and "A woman who wrote novels": Didion quoted in Linda Kuehl, "Joan Didion, The Art of Fiction No. 71," *The Paris Review* 20, no. 74 (Fall-Winter 1978); available at www.theparisreview.org/inter views/3439/the-art-of-fiction-no-71-joan-didion.

55 "big, anonymous place": Didion quoted in Susanna Rustin, "Legends of the Fall," *The Guardian*, May 20, 2005; available at www.theguardian.com/books /2005/May 21/usnationalbookawards.society.

55 "waking up": Didion quoted in Rebecca Meyer, "Berkeley Alumna Discusses Politics After 'Fiction,'" *Daily Californian*, October 19, 2001; available at randomhouse.com/knopf/authors/didion/desktopnew.html.

55 "legitimate resident in any world of ideas": Joan Didion, "Why I Write," originally published in *New York Times Book Review*, December 5, 1976; reprinted in *Joan Didion: Essays and Conversations*, ed. Ellen G. Friedman (Princeton, N.J.: Ontario Review Press, 1984), 6.

55 "The Muse . . . / In distant lands": Bishop George Berkeley, "Verses on the Prospect of Planting Arts and Learning in America," in *Berkeley! A Literary Tribute*, ed. Danielle La France (Berkeley, Calif.: Heyday Books, 1997), 3.

55 "the city of unfinished attics": Ishmael Reed, *The Last Days of Louisiana Red*, cited in ibid., 174.

56 "earthquake weather": Joan Didion, *Run River* (New York: Ivan Obolensky, 1963), 119.

56 "fifteen dentists on fifteen palominos": ibid., 217.

56 "The landscape has a fantastic, strong, and depressing effect": Joan Didion in conversation with Michael Bernstein, the Revelle Forum at the Neurosciences Institute, University of California at San Diego, October 15, 2002.

56 "humorless nineteen-year-old": Joan Didion, *Slouching Towards Bethlehem* (New York: Modern Library, 2000), 127.

57 "It was as if she'd stumbled alone": Didion, *Run River*, 94.

57 "Let us steadfastly love one another": Tri-Delt motto cited at www.trideltaorg /aboutus/tr:_delta_fact_sheet.

57 "I looked at the athletic-looking young people": Simone de Beauvoir, *America Day-by-Day*, trans. Carol Cosman (Berkeley: University of California Press, 1993), 142–43.

58 "I came out of what was called the 'Silent Generation'": Didion quoted in Rustin, "Legends of the Fall."

58 "The mood of Berkeley in those years": Didion, *The White Album*, 207.

58 "provide parking for the faculty": Kevin Starr, *Golden Dreams: California in an Age of Abundance, 1950–1963* (New York: Oxford University Press, 2009), 233.

58 "There are several 'nations' of students": Clark Kerr, *The Uses of the University* (Cambridge, Mass.: Harvard University Press, 1963), 33.

58 led to a specific campus layout: For a discussion of the physical changes to the Berkeley campus in the 1950s, see Max Heirich, *The Spiral of Conflict: Berkeley 1964* (New York: Columbia University Press, 1971), 58–64.

58 "happy home": Kerr, *The Uses of the University*, 124–26.

58 "[T]he undergraduate students are restless": Clark Kerr, "Godkin Lectures at Harvard," April 1963, cited in *The Berkeley Student Revolt: Facts and Interpretations,* ed. Seymour Martin Lipset and Sheldon S. Wolin (Garden City, N.Y.: Anchor Books, 1965), 37. Kerr's remarks also appear in his *The Uses of the University,* 91.

59 "New Dealism": Starr, *Golden Dreams,* 206.

59 "The Bevatron requires": Bruce Cork, "Proton Linear Accelerator for the Bevatron," *Review of Scientific Instruments* 26, no. 2 (1955): 210.

60 "moral force" and "The planet itself seemed less impressive": Henry Adams, *The Education of Henry Adams* (Boston: Houghton Mifflin Company, 1973), 380.

60 "Seize, then, the Atom!": Henry Adams, *Letters to a Niece and Prayer to the Virgin of Chartres* (Boston: Houghton Mifflin, 1920), 130.

60 "ingenious channel": Adams, *The Education of Henry Adams,* 380.

60 "The whole way I think about politics": Meyer, "Berkeley Alumna Discusses Politics After 'Fiction.'"

61 "depends on over-interpreting everything": Connie Brod, *In Depth* interview with Joan Didion, Book TV, C-SPAN 2, 1992.

61 "I still go to the text": Didion in conversation with Bernstein, Revelle Forum.

61 "I was very excited by Sartre in particular": Didion quoted in Rustin, "Legends of the Fall."

61 "Mark Schorer . . . helped me": Kuehl, "Joan Didion, The Art of Fiction No. 71."

61 "form and rhythm imposed" and all other quotes from "Technique as Discovery": Mark Schorer, "Technique as Discovery," first published in *The Hudson Review* 1, no. 1 (Spring 1948); reprinted in Schorer, *The World We Imagine* (New York: Farrar, Straus and Giroux, 1968), 5.

62 "in which we are encamped like bewildered travelers": Joseph Conrad, *Victory* (Garden City, N.Y.: International Collector's Library, 1921), 3.

62 "maybe my favorite book in the world": Als, "Joan Didion, The Art of Nonfiction No. 1."

62 "I am not a central character" and all other quotes from *The Wars of Love*: Mark Schorer, *The Wars of Love* (Sag Harbor, N.Y.: Second Chance Press, 1982), 3, 4.

62 "I tell you this not as aimless revelation": Didion, *The White Album*, 133.

62 "[Y]ou remember the names": Joan Didion, *The Last Thing He Wanted* (New York: Alfred A. Knopf, 1996), 9.

63 *Victory* seems to me a profoundly female novel": Kuehl, "Joan Didion, The Art of Fiction No. 71."

63 "you're seeing [the story] from a distance": Brod, *In Depth* interview with Joan Didion.

63 "We were constantly being impressed": Als, "Joan Didion, The Art of Nonfiction No. 1."

63 "You hoped he would like it" and subsequent Butler quotes: Phyllis Butler in conversation with the author, July 17, 2012.

63 "I was so scared in that class I couldn't speak": Brod, *In Depth* interview with Joan Didion.

63 "there was more to be learned": Kuehl, "Joan Didion, The Art of Fiction No. 71."

63 "[I]t had not yet struck me": Joan Didion, *Telling Stories* (Berkeley, Calif.: Friends of the Bancroft Library, 1978), 3.

63 "A lot of people don't get as excited": Brod, *In Depth* interview with Joan Didion.

64 "mad" and subsequent quotes from Auden: W. H. Auden. "September 1, 1939," *The New Republic*, October 18, 1939, 297.

64 "absolutely terrified": Didion quoted in Rustin, "Legends of the Fall."

CHAPTER 5

66 a boy she referred to in letters: Joan Didion letter to Peggy La Violette, 1955, Bancroft Library, University of California, Berkeley.

66 Four years after World War II: statistics cited in Larry May, *Recasting America* (Chicago: University of Chicago Press, 1989), 148.

66 "rigid," "frozen," and "closed": Simone de Beauvoir cited in Elizabeth Spies, "'Dreaming Houses' and 'Stilled Suburbs': Sylvia Plath Encounters the American Ranch Home"; available at www.iun.edu/~nwadmin/plath/vol4/spies.pdf.

67 "I have, in the space of six days": Sylvia Plath, *Letters Home: Correspondence, 1950–1962*, ed. Aurelia Schober Plath (New York: Harper & Row, 1975), 117–18.

67 "one of the mixed blessings of being twenty": Joan Didion, *Slouching Towards Bethlehem* (New York: Modern Library, 2000), 207.

67 "the city's elite dollhouse" and subsequent quotes about the Barbizon: Michael

Callahan, "Sorority on E. 63rd S," *Vanity Fair*, April 2010; available at www.vanityfair.com/society/features/2010/04/barbizon-hotel-201004 ?printable=true.

68 "I remember Joan": Gael Greene quoted in Linda Hall, "The Writer Who Came In from the Cold," *New York*, September 2, 1996, 31.

68 "I would say, consulting a faulty memory" and other Burroway reminiscences: Janet Burroway to the author, March 21, 2012. Excerpts from Burroway's letters throughout this chapter were provided to the author on March 21, 2012.

69 "creative energy crackled like summer heat lightning": Jane Truslow, "Memo from the Guest Editor," *Mademoiselle*, August 1955, 241.

69 "It was the first time I'd ever worked in an office": "Conversation Between Joan Didion and Meghan Daum," *Black Book*, December 12, 2004; available (2011) at www.meghandaum.com/about-meghan-daum/36-conversation-between -joan-didion-and-meghan-daum.

70 "Joan spends vacations": Ellen Adams, profile of Joan Didion, *Mademoiselle*, August 1955, 249.

70 "seems better suited to the age": Jean Stafford quoted in Joan Didion, profile of Jean Stafford in "We Hitch Our Wagons," *Mademoiselle*, August 1955, 305.

70 "discover[ed] to our delight": Truslow, "Memo from the Guest Editor."

70 "champagne and caviar": Joan Gage, "Bring Back the Mlle. Guest Editor Contest"; available at www.arollingcrone.blogspot.com/2010/05/bring-back-mlle -guest-editor-contest.html.

71 "where fashion scored a touchdown": Truslow, "Memo from the Guest Editor."

71 En route, Didion wrote a series of letters: Joan Didion letter to Peggy La Violette, 1955, Bancroft Library, University of California, Berkeley.

72 "[she] was strong enough to make people take care of [her]": Joan Didion, *Run River* (New York: Ivan Obolensky, 1963), 104.

73 "Capture a man" and other ads: *Mademoiselle*, August 1955, 28–29, 50–51, 174.

74 "beads, cotton cloth": Joseph Conrad, "An Outpost of Progress," in *Joseph Conrad: The Secret Sharer and Other Stories*, ed. John Lawton (London: Orion Publishing Group, 1999), 8.

74 "a form of ugliness so intolerable": Oscar Wilde, "Literary and Other Notes," in *The Woman's World*, vol. 1, ed. Oscar Wilde (New York: Source Book Press, 1970), 39.

74 "A night of memories and sighs": Walter Landor cited in Joan Didion, *The Year of Magical Thinking* (New York: Alfred A. Knopf, 2005), 53–54.

75 "particularly vigorous panty raid": Seymour Martin Lipset and Sheldon S. Wolin, *The Berkeley Student Revolt: Facts and Interpretations* (Garden City, N.Y.: Anchor Books, 1965), 11.

76 "Zen lunatic drunks": Jack Kerouac, *Dharma Bums* (New York: Penguin, 1976), 17.

76 "real poet": Reading at Six Gallery re-creation, March 11, 1956; audio available at https://diva.sfsu.edu/collections/poetrycenter.bundles/191226.

76 "This is very important": Gary Snyder in conversation with the author, October 26, 2012.

76 "clique": Gabriel Rummonds to the author, February 12, 2012.

76 John Ridland agreed: John Ridland to the author, February 17, 2012.

77 "ghostly symposium": Jack Spicer, "One Night Stand," *The Occident*, Spring 1949, 90.

77 "pseudo avant-garde": Joan Didion letter to Peggy La Violette, 1955, Bancroft Library, University of California, Berkeley.

77 "The trouble with you, Didion": Joan Didion, "Movies," *Vogue*, May 1964, 60.

77 "I tried to be friendly with her": Renata "Harriet" Polt to the author, March 6, 2012.

77 "It is not professional": Thomas Parkinson, "Parinson [*sic*] Disects [*sic*], Discusses," *Daily Californian*, Spring 1956.

78 "And that had made all the difference" and subsequent quotes from "Sunset": Joan Didion, "Sunset," *The Occident*, Spring 1956, 21, 22, 24, 26.

79 One night she borrowed a dress: Didion recounted this anecdote in "Making Up Stories," her 1979 Hopwood Lecture at the University of Michigan. The lecture appears in Robert A. Martin, ed., *The Writing Craft* (Ann Arbor: University of Michigan Press), 235–48.

79 "Of course I was awfully jealous": Renata "Harriet" Polt to the author, March 6, 2012.

79 "two wonderful weeks in Paris": *Vogue*, August 1956, 68.

80 "[H]ow crazy I was to get out of California": "Conversation Between Joan Didion and Meghan Daum."

80 "Expect the contest *not* to be a cinch": *Vogue*, August 1956, 68.

80 "poets and idealists": Jacqueline Bouvier, "People I Wish I Had Known," *Vogue*, February 1951, 134.

80 "red, red, red": *Vogue*, August 1954, 98.

80 "[g]ive ideas for a newspaper advertisement": ibid., 71.

80 "unshakable sense of moral righteousness": Aline B. Saarinen, "Four Architects Helping to Change the Look of America," *Vogue*, August 1954, 119.

81 "[Hell] hell hell": Joan Didion letter to Peggy La Violette, 1955, Bancroft Library, University of California at Berkeley.

82 "grayed and obscurely sinister light": Joan Didion, "Why I Write," originally published in *New York Times Book Review*, December 5, 1976; reprinted in

Joan Didion: Essays and Conversations, ed. Ellen G. Friedman (Princeton, N.J.: Ontario Review Press, 1984), 6.

82 "I would like to tell you": Henry Nash Smith letter to Joan Didion, June 2, 1956, Henry Nash Smith Papers, Bancroft Library, University of California at Berkeley.

CHAPTER 6

83 "I can remember asking": "Conversation Between Joan Didion and Meghan Daum," *Black Book*, December 12, 2004; available (2011) at www.meghandaum .com/about-meghan-daum/36-conversation-between-joan-didion-and -meghan-daum.

83 "You lose ninety per cent of your body heat": ibid.

84 "commercial stuff": Linda Hall, "The Writer Who Came In from the Cold," *New York*, September 2, 1996, 31.

84 "I was trying to write a novel": ibid.

84 "in an era": ibid.

84 "ruffled the ends of her semi-pageboy": Rosa Rasiel to the author, August 18, 2012.

84 "liked being there": "Conversation Between Joan Didion and Meghan Daum."

84 "Gorgon always called": Rosa Rasiel to the author.

84 "The late fifties at *Vogue*": Mary Cantwell, *Manhattan Memoir* (New York: Penguin, 1998), 212.

85 "verbals" and "visuals": ibid., 195.

85 "Well, it's a *look*": ibid., 257.

85 "façade" and subsequent quotes about Hawaii: John W. Vandercook, "All Eyes on Hawaii," *Vogue*, February 1941, 67.

86 "opaque bewilderment": Joan Didion, *Where I Was From* (New York: Alfred A. Knopf, 2003), 8.

86 "I was never a fan": Hilton Als, "Joan Didion, The Art of Nonfiction No. 1," *The Paris Review* 48, no. 176 (Spring 2006); available at www.theparisreview .org/interviews/5601/the-art-of-nonfiction-no-1-joan-didion.

CHAPTER 7

89 "in a coma" and "I could quote a lot of English poetry": "Conversation Between Joan Didion and Meghan Daum, *Black Book*, December 12, 2004"; available

(2011) at www.meghandaum.com/about-meghan-daum/36-conversation
-between-joan-didion-and-meghan-daum.

89 "[I was] a good deal of trouble": Didion quoted in Susanna Rustin, "Legends of the Fall," *The Guardian*, May 20, 2005; available at www.theguardian.com/books /2005/may/21/usnationalbookawards.society.

89 "the kind that was sent to stores": Dan Wakefield, *New York in the Fifties* (Boston: Houghton Mifflin/Seymour Lawrence, 1992), 52.

89 "She was a) hard to know": Noel Parmentel quoted in Linda Hall, "The Writer Who Came In from the Cold," *New York*, September 2, 1996, 32.

90 "I . . . tended my own garden": Linda Kuehl, "Joan Didion, The Art of Fiction No. 71," *The Paris Review* 20, no. 74 (Fall-Winter 1978); available at www.the parisreview.org/interviews/3439/the-art-of-fiction-no-71-joan-didion.

90 "I think you're the best movie critic in America": John Gregory Dunne cited in Brian Kellow, *Pauline Kael: A Life in the Dark* (New York: Viking, 2011), 195.

90 "implacable ignorance": John Gregory Dunne, *Quintana & Friends* (New York: E. P. Dutton, 1978), 154.

90 "captures the turbulence": "Jess" at startnarrativehere.com/2010/02/slouching -towards-bethlehem-by-joan-didion-1968.

90 "impose[s] some order": Marc Weingarten, *The Gang That Wouldn't Write Straight: Wolfe, Thompson, Didion, and the New Journalism Revolution* (New York: Crown, 2005), 6.

90 "had her eyes on the nation": Jonathan Yardley, "In a Time of Posturing, Didion Dared 'Slouching,'" *Washington Post*, January 11, 2006; available at kitspsun.com /news/2006/jan/11/in-a-time-of-posturing-didion-dared-145slouching/?print=1.

90 "[In 1969] I was starting a column for *Life*": "Conversation Between Joan Didion and Meghan Daum."

91 "advantages": Kuehl, "Joan Didion, The Art of Fiction No. 71."

91 "At *Vogue*, she worked hard": Noel Parmentel quoted in Hall, "The Writer Who Came In from the Cold," 32.

91 "conned": Joan Didion letter to Peggy La Violette, September 27, 1959, Bancroft Library, University of California at Berkeley.

91 "furnished entirely with things taken from storage": Joan Didion, *Slouching Towards Bethlehem* (New York: Farrar, Straus and Giroux, 1968), 232.

92 "Noel": Joan Didion letter to Peggy La Violette, September 27, 1959, Bancroft Library, University of California at Berkeley.

92 "has never been credited" and "hard-drinking": Hall, "The Writer Who Came In from the Cold," 31.

92 "I owe you an apology": Noel Parmentel in conversation with the author, August 9, 2012.

92 "I had a theory": Hilton Als, "Joan Didion, The Art of Nonfiction No. 1," *The Paris Review* 48, no. 176 (Spring 2006); available at www.theparisreview.org /interviews/5601/the-art-of-nonfiction-no-1-joan-didion.

93 "arch-conservative but a marvelously funny guy": Norman Mailer, "The Writer as Candidate," *New York,* April 6, 1998; available at nymag.com/nymetro/news /people/features/2432.

93 "I must love him": Norman Mailer quoted in Dunne, *Quintana & Friends,* xix.

93 "non-conservative": Kevin J. Smant, *How the Great Triumph: James Burnham, Anti-Communism, and the Conservative Movement* (Lanham, Md.: University Press of America, 1992), 76.

93 "drunk, of course": Julia Reed, excerpt from *The House on First Street,* posted at today.msnbc.msn.com/id/25643400/ns/today-books/t/reporter-reflects-ruin -rebirth-new-orleans.

93 "[A]nyone who knew anything about New York": Wakefield, *New York in the Fifties,* 268.

93 "little Leftist don't-do-it-yourself affair": Noel Parmentel, "Portrait of the Reviewer," *National Review,* January 30, 1962, 68.

93 "Well, Dan had some fun with me": Parmentel in conversation with the author, August 9, 2012.

93 "I could have gotten my Ph.D.": Parmentel in conversation with the author, July 11, 2013.

93 "small, cluttered apartment": Wakefield, *New York in the Fifties,* 269.

93 "about six parties a day": Parmentel in conversation with the author, July 11, 2013.

93 "shock of light brown hair": Wakefield, *New York in the Fifties,* 268.

93 "conservative streak": Jim Desmond in conversation with the author, December 5, 2011.

94 "he'd been a rake-hell": Sam Waterston to the author, November 30, 2011.

94 "His style . . . was that of an axe-murderer": Dunne, *Quintana & Friends,* xix.

94 "As I remember it": Rosa Rasiel to the author, August 18, 2012.

94 "At the party": Parmentel in conversation with the author, July 11, 2013.

94 "Noel was around a lot": Rosa Rasiel to the author, August 18, 2012.

94 "Joan's eminence grise": Rosa Rasiel quoted in Hall, "The Writer Who Came In from the Cold," 31.

94 "the acne and the ecstasy": Wakefield, *New York in the Fifties,* 268.

94 "One evening": Rosa Rasiel to the author, August 18, 2012.

95 "He's too big": Parmentel in conversation with the author, July 11, 2013.

95 "I never saw ambition like that": Noel Parmentel quoted in Hall, "The Writer Who Came In from the Cold," 32.

95 "Action verbs": Connie Brod, *In Depth* interview with Joan Didion, Book TV, C-SPAN-2, 1992.

95 "get very angry": Kuehl, "Joan Didion, The Art of Fiction No. 71."

96 "The first few weeks": Mary Cantwell, *Manhattan Memoir* (New York: Penguin, 1998), 217.

96 "On its own terms": Brod, *In Depth* interview with Joan Didion.

96 "I would have her write": Allene Talmey quoted in Michiko Kakutani, "Joan Didion: Staking Out California," *New York Times,* June 10, 1979; available at www.nytimes.com/1979/06/10/books/didion-calif.html?ref-joandidion.

96 "All through the house" and "It is easy to make light": Joan Didion, *Telling Stories* (Berkeley, Calif.: Friends of the Bancroft Library, 1978), 4, 5.

96 "Run it through again, sweetie": ibid., 5.

96 "We were connoisseurs": ibid.

96 "traditional convention of the portrait": Joan Didion, "An Annotation," introduction to Robert Mapplethorpe, *Some Women* (Boston: Bullfinch Press/Little, Brown, 1989), 5.

97 "part of the texture of life in general" and "drinks for fifty cents": Interviews with Joan Didion and John Gregory Dunne, *New York in the Fifties,* directed by Betsy Blankenbaker (Figaro Films, 2000), film documentary.

97 "it was not long after *Sputnik*" and subsequent quotes from Noel Parmentel in this section: Parmentel in conversation with the author, July 11, 2013.

97 "Noel told her": Dan Wakefield in conversation with the author, May 4, 2013.

98 "I adored Greg": Madeleine Noble (née Goodrich) in conversation with the author, August 3, 2013.

98 "He made me laugh": Didion quoted in Sara Davidson, "Joan Didion—Losing John," *O, The Oprah Magazine,* 2005; available at www.saradavidson.com/joan-didion-losing-john.

98 "I've thought of myself that way": Didion quoted in Leslie Garis, "Didion and Dunne: The Rewards of a Literary Marriage," *New York Times Magazine,* February 8, 1997; available at www.nytimes.com/1987/02/08/magazine/didion-dunne-the-rewards-of-a-literary-marriage.html.

98 "I decided it was pathological": Didion, "Staking Out California."

98 "We talked all night": Dunne quoted in John Riley, "Writers Joan Didion and John Gregory Dunne Play It as It Lays in Malibu," *People,* July 26, 1979; available at people.com/people/archive/article/0,,20066717,00.html.

98 Didion's early *Vogue* pieces: See, for example, Joan Didion, "Take No for an Answer," *Vogue,* October 1961, 132–33; Joan Didion, "Emotional Blackmail: An Affair of Every Heart," *Vogue,* November 1962, 115–16.

99 "the world takes on for me": Didion, "Take No for an Answer," 132.

99 "[W]e are fatally drawn toward anyone": ibid., 133.

99 "direct wire to the PMLA": Joan Didion, "Finally (Fashionably) Spurious," originally published in *National Review*, November 18, 1961, reprinted in *Salinger: The Classic Critical and Personal Portrait*, ed. Henry Anatole Grunwald (New York: Harper Perennial, 2009), 77.

CHAPTER 8

102 "Whatever one may think of them": "Quo Vadis?" *Mademoiselle*, January 1960, 34.

102 "several thousand young women": Joyce Johnson, *Minor Characters: A Beat Memoir* (New York: Penguin, 1999), 118–19.

102 "Everybody should get high": "Quo Vadis?" 34.

102 "plastic, all hues": ibid.

102 "Call it the weather" and subsequent quotes from "Berkeley's Giant": Joan Didion, "Berkeley's Giant: The University of California," *Mademoiselle*, January 1960, 88, 103, 105.

102 "get top jobs": *Mademoiselle*, January 1960, 105.

103 "We were all oblivious": Larry Colton in conversation with the author, April 8, 2013.

103 "yearning for California": Joan Didion, *Where I Was From* (New York: Alfred A. Knopf, 2003), 156–57.

103 "nightmare": Mary Cantwell, *Manhattan Memoir* (New York: Penguin, 1998), 217.

103 "silliest occupations going": Joan Didion letter to Peggy La Violette, September 27, 1959, Bancroft Library, University of California at Berkeley.

104 "leading a rebellion in beauty": "People Are Talking" column, *Vogue*, January 1963, 34.

104 "neither topical nor punchy": "People Are Talking" column, *Vogue*, August 1963, 73.

104 "hair tonic": "People Are Talking" column, *Vogue*, October 1962, 150.

104 "sleepiness of the enlarged": "People Are Talking" column, *Vogue*, October 1963, 81.

104 "Have Wife With Gun Must Travel": "People Are Talking" column, *Vogue*, January 1960, 111.

104 "profoundly moving young woman": "People Are Talking" column, *Vogue*, September 1962, 190.

104 "looking like a man ridden": "People Are Talking" column, *Vogue*, March 1960, 135.

104 "threatened" people: "People Are Talking" column, *Vogue*, March 1962, 111.

104 "satisfying rightness of the baseball phrase": "People Are Talking" column, *Vogue*, November 1959, 129.

104 "double-talk adjective": "People Are Talking" column, *Vogue*, June 1960, 102.

104 "'elliptical'": "People Are Talking" column, *Vogue*, April 1961, 123.

104 "'Flash'": "People Are Talking" column, *Vogue*, April 1960, 85.

104 "zortz": "People Are Talking" column, *Vogue*, July 1962, 48.

104 "developers blast[ing] miles of ski runs": *Vogue*, November 1959, 160.

105 campaign speeches: "The Campaign Speech Writers," *Vogue*, August 1960, 158–59.

105 "the tripping sound of 'plastique'": *Vogue*, January 1963, 39.

105 "young writer with an uncompromising moral intelligence": "People Are Talking" column, *Vogue*, April 1960, 122.

105 "irritating": "People Are Talking" column, *Vogue*, September 1961, 159.

105 "dope dreams": "People Are Talking" column, *Vogue*, January 1963, 102.

105 "what it means to be a Westerner": "People Are Talking" column, *Vogue*, October 1960, 158.

105 "helpless": Joan Didion, "Notes from a Helpless Reader," *National Review*, July 15, 1961, 21–22.

106 "exploring the vagaries of his career": "People Are Talking" column, *Vogue*, November 1961, 117.

106 "fence-sitting": "People Are Talking" column, *Vogue*, March 1960, 94.

106 "our economy": "People Are Talking" column, *Vogue*, December 1961, 110.

106 "part of the boredom": "People Are Talking" column, *Vogue*, November 1959, 120.

106 "forced breaking up of some of the big San Joaquin Valley ranches": *Vogue*, October 1962, 150.

107 "passion for the documentation of irrelevant detail": Joan Didion, "Jealousy—Is It a Curable Illness?" *Vogue*, June 1961, 96.

107 "improvised . . . in two sittings": Joan Didion, comments at the National Book Award ceremony, November 17, 2007, upon receiving the Medal for Distinguished Contribution to American Letters.

107 "the magazine had a piece that had been assigned": Christopher Bollen, "Joan Didion," *V Magazine*; available at christopherbollen.com/portfolio/joan-didion.pdf.

107 "character count": Didion, comments at the National Book Award ceremony.

107 "She was better than all of them": Noel Parmentel in conversation with the author, July 11, 2013.

107 "Joan Didion, the fantastically brilliant writer": quoted in Linda Hall, "The Writer Who Came In from the Cold," *New York,* September 2, 1996, 32.

107 "beat-up desks": Allene Talmey, "Biography of a Musical: 'Damn Yankees,'" *Vogue,* March 1956, 152.

107 "A lot of people read these pieces": Joan Didion in conversation with Sloane Crosley, New York Public Library, November 21, 2011.

CHAPTER 9

108 "[d]istinctively dolorous," "perfect pitch," and "East End Avenue Ophelia": Joan Didion, "Gentlemen in Battle," *National Review,* March 27, 1962; available at old.nationalreview.com/flashback/flashback200604180656.asp.

108 "by the time the battle was done": Joan Didion, "Wayne at the Alamo," *National Review,* December 31, 1960, 414–15.

109 "There was once a day": Joan Didion, "Into the Underbrush," *National Review,* January 28, 1961, 54–55.

109 "lost money and lost families": Joan Didion, "A Celebration of Life," *National Review,* April 22, 1961, 254–55.

109 "Every real American story": Didion, "Gentlemen in Battle."

110 "there are no more great journeys": ibid.

110 "I would remind you": Barry Goldwater, acceptance speech at the twenty-eighth Republican National Convention, San Francisco, July 1964; available at washingtonpost.com/wp-srv/politics/daily/may98/goldwaterspeech.htm.

110 "(correctly) perceived": Priscilla L. Buckley, *Living It Up with National Review: A Memoir* (Dallas: Spence Publishing Company, 2005), 187.

111 "[h]er prose, while always careful": Priscilla Buckley cited in Linda Hall, "The Last Thing She Wanted," *The American Prospect,* October 23, 2005, 19.

111 "My God, did he love and appreciate his daughter": Noel Parmentel in conversation with the author, July 11, 2013.

111 "hysterical smallness" and "good deal of unpleasantness": Joan Didion letter to Peggy La Violette, August 6, 1960, Bancroft Library, University of California at Berkeley.

111 "Nothing if not eclectic!": Joan Didion letter to Peggy La Violette, September 27, 1959, Bancroft Library, University of California at Berkeley.

112 "I just turned a corner": Joan Didion letter to Peggy La Violette, November 9, 1961, Bancroft Library, University of California at Berkeley.

112 "[We] were all Westerners": F. Scott Fitzgerald, *The Great Gatsby* (New York: Charles Scribner's Sons, 1953), 177.

113 A series of short stories: "Coming Home," "The Welfare Island Ferry," and "When Did Music Come This Way? Children Dear, Was It Yesterday?" in Joan Didion, *Telling Stories* (Berkeley, Calif.: Friends of the Bancroft Library, 1978).

113 "everything I saw and heard": Didion, *Telling Stories*, 6.

113 "a romantic figure in . . . white suits": Linda Hall, "The Writer Who Came In from the Cold," *New York*, September 2, 1996, 31–32.

113 "hostile": Noel Parmentel in conversation with the author, July 11, 2013.

113 "That's what we did then": ibid.

113 "In 'Goodbye to All That'": Dan Wakefield in conversation with the author, May 4, 2013.

114 "new people": Noel Parmentel in conversation with the author, July 11, 2013.

114 "rumors of abortions": Mary Cantwell, *Manhattan Memoir* (New York: Penguin, 1998), 199.

115 "tidal surge": Joan Didion, *Blue Nights* (New York: Alfred A. Knopf, 2011), 80.

116 "spent most of every morning in tears": Nicholas Haslam, *Redeeming Features: A Memoir* (New York: Alfred A. Knopf, 2009), 156.

116 "All the fruit's going": Didion, *Telling Stories*, 6.

117 "One incident I remember": Noel Parmentel quoted in Hall, "The Writer Who Came In from the Cold," 32.

117 "What do I want with some little nobody": ibid.

117 "Those Okies she grew up with": ibid., 33.

117 "tapped into a certain vein of discontent": Joan Didion, "Turning Point," in *Nostalgia in Vogue, 2000–2010*, ed. Eve MacSweeney (New York: Rizzoli, 2010), 81–82.

118 "equalizers" and "sedation of anxiety": Joan Didion, *The White Album* (New York: Simon & Schuster, 1979), 180, 186.

118 "I was bored": "Telling Stories in Order to Live," Academy of Achievement interview with Joan Didion, June 3, 2006; available at www.achievement.org /autodoc/page/did0int-1.

118 "bad afternoon": Joan Didion, "A Problem of Making Connections," *Life*, December 5, 1969, 34.

118 "Noel came over to my place": Dan Wakefield in conversation with the author, May 4, 2013.

119 "nothing much touched him" and "Nobody wants to": Didion, "A Problem of Making Connections," 34.

119 "memoir" and "fiction which recalls a time": John Gregory Dunne, *Vegas* (New York: Random House, 1974), frontispiece.

119 "capacity for voyeurism": ibid., 199.

119 In a letter to journalist Jane Howard: John Gregory Dunne letter to Jane Howard, October 17, 1973, Rare Book and Manuscript Library, Columbia University.

119 "large, good-looking woman": Dunne, *Vegas*, 201.

119 "to see if anyone famous had died": ibid., 200.

119 "She required total concentration": ibid., 201.

120 "There must have been five hundred bodies": Dunne quoted in Michiko Kakutani, "How John Gregory Dunne Puts Himself into Books," *New York Times*, May 3, 1982; available at www.nytimes.com/books/97/03/02/reviews /dunne-work.html.

120 "Don't be obtuse": Dunne, *Vegas*, 206.

120 "sat and stared": ibid., 205.

120 "I listened to the way people talked": John Gregory Dunne, *Quintana & Friends* (New York: E. P. Dutton, 1978), xv.

120 "The joke . . . was that the nuns": George Plimpton, "John Gregory Dunne, The Art of Screenwriting No. 2," *The Paris Review* 38, no. 138 (Spring 1996); available at theparisreview.org/interviews/1430/the-art-of-screenwriting-no-2 -john-gregory-dunne.

121 "we divided into the Four Oldest and the Two Youngest": John Gregory Dunne, *Harp* (New York: Simon & Schuster, 1989), 16.

121 "a full cargo of ethnic and religious freight": ibid.

121 "their faces scrubbed and shiny": "Dominick Dunne Biography"; available at www.biography.com/print/profile/dominick-dunne-9542407.

121 "steerage to suburbia": Dunne, *Harp*, 34.

121 "[I was] slightly ashamed of my origins": ibid., 45.

121 "Get mad *and* get even": ibid., 26.

121 "[H]e had an enormous influence" and subsequent quotes from Dominick Dunne: Dominick Dunne, "A Death in the Family," originally published in *Vanity Fair*, March 2004; reprinted in Andrew Blauner, ed., *Brothers: 26 Stories of Love and Rivalry* (San Francisco: Jossey-Bass, 2009), 186.

121 "coloreds," "wayward," and "as my mother was the dispenser of Kotex": Dunne, *Harp*, 45.

121 "sniper fire": ibid., 30.

121 "quick man with a strap": ibid., 16.

122 "would do my crying for me": ibid., 17.

122 "played life on the dark keys": ibid., 18.

122 "I listened for a heartbeat": John Gregory Dunne, *Regards: The Selected Nonfiction of John Gregory Dunne* (New York: Thunder's Mouth Press, 2006), 159.

122 "and worked in the factories": Dunne, *Vegas,* 88.

122 "very worldly": Plimpton, "John Gregory Dunne, The Art of Screenwriting No. 2."

122 Dunne thought the fellow queer: Dunne expressed this suspicion in a letter to Jane Howard on December 30, 1974, Rare Book and Manuscript Library, Columbia University.

122 "pageantry": Dunne, *Vegas,* 107–108.

123 "taint on the human condition": Plimpton, "John Gregory Dunne, The Art of Screenwriting No. 2."

123 "Where you from?": Dunne, *Vegas,* 115.

123 "Though it was three years after Hiroshima": ibid., 116.

123 "cherry": ibid.

123 "Hartford was a Yale town": Dunne, *Harp,* 46.

123 "I was just a tight-assed upper-middle-class kid": Plimpton, "John Gregory Dunne, The Art of Screenwriting, No. 2."

123 "contacts who might help me": Dunne, "The Death of a Yale Man," *The New York Review of Books,* April 20, 1993; available at www.nybooks.com/articles /archives/1993/apr/22/the-death-of-a-yale-man.

124 "swordsmen": ibid., 98.

124 "finally made contact": ibid., 120.

124 "John was always fascinated": Dominick Dunne, "A Death in the Family," 187.

124 "constituency of the dispossessed," "white and black underclass," and "I grew to hate the officer class": Plimpton, "John Gregory Dunne, The Art of Screen-writing No. 2."

124 "to appreciate whores": ibid.

125 "Every failure in New York": Dunne quoted in Dan Wakefield, *New York in the Fifties* (Boston: Houghton Mifflin/Seymour Lawrence, 1992), 57.

125 "tinkling the ivories": John Gregory Dunne, "Catching the Next Trend," *Esquire,* April 1977, 10.

125 "waiters from the Tower Suite": Dunne, *Regards,* 283.

125 "most creative gossip": Calvin Trillin, *Floater* (New Haven, Conn.: Ticknor & Fields, 1980), 30.

125 "was always discovering two people": Wakefield, *New York in the Fifties,* 231.

126 "I was a jerk": Dunne, *Regards,* 350.

126 "I was still trying to run the game": Joan Didion, "In Sable and Dark Glasses," *Vogue Daily,* October 31, 2011; available at www.vogue.com/magazine/article /in-sable-and-dark-glasses-joan-didion.

126 "I want to marry him" and "The minute I got into this house": Didion quoted in Sara Davidson, "Joan Didion—Losing John," *O, The Oprah Magazine,* 2005; available at www.saradavidson.com/joan-didion-losing-john.

CHAPTER 10

127 "couldn't": John Gregory Dunne, *Harp* (New York: Simon & Schuster, 1989), 137–38.

127 "Saigon-watcher": John Gregory Dunne, *Regards: The Selected Nonfiction of John Gregory Dunne* (New York: Thunder's Mouth Press, 2006), 350.

127 "I didn't even know where the countries were": Dunne quoted in Dan Wakefield, *New York in the Fifties* (Boston: Houghton Mifflin/Seymour Lawrence, 1992), 33.

127 "what now seems a constant postcoital daze": Dunne, *Regards*, 351.

127 "I respected these guys": Dunne quoted in Wakefield, *New York in the Fifties*, 331.

127 "set straight the local reporters": Dunne, *Regards*, 235.

127 "all shit": ibid., 351.

128 "I start a book": Linda Kuehl, "Joan Didion, The Art of Fiction No. 71," *The Paris Review* 20, no. 74 (Fall-Winter, 1978); available at www.theparisreview.org /interviews/3439/the-art-of-fiction-no-71-joan-didion.

129 "very complicated chronologically": ibid.

129 "A friend would leave me the key": Joan Didion, *Slouching Towards Bethlehem* (New York: Farrar, Straus and Giroux, 1968), 235.

129 "fifty yards of yellow theatrical silk": ibid., 232–33.

129 "everything in it": ibid., 232.

129 "[T]hese dwarfs would go out into the garden": Chris Chase, "The Uncommon Joan Didion," *Chicago Tribune*, April 3, 1977.

130 "Its specialty is being two blocks away": Calvin Trillin, *Floater* (New Haven: Ticknor & Fields, 1980), 68.

130 "The usual suspects all turned it down": Noel Parmentel to the author, February 5, 2013.

130 "He used to say": Noel Parmentel in conversation with the author, July 11, 2013.

130 "I wrote this book" and subsequent quotes from Ivan Obolensky: Ivan Obolensky in conversation with the author, January 22, 2013.

130 "pounding the sidewalks": Matthew Guinn, "David McDowell: Forgotten Man of Letters," *Publishing Research Quarterly* (Spring 1988): 1.

131 "What does it mean?": "Telling Stories in Order to Live," Academy of Achievement interview with Joan Didion, June 3, 2006; available at www.achievement .org/autodoc/page/did0int-1.

131 "didn't know how to do anything at all": Kuehl, "Joan Didion, The Art of Fiction No. 71."

131 "That's why the last half is better than the first half": ibid.

132 Smith couldn't get anything past him: Noel Parmentel in conversation with the author, July 11, 2013.

132 "I kept trying to run the first half through": Kuehl, "Joan Didion, The Art of Fiction, No. 71."

132 "Obolensky had a wonderful party" and subsequent quotes about the party: Noel Parmentel in conversation with the author, July 11, 2013.

132 *"Things change"*: Joan Didion, *Run River* (New York: Ivan Obolensky, 1963), 47.

133 "Okie voice": ibid., 68.

133 "little interest": ibid., 133.

133 "talk about their diets": ibid., 182.

133 *"lots of land / Under starry skies a-bove"*: ibid., 162.

133 "towns so clean": ibid., 177.

134 "She was not certain": ibid., 264.

134 *"We could make the reasons"*: ibid., 25.

134 *"late for choosing"*: ibid., 33.

135 "The future was being made": ibid., 157.

135 "tenacious": Joan Didion, *Where I Was From* (New York: Alfred A. Knopf, 2003), 160.

135 "not inaccurate characterization": ibid., 166.

135 "while the shrill verve": Robert Lowell, "Man and Wife"; available at www.poets.org/viewmedia.php./prmMID/15283.

136 *"A member of* Vogue's *staff"*: *Vogue*, May 1963, 204.

136 "[T]here are moments": Katherine Mansfield, *The Letters and Journals of Katherine Mansfield*, ed. C. K. Stead (London: Penguin, 1977), 173.

136 "While the scene here is California": *Kirkus Reviews*, June 15, 1963; available at www.kirkusreviews.com/book-reviews/joan-didion/run-river.

136 "the appearance in California": Guy E. Thompson, "California Saga Echoes Faulkner," *Los Angeles Times,* May 19, 1963.

137 "Miss Didion's first novel": *The New Yorker,* May 11, 1963, 178.

137 "seemed to think": Kuehl, "Joan Didion, The Art of Fiction No. 71."

137 "war was not even being fought" and subsequent quotes from David Halberstam: David Halberstam, *The Powers That Be* (New York: Dell, 1979), 642, 644–46.

138 "There's no way *Time"*: Dunne quoted in Wakefield, *New York in the Fifties,* 331.

138 "light at the end of the tunnel": ibid., 332.

139 "dreamed of being an adventurer": Dunne, *Regards,* 244–45.

139 "The longing in man's heart": *Life,* October 19, 1962, 20.

139 "tuneful source": ibid., 117.

139 "modern methods": ibid., 96.

139 "[W]e did not guarantee to each other": John Gregory Dunne, *Quintana & Friends* (New York: E. P. Dutton, 1978), xix.

139 "I don't know of many good marriages": Trudy Owett, "Three Interviews," *New York*, February 15, 1971, 40.

140 "It wasn't so much a romance": Didion quoted in Madore McKenzie, "Joan Didion Is Small but Far from Timid," *Boca-Raton News*, July 21, 1977.

140 "without emotional investment" and "clinically detached": John Gregory Dunne, *Vegas* (New York: Random House, 1974), 4–5.

140 "Who can I turn to?" John Gregory Dunne, *Crooning* (New York: Simon & Schuster, 1990), 17.

140 "Marriage, writing" and subsequent quotes from Robinson: Jill Schary Robinson in conversation with the author, April 23, 2013.

141 "I'm in a serious decline": ibid.

141 "My mother had a party for us": Dunne quoted in Bernard Weinraub, "At Lunch with John Gregory Dunne: The Bad Old Days in All Their Glory," *New York Times*, September 14, 1994; available at www.nytimes.com/1994/09/14 /garden/at-lunch-with-john-gregory-dunne-the-bad-old-days-in-all-their -glory.html?pagewanted=all&src=pm.

141 "by-elections in Liechtenstein": Dunne, *Regards*, 352.

141 "San Francisco's independently owned": Ransohoff's advertisement in the *San Francisco City Directory*, 1963; available at sfgeneaology.com/sanfranciscodirec tory/1963/1963_2853.pdf.

142 "It's when a woman is thirty" and subsequent quotes from this article: *Vogue*, July 1963, 31.

143 "vertigo": Joan Didion, *The White Album* (New York: Simon & Schuster, 1979), 15.

143 "You know those little old ladies": Michiko Kakutani, "Staking Out California," *New York Times*, June 10, 1979; available at www.nytimes. com/1979/06/10/books/didion-calif.htm?ref-joandidion.

143 "The entire John Birch library": Didion, *Where I Was From*, 205.

144 "the classic betrayal": Didion, *Slouching Towards Bethlehem*, 165.

145 "So who *were* those little faggots?": Robert Lipsyte quoting Ali in *Muhammad Ali Through the Eyes of the World*, ed. Mark Collings (London: MPG Books, 2001), 259.

145 "a lot of people talking to [her]": "Telling Stories in Order to Live."

146 "unshirted hell": Noel Parmentel, "Portrait of the Reviewer," *National Review*, January 30, 1962, 68.

146 "[One day] I stopped riding": Didion, *Slouching Towards Bethlehem*, 141.

146 "lilac and garbage": ibid., 228.

146 "[I] could not walk on upper Madison Avenue": ibid., 237.

147 "Its main liability": Joan Didion, "Captain Newman, M.D.: 'Painless Erosion,'" *Vogue*, April 1964, 42.

147 "What disagreements?": Halberstam, *The Powers That Be*, 647.

147 "I could sit through": Joan Didion, "The Guest," *Vogue*, March 1964, 57.

147 *"What a Way to Go"*: Joan Didion, "What a Way to Go: 'A Million and a Half a Laugh,'" *Vogue*, May 1964, 60.

147 "Although I assume": Joan Didion, "The Night of the Iguana: 'The Dream and the Nightmare,'" *Vogue*, September 1964, 106.

148 "Everyone's sitting around": Lynne Sharon Schwartz interview, *New York in the Fifties*, directed by Betsy Blankenbaker (Figaro Films, 2000), film documentary.

148 "The American soil": James Baldwin in *New York in the Fifties*, film documentary.

148 *"Who'd you call"*: Joan Didion, "Doulos—The Finger Man: 'Wild, Scary, Comic,'" *Vogue*, April 1964, 42.

148 "precisely because we know them so well": Joan Didion, "The Organizer: 'A Parlour Trick,'" *Vogue*, July 1964, 35.

148 "She knew exactly what she was doing": Dan Wakefield in conversation with the author, May 4, 2013.

149 "creepy self": Didion quoted in Wakefield, *New York in the Fifties*, 334.

149 "[S]ome things just aren't as funny as they once were": Joan Didion, "Bedtime Story: 'Prolonged Sick Joke,'" *Vogue*, August 1964, 34.

149 "the only seduction": Joan Didion, "The Pink Panther: 'Built-in Comicality,'" *Vogue*, March 1964, 57.

149 "[T]here was a song": Didion, *Slouching Towards Bethlehem*, 226.

150 "If New York is the site": Harold Rosenberg, "The Art World: Place, Patriotism, and the New York Mainstream," *The New Yorker*, July 15, 1972, 52.

CHAPTER 11

154 "Joan definitely had the real estate gene": Josh Greenfeld in conversation with the author, April 6, 2013.

154 "Joan put an ad in the paper": Dominick Dunne, "A Death in the Family," originally published in *Vanity Fair*; reprinted in Andrew Blauner, ed., *Brothers: 26 Stories of Love and Rivalry* (San Francisco: Jossey-Bass, 2009), 187–88.

155 "Feel the swell": Joan Didion, *The Year of Magical Thinking* (New York: Alfred A. Knopf, 2005), 227.

155 "her blue Dacron crepe nightgown": John Gregory Dunne, *Quintana & Friends* (New York: E. P. Dutton, 1978), 34.

156 "nutty idea": Hilton Als, "Joan Didion, The Art of Nonfiction No. 1," *The Paris Review* 48, no. 176 (Spring 2006); available at www.theparisreview.org/interviews/5601/the-art-of-nonfiction-no-1-Joan-didion.

156 "In Hollywood": Jill Schary Robinson in conversation with the author, April 23, 2013.

156 "Hollywood was always a nepotistic society": Tim Steele in conversation with the author, April 29, 2013.

156 "We don't go for strangers in Hollywood": F. Scott Fitzgerald, *The Last Tycoon* (New York: Charles Scribner's Sons, 1941), 18.

156 "[It was] quite rigidly organized": Joan Didion, *After Henry* (New York: Simon & Schuster, 1992), 33.

157 "God, I love to look at movie stars": *Dominick Dunne: After the Party*, directed and produced by Kirsty de Garis and Timothy Jolley (Mercury Media/Road Trip Films/Film Art Docco, 2008), film documentary.

157 "She was totally comfortable": ibid.

157 "People said they were climbers": ibid.

158 "[It] was the best place to be": Dominick Dunne, *The Way We Lived Then: Recollections of a Well-Known Name Dropper* (New York: Crown, 1999), 30.

158 "'Get the girls, Peter'": ibid., 198.

158 "They were careless people": F. Scott Fitzgerald, *The Great Gatsby* (New York: Charles Scribner's Sons, 1974), 120.

158 "Dancing 10:00 p.m.": Dominick Dunne, *The Way We Lived Then*, 114.

159 "The freeway is forever!" and "go gargle razor blades": John Gregory Dunne, *Regards: The Selected Nonfiction of John Gregory Dunne* (New York: Thunder's Mouth Press, 2006), 364, 352.

159 "ribbons of freeway": "Los Angeles in a New Image," *Life*, June 20, 1960, 75.

159 "space between [destination] points": California Assembly Interim Committee on Natural Resources, Planning, and Public Works, *Highway and Freeway Planning* (Sacramento: Assembly of the State California, 1965), 22.

160 "audacious lane changes": Joan Didion, *Play It As It Lays* (New York: Farrar, Straus and Giroux, 1970), 163.

160 "What was happening was": Tim Steele in conversation with the author, April 29, 2013.

160 "When the Old Hollywood fell apart": Jill Schary Robinson in conversation with the author, April 23, 2013.

161 "like a little neighborhood": Marlo Thomas quoted in Todd S. Purdum, "Children of Paradise," *Vanity Fair*, March 2009; available at www.vanityfair.com /style/features/2009/03/Hollywood-kids200903.

161 "too beautiful for high school": Eve Babitz, *Eve's Hollywood* (New York: Delacorte Press, 1974), 79.

161 "unassuming little Beverly Hills restaurant": Valerie J. Nelson, "Beverly Hills Restaurateur Kurt Niklas Dies at 83," *Los Angeles Times*, August 20, 2009; available at articles/latimes.com/2009/aug/28/local/me-kurt-niklas28.

161 "Compared to The Daisy": Dan Jenkins, "Life with the Jax Pack," *Sports Illustrated*, July 10, 1967; available at sportsillustrated.cnn.com/vault/article /magazine/MAG1080051.

161 "evil": Cindy Kadonaga, "The Daisy Discotheque: A Born-Again Nightclub," *St. Petersburg Times*, June 11, 1977.

161 "Oh, Mr. Dunne": Dominick Dunne, *The Way We Lived Then*, 131.

161 "I was the amusement for Sinatra": *Dominick Dunne: After the Party*, de Garis and Jolley, film documentary.

162 "corner banquette": Joan Didion, *Blue Nights* (New York: Alfred A. Knopf, 2011), 62–63.

162 "Kosher Nostra" and subsequent references from Russo: Gus Russo, *Supermob: How Sidney Korshak and His Criminal Associates Became America's Hidden Power Brokers* (New York: Bloomsbury USA, 2006), 34, 282, 284, 285.

163 "Along with his pal Lew Wasserman": Tim Steele in conversation with the author, April 29, 2013.

163 "exactly like a bunch of topflight Chicago gangsters": Frank McShane, *The Life of Raymond Chandler* (New York: E. P. Dutton, 1976), 121.

163 "We were forced to sit in a house together": Joan Didion's remarks at Kelly Writer's House, University of Pennsylvania, March 31, 2009.

163 "I had no idea how to be a wife": Didion quoted in Sam Schulman, "The Year of Magical Thinking by Joan Didion," *Commentary*, December 2005; available at www.commentarymagazine.com/article/the-year-of-magical-thinking-by -joan-didion/.

163 "crapshoot": John Riley, "Writers Joan Didion and John Gregory Dunne Play It as It Lays in Malibu," *People*, July 26, 1976; available at people.com/people /archive/article/0,,20066717,00.htm.

163 "We needed . . . money": Als, "Joan Didion, The Art of Nonfiction No. 1."

164 "like being trapped on a dance floor": Joan Didion, "The Sound of Music: More Embarrassing Than Most," *Vogue*, May 1965, 143.

164 "It will probably be a big success": Pauline Kael, "Cat Ballou: Lumpy, Coy, and Obvious," *Vogue*, September 1965, 180.

164 "This is an old-fashioned action Western": Joan Didion, "The Sons of Katie Elder: Old-fashioned Action," *Vogue,* September 1965, 76.

164 "At the time I began working for *Vogue*": "Conversation Between Joan Didion and Meghan Daum," *Black Book,* December 12, 2004; available (2011) at www .meghandaum.com/about-meghan-daum/36-conversation-between-joan -didion-and-meghan-daum.

164 "I was suffering a fear": Joan Didion, *Telling Stories* (Berkeley, Calif.: Friends of the Bancroft Library, 1978), 9–10.

164 "no talent" and "no ability": ibid., 10.

164 a letter to the actor Buzz Farber: Joan Didion to Buzz Farber, November 28, 1964, Dobkin Collection, Glenn Horowitz Booksellers, Inc., New York.

165 "[S]he had gone": Didion, *Telling Stories,* 31.

165 "When she heard the door close": ibid., 25–26.

165 "When she was almost asleep": ibid., 26.

165 "There's a rush to opinion": Anne-Marie O'Connor, "Joan Didion Re-enters Her Life," *Los Angeles Times,* October 4, 2005; available at article/latimes .com/2005/Oct/04/books/la-bk-joan-didion-2005-10-04/3.

165 "Well, of course": Josh Greenfeld in conversation with the author, April 6, 2013.

165 "you didn't see other writers and editors": O'Connor, "Joan Didion Re-enters Her Life."

165 "sense of impending doom": Dunne, *Quintana & Friends,* 13.

165 "Middle America": ibid., 11.

166 "Respect was grudgingly given": ibid., 13

166 "schmucks with Underwoods": Jack Warner cited in John Gregory Dunne, *Crooning* (New York: Simon & Schuster, 1990), 200.

166 "Show me a hero": F. Scott Fitzgerald cited in Dunne, *Regards,* 18.

166 "reciprocates carnally": ibid., 19.

167 a letter from Dunne to H. N. "Swanie" Swanson: John Gregory Dunne to H. N. Swanson, February 13, 1965. The letter is in the possession of Houle Rare Books in Los Angeles.

167 "constructive criticism": Dunne, *Regards,* 20.

167 "We were coming out of [the Daisy]": Dunne quoted in Leslie Garis, "Didion and Dunne: The Rewards of a Literary Marriage," *New York Times,* February 8, 1987; available at www.nytimes.com/1987/02/08/magazine/didion-dunne -the-rewards-of-a-literary-marriage.html/.

167 "Basically the terminology is easy": ibid.

168 "If you're going to be a whore": Tim Steele in conversation with the author, April 29, 2013.

168 "We were crazy about it": "Telling Stories in Order to Live," Academy of

Achievement interview with Joan Didion, June 3, 2006; available at www
.achievment.org/autodoc/page/did0int-1.

168 "[N]o one goes to a piano bar": John Gregory Dunne, "Catching the Next
Trend," *Esquire*, April 1979, 10.

169 "twenty-five thousand dollars' worth of free publicity": Didion, *After Henry*,
228–29.

169 "You want a different kind of wife": Didion, *The Year of Magical Thinking*, 209.

169 swallowed a phenobarbital: Didion makes reference to taking the medication
in a letter to Mary Bancroft, March 30, 1966, Mary Bancroft Papers, Schlesinger
Library, Radcliffe Institute.

169 "planning meetings": ibid.

169 "white Saint Laurent evening dress": Dunne, *Regards*, 244.

169 "Outsiders . . . had to be thoroughly vetted": ibid.

170 when Nick Gurdin killed a man: ibid., 245.

170 "Everything was changing": Dominick Dunne, *The Way We Lived Then*, 127.

170 "The nanny would have the meal with the kids": *Dominick Dunne: After the
Party*, de Garis and Jolley, film documentary.

170 "A series of such [military] encounters around the world": Susanna Rustin,
"Legends of the Fall," *The Guardian*, May 20, 2005; available at www.the
guardian.com/books/2005/may/21/usnationalbookawards.society.

171 "with the possible exception of Senator Goldwater": Dunne, *Crooning*, 113.

171 "repeated droll allegations": ibid.

171 "The stench of fascism is in the air": Rick Perlstein, "1964 Republican Convention: Revolution from the Right," *Smithsonian*, August 2008; available at
www.smithsonianmag.com/history/1964-republican-convention-revolution
-from-the-right-915921/?all.

171 "The nigger issue": Bruce Watson, *Freedom Summer*, cited at padresteve
.com/2013/05/07/things-havent-changed-too-much-jackie-robinson
-goes-to-the-1964-GOP-convention-and-freedom-summer.

171 "A new breed of Republican": Jackie Robinson cited at ibid.

172 "The throng began tossing garbage": Belva Davis, *Never in My Wildest Dreams:
A Black Woman's Life in Journalism* (San Francisco: Berrett-Koeler, 2011), 4.

172 "crypto-liberals": Perlstein, "1964 Republican Convention."

172 "You know, these nighttime news shows": ibid.

172 "greatest campaign in history": American President: A Reference Resource at
millercenter.org/president/Nixon/essays/biography/3.

172 "stagnate in the swampland of collectivism": "Goldwater's 1964 Acceptance
Speech"; available at www.washingtonpost.com/wp-srv/politics/daily/may98
/goldwaterspeech.htm.

172 "liberal media," "unspoken, unadmitted," "like so much marsh gas," and "[M]onkeys": Joan Didion, "Alicia and the Underground Press," *The Saturday Evening Post*, January 13, 1968, 14.

173 "By the early 60s": Charles Taylor, "The Gipper's Dark Side," *Salon*, June 8, 2004; available at salon.com/2004/06/08/killers_4/.

173 "fake": *Dominick Dunne: After the Party*, de Garis and Jolley, film documentary.

173 "Lotusland" and "You cook New York": Dunne, *Regards*, 354–55.

174 "On nights like [this]": Raymond Chandler cited in Didion, *Slouching Towards Bethlehem*, 218.

CHAPTER 12

175 "Everything was getting wilder": Dominick Dunne, *The Way We Lived Then: Recollections of a Well-Known Name Dropper* (New York: Crown, 1999), 139.

175 "was not important": ibid., 140.

175 "were in the Mercedes": ibid., 143–44.

175 "multipaneled mirrored dining room": ibid., 145.

176 "stop-by": ibid.

176 "came by for a smoke" and other quotes about Morrison: ibid., 145–46.

176 "Hot damn, Vietnam!": Seth Rosenfeld, *Subversives: The FBI's War on Student Radicals, and Reagan's Rise to Power* (New York: Farrar, Straus and Giroux, 2012), 260–61.

177 "mechanism held together": ibid., 207.

177 "There is a time": ibid., 217.

177 "Literature, poetry and history": ibid., 225.

177 To *be* is to be *heard*: ibid., 12.

177 "right things": Joan Didion, "A Social Eye," *National Review*, April 20, 1965, 329.

178 "most serious New York novel": ibid., 330.

178 "[it was an] unmitigatable fact": Norman Mailer excerpt from *An American Dream* in *The Time of Our Time* (New York: Random House, 1998), 499.

178 "[her] breast made its pert way": ibid.

178 "What a marvelous girl Joan Didion must be": Norman Mailer's letter to William F. Buckley (1965) cited in Adam Clark Estes, "Some Literary Advice from Norman Mailer," *The Atlantic*, October 17, 2011; available at thewire.com/entertainment/2011/10/some-literary-advice-norman-mailer/43781/.

178 "She's a perfect advertisement": Mailer quoted by Noel Parmentel in conversation with the author, July 11, 2013.

178 "general erosion of technique": Joan Didion, "Questions About the New Fiction," *National Review,* November 30, 1965, 1101.

178 "[I]mprovisation is no art but a stunt": ibid.

178 "real vacuity": ibid.

178 "follow or think": ibid.

179 "Everyone wants to tell the truth": ibid.

179 "well-dressed, high-strung young woman" and subsequent quotes about *Lilith*: Joan Didion, "Lilith: Emotional Slippage," *Vogue,* November 1964, 64.

180 "What makes Iago evil?": Joan Didion, *Play It As It Lays* (New York: Farrar, Straus and Giroux, 1970), 1.

180 "constitutional inferiority": Joan Didion letter to Mary Bancroft, May 9, 1965, Mary Bancroft Papers, Schlesinger Library, Radcliffe Institute.

181 "in certain ways" and subsequent quotes from "John Wayne: A Love Song": Joan Didion, *Slouching Towards Bethlehem* (New York: Farrar, Straus and Giroux, 1968), 34, 37, 41.

181 "Oh yeah": Ben Stein in conversation with the author, June 6, 2013.

182 "I have found my way around *plenty of museums*": Joan Didion, "New Museum in Mexico: An Assault upon the Imagination," *Vogue,* August 1965, 48.

182 "Two months might be stretching that particular role": ibid.

182 "[S]he cradles herself": Alfred Kazin, "Joan Didion: Portrait of a Professional," *Harper's* magazine, December 1971, 114.

183 She told Mary Bancroft: Joan Didion letter to Mary Bancroft, May 9, 1965, Mary Bancroft Papers, Schlesinger Library, Radcliffe Institute.

183 "traumatic blindness": Kazin, "Joan Didion," 114.

183 "You don't *look* like a migraine personality": Joan Didion, *The White Album* (New York: Simon & Schuster, 1979), 171.

183 "Mountain Greenery": Joan Didion letter to Mary Bancroft, May 9, 1965, Mary Bancroft Papers, Schlesinger Library, Radcliffe Institute.

183 "I had, [at this] time": Didion, *The White Album,* 46.

183 "Joan's husband" and subsequent quotes from "On Going Home": Didion, *Slouching Towards Bethlehem,* 165.

184 "Joan and John were tremendous celebrity-fuckers": Josh Greenfeld in conversation with the author, April 6, 2013.

184 "fairy": Joan Didion letter to Mary Bancroft, August 26, 1965, Mary Bancroft Papers, Schlesinger Library, Radcliffe Institute.

184 "were strivers": Hunter Drohojowska-Philp in conversation with the author, March 27, 2013.

184 "Mrs. Misery and Mr. Know-All": Christopher Isherwood, *Liberation: Diaries*

1970–1983, ed. Katharine Bucknell (New York: HarperCollins Publishers, 2012), 676.

184 "spoke in [a] tiny little voice": ibid., 272.

184 "Those tragic and presumably dying women": ibid., 601.

184 "Well, it was obvious why Chris didn't warm to Joan": Don Bachardy in conversation with the author, April 23, 2013.

185 "Harrison": Eve Babitz in conversation with the author, March 27, 2013.

185 "art groupie/art model": ibid.

185 "In every young man's life": Earl McGrath cited in Lili Anolik, "All About Eve and Then Some," *Vanity Fair,* March 2014, 291.

185 "Mostly, he was supported by his wild Italian wife": Eve Babitz in conversation with the author, March 27, 2013.

185 "Marilyn Monroe was [a] role model": "Oral History Interview with Eve Babitz," 2000 Jun 14, Archives of American Art, Smithsonian Institution.

186 "I mean, it was built for, you know, peccadilloes:" Eve Babitz quoted in A. M. Homes, *Los Angeles: People, Places, and the Castle on the Hill* (Washington, D.C.: National Geographic, 2002), 25.

186 "When I was growing up": Griffin Dunne quoted in ibid., 28.

187 "Someday you will" and "because I wanted a baby": Joan Didion, *Slouching Towards Bethlehem,* 138–39.

187 "like an all-out war zone": Sgt. Ben Dunn quoted at sites.google.com/site/watts riotsofla/the-riot/thumbnailCAOQQ512.jpg?attredirect=0.

187 Noel Parmentel: All details of Noel Parmentel's visit in August 1965 are from Joan Didion in letters to Mary Bancroft, May 9, 1965, and August 26, 1965, and from John Gregory Dunne in a letter to Mary Bancroft, March 30, 1966, Mary Bancroft Papers, Schlesinger Library, Radcliffe Institute.

187 "Black people had been taught non-violence": Huey P. Newton, *The Huey P. Newton Reader,* ed. David Hilliard and Donald Weise (New York: Seven Stories Press, 2002), 49.

188 "goddamned elephant": John Gregory Dunne quoted in "Exploring L.A. Through the Eyes of a Writer," *Los Angeles Times,* January 30, 1994; available at latimes.com/1994-01-30/opinion/op-18357_1_john_gregory_dunne.

188 Parmentel disputes this: Noel Parmentel in conversation with the author, July 11, 2013.

188 "You were wrong": Joan Didion, *The Year of Magical Thinking* (New York: Alfred A. Knopf, 2005), 138.

188 "The Old Duke" was gratified: John Wayne in a letter to Joan Didion, September 28, 1965, cited at the Web site for the 2011 October Personal Property of John Wayne Signature Auction #7045, "A Joan Didion Set of Correspondence, 1965."

CHAPTER 13

189 "his ear to the ground": John Gregory Dunne's notebook, John Gregory Dunne Papers, 1962–1967, Charles E. Young Research Library, UCLA Library Special Collections.

189 "like driving four hundred miles on a pool table": John Gregory Dunne, *Quintana & Friends* (New York: E. P. Dutton, 1978), 115.

190 "Cesar is a mystic": John Gregory Dunne's notebook, John Gregory Dunne Papers 1962–1967, Charles E. Young Research Library, UCLA Library Special Collections.

190 "It was rough in those early years": Cesar Chavez quoted in Luis Valdez, Sister Mary Prudence, and Cesar Chavez, "Tales of the Delano Revolution," *Ramparts,* July 1966, 6.

191 "having or thinking about having": Joan Didion, *Blue Nights* (New York: Alfred A. Knopf, 2011), 59.

191 "[T]he next week I was meeting Blake Watson": ibid.

191 "on Palos Verdes Drive": John Gregory Dunne, *Vegas* (New York: Random House, 1974), 9.

191 "sat in a stall": ibid.

191 "[u]nable to have children of their own": Didion quoted in Susanna Rustin, "Legends of the Fall," *The Guardian,* May 20, 2005; available at www.theguardian.com/books/2005/may/21/usnationalbookawards.society.

191 "not strong enough": John Gregory Dunne, *True Confessions* (New York: Pocket Books, 1977), 343.

191 "incompetent" cervixes: John Gregory Dunne, *The Red White and Blue* (New York: Simon & Schuster, 1987), 213.

191 "a migraine attack": Joan Didion, "A Review of *The Soft Machine,*" *Bookmark,* March 1966, 2–3.

192 "In my beginning is my end": T. S. Eliot, *Four Quartets* (New York: Harcourt Brace Jovanovich 1971), 13, 23.

192 *"L'adoptada"*: Didion, *Blue Nights,* 60.

192 "[e]ither birth parent": California Family Code, Section 8700-8720; available at legalinfo.ca.gov/cgi-bin/displaycode?section=fam&group=08001-09000 &file=8700-8720.

192 "is not open to inspection": California Family Code, 9200 (a); available at law.onecle.com/California/family/9200.html.

192 "troubled lot": Griffin Dunne quoted in Boris Kachka, "I Was No Longer Afraid to Die. I Was Now Afraid Not to Die," *New York,* October 16,

2011; available at nymag.com/arts/books/features/joan-didion-2011-10/index3.html.

193 "I have never gotten over it": Blake Watson quoted in Al Martinez, "For Obstetrician, Life is Not Routine," *Sarasota Herald-Tribune*, August 11, 1974.

193 "I think you should feel": J. Randy Taraborrelli, *Jackie, Ethel, Joan: Women of Camelot* (New York: Warner Books, 2000), 344.

193 "I have a beautiful baby girl": Didion, *Blue Nights*, 55.

193 "did not trust the uncertainties of unknown blood": John Gregory Dunne, *Dutch Shea, Jr.* (New York: Pocket Books, 1983), 13.

194 "an infant with fierce dark hair": Didion, *Blue Nights*, 55.

194 "Once she was born": ibid., 54.

194 "You're safe": Joan Didion, *The Year of Magical Thinking* (New York: Alfred A. Knopf, 2005), 96.

194 "Quintana!": Dunne, *Quintana & Friends*, 5. Didion also tells a version of the nursery story in *Blue Nights*, 56.

194 Dunne used the word *fierce*: Dunne, *Quintana & Friends*, 3.

194 Didion wrote "fierce": Didion, *Blue Nights*, 55.

194 "singularly blessed and accepting child": Joan Didion, *Slouching Towards Bethlehem* (New York: Modern Library, 2000), 132.

194 "[W]atching her journey from infancy": Dunne, *Quintana & Friends*, 3.

195 "Making celebratory drinks": Didion, *Blue Nights*, 56–57.

195 "Saks because if you spend eighty dollars": ibid., 57.

195 "And worse yet, worse by far": ibid., 58.

195 "Quintana, Manuel José": John Gregory Dunne letter to Mary Bancroft, March 30, 1966, Mary Bancroft Papers, Schlesinger Library, Radcliffe Institute.

196 Didion was stunning: ibid.

196 *"What if you hadn't been home"*: Didion, *Blue Nights*, 118.

196 *"Do the peacocks"*: ibid., 163.

196 "I heard them cry—the peacocks": Wallace Stevens, *The Collected Poems of Wallace Stevens* (New York: Alfred A. Knopf, 1975), 8.

196 "Swing up into the apple tree": T. S. Eliot, *The Complete Poems and Plays, 1909–1950* (New York: Harcourt Brace Jovanovich, 1971), 93.

196 "It lay before us": John Lloyd Stephens cited in Joan Didion, "New Museum in Mexico: An Assault upon the Imagination," *Vogue*, August 1965, 48.

196 "I just christened the baby": Didion, *Blue Nights*, 77.

196 phenobarbital: Joan Didion letter to Mary Bancroft, March 30, 1966, Mary Bancroft Papers, Schlesinger Library, Radcliffe Institute.

196 She was also taking ergot: ibid.

197 "finish the book he had contracted": Didion, *Blue Nights*, 71.

197 Dunne told Mary Bancroft: John Gregory Dunne letter to Mary Bancroft, March 30, 1966, Mary Bancroft Papers, Schlesinger Library, Radcliffe Institute.

198 "Mexicans on the run": Didion, *The Year of Magical Thinking*, 118–19.

198 *"L' adoptada"*: Didion, *Blue Nights*, 60.

198 *"Qué hermasa . . . Qué chula"*: ibid., 62.

198 *"[V]ibora* in Los Angeles": ibid., 73.

198 "Why am I dragging myself all the way out to California?": PBS Web site for *The American Experience: Robert F. Kennedy*, "People and Events, Cesar Chavez, 1927–1993"; available at www.pbs.org/wgbh/amex/rfk/peopleevents/p_chavez .htm.

198 "his head [caught] up with his heart": ibid.

198 "The Kennedys sponged up ideas": Dunne, *Quintana & Friends*, 119.

199 it tended to publish "long": John Gregory Dunne letter to Carl Brandt, January 8, 1966, John Gregory Dunne Papers, 1962–1967, Charles E. Young Research Library, UCLA Library Special Collections.

199 He told his agent: ibid.

199 Dunne should test the "desirability": Carl Brandt letter to John Gregory Dunne, June 29, 1966; in ibid.

199 "big waves": John Gregory Dunne letter to Carl Brandt, June 1966; in ibid.

199 "You'll have friends over": Didion, *Blue Nights*, 74.

200 He would be going to Los Angeles for a few days: Henry Robbins letter to John Gregory Dunne and Joan Didion, June 2, 1966, John Gregory Dunne Papers, 1962–1967, Charles E. Young Research Library, UCLA Library Special Collections.

200 "I thought so little of myself as a writer": Joan Didion, *After Henry* (New York: Simon & Schuster, 1992), 16.

200 "we got drunk" and "before the summer was out": ibid.

200 "epic" and subsequent Fox quotes: Margi Fox, "God of Books," *Literal Latté*, Summer 2009; available at www.literal-latte.com/2009/06/god-of-books.

201 "incredibly busy" and "The enclosed check": Henry Robbins letter to Cesar Chavez, July 5, 1966, John Gregory Dunne Papers, 1962–1967, Charles E. Young Research Library, UCLA Library Special Collections.

201 "Anthony Kennedy, attorney": John Gregory Dunne expenses list; in ibid.

202 "this used to be a good town before": John Gregory Dunne, *Delano: The Story of the California Grape Strike* (New York: Farrar, Straus and Giroux, 1967), 11.

202 if "you are working on a book about the strike": Dick Kluger letter to Joan Didion, July 15, 1966, John Gregory Dunne Papers, 1962–1967, Charles E. Young Research Library, UCLA Library Special Collections.

203 "People, issues, and causes": Dunne, *Quintana & Friends*, 117.

203 "In Ingles!": John Gregory Dunne's notebook, John Gregory Dunne Papers, 1962–1967, Charles E. Young Research Library, UCLA Library Special Collections.

203 "The soil [here] has been engineered": Verlyn Klinkenborg. "Lost in the Geometry of California's Farms," *New York Times*, May 4, 2013; available at nytimes.com/2013/05/05/opinion/Sunday/lost-in-the-geometry-of-californias -farms.htm/?_r=0.

203 "largest human alteration of the earth's surface": ibid.

203 "He had proposed a story on Chavez" and subsequent quotes from Streshinsky: Shirley Streshinsky to the author, March 25, 2012.

205 "Who is this fellow": John Gregory Dunne's notebook, John Gregory Dunne Papers, 1962–1967, Charles E. Young Research Library, UCLA Library Special Collections.

205 "the Vietcong": Dunne, *Delano*, 158.

205 "Agriculture is the very foundation of our nation": ibid., 111.

205 "I see you got a sunburn last Monday": ibid., 85.

205 "Because I had been tired too long": Didion, *Slouching Towards Bethlehem*, 187.

205 "In early August 1966": Dunne, *Delano*, 154.

206 "temperament for paradise": Didion, *Slouching Towards Bethlehem*, 188.

206 "[S]omething to see": Joan Didion, *Democracy* (New York: Simon & Schuster, 1984), 11.

206 "They do not describe" and "done Carson": Joan Didion, "Where *Tonight Show* Guests Go to Rest," *Esquire*, October 1976, 77.

206 "pale and bored": ibid.

206 "sleazy festivity": Didion, *Slouching Towards Bethlehem*, 191.

206 "[S]omeone just four years younger than": ibid., 192–93.

207 "girls with hibiscus in their hair": ibid., 194.

207 "Inside were a mother and seven children": Dunne, *Delano*, 98.

208 "California golden girl": Dunne, *Quintana & Friends*, 116–17.

CHAPTER 14

209 "Seldom has a jury": Ruth Reynolds, "A Murder Jury Had to Decide Whether a Pregnant Wife Was Trying to Keep or Get Rid of Her Husband," *Reading Eagle*, September 5, 1965.

209 "lies only an hour east": Joan Didion, *Slouching Towards Bethlehem* (New York: Farrar, Straus and Giroux, 1962), 3.

209 "It was then and there": Marc Reisner, excerpt from *Cadillac Desert*, in Gayle Wattawa, *Inlandia: A Literary Journey through California's Inland Empire* (Berkeley, Calif.: Heyday Books, 2006), 19.

211 "What will I tell the children": Didion, *Slouching Towards Bethlehem*, 6.

211 "October is the bad month": ibid., 3.

211 "It might have been anyone's bad summer": ibid., 9.

211 "[It] was a bright warm day": ibid., 19.

212 "I now learned how others saw us": Susan Straight, "Introduction," in Wattawa, *Inlandia*, xx.

212 "The future always looks good": Didion, *Slouching Towards Bethlehem*, 4.

212 "The guys I worked with": James Fallows, "WigWams, Wittfogel, and Joan Didion: All in One Post," *The Atlantic* online; available at www.theatlantic.com /national/print/2013/08/wigwams-wittfogel-and-joan-didion-all-in -one-post.

212 "full of hot exciting young babes": ibid.

212 "It helped to make you famous but it's my life": letter quoted in Debra J. Miller, "A Mother's Crime," *Los Angeles Times*, April 2, 2006; available at http://arti cles.latimes.com/print/2006/apr/02/magazine/tm-dreams14.

213 "She didn't do it": Reynolds, "A Murder Jury Had to Decide . . ."

213 "I never sleep": Joan Didion's remarks at the 2007 National Book Award ceremony upon receiving the Medal for Distinguished Contribution to American Letters, November 14, 2007, Marriott Marquis Hotel, New York.

CHAPTER 15

217 "I am talking here": Joan Didion, *The White Album* (New York: Simon & Schuster, 1979), 11.

217 "The place [was] vast": John Gregory Dunne, *Crooning* (New York: Simon & Schuster, 1990), 39.

217 "Bette Davis had": ibid.

217 "Now the pimps and junkies": ibid.

217 "Synanon owned one house": These days the Dunnes' old house is itself the home of the Shumei Hollywood Center, which advertises "healing by spiritual light."

218 "a vast Stalinist couch": Didion, *The White Album*, 89.

218 "It is raining in California": Karl Shapiro cited in ibid., 65.

218 "in order to live" and "The princess is caged in the consulate": Didion, *The White Album*, 11.

219 "Everybody knew everybody" and subsequent Phillips quotes: Michelle Phillips, *California Dreamin'* (New York: Warner Books, 1986), 90, 118, 119.

219 "What do you want?": Didion, *The White Album*, 19.

219 "It seems to me": ibid.

220 "the man who will bring a big breath of fresh air": Seth Rosenfeld, *Subversives: The FBI's War on Student Radicals and Reagan's Rise to Power* (New York: Farrar, Straus and Giroux, 2012), 361.

220 "Before this is all over": ibid.

221 "big ticket": handwritten note (author unidentified) to Carl Brandt, February 25, 1966, Farrar, Straus and Giroux Records, Manuscripts and Archives Division, New York Public Library.

221 "troubled time": Joan Didion, *Slouching Towards Bethlehem* (New York: Modern Library, 2000), xvi.

221 "Tell me that my house is burned down": Didion, *The White Album*, 172.

221 "Delano?": Joan Didion letter to Henry Robbins, August 1, 1967, Farrar, Straus and Giroux Records, Manuscripts and Archives Division, New York Public Library.

221 "The door on the Victorian commode" and other quotes about the break-in: John Gregory Dunne, *Quintana & Friends* (New York: E. P. Dutton, 1978), 42–43.

222 "superb job of reporting": Henry Robbins letter to John Gregory Dunne, January 27, 1967, John Gregory Dunne Papers, 1962–1967, Charles E. Young Research Library, UCLA Library Special Collections.

222 "I keep waiting and hoping": Dick Kluger letter to John Gregory Dunne, January 4, 1967; in ibid.

222 "You can run a Greyhound bus": Dunne, *Quintana & Friends*, 112.

223 "was as if Achilles had fallen": ibid., 113.

223 "And now that you're with FSG": Henry Robbins letter to John Gregory Dunne, February 1, 1967, John Gregory Dunne Papers, 1962–1967, Charles E. Young Research Library, UCLA Library Special Collections.

223 "When I started writing": Tom Wolfe cited in Marc Weingarten, *The Gang That Wouldn't Write Straight: Wolfe, Thompson, Didion and the New Journalism Revolution* (New York: Crown, 2005), 95.

224 "I had not been able to work in some months": Didion, *Slouching Towards Bethlehem*, xiii–xiv.

224 "San Francisco was where": ibid., 85.

225 Max Rinkel: For this and subsequent references to the history of LSD's development and distribution, I have drawn upon Jay Stevens, *Storming Heaven: LSD and the American Dream* (New York: Harper & Row, 1987), and

Martin A. Lee and Bruce Shlain, *Acid Dreams: The CIA, LSD and the Sixties Rebellion* (New York: Grove Press, 1985).

225 "I have been born again": Cary Grant quoted in Stevens, *Storming Heaven*, 64.

225 "If the doors of perception": epigraph in Aldous Huxley, *The Doors of Perception* (New York: Harper & Brothers, 1954).

225 "wisdom drugs": Stevens, *Storming Heaven*, 147.

226 "People are beginning to see": Allen Ginsberg quoted in ibid., 146–47.

226 "Hold back the edges of your gowns, Ladies": William Carlos Williams quoted in ibid., 114.

226 "After Delano" and subsequent quotes from Shirley Streshinsky: Shirley Streshinsky to the author, April 1, 2012.

226 Paul Hawken: For a profile of Paul Hawken, see Wes Smith, "The Gardener of Eden," *Chicago Tribune*, January 9, 1989; available at http://articles.chicagotribune.com/1989-01-09/features/8902240351_1_smith-hawken-paul-gardening.

227 "total theater": Didion, *Slouching Towards Bethlehem*, 95.

227 "Somebody is usually doing something interesting" and "garage of a condemned hotel": ibid.

227 "actually an old factory": Jean Allison Young quoted in William Shurtleff and Akiko Aoyogi, *History of Erewhon* (Lafayette, Calif.: Soyinfo Center, 2011), 276–77.

227 "I just stayed around awhile": Didion, *Slouching Towards Bethlehem*, 85.

227 "photos of personal saints": Magic Bus; available at http://magicbussf.com/october-06-1966-love-pageant-rally-in-panhandle.

227 "We wanted to create a celebration of innocence": ibid.

228 "We're in the same business": Ken Kesey quoted in Alice Echols, *Scars of Sweet Paradise: The Life and Times of Janis Joplin* (New York: Henry Holt, 1999), 157.

228 "giant restaurant mayonnaise jar": Linda Gravenites quoted in ibid., 156.

228 "Up until then": ibid., 157.

228 "Pretty little 16-year-old": Didion, *Slouching Towards Bethlehem*, 101.

228 "IF YOU DON'T KNOW": ibid., 125.

229 "a very blond and pale and dirty child": ibid., 95.

229 "High Kindergarten": ibid., 127.

229 "pathetically unequipped": ibid., 122.

229 "The only LSD we could get": Jean Allison Young quoted in Shurtleff and Aoyogi, *History of Erewhon*, 276–77.

229 "Wow": Didion, *Slouching Towards Bethlehem*, 106.

229 "who were never taught": ibid., 84.

229 "less in rebellion": *Joan Didion: Essays and Conversations*, ed. Ellen G. Friedman (Princeton, N.J.: Ontario Review Press, 1984), 123.

229 "These were children": ibid.

230 "Anybody who thinks": ibid., 120.

230 "[T]he peculiar beauty": ibid., 121.

230 "Broken Man" and "*Hello, Quintana*": Joan Didion, *Blue Nights* (New York: Alfred A. Knopf, 2011), 51.

231 "imperative" and "I was . . . as sick": Didion, *Slouching Towards Bethlehem*, xiii, xv.

231 "was a very odd piece to do": "The Female Angst: Anaïs Nin, Joan Didion, and Dory Previn," interview by Sally Davis, Pacifica Radio Archives Preservation and Access Project, KPFK, February 1, 1972; available at www.pacificaradio archives.org/recordings/bc0611.

231 "running so close to deadline": Joan Didion's remarks at the 2007 National Book Award ceremony upon receiving the Medal for Contribution to American Letters, November 14, 2007, Marriot Marquis Hotel, New York.

232 "despondent" and "finished the piece": Didion, *Slouching Towards Bethlehem*, xiv.

232 "I suppose almost everyone who writes": ibid.

232 "unfair": Christopher Bollen, "Joan Didion," *V Magazine*; available at christopher bollen.com/portfolio/joan_didion.pdf.

232 "I want to include a special option clause": Henry Robbins letter to Joan Didion, July 12, 1967, Farrar, Straus and Giroux Records, Manuscripts and Archives Division, New York Public Library.

232 "mindless": Joan Didion letter to Henry Robbins, August 1, 1967; in ibid.

232 "would either prove": Didion quoted in Chris Chase, "The Uncommon Joan Didion," *Chicago Tribune*, April 3, 1977.

232 "inaccuracies" and "protect": David D. Connors, Jr., for Brabeck, Phleger, and Harrison, Attorneys, in a letter to Roger Straus and Henry Robbins, June 28, 1967, John Gregory Dunne Papers, 1962–1967, Charles E. Young Research Library, UCLA Library Special Collections.

232 "alleged errors": ibid.

233 "The author has clearly conveyed" and "The sweet and gentle Chavez": Subscriber letters to Don McKinney at *The Saturday Evening Post*; in ibid.

233 "I've tried several approaches on the DELANO": L. Marvin Craig letter to Roger Straus, August 12, 1967, Farrar, Straus and Giroux Records, Manuscripts and Archives Division, New York Public Library.

233 "a very difficult young man": John Gregory Dunne letter to Henry Robbins, March 22, 1967, John Gregory Dunne Papers 1962–1967, Charles E. Young Research Library, UCLA Library Special Collections.

233 "The [thematic] combinations are endless": Lois Wallace letter to Henry Robbins, September 21, 1967; in ibid.

234 "'as it lays' part": Henry Robbins letter to Joan Didion, August 9, 1967; in ibid.

234 "Will you tell Joan, please": Roger Straus letter to John Gregory Dunne, August 24, 1967; in ibid.

234 "confus[ing] objectivity" and "postscript to Joan": Henry Robbins letter to John Gregory Dunne, September 27, 1967; in ibid.

234 "There was no reason for him": John Gregory Dunne, "Foreword to the New Edition," *The Studio* (New York: Limelight Editions, 1985), unpaginated.

234 "became as anonymous": ibid.

235 "[T]he omniscient cool narrator": ibid.

235 "As a story": ibid.

235 "There was a jasmine vine": Didion, *The White Album*, 41.

235 "She cooked nonstop" and subsequent quotes from Eve Babitz, unless otherwise noted: Eve Babitz in conversation with the author, March 30, 2013.

236 "The two worlds met": Travis Elborough, "Kicking Against the Pricks," interview with Barney Hoskyns in *P.S.*, end section to Barney Hoskyns, *Hotel California: Singer-Songwriters and Cocaine Cowboys in the LA Canyons, 1967–1976* (London: Fourth Estate, 2005), 2.

237 "Folk+Rock+Protest=Dollars": Hoskyns, *Hotel California*, 7.

237 "We put 'Lay Lady Lay' on the record player": Didion, *The White Album*, 41.

237 "Joan and I connected": Eve Babitz quoted in Lili Anolik, "All About Eve and Then Some," *Vanity Fair*, March 2014, 291.

237 "Los Angeles had no modern art museum": Hunter Drohojowska-Philp, *Rebels in Paradise: The Los Angeles Art Scene and the 1960s* (New York: Henry Holt, 2011), xxiii–xxiv.

238 "[T]he book is so curious": Philip Leider, "Books Received: *Twentysix Gasoline Stations*, by Edward Ruscha," *Artforum*, September 1963, 57.

238 "I want absolutely neutral material": Ed Ruscha quoted in John Coplans, "Concerning 'Various Small Fires': Edward Ruscha Discusses His Perplexing Publications," in Edward Ruscha, *Leave Any Information at the Signal*, ed. Alexandra Schwartz (Cambridge, Mass.: MIT Press, 2004), 26.

238 "direct response to life": John Coplans, "The New Painting of Common Objects," in *Pop Art: A Critical History*, ed. Steven Henry Madoff (Berkeley: University of California Press, 1997), 43. For more about Ruscha's work, see Alexandra Schwartz, *Ed Ruscha's Los Angeles* (Cambridge, Mass.: MIT Press, 2010).

238 "contemporary morality": C. D. B. Bryan, "'The Pump House Gang' and 'The Electric Kool-Aid Acid Test,'" *New York Times Book Review*, August 18, 1968; available at www.nytimes.com/1968/08/18/books/1968wolfe-acid.html?_r=0.

239 "There is a very thin line": Ed Ruscha quoted in Coplans, "Concerning 'Small Various Fires,'" 22.

239 "I never ask": Joan Didion, *Play It As It Lays* (New York: Farrar, Straus and Giroux, 1970), 1.

239 "I imagined that my": Didion, *The White Album*, 41.

239 "The first time I dropped acid": Dominick Dunne, "Murder Most Unforgettable," *Vanity Fair,* April 2001; reprinted at sensationalsharontate.blogspot .com/2009/08/one-of-sharons-friends-dies-author.html.

239 "Jay had a private room": ibid.

240 "She wore her blonde hair straight": ibid.

240 "jitters": Didion, *The White Album*, 42.

240 "You could smell the semen": Eve Babitz quoted in Hoskyns, *Hotel California,* 70.

240 "my moon lamp": John Gregory Dunne, *Dutch Shea, Jr.* (New York: Pocket Books, 1983), 195. Didion has said that phrases attributed to Cat in the novel came from Quintana.

240 "We invited one hundred people": Elizabeth Mehren, "Authors Share Personal Footnotes: Joan Didion, Tom Wolfe Speak to Literati at PEN Meeting," *Los Angeles Times,* November 13, 1985; available at articles.latimes.com/print /1985-11-13/news/vw-5406_1_novelist-joan-didion.

240 "It was a fucking zoo": Jemima Hunt, "The Didion Bible," *The Guardian,* January 12, 2003; available at www.theguardian.com/books/2003/jan/12 /fiction.society.

240 "I thought it was Colonel Klink": Griffin Dunne quoted in "Sarasota Film Festival 2013: Closing Weekend," *Sarasota,* April 13, 2013; available at sarasota magazine.com/on-stage/2013/04/15/sarasota-film-festival-2013-closing -weekend.

240 "Chicken salad": Hunt, "The Didion Bible."

240 "[W]hen I gave it to her": Mehren, "Authors Share Personal Footnotes."

240 "She had just done a concert": Didion, *The White Album*, 25.

241 "passed out on the divan": Mehren, "Authors Share Personal Footnotes."

241 "convenience of being close to the street dealers": Echols, *Scars of Sweet Paradise,* 295.

241 "It's so strong": ibid., 300.

CHAPTER 16

242 "We've got entertainment": John Gregory Dunne, *The Studio* (New York: Limelight Editions, 1985), 111.

242 "accept the nomination": Lyndon Johnson quoted in Norman Mailer, *Miami and the Siege of Chicago* (New York: New American Library, 1968), 102.

243 "They find an almost childlike fascination" and "[i]ndoors or outdoors": James Shepley, a letter from the publisher in *Time*, July 7, 1967, photo insert captions (unpaginated).

243 "The only American newspapers": Joan Didion, "Alicia and the Underground Press," *The Saturday Evening Post*, January 13, 1968, 14.

244 "I find that most people east of Nevada": Henry Robbins letter to Robert Coles, October 18, 1967, Farrar, Straus and Giroux Records, Manuscripts and Archives Division, New York Public Library.

244 "A lot of shit": John Gregory Dunne letter to Julie Coryn, April 5, 1968: in ibid.

245 "the Norman Mailers of the Top Forty": Joan Didion, *The White Album* (New York: Simon and Schuster, 1979), 212.

245 "Protest songs are dead": Roger McGuinn quoted in Barney Hoskyns, *Waiting for the Sun: Strange Days, Weird Scenes, and the Sound of Los Angeles* (New York: St. Martin's Press, 1996), 159.

245 "from behind some disabling aphasia," "There was a sense," and "to the fly": *The White Album*, 24–25.

245 Eve Babitz told me: Eve Babitz in conversation with the author, March 30, 2013.

246 "Each of us was mad at the other": Didion quoted in Sara Davidson, "Joan Didion—Losing John," *O, The Oprah Magazine*, 2005; available at www.saradavidson.com/joan-didion-losing-john.

246 "Manifest Destiny": John Gregory Dunne, *Crooning* (New York: Simon & Schuster, 1991), 60.

246 "*Why seek ye the living*": Joan Didion, *Slouching Towards Bethlehem* (New York: Farrar, Straus and Giroux, 1968), 208.

246 "lawns of the men": ibid., 213.

247 "my arena, my stage": Jane Howard cited in the "Biographical Note" to the Jane Howard Papers, ca. 1930–1996, Columbia University Libraries Archival Collections; available at www.columbia.edu/cu/lweb/archival/collections/ldpd_4079538.

247 "so depressing": Joan Didion, *Telling Stories* (Berkeley, Calif.: Friends of the Bancroft Library, 1978), 13.

247 "*2 skirts*": Didion, *The White Album*, 34–35.

248 "payable by the state": ibid., 70.

248 "That, apparently, was my big mistake": Nancy Reagan, *My Turn* (New York: Random House, 2011); available at books.google.com/books?isbn=0307766520.

248 "It was kind of a mean piece": Lou Cannon cited in *The Annotated Script*; available at http://newshour-the-pbs.org/newshour/nancy-reagan/annotated_bib /Act%205%20Annotated%Script%RET.pdf.

248 "My biggest fault": Reagan, *My Turn*.

249 "watch[ing] Nancy Reagan being watched by me": Didion, *The White Album*, 90.

249 "Fake the nip": ibid., 92.

249 "aggressive manipulator" and "not one of Nancy Reagan's greatest admirers": Bernard Weinraub, "The Public's Feelings About Its First Ladies Are Decidedly Mixed," *New York Times*, March 8, 1987; available at www.nytimes .com/1987/03/08/weekinreview/the-public-s-feelings-about-its-first-ladies -are-decidedly-mixed.

249 "It has the feeling of the dust bowl": John Gregory Dunne, *Quintana & Friends* (New York: E. P. Dutton, 1978), 103.

249 "hot and close" and "Dozens of vending machines": ibid., 82–83.

250 "where the rich used to live": ibid., 89.

250 "If Canada is a bummer": ibid., 91.

250 "How many men must the U.S. send?": *Time*, July 7, 1967, 13.

250 "if the Republican Party comes beating at my door": ibid., 14.

251 "I hope we get a look at your next one": Robert Giroux quoted in a letter to Henry Robbins from John Gregory Dunne, March 1, 1968, Charles E. Young Research Library, UCLA Special Collection.

251 "Quintana's mommy" and "mindlessly happy": Joan Didion, "Where *Tonight Show* Guests Go to Rest," *Esquire*, October 1976, 25.

252 "You are at all times prey to subversive elements": Dunne, *Quintana & Friends*, 87.

253 "reality contact" and subsequent quotes from Didion's psychiatric report: Didion, *The White Album*, 14–15.

253 "an inappropriate response": ibid., 15.

253 "Many saw the unleashing": *Time*, June 14, 1968, 15.

254 "It became clear to me:" ibid., 93.

254 "total breakdown" and subsequent quotes from "Singular Voices" questionnaire: rough draft of *Harper's Bazaar* questionnaire, "Singular Voices: 100 Women in Touch with Our Time," Farrar, Straus and Giroux Records, Manuscripts and Archives Division, New York Public Library.

254 King of Beasts: *Aesop's Fables* cited in Hugh Sidey, *Time*, June 28, 1968, 16.

255 "[He offers] a dizzying series": William Gass, "The Leading Edge of the Trash Phenomenon," *The New York Review of Books*, April 25, 1968; available at

www.nybooks.com/articles/archives/1968/apr/25/the-leading-edge-of-the
-trash-phenomenon.

255 "enthusiasm and literary fireworks": C. D. B. Bryan, "'The Pump House Gang'
and 'The Electric Kool-Aid Acid Test,'" *New York Times Book Review*, August
18, 1968; available at www.nytimes.com/1968/08/18/books/1968wolfe-acid
.html?_r=0.

255 "some of the finest magazine pieces": Dan Wakefield, "People, Places, and Personalities" in *New York Times Book Review*, June 21, 1968; available at www
.nytimes.com/1968/06/21/books/didion-bethlehem.html.

255 "Mailer presents this book": Alfred Kazin, "The Trouble He's Seen," *New York
Times Book Review*, May 5, 1968; available at www.nytimes.com/books/97/05/04
/reviews/mailer-armies.html.

256 "The new journalism": Gay Talese quoted in Nicolaus Mills, *The New Journalism:
A Historical Anthology* (New York: McGraw-Hill, 1974), xii.

256 "never dreamed": Tom Wolfe, "The Birth of 'The New Journalism'; Eyewit-
ness Report," *New York*, February 14, 1972; available at nymag.com/news/media
/47353/.

256 "A new kind of journalism": Dwight Macdonald quoted in Marc Weingarten,
*The Gang That Wouldn't Write Straight: Wolfe, Thompson, Didion, and the New
Journalism Revolution* (New York: Crown), 5.

257 "So far nobody in or out of the medical profession": Tom Wolfe quoted in ibid.,
107–108.

257 "The ceiling is moving": ibid., 114.

257 "Despite the skepticism": ibid., 105.

257 "though her own personality": Wakefield, "People, Places, and Personalities."

258 "cat's ass": handwritten note from John Gregory Dunne to Henry Robbins,
October 2, 1967, Farrar, Straus and Giroux Records, Manuscripts and Archives Division, New York Public Library.

258 "I am comfortable": Didion, *Slouching Towards Bethlehem*, 62–63.

258 "I had a strong feeling that it was necessary": "Telling Stories in Order to Live,"
Academy of Achievement interview with Joan Didion, June 3, 2006; available
at www.achievment.org/autodoc/page/did0int-1.

258 "The fiction voice": Didion quoted in Connie Brod, *In Depth* interview with
Joan Didion, Book TV, C-SPAN 2, 1992.

258 her "beauty": Henry Robbins letter to Joan Didion, October 1967, Farrar,
Straus and Giroux Records, Manuscript and Archives Division, New York
Public Library.

258 "hippie" jacket: Joan Didion letter to Henry Robbins, October 2, 1967; in ibid.

259 "pretty shocking": ibid.

259 "bleak and joyless": "Melancholia, U.S.A.," *Time*, June 28, 1968, 84.

259 "Journalism by women": Melvin Maddocks quoted in "Contemporary Reviews of *Slouching Towards Bethlehem*," compiled by Jesse Donaldson for the author; available at http://didion.wikispaces.com/Contemporary+Reviews+of+Slouching+Towards+Bethlehem.

259 "to that bend in the river": *Time*, June 28, 1968, 84.

259 "Defoe, Addison and Steele": Jack Newfield quoted in Mills, *The New Journalism*, xvi.

260 "In the Sixties you kept hearing": Nora Sayre, *Sixties Going on Seventies* (New Brunswick, N.J.: Rutgers University Press, 1996), 5.

260 "The so-called stylistic excesses": Robert Scholes, "Double Perspective on Hysteria," *The Saturday Review*, August 24, 1968, 37.

260 "I am not the society in microcosm": Didion, *The White Album*, 135.

260 "movements of the Army day": ibid., 152.

261 REACH OUT AND GRAB THE GREATEST SUMMER EVER: Sayre, *Sixties Going on Seventies*, 12.

261 "Chicago is a police state": Mailer, *Miami and the Siege of Chicago*, 145.

261 "We will try to develop": ibid., 135.

261 "[J]oy, nooky, circle groups": ibid.

262 "not American": ibid., 103.

262 "time, I think": ibid., 48.

262 "faraway places": ibid., 80.

262 "country had learned an almost unendurable lesson": ibid., 34.

263 "political ideas are reduced": Didion, *The White Album*, 86.

263 "senseless-killing neighborhood": ibid., 15.

263 "someone who can talk": ibid., 17.

264 "since there [were] no winters": Eve Babitz, *Eve's Hollywood* (New York: Delacorte Press, 1974), 126.

264 "We hear sirens in the night": Richard Nixon's acceptance speech, Republican National Convention, Miami, August 8, 1968; available at presidency.ucsb.edu/ws/?pid=25968#axzz2h4V_FXLK.

265 "Where you was?": John Gregory Dunne, *Dutch Shea, Jr.* (New York: Pocket Books, 1983), 23, 25, 369.

265 "I remember watching her weed it": Joan Didion, *Blue Nights* (New York: Alfred A. Knopf, 2011), 150.

CHAPTER 17

266 "an adequate supply": Nora Sayre, in *Sixties Going On Seventies* (New Brunswick, N.J.: Rutgers University Press, 1996), 5.

266 "Mommy's snake book": Joan Didion, *The Year of Magical Thinking: A Play* (New York: Vintage Books, 2007), 37.

266 "I wanna dance": Joan Didion, *Blue Nights* (New York: Alfred A. Knopf, 2011), 68.

267 Mills insisted: John Gregory Dunne letter to Henry Robbins, November 1, 1968, Farrar, Straus and Giroux Records, Manuscript and Archives Division, New York Public Library.

267 "Romeo and Juliet on junk": John Gregory Dunne, *Quintana & Friends* (New York: E. P. Dutton, 1978), 175.

267 "Writing is essentially donkey work": John Gregory Dunne, "Foreword to the New Edition," *The Studio* (New York: Limelight Editions, 1985), unpaginated.

268 "What do they speak there?": ibid., 156.

268 "It is the season . . . of divorce": Joan Didion, *Slouching Towards Bethlehem* (New York: Farrar, Straus and Giroux, 1968), 3.

268 "season of doubt": Joan Didion, "In Praise of Unhung Wreaths and Love," *Life*, December 19, 1969, 28.

268 "We communicated in nuance": John Gregory Dunne, *Vegas* (New York: Random House, 1974), 268.

269 "tell each other about their first wives": Didion, *Slouching Towards Bethlehem*, 224.

269 "Didion's description of Maria's abortion": Barbara Grizzuti Harrison, "Joan Didion: Only Disconnect" (1979); available at writing.upenn.edu/~afilreis/103/didion-per-harrison.html.

269 "You familiar with this area, Maria?": Joan Didion, *Play It As It Lays* (New York: Farrar, Straus and Giroux, 1970), 77.

269 "theatrical temperament": Michiko Kakutani, "Joan Didion: Staking Out California," *New York Times*, June 10, 1979; available at www.nytimes.com/1979/06/10/books/didion-calif.html?ref=joandidion.

269 "John and I were having a fight": Didion, *The Year of Magical Thinking: A Play*, 19.

269 "Did they have trouble?": Eve Babitz in conversation with the author, March 30, 2013.

269 "We . . . refrain": Joan Didion, "A Problem of Making Connections," *Life*, December 5, 1969, 34.

269 *"Why do you always have to be right"*: Joan Didion, *The Year of Magical Thinking* (New York: Alfred A. Knopf, 2005), 141.

269 "Anyway, John and I stayed together": Trudy Owelt, "Three Interviews by Trudy Owelt," *New York*, February 15, 1971, 40.

270 "never worked for us": Dunne, *Vegas*, 270.

270 "If you can make the promise over again": Owelt, "Three Interviews by Trudy Owelt," 40.

270 "What's new with you?" and subsequent quotes about this conversation: Dunne, *Vegas*, 174–75.

270 "familiar season of discontent": ibid., 11.

270 "too high a trouble quotient": ibid., 245.

270 "she'd try harder to make things matter": Didion, "A Problem of Making Connections," 34.

271 "precocious" and "could be construed": Jeff Glor, *"Blue Nights* by Joan Didion," *Author Talk*, CBS News, January 28, 2012; available at cbsnews.com/videos /author-talk-blue-nights-by-joan-didion.

271 "She claimed": Dunne, *Vegas*, 269–70.

271 "a sleepwalker": Didion, "A Problem of Making Connections," 34.

271 "I am reminded that we laugh at the same things": ibid.

271 "That child is the picture of Ginger Rogers": Didion, *The Year of Magical Thinking*, 110.

272 "There were simply too many drugs": Noel Parmentel in conversation with the author, July 2013.

272 "Cass used to send a limo": ibid.

273 Michelle Phillips told Didion a stunning story: Eve Babitz in conversation with the author, March 30, 2013. A version of the story appears in Phillips's memoir, *California Dreamin'* (New York: Warner Books, 1986), 22–23.

273 "She closed her eyes against the light": Didion, *Play It As It Lays*, 215.

273 "quite paranoid": Phillips, *California Dreamin'*, 187.

273 "heard sounds one night": ibid.

274 "lit biz": John Gregory Dunne letter to Henry Robbins, April 7, 1969, Farrar, Straus and Giroux Records, Manuscripts and Archives Division, New York Public Library. All details of Dunne's New York book party are from documents in these records.

275 "much darker than it was anyplace else": "Telling Stories in Order to Live," Academy of Achievement interview with Joan Didion, June 3, 2006; available at www.achievement.org/autodoc/page/did0int-1.

275 "Although it is not necessary": John Gregory Dunne, *Harp* (New York: Simon & Schuster, 1989), 49.

275 "scattered to the four winds": Dunne, *Quintana & Friends*, 13.

275 "May all the one-eyed critics": Philip H. Dougherty, "Postmortem on *Saturday Evening Post*," *New York Times*, March 30, 1969; available at select.nytimes.com/gst/abstract.html?.

275 "did the LaBianca murder": "Telling Stories in Order to Live."

276 "drinking beer and smoking grass": Tex Watson quoted at mansonsbackporch.com/library.html.

276 "I can remember we had a baby-sitter": "Telling Stories in Order to Live."

276 "Darling, put the gun away": Dominick Dunne, "Murder Most Unforgettable," *Vanity Fair*, April 2001; available at sensationalsharontate.blogspot.com/2009/08/one-of-sharons-friends-dies-author.html.

276 "It was the most bizarre period of my life": Michelle Phillips quoted in ibid.

276 "a kind of a conflicting sense": "Telling Stories in Order to Live."

277 "[T]his investigation": William "Billy" Doyle interviewed by LAPD lieutenant Earl Deemer, August 30, 1969; available at cielodrive.com/updates/?cat=3.

277 "were garbled and contradictory": Joan Didion, *The White Album* (New York: Simon & Schuster, 1979), 42.

277 "His rose garden was lovely": Dominick Dunne, "Murder Most Unforgettable."

277 "People were sending their children out of town" and "Steve McQueen packed a gun": ibid.

277 "Many people I know in Los Angeles": Didion, *The White Album*, 47.

277 "The tension broke that day": ibid.

278 "greatest peaceful event in history": Spencer Bright, "Forty Far-Out Facts You Never Knew about Woodstock," *The Daily Mail*, August 8, 2009; available at dailymail.co.uk/tvshowbiz/article-1204849/forty-far-facts-knew-woodstock.html.

278 "Commedia dell'Artestyle group": posted at rootsofwoodstock.com/2013/03/28/gerry-michael-and-the-bummers.

278 "kind of the spark for the Festival": Weston Blalock and Julia Blalock, eds., *Roots of the 1969 Woodstock Festival: The Backstory to "Woodstock"* (Woodstock, N.Y.: WoodstockArts, 2009), 27–28.

278 whom Michael's son said he met in a bar: Sean Day Michael to the author, November 4, 2013.

279 "wheel person": "Telling Stories in Order to Live."

279 "In fact we never talked about 'the case'": Didion, *The White Album*, 43.

279 "I was at the time the vice president" and subsequent quotes about Katleman: Dominick Dunne, *The Way We Lived Then: Recollections of a Well-Known Name Dropper* (New York: Crown, 1999), 172, 175–76, 177.

280 "The numbers of the dead": posted at time.com/history/faces-of-the-american-dead-in-vietnam-life-magazine-june-1969/#1.

281 "nibbled to death by ducks": Didion, *The Year of Magical Thinking*, 111.

281 "to put me out in a world of revolution": Didion quoted in Linda Hall, "The Writer Who Came In from the Cold," *New York*, September 2, 1996, 33.

281 "William L. Calley, Jr.": Seymour Hersh, "Lieutenant Accused of Murdering 109 Civilians," *St. Louis Post-Dispatch*, November 13, 1969; available at pierre tristam.com/Bobst/library/wf-200.htm.

281 "outstanding action": Maurice Isserman, *Vietnam War* (New York: Infobase Publishing, 2009), 134.

281 "These factors are not in dispute": Hersh, "Lieutenant Accused of Murdering 109 Civilians."

281 "He's watching the NFL game": Didion, *The Year of Magical Thinking*, 111.

282 "Some of the guys are going out": ibid.

282 "Where did the morning went?": Didion, *Blue Nights*, 89.

282 "It was point-blank murder": Seymour Hersh, "Hamlet Attack Called 'Point-Blank Murder,'" *St. Louis Post-Dispatch*, November 20, 1969; available at pierretristam.com/Bobst/library/wf-200.htm.

282 "The American way of war": ibid.

282 "There was a lot of illusion in our national history": ibid.

282 "I had better tell you where I am, and why": Joan Didion, "A Problem of Making Connections," 34.

283 "At the Western Union office": Didion, *The Year of Magical Thinking*, 112.

283 "didn't get it": Dan Wakefield quoted in Hall, "The Writer Who Came In from the Cold," 32.

283 "I am not the society in microcosm": Didion, *The White Album*, 135.

283 "It was a big shock": Didion quoted in Hall, "The Writer Who Came In from the Cold," 32.

283 "We saw you on the David Frost Show": Henry Robbins letter to Jane Fonda, December 31, 1969, Farrar, Straus and Giroux Records, Manuscripts and Archives Division, New York Public Library.

CHAPTER 18

284 she told her mother: Joan Didion, *Blue Nights* (New York: Alfred A. Knopf, 2011), 6.

284 "'In lieu of divorce!'": Didion quoted in Leslie Garis, "Didion and Dunne: The Rewards of a Literary Marriage," *New York Times Magazine*, February 8, 1987; available at www.nytimes.com/1987/02/08/magazine/didion-dunne-the -rewards-of-a-literary-marriage.html.

285 "narcotized": Joan Didion, *The White Album* (New York: Simon & Schuster, 1979), 159.

286 "Miss Didion": Joan Didon, "In Praise of Unhung Wreaths and Love," *Life*, December 19, 1969, 28.

286 "I'll be there around noon": ibid.

286 "I had wanted to make this Christmas": ibid.

286 "[m]y husband and I see our lawyer": ibid.

286 Could he have a small role in the movie?: Eileen Peterson, "They Dunne It Right!," Twentieth Century–Fox press release, January 8, 1971, Dominick Dunne papers, Harry Ransom Center, University of Texas.

287 "I tell myself that I am crying": Didion, "In Praise of Unhung Wreaths and Love," 28.

287 "There hasn't been another American writer": John Leonard, "The Cities of the Desert, the Desert of the Mind," *New York Times,* July 21, 1970.

287 "A new novel by Joan Didion": Lore Segal, "Maria Knew What 'Nothing' Meant" in *New York Times Book Review,* August 8, 1970; available at www .nytimes.com/1970/08/08/books/didion-play.html?_r=0.

287 "I just wanted to write a fast novel": "Telling Stories in Order to Live," Academy of Achievement interview with Joan Didion, June 3, 2006; available at www .achievement.org/autodoc/page/did0int-1.

288 "I wanted to make it all first person": Linda Kuehl, "Joan Didion, The Art of Fiction No. 71," *The Paris Review* 74 (Fall-Winter 1978); available at www.the parisreview.org/interviews/3439/the-art-of-fiction-no-71-joan-didion.

288 "pull-back third person": Joan Didion Papers, Bancroft Library, University of California at Berkeley.

288 "in her essays [Didion] chooses to speak": Segal, "Maria Knew What 'Nothing' Meant."

288 "The water in the pool": Joan Didion Papers, Bancroft Library, University of California at Berkeley.

288 "Grammar is a piano I play by ear": Joan Didion, "Why I Write," *New York Times Book Review,* December 5, 1976; reprinted in *Joan Didion: Essays and Conversations,* ed. Ellen G. Friedman (Princeton, N. J.: Ontario Review Press, 1984), 7.

288 "'character' or 'plot' or even 'incident'": ibid.

289 "all eyes": Joan Didion Papers, Bancroft Library, University of California at Berkeley.

289 "I showed [the novel] to John": Kuehl, "Joan Didion, The Art of Fiction No. 71."

289 Lines of dialogue: Joan Didion Papers, Bancroft Library, University of California at Berkeley.

289 "Henry . . . and John and I sat down": Kuehl, "Joan Didion, The Art of Fiction No. 71."

289 "I try not to think of dead things and plumbing": Joan Didion, *Play It As It Lays* (New York: Farrar, Straus and Giroux, 1970), 8.

289 "a narrative strategy": Kuehl, "Joan Didion, The Art of Fiction No. 71."

290 "very arbitrary" and "I remember writing a passage": ibid.

290 "By the time I finished it": Michael Silverblatt, "The KCRW Bookworm Book Club"; available at https://soundcloud.com/KCRW/joan-didion-for-bookworm-book.

290 "This isn't going to": Sheila Heti, "Joan Didion," *The Believer*, December 2011; available at believermag.com/exclusives/?read=interview_didion.

290 "And I didn't think": ibid.

290 "I told them both I wished to God": Dunne quoted in Linda Hall, "The Writer Who Came In from the Cold," *New York*, September 2, 1996, 32.

290 "other man": Joan Didion Papers, Bancroft Library, University of California at Berkeley.

291 "She would never": Didion, *Play It As It Lays*, 137.

291 "two glands of neurotoxic poison": ibid., 1.

291 "To look for 'reasons'": ibid.

291 "I might as well lay it on the line": ibid., 5.

291 "[my name] is pronounced Mar-*eye*-ah": ibid., 2.

291 "We had a lot of things and places": ibid., 3.

291 "What makes Iago evil?": ibid., 1.

292 "You got a map of Peru?": ibid., 183.

292 "In the preface to her essays": Segal, "Maria Knew What 'Nothing' Meant."

293 "an ephemeral form of survival kitsch": *Kirkus Reviews*, July 13, 1970; available at www.kirkusreviews.com/book-reviews/joan-didion/play-it-as-it-lays/.

293 "hurt" and "shattering": Herman Briffault letter to Henry Robbins, undated (July 1970), Farrar, Straus and Giroux Records, Manuscripts and Archives Division, New York Public Library.

293 "the heroine, like the author herself": Henry Robbins letter to Herman Briffault, July 22, 1970; in ibid.

293 "high intelligence" and "When Maria speaks": Segal, "Maria Knew What 'Nothing' Meant."

293 "I can't believe": Dan Wakefield quoted in Hall, "The Writer Who Came In from the Cold."

293 "There was a certain tendency": Keuhl, "Joan Didion, The Art of Fiction No. 71."

CHAPTER 19

297 "This . . . house on the sea": Joan Didion, *The White Album* (New York: Simon & Schuster, 1979), 47–48.

297 "She still had parties": Eve Babitz in conversation with the author, March 30, 2013.

298 "The hills are scrubby and barren": Didion, *The White Album*, 209.

298 "There are not only no blacks in Malibu": John Gregory Dunne, *Harp* (New York: Simon & Schuster, 1989), 80.

298 "They were the most sophisticated people I knew": Carolyn Kellogg, "PEN's Joan Didion Event Lacked Just One Thing: Joan Didion," *Los Angeles Times,* October 15, 2013; available at latimes.com/books/jacketcopy/le-et-jc-pen-joan -didion-event-lacked-just-one-thing-joan-didion-2013015,06823645.story.

298 "[W]hat had started as a two-month job": John Gregory Dunne, *Vegas* (New York: Random House, 1974), 231.

299 "look of the horizon": Tom Brokaw interview with Joan Didion for NBC tele-vision, mid-1970s; available at youtube.com/watch?v=4qrsozdFKSU.

299 "a new kind of life": Connie Brod, *In Depth* interview with Joan Didion, Book TV, C-SPAN 2, 1992.

300 "Free the Strip!": Mike Davis, "Riot Nights on Sunset Strip," *Labour / Le Travail* 59 (Spring 2007): 212.

300 "I was so unhappy": Brod, *In Depth* interview with Joan Didion.

300 "the finest woman prose stylist": James Dickey quoted in Alfred Kazin, "Joan Didion: Portrait of a Professional," *Harper's* magazine, December 1971, 113.

300 "One thinks of the great *performers*": Mark Schorer, quoted in ibid.

300 "ripple": Alfred Kazin's journal, posted at theamericanscholar.org/the -passionate-encounter.

300 "most interesting personality": Kazin, "Joan Didion," 112.

301 "People who live in a beach house": ibid., 114.

301 "very vulnerable": ibid.

301 "subtle," "alarmed fragility," and "many silences": ibid., 116, 120.

301 "full of body language": Alfred Kazin's journal.

301 "the academic-community-Moratorium": Joan Didion, "On the Last Frontier with VX and GB," *Life,* February 20, 1920, 22.

301 "mutilated the land": ibid.

302 "not in a frontier town" and "cut free from the ambiguities of history": ibid.

302 "Pretty healthy rabbit": ibid.

302 "If you can't believe you're going to heaven": ibid.

302 "[M]y child mourned Bunny Rabbit's cruel fate": Joan Didion, *Blue Nights* (New York: Alfred A. Knopf, 2011), 181.

303 "We had a lawn": *The Panic in Needle Park,* directed by Jerry Schatzberg (Twentieth Century–Fox, 1971).

303 "Basically, we just reported": Film Forum podcast on *The Panic in Needle Park,* January 30, 2009; available at digitalpodcast.com/items/1526291. See also "Joan Didion Remembers 'The Panic in Needle Park,'" posted at ifc.com/news/2009 /01/joan-didion-on-the-panic-in-ne.php.

303 "We rehearsed it as though it were a stage play": Joshua Rothkopf, "Junk Bonds," *Time Out New York,* January 22, 2009; available at timeout.com/newyork/film /junk-bonds.

303 "It was a fantastic script": Film Forum podcast on *The Panic in Needle Park.*

303 "I didn't see it as a happy ending": ibid.

303 "I never found out what [he] saw": Rothkopf, "Junk Bonds."

303 "I'd seen Al four years earlier": ibid.

303 "When you come from a gray, grimy Communist country": ibid.

304 "[We were] a group of improbables": Film Forum podcast on *The Panic in Needle Park.*

304 "'We didn't have money for heroin'": ibid.

304 "The thoroughness": ibid.

304 "drunk and stoned": Dominick Dunne, *The Way We Lived Then: Recollections of a Well-Known Name Dropper* (New York: Crown, 1999), 184.

304 "knew exactly how to launch a production": Eileen Peterson, "They Dunne It Right!" Twentieth Century–Fox press release, January 8, 1971, Dominick Dunne papers, Harry Ransom Center, University of Texas.

304 "Neither of us likes to come back here": Bruce Cook, "For the Dunnes, the Future Begins in L.A.," *The National Observer,* March 8, 1971, 21.

305 "writing the film was great fun for us": ibid.

305 "When a picture is shooting": "Joan Didion Remembers 'The Panic in Needle Park.'"

305 "All loss is loss": Film Forum podcast on *The Panic in Needle Park.*

305 "I never thought this was a picture about drugs": ibid.

305 "You can kill me now!": Jeff Guinn, *Manson: The Life and Times of Charles Manson* (New York: Simon & Schuster, 2013), 353. For details about the Manson trial in general, I have drawn on Guinn's excellent book.

305 "there is a minimum of client control": ibid.

305 A young man in Berkeley: Ed Sanders, *The Family* (New York: New American Library, 1989), 418.

306 "Death is psychosomatic": Guinn, *Manson,* 354.

306 "You have created the monster": ibid., 357.

306 "coverage of the Charles Manson case": ibid., 362.

306 "Your Honor, the President": ibid., 363.

306 "demure," "pigtailed," "author Joan Didion," and "straight": Yvonne Patten, "Linda Kasabian on Stand for Third Day of Cross-Examination in Manson Murder Trial," *Los Angeles Times*, August 4, 1970; available at cielodrive.com /archive/?p=6660.

306 "long is for evening": Guinn, *Manson*, 360.

306 "Size 9 Petite": Didion, *The White Album*, 45.

306 "little death": ibid., 43.

307 "have two drinks": ibid.

307 "You'll kill us all": Guinn, *Manson*, 360–61.

307 "In the name of Christian justice": ibid., 371

307 "I am only what you made me": ibid., 374–75.

307 "On August 13": Sanders, *The Family*, 419.

308 "You abandoned your child": Patten, "Linda Kasabian on Stand for Third Day of Cross-Examination in Manson Murder Trial."

308 Didion and FSG received letters: Nathaniel J. Friedman to Henry Robbins and Joan Didion, February 11, 1971, Farrar, Straus and Giroux Records, Manuscripts and Archives Division, New York Public Library.

308 Robbins replied: Henry Robbins letter to Nathaniel J. Friedman, February 26, 1971; in ibid.

308 "Pussy": Henry Robbins letter to Victor Temkin, August 11, 1970; in ibid.

309 "The idea was": Dunne, *Harp*, 139.

309 "most interesting place[s]": Hilton Als, "Joan Didion, The Art of Nonfiction No. 1," *The Paris Review* 48, no. 176 (Spring 2006); available at www.theparis review.org/interviews/5601/the-art-of-nonfiction-no-1-joan-didion.

309 "weird stories": Don Swaim's audio interview with Joan Didion, October 29, 1987; available at www.wiredforbooks.org/joandidion.

309 "This was a time": Brod, *In Depth* interview with Joan Didion.

309 "gateway to the Caribbean": ibid.

310 "triangulation of crossfire": testimony of Perry Raymond Russo, *State of Louisiana v. Clay L. Shaw*, February 10, 1969, posted at jfk-online.com/pr01.html.

310 "whole underbelly": Als, "Joan Didion, The Art of Nonfiction No. 1."

310 "had taken the American political narrative seriously": Joan Didion, *After Henry* (New York: Simon & Schuster, 1992), 85.

310 "testimony of a number of witnesses" and subsequent quotes from the House Select Committee on Assassinations: excerpt, volume 10, House Select Committee on Assassinations; available at mcadams.posc.mu.edu/544camp.txt.

310 "one of those occasional accidental intersections": Didion, *After Henry,* 86.

310 "road glass": Dunne, *Harp,* 140.

311 "in the South they remained convinced": Didion, *Where I Was From* (New York: Alfred A. Knopf, 2003), 71.

311 In a letter to Marc Joffe: Henry Robbins letter to Marc Joffe, May 17, 1971, Farrar, Straus and Giroux Records, Manuscripts and Archives Division, New York Public Library.

311 "I had a year's contract": Joan Didion in conversation with Sloane Crosley, New York Public Library, November 21, 2011.

311 "Napalm has become 'Incender-Jell'": Mary McCarthy, *Vietnam* (New York: Harcourt, Brace & World, 1967), 3.

312 "the all-time top-seeded Hollywood bully boy"; John Gregory Dunne, *Monster: Living Off the Big Screen* (New York: Random House, 1997), 75.

312 "the antithesis" and subsequent quotes about this meeting unless otherwise noted: David Patrick Columbia, "Remembering John Gregory Dunne," New York Social Diary, January 7, 2004; available at newyorksocialdiary.com/the -list/2007/john-gregory-dunne.

312 "if Otto thought": Dunne, *Monster,* 76.

312 "rage was never far beneath the surface": ibid.

312 "grimy, roach-infested": ibid.

313 "Studio executives": John Gregory Dunne, *Regards: The Selected Nonfiction of John Gregory Dunne* (New York: Thunder's Mouth Press, 2006), 23.

313 "nice lesbian relationship": Didion, *The White Album,* 154.

313 "If he got angry with us" and "[W]ith elaborate politeness": Dunne, *Monster,* 76.

313 "Miss Universe contestants": Dunne, *Regards,* 50.

313 "I forbid you to go": Dunne, *Monster,* 76.

313 "My blessed cancer": Trudy Dixon quoted by David Chadwick; available at cuke .com/Crooked%20Cucumber/cc%20excerpts/zmbm_excerpt_from_cc.htm.

314 "Trudy had been struggling": Willard Dixon to the author, November 13, 2013.

314 "She was totally inspiring": Didion quoted in Sara Davidson, *Joan: Forty Years of Life, Loss, and Friendship with Joan Didion* (San Francisco: Byliner, 2011).

314 "every night to relax": ibid.

314 "I didn't like [meditation]": ibid.

314 "[W]e should not do [something]": Shunryu Suzuki, *Zen Mind, Beginner's Mind,* ed. Trudy Dixon (New York: Weatherhill, 2003), 53.

315 "In the beginner's mind": ibid., 21.

315 "As it was in the beginning": Didion quoted in David Swick, "The Zen of Joan Didion," *Shambhala Sun,* January 2007; available at www.lionsroar.com/the -zen-of-joan-didion.

315 "personal God": ibid.

315 "vast indifference": ibid.

315 "I found earthquakes": ibid.

316 "What I have made for myself": Didion, *The White Album,* 208.

316 "couldn't do that to him": Joan Didion, *The Year of Magical Thinking: A Play* (New York: Vintage, 2007), 19.

316 "lit a joint": Dunne, *Vegas,* 231–32.

316 "I stopped": Didion, *Where I Was From*, 218.

316 "the weather": Dunne, *Vegas,* 169–70.

316 "Halfway home": Jonathan Yardley, "John Gregory Dunne," *Washington Post,* January 22, 2006; available at washingtonpost.com/wp-dyn/content/article /2006/01/19/AR2006011902698.html.

317 "Frank E. Campbell": Dunne, *Vegas,* 13.

317 "[S]he was lonely and depressed": ibid., 174–75.

317 "living with [a] piranha": ibid., 11.

317 "It was like all those terrible parties": ibid., 232.

317 "kilo of marijuana": ibid.

317 "[w]hatever minimal impulse I had": ibid., 246.

317 "When are you coming home?": ibid., 269.

317 "bad season . . . was over": ibid., 287.

317 "He has on a blue work shirt": Didion, *Blue Nights,* 51.

318 "Don't let the Broken Man catch me": Joan Didion, *The Year of Magical Thinking* (New York: Alfred A. Knopf, 2005), 51.

318 "I realized my fear of The Broken Man": Didion, *Blue Nights,* 52.

318 "the hall porter": Dunne, *Regards,* 24–25.

319 "To me" and Dominick Dunne's subsequent remarks: John J. Massaro, "Dunne Film Is Cannes Festival Entry," *Hartford Courant,* December 22, 1970.

319 "disappointing": "The Panic in Needle Park," *Women's Wear Daily,* May 15, 1971.

319 "Are you doing the hard stuff?": Film Forum podcast on *The Panic in Needle Park.*

319 "[I]t must be considered": Archer Winster, "The New Movies," *New York Post,* July 14, 1971.

319 "When a reporter": Kitty Winn quoted in "The Midnight Earl" syndicated newspaper column; available at zebradelic.blogspot.com/2012/01/kitty-winn -1971-press-coverage.html.

319 "The idea of stardom I find frightening": Kitty Winn quoted in William Otterburn-Hall, "Actress Wants Own Life Style"; available at ibid.

CHAPTER 20

320 "a cold leek soup": John Gregory Dunne, *Regards: The Selected Nonfiction of John Gregory Dunne* (New York: Thunder's Mouth Press, 2006), 27.

320 "listen to Joan Didion": Leslie Caron, *Thank Heaven: A Memoir* (New York: Penguin, 2009); available at books-google.com/books?id=0dp-ycQ01ocC&pg=p.

320 "very heady": Joseph McBride, *Steven Spielberg: A Biography* (London: Faber and Faber, 2012), unpaginated; available at books-google.com/books?isbn -0571280552.

320 "[T]he spirit of the place": Joan Didion, *The White Album* (New York: Simon & Schuster, 1979), 222.

321 "acid yellow": ibid., 157.

321 "last stable society": ibid., 155.

321 "hangover": ibid., 159.

321 "all the terrific 22-year-old directors": ibid.

321 "looking for the action": ibid.

322 "a personality before she was entirely a person": Joan Didion, *Slouching Towards Bethlehem* (New York: Farrar, Straus and Giroux, 1968), 47.

322 "invention of women as a 'class'" and "To make an omelette": Didion, *The White Album*, 109–110.

322 "Her attitudes pose a problem": Catharine Stimpson, "The Case of Miss Joan Didion," *Ms.*, January 1973, 36–40.

322 "The idea that fiction": Didion, *The White Album*, 112.

322 "I think sex": Trudy Owelt, "Three Interviews by Trudy Owelt," *New York*, February 15, 1971, 40.

322 "I agree": ibid.

322 "Everywoman": Didion, *The White Album*, 114–15.

323 "fine time for writers in Hollywood": Tim Steele in conversation with the author, April 29, 2013.

323 "an extension of *The Graduate*": Dunne, *Regards*, 30.

323 "Write me a Western": ibid., 31–32.

323 "hot idea": ibid., 30.

323 "What if": ibid., 27.

324 "attraction of borrowed luxury": ibid., 32.

324 "Hollywood is largely a boy's club" and "[F]or years Joan was tolerated": Dunne, *Regards*, 77.

324 "You're a Mel": ibid., 27–28.

324 "She was perched": ibid., 251.

324 "She had despised": ibid., 252.

324 "circled each other warily": ibid.

324 During the course: Brian Kellow, *Pauline Kael: A Life in the Dark* (New York: Viking, 2011), 194–95.

325 "studios reacted to Sam's": ibid.

325 "the most important voice writing in English": Anitra Earle, "Director's Appraisal of Joan Didion," *San Francisco Chronicle,* December 21, 1971.

325 "ultimate princess fantasy" and subsequent quotes from Kael: Pauline Kael, "The Current Cinema: Anarchic Laughter," *The New Yorker,* November 11, 1972, 155–58.

325 "ludicrous": Dunne, *Regards,* 252.

326 "The four of us": Roger Ebert interview with Frank Perry, cited at Alt Screen, "Wednesday Editor's Pick: Play It As It Lays (1972)"; available at altscreen .com/09/15/2011/wednesday-editors-pick-play-it-as-it-lays-1972/.

326 "cutting": ibid.

326 "mosaic": "Perry Will Shoot 'Play It As It Lays' in Mosaic Fashion" *Variety,* November 19, 1971.

326 "dreadful Los Angeles freeway": Vincent Canby, "'Play It As It Lays' Comes to the Screen," *New York Times,* October 30, 1972; available at www.nytimes.com /movie/review?res=9D02EFDB173FE53ABC4850DFB6678389669EDE.

326 "I wanted Lichtenstein": Paul Gardner, "Perry Making Hollywood Film—His Way," *New York Times,* February 10, 1972.

327 "[W]e had a studio chief": posted at Hollywood-elsewhere.com/2009/08 /as-dominick-dun/.

327 "I know what nothing is": Joan Didion, *Play It As It Lays* (New York: Farrar, Straus and Giroux, 1970), 216.

327 "a lot of puckers": Kael, "The Current Cinema," 157.

327 "incredibly essential statement[s]": Earle, "Director's Appraisal of Joan Didion."

327 "pretentious": Stanley Kauffmann, "Play It As It Lays," *The New Republic,* December 9, 1972, 22.

327 "the year's most effective capturing": Charles Champlin, "Top 10 Films—and Then Some—in an Actor's Year," *Los Angeles Times,* December 31, 1972.

327 "profound": Rex Reed, "The Goodies and Baddies of '72 Films," New York *Daily News,* December 31, 1972.

327 "his mother and my grandmother": Jon Carroll in conversation with the author, April 1, 2013.

328 "Jann Wenner gave me a copy": Ricky Fedora, "The Uncool Exclusive Interview with Cameron Crowe," posted at theuncool.com/press/the-uncool -exclusive-interview/.

328 "with rock stars" and "broke our hearts": Jon Carroll quoted in Robert Draper, *Rolling Stone Magazine: The Uncensored History* (New York: HarperPerennial, 1991), 15.

328 "I left *Rolling Stone*": Jon Carroll in conversation with the author, April 1, 2013.

328 "finish each other's sentences": Sara Davidson, *Joan: Forty Years of Life, Loss, and Friendship with Joan Didion* (San Francisco: Byliner, 2011).

328 "the Didion-Dunnes": Eve Babitz, *Eve's Hollywood* (New York: Delacorte Press, 1974), dedication page.

329 "Before Quintana was born": Stephen Nessen, "Joan Didion Explores the Death of a Daughter in 'Blue Nights,'" WNYC News, November 2, 2011; available at wnyc.org/story/168270-joan-didion-explores-death-daughter/.

329 "I wish I could have stopped Quintana": Jeff Glor, "*Blue Nights* by Joan Didion," *Author Talk*, CBS News, January 28, 2012; available at cbsnews.com/videos /author-talk-blue-nights-by-joan-didion.

329 "already a health worry": Caron, *Thank Heaven*.

329 "dizzying alterations": Joan Didion, *Blue Nights* (New York: Alfred A. Knopf, 2011), 83.

329 "strenuousness": ibid., 88.

329 "sundries": ibid., 83.

329 "projection room": ibid., 85–86.

329 "I just noticed I have cancer": ibid., 84.

329 "quicksilver changes of mood": ibid., 36.

329 "the hospital in which Charlie Parker once detoxed": ibid., 40.

330 "was always very sweet": Josh Greenfeld in conversation with the author, April 6, 2013.

330 "[We] would sit on the couch": James Oakley, "Susan Traylor's LA Story," *Interview*, July 11, 2012; available at interviewmagazine.com/film/susan-traylor -the-casserole-club.

330 "I've loved Donny Osmond": Davidson, *Joan*.

330 "Who drew it": Didion, *The White Album*, 126.

331 "*Brush your teeth*": Didion, *Blue Nights*, 35.

331 "Mom's Sayings": ibid., 36.

331 "*Dear Mom*": Joan Didion, *The Year of Magical Thinking* (New York: Alfred A. Knopf, 2005), 88.

331 "*Roses are red*": ibid., 148.

331 "The world": Didion, *Blue Nights*, 38.

331 "Dry winds and dust": Joan Didion, *After Henry* (New York: Simon & Schuster, 1992), 218.

331 "Joan was trying to finish a book": Dunne quoted in Didion, *Blue Nights*, 28–29.

332 "was already a person": ibid., 41.

332 "apprehensive about everything": "The Female Angst: Anaïs Nin, Joan Didion, and Dory Previn," interview by Sally Davis, Pacifica Radio Archives Preservation and Access Project, KPFK, February 1, 1972; available at www .pacificaradioarchives.org/recordings/bc0611.

332 "She was pregnant": Didion quoted in Chris Chase, "The Uncommon Joan Didion," *Chicago Tribune*, April 3, 1977.

332 "I was not one who learned my lesson": Dominick Dunne, *The Way We Lived Then: Recollections of a Well-Known Name Dropper* (New York: Crown, 1999), 183.

332 "stranger's closet": ibid., 184.

333 "rose too high": *Dominick Dunne: After the Party*, directed and produced by Kirsty de Garis and Timothy Jolley (Mercury Media/Road Trip Film/Films Art Docco, 2008), film documentary.

333 "written . . . with all the fearlessness": Vincent Canby, "Ash Wednesday," *New York Times*, November 22, 1973; available at www.nytimes.com/movie/review? res=9A04EFDA1F3CE13BBC4A51DFB7678388669EDE.

333 "the most powerful woman in Hollywood": ibid., 161.

334 "It's a minor film": C. David Heymann, *Liz: An Intimate Biography of Elizabeth Taylor* (New York: Simon & Schuster, 2004), 336.

334 "If the history of this movie": *Dominick Dunne: After the Party*, de Garis and Jolley, film documentary.

334 "He just said to me": ibid.

334 "Joan Didion's brother-in-law": Dominick Dunne, *The Way We Lived Then*, 186.

334 "I don't remember": ibid.

334 "I was flattered": ibid.

334 "John Woolf jewel": Graydon Carter, "Remembering Sue Mengers: Everybody Came to Sue's," *Vanity Fair*, October 18, 2011; available at www.vanityfair.com /online/daily/2011/10/sue-mengers-in-memoriam.

334 "What do you think of fidelity in marriage?": Dunne, *Regards*, 41.

334 "sort of new for the movie world": Susanna Rustin, "Legends of the Fall," *The Guardian*, May 21, 2005; available at www.theguardian.com/books.2005/may /21/usnationalbookawards.society.

335 "In the background": Dunne, *Regards*, 371.

335 "Someday I'm going to kill that kid": Josh Greenfeld quoted in John Gregory Dunne, *Quintana & Friends* (New York: E. P. Dutton, 1978), 52.

335 "When John got too loud": Eve Babitz in conversation with the author, March 30, 2013.

335 "Writers don't compete with each other": Josh Greenfeld in conversation with the author, April 6, 2013.

335 "shack on the Pacific": Patricia Craig, *Brian Moore: A Biography* (London: Bloomsbury, 2002), 196.

335 "show-business people": Denis Sampson, *Brian Moore: The Chameleon Novelist* (Toronto: Doubleday Canada, 1999), 139.

336 "abruptly became a shambles": Joan Didion, "An Introduction," in Tony Richardson, *The Long-Distance Runner: A Memoir* (New York: William Morrow, 1993), 15.

336 "I remember the first time": Julia Phillips, *You'll Never Eat Lunch in This Town Again* (New York: Signet Books, 1991), xx.

336 "All prescribed (in vain)": Dunne, *Regards,* 268.

336 "I recall invoking": Joan Didion, "Why I Write," originally published in *New York Times Book Review,* December 5, 1976, reprinted in *Joan Didion: Essays and Conversations,* ed. Ellen G. Friedman (Princeton, N.J.: Ontario Review Press, 1984), 8.

336 "Why had the American film industry": Didion, *The White Album,* 192.

337 "[I] bought a paper": ibid., 188.

337 "whole history of the place": ibid.

337 "room service and Xerox *rápido*": ibid., 187.

337 "dislocation of time": ibid., 190.

337 "I was aware of being an American": ibid., 191.

338 "local color": ibid., 190.

339 three whiskies and a coco martinique: receipt in Joan Didion Papers, Bancroft Library, University of California at Berkeley.

339 "That was what she *had to know*": Didion, *Blue Nights,* 99.

339 "I [made] graphs": Leslie Garis, "Didion and Dunne: The Rewards of a Literary Marriage," *New York Times Magazine,* February 8, 1987; available at www .nytimes.com/1987/02/08/magazine/didion-dunne-the-rewards-of-a-literary -marriage.html.

340 "I love Joan's work!": Josh Greenfeld in conversation with the author, April 6, 2013.

340 "sixteen words": Dunne, *Regards,* 37.

340 "James Taylor and Carly Simon": ibid.

CHAPTER 21

341 "a parable for the period": Joan Didion, *After Henry* (New York: Simon & Schuster, 1992), 96.

341 The facts were improbable and bizarre: For the Patty Hearst backstory, I have

drawn upon the following sources, in addition to others listed below: David Talbot, *Season of the Witch: Enchantment, Terror, and Deliverance in the City of Love* (New York: Free Press, 2012), 169–203; Paul Morantz, "Escape from the SLA," posted at paulmorantz.com/cult/escape-from-the-sla/; Paul Krassner, "Symbionese Liberation Army: Historical Essay," posted at foundsf.org/index .php?title=Symbionese_Liberation_Army; Paul Krassner, "The Parts Left Out of the Patty Hearst Trial, Part Two," posted at disinfo.com/2013/01/the-parts -left-out-of-the-patty-hearst-trial-part-2; "Who Were the Symbionese, and Were They Ever Liberated?", posted at straightdope.com/columns/read/2004 /who-were-the-Symbionese-and-were-they-ever-liberated; *American Experience* segment, "Guerrilla: The Taking of Patty Hearst," posted at pbs.org/wgbh /amex/guerrilla/peopleevents/e_kidnapping.html.

343 "an unusually high number of savage murders": Barry Farrell, *How I Got to Be This Hip*, ed. Steve Hawk (New York: Washington Square Press, 1999), 94–95.

343 "overkills": ibid., 95.

343 "curse of the Donner Party": ibid., 91.

343 "nation's most dysfunctional prison system": Talbot, *Season of the Witch*, 170.

343 "spying on law-abiding individuals": David Johnston, "L.A. Police Officials Allegedly Hid Crimes; An Ex-Officer's Book Says a Spy Unit Also Looked into the Sex Lives of State Officials," *Philadelphia Inquirer*, July 13, 1992, available at articles.philly.com/1992-07-13/news/26026052_1_organized-crime-intelligence -division. See also "A Timeline of LAPD Spying and Surveillance," posted at stoplapdspying.org; and David Cay Johnston, "Daryl Gates' Real Legacy," posted at laobserved.com/visiting/2010/04/daryl_gates_secret_legacy.php.

343 "incidents of conspiracy to commit murder": Johnston, "L.A. Police Officials Allegedly Hid Crimes."

344 "government agent": Krassner, "Symbionese Liberation Army."

344 "tried to keep his military": Talbot, *Season of the Witch*, 173.

344 "the gentlest, most beautiful man": Patty Hearst quoted in Krassner, "Symbionese Liberation Army."

344 Lake Headley: Talbot, *Season of the Witch*, 193–95.

344 "kind, honest person": Sara Davidson, "Patty Hearst in the Land of the Cobra," *New York Times Magazine*, June 2, 1974; available at www.saradavidson .com/articleD3.html.

345 "[T]he name 'symbionese'": "Who Were the Symbionese, and Were They Ever Liberated?"

345 "[d]iscussions were held": Krassner, "The Parts Left Out of the Patty Hearst Trial, Part Two."

345 "Declaration of Revolutionary War": "Who Were the Symbionese, and Were They Ever Liberated?"

345 "hatred, fear and disunity": Talbot, *Season of the Witch*, 179.

345 "palsy-walsy with everybody in the glass house": The Jonestown Institute, Jonestown Audiotape Primary Project, tape number Q 622, transcribed by Fielding M. McGehee III; available at jonestown.sdsu.edu/?page-id-27498.

346 "brilliant" and "leader": Talbot, *Season of the Witch*, 182.

346 "shot on sight": ibid.

346 "extortion": ibid., 185.

347 "75% slop": Mae Brussell, "Why Was Patty Hearst Kidnapped?" *The Realist*, July 1974; available at prouty.org/brussell/hearst_1.html.

347 "hog feed": Linda Kramer, "Progress Report Due on Hearst Kidnapping," *Nashua Telegram* (Associated Press), March 18, 1975.

347 "It's just too bad": Calvin Welch, "The Legacy of the SLA," posted at foundsf .org/index.php?title=The_Legacy_of_the_SLA.

347 "I have been given the name Tania": Morantz, "Escape from the SLA."

347 "One thing I learned": Talbot, *Season of the Witch*, 191.

347 "We love you Tania": ibid.

347 "one California busy being born": Didion, *After Henry*, 98.

347 "looking for a stake": ibid., 99.

347 one of the strangest proposals: Joan Didion letter to Jann Wenner, October 20, 1975, Lois Wallace Literary Agency Records, Harry Ransom Center, University of Texas at Austin.

348 "California experience" and subsequent quotes from letter: Lois Wallace letter to James Silberman, October 20, 1975; in ibid.

349 Cinque was the nation's first black Lee Harvey Oswald: Stephanie Caruana, "About Women . . ." *Playgirl*, August 1974; available at prouty.org/brussell/play girl.html.

349 "He'll be killed, probably in a shootout": Talbot, *Season of the Witch*, 194.

349 "an art form": Mae Brussell, "From Monterey Pop to Altamont: Operation Chaos, the CIA's War Against the Sixties Counter-Culture," November 1976 (unpublished); available at maebrussell.com/Mae%20Brussell%20Articles/ Operation%20Chaos.html.

349 "abrupt sloughing of the past": Didion, *After Henry*, 102.

350 "Don't examine your feelings": ibid., 103.

350 "seemed to project an emotional distance": ibid., 104.

350 "This was a California girl": ibid., 107–108.

350 "happened" and "minister": ibid., 108–109.

351 an anecdote that Lewis Lapham: Joan Didion letter to Jann Wenner, January

7, 1976, Lois Wallace Literary Agency Records, Harry Ransom Center, University of Texas at Austin.

351 "marginal titles": Boris Kachka, *Hothouse: The Art of Survival and the Survival of Art at America's Most Celebrated Publishing House, Farrar, Straus & Giroux* (New York: Simon & Schuster, 2013), 199.

352 "touch and go," "frightened the whiskers," and "had to try": ibid., 198.

352 "[f]inancial considerations": ibid., 200.

352 "such major writers": Sarah Gallick, "Some Gossip," *Harper's* magazine, September 30, 1974, 4.

352 "None of [my] authors": Kachka, *Hothouse*, 201.

352 "surrogate father": ibid., 202.

352 "to our part of town": Roger Straus letter to Lois Wallace, July 25, 1974, Farrar, Straus and Giroux Records, Manuscripts and Archives Division, New York Public Library.

353 "the new novel is going well": Roger Straus letter to Joan Didion, November 11, 1975, Lois Wallace Literary Agency Records, Harry Ransom Center, University of Texas at Austin.

353 "not the kind of writer that should be put on the block": Kachka, *Hothouse*, 203.

353 "terribly impressed" and subsequent quotes about Wharton: Didion quoted in Madore McKenzie, "Writer Joan Didion: A Laugh Like a Silver Bell," *Boca Raton News*, July 21, 1977.

353 "an uncertain but determined adolescent": Joan Didion, *Blue Nights* (New York: Alfred A. Knopf, 2011), 19.

354 "some gynecological detective work" and "This is not . . . feasible": Sara Davidson, *Joan: Forty Years of Life, Loss, and Friendship with Joan Didion* (San Francisco: Byliner, 2011).

354 "to make it all one book": McKenzie, "Writer Joan Didion."

354 "Maybe because he thought": ibid.

355 "[T]hree weeks of one-night stands": John Gregory Dunne, *Regards: The Selected Nonfiction of John Gregory Dunne* (New York: Thunder's Mouth Press, 2006), 40.

355 "You'd find yourself": "Telling Stories in Order to Live," Academy of Achievement interview with Joan Didion, June 3, 2006; available at www.achievement.org/autodoc/page/did0int-1.

355 "the better part of an afternoon": Dunne, *Regards*, 40.

355 "Call KL 5-2033": ibid.

355 "a groupie": ibid.

355 "roomy suite": Robert Lamm, "Memoir 4: Joan Didion, John Gregory Dunne, and Colonel Klink," posted at ChicagoTheBand.us/forum/topics/memoir-4-joan-didion-john?commentID=5536203%3AComment%3A31058.

356 "ate caviar for the first time": Joan Didion, *Blue Nights* (New York: Alfred A. Knopf, 2011), 89.

356 "onstage, on one of the amps": ibid.

357 "the crowd had rocked the car": ibid.

357 "did not want to go to her grandmother's": ibid., 90.

357 "I crave the power Charlie Manson had": Talbot, *Season of the Witch*, 176.

357 "an ongoing program": ibid., 128.

357 "blasting off": ibid.

357 "If everybody is willing to accept the fact": "Wayne Says Patty Hearst Should Be Granted Freedom," *Eugene Register-Guard*, December 2, 1978.

358 "bad energy": Stephen Davis, "Power, Mystery, and the Hammer of the Gods: The Rise and Fall of Led Zeppelin," *Rolling Stone*, July 4, 1985; available at http://boards.atlantafalcons.com/topic/2988594-the-rise-and-fall-of-led-zeppelin-power-mystery-and-the-hammer-of-the-gods/.

358 "greatest domestic firefight": Farrell, *How I Got to Be This Hip*, 71.

358 "[I]t was clear": ibid., 81.

358 "police shoot-out": Talbot, *Season of the Witch*, 194.

358 "It Took 500 Cops": Miles Corwin, "The Shootout on East 54th Street," *Los Angeles Times*, May 18, 1994; available at articles.latimes.com/1994-05-18/local/me-59109_1_east-54th-street.

359 "The LAPD was making a statement": ibid.

359 "homage of a coast-to-coast auto-da-fe": Farrell, *How I Got to Be This Hip*, 71–72.

359 "President Nixon Vietnam Watergate": John Gregory Dunne, *Quintana & Friends* (New York: E. P. Dutton, 1978), 6.

CHAPTER 22

360 "[T]here was a sense that something was happening": This and subsequent quotes in this chapter are from Caitlin Flanagan's article "The Autumn of Joan Didion," *The Atlantic*, January/February 2012, 95–100.

361 "Certainly I have nothing in common with Hunter": Didion quoted in Susanna Rustin, "Legends of the Fall," *The Guardian*, May 20, 2005; available at www.theguardian.com/books/2005/may/21/usnationalbookawards.society.

361 "This may be the year": Hunter S. Thompson, "Fear and Loathing: The Fat City Blues," cited in Marc Weingarten, *The Gang That Wouldn't Write Straight: Wolfe, Thompson, Didion, and the New Journalism Revolution* (New York: Crown, 2005), 267.

362 "At night I would be the only person on the campus": Don Swaim's audio interview with Joan Didion, October 29, 1987; available at www.wiredforbooks. org/joandidion.

362 "[I] wrapped myself in my bedspread": Joan Didion, *After Henry* (New York: Simon & Schuster, 1992), 115–16.

362 "I'm not telling you to make the world better": Didion quoted in Rachel Donadio, "Every Day Is All There Is," *New York Times*, October 9, 2005; available at www.nytimes.com/2005/10/09/books/review/09donadio.html?pagewanted=all.

363 "Drink": John Gregory Dunne, *Harp* (New York: Simon & Schuster, 1989), 31–32.

363 "I had always thought body bags were black": ibid., 33.

364 "a dozen or so students in the English Department": Joan Didion, *Democracy* (New York: Simon & Schuster, 1984), 71–72.

364 "in the face of definite annihilation": Didion, *After Henry*, 123.

364 "blue in the glass at Chartres": ibid., 124.

364 "the blue that is actually a shock wave in the water": ibid.

364 "question of whether one spoke of Saigon 'falling'": ibid., 117.

365 "plotting of *Vanity Fair*": ibid.

365 "Tank battalions vanished": Didion, *Democracy*, 73.

365 "colors of the landing lights": ibid.

365 "amount of cash burned": ibid., 73–74.

365 "formed a straight line": Hilton Als, "Joan Didion, The Art of Nonfiction No. 1," *The Paris Review* 48, no. 176 (Spring 2006); available at www.theparisreview .org/interviews/5601/the-art-of-nonfiction-no-1-joan-didion.

365 "I'm a writer" and subsequent quotes regarding this encounter: Didion, *After Henry*, 118.

366 "At nineteen I had wanted to write": ibid.

366 "large numbers of . . . Vietnamese": George Esper, "Evacuation from Saigon Tumultuous at the End," *New York Times*, April 30, 1975; available at www .nytimes.com/learning/general/specials/Saigon/evacuation.html.

367 "Americans can [now] regain the sense of pride": Gerald Ford's speech at Tulane University, April 23, 1975, posted at historyplace.com/speeches/ford-tulane.htm.

367 "number of Vietnamese soldiers": Didion, *Democracy*, 74.

368 "[E]ditors do not, in the real world": Didion, *After Henry*, 21.

368 Didion said she had worked up the nerve: Joan Didion letter to Lois Wallace, August 7, 1976, Lois Wallace Literary Agency Records, Harry Ransom Center, University of Texas at Austin.

369 "I've been sitting here": Didion quoted in Susan Braudy, "A Day in the Life of Joan Didion," *Ms.*, February 1977, 108.

369 "[T]here's no getting around the fact": Joan Didion, "Why I Write," *New York Times Book Review*, December 5, 1976; reprinted in *Joan Didion: Essay and Conversations*, ed. Ellen G. Friedman (Princeton, N.J.: Ontario Review Press, 1984), 5.

369 "By which I mean": ibid.

369 "You just lie low": ibid.

CHAPTER 23

370 "I don't mean physically": Susan Stamberg, "Cautionary Tales," in *Joan Didion: Essays and Conversations*, ed. Ellen G. Friedman (Princeton, N.J.: Ontario Review Press, 1984), 22.

370 "*A Book of Common Prayer* to some extent": ibid., 23.

371 "What I work out in a book": ibid.

371 "congealed into a permanent political class": Joan Didion, *Political Fictions* (New York: Alfred A. Knopf, 2001), 9.

372 "In North America": Didion quoted in Sara Davidson, "A Visit with Joan Didion," in Friedman, ed., *Joan Didion*, 14.

372 "fantastic researcher": Hilton Als, "Joan Didion, The Art of Nonfiction No. 1," *The Paris Review* 48, no. 176 (Spring 2006); available at www.theparis review.org/interviews/5601/the-art-of-nonfiction-no-1-joan-didion.

372 "intercutting": ibid.

372 "big set-piece": ibid.

372 "still hadn't delivered [the] revolution": Linda Kuehl, "Joan Didion, The Art of Fiction No. 71," *The Paris Review* 20, no. 74 (Fall-Winter 1978); available at www.theparisreview.org/interviews/3439/the-art-of-fiction-no-71-joan-didion.

373 "romance": ibid.

373 "power and beauty": Henry Robbins letter to Joan Didion, March 24, 1976, Lois Wallace Literary Agency Records, Harry Ransom Center, University of Texas at Austin.

373 magic objects: This list of objects and texts can be found among the Joan Didion Papers, Bancroft Library, University of California at Berkeley.

373 "low dread": Davidson, in Friedman, ed., *Joan Didion*, 15.

373 "The oil rainbow slick" and "He runs guns": ibid.

373 "When I heard Charlotte say this": Kuehl, "Joan Didion, The Art of Fiction No. 71."

373 "I don't want to be tired alone": Pablo Neruda, "A Certain Weariness,"

clipping found in the Joan Didion Papers, Bancroft Library, University of California at Berkeley.

374 "As a child of comfortable family": Joan Didion, *A Book of Common Prayer* (New York: Simon & Schuster, 1977), 59.

374 "I tell you . . . about myself": ibid., 21.

374 "child of the western United States": ibid., 59–60.

374 "Some women": ibid., 84.

374 "So you know the story": ibid., 11.

374 "underwater narrative": Joan Didion, *Vintage Didion* (New York: Vintage Books, 2004), 50.

374 "no history": Didion, *A Book of Common Prayer*, 14.

374 "occasional mineral geologist": ibid., 26.

375 "alone in the dark": ibid., 24.

376 "in a dirty room in Buffalo": ibid., 258.

376 "I have not been the witness I wanted to be": ibid., 272.

376 The way to sell a literary novel: Joan Didion letter to Lois Wallace, August 7, 1976, Lois Wallace Literary Agency Records, Harry Ransom Center, University of Texas at Austin.

377 "capable of having sex with a venetian blind": ibid.

377 "I just think he was a saint!": Caitlin McDermott Click, "People Watching in Washington," *Politico*, April 2013; available at politico.com/blogs/click/2013/94/ben-stein-nixon-was-a-saint-162102.html.

377 "I just didn't have": Alicia C. Shepard, "People and Politics: Woodward and Bernstein Uncovered," *The Washingtonian*, September 1, 2003; available at washingtonian.com/articles/people/woodward-and-bernstein-uncovered.

378 "I remember going to a party": Ben Stein in conversation with the author, June 6, 2013.

378 "I wasn't invited": Dominick Dunne, *The Way We Lived Then: Recollections of a Well-Known Name Dropper* (New York: Crown, 1999), 199.

378 "Put it this way, it's our beads": Susan Braudy, "A Day in the Life of Joan Didion," *Ms.*, February 1977, 66.

378 "I wasn't crazy about their playing in the cage": John Gregory Dunne, *Regards: The Selected Nonfiction of John Gregory Dunne* (New York: Thunder's Mouth Press, 2006), 41–42.

379 "It should make us a lot of money": James Kimbrell, *Barbra: An Actress Who Sings: An Unauthorized Biography* (Wellesley, Mass.: Branden Books, 1984), 198.

379 "I had seen Barbra": ibid., 195.

379 "Jon has a way of seeing me": ibid., 196.

379 "Jon's brainstorm": excerpts of Peters's book proposal, posted at deadline

.com/2009/05/it-should-be-called-dickhead-jon-peters-book-proposal-sets -new-low.

380 "*A Star Is Born* was becoming a career": Dunne, *Regards,* 41.

380 "We couldn't . . . quit": ibid., 42.

380 "Put a band behind me": Kimbrell, *Barbra,* 198.

380 "The Didion/Dunne third draft": Frank Pierson, "My Battles with Barbra and Jon," *New West,* November 22, 1976; available at barbra-archives.com/bjs_library /70s/new_west_battles_barbra_jon.html.

380 "People are curious": ibid.

381 "We are going to miss planes": Didion quoted in Sara Davidson, *Joan: Forty Years of Life, Loss, and Friendship with Joan Didion* (San Francisco: Byliner, 2011).

381 "for absolutely no reason": Joan Didion, *Blue Nights* (New York: Alfred A. Knopf, 2011), 87.

381 "I would drive past Zuma": Joan Didion, *The White Album* (New York: Simon & Schuster, 1979), 211.

381 "some grave solar dislocation": ibid.

381 "most aqueous filtered light": ibid., 216.

382 most fertile at "full moon": ibid., 218.

382 "I had never talked to anyone so direct": ibid., 221.

382 she felt she had become impossible to live with: Chris Chase, "The Uncommon Joan Didion," *Chicago Tribune,* April 3, 1977.

382 "I'm like a child in my parents' house": Didion quoted in Davidson, *Joan,* 17.

382 "*A Book of Common Prayer* was an evil impulse" and subsequent quotes from Noel Parmentel unless otherwise noted: Noel Parmentel in conversation with the author, July 11, 2013.

383 "calumny": Noel Parmentel letter to Dick Snyder, January 28, 1977, Lois Wallace Literary Agency Records, Harry Ransom Center, University of Texas at Austin.

383 "[S]he was incapable": Didion, *Book of Common Prayer,* 85.

383 "it would [not] be legally improper": Rachel Ulell letter to Noel Parmentel, February 7, 1977, Lois Wallace Literary Agency Records, Harry Ransom Center, University of Texas at Austin.

384 "Where are we heading": Didion, *The White Album,* 173.

384 "She's remarkably well-adjusted": Dominick Dunne quoted in John Gregory Dunne, *Quintana & Friends* (New York: E. P. Dutton, 1978), 6.

384 "We go out to dinner in Tucson": Didion, *The White Album,* 162.

385 "The Hilton Inn": Didion, *Blue Nights,* 90.

385 "[S]he had no business in these hotels": ibid., 88.

385 "[U]nder no condition" and "I believed as I did": ibid., 126.

385 "How do you like our monuments?": ibid., 91.

385 "Had an interesting talk with Carl Bernstein": Didion, *The White Album*, 177.

385 "all white": Didion, *Blue Nights*, 91.

386 most Americans were too soft: Rachel Donadio, "Every Day Is All There Is," *New York Times*, October 9, 2005; available at www.nytimes.com/2005/10/09 /books/review/09donadio.html?pagewanted=all.

386 "[W]e were often, my child and I": Didion, *The White Album*, 176.

386 "more sad songs": *Kirkus Reviews*, March 1, 1977; available at www.kirkus reviews.com/book-review/joan-didion/a-book-of-common-prayer/.

386 "its own capacity to come up with the truth": Russell Davies, "Then and Now, 1977," *Times Literary Supplement*, July 8, 1977, available at the-tls.co.uk/tls /public/article833615.ece.

387 "a not untypical North American": Joyce Carol Oates, "A Taut Novel of Disorder," *New York Times Book Review*, April 3, 1977; available at www.nytimes .com/1977/04/03/books/didion-prayer.html?_r=0.

387 "The oft-rewritten script": John Simon, "May, Bogdonovich, and Streisand: Varieties of Death Wish," *New York*, January 10, 1977, 56.

387 "A concert sequence": Jay Cocks, "Barbra: A One-Woman Hippodrome," *Newsweek*, January 3, 1977, 68.

387 "During the filming": Simon, "May, Bogdonovich, and Streisand," 56.

387 "windfall": John Gregory Dunne, *Crooning* (New York: Simon & Schuster, 1990), 179.

388 "Quintana just said": Dunne, *Quintana & Friends*, 6.

CHAPTER 24

389 "I knew doom when I saw it": Mike Davis, "Let Malibu Burn: A Political History of the Fire Coast," posted at ic.unicamp.br/~stolfi/misc/misc/SoCal Fires.html.

389 "The seven million people": ibid.

390 "But when do you give her the money?": Joan Didion, *Blue Nights* (New York: Alfred A. Knopf, 2011), 92.

390 "[A]s little girls do": John Gregory Dunne, *Quintana & Friends* (New York: E. P. Dutton, 1978), 6.

390 "other mother": ibid.

390 "What do you think?": Sara Davidson, *Joan: Forty Years of Life, Loss, and Friendship with Joan Didion* (San Francisco: Byliner, 2011).

390 "something obscene about rolling pastry": Chris Chase, "The Uncommon Joan Didion," *Chicago Tribune,* April 3, 1977.

391 "combat intelligence": ibid.

391 "She fucked her way to the middle": ibid.

391 "Saturday jits": Sara Davidson, "A Visit with Joan Didion," in *Joan Didion: Essays and Conversations,* ed. Ellen G. Friedman (Princeton, N.J.: Ontario Review Press, 1984), 13.

391 "ideal writer's wife": Josh Greenfeld in conversation with the author, April 6, 2013.

391 "They were like one person": Dominick Dunne quoted in Susanna Rustin, "Legends of the Fall," *The Guardian,* May 20, 2005; available at www.the guardian.com/books/2005/may/21/usnationalbookawards.society.

391 "[F]rankly, I'm in the office most of the time": Emily Stokes, "Lunch with the FT: Robert B. Silvers," *Financial Times,* January 25, 2013; available at ft. com/cms/s/2/091b61b6-11e2-a3db-00144feab49a.html.

392 "whose lobby smelled of the Chinese food" and subsequent Wanger quotes from this article: Shelley Wanger, "It Was 1975 . . . ," posted at www.nybooks .com/blogs/50-years/2013/apr/17/shelley-wanger-it-was-1975/.

392 "Even the telephone sex": Andrew Brown, "The Writer's Editor," *The Guardian,* January 23, 2004; available at www.theguardian.com/books/2004/jan/24 /society.

392 "I just thought she was a marvelous observer": Robert Silvers quoted in Rachel Donadio, "Every Day Is All There Is," *New York Times,* October 9, 2005; available at nytimes.com/2005/10/09/books/review/09donadio.html?page wanted=all.

392 "by no means predictable": Robert Silvers quoted in Rustin, "Legends of the Fall."

392 "with lunch at Patsy's" and "If he doesn't know": John Gregory Dunne, *Crooning* (New York: Simon & Schuster, 1990), 12–13.

393 Agoura fire alarms: For details on the Agoura fire, see Molly Burell, "The Hour-by-Hour Battle of $70 Million Holocaust," Los Angeles Fire Department Historical Archive; available at lafire.com/famous_fires/1978-1000 _MandevilleCanyonFire/102978_mandeville_LBpresstele.htm.

393 "a house in West Hartford": Davidson, *Joan.*

394 "suburbia house": Didion, *Blue Nights,* 50.

394 "house on a hill above Sunset": Joan Didion, *After Henry* (New York: Simon & Schuster, 1992), 210.

394 "I lost three years": Joan Didion, *The White Album* (New York: Simon & Schuster, 1979), 223.

394 "I thought we both would cry": ibid.

394 "You want today to see flowers": ibid.

394 "The fire had come": ibid.

CHAPTER 25

397 "Poor dope": Lines from *Sunset Boulevard* cited in Ryan Reft, "A Dive in the Deep End: The Importance of the Swimming Pool in Southern California," posted at kcet.org/socal/departures/columns/intersections/a-dive-in-the-deep -end-the-importance-of-the-swimming-pool-in-southern-california-culture. I have drawn upon Reft's insightful observations for the opening section of this chapter.

397 "Water in a swimming pool": David Hockney quoted in Christopher Simon Sykes, *Hockney: The Biography,* vol. 1 (New York: Random House, 2011).

398 "control of the uncontrollable" and "pool is, for many of us in the West": Joan Didion, *The White Album* (New York: Simon & Schuster, 1979), 64.

398 "apparent ease": ibid.

398 "John in his office" and "room was cool": Joan Didion, *The Year of Magical Thinking* (New York: Alfred A. Knopf, 2005), 24.

398 "we'll have a better life": Sara Davidson, *Joan: Forty Years of Life, Loss, and Friendship with Joan Didion* (San Francisco: Byliner, 2011).

399 "white Americans": John Gregory Dunne, *Regards: The Selected Nonfiction of John Gregory Dunne* (New York: Thunder's Mouth Press, 2006), 173.

399 "quintessential intimate stranger" and Dunne's subsequent quotes about Simpson: ibid., 172.

399 "If you don't know Los Angeles": Rodney King quoted in Aisha Sabatini Sloan, "A Clear Presence," June 17, 2013, posted at guernicamag.com/features/a-clear -presence/.

400 "All the time we were living at the beach": Didion quoted in Michiko Kakutani, "Joan Didion: Staking Out California," *New York Times,* June 10, 1979; available at www.nytimes.com/1979/06/10/books/didion-calif.html?pagewanted =all&_r=O.

401 "to shed their leaves": Dunne, *Regards,* 174.

401 "newly arrived": Leslie Garis, "Didion and Dunne: The Rewards of a Literary Marriage," *New York Times,* February 8, 1987; available at www.nytimes .com/1987/02/08/magazine/didion-dunne-the-rewards-of-a-literary-marriage .html.

401 "cain't" and "youse": Davidson, *Joan.*

401 "You don't know White Trash": Dunne quoted in ibid.

401 "I'm going to have a 'me' decade": Didion quoted in ibid.

402 "Kids grow up": Tim Steele in conversation with the author, April 29, 2013.

402 "Writers do not get gross": Joan Didion, *After Henry* (New York: Simon & Schuster, 1992), 163.

403 "In those days, public schools": Tim Steele, in conversation with the author, April 29, 2013.

403 "This place never changes": Kakutani, "Joan Didion."

403 "[W]e encourage them to remain children": Joan Didion, *Blue Nights*: (New York: Alfred A. Knopf, 2011), 53.

403 "She was already a person": ibid, 41.

403 "It bothered her father": Jeff Glor, interview with Joan Didion on *Author Talk*, CBS News, January 28, 2012; available at cbsnews.com/video/author-talk -blue-nights-by-joan-didion.

404 "just to show you" and the quotes from Quintana's novel: Didion, *Blue Nights*, 49–50.

404 "Some of the events": ibid., 50.

404 "Day-to-day living": Dominick Dunne, *The Way We Lived Then: Recollections of a Well-Known Name Dropper* (New York: Crown, 1999), 186.

404 "I sold my West Highland terrier": ibid., 187.

404 "Desperate to save myself": ibid., 188.

405 "I had heard the word[s]": ibid., 199.

405 "He did tell me that a lady": David Jasper, "Camp Sherman Gets a Visit from Dominick Dunne Documentarians," *Bend Bulletin*, September 23, 2007; available at bendbulletin.com/csp/mediapool/sites/BendBulletin/News/story.csp?cid =1491.

405 "There were 150-foot-high pine trees": Dominick Dunne, *The Way We Lived Then*, 201.

405 "You're dead meat": ibid., 206.

405 "licked [his] wounds": James H. Hyde, "Dominick Dunne: An Inveterate Connecticut Yankee Tells Us About His Remarkable Life," posted at new englandtimes.com/dominick_dunne/dd_index.shtml.

405 "All that bullshit": ibid.

406 "But remember this": Truman Capote quoted in Dominick Dunne, *The Way We Lived Then*, 210.

406 "I felt sure": ibid.

406 "I fed them a lot of popcorn": Scot Haller, "According to Critics and His Famous Female Fans, Griffin Dunne Does His Best Work in *After Hours*," *People*, September 30, 1985; available at people.com/people/article/0,,20091842,00.html.

406 "It was like seeing three of my characters": Ann Beattie quoted in James Atlas,

"How 'Chilly Scenes' Was Rescued," *New York Times Book Review*, October 10, 1982; available at www.nytimes.com/books/98/06/28/specials/beattie-chilly .html.

406 "A terrible resentment": Dominick Dunne, "A Death in the Family," originally published in *Vanity Fair*, March 2004; reprinted in *Brothers: 26 Stories of Love and Rivalry* (San Francisco: Jossey-Bass, 2009), 189.

406 "epiphany" and "long, artful" letters: John Gregory Dunne, *Harp* (New York: Simon & Schuster, 1989), 19.

407 "I had the uneasy feeling," "Fuck you!" and "[M]y note": ibid., 19–20.

407 *I wake and feel the fell of dark*: Gerard Manley Hopkins cited in ibid., 23.

407 "bleakness": ibid., 19.

407 "played life on the dark keys": ibid., 18.

408 "wanton and insensitive": ibid., 19.

408 "mutual disaster": ibid., 20.

408 *O the mind, mind has mountains*: Gerard Manley Hopkins cited in ibid., 23.

408 "under Roger's gaze": Boris Kachka, *Hothouse: The Art of Survival and the Survival of Art at America's Most Celebrated Publishing House, Farrar, Straus & Giroux* (New York: Simon & Schuster, 2013), 223.

408 "lot of publishing houses": ibid., 219.

408 "I think his opinion": ibid.

408 "[W]e are all terminal cases": John Irving quoted in Margi Fox, "God of Books," *Literal Latte*, Summer 2009; available at literal-latte.com/2009/06/god -of-books/.

409 "Because of [Henry's] importance": ibid.

409 "Henry's orphan sister": Didion, *After Henry*, 19.

409 Robbins's real sister: Fox, "God of Books."

409 of all the speakers at the service: ibid.

409 "I would be less than honest": Roger Straus letter to Joan Didion, August 8, 1979, Farrar, Straus and Giroux Records, Manuscripts and Archives Division, New York Public Library.

409 "benign climate": Davidson, *Joan*.

410 "It's part of the exaggerated politeness": Dunne, *Harp*, 91.

410 "children with bright scarlet rashes": Didion, *After Henry*, 139.

410 "11,573 Vietnamese": ibid., 142.

410 "*Mes filles, mes filles!*": ibid., 143.

410 "[The] events of the last few years": Dominick Dunne, *The Way We Lived Then*, 211.

411 "I had no money": ibid.

411 "She stayed by my side": ibid., 213.

411 "I'll never forget that": Hyde, "Dominick Dunne."

411 "It was smaller than the cabin": Dominick Dunne, *The Way We Lived Then*, 213.

411 "Simon & Schuster": Lois Wallace letter to Anthony Sheil, November 30, 1979, Lois Wallace Literary Agency Records, Harry Ransom Center, University of Texas at Austin.

411 "montage": Lynn Marie Houston and William V. Lombardi, *Reading Joan Didion* (Santa Barbara, Calif.: Greenwood Press, 2009), 81.

412 "smells of the Sixties": Didion, *The White Album*, 58.

412 "Something [about the new Getty Museum]": ibid., 75.

412 "learning" and "unremittingly reproachful": ibid.

412 "set the natural child in each of us free": ibid., 76.

412 "pay for any" and "flouting": ibid., 77.

412 "large numbers" and "as its founder": ibid.

413 "On the whole, 'the critics'": ibid., 78.

413 "equipped early": ibid., 129.

413 "If I could believe that going to a barricade": ibid., 208.

413 "Her nervous system is a San Andreas Fault": John Leonard, "The White Album," *New York Times*, June 5, 1979; available at www.nytimes.com/menu/archive/pdf?res=F20F10FA3L5A12728DDDACO894DE405B898BF1D3.

414 "In her relatively self-effacing preface": Martin Amis, "Joan Didion's Style," *London Review of Books*, February 1980, 3–4.

414 "adolescent" and subsequent quotes from Didion's Woody Allen piece: Joan Didion, "Letter from Manhattan," *The New York Review of Books*, August 16, 1979; available at www.nybooks.com/articles/archives/1979/aug/16/letter-from-manhattan/.

415 "When I am asked" and subsequent quotes from this article: Barbara Grizzuti Harrison, "Joan Didion: Only Disconnect," *The Nation*, October 1979; available at writing.upenn.edu/~afilreis/103/didion-per-harrison.html.

415 "I knew I wasn't going to get a break": Brod, *In Depth* interview with Joan Didion, Book TV, C-Span 2, 1992.

415 "I was sorry": ibid.

CHAPTER 26

417 "I have a feeling": Ronald Reagan quoted in Joan Didion, *After Henry* (New York: Simon & Schuster, 1992), 43.

417 "The gruesome quiet": Hannah Arendt quoted in Joan Didion, *Miami* (New York: Simon & Schuster, 1987), 159.

418 "Get him off his feet!": Bob Colacello, "Ronnie and Nancy," *Vanity Fair,* July 1998; available at www.vanityfair.com/magazine/archive/1998/07/ronnie -and-nancy199807.

418 "You know, we need more money for the campaign": Bob Colacello cited in *Nancy Reagan: The Role of a Lifetime* (PBS documentary); available at pbs.org /newshour/nancy-reagan.

418 "There was a lot of ideological fervor": Joan Didion in conversation with Michael Bernstein, the Revelle Forum at the Neurosciences Institute, University of California at San Diego, October 15, 2002.

418 "is not going to have sources": ibid.

418 "these are books": Joan Didion, *Political Fictions* (New York: Alfred A. Knopf, 2001), 194. Of Didion's assessment of Woodward, Carl Bernstein said, "I've had two good friends who have attacked Bob's work—Joan Didion and Renata Adler. I let them both know they were wrong. Whatever the criticism of Bob's methods in terms of getting too close to sources, there's a context that ignores his contributions. We know more about the presidencies from Nixon through both Bushes than we ever would have because of Bob's work." Bernstein quoted in Alicia C. Shepard, "People and Politics: Woodward and Bernstein Uncovered," *The Washingtonian,* September 1, 2003; available at washingtonian .com/articles/people/woodward-and-bernstein-uncovered.

419 "critical reading faculty": ibid.

419 "ghost resorts": Joan Didion, *Salvador* (New York: Simon & Schuster, 1983), 13.

419 "is to plunge directly": ibid.

420 "I'm not sure that I have a social conscience": Didion quoted in Jemima Hunt, "The Didion Bible," *The Guardian,* January 11, 2003; available at www.theguard ian.com/books/2003/jan/12/fiction.society.

420 "expressed interest in having one or both of us": Hilton Als, "Joan Didion, The Art of Nonfiction No. 1," *The Paris Review* 48, no. 176 (Spring 2006); available at www.theparisreview.org/interviews/5601/the-art-of-nonfiction-no-1 -joan-didion.

420 "desperate to go" and "he'd been in Beirut": Leslie Garis, "Didion and Dunne: The Rewards of a Literary Marriage," *New York Times,* February 8, 1987; available at www.nytimes.com/1987/02/08/magazine/didion-dunne -the-rewards-of-a-literary-marriage.html.

421 "making a concerted and significant effort": Joan Didion, "'Something Horrible' in El Salvador," *The New York Review of Books,* July 14, 1994; available at

www.nybooks.com/articles/archives/1994/jul/14/something-horrible-in-el
-salvador/.

421 "woke up in the middle of the night": Garis, "Didion and Dunne."

421 "What's *she* doing here?": Paul VanDevelder in conversation with the author, February 21, 2013.

421 "large sunglasses and sun hat": John Newhagen to the author, April 2, 2013.

421 "We all wore T-shirts": Paul VanDevelder in conversation with the author, February 21, 2013.

422 "concerted and significant effort" and "revise": Didion, "'Something Horrible' in El Salvador."

422 "have credibility": ibid.

422 "Consider the political implications": Joan Didion, *Democracy* (New York: Simon & Schuster, 1984), 72.

422 "The consciousness of the human organism": Joan Didion, *A Book of Common Prayer* (New York: Simon & Schuster, 1977), 234.

422 ammunition manufactured: Mark Danner cited in Didion, "'Something Horrible' in El Salvador."

422 "El Mozote entered the thin air": ibid.

422 "only six years" and "most of us": ibid.

422 "I was just panicked": Didion quoted in Garis, "Didion and Dunne."

422 "But it's the only way": Dunne quoted in ibid.

423 Maria Ynez Camacho: Matthew Specktor to the author, June 5, 2013.

423 "repeated instructions": Didion, *Salvador*, 77.

423 "[W]e went out to the body dump" and Didion's description: Garis, "Didion and Dunne."

423 "Nothing fresh": Didion, *Salvador*, 20.

423 in the military zone: John Gregory Dunne, *Harp* (New York: Simon & Schuster, 1989), 94–95.

423 pocket notebook: Joan Didion Papers, Bancroft Library, University of California at Berkeley.

424 "noble words": Joseph Conrad's *Heart of Darkness* cited in Didion, *Salvador*, 12.

424 "the models and colors": ibid., 14.

424 "is the given of the place": ibid.

424 "mechanism[s] of terror": ibid., 21.

424 "names are understood locally": ibid., 63.

425 "refining . . . artistic expression": "Bennington College Summer Program Expands Horizons," posted at iberkshires.com/story/4171/Bennington-College -summer-program-expands-horizons.html.

425 "great ability": Quintana Roo Dunne quoted in Jill Krementz, *How It Feels to Be Adopted* (New York: Alfred A. Knopf, 1982), 58.

425 "terrific": Christopher Dickey to the author, June 3, 2013.

426 Michael Korda: Korda cited in a letter from Lois Wallace to Anthony Sheil, October 4, 1982, Lois Wallace Literary Agency Records, Harry Ransom Center, University of Texas at Austin.

426 "gratifying to write something so topical": interview notes, Joan Didion Papers, Bancroft Library, University of California at Berkeley.

426 "color": Didion, *Salvador*, 36.

426 "According to the text": Sandra Braman, "The 'Facts' of El Salvador According to Objective and New Journalism," *Journal of Communication Inquiry* 13, no. 2 (1985): 82.

426 "She attended to information": ibid., 84.

426 "geographic source of news": ibid., 82.

426 "participated in informal and formal social gatherings": ibid., 84.

427 "Bonner and *The New York Times*": ibid., 87.

427 "disjointed": ibid., 83.

427 "[c]ollecting facts": ibid., 87.

427 "the passage of bureaucratically recognized events" and "perpetual frontier": ibid., 88–89.

427 "diction that won't be outflanked by events": Terrence Des Pres cited in Noel Valis, "Fear and Torment in El Salvador," *Massachusetts Review* 48, no. 1 (Spring 2007): 122. Valis's meditation on El Salvador proved enormously helpful to me in composing this chapter.

427 "what is quite literally at stake" and subsequent quotes from Scarry: Elaine Scarry, *The Body in Pain: The Making and Unmaking of the World* (New York: Oxford University Press, 1985), 23, 145, 306.

428 saying she had just received three copies: Joan Didion letter to Michael Korda and Lois Wallace, August 8, 1987, Lois Wallace Literary Agency Records, Harry Ransom Center, University of Texas at Austin.

428 "I'm crazy about Miami" and subsequent quotes from the Atlas profile: James Atlas, "Slouching Towards Miami," *Vanity Fair*, October 1987; available at www.vanityfair.com/culture/features/1987/10/joan-didion-on-miami.

429 "underwater narrative": Didion, *Miami*, 38.

429 "liquidity": ibid., 31.

429 "cognitive dissonance": ibid., 99.

430 "[I]n 1959": ibid., 13.

430 "disposal problem": ibid., 83.

430 "teeming, incomprehensible presence": ibid., 55.

430 "healing process": ibid., 202.

430 "That *la lucha* had become": ibid., 20.

430 "social dynamic": ibid., 47.

430 "women in Chanel": ibid.

431 "most theatrical possible": ibid.

431 "provisional," "individuals," and "affect events directly": ibid., 13.

431 "largest CIA installation" and "who left Miami": ibid., 93.

432 "As it happens": Joan Didion, *Slouching Towards Bethlehem* (New York: Farrar, Straus and Giroux, 1968), 157.

432 "You can't just leave a body": ibid., 158.

433 "We tell ourselves stories in order to live": Joan Didion, *The White Album* (New York: Simon & Schuster, 1979), 11.

433 "granddaughter of a geologist": Didion, *Democracy*, 18.

433 "write anything down": ibid., 12.

433 "[c]olors, moisture, heat": ibid., 16.

433 "The light at dawn": ibid., 11.

433 "Call me the author": ibid., 16.

433 "I began thinking": ibid., 17.

433 "When novelists speak of unpredictability": ibid., 215.

434 "In the spring of 1975": ibid., 71.

434 "family in which the colonial impulse": ibid., 26.

434 "various investigations into arms and currency": ibid., 217.

435 "nothing in this situation": ibid., 233.

435 "sudden sense of Inez": ibid., 234.

435 "flotsam of some territorial imperative": ibid., 228.

435 "When I started thinking about the novel": Joan Didion, "Second Thoughts: Tyranny in the Tropics: Joan Didion on a Novel That Began with an Angel and Ended with Saigon," *The Independent*, October 29, 1994; available at independent.co.uk/arts-entertainment/books/books-second-thoughts -tyranny-in-the-tropics-joan-didion-on-a-novel-that-began-with-an-angel- and-ended-with-saigon-1445563.html.

435 "weeping": Christopher Bollen, "Joan Didion," *V Magazine*; available at chris- topherbollen.com/portfolio/joan-didion.pdf.

435 "[I]f man should continue": Henry Adams, *The Degradation of the Democratic Dogma* (New York: Peter Smith, 1949), 309.

435 "What Adams really meant": Timothy Parrish, *From the Civil War to the Apoc- alypse: Postmodern History and American Fiction* (Amherst: University of Mas- sachusetts Press, 2008), 194.

436 "must submit": Adams, *The Degradation of the Democratic Dogma*, 206.

436 "within the Democratic Party": Michael Szalay, *Hip Figures: A Literary History of the Democratic Party* (Stanford: Stanford University Press, 2012), 251.

436 "thinly veiled Jackie Kennedy" and "a left-leaning liberal": ibid., 252. Szalay's remarks about Harry Victor use quotes from another literary critic, John McClure. I owe Szalay the insight about the Democratic Leadership Council.

436 "asshole": Didion, *Democracy*, 173.

436 Didion claimed: See, for example, Didion, "Second Thoughts."

436 "Let me die": Didion, *Democracy*, 60.

437 *"Let me just be in the ground"*: Joan Didion, *Blue Nights* (New York: Alfred A. Knopf, 2011), 49.

437 "After I finished my first novel": Didion, *Democracy*, 39.

437 "kept a copy": ibid., 193.

437 "[D]espite an appearance of factuality" and subsequent quotes from McCarthy: Mary McCarthy, "Love and Death in the Pacific," *New York Times Book Review*, April 22, 1984; available at www.nytimes.com/books/00/03/26/specials/mccarthy-didion.html.

437 "Miss McCarthy": John Gregory Dunne, "Conrad's 'Victory,'" *New York Times*, May 6, 1984; available at www.nytimes.com/1984/05/06/books/l-conrad-s-victory-168073.html.

438 "[J]argon ends": V. S. Naipaul quoted in Joan Didion, "Without Regret or Hope," *The New York Review of Books*, June 12, 1980; available at www.nybooks.com/articles/archives/1980/jun/12/without-regret-or-hope/.

438 "The wisdom of the heart": ibid.

438 "absolutely against regulations": John Gregory Dunne, *Regards: The Selected Nonfiction of John Gregory Dunne* (New York: Thunder's Mouth Press, 2006), 394.

439 "the arteries to the pump are shot" and "In a way": *True Confessions* movie dialogue cited in Richard Grenier, "Our Lady of Corruption," *Commentary*, December 1, 1981; available at commentarymagazine.com/article/our-lady-of-corruption/.

439 a public slap from William F. Buckley, Jr.: ibid.

439 "Oddly enough": John Gallagher, *Film Directors on Directing* (Los Angeles: ABC-CLIO, 1989), unpaginated.

439 "[He] has established a distinctive voice": Michiko Kakutani, "How John Gregory Dunne Puts Himself into His Books," *New York Times*, May 3, 1982; available at www.nytimes.com/books/97/03/02/reviews/dunne-work.html.

439 "I've always thought a novelist": Dunne, *Regards*, 384.

439 "What I mean is": Dunne quoted in Kakutani, "How John Gregory Dunne Puts Himself into His Books."

439 "the loss of public honor": Paul Schrader, "Notes on Film Noir," posted at mon-tevallotimetravel.files.wordpress.com/2012/04/notes-on-noir.doc.

440 "Miss Didion's dust-jacket image": Christopher Lehmann-Haupt, "Critic's Notebook: Pondering the Secrets Photographs Reveal," *New York Times,* July 5, 1984; available at www.nytimes.com/1984/07/05/arts/critic-s-notebook -pondering-the-secrets-photographs-reveal.html.

440 "It just shows somebody": ibid.

440 In his letter: John Gregory Dunne letter to Christopher Lehmann-Haupt, August 1, 1984, Lois Wallace Literary Agency Records, Harry Ransom Center, University of Texas at Austin.

441 "history of an investigation" and "absurd daintiness": Dunne, *Regards,* 394–95.

CHAPTER 27

442 "In truth, she and I" and subsequent quotes from Connolly: Anna Connolly to the author, March 20, 2013.

443 "There were always open bars": Tim Steele in conversation with the author, April 2, 2013.

443 "I knew a lot of privileged kids" and subsequent quotes from Matthew Speck-tor: Matthew Specktor to the author, June 6, 2013.

444 "socially vicious" and subsequent quotes from Greenfeld: Karl Taro Green-feld, *Boy Alone: A Brother's Memoir* (New York: HarperCollins, 2009), 125, 134–35.

444 "Karl knew some of the same people": Josh Greenfeld in conversation with the author, April 6, 2013.

445 Josh Greenfeld said: ibid.

445 "wishing for death": Joan Didion, *Blue Nights* (New York: Alfred A. Knopf, 2011), 49.

445 "She was depressed": ibid., 48.

445 "depths, shallows": ibid., 47.

445 "borderline personality disorder": ibid., 48.

445 "Borderline individuals": Marsha Linehan quoted in Scott O. Lilienfeld and Hal Arkowitz, "Diagnosis of Borderline Personality Disorder Is Often Flawed," *Scientific American,* January 4, 2012; available at scientificamerican.com/article .cfm?id=the-truth-about-borderline&print=true.

445 "I have not yet seen that case": Didion, *Blue Nights,* 47.

445 *"Let me just be in the ground"*: ibid., 49.

445 Susanna Moore wrote Quintana: Susanna Moore letter to Quintana Roo

Dunne, November 17, 1982; Susanna Moore Papers, Department of Rare Books and Special Collections, Princeton University Library.

446 "I killed my girlfriend": Brad Darrach, "An American Tragedy That Brought Death to Actress Dominique Dunne Now Brings Outrage to Her Family," *People,* October 10, 1983; available at people.com/people/archive/article/0,, 20086105,00.html.

446 "I need you" and subsequent dialogue: Dominick Dunne, *Justice: Crimes, Trials, and Punishments* (New York: Crown, 2001), 2.

447 "The news is not good," "brain damage," and "permission to insert": ibid., 4–5.

447 "She looks even worse than Diana did": Lenny Dunne quoted in Didion, *Blue Nights,* 67.

447 "It's not black and white": Dominick Dunne, *Justice,* 6.

447 "It's not necessarily an either-or situation": Joan Didion, *Democracy* (New York: Simon & Schuster, 1984), 151–52.

447 "Give me your talent": *Dominick Dunne: After the Party,* directed and produced by Kirsty de Garis and Timothy Jolley (Mercury Media/Road Trip Films/Film Art Docco, 2008), film documentary.

447 "Oh, what difference does it make?" and subsequent dialogue: Dominick Dunne, *Justice,* 7–8.

447 "two television programs": ibid., 9.

448 "Most people I know at Westlake": Joan Didion, *The Year of Magical Thinking* (New York: Alfred A. Knopf, 2005), 172–73. See also John Gregory Dunne, *Harp* (New York: Simon & Schuster, 1989), 106.

448 "It all evens out in the end": Didion, *The Year of Magical Thinking,* 173. See also Dunne, *Harp,* 106.

448 "I have watched too many murder trials": Dunne, *Harp,* 107.

448 "John, who knew his way around": Dominick Dunne, "A Death in the Family," originally published in *Vanity Fair,* March 2004; reprinted in Andrew Blauner, ed., *Brothers: 26 Stories of Love and Rivalry* (San Francisco: Jossey-Bass, 2009), 191.

448 "Lenny, Griffin, Alex and I": ibid.

449 "When Miss Dunne got in from the bars": Dominick Dunne, *Justice,* 13.

449 "prejudicial": ibid., 21.

449 "opened first one envelope" and subsequent courtroom dialogue: ibid., 30–31.

449 "Dominick, you don't want to do this": Kim Masters, "You Don't Want to Do This," posted at slate.com/articles/arts/hollywoodland/2007/08/you-don't-want -to-do-this.html.

450 He told the story this way: Dominick Dunne, *The Way We Lived Then:*

Recollections of a Well-Known Name Dropper (New York: Crown, 1999), 215. See also James H. Hyde, "Dominick Dunne: An Inveterate Connecticut Yankee Tells Us About His Remarkable Life," posted at newenglandtimes.com/dominick_dunne/dd_index.shtml; Marie Brenner, "Behind the Big Round Glasses," *Vanity Fair*, August 20, 2009; available at www.vanityfair.com/online/daily/2009/08/marie-brenners-dominick-dunne-tribute.

450 "If I hadn't kept that journal": Dominick Dunne quoted in Mick Brown, "Dominick Dunne: Lost and Found," *The Telegraph*, October 18, 2008; available at telegraph.co.uk/culture/film/3562275/Dominick-Dunne-lost-and-found.html.

450 "Tina . . . saw something": Dominick Dunne, *The Way We Lived Then*, 215.

450 "For the first time in my life": Dominick Dunne, *Justice*, xi.

450 "great, highbrow, bling-bling": Hyde, "Dominick Dunne."

450 "Wealthy people aren't quite shooting themselves": Graydon Carter quoted in *Dominick Dunne: After the Party*, film documentary.

450 "I had an exciting revelation": Didion, *Blue Nights*, 131.

451 "The guests, gathered on a terrace": Leslie Garis, "Didion and Dunne: The Rewards of a Literary Marriage," *New York Times Magazine*, February 8, 1987; available at www.nytimes.com/1987/02/08/magazine/dunne-didion-the-rewards-of-a-literary-marriage.html. See also David Rieff, *Los Angeles: Capital of the Third World* (New York: Touchstone, 1992), 92–93.

451 "The last time I saw Joan": Don Bachardy in conversation with the author, April 23, 2013.

451 "You still have not taken my advice": Dunne, *Harp*, 72.

452 "BRENTWOOD PARK STEAL!": John Gregory Dunne letter to Tom Johnson, September 8, 1981, Lois Wallace Literary Agency Records, Harry Ransom Center, University of Texas at Austin.

452 "That's Rupert Murdoch for you": John Gregory Dunne quoted in Lois Wallace letter to Anthony Sheil, September 18, 1983; in ibid.

452 "At some point . . . I think I twigged to the fact": Hari Kunzru, "Joan Didion's Yellow Corvette," posted at harikunzru.com/archive/joan-didion-yellow-corvette-interview-transcript-2011.

453 "a stressful time," "adolescent substance abuse," and the subsequent dialogue exchange: Didion, *Democracy*, 61–63.

453 "reminded me of you" and "Cuddling on the ice floe": Didion, *Blue Nights*, 151.

453 *"Like when someone dies"*: ibid., 168.

453 "foundered on the twin rocks": John Gregory Dunne, *Regards: The Selected Nonfiction of John Gregory Dunne* (New York: Thunder's Mouth Press, 2006), 61.

454 "the pay is good": John Gregory Dunne, *The Red White and Blue* (New York: Simon & Schuster, 1987), 34.

454 "celebrity and political action": ibid., 15.

454 "not guilty by reason of insanity": ibid., 474.

454 "There is in the development of every motion picture": Joan Didion, *Political Fictions* (New York: Alfred A. Knopf, 2001), 111.

454 "a lovely little war": posted at pbs.org/wgbh/americanexperience/features/general -article/reagan-grenada/.

455 "the number of medals": Didion, *Political Fictions*, 101.

455 "new generation with no alternative source of information": ibid., 96.

455 "slime": John Gregory Dunne, *Crooning* (New York: Simon & Schuster, 1990), 271.

456 "Two things the Irish would think": Elizabeth Venant, "Pages Open for Dunne, Didion," *Los Angeles Times*, February 2, 1987.

456 "odd waters" and "very tedious": ibid.

457 "in light of the many changes" and subsequent details and quotes regarding Dunne's health tests: Dunne, *Harp*, 110–114.

CHAPTER 28

461 "*I now know*" and "*You no more know*": Joan Didion, *The Year of Magical Thinking* (New York: Alfred A. Knopf, 2005), 203.

461 "I know Jim" and "pretentious asshole": John Gregory Dunne, *Harp* (New York: Simon & Schuster, 1989), 119.

461 "Milk it": ibid., 121.

461 "I was ever aware": ibid.

462 "the little widow": ibid., 122.

462 "He's too terrible to die": ibid., 124.

462 "Bye, bye, life" and subsequent details of Dunne's angioplasty and its aftermath: ibid., 126–129.

463 "Twenty-four years": ibid., 132.

464 "I don't know why we moved back to New York": Rachel Donadio, "Every Day Is All There Is," *New York Times*, October 9, 2005; available at www.nytimes .com/2005/10/09/books/review/09donadio.html.

464 "hetero-coastal": Elizabeth Mehren, "Why They Left," *Los Angeles Times*, May 9, 1988; available at articles.latimes.com/print/1988-05-09/news/vw-1725_1 _didion-and-dunne.

464 "I don't know": "Telling Stories in Order to Live," Academy of Achievement

interview with Joan Didion, June 3, 2006; available at www.achievement.org/autodoc/page/did0int-1.

464 "[We've] stayed too long at the fair": Dunne, *Harp,* 132.

464 In their conflicting accounts: See, for example, Bernard Weinraub, "At Lunch with John Gregory Dunne: The Bad Old Days in All Their Glory," *New York Times,* September 14, 1994, available at www.nytimes.com/books/97/03/02/reviews/dunne-lunch.html; Andrew O'Hehir, "Golden State of Hypocrisy," posted at salon.com/2003/10/18/didion_4/.

464 "cocaine days" and "scandal-plagued faculty": Jonathan Lethem, *The Ecstasy of Influence* (New York: Doubleday, 2011), 23.

464 "about youth culture in L.A" and "very much in the style": Jaime Clarke, "An Interview with Bret Easton Ellis," posted at geocities.com/Athens/forum/8506/Ellis/clarkeint.html.

465 "It was inconvenient that I liked him": Lethem, *The Ecstasy of Influence,* 23.

465 "I would rewrite paragraphs of hers": Carl Swanson, "The Haunting of Bret Easton Ellis," *New York,* June 6, 2010; available at nymag.com/arts/books/features/66447/index1.html.

465 "Quintana seemed spooky to me": Jonathan Lethem to the author, March 9, 2012.

465 One fellow resident: Anonymous to the author, March 12, 2012.

466 "it was upsetting to her": Jeff Glor, *"Blue Nights* by Joan Didion," *Author Talk,* CBS News, January 28, 2012; available at cbsnews.com/videos/author-talk-blue-nights-by-joan-didion.

466 "I have a child in college now": Don Swaim's audio interview with Joan Didion, October 29, 1987; available at wiredforbooks.org/joandidion.

466 "I have a highly developed capacity for denial": Didion quoted in O'Hehir, "Golden State of Hypocrisy."

466 "The 'bones' of the house": Carol Herman to the author, April 1, 2013.

467 "man who was buying the house": Joan Didion, *Blue Nights* (New York: Alfred A. Knopf, 2011), 8.

467 "have to arrange to get the windows washed": Hilton Als, "Joan Didion, The Art of Nonfiction, No. 1," *The Paris Review* 48, no. 176 (Spring 2006); available at www.theparisreview.org/interviews/5601/the-art-of-nonfiction-no-1-joan-didion.

467 "Oh no," friends told them: Dunne, *Harp,* 134–35.

467 "There weren't too many ways I was going to do it": Mehren, "Why They Left."

467 "[Y]ou took all those years": ibid., 139.

468 "I hope you're not going to move back east": Dunne, *Harp,* 133.

468 "When they left": Josh Greenfeld in conversation with the author, April 6, 2013.

468 "You ready?": Mehren, "Why They Left."

469 "underwater color": Didion quoted in Sara Davidson, *Joan: Forty Years of Life, Loss, and Friendship with Joan Didion* (San Franciso: Byliner, 2011).

469 "I just tried to ignore": Mehren, "Why They Left."

469 "All ready in case of a storm": ibid.

469 "Californian": ibid.

469 "pain in the ass": Dunne, *Harp*, 232.

470 "city's rage at being broke": Als, "Joan Didion, The Art of Nonfiction No. 1."

470 "stories the city [told] itself": ibid.

470 "distortion and flattening of character" and "Lady Liberty": Joan Didion, *After Henry* (New York: Simon & Schuster, 1992), 279–80.

470 "market economy": ibid., 285.

470 "enemy of the city": ibid., 222.

471 "telephones ringing": Helen Peterson, "Beauty in Ugly Lawsuit," New York *Daily News,* January 17, 2001; available at nydailynews.com/archives/news/beauty -ugly-lawsuit-crawford-hubby-noise-row-article-1.911801.

471 "social and economic phenomena": Didion, *After Henry,* 283.

471 "who could in turn inspire": ibid.

CHAPTER 29

472 "[W]e had not stayed married": John Gregory Dunne, *Harp* (New York: Simon & Schuster, 1989), 233.

472 "I was quite desolate for about a year": "Telling Stories in Order to Live," Academy of Achievement interview with Joan Didion, June 3, 2006; available at www.achievement.org/autodoc/page/did0int-1.

473 "Bob kept pushing": Hilton Als, "Joan Didion, The Art of Nonfiction No. 1," *The Paris Review* 48, no. 176 (Spring 2006); available at www.theparisreview .org/interviews/5601/the-art-of-nonfiction-no-1-joan-didion.

473 "Who's she?": Joan Didion, *Political Fictions* (New York: Alfred A. Knopf, 2001), 5–6.

473 "Give me a guesstimate": ibid., 6.

473 "I was just in tears": "Telling Stories in Order to Live."

474 "He's a fucking snake": Dunne, *Harp,* 190.

474 "political groupie," "She still has that insane glitter," and "It comes from trying": ibid., 161.

474 "An artful presentation" and ensuing dialogue: ibid., 190.

474 "Pat Curtin's ma" and ensuing dialogue: ibid., 202.

474 "small but highly visible group": Didion, *Political Fictions*, 279.

474 "They report the stories": ibid.

475 "I don't know how good an idea" and subsequent quotes regarding Quintana's Latin American trip: Quintana Roo Dunne, "Photographer's Notebook: Exploring Guatemala and Nicaragua," *Columbia Spectator*, November 14, 1988.

477 "had gone immediately to bed": Joan Didion, *Blue Nights* (New York: Alfred A. Knopf, 2011), 34.

477 "exactly yesterday" and "I did not ask": ibid., 34–35.

477 "*For Mom and Dad*": ibid., 35.

478 "the characteristic surface wrinkles" and "found in her vagina": Joan Didion, *After Henry* (New York: Simon & Schuster, 1992), 254.

478 "ultimate shriek of alarm": ibid., 255.

478 "Teen Wolfpack" and "One [assailant] shouted": ibid.

478 "[C]rimes are universally understood": ibid., 255–56.

478 "probably one of the top four or five students" and "fun-loving": ibid., 258.

478 "Bacharach bride": ibid.

478 "protect," "magical," and "nature best kept secret": ibid., 260–61.

478 "no matching semen": ibid., 258.

479 "The accounts given": "Affirmation in Response to Motion to Vacate Judgment of Conviction: *The People of the State of New York Against Kharey Wise, Kevin Richardson, Antron McCray, Yusef Salaam, and Raymond Santana, Defendants*," posted at manhattanda.org/whatsnew/press/2002-12-05a.pdf.

479 "taking back": Didion, *After Henry*, 278–79.

479 "Lady Courage" and quotes from the other two newspapers: ibid., 259.

479 "You're going to get it right": Joan Didion's remarks made at Kelly Writers House, University of Pennsylvania, March 31, 2009.

479 "What you do in the United States of America": Calvin O. Butts quoted in Didion, *After Henry*, 265.

479 "logical": "Telling Stories in Order to Live."

479 "grown steadily less inflammatory": David Blum, "Literary Lotto," *New York*, January 21, 1985, 39.

480 "savvy ad campaign" and "plain clothing": "Everybody's Falling into the Gap," *Businessweek*, September 22, 1991; available at businessweek.com/stories /1991-09-22/everybodys-falling-into-the-gap.

480 "contribution" and "financial community": Peter Minichiello letter to Joan Didion, March 30, 1984, Lois Wallace Literary Agency Records, Harry Ransom Center, University of Texas at Austin.

480 "Some years back": Joan Didion's remarks in the 1984 Gulf & Western share-holders' report; in ibid.

480 "anticipate[d] a terrifically positive response": Peter Minichiello letter to Joan Didion; in ibid.

481 He was the CEO: *Businessweek* executive profile for James J. Didion, posted at investing.businessweek.com/research/stocks/people/person.asp?personID=21574&ticker=CY&previousCId=13513368&previousTitle-Bancroft%20Capital.

481 "Hollywood ratfuck": John Gregory Dunne, *Monster: Living Off the Big Screen* (New York: Random House, 1997), 82.

481 "so much to read a script": ibid., 52.

481 "[A]fter each of us": ibid., 52–53.

482 "venomous": ibid., 8.

482 "[I]t was a class issue": Didion, *After Henry*, 159.

482 "Fuck 'em": ibid., 163.

482 "Not until July of 1988" and subsequent quotes about the convention: ibid., 172–73.

482 "We feel this project has a lot of potential": Dunne, *Monster*, 10.

482 "full of so many silences," "White Christmas," and "it's time to cut our losses": ibid., 61–62.

483 "whammy picture": ibid., 36.

483 "concept line" and "When terrorists threaten": ibid., 53.

483 "did not seem the most fortuitous moment": ibid., 55.

483 "'Saturday Night Live' skit": ibid., 60.

483 "visualize what you see": ibid., 55.

483 "You have open-heart surgery": ibid., 62.

484 "The children talked": Dominick Dunne, "Fatal Charm: The Social Web of Claus von Bülow," *Vanity Fair*, August 1985; available at www.vanityfair.com/magazine/archive/1985/08/vonbulow198508.

484 "Tin Man": Dunne, *Monster*, 62.

CHAPTER 30

485 "Hi, this is Bill Clinton": John Gregory Dunne, *Monster: Living Off the Big Screen* (New York: Random House, 1997), 86–87.

485 "bobbing, weaving target": Sara Davidson, "Travels with Jerry," posted at www.saradavidson.com/travels-with-jerry.

485 "reservoir of self-pity": Joan Didion, *Political Fictions* (New York: Alfred A. Knopf, 2001), 215.

485 "guerrilla": ibid., 128.

485 "He seemed to be the most left-wing and right-wing man": Jesse Walker, "Five Faces of Jerry Brown," *The American Conservative,* November 1, 2004; available at theamericanconservative.com/articles/five-faces-of-jerry-brown/.

486 "Jerry rubs people the wrong way": Dunne quoted in Davidson, "Travels with Jerry."

486 Dunne said most of the guests patronized Brown: ibid.

486 "What did you know?": ibid.

486 "If he gets New York": ibid.

486 "He's apologized" and "powerful leader": ibid.

487 Dunne told him that most of the Irish help: Dunne, *Monster,* 87.

487 "There's an old saying": ibid.

487 "an experiment": ibid.

487 "We're change agents" and "full of gooey": George Skelton, "'92 Democratic Convention: Jerry Brown Vows He'll Have His Say at Podium," *Los Angeles Times,* July 12, 1992; available at articles.latimes.com/1992-07-12/news/mn -4293_1_jerry-brown.

487 "blinding fight" and subsequent quotes from Rupert Everett: Rupert Everett, "A Last Hug, Then Days Later Natasha Lay Dead," *Daily Mail,* September 17, 2012; available at dailymail.co.uk/femail/article-2204811/Death -Natasha-Richardson-plunged-Rupert-Everett-strangest-scene-life.html.

487 "I never knew anyone who so loved to make things": Joan Didion, "An Introduction," in Tony Richardson, *The Long-Distance Runner: A Memoir* (New York: William Morrow, 1993), 13.

488 "As far as I know": dialogue from *Hills Like White Elephants,* posted at may-on -the-short-story.blogspot.com/2009/03/more-on-short-fiction-and-film.html.

488 "what is going to happen in this picture": Dunne, *Monster,* 17.

488 "a small-town girl": ibid., 14.

489 Didion remained convinced that Simon & Schuster: The correspondence paraphrased in this section is all in the Lois Wallace Literary Agency Records, Harry Ransom Center, University of Texas at Austin.

490 "This book is dedicated to Henry Robbins": Joan Didion, *After Henry* (New York: Simon & Schuster, 1992), dedication page.

490 "were on different channels" and "The dedication speaks for itself": Esther B. Fein, "Book Notes: A Talked-About Dedication," *New York Times,* April 29, 1992; available at www.nytimes.com/1992/04/29/books/book-notes-815492 .html.

490 "I'd never thought of Joan Didion as dependable": Constance Casey, "When

the Writer Is Also a Good Reporter," *Los Angeles Times*, May 5, 1992; available at articles.latimes.com/print/1992-05-05/news/vw-1272_1_joan-didion.

490 "[S]he's truly one of the premier essayists": *Kirkus Reviews*, May 1, 1992; available at www.kirkusreviews.com/book-reviews/joan-didion/after-henry/.

490 "regular guy": Didion, *After Henry*, 62.

491 "marketing people" and "deliberate dumb-down": ibid., 239.

491 "systematically ruined": ibid., 300.

491 "an exact representation": ibid.

491 "subversion of authority": Didion, *Political Fictions*, 269.

491 "not far from that of the Taliban": ibid., 302.

491 "the old-time religion": ibid., 143.

491 "entitlement" and "empowerment": ibid., 123.

491 "welfare as we know it": "Clinton Signs Welfare Reform Bill, Angers Liberals," posted at cgi.cnn.com/ALLPOLITICS/1996/news/9608/22/welfare.sign/.

491 "Vietnam base": Didion, *Political Fictions*, 143.

491 "The choice we offer" and subsequent quotes on the New Covenant: ibid., 120–21.

492 "Instead of talking about Democrats": ibid., 146.

492 "crisis" and "structural malfunction": ibid., 207.

492 "At Madison Square Garden": ibid., 119–20.

493 On December 22: Lois Wallace letter to Joan Didion, Lois Wallace Literary Agency Records, Harry Ransom Center, University of Texas at Austin.

493 "Are we on the right road?": Joan Didion, *Where I Was From* (New York: Alfred A. Knopf, 2003), 215.

493 "She meant where did Gilroy go": ibid.

493 "all San Jose": ibid., 216.

493 "with the son of a rancher": ibid.

493 "in front of everybody" and subsequent dialogue: ibid., 216–17.

CHAPTER 31

494 "adorable": Dominick Dunne, *Justice: Crimes, Trials, and Punishments* (New York: Crown, 2001), 108.

494 $700,000: ibid., 85.

494 "endemic" and "remarkably stupid": Susie Linfield, "Big Girls Don't Cry," *Los Angeles Times*, February 16, 1997; available at articles.latimes.com/1997-02-16/books/bk-29251_1_big-girls-don-t-cry.

494 "Leslie Abramson's curly blond hair": Dominick Dunne, *Justice,* 134.

494 "venomous little pieces": Terrence Butcher, "Dominick Dunne: After the Party," posted at popmatters.com/review/95250-dominick-dunne-after-the-party/.

494 "admired her, and she doted on him": Dominick Dunne, "A Death in the Family," originally published in *Vanty Fair,* March 2004; reprinted in Andrew Blauner, ed., *Brothers: 26 Stories of Love and Rivalry* (San Francisco: Jossey-Bass, 2009), 191.

494 "a believer": John Gregory Dunne, *The Red White and Blue* (New York: Simon & Schuster, 1987), 80.

494 "curious": George Rush, Joanna Molloy, and Baird Jones, "Contempt Citation Refuels Dunne-ybrook," New York *Daily News,* March 5, 1997; available at nydailynews.com/archives/gossip/contempt-citation-refuels-dunne-ybrook -article-1.750652.

495 "complicated": ibid.

495 "at the very time": Dominick Dunne, "A Death in the Family," 191–92.

495 "All O.J.": Dominick Dunne, *Justice,* 144.

495 "a second-rate Brentwood restaurant": John Gregory Dunne, *Regards: The Selected Nonfiction of John Gregory Dunne* (New York: Thunder's Mouth Press, 2006), 176.

495 "Ninety-five million Americans": ibid., 180.

495 "On a wet Sunday morning": Dominick Dunne, "Three Faces of Evil," *Vanity Fair,* June 1996; available at www.vanityfair.com/magazine/archive/1996/06 /dunne199606.

495 "O.J. will never be accepted": ibid.

496 "a third-rate middlebrow Depends ad": Alex Ross, "Hollywood Babylon: Dominick Dunne, Gary Indiana, and the Whole Shebang," posted at slate.com /articles/arts/books/1997/12/Hollywood_babylon.html.

496 "Can you imagine": Matthew DeBord, "Keyed Up," posted at weeklywire.com /ww/04-06-98/boston_books_2.html.

496 "novel in the form of a memoir": Celia McGee, "Dunne In: Society Scrivener Throws Fit Over Harsh Review," *New York Observer,* January 26, 1998; available at observer.com/1998/01/dunne-in-society-scrivener-throws-fit-over-harsh -review/.

496 "litany of show-business": Ross, "Hollywood Babylon."

496 "I am not aware of any animus": McGee, "Dunne In."

496 "Wasserman is a fucking liar" and subsequent quotes regarding the Dunne-Indiana feud: ibid.

497 "sensitive and shy and incredibly spiritual": Kevin Gray, "A Kind of Deliverance," *People,* August 25, 1995; available at people.com/article/0,,20101426,00.html.

497 "I thought he was dead": ibid.

497 "transcendental experience" and "It's a little less than plausible": ibid.

497 "We've lost Alex in our lives": James H. Hyde, "Dominick Dunne: An Inveterate Connecticut Yankee Tells Us About His Remarkable Life," posted at newenglandtimes.com/dominick_dunne/dd_index.shtml.

497 "in lieu of flowers": "Deaths: Dunne, Ellen Griffin," *New York Times*, January 13, 1997; available at www.nytimes.com/1997/01/13/classified/paid-notice-deaths -dunne-ellen-griffin.html.

498 "*We had a real life*": Joan Didion, *The Last Thing He Wanted* (New York: Alfred A. Knopf, 1996), 42.

498 "She was twenty-nine or thirty" and "She drank too much": Adam Higginbotham, "Joan Didion on Love, Loss, and Parenting," *The Telegraph*, October 30, 2011; available at telegraph.co.uk/culture/8852890/Joan-Didion-on-love-loss -and-parenting.html.

498 "It's like a Big Ten campus": "The Rehab Review: Hazelden," posted at thefix .com/content/hazelden.

499 "It's about two movie stars": John Gregory Dunne, *Monster: Living Off the Big Screen* (New York: Random House, 1997), 105.

499 She apologized: Quintana Roo Dunne letter to Susanna Moore, May 9, 2001, Susanna Moore Papers, Department of Rare Books and Special Collections, Princeton University Library.

499 "Of course, mine was more serious" and "exclaim in outrage": Dunne, *Monster*, 156.

500 "uncritical endorsement of": Michael Medved quoted in ibid., 202.

CHAPTER 32

501 "Some real things have happened lately": Joan Didion, *The Last Thing He Wanted* (New York: Alfred A. Knopf, 1996), 3.

501 "interestingly described": ibid., 3–4.

501 "You know me" and "I wanted to come at this straight": ibid., 5.

502 "History's rough draft": ibid., 11.

502 "You may recall the rhetoric": ibid., 13.

502 "weightless": ibid., 3.

502 "picking out with one hand": Joan Didion, *A Book of Common Prayer* (New York: Simon & Schuster, 1977), 24.

502 "I still believe in history": Didion, *The Last Thing He Wanted*, 33.

502 "If you remember 1984" and "You know the context": ibid., 9.

503 "I want[ed] those two": ibid., 227.

503 "The hotel was pink": ibid., 225–226.

503 "I wanted to do a very, very tight plot": Dave Eggers, "The Salon Interview: Joan Didion," October 28, 1996, available at salon.com/1996/10/28/inter view_11/.

504 "sketching in a rhythm" and "The arrangement was the meaning": Joan Didion, *Blue Nights* (New York: Alfred A. Knopf, 2011), 104.

504 "I knew the end": "Telling Stories in Order to Live," Academy of Achievement interview with Joan Didion, June 3, 2006; available at www.achievement.org /autodoc/page/did0int-1.

504 "tended to appear": Didion, *The Last Thing He Wanted*, 67.

504 "conspiratorial view of history": Michiko Kakutani, "From a Life of Wealth into a Life of Danger," *New York Times*, September 3, 1996; available at www .nytimes.com/1996/09/03/books/from-a-life-of-wealth-into-a-life-of -danger.html.

504 "strangle liberty in the night": "Death Plot in El Salvador," *St. Petersburg Times*, July 26, 1984.

505 "hard to buy": Kakutani, "From a Life of Wealth into a Life of Danger."

505 "[i]f you put an assassination plot into play": Didion, *The Last Thing He Wanted*, 185.

505 "I'm not sure I know what business": ibid., 200.

505 "What . . . occurred was": Joan Didion, *Political Fictions* (New York: Alfred A. Knopf, 2001), 281.

505 "He came in here and he trashed the place": David Broder quoted in ibid., 287.

505 "The question of 'impeachment'": Joan Didion in conversation with Michael Bernstein, the Revelle Forum at the Neurosciences Institute, University of California at San Diego, October 15, 2002.

506 "quandary" and "No analysis can absolve": Don Eberly quoted in Didion, *Political Fictions*, 278.

506 "non-governmental institutions": posted at activistcash.com/organizations/496 -civil-society-project/.

506 "He's the luckiest man alive": Eggers, "The Salon Interview."

506 "an unreliable first person narrator": Didion, *Political Fictions*, 243.

506 "who don't have a very deep commitment": Didion quoted in Rebecca Meyer, "Berkeley Alumna Discusses Politics After 'Fictions,'" *Daily Californian*, October 19, 2001; available at randomhouse.com/knopf/authors/didion/desk topnew.html.

506 "basic craft error[s]": Didion, *Political Fictions*, 244.

506 "voting as a consumer transaction": Didion, *Political Fictions*, 12.

506 "choice": ibid., 9.

506 "sentimentally does 'the vote' give": ibid., 12.

506 "It was a perfect thing": Didion quoted in J. Hale Russell, "Joan Didion Takes On the Political Establishment," in *The Harvard Crimson,* October 19, 2001; available at thecrimson.com/article/2001/10/19/joan-didion-takes-on-the-political/.

507 "fact that the 2000 presidential election in Florida": Didion, *Political Fictions,* 14.

507 "I think people do think": Cokie Roberts quoted in ibid., 15.

507 "'rule of law'": ibid., 16.

507 "Assassins": "Federal Agents Seize Elian in Predawn Raid: Boy to Be Reunited with His Father in Maryland," CNN, April 22, 2000; available at archives.cnn .com/2000/US/04/22/cuba.boy.05/index.html.

508 "Many underground operatives": Victor Triay quoted in Yenisel Porro Delgado, "Operation Pedro Pan and Its Political Implications in the U.S. Peter Pan: The Fairy Tale That Became a Reality," posted at writing.uncc.edu/student-writing /operation-pedro-pan-and-its-political-implications-us-fairy-tale-became -reality.

508 "He's a very mysterious figure to me": Didion quoted in Meyer, "Berkeley Alumna Discusses Politics After 'Fictions.'"

508 "faith-based": Didion, *Political Fictions,* 293.

508 "redemption" and "reform": ibid., 313.

508 "personal transformation": ibid., 334.

508 "hearts": ibid., 309.

CHAPTER 33

509 "It's been very up and down": Quintana Roo Dunne quoted in Celia McGee, "State Editions for American Lawyer," New York *Daily News,* October 22, 1998; available at nydailynews.com/archives/money/state-edition-american -lawyer-article-1.810034.

509 "At *Elle Décor* magazine": ibid.

509 "[O]n a Saturday morning": Joan Didion, *Blue Nights* (New York: Alfred A. Knopf, 2011), 120.

509 "The sister had agreed": ibid., 121.

509 "I cannot easily express": ibid., 123–24.

510 "Saturday delivery" and "as if maintaining focus": ibid., 122.

510 "12-step recovery community" and subsequent quotes from Kaufman: Sue Kaufman to the author, March 10, 2012.

510 "she was so excited to see you" and subsequent quotes from Cooper: Amy Cooper to the author, May 11, 2013.

511 "[m]argaritas were mixed": Didion, *Blue Nights,* 127.

511 "she had seemed distraught": ibid.

511 "What a long strange journey": ibid., 130.

511 "On top of everything else": ibid.

CHAPTER 34

515 "half the nation's citizens": Joan Didion, *Political Fictions* (New York: Alfred A. Knopf, 2001), 18.

515 "postmodern": Edward Rothstein, "Attacks on U.S. Challenge the Perspectives of Postmodern True Believers," *New York Times,* September 22, 2001, available at www.nytimes.com/2001/09/22/arts/connections-attacks-us-challenge-perspec tives-postmodern-true-believers.html.

515 "moral clarity": Joan Didion, *Fixed Ideas: America Since 9.11* (New York: New York Review of Books, 2003), 11.

515 "One good thing": Roger Rosenblatt quoted in ibid., 10.

516 "frightened and fragmented world": Michiko Kakutani, "The Age of Irony Isn't Over After All; Assertions of Cynicism's Demise Belie History," *New York Times,* October 9, 2001; available at www.nytimes.com/2001/10/09/arts/critic-s -notebook-age-irony-isn-t-over-after-all-assertions-cynicism-s-demise.html.

516 "*mujaheddin* in Afghanistan": Joan Didion, *Miami* (New York: Simon & Schuster, 1987), 205.

516 "nothing to be gained": Didion, *Political Fictions,* 61.

516 "broad strokes": Joan Didion, *After Henry* (New York: Simon & Schuster, 1992), 67.

516 "not new in New York": ibid., 279–80.

516 "I will try to get": Samuel Byck quoted in Matthew C. Duersten, "The Man in the Santa Claus Suit," *L.A. Weekly,* September 12, 2001; available at laweekly. com/news/the-man-in-the-santa-claus-suit-2133809.

516 "deal broker" and "alleged associations": James Hatfield, "Why Would Osama bin Laden Want to Kill Dubya, His Former Business Partner?" posted at www.onlinejournal.com/Attack.

517 "specializing in personal": See www.rloatman.com.

517 "Humanity learned how to destroy": Matthys Levy and Mario Salvadori, *Why Buildings Fall Down* (New York: W. W. Norton, 2002), 239.

517 "Everyone's . . . talking": Didion quoted in Tom Christie, "The Secret Agent: Joan Didion Talks," *L.A. Weekly,* October 3, 2001; available at laweekly.com /news/the-secret-agent-2133880.

518 "had been just too frail": Joan Didion, *Where I Was From* (New York: Alfred A. Knopf, 2003), 204.

518 "when she died": Hari Kunzru, "Joan Didion's Yellow Corvette," posted at harikunzryu.com/archive/joan-didions-yellow-corvette-interview-tran script-2011.

518 "two pieces of silver flatware": Didion, *Where I Was From,* 225–26.

518 "lightening of spirit": ibid., 204.

519 "I took one bite": ibid., 207.

519 "call-to-action": ibid., 205.

519 *"[W]ho will remember me"*: ibid., 204.

519 "[I]t's fine": ibid., 206.

519 "I insisted to my brother": Kunzru, "Joan Didion's Yellow Corvette."

519 *"Joan Didion and Nancy Kennedy"*: Didion, *Where I Was From,* 224.

520 "When my father died": ibid., 225.

520 "I dare you to spit on my flag!": John M. Hubbell, "A Sharp Eye on Politics: Joan Didion Reflects on New York's Tragedy, Washington's Elite," *San Francisco Chronicle,* September 25, 2001; available at sfgate.com/entertainment /article/A-sharp-eye-on-politics-Joan-Didion-reflects-on-2874929.php.

520 "an infinitely romantic notion": cited in ibid.

520 "The last of the sentence": ibid.

520 "encounter with an America": Joan Didion, *Fixed Ideas,* 5.

520 "good deal of opportunistic ground": ibid., 6.

521 "[T]he words 'bipartisanship'": ibid.

521 "Washington was still talking": ibid., 7.

521 "These people got it": ibid.

521 "Bush says the country needs to be reborn" and ensuing dialogue: Christie, "The Secret Agent."

521 "view of our cold war victory": Thomas Mallon, "On Second Thought," *New York Times,* September 25, 2005; available at www.nytimes.com/2003/09/28 /books/on-second-thought.html.

522 "notion that non-voters are a seething, alienated mass": Joe Klein, "Bulworthism," *The New Republic,* November 15, 2001; available at powells.com /review/2001_11_15.html.

522 "Remember Mencken?": Linda Hall, "The Writer Who Came In from the Cold," *New York,* September 2, 1996, 30.

522 "My responses are pretty much the same": Didion quoted in Christie, "The Secret Agent."

522 "I don't know who is represented": ibid.

522 "political trajectory": Rachel Donadio, "Every Day Is All There Is," *New York Times,* October 9, 2005; available at www.nytimes.com/2005/10/09/books /review/09donadio.html.

522 "I think of political writing": Didion quoted in ibid.

522 "[P]eople, if they got it": Didion, *Fixed Ideas,* 7.

522 "was being processed, obscured, systematically leached": ibid., 8–9.

523 "evildoers," "moral clarity," and "America's New War": Frank Rich, "Preface" to ibid., ix.

523 "[T]his reinvention of Bush as a leader": Didion quoted in J. Hale Russell, "Joan Didion Takes On the Political Establishment," *The Harvard Crimson,* October 19, 2001; available at thecrimson.com/article/2001/10/19/joan-didion-takes -on-the-political/.

523 "You know that famous Vietnam thing": Didion quoted in Christie, "The Secret Agent."

523 "[W]e have been instructed": Rich, "Preface" to Didion, *Fixed Ideas,* vii.

523 "discussion got short-circuited": Steven Weber quoted in Didion, *Fixed Ideas,* 20–21.

523 "discussion with nowhere to go": ibid., 21.

524 "I made up my mind": George W. Bush quoted in ibid., 36.

524 "Given all we have said": ibid.

524 "It draws you toward it": ibid.

524 "I think that democracy has shallow roots": Jonah Raskin, "Joan Didion"; available at Sonoma.edu/users/r/raskin/interview_didion.htm.

524 "Stall. Keep the options open": Didion, *Fixed Ideas,* 21–22.

524 "Jesus Christ": Joan Didion, *The Last Thing He Wanted* (New York: Alfred A. Knopf, 1996), 61.

CHAPTER 35

525 as one critic pointed out: Thomas Larson, "Music, Memory, and Prose: On Joan Didion's Memoirs," *Puerto del Sol* 47, no. 1 (Summer 2012); available at thomaslarson.com/publications/essays-and-memoirs/242-music-memory -prose.html.

525 "There is no real way to deal with everything we lose": Joan Didion, *Where I Was From* (New York: Alfred A. Knopf, 2003), 225.

525 "All of the great English fiction": Meghan Daum, "Conversation Between Joan Didion and Meghan Daum," *Black Book*, December 12, 2004; available (2011) at meghandaum.com/about-meghan-daum/36-conversation-between-joan-didion-and-meghan-daum.

526 "I think specifically novels": ibid.

526 "My great-great-great-great-great-grandmother": Didion, *Where I Was From*, 3.

526 "California likes to be fooled": Frank Norris quoted in Andrew O'Hehir, "Golden State of Hypocrisy"; available at salon.com/2003/10/18/didion_4/.

527 "willingness to abandon": ibid.

527 "Well, it is hard to know": ibid.

527 "towns I knew": Didion, *Where I Was From*, 183.

527 "[w]e were seeing nothing 'new' here": ibid.

527 "[W]hen the families of inmates": ibid., 186–87.

528 "It was only Quintana who was real": ibid., 219.

528 "saying goodbye" and "It's a love song": O'Hehir, "Golden State of Hypocrisy."

528 "about being older": Adair Lara, "You Can't Keep the California Out of Joan Didion," *San Francisco Chronicle*, January 6, 2004.

528 "Be a better person" and "[N]obody can ever be nice enough": ibid.

CHAPTER 36

529 "My father likes nobody": Rosemary Breslin, *Not Exactly What I Had in Mind* (New York: Villard Books, 1997), 64.

529 "was dating some anemic offspring" and "children of successful parents": ibid.

529 "the chronicler of the society set" and "who [said] in all his years": ibid.

530 "an extremely rare occurrence": ibid.

530 "someone with a center made of steel" and subsequent quotes by Rosemary Breslin: ibid., 88.

530 "I remember being dazzled": Dominick Dunne quoted in Chris Smith, "Dominick Dunne vs. Robert Kennedy," *New York*; available at nymag.com/nymetro/news/crimelaw/features/n_8816.

530 "Joe Kennedy be so": ibid.

531 "pathetic creature" and "The formula": ibid. In 2012 a Connecticut judge overturned Skakel's murder conviction and recommended he be retried. See Mike Hogan, "Michael Skakel Retrial Order Would Have Infuriated Dominick Dunne," *Vanity Fair*, October 24, 2013; available at www.vanityfair.com/online/daily/2013/10/michael-skakel-retrial-dominick-dunne.

531 "I don't give a fuck": Smith, "Dominick Dunne vs. Robert Kennedy."

531 "friendship" and Nick's subsequent story: ibid.

532 "I've had prostate cancer": ibid.

532 "by happenstance" and Nick's subsequent comments on the brothers' reconciliation: Dominick Dunne, "A Death in the Family," originally published in *Vanity Fair*, March 2004; reprinted in Andrew Blauner, ed., *Brothers: 26 Stories of Love and Rivalry* (San Francisco: Jossey-Bass, 2009), 192–93.

532 "He had these big, arty glasses": Meghan Daum to the author, March 29, 2013.

532 "John was having problems with his heart": Dominick Dunne, "A Death in the Family," 193.

533 not for eleven million dollars: Fox News, March 14, 2005; available at foxnews.com/story/2005/03/14/condit-settles-lawsuit-against-writer-dunne/.

533 "being found": Joan Didion, *Blue Nights* (New York: Alfred A. Knopf, 2011), 128.

533 "shattering": ibid., 129.

533 "I phoned her once or twice": Anna Connolly to the author, March 20, 2013.

534 "It was a meeting by proximity" and all subsequent quotes from Sean Day Michael: Sean Day Michael to the author, November 2, 2013.

534 "vacuum": Joan Didion, *Slouching Towards Bethlehem* (New York: Farrar, Straus and Giroux, 1968), 122–23.

535 "no longer pretend": ibid.

535 early career start: For details about Gerry Michael and the Bummers, I have drawn on Weston Blalock and Julia Blalock, remarks posted at rootsofwoodstock.com/2013/03/28/gerry-michael-and-the-bummers. I am grateful to Weston Blalock for his help.

CHAPTER 37

536 *"When something happens to me"*: Joan Didion, *The Year of Magical Thinking* (New York: Alfred A. Knopf, 2005), 196.

537 reminded Didion of a night alone: ibid., 131.

537 "What exactly do those wit-nits": Joan Didion e-mail to Susanna Moore, April 16, 2005, Susanna Moore Papers, Department of Rare Books and Special Collections, Princeton University Library.

537 "Not our friend from the bridge": Didion, *The Year of Magical Thinking*, 38.

538 "[Didion's] place in American letters": Linda Hall, "The Writer Who Came In from the Cold," *New York*, September 2, 1996, 30.

538 "quick sunlight dappling" and "apprehension of death": Didion, *The Year of Magical Thinking*, 76.

538 "[O]n the contrary": ibid., 77.

539 "Let's do it": Joan Didion, *Blue Nights* (New York: Alfred A. Knopf, 2011), 5.

539 "I remember how unhappy John was that day": Josh Greenfeld in conversation with the author, April 6, 2013.

540 "Wasn't that just about perfect": Didion, *The Year of Magical Thinking*, 71.

540 "That settles it then": ibid., 80.

540 Episcopalians "took" Communion: ibid., 81.

540 "Joan Didion," "hack," and "bitch": John Gregory Dunne e-mail to Susanna Moore, December 7, 2003, Susanna Moore Papers, Department of Rare Books and Special Collections, Princeton University Library.

540 "You were right about Hawaii": Didion, *The Year of Magical Thinking*, 82.

541 "fritter[ed] away": ibid., 186.

541 "You can use it if you want to": ibid., 23.

541 "Goddamn. Don't ever tell me again you can't write": ibid., 166.

541 Didion said she envied her friend: Joan Didion e-mail to Susanna Moore, December 24, 2003, Susanna Moore Papers, Department of Rare Books and Special Collections, Princeton University Library.

CHAPTER 38

542 "fell into a kind of semi-conscious state": Amy Ephron, "Kind of Blue," *Los Angeles Review of Books*, October 27, 2011; available at tumblr.lareviewofbooks .org/post/11988483028/kind-of-blue.

542 "*How does 'flu' morph into whole-body infection*": Joan Didion, *The Year of Magical Thinking* (New York: Alfred A. Knopf, 2005), 67.

542 "There really was no explanation given": Didion quoted in Adam Higginbotham, "Joan Didion: A Mother's Journey Into Grief," *Belfast Telegraph*, November 14, 2011; available at belfasttelegraph.co.uk/woman/life/joan-didi on-a-mothers-journey-into-grief-28680460.html.

543 "walking pneumonia" and "nothing serious": Didion, *The Year of Magical Thinking*, 64.

543 "feeling terrible": ibid., 63.

543 "I was in town": Sean Day Michael to the author, November 2, 2013.

543 "Do I think her lifestyle contributed to her death?": Sean Day Michael to the author, November 4, 2013.

544 "She's still beautiful": Didion, *The Year of Magical Thinking*, 218.

544 "More than one more day": ibid., 68.

544 "sobbed about his daughter": Dominick Dunne, "A Death in the Family,"

originally published in *Vanity Fair*, March 2004; reprinted in Andrew Blauner, ed., *Brothers: 26 Stories of Love and Rivalry* (San Francisco: Jossey-Bass, 2009), 184.

544 *"which way this is going"*: Didion, *The Year of Magical Thinking*, 62.

544 "Why did I waste time": ibid., 82.

544 *"I don't think I'm up for this"* and *"You don't get a choice"*: ibid., 217.

545 *"Don't do that"*: ibid., 10.

545 Quintana's dreams about the Broken Man: ibid., 219.

545 "The minute I got to him": Didion quoted in Dominick Dunne, "A Death in the Family," 184–85.

545 Didion took a taxi home: For details of the night of Dunne's death, see Didion, *The Year of Magical Thinking*, 3–23.

546 "leaden": ibid., 31.

546 The obituary in *The New York Times*: Richard Severo, "John Gregory Dunne, Novelist, Screenwriter, and Observer of Hollywood Is Dead at 71," *New York Times*, January 1, 2004; available at www.nytimes.com/2004/01/01/arts/john -gregory-dunne-novelist-screenwriter-and-observer-of-hollywood-is-dead-at -71.html.

547 "I knew he had heart trouble": Hari Kunzru, "Joan Didion's Yellow Corvette," posted at harikunzru.com/archive/joan-didions-yellow-corvette-interview -transcript-2011.

547 "I couldn't help drawing a line": Sean Day Michael to the author, November 2, 2013.

547 "Then when is she coming in?": Didion, *The Year of Magical Thinking*, 84.

547 "Where's Dad?": ibid.

547 "How's Dad?": ibid.

547 "But how is he *now*?": ibid.

CHAPTER 39

549 "sunny room" and "[c]old milk": Emily Post quoted in Joan Didion, *The Year of Magical Thinking* (New York: Alfred A. Knopf, 2005), 58.

549 "Don't tell me your dream": ibid., 159.

549 "a very new-on-the-scene blood thinner": Sean Day Michael to the author, November 2, 2013.

549 "For nothing now can ever come to any good": W. H. Auden's "Funeral Blues" cited in Joan Didion, *Blue Nights* (New York: Alfred A. Knopf, 2011), 156–57.

549 "wrong" and "vehement": ibid., 157.

549 "place to be": Liz Smith cited in an e-mail from Joan Didion to Susanna Moore,

March 5, 2004, Susanna Moore Papers, Department of Rare Books and Special Collections, Princeton University Library.

550 "When John was alive": Hari Kunzru, "Joan Didion's Yellow Corvette," posted at harikunzru.com/archive/joan-didion-yellow-corvette-interview-transcript-2011.

550 Dunne's memorial: all quotes regarding the memorial service are from Jane Gross, "John Gregory Dunne Eulogized in Cathedral," *New York Times*, March 24, 2004; available at www.nytimes.com/2004/03/04/nyregion/john-gregory-dunne-eulogized-in-cathedral.html.

551 "I had encouraged this": Didion, *The Year of Magical Thinking*, 86.

551 "[My dad] said she was fine walking one minute": Sean Day Michael to the author, November 4, 2013.

552 "reliable" folks: Claire Potter, "Slouching Towards Joan Didion," posted at chronicle.com/blognetwork/tenuredradical/2012/01/slouching-towards-joan-didion/.

552 "Do I know if she was drinking": Sean Day Michael to the author, November 4, 2013.

552 "happened to be in New York": Sean Day Michael to the author, November 2, 2013.

552 "*You're safe*": Didion, *The Year of Magical Thinking*, 96.

552 "When do you have to leave?": ibid.

552 For the next five weeks: For details of this period and "the vortex effect," see ibid., 107–118.

552 "suspicious violation of boundaries": ibid., 106.

554 "suggesting trauma all over Southern California": ibid., 135–36.

554 "cornfield": ibid., 138.

554 "Am I going to make it?" and "Definitely": ibid., 140.

554 "It was a Quarter Pounder": ibid.

555 "systematic . . . sadistic," "[b]reaking chemical lights," and "almost went into cardiac arrest": Seymour Hersh, "Torture at Abu Ghraib," *The New Yorker*, May 10, 2004, 43.

555 "senior military officers": ibid., 46.

555 "enhanced interrogation techniques": ibid., 47.

556 "collective wrong-doing": ibid.

556 "Army intelligence officers": ibid., 45.

556 "Do you really think": ibid., 44.

556 "tell you what you want to hear": ibid., 47.

556 Cheney said simply: See Chris McGreal, "Dick Cheney Defends Use of Torture on al-Qaida Leaders," *The Guardian*, September 9, 2011; available at www.theguardian.com/world/2011/sep/09/dick-cheney-defends-torture-al-qaida.

556 A caller to Rush Limbaugh's radio talk show: See "Rush: MPs Just 'Blowing Off Steam,'" CBS News, May 6, 2004; available at www.cbsnews.com/stories /2004/05/06/opinion/meyer/main616021.shtml.

556 "The photographs are us": Susan Sontag, "Regarding the Torture of Others," *New York Times*, May 23, 2004; available at www.nytimes.com/2004/05/23 /magazine/regarding-the-torture-of-others.html.

556 "image of a frightened, naked man": Elaine Scarry quoted in Linda Myers, "Torture Can Never Be Defended as a Military Necessity, Asserts Harvard Professor and Iraq War Critic Elaine Scarry," *Cornell Chronicle*, March 6, 2014; available at news.cornell.edu/stories/2006/05/torture-can-never-be-defended -military-necessity-says-harvard-prof.

557 Gerry Michael's insurance stopped paying: Didion expressed these concerns to Susanna Moore in e-mails in April 2005, Susanna Moore Papers, Department of Rare Books and Special Collections, Princeton University Library.

557 "shadowy silhouettes": Didion, *The Year of Magical Thinking*, 178.

557 "attempt to make sense": ibid., 7.

557 "*Life changes in the instant*": ibid., 3.

558 "Primitive men and neurotics": Freud's *Totem and Taboo* cited in Jeffrey Berman, *Companionship in Grief: Love and Loss in the Memoirs of C. S. Lewis, John Bayley, Donald Hall, Joan Didion, and Calvin Trillin* (Amherst: University of Massachusetts Press, 2010), 205.

558 "pathological condition": Didion, *The Year of Magical Thinking*, 34–35.

558 "Let them become the photograph on the table": ibid., 226.

558 "as January becomes February": Didion, *The Year of Magical Thinking*, 225.

558 she had an image: Joan Didion e-mail to Susanna Moore, December 2, 2004, Susanna Moore Papers, Department of Rare Books and Special Collections, Princeton University Library.

CHAPTER 40

559 "[V]ery good. Really interesting": Joan Didion, *The Year of Magical Thinking: A Play* (New York: Vintage, 2007), 53.

559 Didion started to venture out in public: Details about Didion's activities are from correspondence between Didion and Susanna Moore in the early months of 2005, Susanna Moore Papers, Department of Rare Books and Special Collections, Princeton University Library.

560 "anybody" was at "home" and "No one who has had even a passing exposure": Joan Didion, "The Case of Theresa Schiavo," *The New York Review of Books*,

June 9, 2005; available at nybooks.com/articles/archives/2005/jun/09/the
-case-of-theresa-schiavo.

561 "unassuageable grief": ibid.

561 At the end of April 2005: Joan Didion e-mail to Susanna Moore, April 30,
2005, Susanna Moore Papers, Department of Rare Books and Special Collections, Princeton University Library.

561 Ten days later: Joan Didion e-mail to Susanna Moore, May 10, 2005, in ibid.

561 "entered the hospital": Joan Didion, *Blue Nights* (New York: Alfred A. Knopf,
2011), 158.

561 "had been at home": Didion, *The Year of Magical Thinking: A Play*, 53.

561 "Your daughter wasn't in great condition," "five surgical interventions," and
"ventilated": Didion, *Blue Nights*, 159.

561 acute pancreatitis: Didion, *The Year of Magical Thinking: A Play*, 53.

561 "probably intertwined": Susan Traylor quoted in Boris Kachka, "I Was No
Longer Afraid to Die. I Was Now Afraid Not to Die," *New York*, October 16,
2011; available at nymag.com/arts/books/features/joan-didion-2011-10.

561 "Alcohol has its well-known defects": Didion, *Blue Nights*, 48.

561 "torchy" and "The power of cheap music": ibid., 160.

561 "an important moment": Sean Day Michael to the author, March 7, 2014.

561 "She asked specifically for the word 'Ambivert'": ibid.

562 At Quintana's memorial service: For details about the service, see Didion, *Blue
Nights*, 162–64.

562 "Woodstock wasn't in his plans": Sean Day Michael to the author, March 7,
2014.

562 "My dad lost a wife": Sean Day Michael to the author, November 2, 2013.

562 "I promised myself that I would maintain momentum": Didion, *Blue Nights*, 165.

562 "[I]t did not cross my mind to cancel it": Hari Kunzru, "Joan Didion's Yellow
Corvette," posted at harikunzru.com/archive/joan-didions-yellow-corvette-
interview-transcript-2011.

563 "very strong emotional response" and subsequent quotes in this paragraph:
Hilton Als, "Joan Didion, The Art of Nonfiction No. 1," *The Paris Review* 47,
no. 176 (Summer 2006); available at www.theparisreview.org/interviews/5601
/the-art-of-nonfiction-no-1-joan-didion.

563 "You're the awesomest": David Swick, "The Zen of Joan Didion," *Shambhala
Sun*, January 2007; available at www.lionsroar.com/the-zen-of-joan-didion.

563 "she in no way ingratiates herself": Mark Feeney, "Amid Unbearable Sorrow,
She Shows Her Might," *Boston Globe*, October 26, 2005; available at boston.
com/ae/books/articles/2005/10/26/amid_unbearable_sorrow_she_shows_her
_might/?page=full.

563 "I don't think she's changed much": Robert Silvers quoted in ibid.

563 "I think my view of death didn't change": Didion quoted in ibid.

564 The judges' citation: The citation and Didion's remarks are posted at national book.org/nba2005_nf_didion.html.

564 "There is hardly anything I can say": ibid.

564 "Hats by John Frederics": Joan Didion, "Joan Didion's Year of Magical Thinking," *The Telegraph*, April 19, 2008; available at telegraph.co.uk/culture/the atre/3672742/Joan-Didions-Year-of-Magical-Thinking.html.

565 "Absolutely too short for the stage": ibid.

565 "The movement . . . should build": ibid.

565 "I knew that the play would be about language": ibid.

566 "sexually simmering suburban scenes" and "bad boy": Celia McGee, "A World and an Artist Transformed," *New York Times*, May 15, 2013; available at www .nytimes.com/2013/5/16/fashion/eric-fischl-goes-back-to-his-future,html?_r=0.

566 "Only when I realized": Didion, "Joan Didion's Year of Magical Thinking."

566 "I remember liking the entire process": Didion, *Blue Nights*, 166.

567 "Cheney did not take the lesson": Joan Didion, "Cheney: The Fatal Touch," *The New York Review of Books*, October 5, 2006; available at www.nybooks .com/articles/archives/2006/oct/05/cheney-the-fatal-touch/.

568 "separated from [his] body": Mark Danner, "In the Darkness of Dick Cheney," *The New York Review of Books*, March 6, 2014; available at www.nybooks.com /articles/archives/2014/mar/06/darkness-dick-cheney/.

568 "Vanessa Redgrave is not playing me": Didion, "Joan Didion's Year of Magical Thinking."

568 "You think I'm crazy": Didion, *The Year of Magical Thinking: A Play*, 44.

569 "I liked watching the performance[s]": Didion, *Blue Nights*, 167.

569 "I did not want the yellow roses touched": ibid., 169–70.

570 "There are a handful of writers": Transcription of Michael Cunningham's remarks at the National Book Awards Ceremony, November 14, 2007, Marriott Marquis Hotel, New York.

570 "I didn't start writing": Transcript of Joan Didion's remarks at the National Book Awards Ceremony, November 14, 2007, Marriott Marquis Hotel, New York.

570 "children of Gaza": Ellen Gamerman, "An Encore of Magical Thinking," *Wall Street Journal*, October 23, 2009; available at online.wsj.com/articles/SB1000 142405274870450060457448370173524538 2.

570 "This was never supposed to happen to her": Didion, *The Year of Magical Thinking: A Play*, 42.

570 "[S]omebody failed Quintana": Didion quoted in Adam Higginbotham, "Joan Didion: A Mother's Journey into Grief," *Belfast Telegraph*, November 14,

2011; available at belfasttelegraph.co.uk/woman/life/joan-didion-a-mothers
-journey-into-grief-28680460.html.

571 "Did I lie to you?": Didion, *The Year of Magical Thinking: A Play*, 55.

571 "five evenings and two afternoons a week": Didion, *Blue Nights*: 167.

CHAPTER 41

572 "[Y]ou kind of grow into the role": Didion quoted in Sheila Heti, "Joan Didion," *The Believer*, December 2011; available at believermag.com/exclusives/read
=interview_didion.

572 "I can hardly stay awake": Didion quoted in Carrie Tuhy, "Joan Didion: Stepping into the River Styx, Again," *Publishers Weekly*, September 30, 2011; available at www.publishersweekly.com/pw/by-topic/authors/profiles/article/48908
-joan-didion-stepping-into-the-river-styx-again.html.

573 "It got closer to my brother-in-law" and all subsequent comments from the
screening of *Dominick Dunne: After the Party*: "Joan Didion on Obama: We
All Have High Hopes, But Who Knows?" *New York Observer*, November
2008; available at observer.com/2008/11/joan-didion-on-obama-we-all-have
-high-hopes-but-who-knows/.

573 "I couldn't count" and subsequent quotes from this article: Darryl Pinckney
and Joan Didion, "Obama: In the Irony-Free Zone," *The New York Review of
Books*, December 18, 2008; available at www.nybooks.com/articles/archives
/2008/dec/18/Obama-in-the-irony-free-zone/.

574 Obama's acceptance speech: Susanna Moore e-mail to Joan Didion, November 5, 2008, Susanna Moore Papers, Department of Rare Books and Special
Collections, Princeton University Library.

574 "national coma" and subsequent quotes in this paragraph: Didion's remarks at
a Brooklyn Book Fair panel, "Consequences to Come," September 2008,
sponsored by *The New York Review of Books*, www.nybooks.com/podcasts
/events/2008/sep/24/consequences-come.

574 "made an inadequate adjustment" and Didion's reply: Joan Didion, *Blue Nights*
(New York: Alfred A. Knopf, 2011), 137.

575 "Your cardiac problem": ibid., 144–45.

575 "[e]veryone agreed": ibid., 148.

575 "No good at human relationships": Frank Langella, *Dropped Names: Famous
Men and Women As I Knew Them* (New York: HarperCollins, 2012), 303.

575 "practiced reporter's skill": ibid., 302.

576 "So, are you gay" and the ensuing conversation: ibid., 303–304.

576 "a great friend of my sister's": "Griffin Dunne: Reflections on His Father, Dominick," *Fresh Air*, National Public Radio, December 15, 2009; available at wbur.org/npr/127862990/griffin-dunne-reflections-on-his-father-dominick.

576 "Dominick and I met" and subsequent Carby quotes: Norman Carby to the author, March 23, 2014.

576 "Sweeney attacked her": Jim Hyde, "Dominick Dunne: An Inveterate Connecticut Yankee Tells Us About His Remarkable Life," posted at newenglandtimes.com/dominick_dunne/dd_index.shtml.

577 "looking after" and "I don't think he'd mind": "Griffin Dunne: Reflections on His Father, Dominick."

577 "I saw the": ibid.

577 "Can't die with a secret": Dominick Dunne, *Too Much Money* (New York: Random House, 2009), 214.

577 "I call myself": Tim Teeman, "It Isn't Over, Not When It's Dunne," *Times* (London), February 12, 2009.

577 "Frank. I did it": Langella, *Dropped Names*, 306–307.

577 "even on his deathbed": ibid.

579 "Nowadays the substance rendered here": Guy Trebay, "Trading on Sentiment at Dominick Dunne's Estate Sale," *New York Times*, November 24, 2010; available at www.nytimes.com/2010/11/25/fashion/25Gimlet.html?_r=0.

EPILOGUE: LIFE LIMITS

580 "a work of stunning frankness": Joan Didion, *Blue Nights* (New York: Alfred A. Knopf, 2011), jacket copy.

580 "[T]here's a discernible remoteness": Meghan Daum, "Having, or Making, or Thinking about Making a Drink," *The Los Angeles Review of Books*, October 28, 2011; available at lareviewofbooks.org/review/having-or-making-or-thinking-about-making-a-drink.

580 "twilights turn[ing] long and blue": Didion, *Blue Nights*, 3.

581 "When we talk about mortality": ibid., 13.

581 "Fade as the blue nights fade" and "there is no day in her life": ibid., 188.

581 "morality and culture": Carrie Tuhy, "Joan Didion: Stepping into the River Styx, Again," *Publishers Weekly*, September 30, 2011; available at www.publishersweekly.com/pw/by-topic/authors/profiles/article/48908-joan-didion-stepping-into-the-river-styx-again.html.

581 "It is often said": Joan Didion, *Slouching Towards Bethlehem* (New York: Modern Library, 2000), 227.

582 "Earl's job these days": Eve Babitz in conversation with the author, March 30, 2013.

582 "unflinching": Richard Levine's remarks, Yale University, May 23, 2011.

582 "I'm surprised": Barack Obama's remarks at the White House, July 10, 2013; available at thewire.com/politics/2013/07/obama-honors-joan-didion-and-others-well-their-us-policy-criticism/67056.

583 "really love Joan Didion": Caitlin Flanagan, "The Autumn of Joan Didion," *The Atlantic,* January/February 2012; available at www.theatlantic.com/magazine/archive/2012/01/the-autumn-of-joan-didion/308851.

583 "There are . . . male writers": Katie Roiphe, *In Praise of Messy Lives: Essays* (New York: Random House, 2012), 115.

583 "absolutely essential": Matthew Specktor to the author, June 5, 2013.

584 "Sociology is not literature": Timothy Sedore, "Violating the Boundaries: An Interview with Richard Rodriguez," *The Michigan Quarterly Review* 38, no. 3 (Summer 1999); available at quod.lib.umich.edu/cgi/text/text-idx?cc=mqr;c=mqr;c=mqrarchive;idno=act2080.0038.308;cgn=main;view=text;xc=1;g=mqrg.

584 "Sometimes I feel": Robert Caro quoted in ibid.

584 "Memories are what you no longer want to remember": Didion, *Blue Nights,* 64.

585 "like sitting down at the typewriter": Sara Davidson, *Joan: Forty Years of Life, Loss, and Friendship with Joan Didion* (San Francisco: Byliner, 2011).

585 "I wouldn't get married again": Didion quoted in Mark Matousek, *When You're Falling, Dive* (London: Hay House, 2009), 22.

585 "I just jumped ship" and Didion's subsequent remarks to Davidson: Davidson, *Joan.*

586 "[I]t's an enterprise" and "There's something missing in survival": Didion quoted in Andrew O'Hehir, "Golden State of Hypocrisy," posted at salon.com/2003/10/18/didion_4/.

Selected Bibliography

BOOKS BY JOAN DIDION

Run River (novel). New York: Ivan Obolensky, 1963.

Slouching Towards Bethlehem (essays). New York: Farrar, Straus and Giroux, 1968.

Play It As It Lays (novel). New York: Farrar, Straus and Giroux, 1970.

A Book of Common Prayer (novel). New York: Simon & Schuster, 1977.

The White Album (essays). New York: Simon & Schuster, 1979.

Salvador (nonfiction). New York: Simon & Schuster, 1983.

Democracy (novel). New York: Simon & Schuster, 1984.

Miami (nonfiction). New York: Simon & Schuster, 1987.

After Henry (essays). New York: Simon & Schuster, 1992.

The Last Thing He Wanted (novel). New York: Alfred A. Knopf, 1996.

Political Fictions (essays). New York: Alfred A. Knopf, 2001.

Fixed Ideas: America Since 9.11 (essay). New York: New York Review of Books, 2003.

Where I Was From (nonfiction). New York: Alfred A. Knopf, 2003.

The Year of Magical Thinking (nonfiction). New York: Alfred A. Knopf, 2005.

Blue Nights (nonfiction). New York: Alfred A. Knopf, 2011.

SELECTED BOOKS ON JOAN DIDION'S WORK

Berman, Jeffrey. *Companionship in Grief: Love and Loss in the Memoirs of C. S. Lewis, John Bayley, Donald Hall, Joan Didion, and Calvin Trillin.* Amherst: University of Massachusetts Press, 2010.

Davidson, Sara. *Joan: Forty Years of Life, Love, and Friendship with Joan Didion*. San Francisco: Byliner, 2011.

Felton, Sharon, ed. *The Critical Response to Joan Didion*. Westport, Conn.: Greenwood Publishing Group, 1993.

Friedman, Ellen G., ed. *Joan Didion: Essays and Conversations*. Princeton, N.J.: Ontario Review Press, 1984.

Henderson, Katharine Usher. *Joan Didion*. New York: Frederick Ungar, 1981.

Houston, Lynn Marie, and William V. Lombardi, eds. *Reading Joan Didion*. Westport, Conn.: Greenwood Press, 2009.

Loris, Michelle Carbone. *Innocence, Loss and Recovery in the Art of Joan Didion*. New York: Peter Lang, 1989.

Parrish, Timothy. *From the Civil War to the Apocalypse: Postmodern History and American Fiction*. Amherst: University of Massachusetts Press, 2008.

Stout, Janis P. *Strategies of Reticence: Silence and Meaning in the Works of Jane Austen, Willa Cather, Katharine Anne Porter, and Joan Didion*. Charlottesville: University Press of Virginia, 1990.

Szalay, Michael. *Hip Figures: A Literary History of the Democratic Party*. Redwood City, Calif.: Stanford University Press, 2012.

Weingarten, Marc. *The Gang That Wouldn't Write Straight: Wolfe, Thompson, Didion and the New Journalism Revolution*. New York: Crown, 2006.

Winchell, Mark Royden. *Joan Didion*. Boston: Twayne, 1980.

SELECTED CRITICAL ARTICLES AND PROFILES OF JOAN DIDION

Atlas, James. "Slouching Towards Miami." *Vanity Fair*, October 1987; www.vanityfair.com/culture/features/1987/10/joan-didion-on-miami.

Brady, Jennifer. "Points West, Then and Now: The Fiction of Joan Didion." *Contemporary Literature* 20 (1979): 452–470.

Braman, Sandra. "The 'Facts' of El Salvador According to Objective and New Journalism." *Journal of Communication Inquiry* 13, no. 2 (1985): 75–96.

Braudy, Susan. "A Day in the Life of Joan Didion." *Ms.*, February 1977, 65–68, 108–109.

Chabot, Barry C. "Joan Didion's *Play It As It Lays* and the Vacuity of the Here and Now." *Critique: Studies in Modern Fiction* 21, no. 3 (1980): 53–60.

Coale, Samuel. "Didion's Disorder: An American Romancer's Art." *Critique: Studies in Modern Fiction* 25, no. 1 (1984): 160–170.

Garis, Leslie. "Didion and Dunne: The Rewards of a Literary Marriage." *New York Times Magazine,* February 8, 1987; www.nytimes.com/1987/02/08/magazine /didion-dunne-the-rewards-of-a-literary-marriage.html.

Geherin, David J. "Nothingness and Beyond: Joan Didion's *Play It As It Lays.*" *Critique: Studies in Modern Fiction* 16, no. 1 (1974): 64–78.

Gornick, Vivian. "The Prose of Nothingness." *The Women's Review of Books* 29, no. 34 (1999): 28.

Hall, Linda. "The Writer Who Came In from the Cold." *New York,* September 2, 1996, 28, 31–32.

Hanley, Lynne T. "To El Salvador." *Massachusetts Review* 24, no. 1 (1983): 13–29.

Harrison, Barbara Grizzuti. "Joan Didion: The Courage of Her Afflictions." *The Nation,* September 29, 1979, 277–86.

Kachka, Boris. "I Was No Longer Afraid to Die. I Was Afraid Not to Die." *New York,* October 16, 2011; www.nymag.com/arts/books/features/joan-didion-2011-10/.

Kakutani, Michiko. "Joan Didion: Staking Out California." *New York Times Magazine,* June 10, 1979, 44–50.

Kazin, Alfred. "Joan Didion: Portrait of a Professional." *Harper's* magazine, December 1971, 112–14.

Mallon, Thomas. "The Limits of History in the Novels of Joan Didion." *Critique: Studies in Modern Fiction* 21, no. 3 (1980): 43–52.

Reft, Ryan. "A Dive in the Deep End: The Importance of the Swimming Pool in Southern California"; kcet.org/socal/departures/columns/intersections/a-dive -in-the-deep-end-the-importance-of-the-swimming-pool-in-southern-califor nia-culture.

Romano, John. "Joan Didion and Her Characters." *Commentary,* July 1977, 61–63.

Schorer, Mark. "Novels and Nothingness." *American Scholar* 40 (Winter 1970–1971): 168–74.

Stimpson, Catharine. "The Case of Miss Joan Didion." *Ms.,* January 1973, 36–41.

Index